The Book of
Common
Fallacies

D1649160

BOOKS BY PHILIP WARD

Poetry
Collected Poems, 1960
Seldom Rains, 1967
At the Best of Times, 1968
The Poet and the Microscope, 1969
Maps on the Ceiling, 1970
A House on Fire, 1973
Impostors and their Imitators, 1977
The Keymakers, 1977

Drama
A Musical Breakfast, 1968
Garrity and other Plays, 1970
Pincers, 1973
Television Plays, 1976

Travel
Touring Libya, 3 vols., 1967-9
Tripoli, 1969
Touring Iran, 1970
Sabratha, 1970
Motoring to Nalut, 1970
Touring Cyprus, 1971
The Way to Wadi al-Khail, 1971
Touring Lebanon, 1971
Come with me to Ireland, 1972
The Aeolian Islands, 1973
Bangkok, 1974
Indonesia: a Traveler's Guide
(as "Darby Greenfield"), 2 vols., 1975-6

Fiction and Essays
The Okefani "Song of Nij Zitru," 1966
Ambigamus, or The Logic Box, 1967
Apuleius on Trial at Sabratha, 1968
The Quell-Finger Dialogues, 1969
A Lizard and other Distractions, 1969
A Maltese Boyhood, 1976

Librarianship
Simplified Cataloguing Rules (with R. Cave), 1959
A Survey of Libyan Bibliographical Resources, 1964
The Libyan Research Library Catalog, 1970
Planning a National Library Service, 1973
Indonesia: the Development of a National Library
Service, 3 vols., 1976

Literature
Spanish Literary Appreciation, 1969
Indonesian Traditional Poetry, 1975
The Oxford Companion to Spanish Literature, 1978

The Book of
Common
Fallacies

*Falsehoods, Misconceptions, Flawed
Facts, and Half-Truths
That Are Ruining Your Life*

Philip Ward
with Julia Edwards

Skyhorse Publishing

www.skyhorsepublishing.com

10 9 8 7 6 5 4 3 2 1

Library of Congress Cataloging-in-Publication Data

Ward, Philip, 1938-
 The book of common fallacies : falsehoods, misconceptions, flawed facts, and half-truths that are ruining your life / Phillip Ward ; with Julia Edwards.
     p. cm.
Updated ed. of author's: Dictionary of common fallacies, c1988.
 ISBN 978-1-61608-336-6 (alk. paper)1. Common fallacies--Dictionaries. I. Edwards, Julia. II. Ward, Philip, 1938- Dictionary of common fallacies. III. Title. AZ999.W36 2012 001.9'6--dc23
                    2012006614

Printed in the United States of America

Editor's Note to the 2012 Edition

Originally published more than three decades ago, *The Book of Common Fallacies* sought to educate, entertain, and enlighten at a time when there was no internet, personal computers were extremely rare, and smartphones and internet-connected tablets only existed in the minds of science fiction writers. Nevertheless, Philip Ward managed to pack the original two volumes full of myth-debunking knowledge, much of it still relevant even today in our always-connected, instant-answers-at-our-fingertips world.

In this new single-volume edition, we have left the majority of Ward's original text and style unchanged, only deleting those entries that were truly outdated (though we retained those entries that were outdated but histotrically interesting). In addition, we have added more than a hundred brand-new entries to address some of the myths, urban legends, and common misconceptions that plague modern society today. You'll find these entries in gray boxes.

Philip Ward's Preface to the Original Edition

The Book of Common Fallacies deals not only with the narrow field of purely logical fallacies, but also with a number of important ideas or theories common either now or in the past which have been proved wrong by scientific experiment or observation, or are so intrinsically improbable that their widespread acceptance should be questioned.

The Latin word "fallere" (to escape from, deceive) gave the Vulgar Latin "fallire" (to commit a fault, deceive, fail), and the adjective "fallax" (deceptive), which provided the English adjective fallacious through "fallaciosus." In classical logic, a fallacy is understood to denote an argument violating the laws of correct demonstration; more generally, it refers to any mistaken statement used in argument, while in common parlance is understood in the even wider sense of a mistaken view which is held by a relatively large number of people in spite of its having been disproved by some form of scientific or logical test.

"For a mind, let us not say exactly ignorant, but shall we say superficial, a work on popular errors might appear quite useless. Why, indeed, he might complain, give the slightest attention, the least emphasis to those daydreams which occupy the brain of the common people, old wives, nurses, and children?" asked Louis Pierre Francois Adolphe, Marquis de Chesnel de la Charbouclais, in mock despair, before contributing 1360 closely printed columns of popular fallacies to Migne's *Troisième et dernière encyclopédie théologique*... (Paris, 1856, vol. 20).

Why indeed! As if it were not provocation enough to read newspapers and magazines still containing horoscopes in the 1970s, to see shelf upon shelf of fashionable occult "literature" in otherwise reputable bookshops, fanatic religious sects springing up to make claims of miracle-working and Messianity, extremist political groups seeking converts among the badly educated and the confused, and pseudo-sciences making untestable and incredible claims. However, a dictionary which exhaustively attempted to examine all the various fallacies which have bewitched, beguiled, and bemused the minds of men (and women) would fill an anti-encyclopedia more voluminous than that of the Marquis de Chesnel de la Charbouclais. The intention of the present work is not so ambitious: it merely offers to anatomize some of the popular beliefs which have been shown to be false by those without a vested interest in deceiving the multitude for power, wealth or prestige.

The compiler has taken to heart the three mildly skeptical attitudes proposed by Bertrand Russell in *Let the people think* (London, 1941, p. 2):

1. That when the experts are agreed, the opposite opinion cannot be held to be certain;
2. That when they are not agreed, no opinion can be regarded as certain by a non-expert;
3. That when they all hold that no sufficient grounds for a positive opinion exist, the ordinary man would do well to suspend his judgment.

"These opinions may seem mild," wrote Russell, "yet, if accepted, they would absolutely revolutionize human life. The opinions for which people are willing to fight and persecute all belong to one of the three classes which this skepticism condemns. When there are rational grounds for an opinion, people are content to set them forth and wait for them to operate. In such cases, people do not hold their opinions with passion; they hold them calmly, and set forth their reasons quietly. The opinions that are held with passion are always those for which no good ground exists; indeed the passion is the measure of the holder's lack of rational conviction."

There is no sign that impostors, charlatans, and the plain misguided have diminished in numbers since the Middle Ages. The steep rise in population since the Crusades has been accompanied by the fragmentation of a greatly increased quantity of scientific knowledge, so that fewer and fewer possess a clear understanding of a smaller segment of knowledge and their skepticism about their own "truths," healthy as it is, leaves ample scope for the less scrupulous to protest the truth of new "religions," occultist movements varying in integrity and intelligence, pseudo-sciences, and obsessions touted as facts.

Excluded from this catalogue of common fallacies are a majority of the phenomena generally classified as *hallucinations and delusions* of an individual or of a closely knit group which are evidently not shared by the generality of mankind; *hoaxes* except insofar as they have led to fallacious conclusions; mere *ignorance* before major discoveries, inventions, or new patterns of awareness pervade the times; *miracles* of the various churches which have a vested interest in advertising the power of their magic or the ease with which they can obtain favors from a deity; simple *mistakes* which are subsequently recognized and rectified; *occult* beliefs which appeal, however irrationally, to a sector of the consciousness allegedly different from that to which known scientific principles can be seen to apply; *religious systems* which, through their dogma of faith, claim to be immune from the process of verification which is logically applicable to them as to everything else; *superstitions,* which are by their nature irrational and, as their name suggests, constitute survivals of religious systems now abandoned; and *unsolved mysteries,* which are stated with data that are normally either incomplete or prejudiced.

The compiler has not fallen into the predictable trap of believing that his is the whole truth, or even most of it (whatever "truth" is). He would be very grateful for suggestions as to ways in which the book might be improved by omission, correction, or addition. Describing an idea as a "common fallacy" does not of course thereby automatically make it so; the intention is merely to reflect the best scholarly opinion currently available and the reader's indulgence is craved for mistakes and distortions which, regrettably, as the book demonstrates, are all too obviously part of the human condition.

How to Use the Book

A. Readers not looking for any subject in particular may start anywhere and find cause for amusement or concern, depending on
   their temperament.
B. Readers interested in one particular subject should:
   1. Look up that name or subject in the INDEX. If no reference
      seems to be present, seek synonyms or heteronyms.
   2. Should there be no reference at all, check the PREFACE for
      the categories deliberately omitted from the book.
   3. Should there be a reference, consult the TEXT of the dictionary
      and, if desired, note the source (where given) for verification.
   4. Refer to the BIBLIOGRAPHY for general or specialized stud-
      ies on fallacies in your field of interest.

A

"Are you clear in your mind in regard to the following (some people would call them platitudes)?

That an idea or belief is not necessarily true or false because your parents, your friends, or you or your children have believed it.

That an idea is not necessarily false because you would hate to believe it, or true because you would like to believe it.

That an idea is not necessarily true or false because it is new, or because it is old.

That asserting a statement an infinity of times does not in itself make that statement true.

That the repeated denial of the existence of a thing does not dispose of its existence."

—ABEL J. JONES, *In search of truth* (London, 1945)

"The age of miracles is past; the age of miracles is forever here."

—THOMAS CARLYLE

ABSINTHE IS A HALLUCINOGEN

Absinthe, to most people, is fascinating and desirable, both for its literary and cultural prevalence, as well as for the fact that it is said to possess hallucinogenic properties. However, this isn't necessarily true. Absinthe as a hallucinogenic drug that drives people to insanity has been greatly exaggerated, while its dangers related to high alcohol content have gone, by and large, under the radar.

Extracts of one of absinthe's most notable ingredients, wormwood, were said to have been used as medical remedies as far back in time as the ancient Egyptian period (for gastrointestinal worms). Apparently, wormwood oil in itself is used as an herbal cure for loss of appetite, liver and gallbladder problems, and dyspeptic disorders.

(Continued)

1

The rise of absinthe as an alcoholic beverage appeared and took off in the late 19th century in Europe. The beverage was "invented" by a doctor in Switzerland, whose recipe was subsequently obtained by Henri-Louis Pernod, who began the commercial production of absinthe in 1797 and soon after brought it to the French market.

Due to an increased public interest, advertising, and a temporary decrease in red wine production due to a vine-pest, Pernod increased absinthe production from 16 liters per day to 125,000 liters in the span of 100 years. Not to mention, annual capita per consumption of absinthe in France increased a whopping fifteenfold in a mere thirty-eight years (between 1875 and 1913). Pure alcohol consumption in France was so high that if the product was spread evenly among the population, each French citizen would have been consuming 60 liters (that's almost 16 U.S. gallons) per year. In other words, if you lived in France in this time period, it would be standard practice for you to singlehandedly finish a personal gallon of straight liquor every three weeks or so.

Not surprisingly, representatives from a number of different professional backgrounds (the church, the medical field, winegrowers... etc.) took action around the same period to ban alcohol consumption. Medical studies began to provide proof that absinthe caused mental and other illness (insanity). The movements to ban alcohol were ironically backed by winegrowers and the wine industry in order to "stop alcoholism" but obviously just to eliminate the domination of absinthe in the marketplace.

Although the French government ignored the protests at first, anti-alcohol campaigns became widespread through educational programs and public awareness demonstrations, so a bill was passed in 1908. But once again, instead of banning alcohol because of its growing dangers to human health that everyone was so concerned about, the alcohol content in absinthe was raised, the logic being that if absinthe makers had to use more pure alcohol, there would be less potential for other more "artificial" ingredients to be added, and the strength of the pure alcohol would eliminate other negative additives.

Finally, not public health concerns but rather the weakening strength of the French military army due to absinthe consumption triggered the government to ban absinthe altogether in 1915. A bunch of other countries, including the United States, had already banned the drink. Not shockingly, the French public health did not improve much after this action, as they simply just switched over to other alcoholic drinks.

Before the ban on absinthe, the beverage was originally categorized officially as any drink that contained compounds taken from wormwood. Thujone was the main compound taken from wormwood and put in absinthe. This compound was said by some to be the cause for the hallucinogenic properties of absinthe back in the late 1800s/early 1900s. Thujone, not alcoholism and mental instability, was blamed for driving Pablo Picasso and Vincent Van Gogh to insanity and Edgar Allen Poe to death. Oscar Wilde drank absinthe and so therefore was clearly delusional. "We lost another great one to absinthism," fine people would lament.

However, there is still really no concrete evidence that proves thujone, or even wormwood in general, leads to hallucination. In popular culture, absinthe was extremely demonized. Doctors attributed absinthe specifically as the cause of everything from auditory and visual hallucinations and loss of consciousness to seizures and cancer. At the First International Eugenics Conference, the differences were laid out plain and clear between the alcoholic and the "absinthe-oholic." For the latter, hallucinations were said to be more extreme, terrifying, sudden in onset, and often provoking serious and dangerous acts of violence. Sounds a little like the typical raging alcoholic symptoms, if you ask us.

Furthermore, between 1867 and 1912 in Paris, 16,532 people were treated for alcoholic intoxication. Of them, 70 percent were diagnosed as chronic alcoholics, while only 1 percent were reported to have cases of "absinthism."

Absinthe is now allowed again in some European countries and the United States. It is basically made the same way with the same herbal ingredients, but there are limits in place on how much thujone can be included. Kids order absinthe online or smuggle it back from their family trip abroad in Listerine bottles in the hopes of drinking it and seeing all kinds of green fairies and psychedelic visuals as if they were tripping on LSD. However, it is not at all surprising that no one has reported hallucinatory effects of absinthe since it has been recirculated on the market. Although there is less thujone than previously, which is the factor that most young thrill seekers blame their nonexistent psychedelic trips on, people continue to get significantly more intoxicated more rapidly from drinking absinthe. This is probably because thujone alone cannot be consumed with the inclusion of copious amounts of ethyl alcohol as well.

In conclusion, drinking tons of ethyl alcohol, with or without thujone, is an obvious enough explanation for why people tended

(*Continued*)

to go crazy, experience bodily dysfunctions, and remember seeing things that were never there.

Sources: BioMed Central: *Substance Abuse Treatment, Prevention, and Policy,* "Absinthism: a Fictitious 19th Century Syndrome with Present Impact," Stephan A Padosch, Dirk W Lachenmeier, Lars U Kroner, 2006; *Science News,* "Toxin in Absinthe Makes Neurons Run Wild," Corinna Wu, 2000.

USING **ACCUTANE** LEADS TO SUICIDE

As far back as the 1980s, experts and scientists have been looking into the effects of the active ingredient in acne treatment product, Accutane, on depression, psychological disorders, and suicides. The main drug in the product, Isotretinoin, has been accused by many of actually causing or triggering depression in those who use Accutane on a daily basis.

According to the FDA, Isotretinoin has been directly linked with reported suicides and those suffering from depression. Between 1982 and 2000, the FDA recorded 37 suicide cases, 110 hospitalizations based on patients who had attempted suicide, and over 200 other reports of nonhospitalized depression patients related to this drug. However, there was still no concrete evidence proving that Accutane was the sole cause.

Depressingly, there are some who continue to stand by the conclusion that it is not the drug that causes teens and other people to become suicidal, but the severity of their acne. For instance, a fairly recent study by researchers in Sweden reviewed almost 6,000 cases of people who had been using Accutane in the 1980s compared to people who had been hospitalized. Of the 150ish people who were hospitalized, 32 of them had attempted suicide before they began acne treatment, while only 12 were reported to have done so afterwards.

The issue is controversial, as teen suicide is tragic and all measures possible should be taken to prevent it. But that an acne medication changes brain chemistry so drastically that its users suddenly become suicidal seems less likely than the frightened public assumes it to be. But for the record, we advise switching to Proactiv.

Sources: Diane K. Wysowski, PhD., "An analysis of reports of depression and suicide in patients treated with isotretinoin," *Journal of the American Academy of Dermatology*, 2001; Traci Pedersen, "Severe Acne, Not Accutane, Related to Increased Suicide Risk," *Psych Central*, 2010.

FALLACIES ON WHAT CAUSES ACNE

Here is a list of some common misconceptions on how daily habits influence pimples:

1) Chocolate

As discussed later in CHOCOLATE IS UNHEALTHY, chocolate has a pretty bad reputation in the health world. Worse than it should, we have seen. Here we go with another defense in the name of chocolate. Consuming chocolate and other sugary foods really contributes very little to the rate or severity of acne. In fact, diet itself is said to have little effect on pimple occurrence overall, or at least, there is hardly evidence to prove whether it does or does not. Therefore, we figure there are already a number of reasons to restrict diet, many of them artificial in motivation, so, why add another?

2) Stress

Stress is always problematic. Who wants to spend time stressing about arbitrary things that you are probably unable to change? No one. So the fact that psychological stress is so often listed as a trigger for physiological health issues is not just sometimes over-emphasized, but it is also frustrating, as it is not an emotion that anyone adopts by choice (as far as we know). That being said, cutting out excess stress will probably not do much to prevent acne. Although stress can be related to hormonal change, which can bring about acne, stress itself is not the cause. So, if you do try and fit thirty minutes of meditation into your stress inducing daily schedule, it should be motivated by a search for peace of mind rather than a way to clear up blemishes.

3) Smoking

Obviously, smoking is bad for you. Smoking has been shown to cause wrinkles and premature signs of aging. It is also proven to have negative effects on teeth, gums, and a number of other less appearance based health problems. However, when it comes to smoking and pimples, the correlation is less clear cut.

In fact, recent studies have shown that smokers are just as likely, if not less likely, than nonsmokers to break out. For instance, a notable study was conducted in 2006 and published in the *Journal of Investigative Dermatology*, where it was found that in men, there was no correlation between acne and smoking, while in girls, smokers actually had significantly less acne than non-nicotine addicts. Supposedly, the reason for this is the nicotine. Nicotine itself is not harmful to skin, while smoking tobacco and its additives obviously are. But experts speculate that

(Continued)

5

the reason some smokers have less acne is because of the drug, as it constricts blood vessels.

There you have it and there we said it.

Sources: *Acne.org*, "Acne Myths Explained" and "Smoking and Acne – How Cigarettes Affect the Skin"; *Acne Treatment.org*, "Does Eating Chocolate Cause Acne?"; NIAMS, "Acne."

ATHENS HAS THE ONLY **ACROPOLIS**

Many Greek cities, whether on the mainland of Greece and Asia Minor, or on the islands, had an akropolis, largely for purposes of military defence. One thinks of Tiryns on the mainland, say, or Lindos on Rhodes. *Akros* is the Greek for "topmost, highest," and *polis* means "city," so the akropolis is that upper city which is most easily defended against a besieging force. The example at Athens is merely the best-known of hundreds.

BRAIN ACTIVITIES AND OTHER ABILITIES ARE IMPAIRED WITH INCREASING **AGE**

Though aging is of course a process which often involves deterioration of certain abilities, there are brilliant exceptions which make this observation no reason for complacency among the elderly.

Mrs. Winifred A. Mould took the BA at London University at the age of seventy and was reported in the *Times of London* July 6, 1976 to be continuing her studies, while Havergal Brian wrote his Symphony no. 30 in 1967 at the age of ninety-one (one of three written that year).

Some of Robert Graves's most passionate and sensitive love poems were written in his sixties and seventies.

These examples could be multiplied a hundredfold.

BRIDES WALK UP THE **AISLE**

Not unless they lose their way they don't. "Aisle" (from the French *aile*, wing) is one of the lateral passages of a church. The bride walks along the central passage.

ALGEBRA FALLACIES

1) Algebra Is an Invention Particularly Useful to the Army

We owe to the breathtaking fantasy of Jean de Beaulieu (who of course intended it for fact) the notion that "Algebra is the curious science of scholars, and particularly for a general of an army, or a captain, in order to draw up an army quickly into battle array, and to number the musketeers and pikemen who compose it, without using arithmetic."

How does the celebrated 17th-century French mathematician, engineer, and royal geographer arrive at this conclusion? "This science has five special figures: P means plus in commerce and pikemen in the army; M means minus in commerce, but musketeers in the art of war; R signifies root in the measurement of a cube, and rank in the army; Q means square [then spelled quaré in French] in both commerce and the army; C means cube in calculation, but cavalry in the army." And how then might this dual-purpose algebra work?

"As for the operations of algebra, they are as follows: if you add a plus to a plus, the sum will be plus; to add minus to plus, take the lesser from the greater, and the remainder will be the number required. I say this only in passing, for the benefit of those who are wholly ignorant of it."

Among whom, presumably, is the Sieur de Beaulieu himself, who indeed goes on to attempt the impossible—squaring the circle—in the same remarkable book. He also wrote *La lumière des mathématiques* (Paris, 1673), and *Nouvelle invention d'arithmétique* (Paris, 1677).

2) That by algebra one can make 2 = 1
The notion has been current since George Bernard Shaw first admitted to being hoodwinked by a schoolboy friend.

Mr. Shaw's youthful experience about x and a are so highly instructive that I cannot refrain from dwelling upon them for a moment. His friend induced him to "let x = a" and Mr. Shaw—not expecting that x would take any mean advantage of the permission—granted the request. But he did not understand that in letting x = a he was also letting xt −a = 0, and the proof (of the proposition, 2 = 1) that "followed with rigorous exactness," assumed that x −a did not equal 0.

3) The algebra of William Frend
William Frend (1757-1841) was a famous Cambridge figure, who denounced the abuses of the Church and was banished (not expelled) from the University for sedition and opposition to the Liturgy following his trial of 1792. Though a mathematician of ability, Frend wrote a peculiar treatise, *The principles of algebra* (2 vols., London, 1796-9) in which he refused to use negative quantities in algebraic operations.

Indeed, Frend objected to algebra itself and—in the words of Augustus de Morgan—made "war of extermination upon all that distinguishes algebra from arithmetic." In this he was following the same line of attack as were Robert Simson (1687-1768) and Baron Francis Maseres (1731-1824).

George Peacock (1791-1858), Lowndean Professor of Astronomy at the University of Cambridge, poked gentle fun at Frend's Algebra for its "great distrust of the results of algebraical science which were in existence at the time when it was written."

Sources: Jean de Beaulieu, La géométrie françoise . . . (Paris, 1676); Philip H. Wicksteed, *The common sense of political economy* (Rev. ed., 2 vols., London, 1948, vol. II, p. 726); Augustus de Morgan, *A budget of paradoxes* (2nd ed., 2 vols., Chicago, 1915).

ALMANACS

The U.S. Weather Bureau, attacked for its inability to provide weather forecasts for more than a day or two in advance by irate individuals who use popular, fallacious almanacs such as Hicks' (U.S.) or Old Moore's (U.K.), replied in E. B. Garriott's Long range weather forecasts (Bulletin 35 of the U.S. Weather Bureau), brought up to date since. As Hering observes, "the futility of protesting in that way against the almanac forecasts is plain, since the latter keep on appearing at short and regular intervals, with constant reiteration, while the reports of scientific tests or investigations are published but once, and then meet the eyes of few readers—perhaps of none who especially ought to see them."

Source: Daniel Webster Hering, *Foibles and fallacies of science* (New York, 1924, pp. 38-57).

ALTARS

1) Altars Are of Christian Origin
Quite the reverse. The earliest Christians had no altars, and were taunted for this by the pagans, who used them for offerings to pre-Christian deities. Celsus charged the Christians with being a secret society for their refusal to build temples or raise altars, to which Origen replied that the altars were the heart of every Christian.

Altars have been found from the earliest remains of Babylonian cities, from Egypt and from Palestine.

Source: *Encyclopaedia Britannica*, 11th ed. (1910-11), art. Altar.

2) All Churches Have Their Altar in the East End
Many West European churches are built in relation to the rising sun, hence the term "orientation," with the altar at the east end. The main façade is consequently often spoken of as the West Front.

However, there is no necessity for this, and hundreds of churches have their main altar at the west end, including St. Peter's in Vatican City.

AMPHIBOLY

A linguistic fallacy due to double meanings of words, or phrases or sentences including words with double meanings.

Abraham Fraunce, in The lawiers logike, exemplifying the praecepts of logike by the practice of the common lawe (London, 1588) defined amphiboly as any case "when the sentence may be turned both the wayes, so that a man shall be uncertayne what waye to take, . . . as that olde sophister the Devill deluded Pyrrhus by giving him such an intricate answere: Aio te, Aeacida, Romanos vincere posse."

The Latin sentence can be construed both "I say that the Romans can conquer you" and "I say that you can conquer the Romans," Aeacida referring to King Pyrrhus. (This cunning use of the Latin accusative-and-infinitive construction also helps to demonstrate the fallaciousness of a Latin teacher's argument that the correct application of case-endings will wholly prevent ambiguity in a Latin text).

Note further that Fraunce's example is doubly ambiguous by the use of posse ("can"), implying that the prediction is equally true if either of the eventualities cunningly prophesied fail to occur.

However, I prefer the wartime austerity slogan offered by Irving Copi, in his *Introduction to logic* (2nd ed., New York, 1961) to illustrate amphiboly: *Save Soap and Waste Paper*.

AMULETS

An amulet is a charm worn on some part of the body, usually around the neck or wrist. Most of the ancient amulets are of ancient Eastern provenance, but E. A. W. Budge showed (*Amulets and Talismans*, New York, 1961) that all cultures have suffered the delusions of the amulet's power. "The truth seems to be," wrote Budge, "that primitive man believed that every object which he used as an amulet possessed, either as a result of its natural formation or through the operation of some supernatural spirit which had incorporated itself in it, a power which to him was invisible. It was this power which, existing in everything, animate and inanimate, turned every object into an amulet, and as such it became a prized possession."

A detailed study of American servicemen by social psychologists recorded that Americans normally carry into battle such amulets as crosses, Bibles, four-leafed clovers, rabbit's-foot charms, billikens, kewpie dolls and dice.

Italian troops by contrast were discovered to favor miniature sucking-pig amulets; Japanese soldiers engraved black carp on their sword-guards; and Indian infantrymen preferred animal or human teeth set in gold mounts. All amulets are equally useless in themselves.

The amulet is merely a superstitious object, but the real belief in its efficacy, which seems widespread not only in the miscalled "primitive" cultures but also in the literacy-based cultures, is a fallacy.

Source: Raymond Lamont Brown, *A casebook of military mystery* (Cambridge, 1974).

DERYAGIN AND **ANOMALOUS** WATER

In the early 1960s, a Russian physical chemist called Boris Deryagin reported to a puzzled scientific press certain unusual phenomena in water condensed from the vapor in fine glass capillaries. His view that the compound H_2O has more than one liquid form was apparently confirmed by the strange behavior on melting, unusual Raman spectrum, and high viscosity. Hundreds of detailed experiments were carried out in the United States, the Soviet Union and elsewhere to explore this discovery; it was argued that it must be a polymer of ordinary water and was accordingly called "polywater."

However, there is no such thing as "anomalous water" or "polywater." The anomalous properties of the condensate must have been due to a number of chemical impurities dissolved from the glass: one such impurity was human sweat!

Source: Leland Allen, in *New Scientist*, August 16, 1973, p. 376.

WATER IS AN **APHRODISIAC**

Not many substances are aphrodisiac (sex appeal is after all rather a subjective matter, not easily induced unless there is a marked propensity for it) but Nicolas Venette, in *La génération de l'homme* (Paris, 1690) went altogether too far: "After all," he wrote, "the celebrated Tiraqueau could not have engendered thirty-nine legitimate children, if he had not been a drinker of water: and the Turks would not have had several wives today, if wine had not been prohibited to them."

Alcohol is often thought to have aphrodisiac qualities, but alcohol does not so much increase the appetite for love as decrease the fear of its consequences. Modern aphrodisiac lore places the mistaken faith in raw eggs that Casanova placed in oysters, the Elizabethans in prunes, potatoes and tobacco, and classical antiquity in onions. All the remedies are thought to be inefficacious of themselves.

APPORTS

In the psychic world that occultists claim we live in, "apports" are alleged to be material objects transmitted by the will of a medium or psychic from one place to a distant place by means other than those allowed by materialistic science.

The most widely reported "apport" in the history of the world so far is the Uri Geller—Andrija Puharich banknote case of 1973. Psychic magazine published the following words by Geller in their June 1973 issue: "One experiment I did with Andrija Puharich was when he asked me to go to Brazil out of the body. I got to this city and asked a person where I was and he told me it was Rio de Janeiro. Then someone came up to me and pressed a brand new one-thousand cruzeiro note in my hand on the couch by Andrija—to prove I was there."

At last we have a testable story! Every banknote of course carries a consecutive running number, allowing us to date the note with absolute precision. One reader decided to check up on this story, and G. L. Playfair published the results of his investigation for all to read in *The New Scientist* of November 14, 1974.

The 1000-cruzeiro banknotes went into circulation in 1963, so could not conceivably have been "brand new" ten years later: they were in fact no longer in circulation in 1973. We know that Andrija Puharich himself visited Brazil in 1963, when a 1000-cruzeiro note was worth about 40 pence and thus not worth changing at a bank on departure.

Since G. L. Playfair's deductions were unacceptable to those temperamentally susceptible to claims for the paranormal, the fact remains that psychics and their supporters regularly claim that "apports" may occur, despite physical laws which seem to rule them out. The crux must lie in the size of the apports. If psychic laws are different from physical laws, and "apports" are genuine, then the weight and size of the apports should be limitless. In fact—as far as records are available—"apports" are invariably of a size easily portable by a medium or a medium's assistant, or easily purveyed by a conjuror of normal attainment.

THE **ARCTIC** IS SIGNIFICANTLY COLDER AND SNOWIER THAN THE REST OF THE WORLD COLD

These popular errors stem from an ignorant assumption that cold increases in close proportion to distance north (or south) of the Equator. But more snow falls in Virginia, U.S.A., than in the Arctic lowlands. Reykjavik, Iceland's capital, is only just below the Arctic Circle, but its mean annual temperature is actually higher than that of New York City. Montana has recorded a temperature 10 degrees Fahrenheit colder than the North Pole's record.

Sources: Merle Colby, *A guide to Alaska* (New York, 1939, p. xliv).

JOHN LOCKE ON **ARGUMENTS**

In his Essay concerning human understanding (London, 1690; ed. by John W. Yolton, 2 vols., London, 1961), John Locke (1632-1704) deals with the imperfections of ideas—clear and obscure, distinct and confused, real and fantastical, adequate and inadequate; with the imperfections of words; and with knowledge and opinion, the last-named comprising Book IV. Perhaps the most cogent passage is one occurring near the end of the chapter "Of Reason":

"It may be worth our while a little to reflect on four sorts of arguments that men, in their reasonings with others, do ordinarily make use of to prevail on their assent, or at least so to awe them as to silence their opposition.

First, The first is to allege the opinions of men whose parts, learning, eminency, power, or some other cause has gained a name and settled their reputation in the common esteem with some kind of authority. When men are established in any kind of dignity, it is thought a breach of modesty for others to derogate any way from it, and question the authority of men who are in possession of it. This is apt to be censured as carrying with it too much of pride, when a man does not readily yield to the determination of approved authors which is wont to be received with respect and submission by others; and it is looked upon as insolence for a man to set up and adhere to his own opinion against the current stream of antiquity, or to put it in the balance against that of some learned doctor or otherwise approved writer. Whoever backs his tenets with such authorities thinks he ought thereby to carry the cause, and is ready to style it impudence in anyone who shall stand out against them. This I think may be called argumentum ad verecundiam.

Secondly, Another way that men ordinarily use to drive others and force them to submit their judgements and receive the opinion in debate is to require the adversary to admit what they allege as a proof, or to assign a better. And this I call argumentum ad ignorantiam.

Thirdly, A third way is to press a man with consequences drawn from his own principles or concessions. This is already known under the name of argumentum ad nominem.

Fourthly, The fourth is the using of proofs drawn from any of the foundations of knowledge or probability. This I call argumentum ad judicium. This alone of all the four brings true instruction with it and advances us in our way to knowledge. For: (1) It argues not another man's opinion to be right because I, out of respect or any other consideration but that of conviction, will not contradict him. (2) It proves not another man to be in the right way, nor that I ought to take the same with him, because I know not a better. (3) Nor does it follow that another man is in the right way because he has shown me that I am in the wrong. I may be modest and therefor not oppose another man's persuasion; I may be ignorant and not be able to produce a better; I may be in an error and another may show me that I am so. This may dispose me, perhaps, for the reception of truth but helps me not to it; that must come from proofs and arguments and light arising from the nature of things themselves, and not from my shamefacedness, ignorance, or error."

THE "MIRACULOUS CURES" OF ZE **ARIGÓ**

John G. Fuller, in a sensationally written and credulous book entitled *Arigó: Surgeon of the Rusty Knife* (New York, 1974), has described how Sao Paulo in Brazil is a center for doctors who believe in the ideas of "Allan Kardec." A French mystic whose real name was Leon Dénizard Hippolyte Rivail had taught that it is possible for unqualified and unskilled "doctors" to receive instructions about the symptoms and treatment of patients through mediums who are in contact with deceased doctors and surgeons. Fuller quotes the following words of Kardec: "The spiritual world is in constant contact with the material world, each reacting constantly on the other. This is what the spirits themselves have dictated. If your reason says "no," then reject it." [All dogmas bear this same postscript, whether overt or covert.]

The most famous of the Kardecist doctor-surgeons who possess no medical qualifications at all was the late Jose de Freitas, known as Ze Arigó, who lived in the village of Con-gonhas do Campo, in the state of Minas Gerais. Arigó, who was sentenced to sixteen months in jail for witchcraft in 1964, claimed that it was not he who diagnosed and treated the ailments of his patients; he was merely the recipient of guidance from a German physician, one Adolf Fritz, who had died in 1918, and was passing his secrets on to Arigó. When asked "Does the voice speak to you in German or Portuguese?" the healer replied, "I always hear it in Portuguese. I don't know German. I don't understand what I'm saying."

The following which Arigó had enjoyed among the Brazilian peasants, who are desperate for any medical treatment in a nation without a free health service, led to his becoming an important figure in the rural communities of Minas Gerais, and his pronouncements were awaited with bated breath. One such edict was that a husband was justified in taking a fresh wife if his first wife smoked a cigarette.

Arigó has been filmed for television. Viewers apparently saw him extract a patient's eye, seemingly without anaesthetic and without the patient's feeling any considerable pain. The healer then seemed to put the eye back in.

A Western doctor familiar with eye surgery, however, cast grave doubt on the "operation." He claimed that the eye filmed must have been a rubber demonstration eye used for teaching purposes, since the optic nerve is completely floppy after a real eye is removed, whereas viewers in the film saw a stiff nerve.

13

Nobody can deny that, by an extraordinary effort of autosuggestion, it is possible for a patient to overcome certain physical disabilities, or to minimize the amount of pain they are suffering. It is equally true that roughly 70 percent to 75 percent of all medical problems clear themselves up without any form of medication. But it has not yet been proved that Kardecism works, that Arigó's "cures" had any lasting effects, and that fraud in faith healing is always absent.

See also **Philippine Psychic Surgery** under PSYCHIC FALLACIES.

ARISTOTLE COMMITTED SUICIDE BY DROWNING

One of the two greatest philosophers that classical Greek civilization produced, Aristotle, died in the year 322 B.C., a year after the death of Alexander (one of his pupils) and of his own retirement to Euboea. His prior and posterior analytics ("analytics" being his word for what we know as logic), written probably between 350 and 344, are still available in a handy edition and translation by John Warrington (London, 1964), who has called the book "one of the greatest achievements of the human intellect; [it] served for more than two thousand years as the controlling instrument of western thought in every department of knowledge, human and divine."

There is absolutely no reason for thinking that Aristotle died any other than a natural death according to Ingemar During, but Procopius, Justin Martyr and others passed on the mistaken belief that Aristotle drowned himself in the narrow strait of Euripus, separating Boeotia from Euboea by only forty meters or so near the town of Chalkis.

Let the inimitable Sir Thomas Browne take up the story: "That Aristotle drowned himselfe in Euripus as despairing to resolve the cause of its reciprocation, or ebbe and flow seven times a day, with this determination, *Si quidem ego non capio te tu copies me* ['If I don't understand (lit. "seize") you, you will seize me,'] was the assertion of Procopius, Nazianzen, Justin Martyr, and is generally beleeved amongst us; wherein, because we perceive men have but an imperfect knowledge, some conceiving Euripus to be a River, others not knowing where or in what part to place it. . . ."

Sources include: Sir Thomas Browne, *Pseudodoxia epidemica* (London, 1646); and Ingemar During, *Aristotle in the ancient biographical tradition* (Gothenburg, 1957).

FALLACIES IN ART

The best general work on such topics as false perspective and optical illusions in art is E. H. Gombrich's *Art and illusion: a study in the psychology of pictorial representation* (London, 1960; 2nd ed., 1962).

Gombrich illustrates the "Fraser spiral" which is a fallacy, since it only appears to be a spiral: closer examination reveals a series of concentric circles. This illusion operates through the spectator's tendency to take on trust the continuation of a series which turns out to be less simple than one had thought. Leonardo da Vinci's sfumato, the deliberately blurred image, works on the same principle of reducing the amount of information on a canvas to stimulate the spectator's powers of projection. Titian's contemporary, Daniele Barbara, writes of the technique of sfumato which leads us to "understand what one does not see." The fallacy is that one could often be persuaded to swear that what one imagines is actually "there," a technique used by certain film directors too.

Trompe l'oeil (deception of the eye) relies on the spectator's reinforcement of expectation over the artist's illusion. Dutch art is full of such effects, in still life and in architectural compositions, the most interesting perhaps being the peepshow box painted by Samuel van Hoogstraten (1627-1678) in the National Gallery, London. One can see, through two peepholes at opposite ends of the box, typical tiled floors and various "rooms" with a range of illusionistic effects including coats and hats "hung up" and a "dog" awaiting the visitor who is presumably oneself.

The most ingenious trompe l'oeil demonstrations yet devised are probably those by Adelbert Ames, Jr. In one peepshow he allows us three peepholes, through each of which we apparently see a chair: we recognize the apparent shape of a chair, and because we recognize it we wish it to be a chair. However, only the first is a chair-object; the right-hand object is a distorted object which assumes the appearance of a chair only from the one angle at which we viewed it through the peephole; the middle object is merely a variety of wires extended in front of a backdrop on which is painted what we took to be the seat of a chair.

William Hogarth's engraving False perspective (1754), said to be a satire on a dilettante nobleman whom he wished to ridicule, indicated a number of visual fallacies against the laws of perspective. Maurits Cornells Escher, a Dutch artist born in 1898, has devoted much of his life to creating impossible (and hence fallacious) waterfalls, buildings, staircases, and spiral forms which can exist in the two dimensions of the print but are incapable of reproduction in three dimensions (see his *Graphic work*, 2nd ed., London, 1967 for reproductions and the artist's commentary). A cube-shaped building, for instance, has openings in five visible walls on to three different landscapes. "Through the topmost pair one looks down, almost vertically, on to the ground; the middle two are at eye-level and show the horizon, while through the bottom pair one looks straight up to the stars. Each plane of the building, which unites nadir, horizon and zenith, has a threefold function. For instance, the rear plane in the centre serves as a wall in relation to the horizon, a floor in connection with the view through the top opening, and a ceiling so far as the view up towards the starry sky is concerned."

Fakes and forgeries in art, such as the "Vermeers" passed off by van Meegeren to Hermann Goering as original during World War II, show the fallacy that it is possible for an expert to detect the difference between an original and a fake. Alceo Dossena (1878-1937) had forged a vast number of sculptures from Greek to Gothic and Renaissance styles before the characteristics of his style were detected, and even now it is almost certain that much of his work is still at large, credited to the period which he was copying. Jean-Baptiste-Camille Corot's landscapes were and are among the easiest masterpieces to copy. The Jousseaume collection of 2,414 spurious Corots was acquired over many years, mainly from obscure dealers and at very low prices: none appeared in Robaut's catalogue of Corot's works published in 1905 and so a mysterious rumor about Corot's "secret" output was invented and the worthless legacy of Jousseaume was turned into a goldmine.

ASTROLOGY FALLACIES

1. Astrology is Scientific

A former Astronomer Royal, Sir William Christie, sent the following duplicated reply to those who plagued him with questions on astrology:

Sir or Madam,
I am directed by the Astronomer Royal to inform you that he is unable to rule your planets. Persons professing to do so are rogues and vagabonds.
I am, yours faithfully,

(Secretary).

If you or anyone in your household has ever tempted to "read the stars" or "have your fortune told, dearie," please recall the stern legal warning from 5 Geo. IV c. 83 which is still in force:

"And be it further enacted that . . . every Person pretending or professing to tell Fortunes, or using any subtle Craft, Means, or Device, by Palmistry or otherwise, to deceive and impose on any of His Majesty's Subjects . . . shall be deemed a Rogue and Vagabond, within the true Intent and Meaning of this Act; and it shall be lawful for any Justice of the Peace to commit such Offender . . . to the House of Correction, there to be kept to hard Labor for any Time not exceeding Three Calendar Months. . . ."

Those who smile at astrologists and excuse them on the grounds that we should not have had astronomy without an interest in superstitious astrology are forgetting that ignorance is excusable only before the state of knowledge has so advanced that further preying on ignorance can be construed only as fraud.

There is of course no possible correlation between the stars or the planets in their movements and the fate of human beings on earth, their character, or their luck. The ignorance characteristic of all earnest astrologers can be illustrated from the modern prediction that a man will catch cold with unusual frequency if he was born when Saturn is opposite the sun in the sky because Saturn is the coldest planet! Even if there were any connection between a man's health and the planets (which there is not), it must now be told that Saturn was only the coldest planet known until the discovery of Uranus, Neptune and Pluto. . . .

The fallacy in the study of cosmic objects and events is their "interpretation" as portents and heralds of human fate. The study of the heavens with this intent developed astrology. It required the study of the celestial positions and movements for interest in their laws alone to establish astronomy. Not only motive but the level of logical method shapes inquiry; the beliefs of astrology proceed on the folklore level, elaborated by learned doctrines; the conclusions of astronomy are framed—with whatever measure of error and imperfection—on the scientific level of investigation.

Patrick Moore wrote a simple, careful explanation of the fallacy of astrology in *Can you speak Venusian?* (London, 1976, pp. 121-8).

"The horoscope remains as the blue ribbon exhibit of the misuse of intelligence," concluded Joseph Jastrow in his *The story of human error* (New York, 1936).

One frightening feature of superstitious astrology (which is the only kind of astrology there is) is the unknown degree of its power over every human mind—not only mine but his, hers, and yours. Even the most intelligent skeptic glances cynically yet compulsively over any horoscope he is shown. In *The dawn of magic* (London, 1963), Louis Pauwels and Jacques Bergier offer unsubstantiated figures which, if correct, constitute a terrible indictment of human credulity. In the early 1960s there were "in the United States more than 30,000 astrologers, and 20 magazines exclusively devoted to astrology, one of which [had] a circulation of 500,000." More than 2,000 newspapers had an astrological column, and it is reasonable to suppose that if that number has been reduced, it is because of the mortality among newspapers rather than among astrological columns. Pauwels and Bergier claimed that in 1943 five million Americans followed the advice of these "prophets" and spent

17

U.S. $200 million on buying prophecies and advice based on these prophecies,

Francois Le Lionnais has studied this problem in *Une maladie des civilisations: Les fausses sciences in La Nef* (no. 6, June 1954), finding that in France during the mid-fifties there were 40,000 "healers" and 50,000 practising occultists of all types. Le Lionnais estimated that fees paid to "prophets," radiesthetists, clairvoyants and such amounted to Frs. 50,000 million a year in Paris alone and probably Frs. 300,000 million a year throughout the nation, which was far more than the total budget for scientific research.

Pauwels and Bergier are "sure that the fact that occultism and the pseudo-sciences are at present in such high favor with an enormous public is an unhealthy symptom. It is not cracked mirrors that bring bad luck, but cracked brains." Sources include: Rupert T. Gould, *Oddities*, 2nd ed. (London, 1944) and *The Humanist* (Buffalo, N.Y.), September-October 1975 (studies by Bart J. Bok and Lawrence E. Jerome), with signatures against astrology by 186 leading scientists, including eighteen Nobel Prizewinners.

2. Belomancy

Divination by arrows. Various admonitions were attached to arrows and then given to archers, who let them fly. The label on the arrow which flew the farthest was then read and, in theory at least, the advice on it was carried out.

Evidence for this form of divination occurs in Sir Thomas Browne's magnificent compendium of vulgar errors, *Pseudodoxia epidemica* (V, 23), where he describes the use of belomancy (Gk. belos=arrow) "with Scythians, Alanes, Germans, with the Africans and Turks of Algier."

A moment's reflection will show that one simply wrote a label with the advice that one wanted to follow and gave it to the strongest and most practiced archer, much as the modern reader of *Woman's Own* looks up her horoscope, and then follows just that advice which seems to her the most desirable.

3. Horoscopes in Diaries

Michael Watts, of the London *Sunday Express,* has drawn attention to the hilarious error in the *Ladies Diary* discovered by Mrs. Ann Palmer, of Ash, near Aldershot.

Mrs. Palmer checked on her horoscope (Libra) in the 1977 diary and found that it read "You are an excellent organizer and may find yourself concerned with local affairs. Take care this year that you do not overwork. You will have a full social life which you will enjoy immensely." Mrs. Palmer recollected reading something like that before. The Libra horoscope in the 1976 *Ladies Diary* ran: "You are an excellent organizer and may find yourself concerned with local affairs . . . " word for word identical with the new horoscope. So were all the others. Michael Watts challenged the publishers of the diary, T. J. & J. Smith, who told him: "To our horror you're right. The predictions from the 1976 diary have been used again this year by mistake. We've sold many, many thousands already, but nobody has spotted the error until now. However, all our diaries contain a clause which says: "Whilst great care has been taken in compiling the information in this diary, the publishers cannot accept responsibility for any errors."

"Still," concludes Michael Watts, "you ladies might as well follow that horoscope advice in your 1977 diaries, and believe the predictions. For they are just as likely to hold true for this year as for last. Or not, as the case may be."

4. Making Love With the Use of Astrology
Planets in love: exploring your emotional and sexual needs (Rockport, Ma., 1978) is a book by John Townley published by Para Research Inc., Whistlestop Mall, Rockport, Ma. 01966.

Katherine de Zengotita, reviewing this guide to making love by the expert use of a particular kind of astrology, has said: "This is the latest in a series of astrological reference books by this publisher. The others have been inoffensive, if uninspired. This one, with a long appendix on sado-masochism as a "road to spiritual transcendence," is offensive and uninspired."

Source: *Library Journal* (New York), October 1, 1978.

5. The Zodiac Has Thirteen Signs
The "zodiac" (Gk. *o zodiakos kuklos,* "the zodiacal zone," *zodion* meaning "a little animal") is an astrological area in which lie the paths of the sun, the moon, and the chief planets of our solar system. The art of divining the fate or future of persons from the relative positions of the sun, moon and planets is astrology (technically, "judicial astrology").

However, the twelve constellations which corresponded at the time of Hipparchus (fl. 161-127 B.C.) to the signs Aries, Taurus, Gemini, Cancer, Leo, Virgo, Libra, Scorpio, Sagittarius, Capricorn, Aquarius, and Pisces, so that the sign Aquarius corresponded to the constellation Aquarius, no longer correspond, as a result of equinoctial precession. The system was based on March 21 as the first point in Aries, whereas it is now in Aquarius, so all the signs are wrong. As the whole of astrology is based on the fallacious idea of correspondence between heavenly bodies and earthly lives, this further error in astrological predictions and assumptions is perhaps not as crucial as a comparable error would be in a serious discipline.

What is perhaps astonishing is that an author has recently discovered a "thirteenth" sign of the zodiac which had escaped the notice of all previous writers. James Vogh, in *Arachne rising: the thirteenth sign of the zodiac* (London, 1977), suggests that a thirteenth sign was in fact "lost" in the mists of history. Needless to say, if the hypothesis were true it would be useless, but it is almost certainly false.

THE **ATLANTIC** OCEAN IS NARROW

The first fallacy is that we mean the same "atlantic" as did the ancient geographers. For us, the Atlantic Ocean is definable as that stretch of water dividing the eastern coasts of the American continent from the western coasts of Western Europe and Africa. Throughout the classical period, however, the term denoted the waters between the western and eastern extremities of the Old World, for they had no conception of the New. Their view that the Mediterranean was the center of the world pervaded medieval geography up to and including Columbus.

Briefly, in the 3rd century B.C. Eratosthenes of Alexandria solved the problem of calculating a line on Earth by the rules of spherical geometry, given the measure in units of distance of the length of an arc of a great circle (whether equator or meridian circle) on the Earth's surface. Eratosthenes discovered that at Aswan (then called Syene) the sun is at zenith at noon on the summer solstice, so the town must be situated on the Tropic of Cancer. Measuring the angle between zenith and the noon position of the sun on the summer solstice at Alexandria, he found it to be one fiftieth of a circle, corresponding to seven and one-fifth degrees. Supposing that Syene and Alexandria were on the same meridian, 5,000 stadia apart, the length of a meridian circle (and hence the length of any great circle on the earth) was found by multiplying 5,000 stadia by 50, or a total of 250,000 stadia. To obtain a number divisible by 360, he added 2,000 stadia, a grand total of 252,000 stadia, so that by modern units of measurement he estimated the circumference of the Earth at 25,740 miles. It is now known that the Equator measures 24,900 miles, but the high degree of accuracy is only apparent due to the cancelling out of errors in the original data.

Now Eratosthenes faced the problem of assigning a dimension to the lands then known, and placing them on a map. He assumed that the longest piece of land lay at about latitude 36°N, on the parallel of Rhodes. He estimated—again more by the luck of cancelling errors than by his own geographical knowledge—that the length of the lands along this parallel was enough to stretch through an arc of 130° of longitude. The final figure was again remarkably close to current knowledge.

Columbus did not know of Eratosthenes, but only of Ptolemy, whose mistakes derived from Posidonius (2nd century B.C.) through Marinus of Tyre. Posidonius had shown a difference in latitude of one and one-half degrees between Alexandria and Rhodes, corresponding to about 3,750 stadia. His arc of the meridian between the two cities was one forty-eighth of the Earth's circumference, the total circumference therefore being $48 \times 3,750$ stadia, a total of 180,000 stadia and consequently very far from the true figure.

By the time of Marinus, news was available of lands east of India: that is to say, at the easternmost part of the known world. Marinus therefore estimated that the land mass extended through 225° of longitude on the parallel of Rhodes. Ptolemy disagreed, and reduced the estimate of Marinus by half, but he recorded the views of his predecessor, and both views came down to Columbus, together with the view of the Arab astronomer al-Farghani (known in Europe as Alfragan), transmitted through Roger Bacon and Pierre d'Ailly, that the Earth was actually smaller still. D'Ailly repeatedly asserts that the Atlantic (or western sea) is very narrow, though no specific width is mentioned in his tract (Louvain, 1483), commonly known as the Imago mundi.

Columbus paid no heed to the correction of Marinus by Ptolemy, but made his own corrections, narrowing even further the estimated gap between the west coast of Europe and the east coast of "asia." Columbus was impressed by Marco Polo's expansive notions of Asia, and by Portuguese reports of the Azores and the Cape Verde Islands, two factors which combined to reduce once more the estimated width of the Atlantic. Columbus believed the waters to extend no wider than 120 degrees of longitude, or a third of the length of the parallel along which he intended to sail westward. (In fact he sailed roughly on the parallel of the Canary Islands: about 28°N.)

If Columbus had believed Ptolemy, he would have been much closer to the truth in planning to cross the wide ocean and would have had to carry far more stores than his ships could bear.

Source: John Leighly, "Error in geography" in Joseph Jastrow, ed., *The story of human error* (New York, 1936).

ATLANTIS

The myth that an "atlantis" once existed occurs first in Plato, where the imaginary island, full of pomp and luxury, is sited near the Straits of Gibraltar, "beyond the Pillars of Hercules." Plato says he heard of Atlantis from Solon, who had heard it from Egyptian priests, who dated the flooding of Atlantis to 9,000 years before Solon's birth. Regrettably for this theory, the present level of the Atlantic Ocean has remained constant for several million years, according to geologists and oceanographers. The civilization described by Plato is not altogether dissimilar to the Minoan culture centered on Crete, which disappeared abruptly late in the 15th century B.C. But recent archaeological findings suggest that the Minoan Empire was destroyed by a single volcanic explosion. Thera (the largest of three islands in the small archipelago now called Santorini) is a volcanic island in the Eastern Mediterranean which suffered an eruption in 1470 B.C., its mountain about 4,900 feet high exploding so violently that the center of the island dropped into a hole about 1,200 feet below sea level. The island was covered in a hundred feet of volcanic ash, but this was 900 not 9,000 years before Solon's birth, so that both time and place are radically different from Plato's story in the Critias and the Timaeus.

The most remarkable fantasies concerning the fallacious belief in an actual Atlantis were perpetrated by the Minnesota Irishman Ignatius Donnelly, known as the U.S. Prince of Cranks, in *Atlantis: the Antediluvian World* (New York, 1882), a work of immense popularity not only in Victorian times (when it was absorbed by Madame Blavatsky into her *Secret Doctrine* of 1888) but right up to the present day, when successive editions are appearing with the enthusiastic revisions of Egerton Sykes (the latest in 1970).

Briefly, Donnelly asserted that Atlantis was the Biblical Paradise which existed on a huge continent in the Atlantic Ocean. Mankind there arose from barbarism after a glacial epoch and developed the world's first civilization which worshipped the sun. Colonizers from Atlantis spread their advanced technological knowledge all over the world, and were the first to inhabit Asia, Europe, and the Americas. Atlantean kings and queens became the gods and goddesses of the ancient religions. Atlantis was entirely submerged about 13,000 years ago by floods which followed a volcanic cataclysm.

William Ewart Gladstone, whose logical abilities may be assessed from his argument that the ancient Greeks were colorblind because few color-words occur in Homer, asked the British Cabinet for funds to send a ship into the Atlantic to trace the outline of the sunken continent. The otherwise eminent folk-lorist Lewis Spence, a Scottish Presbyterian, thought that the Atlanteans were a composite race with large brains, and that their first colonists of Europe were of the Cro-Magnon type. "If a patriotic Scotsman may be pardoned the boast," he wrote in *The problem of Atlantis* (London, 1924), "I may say that I devoutly believe that Scotland's admitted superiority in the mental and spiritual spheres springs almost entirely from the preponderant degree of Cro-Magnon blood which certainly runs in the veins of her people ... " Of the thousands of books and pamphlets on Atlantis which have gushed from the presses of the world since the Middle Ages, Spence's *Atlantis in America* (London, 1925) and *The History of Atlantis* (London, 1926) are among the least peculiar.

The connections between the occultists and Atlantis, fostered by Blavatsky and the Theosophists, were strengthened by the clairvoyant methods of Rudolf Steiner and the Anthroposophists, whose theories of Atlantis were based on W. Scott-Elliot's *The story of Atlantis and the lost Lemuria* (1914), a theosophical work speculating on the seven sub-races whom Scott-Elliot believed to have inhabited Atlantis in succession.

Steiner's own *Atlantis and Lemuria* (1923) claimed occult knowledge from the Akashic record (a hypothetical bank of all events, ideas and emotions that have ever occurred said by some occultists to be preserved in the "astral plane") to describe Atlantean history. According to Steiner, the Atlanteans used the energy latent in plants to drive airships.

The occultist Edgar Cayce predicted that Atlantis would rise again in 1968 or 1969.

The British witch Alex Sanders, in reviewing Francis King's *Ritual magic in England* (London, 1970), claimed that the book's appendices had been "brought through by the Hidden Masters from Atlantis."

The search for Atlantis is never-ending because there is nothing to find. If the continent was totally destroyed, how is it possible for enthusiasts to demonstrate that artefacts claimed to be Atlantean do in fact survive? Exactly how is their knowledge obtained if all Atlanteans perished with Atlantis? If it is all a parable or metaphor, why does not somebody, somewhere, say so? Jürgen Spannuth's quest for Atlantis, published in 1956, ended "off Heligoland."

Karl Georg Zschaetzsch believed the Atlanteans to have been the original Aryans, and the only survivors of the destruction of Atlantis to have been Wotan, his daughter, and his pregnant sister, who sought refuge in a cave among the roots of a giant tree beside a cold geyser. Wotan's sister died in childbirth and a she-wolf suckled her infant. The pure, noble "blood" of these Wagnerian characters was inevitably mingled with that of non-Aryans on the European continent; Zschaetzsch's pernicious nonsense was merely one of the strands in Hitler's occultist mania to purify the world.

Another hypothesis identifying Atlantis with Corsica was answered at the Congress of the Society for Atlantis Studies held in Paris in 1929 by the hurling of tear-gas bombs.

Thus is the irrational answered by the irrational.

Robert J. Scrutton has claimed that there is not only the Atlantis known from fantasy since the time of Plato, but also a second Atlantis that we did not know about.

According to Scrutton, a large semi-circular land mass (a sort of silhouette halo around the North and East of the British Isles), was contemporary with the better-known Atlantis. However, it survived its famous namesake by many thousands of years. Its name was "Atland"

and, although situated between the storm-racked Hebrides and the Greenland "permafrost' [this notion is itself incorrect—Ph.W.], Atland was no impoverished continent, but enjoyed a sub-tropical climate, yielding all that was required for a contented human life. In the year 2193 a cosmic calamity struck the Earth, in Scrutton's view perhaps that imbalance noted by Velikovsky, or collision with an asteroid. In either event, within three days climatic changes of "overwhelming severity took place. Atland was submerged and her history lost . . . or nearly so."

In 1256 (again to quote the extraordinary pages of Scrutton's book), Hiddo Over de Linda of Friesland recopied all existing material on Atland on to the new cotton-based paper which the Arabs had recently brought to Spain. Copies were made in each succeeding generation so that the secrets of Atland were always available to a select few until 1848, when A. Meylhof (née Over de Linden) handed it to her nephew Cornelius Over de Linden. He decided to allow a copy of the document to be made by Dr. E. Verwijs, Librarian of the Provincial Library of Leeuwarden, the provincial capital of Friesland. However, the Frisian Society rudely declined to finance the translation, edition, printing and publishing of *Thet Oera Linda Bok*, stating that in their opinion the document was a hoax.

M. de Jong, in *The secret of the Oera Linda Book* (1927), claimed that Dr. Verwijs was the forger, while J. F. Hof believed that Verwijs collaborated with Over de Linden in the fraud, and R. C. J. A. Boles expressed the view that Over de Linden was the sole perpetrator of the whole absurd story. The Oera Linda Book, with the original Frisian text, and an English version of Dr. Ottema's Dutch translation by W. R. Sandbach, was published by Trubner's of London in 1876. Scrutton even now—unless he has recently changed his mind—assumes the book to be authentic, and says that "athens" (yes, the capital of Greece) is a word meaning "friends" in Old Frisian, and that Athens was a colony of Atland founded by Frisians.

If you need any more, Secrets of Lost Atland is announced as a sequel to The other Atlantis. Would anyone who actually believes any of it please let us know?

Sources include: Martin Gardner, *Fads and fallacies in the name of science* (New York, 1957) and A. G. Galanopoulos and Edward Bacon, *Atlantis: the truth behind the legend* (London, 1965); Robert J. Scrutton, *The other Atlantis*, edited by Ken Johnson (St. Helier, Jersey, 1977).

AUBURN ORIGINALLY MEANT REDDISH-BROWN

The Latin "albumus" (whitish, nearly white) passed through many forms in English, from the Old French "alborne, auborne," to reach its present spelling.

It was as late as the 16th century that we find the common forms like "abroun" which induced many English-speakers to compare and even to derive the word from the root for "brown," and thus pervert the original meaning of a color related to white to that of a color related to brown.

By the time we come to Scott's "Marmion" (1808), the poet can write (v., ix): "And auburn of the darkest dye, His short curled beard and hair. . . ."

Source: *Oxford English Dictionary*.

AUTOBIOGRAPHICAL FALLACIES

"It is doubtful whether it is humanly possible to write an entirely true autobiography. If a man deals frankly with his weaknesses he may be merely an exhibitionist. Dr. Johnson once said that all condemnation of self was oblique praise: it was to show how much a man can spare. On the other hand most men are too modest to speak openly of their achievements.

"Volumes of reminiscences are often full of inaccuracies, due to their being written, for the most part, many years after the events. E. F. Benson, in his last work, *Final edition* (published posthumously), gives several examples from published reminiscences of reported incidents that could never have occurred. On one of these writers he commented: 'It is not his memory that had failed, but his imagination that had flowered.'

"I am fond of reading autobiographies, but I read them for their anecdotes and the glimpses they afford into the character of the writer; I realize that they are among the least reliable of historical literature so far as truth is concerned."

See also HISTORICAL FALLACIES.

Source: Abel J. Jones, *In search of truth* (London, 1945, pp. 110-1).

B

"By the communication of general and popular Science, Vulgar Errors and Common Prejudices are constantly diminished."

—SIR HUMPHRY DAVY

"Believe nothing on the faith of traditions, even though they have been held in honor for many generations, and in diverse places. Do not believe a thing because many speak of it. Do not believe on the faith of the sages of the past. Do not believe what you have imagined, persuading yourself that a god inspires you. Believe nothing on the sole authority of your masters or priests. After examination, believe what you yourself have tested and found to be reasonable, and conform your conduct thereto."—Buddhist Scriptures.

LUKAS THE **BABOON-BOY**

Lukas, the South African baboon-boy explained in Afrikaans to eager audiences in the late 1930s and early 1940s how he had lived among the baboons. His tale was apparently accepted because he could (and did) eat cacti. A similar story of life among the baboons was told by a rival, Ndola, exposed in the *American Journal of Psychology* as "merely a case of neglected paralysis provoking the quadrupedal posture," and seven months later Lukas's imposture was also exposed: he had in fact not lived with baboons at all, but among fellow-convicts in the Burghersdorp jail.

The credulity of the scientists can be found in the *American Journal of Psychology* (January 1940, pp. 128-33) and their honorable recantation in the same journal (July 1940, pp. 455-462).

The unfortunate Lukas was put away in an institution for the feeble-minded.

Source: Bergen Evans, *The natural history of nonsense* (London, 1947, pp. 87-88).

BACTERIA ARE HARMFUL

This is an extraordinary fallacy: it is true only of a very few species of bacteria known as pathogens, but most bacteria are quite harmless and not all parasitic bacteria cause disease. The skin and the openings of the body are crowded with harmless bacteria which seem to prevent the growth of harmful species. Some bacteria even synthesize vitamins in the intestine and thus drugs which destroy bacteria indiscriminately may do more harm than good. If all bacteria were to be destroyed by some malignant power most other forms of life would also disappear, because throughout the course of evolution so many important duties have been taken over by microbes. For example, herbivores rely on bacteria in their digestive organs to break down plant cellulose into digestible sugars and it is because humans lack such bacteria that they cannot survive on a diet of grass.

THE **BAGPIPE** IS A SCOTTISH INSTRUMENT

An instrument of great antiquity, known to the ancient Greeks as the askaulos or symphoneia, and to the Romans as tibia utricularis. It is the French cornemuse, the Italian cornamusa, and the German Sackpfeife. The bagpipe appears on a coin of Nero's time and Nero himself is reputed (by Suetonius and Dion Cfary-sostomos) to have played it. Chaucer's miller performed on it: "A bagpipe well couth he blowe and sowne." The Highland bagpipe is just one of a hundred variants.

Source: George Grove, *Dictionary of music and musicians* (4th ed., London, 1940, vol. I).

THERE IS A **BALCONY** SCENE IN SHAKESPEARE'S ROMEO AND JULIET

Shakespeare's so-called "Balcony Scene" in Romeo and Juliet was probably known to him and his fellow-actors and audience as the "Orchard Scene" or the "Gallery Scene," for the word balcony was imported from Italy (*balcone*, a gallery) later in the 17th century. Incidentally, the stress was, as usual in Italian, on the penultimate syllable (as in Marconi), and the 19th-century writer Samuel Rogers complained that "'contemplate' is bad enough, but 'balcony' makes me sick."

Sources include: Ivor Brown, *I give you my word* (London, 1945).

BALDNESS CAN BE CURED BY RECOGNIZED TREATMENTS

There is no cure for the average loss of a hundred or so hairs every day, and the condition is perfectly normal as a part of aging, though of course loss of hair can also be a symptom of illness. Symptomatic baldness occasionally recovers of its own accord, and some loss of hair occurring as a symptom of pituitary or thyroid gland deficiency can be corrected by hormone threatment.

Baldness as such, except for the disease alopecia areata (in which all the hair drops out and later grows back again naturally and completely) is a strictly hereditary matter, usually (but by no means exclusively) in the male line. Logan Clendening, in *The human body* (New York, 1938), states: "The degeneration of the hair follicles on top of the head is laid down in the germ plasm to begin at a definite time in life, usually not in youth."

There are thousands of patent medicines and techniques for curing baldness even now, but not one of them can be stated to be efficacious.

Among these mistaken ideas, some of which have provided sufficient profit for a quack to make a sizeable income from the ever-gullible public, is the opinion that the common house-fly is "a counter-irritant," and "makes the hair grow if, after crushing flies, one applies them to the bald patch," according to Friedrich-Christian Lesser, in his *Théologie des insectes* (1742) translated into English as Insecto-theology: or, a demonstration of the being and perfection of God, from a consideration of the structure and economy of insects . . . (Edinburgh, 1799).

MALE **BALDNESS** IS PASSED DOWN FROM FATHER TO SON

It makes sense for a young man in his late teens and early twenties to judge whether or not his receding hairline is temporary or permanent based on how bald his father is, and how young he was when he started losing his locks. Like father like son, right?

Research has shown that this correlation is actually typically inaccurate. According to a study by a German University, there is a gene variation that interrupts the direct transfer of this lovely genetic factor from father to son. This "variation" gene sits on the X chromosome, and therefore is transferred solely from mother to son. And since males definitely tend to go balder earlier and more frequently than females, the way in which a young lad should judge his chances of going bald earlier than average (in his fifties), is by figuring out when his maternal grandfather started losing his hair.

If he's lucky, our hypothetical thirty-something-year-old's grandpa carried a full head of salt n' pepper hair with him into his sixties. Otherwise, here's to hoping there's something more reliable than Rogaine come 2020.

Sources: "Going Bald? Blame Mom," CBS News, 2005; James Sturcke, "Mothers' Genes Contain Bald Truth about Hair Loss," *The Independent*, 2005.

A **BANISTER** IS A HANDRAIL ON A STAIRCASE

The whole construction protecting those on an upper floor from falling is a balustrade. A banister is one of the bars running from the handrail to the steps. A stone balustrade's bars are more accurately termed balusters or colonets.

BARBIE WOULD BE 7 FEET TALL IF SHE WERE A REAL PERSON

This unassuming doll named Barbie, created back in 1959, has faced a lifetime of controversy and criticism. The most popular opposition to Barbie is her idealized and unrealistic proportions. Her blonde hair, blue eyes, and "perfect" body has increasingly been contested by parents, activists, researchers and the common man (so as not to assume it's always women) as a misleading and counterproductive image and role model for young girls.

Aside from issues of body image, Barbie has also been accused of political incorrectness, as, clearly, not all young girls are blonde, blue-eyed, tall, and more importantly, white. Although African American Barbie dolls were manufactured and marketed in 1967, 1968, and 1980, all of these models used the same models as the original white Barbie, and therefore were unrealistic, as the only difference between the two were the skin tones.

But Barbie's proportions are unrealistic regardless of ethnicity. She is too tall to be as skinny as she is. Keeping that in mind, however, the distortion of Barbie's body on a real life scale has definitely been exaggerated by the general public. The most common rumor generated by the anti-Barbie campaign is that Barbie would be seven feet tall, anorexic, and unable to even stand up straight if she were a real person. According to one of several sources, real-life Barbie would be seven feet, six inches tall, with a waist size of 40 inches. However, these statistics only measure up if we take a woman of fairly average height and weight (like in the above mentioned scenario) and apply Barbie's proportions to her.

But if Barbie's proportions are measured out on a general math scale (1/6 scale), she would be a five foot 6-inch woman weighing 110 pounds, with a 39-inch bust size, 18-inch waist, and 33-inch hips. So, although this may certainly be considered unhealthy, the unrealistic part about it is really the very unusual proportions throughout her body rather than just the height vs. weight factor.

(Continued)

One avid Barbie fan is quoted on one source with the counter-argument that to say Barbie is so unrealistically tall and skinny that she would have to crawl around rather than walk upright if she were real is actually quite misogynistic, as it conjures up the image of a weak, helpless, sexually vulnerable female.

Recently, Barbie has made all kinds of adaptations to an increasingly modern world, our favorite being the new line of Totally Tattooed Barbies. Nowadays everybody needs a role model to hate, especially one who can't talk back, right?

Sources: Denise Winterman, "What Would a Real Life Barbie Look Like?" *BBC News Magazine*, 2009; "Deconstructing the Barbie Myth," *Berkeley University Newspaper*, 1998; "Mattel Introduces Black Barbies, Gets Mixed Reviews," Fox News, 2009; Sean Poulter, "Barbie Given Tattoos by Makers to Mimic High-Profile Celebrities like Amy Winehouse," UK *Daily Mail Newspaper Online*, 2009.

BASEBALL WAS FIRST PLAYED IN THE U.S.A.

The first game of baseball played under the Cartwright rules was played at Hoboken (New Jersey) on June 19, 1846, but there is a woodcut of "Base-Ball" printed in England as early as 1744, and the Russians too claim to have preceded Americans in playing the game. The "Baseball Ground" in Derby was the scene of experimental baseball games in Britain, but the sport never became popular, and from 1895 the ground has been the home of Derby County Football Club, founded in 1884 and one of the original members of the Football League.

FREQUENT BATHING WILL KEEP THE PORES OPEN AND PROTECT THE SKIN

"Wash with our soap and let your pores breathe" run the popular advertisements by soap manufacturers who should know better and probably do.

Vilhjalmur Stefansson exploded this fallacy in *The standardisation of error* (1928), but of course the error remains standard: "The skin does not excrete any appreciable amount of harmful substances from the body, nor do the pores 'breathe.' Therefore your system is not purified by 'keeping the pores open.'" Stefansson goes on to defy the three-baths-a-day-fanatics: "A chief function of the skin is to protect the body; poisons, such as mercury, will not penetrate if the skin is oiled with its own secretions, but will penetrate if the natural lubricants have been washed away with warm water, soap, or other methods. . . ."

Put simply, the pores of the human skin do not breathe, and the skin does not excrete an appreciable amount of harmful substances from the body, so this argument for bathing frequently is fallacious.

So too is the belief that bathing protects the skin. A major function of the skin is to protect the body; such poisons as mercury will not penetrate if the skin is oiled with its own secretions, but will penetrate if the natural lubricants have been washed away with warm water, or soap.

Source: Vilhjalmur Stefansson, *The standardisation of error* (London, 1928).

THE **BAYEUX TAPESTRY** IS A TAPESTRY MADE AT BAYEUX

The "Bayeux tapestry" is not a tapestry at all, but a long embroidered hanging worked in colored wools on a plain background of bleached linen. It was commissioned by the half-brother of William the Conqueror, Bishop Odo of Bayeux (hence the designation), but it was made, between about 1067 and 1070, in England (where Odo was residing at the time), and not in France, as is commonly supposed.

Signs to the "tapestry" in Bayeux today are to "La tapisserie de la Reine Mathilde," crediting William's wife Mathilde with the embroidery, an attribution discredited today by all French historians.

Source: C. H. Gibbs-Smith, *The Bayeux tapestry* (London, 1973).

BEE FALLACIES

In general, bees as a whole category of species are misunderstood as much as they are feared. Imagine a scenario where a group of people are eating a Memorial Day meal at an outdoor picnic table: In the event that a fly comes over, it will typically be swatted away. If a mosquito lands on the table, or someone's exposed arm, it will probably get hit with a hand or crushed dead by the nearest heavy object. However, when a bee hovers its way over, at least half the table's human occupants will jump up and run for shelter, while the other half may wait unblinkingly and helplessly for the creature to take whatever resources it needs and be on its way. Because bees don't just bite us, they *sting* us. Here are some clarifications on bee myths that might help to ease the pain (emotionally) once we clear them up:

1. All Bees Sting (types and gender)

Like mosquitoes, and really a lot of other insects, the female bees are the sole human injurers (i.e., stingers). The stinger is meant to

(Continued)

31

be a reproductive organ. So in queen bees, their stinger allows them to either lay eggs or defend with this mechanism. But the worker female bees are the ones you typically see flying around collecting honey, and they have stingers which they use more for defense than for laying eggs. Female wasps are also the sole stingers.

2. Bees Sting Once Then Die

This is true for bumble bees. However, it's only sometimes true for honey bees. Both these types (aside from queen bee) use their stingers for defense. The honey bees typically are only able to sting once before they die because their stinger is "barbed." So, while the bumble bee can sting as many times as it would like because its stinger is smooth and can be inserted and removed like a needle prick, the honey bee's stinger gets ripped out of its body once it is injected into human skin, bringing with it the major glands attached to the stinger (venom gland and dufour's gland). These glands produce venom, which keeps releasing into human bloodstream long after the bee is dead. As honey bees mostly just live to work and keep up their colonies, maybe sacrificing their lives to inflict pain upon the little boy who whacks their honey-comb data centers with a stick seems like a valuable tradeoff.

3. Bees vs. Wasps

Wasps are not bees. Actually, bees evolved from predatory wasps. There are subtle differences in appearance and behavior between the two species. For instance, wasps tend to be hairless and have more elongated bodies, while bees are hairier and more compact. While bees mainly collect honey and beeswax for pollination, wasps come to gardens, and even land on flowers and plants primarily to prey on other insects they want to eat. Another common mistake people make is that yellow jackets are bees. They are actually wasps, and like bumble bees, are able to sting repeatedly because they do not lose their stingers when they attack. They will spend lots of time hovering around food and sweet things like soda cans because they have developed a taste for human foods. However, yellow jackets are much more likely to sting and eat other insects than prey upon than humans, and are only really interested in getting food for their young from both sources. Bees, on the other hand, will rarely join your family for a celebratory outdoor BBQ.

4. Bees Seek Out Humans to Bite/Sting Them (like mosquitoes)

Not really, because their stingers are both used as reproductive tools (to lay eggs) and as defense mechanisms, varying on the type and place. Only if you threaten their grounds and their life-style will they actively want to sting you, but otherwise they don't really want to. As they don't spend much time around people's food, or people in general, there's no reason that a bee would sting you unless you stepped into its line of pollination work or into hive territory.

Sources: Urban Bee Gardens @ *nature.berkley.edu*. Urban Bee Garden Research and Findings, since 1987, University of California; University of Illinois at Urbana-Champaign Dept. of Entomology. "Bee Stings" on Bee Spotter site.

THE TRUMPETER **BUMBLE-BEE**'S FUNCTION IS TO SOUND A REVEILLE EVERY MORNING

A Dutchman, J. Gordart, stated in 1700 that every morning a bumble-bee roused the nest by sounding a reveille with its rapidly beating wings, like an army bugler.

This fallacy was unchallenged until, in the 20th century, H. von Buttel-Reepen proved that the real function of the Trumpeter bumble-bee was the same as that observed in his equivalent among the hive-bees: to ventilate the nest by creating a current of air.

Source: Maurice Richardson's review article "the formic community," on M. V. Brian's Ants (London, 1977), in *The Times Literary Supplement*, November 25, 1977, p. 1375.

"BEEFEATERS" DERIVE THEIR NAME FROM "BUFFET"

Mrs. Markham's *History of England* (1823) was, with the same author's *History of France* (1828), one of the most influential schoolbooks ever written. "Mrs. Markham" was the pseudonym of Elizabeth Penrose (1780-1837), nee Cartwright. Any errors in "Mrs. Markham" were remembered and repeated parrot-fashion for many decades by generations of schoolchildren who learned nothing better, and there were errors in Mrs. Markham.

One of the classic mistakes in her *History of England* concerned the "Beefeaters" of Olde England. Mrs. Markham connected their name with the French word *buffet* (sideboard) to invent buffetier (a waiter at the sideboard).

Alas for all such picturesque folk-etymology! The *Oxford English Dictionary* takes into account this error and corrects it. The real meaning of "beefeaters" is, believe it or not, "eaters of beef, and occurs as early as 1610 with this significance, implying a well-fed menial, who should perform his duties adequately because he is splendidly provided for.

"Beefeaters," in popular parlance, is the term used for the Yeomen of the Guard, in the household of the Sovereign of Great Britain, instituted at the accession of Henry VII in 1485 and also for the Yeomen Extraordinary of the Guard in the reign of Edward VI now known as the Warders of the Tower of London.

IT TAKES 44 GALLONS OF WATER TO PRODUCE A PINT OF **BEER**

The National Water Council of Great Britain stated the above in a leaflet distributed at the beginning of the drought of 1976. It subsequently retracted the statement, however, agreeing that the figure should have been between 3½ and 10 pints of water, mostly used for cleaning equipment and bottles.

The same leaflet claimed that 44,000 gallons of water were used to make a single car tire. Since these figures are widely quoted and believed, it is worth pointing out that the Council later admitted that the true figure for making a car tire is in fact only 15 gallons.

BEER BEFORE LIQUOR, NEVER BEEN SICKER. LIQUOR BEFORE BEER, YOU'RE IN THE CLEAR

In slightly varying forms, this catch phrase is one that young people (and perhaps older people as well) abide by religiously. How often have you heard one of your peers use the reasoning that you should always start off the night with liquor, and then wind down and pace yourself afterwards with beer to avoid being as hung-over the next day as you would the other way around?

Even adults and parents, whether or not they want to believe it, reason this way. Why else would cocktail parties be such a commonplace convention? They take place at five o'clock, before dinner. Then most likely, everyone moves into wine or beer with their meals, at least those of us with moderate drinking habits do.

Truth be told, it makes no difference at all, regarding sickness or intoxication level, whether you begin the night with liquor or beer. It all depends on how much alcohol you consume in a night and the rate of consumption. What type of alcohol you are drinking really makes very little difference.

According to some experts, the myth probably originates from the theory that carbonated beverages like beer irritate the stomach lining, absorbing alcohol faster, and therefore could possibly lead to slightly quicker intoxication if liquor is subsequently consumed.

> But the consensus seems to be the order that liquor or beer is consumed, and whether or not they are mixed, is quite irrelevant. Plus, taking shots before moving over to beer is hardly likely once you are too drunk to remember whether beer or liquor is supposed to come first anyway.
>
> **Sources:** Anahad O'Connor, *Really?* Blog, "The Claim: Mixing Types of Alcohol Makes You Sick," *New York Times*, 2006; Dr. Keri Peterson, "Liquor Before Beer, Never Fear? Hangover Myths Exposed," MSNBC Today, 2010.

DATES "BEFORE CHRIST" AND "ANNO DOMINI" HAVE LONG BEEN USED

We began to think in terms of years "in the year of our Lord" (Anno Domini) in Christian Europe as late as AD 525 taking up the suggestion of that year from Dionysius Exiguus.

However, years "Before Christ" were only cited thus as recently as the 17th century, and the first to have used it may have been Jacques-Bénigne Bossuet (1627-1704) in his *Discours sur l'histoire universelle* (Paris, 1681). Bossuet's work is the last in the long series of world histories leading from the Creation by God to the divine choice of the writer's homeland as the culmination of the historical process, a tendency leading to feudal ideas, caste or class divisions, extreme patriotism, and theocentric absolutism. Bossuet was duly rewarded with a bishopric and the lavish rewards of Louis XIV. Voltaire refuted Bossuet's errors in his *Essai sur l'histoire generate et sur les moeurs et l'esprit des nations* (Geneva, 1756), which rejected biblical teleology in favor of a philosophical approach to history, and began the modern school of comparative historiography which replaces divine guidance and Eurocentrism with scientific explanations based on observation and the inclusion of other continents, other ways of life than those immediately familiar to the writer.

JASTROW AND THE VAGARIES OF BELIEF

Joseph Jastrow's books are among the most fascinating ever written on the subject of gullibility and the human propensity to error. However, his classification of errors is less than satisfactory because the seven categories are by no means mutually exclusive.

His first class is Credulity, his examples including Professor Beringer and Sir Arthur Conan Doyle. Then come Magic and Marvel (Theosophy and the cult of the magnet); Transcendence (Ouija Board and Hélene Smith); Prepossession (Thought forms); Congenial

Conclusions (Numerology and palmistry); Cults and Vagaries (Psychometry and phrenology); and Rationalization (Auras and ectoplasm).

In fact, one can be credulous, prepossessed toward a congenial conclusion, and at the same time rationalize a cult such as phrenology. There is still no wholly adequate classification of errors apart from the existing classifications of knowledge itself.

BELLY BUTTON FALLACIES

1. Belly Button Shape Is Based on Where the Umbilical Cord Was Cut

Navels are classified in two genres: innie or outie. Within either category, there are different variations in depth or protrusion of the so-called belly button. "Innies" are more common than "outies," and they are apparently considered the more attractive version of the two. As a result, people sometimes even request a simple surgery to make their overall stomach aesthetic more beautiful, according to the wisdom of Dr. Curtis Cetrulo of Massachusetts General Hospital.

As people do go to such great lengths to push their outies inward, one might think the surgeons who cut their cords at birth would be receiving enough angry calls from the grown babies who they brought into this world in order to change their practices.

As it turns out, these surgeons are not the culprits. Instead, whether you have an innie or an outie belly button depends on how much space there is on each individual person between his and her skin and abdominal wall beneath it. Once the stalk from the umbilical cord (what is cut) dries up, there is a scar remaining above the abdominal wall. If the tissue from the abdomen protrudes upward, it pushes the scar upward, creating the existence of an "outie."

Also, an innie can become more of an outie in a woman post-pregnancy. Because during pregnancy her stomach obviously expands significantly larger than her usual size, her abdominal wall may stretch to the point where the belly button is no longer so far indented as it would be in the case of innie.

So, basically, belly button shape and size is arbitrary, and arguably quite an unimportant component to consider as negative in the overall process of the miracle of life.

2. Belly Button "Lint"

Hey world, we know you've been waiting at the edges of your seats to hear the results of the age-old question: "What are those pesky pieces of 'fluff' or lint that sticks to my finger every time I stick it inside my belly button?" Well, never fear, folks, Australian chemist Georg Steinhauser has an answer for you. And it only took him three years of intensive "navel-gazing"!

In 2009 this dedicated man finally figured out that the existence of so-called lint in belly buttons is not so much the result of one's stomach rubbing up against his or her jeans on a particularly sticky and sweaty day. In fact, there is actually a type of body hair, typically found in males, that literally traps stray pieces of lint on one's body and sucks them into the belly button region.

Dr. Steinhauser was able to come up with this discovery primarily by studying over 500 extracts of "lint" he removed from his belly button daily. In observing and testing these samples, he was eventually able to reach the conclusion that there were not just traces of lint and clothing particles in these extracts. No, sir, there were instead even tinier flakes of skin and dust, and even more charmingly, miniscule pieces of fat and sweat.

This doctor explained that this type of body hair acts as a kind of barbed hook, trapping unwanted, excess flakes of body and likewise, clothing, and pushing it back into the belly button, where it belongs!

He did not use himself as the only subject, mind you. He also surveyed a group of roughly 500 Australian samples, finding that the most common bearer of excess belly button lint was, on average, those who were middle-aged, male, slightly overweight, and possessing a notably hairy abdomen.

It is relatively natural for hairs on the body to catch microscopic particles of skin and sweat so that they don't go back into the skin or cause infection or irritation. They remain there, presumably, only until one takes a shower before the process begins again. But for those who have a particularly distinguishable lint problem, Dr. Steinhauser recommends shaving and/or getting a belly button piercing. However, he adds, once the hair grows back, the problem of lint collecting will recur once more at its usual pace. We'll go ahead and add that a belly button piercing on said demographic of navel lint wearers might add more problems than it would divert us from the initial one.

Sources: Daily Mail UK, "The 'Mystery' of Belly Button fluff is finally solved by navel-gazing scientist," 2009; Fox News, SciTech, "Scientist Solves Mystery of Belly-Button Lint," 2009. Cari Nierenberg, "What Makes an innie and inne? And more Bellybutton mysteries," *Body Odd* blog, MSNBC, 2011.

BELL-RINGING CAN SAVE CITIES FROM LIGHTNING

The Middle Ages in Europe was a period when it was almost ubiquitously believed that the ringing of church bells would diminish the damage done by storms, and even prevent lightning.

Descartes (in De meteoribus) and Francis Bacon (in his Natural history) both refer to the belief with respect as late as the 17th century, suggesting that the bells may fulfil this function by their concussion of the air!

The main written source of the fallacy is *De gentibus septentrionalibus* (Rome, 1555) by the Primate of Sweden, Olaus Magnus, who declares it a well-established fact that cities and harvests may be saved from lightning by the ringing of bells, and incidentally also by the burning of consecrated incense, accompanied by prayers. The fact that nobody ever reported a case when lightning had not been stopped by such measures does not mean that there were no such cases!

BENTHAM ON FALLACIES

The standard work is still *The book of fallacies* (London, 1824) by Jeremy Bentham, in its revision by Harold A. Larrabee (Baltimore, 1952).

Bentham defines a fallacy as "any argument employed or topic suggested for the purpose, or with the probability of producing the effect of deception, or of causing some erroneous opinion to be entertained by any person to whose mind such an argument may have been presented."

He lists four causes of fallacies: self-conscious sinister interest, interest-begotten prejudice, authority-begotten prejudice, and self-defence against counter-fallacies.

There are four major types of fallacy in Bentham's view: fallacies of authority (including our ancestors); of danger (including distrust of innovation); of delay (including the procrastinator's argument); and of confusion (including sham distinctions, allegorical idols, and question-begging epithets).

THE BERMUDA TRIANGLE

The vogue for thrillers, detective stories, and the like which has been a feature of European and American literary life since Edgar Allan Poe and Wilkie Collins has thrown up a parallel library of non-fiction "mysteries," such as the alleged sightings of ghosts, the pseudo-archaeological "search" for secrets of the Easter Island standing figures or Stonehenge which are not always secrets to those who prefer reading serious, detailed studies by subject experts acknowledged as leaders in the field.

No subject, other than perhaps the "Holy Shroud of Turin" or "alien visitors from outer space," has been more surrounded with mystery in recent years than "the Bermuda triangle." The book of that title written by Charles Berlitz (with the collaboration of J. Manson Valentine) is only the best-seller: there is a whole Bermuda Triangle bibliography compiled by Larry Kusche and Deborah Blouin and published in 1973 by Arizona State University Library.

The hoary legend is that a particular area of the Western Atlantic, near the southeast coast of the United States, has experienced more inexplicable disasters than any other area of the same size. The zone in question is roughly triangular from Bermuda in the north to southern Florida, and in the east to a point passing through the Bahamas past Puerto Rico to a point about 40° West longitude. The authors add, pityingly, that there are "many marine or aeronautical authorities who would observe that it is perfectly natural for planes, ships, or yachts to disappear in an area where there is so much sea and air travel, subject to sudden storms and the multiple possibilities of navigational mistakes and accidents. These same authorities are likely to make the comment that the Bermuda Triangle does not exist at all, and that the very name is a misnomer, a manufactured mystery for the diversion of the curious and imaginative reader."

Certainly, there seems a great deal of disagreement among the mystery-mongers as to where the disaster area is. John Godwin, in *This baffling world* (New York, 1968), called the hoodoo area "a rough square," while Ivan Sanderson, in *Invisible residents* (New York, 1970), described the zone as after all an ellipse or lozenge, and suggested that there are eleven more such scattered throughout the world's oceans.

Regrettably for the fantasy-spinners, a detailed B.B.C. television program by Graham Massey entitled "The Case of the Bermuda Triangle" (February 1976) and an equally detailed article in *The New Scientist* (July 14, 1977) showed clearly—as in all known cases of the "paranormal" which are capable of being analysed as well as merely stated—that Berlitz's book and similar works suffer by omissions, by the favoring of hypothesis over research, by prejudiced reporting, by ignoring sober witnesses when unbalanced witnesses offer more sensational versions of the same events, and so on.

To give an example cited by Stan Gooch, in *The Paranormal* (London, 1978), the super-tanker Berge Istra was reported missing in the Pacific on December 29, 1975. No trace whatsoever was found of this massive ship—one of the largest in the world—not even an oil slick. Air rescue having apparently failed, attempts to locate the missing ship were abandoned on January 14. Yet on January 19, two survivors were found by the slimmest of chances, drifting on a raft. The fact they told was that three sharp explosions on the tanker had broken it up so quickly that the Berge Istra sank almost at once. How many similar occurrences, one wonders, would have gone unreported for lack of survivors?

The most celebrated Triangle story (described in both *The Bermuda Triangle* and its sequel *Without a Trace*) concerns the loss of Flight 19, which set off on a routine training mission from Fort Lauderdale Naval Air Base on December 5, 1945. The weather was fine and no problem was suspected until a quarter of an hour before the five U.S. Navy Avenger bomber aircraft with their crew of experienced flyers were due to land. The story goes that a message then came through from Lt. Charles Taylor: "We seem to be off course . . . we cannot see land . . . we don't know which way is west . . . everything is wrong, strange . . . even the ocean doesn't look as it should . . . it looks like we are . . ." then silence. A rescue airplane with thirteen men on board immediately took off to look for the bombers, but it too vanished. A widespread air-sea rescue operation failed to discover the six planes or any of the crew.

This represents the "scary picture" which has sold more than six million copies of Berlitz's books and continues to do so. Now let Graham Massey, of B.B.C. Television's *Horizon* have his say: "Almost everything about this story is wrong. In the first place the strange message from Taylor, on which much of the Triangle mystery is based, never happened: none of the bases in touch with Flight 19 have it in their comprehensive radio logs; none of the people at the naval base at the time listening to Taylor heard him say such things; even the person whom Berlitz quotes as his firsthand authority for the message, a Commander Wirshing, denies that he heard such a message. The message originates word for word, like so many other Triangle stories, from Vincent Gaddis's article in *Argosy* [in 1964], and Gaddis got it secondhand from a journalist who cannot provide any sources.

"The planes did not disappear at 4:25 in daylight in calm weather as the legend has it, but were still flying after 7:00 p.m. in the dark when the weather had turned stormy with rough seas. The crew men were not "experienced flyers"—with the exception of Taylor they were trainee pilots, many of them new to the area. The official Navy report reveals that Taylor had completely mistaken his position. He believed that he was flying over the Florida Keys—a chain of islands to the south of Florida; in fact, he was over the very similar Bahamas chain to the east. He therefore set a course north and east to return him to base—a course that took him and Flight 19 out into the Atlantic. The planes ran out of fuel and crash landed at night in rough seas. The Avenger's maximum "surface time" after crash landing is forty-five seconds. It's not surprising then that a search that began only hours later, in the dark, should find nothing."

Nor is that all: Berlitz's tale of the disappearance of the Mariner rescue airplane is disproved by eyewitnesses on a ship who saw it explode at the time when it vanished on tracking radar. The Mariners are known as "flying gas tanks" because of the large amount of fuel they carry, and any careless or unlucky spark can cause an explosion. Berlitz says that the Mariner in question took off and disappeared around 4:25—some three hours before it actually left base!

Critical readers are indebted to Lawrence Kusche's book *The Bermuda Triangle Solved*, which provides disproof of more than fifty legends of the "Bermuda Triangle." It is as well that disproof exists, for the U.S. 7th Coastguard district morale would be low indeed if unexplained losses occurred at a very high rate. In fact, in 1976 twenty-eight vessels were lost off the U.S. coast, but only six of them were in the Triangle area. Lloyds of London confirms that there is no evidence that the Triangle is a disaster area: no commercial airliner was lost over the Triangle in the decade prior to the publication of *Without a Trace*, and the safety record of airliners in the Triangle is actually better than that over the continental United States.

What else does Berlitz get wrong? Well, the Greenbank conference on extraterrestrial intelligence did not state that 40 or 50 million worlds are trying to signal us or to hear messages from Earth. It is not conclusively proved that Atlantis has been found off Bimini (or anywhere else for that matter). The U.S. Navy and the Soviet Navy are not combining to explore the Triangle. And the reported landing of a UFO in Hudson City Park, New Jersey, is not evidence for the existence of a fatal zone off the shores.

Sources include: Lawrence Kusche, *The Bermuda Triangle mystery solved* (London, 1975); and Graham Massey, "The meretricious triangle," in *New Scientist*, July 14, 1977.

"BETWEEN" IS CORRECTLY USED OF TWO, AND "AMONG" OF MORE THAN TWO

I suppose most of us were taught that it is wrong to say "there was a discussion between the five of us," but the standard *Oxford English Dictionary* states that from the earliest appearance of the word it has been "extended to more than two"; Fowler concurs, as do *Merriam Webster's 3rd edition* and Theodore M. Bernstein in *The careful writer* (New York, 1965). Bernstein adds, "To speak of a treaty between nine powers would be completely proper and exact."

BIRD FALLACIES

1) Birds Can Foretell Weather Conditions

Country folk are full of stories to "prove" that by their actions birds are able to predict the weather. T. A. Coward, in *The migration of birds* (Cambridge, 1929) stresses that this folk belief is not "supported by any satisfactory evidence." It is also clearly open to challenge by the fact that birds in long flights often fly directly into weather that causes their death or injury.

2) Birds Die of Cold
Because country people find the bodies of birds frozen by hedges and fields in midwinter, they have often been inclined to fancy that the birds have died of cold. But they are frozen after death, not before, the reason for death normally being starvation due to the rapid diminution of the food supply in freezing or snowy weather. So always remember to increase your provision of food to birds during the worst weather.

3) Birds Give Milk
This popular error arose in Vietnam when the health authorities, trying to overcome the natural antipathy of the Vietnamese to milk as a product from cows, introduced sweetened condensed milk in cans as 'birds' milk." Milk then became acceptable and came into general use.

4) Birds Sleep With Their Heads Under Their Wings
A fallacy which gave rise to a popular nursery rhyme and has in turn been reinforced by the rhyme; "The north wind doth blow, and we shall have snow; And what will Cock Robin do then, poor thing? He'll fly to the barn, To keep himself warm, And hide his head under his wing, poor thing." A bird's method of going to sleep can be roughly described as turning its head round, putting it on its back with the beak concealed, and often in the process almost concealing the head, but never in any case so far recorded placing the head under the wings.

5) Birds Migrate on the Same Day Each Year
Dozens of fallacies concerning bird migration can be found in standard works such as A. Landsborough Thompson's *Bird migration* (London, 1949) or J. Dorst's *Les migrations des oiseaux* (Paris, 1956), but it will be sufficient to explode one of the commonest which, despite regular scientific refutation by one ornithologist after another, recurs annually. According to Californian newspapers, the cliff swallows nesting at the San Juan Capistrano Mission there always leave the Mission on October 23 for their southward migration and return on March 19, even taking account of leap years! The fact remains that their departure date varies from year to year.

6) Birds Sleep in Their Nests
It has been observed that a mother bird will infrequently doze off while sitting on her eggs, but of course birds are as clean as pigs in their habits and leave their nests at dusk to sleep in tree branches, Town children often imagine birds asleep in their nests at night.

Sources: Thompson, head-keeper at Zoological Gardens during the terribly severe winter of 1894-5, reported in Pearson's Weekly (May 1, 1897); S. and V. Leff, Medicine fights superstition, in *The Humanist*, September 1959; Osmond P. Breland, *Animal facts and fallacies* (London, 1950, pp. 113-14).

BLACK-BEETLES ARE BLACK BEETLES

They are dark brown, not black. And while beetles form the order Coleoptera, black-beetles belong to the order Orthoptera which also includes locusts and grasshoppers.

BLACKHEADS ARE DUE TO POOR HYGIENE

Blackheads are the little black spots that freckle the surface of the nose, forehead, and other "t-zone" areas on our faces we were told about as adolescents. We know them and loathe them. And it seems, particularly for those of us who have combination and/or oily skin, they never fully go away.

Blackheads differ from white heads visually, because they appear to be black in color. Thus arises the misconception that blackheads form as a result of little specks of dirt getting stuck under the skin. And furthermore, we assume that whenever blackheads are present, we are slacking in our hygienic routines, and need to scrub our faces more often and more rigorously in order to get rid of these guys.

But try as you might, doubling, tripling, or quadrupling the amount of times per day you wash your face will not rid you of your blackheads (also known as "open comedos" in the medical world). Blackheads, like pimples proper, are open pores, where excess oil accumulates in the sebaceous gland's duct and combines with dead skin cells to clog up and produce these little bumps on the skin. The reason blackheads appear darker than whiteheads is because there is a little opening in the pore so it is able to oxidize, while whiteheads are totally stopped up and therefore not only look worse, but remain white even on the surface because they are unable to "breathe."

In addition to washing the face excessively being a futile technique in eliminating blackheads, trying to extract them on your own is just as ineffective. Although it does seem incredibly satisfying to go to town on your blackheads, and though you generally do see little white "strings" come out via extraction, it is sadly, only temporary. As you are only removing surface "cloggage," the

(Continued)

pore will still remain open and the bacteria beneath the skin will still build up quickly and re-clog it in a matter of days.

Most sources recommend that if you really want to get rid of blackheads, you should seek out professional help. So much for self-help, and say sayonara to naturally smooth skin.

Sources: National Institute of Arthritis and Musculoskeletal and Skin Diseases (NIAMS), "Acne," 2010; Elizabeth Whitmore, "Can I Wash My Face Too Much?" Discovery Health; "Definition of a Blackhead," *Medicine Net.*

FULL **BLADDER** FALLACIES

1. Frequent Urination Is Only for Those with Small Bladders

It makes sense logically and physiologically that people who have to pee more often are generally smaller people and typically are thought to have smaller bladders. You also don't need half a brain to figure out that people who consume more liquids have to pee more often. Additionally, as people get older they have less control over their bladders and biologically have to urinate more frequently.

But these physiological factors are not the explanations for God putting on earth those annoying people who keep needing to squeeze by you in the movie theatre, blocking your view and knocking over your popcorn. For those of you who *are* one of those hated people, you might like to know that having the urge to pee suddenly may very well stem from the fact that you are put in a situation where you know you are not able to, such as on a long car ride, during a performance, or in the middle of an exam.

These situations are better thought of as nervous peeing. That is, being nervous triggers the urge to urinate even when you might not feel like you need to otherwise. Having anxiety means tensing up muscles, and tense muscles means more frequent urination urges. Not rocket science, but citable science.

2. Having to Pee Is Distracting

Having made the argument above, we can now say that anyone who has been stuck on a long bus ride with no bathrooms on board or in an important meeting with the overwhelming urge to urinate knows how impossible it seems to focus on anything aside from your full bladder.

According to us, it is more than appropriate to wait until the next pit stop before playing our favorite songs on the stereo so that we can fully enjoy the experience of hearing it. Along the same lines, why not use the bathroom in the office building right before embarking upon a mere 30-minute interview, "just in case?" While perhaps not everyone is so adamant about emptying their bladders at every meaningful move, priorities definitely seem to shift when a toilet seat is your greatest fantasy.

However, recent research suggests that the urge to pee is not so much a distraction as it is a beneficial tool in certain more or less crucial situations. This research is somewhat controversial because it challenges the established theory of "ego depletion." This theory holds that we only have a limited pool of self-control. Thus, every time we deny ourselves something we desire, we use up some of our personal self-control resources. In other words, restraint takes a good amount of brain energy and power and the more urges we deprive ourselves of, the less self-control we will have. For instance, studies have shown that other urges, such as hunger and desire, skew decision making (people who are hungrier are more likely to buy unhealthy food at the grocery store and people who are sexually repressed are more likely to have unprotected sex).

The studies conducted consisted of measuring impulsivity restraint levels compared to levels of bladder fullness. For example, one study had subjects identify the names of words that were in different colors than what they read (i.e., the word "blue" might be green in color and the idea is for the person to be able to simply read the word blue while suppressing the urge to identify it as green based on its appearance). Likewise, they were asked to choose between getting a small reward in money and a larger sum in a longer amount of time (i.e., patience vs. instant gratification). It turned out that subjects who had stronger urges to pee were better at controlling their impulsive urges and making more informed, accurate decisions.

This is quite counter-intuitive. But maybe it makes sense on some level: all you want to do is to empty your bladder but you simply cannot at the current time. Perhaps, focusing your energy instead onto a decision at hand is easier because you know getting distracted will only lead back to a desire you cannot fulfill. Also, maybe peeing is the incentive. If you get the question right, you finally get to let sweet Mother Nature take its natural course, out of your body. Bizarre, but possible.

Sources: Sian Beilock, PhD, "Needing to Pee Enhances Decision Making . . . Really," *Choke* Blog, *Psychology Today,* 2011; B.R.,

(*Continued*)

"How, and When, to Make a Decision," *The Economist*, 2011; Association for Psychological Science, "Full Bladder, Better Decisions? Controlling Your Bladder Decreases Impulsive Choices," Tiffany Harrington, 2011.

BATS ARE BLIND

Considering the fact that bats are nocturnal and thus should technically have better sight than humans or other mammals, it's a bit surprising that this fallacy is so commonplace; perhaps because of the small size of their eyes.

It is true that bats don't really depend on their sense of sight to conduct their daily (or more appropriately, nightly) lives. Though their vision is not great, they are in fact quite sensitive to light, as they need to know when it is daytime and when it is nighttime.

Instead of relying on their regular sight as we humans consider it, bats mainly utilize echolocation, a kind of sonar sight, to spot and kill their prey, dodge predators, and navigate their way back home in the dark hours of the night.

So don't feel guilty. Being bats, they probably wouldn't use a human's sense of sight to peacefully observe their cave or forest-like surroundings anyway. Luckily, they don't know what they're missing.

"Blind as a mole" is equally fallacious, since though their eyes are very small (like the eyes of other creatures that burrow underground), moles are perfectly capable of seeing.

BLOOD IS BLUE IN THE BODY BUT TURNS RED ONCE IT TOUCHES THE AIR

This is definitely a commonly believed fallacy. It is also perpetuated by media sources, such as in the song *Blue Veins* by Jack White's other band, The Raconteurs. Although there seems to be no rhyme or reason to this widely circulated mistake, there may actually be a fairly simple and logical explanation for how and why it came about.

Rumor has it (and readers will probably relate once we mention it), that elementary school science textbooks are the heart of the problem. Most of these textbooks that contain pictures and visual diagrams of the inner workings of the human body color code the different devices, so to speak, in a manner which was intended to be arbitrary. This was not the case upon reception, evidently. Arteries were generally color coded in red, whereas veins were in blue, thus the idea that young children developed: organs are really red, so blood in veins must really be blue before it comes out of your body.

Another reason why this myth is falsely reinforced is because venous blood tends to look blue under the skin due to its low oxygen content, despite the fact that it is actually dark red. Veins also look blue because red light travels to a certain point deep enough into the skin (the subcutaneous fat), where it then gets absorbed. As the low frequency light has been absorbed, only the highly energetic blue wavelengths are able to penetrate through to the vein and reflect out toward the surface. That's why the veins look blue!

Although it would be more fun and perhaps more artistically inspiring, blood is always red, and veins are never blue, at least colorwise.

Sources: Michigan State University, "Students" Misconceptions in Science: The Color of Blood;" Mayo Clinic, 1998-2003, Mayo Foundation for Medical Education and Research (MFMER); Kienle, Alwin; Lothar Lilge, I. Alex Vitkin, Michael S. Patterson, Brian C. Wilson, Raimund Hibst, and Rudolf Steiner, "Why do veins appear blue? A new look at an old question," *Applied Optics*, 1996.

BLUE STOCKINGS WERE ONCE WORN BY LADIES OF INTELLECTUAL PRETENSIONS

About 1750, a few ladies grew tired of the endless round of cards, gossip, and intrigue in London society. Mrs. Montague, Mrs. Vesey and Mrs. Ord were among those who acted hostess to those (such as eminent men of letters) interested more in literary themes. Many who attended such serious evening parties disparaged the full formal dress of the period, and appeared in plain, simple worsted as a form of protest. Mr. Benjamin Stillingfieet, who habitually wore grey or "blue" worsted, instead of the black silk stockings usual in society, was a particular butt. Sir W. Forbes, in his *Life of Beattie* (1806), quotes Admiral Boscawen as jeering at "the Blue Stocking Society" but of course he was jeering at a man (Stillingfieet), and the usage "blue Stockingers," later "Blue Stocking Ladies," "Bluestockings" and "Blues" referred to all who attended such gatherings, and had no (accurate) reference to the attire of the ladies. Hazlitt wrote in 1882: "I have an utter aversion to bluestockings"; and in his autobiography de Quincey referred to "The utter want of pretension, and of all that looks like Bluestockingism, in the style of her habitual conversation." The term has become a form of sexist abuse aimed at women, when it was in fact coined by a man about another man.

Sources: *Oxford English Dictionary*.

THE HUMAN **BODY** IS RENEWED EVERY SEVEN YEARS

Professor Sir J. Arthur Thomson writes: "This is what is meant by a credulity—almost universally accepted and yet a nonsensical guess. In a way, the biggest fact about a living body is that it is always changing. It is continually breaking down and almost as continually being built up again . . . Some tissues, like bone, change slowly after growing stops; others, like those of the liver, the seat of bustling activity, change very rapidly . . .

"What, then, is the credulity? It is in fixing the time of replacement at seven years. There is no warrant for this arbitrary estimate, which was doubtless based on the fact that seven is the perfect number."

Source: J. Arthur Thomson, *Scientific riddles* (London, 1938).

BOILING POINT IS ALWAYS 212 DEGREES FAHRENHEIT

If you can recall, you might remember that your elementary school science teacher told you that boiling point is 212 degrees Fahrenheit. However, not everything boils at this specific temperature. In fact, only water is more or less guaranteed to boil at this point. Not to mention, the rule only goes for water under normal pressure conditions. Meaning, the degree at which water boils at a higher altitude will be slightly lower than at sea level.

Additionally, other substances, such as different elements in liquid form (or when converted to liquid form) boil at varying temperatures regardless of whether or not the boiling is happening on top of a mountain or underground.

Something else interesting to note is that, under normal circumstances, one should not be able to boil water above its calculated boiling point (212 degrees). However, because modern inventions such as the pressure cooker came into play, water can now boil more quickly and reach higher temperatures in its liquid form due to controlled pressure from without.

Sources: "Melting Point, Freezing Point, Boiling Point," Bodner Research Group at Purdue.

MOVE YOUR **BOWELS** TWICE A DAY!

The romantic novelist Barbara Cartland, in her pseudo-scientific book *The youth secret* (London, 1968), advises against constipation, to which she attributes "every sort of disease that it's possible to have." In fact, J. A. C. Brown assures us all (*Pears medical encyclopaedia*, London, 1967) that constipation "is a disease largely invented by the individual himself and "is complained of by those who take far too much care of themselves." Ms. Cartland recommends inducing a bowel movement every twelve hours for the sake of health and inner cleanliness, but August Thomen, in his amusing swipe at the health-cranks *Doctors don't believe it! why should you?* (New York, 1935), indicates that man may be safer from auto-intoxication from intestinal poisons when he is constipated, since bacteria would tend not to increase under such conditions, but would do so rapidly under the more moist conditions in the intestinal contents introduced by laxatives. This is also nonsense: there is certainly discomfort during prolonged bouts of constipation, but this is due to mechanical pressure (fullness in the large intestine) and not to any effect of poison.

Let Professor Samson Wright have the last word. In his *Applied physiology* (11th ed., 1965), he writes: "The symptoms of constipation are largely due to distension and mechanical irritation of the rectum," and the average period of constipation is said to be two days, but Professor Wright states from his experience that quite a number of people have bowel movements only about five or six times a year, yet their general health remains good, and certainly better than those sad cases following Ms. Cartland's advice who end up with mucous colitis caused by purgatives.

GOING **BRA-LESS** MEANS HIGHER CHANCES OF DEVELOPING SAGGY BREASTS

Some may contemplate why it is the norm for women to wear bras. Some girls and ladies don't always wear them. Many probably don't question it, while others might argue that wearing a bra is helpful or necessary for women to always wear them, if only to be sure to prevent sagginess in later life, when youth is no longer on their sides.

Yes, some women do truly feel less physically comfortable with no bra than with one on. But, arguably, more so today than ever, wearing a bra is reinforced by society and lingerie marketing companies as a necessary item for women that is not just practical but also sexy. In order to counter at least the former

(Continued)

argument, we think it's valuable to inform our readers who don't already know, particularly women, that there are truly very few actual health benefits to wearing a bra.

In the past, researchers and doctors have proven (or tried to prove inaccurately) that bras really help in keeping breasts firm, and if left unattended, they would become stretched out, due to the gravitational pull on the fibrous tissue attaching the breasts to the chest.

But according to Christine Haycock, a doctor who actively refuted the previous claim, these fibrous tissues (also known as Cooper's Ligaments) are not actually the tissues that make up the breasts themselves. Their only function is to separate the female chest into two separate sections. The rate at which breasts lose firmness is almost entirely based on genetics, and sometimes, in the case of particularly busty women, on size.

There are other medical sources which go so far as to say that wearing a bra is not only falsely advertised as a tool for breast improvement, but that wearing them regularly can actually be a negative thing. In one scenario, the constricting effects of the constant bra wearer would ultimately cause cysts to appear on her chest, as normal flow became blocked from the lymph to the draining system.

Additionally, bra companies have admitted that the bra's effects on preventing sagginess only holds true when the bra is actually being worn. So, in conclusion, there is at least one more reason for ladies throughout Western civilization to ask, why the hold?

Sources: "Bras, the Bare Facts," Transcribed version of a Channel Four British documentary, 2000; Deborah Franklin, "Busted! Let's Uplift The Truth And Separate The Myth From All Those Reasons Mother Gave Us For Wearing A Bra," *Health Magazine*, 1993.

BRAIN CELLS DIE AND NEVER RETURN

Scientists believed up until quite recently that brain cells, once lost, could never be regenerated. Even though we have a ton of brain cells, avoiding the loss of any of them through activities that could easily be avoided (see list below) was still considered important. Yet, in 1998, lo and behold, scientists realized cells could grow back in mature brains. However, rumors about what voluntary (or in some cases, involuntary) human actions contribute to brain cell loss are still prominent. Here are some toppers:

1. Snorting When You Laugh

Often in grade school, children get a kick out of making fun of their friends who accidentally snort while laughing. However, snorting does not make it worse (unless you're snorting drugs, obviously).

Apparently, we typically are losing roughly 9,000 brain cells a day anyway (we can have 100 trillions of them), and recent research shows that we are able to generate them. So, something like snorting or moving your head rapidly does not make a huge difference in the grand scheme of things.

2. Alcohol

This is one of the most popular misconceptions: You wake up from a night of heavy drinking and feel like a plastic bag is wrapped around your brain. You forget where your shoes are. And for that matter, where your dignity went. "I must have lost a good amount of brain cells last night," you might murmur to yourself as you hazily squint around the room trying to block out the noonday sunlight coming in full throttle solely to mock you.

Well, as destructive as alcohol can be in many physical and psychological ways, it does not actually kill brain cells (at least in what the professionals call "moderate" amounts of consumption). Recent studies have shown that only long-term heavy drinking can potentially kill some brain cells. And at that, only white brain cells are killed, and in some cases, a limited section of gray cells. To clarify, white brain cells are the unimportant ones, i.e., the tissue in which messages are passed between gray cells and the central nervous system. The gray cells, which are responsible for thinking, feeling, and decision making (that about covers it, right?), are much more resilient to mind-altering substances. Only a year or two ago a study was conducted which proved that gray cells located in the parietal lobe of the brain, and which are primarily responsible for spatial processing, do sometimes get destroyed over time in the brains of frequent and heavy drinkers.

Likewise, the brain cells do shrink with repeated alcohol consumption over a long period of time. However, once said alcoholic stops drinking or even if he somehow figures out how to become a moderate social drinker, the brain already begins the healing process, unshrinking itself and making up for lost brain cells.

Yet another reason why we can prove that alcohol at parties is 100 percent necessary for small talk and at family dinners as a coping mechanism.

(Continued)

3. Marijuana

Even more so than alcohol, smoking marijuana has been known to kill brain cells. The logic tends to stem from the idea that most people who smoke a lot of weed (nicknames including, "stoners," "washers," "burnouts," "potheads" . . . you get the idea) do not come across as being especially quick witted or sharp. There was also definitely a period in the late '90s/early 2000s where the quintessential stoner character was often portrayed in popular media as someone who wore a beanie, bummed around, ate a lot of fast food, and said things like "radical, dude" a lot at not so notably radical moments.

However, smoking weed does not, in fact, cause irreversible brain damage. The reason this was originally thought to be the case is from a series of experiments on monkeys. The monkeys were given large quantities of marijuana and their brains were observed. Scientists noted alterations in their brain cells, but did not actually prove that the cells were killed. Since then, no evidence has been found to support these notorious monkey trials.

Even more recently, they have been disproved by two scientists, Dr. William Slikker and two others of the SRI International. Using a larger pool of monkeys and more effective controls, these findings determined no physical destruction of brain cells in brains that were exposed to marijuana for one full year. Also, surveys of heavy marijuana users in Costa Rica and Jamaica also showed no evidential "abnormalities" in brain structure.

Not too shockingly, there is still notable loss of short-term memory functioning even in marijuana users who have stopped smoking for up to twelve weeks prior. But no evidence is shown as to link permanent brain damage with smoking too much weed. We've come a long way from *Reefer Madness*, America.

4. Head Banging

This just in: swinging your head around in rapid, abrupt movements in full force to death metal is not actually good for your brain or body. Or, moreover, your self-image and debatably, self-esteem. Head banging, the gesture of whipping your head forward and back to the beat of some bass heavy music and more rapidly with guitar shredding, originated in 1968 with Led Zeppelin. For most of its existence, there had not been much medical attention focusing on the consequences of this phenomenon . . . until now.

Although there is nothing specific cited about brain cells being destroyed, recent research has revealed several ways in which head banging can potentially cause harm to your physical being. Two Australian researchers came up with the brilliant idea to understand the risks involved with head banging by studying the techniques of the gesture in their prime element: rock concerts.

From their observations, they then simulated a "theoretical head-banging model" into which they inserted various head angles and intensities. They incorporated something like the general consensus of top ten best head banging songs, measured beats per minute (average of 146) and assessed different angles accordingly. What they discovered?

Well, if the head-banging arc is forty-five degrees or more, the head-banger will most likely develop mild head and neck injury.

But there's light at the end of the tunnel: just don't arc more than forty-five degrees in a given head bang and you'll be sure to preserve those brain cells and maybe even have a moderately good time actually listening (rather than thrashing) to the band you came to see for a bit.

5. Sneezing

Like snorting when you laugh, sneezing is another somewhat uncontrollable human mechanism that is rumored to lead to brain cell loss. General public consensus appears to prove this wrong. What a triumph for common sense (and the ability to make painfully obvious jokes about how believing in this rumor means you have less brain cells than those of us who use our brains to see its obvious flaw).

Additionally, one Oregon doctor cited in a local newspaper explores the origins of this myth. The truth be told, he says, sneezing does slightly increase the pressure inside the skull (of the brain). The worries come from the fact that brain pressure increases in severe cases do lead to things like stroke. However, never fear, Dr. Koller claims, the pressure on the brain from a sneeze is so brief, infrequent, and mild that it does not destroy any of those precious brain cells of ours.

Sources: HAMS: Harm Reduction for Alcohol, "Myths and Facts about Alcohol and Brain Damage"; *The Thistle*, "Myths about Marijuana," MIT journal via the National Organization for the Reform of Marijuana Laws, 2000; *The Bend Bulletin*, "Sneezing Kills Brain Cells," Dr. Richard Koller, neurologist, 2010; *Discover Magazine*, "Health Hazard Alert: Head-Banging May Hurt Your Brain," 2009.

WE ONLY USE TEN PERCENT OF OUR **BRAINS**

As the legend goes, Albert Einstein was such a genius because while normal people only use 10 percent of their brains, Einstein figured out a way to activate the whole, or at least a higher percentage of his brain to make such profound advances in mathematics. Although the 10 percent myth can be molded into words of encouragement in some lights and a depressing reality in others, it is indeed a fallacy. While not every function of the brain is known, essentially every part of the brain that scientists have identified has a particular function.

The origin of this myth may have come simply from the inability of early neurologists to figure out all the things the brain did. According to one source, these neurologists had trouble figuring out the function of the brain when experimenting with mice, probably, shockingly, because mice don't have quite the same mental capabilities as humans. Still, earlier scientists seemed to have the misunderstanding that if those unknown areas were damaged, or the damage couldn't be assessed, then there must be large amount of areas where brain activity doesn't exist, or areas where damage would be irrelevant because they are void of activity.

This theory was later proved to be misguided. Even if small areas of the brain are damaged, cognitive ability has been proven to be greatly affected, and if only 10 percent of the brain were active, brain trauma would not so often evoke such dire consequences. Also, interestingly, although not all functions of the brain have been mastered, the 10 percent myth can be countered by taking into account the human brain's energy levels.

According to Barry Beyerstein of the Brain Behavior Laboratory, the brain requires a great deal of nutrients and oxygen and therefore can consume 20 percent of the whole body's energy output, despite the fact that it only takes up roughly 2 to 3 percent of a person's overall body weight. So, as scientists have also proven that the amount of energy the brain requires from the body corresponds to brain functions, if 90 percent of the brain were inactive, so much power would not be used to keep fuelling it.

Moral of the story: Einstein may have just been a little smarter than the rest of us.

Sources: Sandra Aarnodt and Sam Wang (both PhD), *Welcome to Your Brain*, 2008; *Scientific American*, "Do We Really Only Use 10 Percent of our Brains?" 2004.

A PENNY UNDER THE TONGUE TRICKS THE **BREATHALYZER** TEST

So, you're driving down the freeway ramp after a couple of drinks on a night out. You get off at your exit in order to go home and hit the hay, when you unexpectedly run into a "checkpoint," or rather, randomized drunk driving test conducted by your local county police officers. Unfortunately, you won't pass the sobriety test. But then you remember hearing that putting a penny under your tongue will throw off the machine. Something along the lines of, "the copper in the penny combined with alcohol I drank will trigger an outrageously high number on the breathalyzer, the breathalyzer will explode, and I'll be off scot free," is the comforting reasoning you may give yourself. Being out of any other options, you futz around in all your car's compartments for a penny and place it under the tongue.

Sorry to say, but this logic is completely unfounded, and was probably invented by a drunk driver in a desperate scenario not unlike the one we just described. Hopefully it doesn't sound familiar. According to a trustworthy source, State Patrolman Keith Trowbridge, this is, first of all, not a reasonable explanation because since 1982, U.S. pennies have been made mostly of zinc (with the exception of the plating, which is 2.7 percent copper).

Secondly, the police are allowed fifteen minutes to investigate/administer a test. They also check your mouth beforehand. So, even if the penny were to really foil the machine, you still can't fool the man working for it.

Sources: *breathalyzer.org*, *Seattle Pi* blog, "Is it Possible to Beat a Breathalyzer by Sucking on a Penny?"

THE GOLDEN GATE **BRIDGE** IS PERPETUALLY REPAINTED

This bridge has some pretty remarkable qualities, ranging from it being called one of the great modern wonders of the world to it ranking number two on the world's most popular suicide destinations list. One of the reasons this bridge is so notable is because of its attention-grabbing color. In order to maintain its vibrancy and live up to its name, popular rumors suggest,

(Continued)

the bridge needs to constantly be repainted. In extremity, some people believe that the job is full time. In other words, by the time a full new coat of paint is applied from one end to the other, the beginning end has already begun to rust or peel, and thus, the next coating commences immediately. And the cycle repeats itself till the end of time.

Although the Golden Gate Bridge does require a fair amount of maintenance, it does not need to be perpetually painted over and over again. When the bridge was first constructed in 1937, its paint was made with red lead primer and lead-based top coat. For the next twenty-seven years following, only touch-ups were required. In 1968, corrosion on the bridge lead a team to take initiative and change the paint to one made of inorganic zinc silicate primer and vinyl topcoats, completed in 1995 (top coat changed to acrylic emulsion to meet air quality standards in 1990). Since, the bridge has only needed touch-ups in the most severe areas of corrosion.

While the Golden Gate Bridge does receive the highest levels of corrosion from air and bay salt in the bay area compared to other bridges, it is certainly not the only bridge that requires some level of maintenance. In fact, the Fourth Bridge in Edinburgh, Scotland, built in the 19th century, and also painted a red color (so that rust won't show vs. GG's intention: so it complements the landscape) has the honor of beginning the never ending paint rumor. Although, perhaps, the bridge required many and constant touch-ups, as of 2008, the newest layer of paint is meant to last a whopping twenty-five to forty years without need of renovation.

Humorously, the perception that this bridge needed to be repainted over and over again turned itself into a nationally recognized British idiom: "like painting the Fourth Bridge," to refer to a task that takes so long that once it is completed, it needs to be started over again.

So, although the Golden Gate may be no more practical in its choice of color or construction than the Fourth Bridge, the former has definitely been given a much more glorious reputation.

Sources: *GoldenGateBridge.org*, "Painting the Golden Gate Bridge," Golden Gate Bridge Highway and Transportation District; *The Telegraph*, "Non-Stop Job of Painting Forth Bridge to End," Auslan Cramb, 2008 and "The Forth Bridge: How about a Hint of Lavender Next time?" David Leafe, 2008; *Freedictionary.org*, "Idioms."

BRITAIN IS RICH IN NATIVE FRUITS AND VEGETABLES

As A. H. Halsey, Professor of Social and Administrative Studies at Oxford University, has said, horticulture as both art and science is a matter of importation into Britain. Six thousand years ago an early form of wheat was introduced into Britain, and the only native English fruits are almost inedible when raw: they include the sloe, elderberry, damson and crab-apple. Fuchsias come from Chile, chrysanthemums from India and roses from China. An English housewife is likely to bring back from the shops French beans, Spanish onions, Jaffa oranges, Caribbean bananas, and New Zealand lamb.

Source: A. H. Halsey, "What books I please," broadcast on B.B.C. Radio 3, December 27, 1979.

BOOMERANGS ARE USED BECAUSE THEY RETURN TO THE THROWER

The great majority of boomerangs, used predominantly by Australian aborigines in war and hunting, will not return and are not intended to do so. The returning boomerang is completely unknown in Central Australia and Northern Territory. It is used in tests of skill, and its main use is in throwing above flights of duck, which mistake it for a hovering hawk and consequently fly low into nets placed by the aborigines.

Source: Museum of Mankind exhibition (London), 1976.

BULLS ARE INFURIATED BY THE COLOR RED

No: bulls are infuriated by a cruel posturing mercenary "fighter" waving a cloth in front of him to the accompaniment of merciless cheering by bloodthirsty spectators. Bulls cannot distinguish red from any other color, and matadores who experimentally used white capes in their antics produced an identical reaction. While visiting Palma de Mallorca in 1976 I found a poster advertising bloodless bullfights for the benefit of squeamish tourists, and Portuguese bullfights are traditionally bloodless. The color red was probably first used partly because in strong sunlight it is the most brilliant color, and partly because it does not show blood so clearly.

SKIN CAN'T **BURN** IN CLOUDY WEATHER

Those of us with pasty pale skin know from experience that if there's even a little sun in the forecast, some SPF is probably in order. Presumably, if you have fairly bronzed skin naturally, you won't burn as easily, and therefore assume there's less to zero reason to apply sunscreen unless you are planning for a day of serious sun exposure. Well, think again, Caucasians.

There are, according to the FDA, six general types of skin tone. Types one to four cover the very pale with freckles who burn easily through the generally tan to moderate brown skin types (probably Caucasian of Mediterranean descent, or of African, Asian, Hispanic, Indian, or Middle Eastern ancestry). For these skin types in particular, it is imperative to wear sun screen even when it looks cloudy or overcast outside.

An explanation for this seemingly illogical phenomenon can be provided through a definition of what a sunburn is. A sunburn on one's skin is due to the ultraviolet radiation (UV rays) in sunlight. These "rays" are distinct from sunlight itself, as they cannot be seen or felt directly by us humans here on earth. UV rays are not blocked from reaching us by clouds, and they are also able to scatter in the air and are reflected via smooth surfaces such as buildings, concrete, sand, and snow.

While we are only really susceptible to two of the three types of UV rays, the effects of the two that do reach us are quite dangerous and damaging to skin. UVA penetrates into deep layers of skin and damages the place where new skin cells are generated. Too much exposure to UVA radiation can lead to dryness, roughness, wrinkling, blotching, and sagging of skin. Especially high doses of UVA can lead to bad sunburn, and even skin cancer.

Interestingly, the more dangerous UV ray (UVB), affects the surface layer of skin. The skin then responds to rays by releasing chemicals that dilate vessels of blood, which in part triggers fluid leakage and inflammation (sunburn).

Certain types of UV rays are projected through not just sunlight but through all natural light. Therefore, you are never safe from UV rays, sunburn, or damage to the insides of your skin that you are quite unaware of. And now that you are aware, best to wear sunscreen in all day light!

Sources: Better Health Channel via Victorian Government Department of Health, "Sunburn"; Dr. Judith Reichman, "It's a Cloudy day. Should I still use Sunscreen?" MSNBC Today, 2004.

COWS THAT EAT BUTTERCUPS GIVE THE YELLOWEST **BUTTER**

A folk fallacy found in several parts of the British Isles. Buttercups grow only on good pastureland, the surrounding grass of which is likely to improve butter (and milk) quality by giving the best quality feed to the cow. Cows will not eat the buttercups, a nauseous, bitter weed. Source: The Field, June 9, 1906.

C

"A common error is the greater and more mischievous for being so common."

—CLARENDON

"La causa mas universal de los errores comunes es que los más de los hombres no pasan con el discurso más allá de la superficie de las cosas." (The most frequent cause of common errors is the fact that most people never delve beneath superficialities).

—FRAY BENITO JERONIMO FEIJOO

THE **CAESAREAN SECTION** WAS FIRST PERFORMED AT THE BIRTH OF JULIUS CAESAR

The Caesarean section, in earlier times, involved saving the life of a newborn child at the expense of its mother by removing the child through a cut made in the front of the abdomen. The operation, known as Caesarean section, is popularly believed to have been first performed on Julia, mother of Julius Caesar, but the operation is not recorded as early as 100 B.C., and Julia lived many years after the birth of the future Dictator.

The name "Caesarean section" probably derives from the so-called "Lex Regia" or "Lex Caesarea," which decreed that the child should be removed from every woman who died when far advanced in pregnancy, even in cases where the child stood no chance of survival, so that mother and child might be buried separately. Such a case is obviously inapplicable to Julia and her son.

Incidentally, Caesar was never Roman Emperor (there was no "Empire" as such until after his time), but first Consul (five times) and eventually Dictator.

Source: Howard W. Haggard, *Devils, drugs and doctors* (London, 1929, pp. 40-1).

CAFFEINE FALLACIES

1) Coffee Stunts Your Growth

As kids, we were told that drinking coffee was a bad idea because it could hinder the growing process. Although there are a fair amount of legitimate reasons why parents should discourage kids from consuming too much caffeine (such as the drug's tendency to increase feelings of anxiety, increase heart rate, insomnia, and sour stomach), height restriction is not one of them.

The myth that coffee stunts growth resulted from misinterpreted data from years ago, when it was thought that caffeine in coffee had some contribution in osteoporosis in later life and loss of bone mass. Now experts have realized (hallelujah!) that the studies previously conducted did not factor in lack of calcium in finding these results.

Let's drink to celebrate another victory for Starbucks' double chip mocha frappuccinos (in other words, candy crack for kids).

2) Caffeine Causes Dehydration

Like all "drugs," there are pros and cons to caffeine, perhaps depending on your age, ethics, and/or personal experience. According to word on the street (and personal experience), caffeine is the culprit of dehydration, if not properly monitored and/or countered with water.

The reason caffeine is said to cause dehydration comes from the fact that it is a stimulant, moreover, naturally diuretic. But according to recent findings, caffeine is found to actually be quite mild in its diuretic properties, so mild, one source argues, that it is comparable to that of water. After an investigation of ten different studies on the topic, it was concluded that in all ten cases, consuming caffeine led to a zero to 84 percent urine volume retention rate, while drinking water was zero to 81 percent retention of initial urine volume.

Other reports indicate that there is no evidence to show that consuming caffeinated beverages leads to a fluid-electrolyte imbalance. Also, it is possible to develop immunity to the mild diuretic qualities of caffeine over time, if consumed regularly. Not unlike smoking cigarettes; both of which begin to have no real effect on their consumers if they become routine habits anyway.

Additionally, it is said that if people sustain healthy diets alongside drinking a normal amount of caffeine (something like one to four cups of coffee or tea per day), there is really no risk of serious dehydration, or losing any more urine volume than in

(Continued)

drinking lots of water (see YOU SHOULD DRINK 8 OR MORE GLASSES OF WATER PER DAY). Again, your frequent coffee fixes are still innocent until proven guilty.

3) Carbonation in Caffeinated Drinks Is Harmful to Bones

If you get your daily caffeine fix from colas and/or energy drinks, your health may be slightly more at risk. But as you may assume that the main differentiating factor between these beverages and coffee and tea (carbonation) is the culprit, this is not really so.

According to a number of fairly recent studies, there is no significant decrease in bone density loss in people who regularly drink carbonated beverages, but there is a slight decrease in those who drink cola carbonated drinks. The way in which this can be understood is through comparing the carbonation in seltzer water to that of soda (cola). Carbonated water in its "natural" state is created by dissolving carbon dioxide in water, thus resulting in carbonic acid as its main ingredient. Soda products are also typically made with the same process. However, there are also small amounts of phosphoric and citric acid in them (along with loads of sugar and chemicals). Although both forms of carbonation can be mildly erosive to bones, the risk of bone loss in soda drinkers is still more significant than in club soda drinkers (though it's advisable to pay attention to how much sodium is included in the soda water you are buying because it varies).

Also, the health risks involved with drinking soda are much more clearly proved in regards to obesity from the sugar rather than in bone deterioration due to carbonation. Even in cases where soda was proven to have slightly harmful effects on calcium levels in bones, those affected were only really older women who tend to suffer bone loss at a certain age regardless of what they are consuming. Plus, the acids in the stomach are exponentially higher than the acids in seltzer water and in soda, so unless you drink more than one can of soda a day and have been doing so all your life, it probably won't make much of a difference in your stature.

Sources: CNN Health, "Is Carbonated Water Safe to Drink?" Dr. Melina Jampolis, 2011; *9Med Journal*, "Colas but not other carbonated beverages are associated with low bone mineral density in older women: The Framingham Osteoporosis Study," 2008; MSNBC Today Health, "Fact or Fiction: Common Diet Myths Dispelled," 2006; Anahad O'Connor, *Really* blog, "The Claim: Caffeine Causes Dehydration," *New York Times*, 2008; *Advance* (University of Connecticut), "Armstrong's Study Shows Caffeine Does Not Increase Dehydration," Janice Palmer, 2002.

THE **CALIFORNIAN COAST** SLIPPED INTO THE OCEAN IN APRIL 1969

Thousands of people deserted California in April 1969 after hundreds alleged having received prophecies through ouija boards, dreams and spiritualistic seances united to the effect that the West Coast of the United States was about to slip forthwith, with loss of life and property, into the Pacific Ocean.

When the predicted event did not happen, where were the shame-faced prophets? Will they stop attending, to false mediums, and to their debris of their dreams? Will they, can they possibly, desert their homes and their reason when the panic strikes again?

Why not? For the churches of California continue to bewitch their gullible congregations, as Nathanael West wrote of his hero and alter ego, Tod Hackett, in his novel *The day of the locust* (1939): "He spent his nights at the different Hollywood churches, drawing the worshippers. He visited the "Church of Christ, Physical" where holiness was attained through the constant use of chestweights and spring grips; the "Church Invisible" where fortunes were told and the dead made to find lost objects; the "Tabernacle of the Third Coming" where a woman in male clothing preached the "Crusade Against Salt"; and the "Temple Moderne" under whose glass and chromium roof "Brain-Breathing, the Secret of the Aztecs" was taught.

As he watched these people writhe on the hard seats of their churches, he thought of how well Alessandro Magnasco would drama-tize the contrast between their drained-out, feeble bodies and their wild, disordered minds. He would not satirize them as Hogarth or Daumier might, nor would he pity them. He would paint their fury with respect, appreciating its awful, anarchic power and aware that they had it in them to destroy civilization.

One Friday night in the "Tabernacle of the Third Coming," a man near Tod stood up to speak. Although his name most likely was Thompson or Johnson and his hometown Sioux City, he had the same countersunk eyes, like the heads of burnished spikes, that a monk by Magnasco might have. He was probably just in from one of the colonies in the desert near Soboba Hot Springs where he had been conning over his soul on a diet of raw fruit and nuts. He was very angry. The message he had brought to the city was one that an illiterate anchorite might have given decadent Rome. It was a crazy jumble of dietary rules, economics, and Biblical threats. He claimed to have seen the Tiger of Wrath stalking the walls of the citadel and the Jackal of Lust skulking in the shrubbery, and he connected these omens with "thirty dollars every Thursday" and "meat eating."

CALORIC

The most important fallacy concerning heat in the 18th century centered on the idea that heat was a material substance capable of being poured or otherwise transferred from one substance to another. Caloric (from the Latin calor, "heat") was supposed to pass from burning paper into the flame. A boiling saucepan, for example, transferred caloric from the wood or charcoal below it into the flame, then through the surface of the saucepan into the water. When the water received the caloric, it was converted into steam.

The fallacy was exploded for the first time by an American, Benjamin Thomson, who fled his country during the Civil War and worked as a physicist in charge of the arsenal of the Elector of Bavaria. In 1798, while supervising the boring of brass cannon, he noted that a great deal of heat was being produced—in excess of that which could be expected by the caloric theory. Enough heat was in fact being generated to bring eighteen pounds of water to boiling point in under three hours. He deduced that heat must be a vibration generated and intensified by the friction (and communicated by the motion) of the borer against the cannon, and not a material substance.

Though clearly fallacious, the caloric theory remained popular and was taught in schools all over Europe for half a century after it was proved wrong. Heat has long been known as a form of energy, like electricity and magnetism.

CAMELHAIR BRUSHES ARE MADE FROM THE HAIR OF CAMELS

Camelhair brashes are made for artists and architects from the hair of the tails of Russian squirrels. The hair of camels, on the other hand, was used for making carpets, tent-cloths, and for mixing with silk. But the advent of synthetic fibers has vastly reduced the use of the hair of camels, as well as that of "camel-hair."

CAMELS HAVE A HUMP FOR STORING WATER

Camels have a hump (or two humps in the case of a Bactrian) which does not have a hollow reservoir for water inside. Excess food and drink that the camel does not need at once are stored in the body as fat and other substances, to be drawn on in time of need. Water is present not only in the hump (together with the fat) but is stored also in other body tissues and in the stomach pouches, allowing the animal to survive without drinking for seven days (if working quite actively) or ten to twelve days (if inactive).

Source: Osmond P. Breland, *Animal facts and fallacies* (London, 1950).

CANARY BIRDS GAVE THEIR NAME TO THE CANARY ISLANDS

Quite the reverse! The Latin name insula Canada derived from the large canes or dogs found there. Birds exported from these islands off the western coast of Morocco were called "canaries" from the place they came from, not the other way round.

CARROTS IMPROVE VISION

The method of parents dropping this line in front of their children in order to get them to eat vegetables is, in our opinion, 100 percent justified. However, like most enticing elements of healthy foods aside from the plain and simple fact that they're better for you than Taco Bell or Sloppy Joes, carrots do not possess magic vision enhancing qualities.

The reason this myth about carrots and their link to vision came about is because they are associated with Vitamin A. Carrots, and other vegetables, don't have Vitamin A directly in them, unlike fish and liver. However, carrots have carotene, and when you eat them, carotene gets converted in your liver to Vitamin A. Vitamin A is important for a number of things such as immune system, skin, etc., but also, apparently, for vision. Vitamin A travels in one's blood to the retina, where it is converted to a chemical called retinal. Once light hits the retinal, communication between retina and other parts of the brain that evoke vision are triggered.

It's a little convoluted, but maybe in some way carrots are helpful, if you can keep the end in sight!

Sources: Karl S. Kruszelnicki, ABC Science, "Carrots & Night Vision," 2005.

CAT ALLERGIES IN HUMANS ARE CAUSED BY CAT FUR

Having an allergy to cats is quite common, albeit inconvenient in some pet loving households. According to medical sources, people with pet allergies are twice as likely to be allergic to cats than dogs.

Despite what one might think, the allergies are not triggered by cat fur (rest assured, cat household hosts, no need to vacuum up all the traces of fur on the tapestries before the guests come over). Instead, the flu, cold and/or asthmatic-like symptoms that

(Continued)

occur in cat allergics are products of a hypersensitive immune system's reaction to the proteins in a cat's saliva, urine, and dander (dry flakes of skin; think dandruff).

As one probably wouldn't ingest an animal's saliva or urine, these lovely microscopic pieces of dead skin are all you've got to worry about. But beware: dander can collect on cat fur, in addition to other types of common allergens such as dust and pollen. Furthermore, dander can cling to articles of clothing, such as wool sweaters. So, although the cat hair itself is not the direct culprit of human cat allergies, maybe the hairless Sphynx is a prime choice for those easily prone to allergic reactions.

Sources: *webmd.com / allergies / cat-allergies;* Asthma and Allergy Foundation of America, "Pet Allergies."

CATS ALWAYS LAND ON THEIR FEET

We think it's fair to assume that no one really believes the myth that cats are able to get into otherwise fatal situations on nine separate occasions. By comparison, the theory that cats, being fairly nimble creatures, could manage to land upright on all fours after falling from any height is not so outrageous. But still.

Cats do have a physiological advantage over other animals in terms of the likelihood of them being able to survive a bad fall. The middle of a cat, according to experts, is a kind of universal joint, which makes the vertebrae in their backbones allow for more flexibility. When they fall, cats automatically "right" themselves, meaning they can twist their bodies to make it so that they are going to land feet first, cushioning their fall.

Although it is more than reasonable to assume that cats, like other animals, despite their flexible bodies, are not invincible, and would probably die if they fell from something as tall as, say, a New York skyscraper. Still, according to a popular-for-cat-enthusiasts study published in the '80s in the *Journal of American Veterinary Medical Association*, our feline friends are actually more likely to survive after falling from taller heights. Here, two vets drew from 132 instances where cats had been taken to the hospital after falling out of a high-rise building. According to these findings, on average, cats fell 5.5 stories, and 90 percent of them survived.

These results are impressive, but believable. However, more questionable are the other findings in the abovementioned study.

As you might expect, the number of injuries and broken bones in these cats increased as the buildings from which they fell got taller ... but only up until seven stories. In other words, the cats that had fallen from buildings higher than seven stories were left with significantly fewer injuries. To justify this phenomenon, the vets explained that the reason cats are better off falling from taller heights is because after they fall five stories, they reach terminal velocity (or, maximum downward-falling speed), at sixty miles per hour. Afterwards, they are able to manipulate and stretch their bodies to form a kind of parachute, thus, softening their landing upon impact with the ground.

Perhaps because this study is often used as evidence to support the almost entirely useless theory that cats are naturally fond of heights (high-rise syndrome), it stands, more or less, uncorrected. However, there are, thankfully, doctors who affirmately say that after cats fall from more than two or three stories up, even if they do try to land on their feet, their legs and feet will not be able to absorb the shock alone, so their heads might instead hit the ground first.

So, really, if cats do for some reason more often survive falls from over seven stories up, it is not related to their body's tendency to land feet first. Besides, if cats are likely to survive a fall from two to three stories up because they can "right themselves," and also from seven stories and above due to the explanation above, then why would firefighters and elderly people make such a big fuss about these pets getting stuck in elm trees planted on suburban lawns?

Sources: John Stossel and Frank Mastropolo, "Does a Falling Cat Always Land on Its Feet?" ABC News, 2007; Doctors Foster and Smith, "Do Cats Always Land on Their Feet?" *Pet Education*; US National Library of Medicine, "Feline high-rise syndrome: 119 cases (1998-2001)."

CAT FALLACIES

1. Black or White Cats are Bad or Good Luck

In the United States, Spain, and some other countries, a white cat is considered lucky, and a black cat unlucky. In Britain, the opposite fallacy prevails. Neither has of course a grain of truth in it. Both go back to the time when "witches" were assumed to have "familiars" and most old ladies living alone kept a cat for company, so the "familiar" must have been a cat. A black cat's green eyes, seen apparently "disembodied" in the dark, have been a source of fear to the ignorant and nervous.

2. Color and Gender of Cats Are Related

Charles Darwin, no less, wrote in *The descent of man* that "the tortoise-shell colour, which is confined to female cats, is quite distinct at birth." But Kit Wilson's *Cat encyclopedia* (Kingswood, Surrey, 1951) disagrees. "There have been statements that sexual difference of colouring has been found in the cat tribe. This is a fallacy, and probably arose over the question of the red male being the counterpart of the tortoiseshell female. This theory has been exploded very successfully; there are as many red females on the show bench today as males, also some tortoiseshell males have made their appearance."

3. Cats Can See in the Dark

Cats can see in the dark, but only if the dark is not complete. In pitch blackness, the cat is as helpless as you or I.

4. Certain Cats Are Better "Quality" Than Others:

It is also a fallacy that "pedigree" cats are of outstanding quality. In *Cats* (Harmondsworth, 1957), Brian Vesey-Fitzgerald observes: "It should be pointed out that every cat, that every living creature, has a pedigree. It may not always be known, and it may be very disreputable, but it is a pedigree. What is meant by the term "pedigree cat" is a cat whose ancestry on both sides is known for some generations back, a cat with the unadulterated blood of a particular breed. This does not necessarily mean that it is a cat of outstanding quality. No breeder can say what qualities are going to appear in the kittens of any particular mating."

5. Cats Have a Bad Sense of Smell

The cat's sense of smell is commonly thought to be poor. "Indeed," writes Vesey-Fitzgerald, "you do sometimes meet people who maintain that the cat has no sense of smell. In fact, the cat has an exceptionally acute and delicate sense of smell—much more delicate than has the dog."

6. Cats Have Nine Lives

Regrettably not. They have the regulation issue of one. However, the cat's good sense, caution, and shrewdness have given it the reputation of surviving when any other animal would have perished, particularly when falling on its feet from a reasonable height,

We are indebted to Dean Inge, writing in the *Evening Standard* of July 8, 1936, for immortalizing the child's essay on cats: "The cat is a quadruped, the legs as usual being at the four corners . . . Do not tease cats, for, firstly, it is wrong to do so, and, secondly, cats have claws, which are longer than people think. Cats have nine lives, but which are seldom required in this country, because of Christianity."

CATGUT

is not that at all, but the fibrous layer of sheep's intestine, toughened with chromic acid. The strings of musical instruments owe nothing whatsoever to the domestic cat.

EDGAR CAYCE AND MEDICAL DIAGNOSIS BY REMOTE CONTROL

A small library and a great cult have formed around the person and alleged powers of Edgar Cayce, who was born in Hopkinsville, Kentucky, in 1877, and died in 1945. The Association for Research and Enlightenment Inc. (ARE) was founded in 1932 at Virginia Beach, Virginia to preserve, study and publish the so-called readings of Edgar Cayce. ARE is now run by Cayce's sons. Hugh Lynn Cayce writes in Doris Agee's *Edgar Cayce on E.S.P.* (New York, 1969): "when Edgar Cayce died . . . , he left well over 14,000 documented stenographic records of the telepathic-clairvoyant statements he had given for more than six thousand different people over a period of forty-three years. These documents are referred to as 'readings.'"

The readings are considered important by Hugh Lynn Cayce, because they "constitute one of the largest and most impressive records of psychic perception ever to emanate from a single individual."

However, no qualified doctor (and Cayce had no orthodox medical qualifications of any kind—indeed he left school after seventh grade) would agree that it is reputable to diagnose an illness or disease without a careful physical examination coupled with an interview with the patient concerning signs and symptoms.

Cayce's method of diagnosis was to enter a (probably genuine) self-hypnotic trance, lying on his back facing south (or later north). In trance, whether the patient was absent or present, Cayce would give, in Martin Gardner's words "a rambling diagnosis of the cause of the disorder, in terms borrowed largely from osteopathy and homeopathy. Most of Cayce's early trances were given with the aid of an osteopath who asked him questions while he was asleep, and helped later in explaining the reading to the patient."

The origin of Cayce's readings can, therefore, be ascribed to associations with osteopaths and fundamentalist religion which favored an unenquiring, uncritical approach. In *There is a river* (1943), the Roman Catholic writer Thomas Sugrue suggested that, if a patient "doubted" Cayce's ability to diagnose his ailment correctly, the diagnosis would not be good. The gullible are thereby satisfied and the skeptical are silenced. But J. B. Rhine of Duke University, a believer in clairvoyance, was critical of Cayce when the reading for Rhine's daughter failed to fit the facts, and there is no doubt that there was never any real medical value in a Cayce reading other than inspired guesswork. The remedies included spinal massage, herbal concoctions, special diets, tonics, electrical treatments and such bizarre notions as "oil of smoke" for a leg sore and almonds for cancer.

Cayce was eventually persuaded by supporters that he enjoyed occult powers, though he was a kindly man by all accounts, with a charming smile, and a willingness to listen to those interested in theosophy, pyramidology, and Atlantis. He believed, or at any rate said he believed, that Atlantis would rise again in 1968-9, but the failure of yet another prediction has not daunted the many study groups formed specifically to consider Cayce's readings. Cayce taught that Arcturus is the next abode of souls leaving the solar system and, in his *Auras* (1945), stated that throughout his life he had been able to diagnose a patient's health and character from the colored aura which he could see surrounding everybody's head and shoulders.

There is no sense in which Cayce, honestly trying to help people who for one reason or another repudiated orthodox medical diagnosis, deliberately deceived anyone, at least as far as is known at present. Certainly his "cures" were demonstrably ineffective in many cases, and nonsensical in others, but there is a residue of readings which, by a process of luck or experience or a combination of both, actually helped the patient.

The danger is that the gullible will be tempted to infer that, because some treatments were successful, so the methods must be successful in other situations. This is not the case, but there has arisen a vast new pseudo-medical field called "paradiagnostics," which claims to make use of clairvoyance in which there is no physical contact with the patient.

It was after reading Joseph Millard's *Edgar Cayce: mystery man of miracles* (Greenwich, Conn., 1961) that Dr. Shafica Karagulla, a Christian Turk, decided that Cayce was a genuine clairvoyant and started to explore for others with his "powers." Dr. Karagulla, who is president and director of the Higher Sense Perception Research Foundation, 8668½ Wilshire Boulevard, Beverly Hills, has worked largely with Dora van Gelder, and has described her work in *Breakthrough to creativity: your higher sense perception* (Santa Monica, 1967). In *Psychic* (vol. IV, no. 6, July-August 1973), Dr. Karagulla indicated her belief in "energy sappers," or people who can steal energy from others. She states that energy sappers are self-centered, their flow of energy being inward, not outward.

Sources include: Martin Gardner, *Fads and fallacies in the name of science* (New York, 1957, pp. 216-9).

A PERSON WITH A TATTOO CANNOT BE BURIED IN A JEWISH **CEMETERY**

You probably have had a Jewish friend who debates getting a tattoo because he knows that once he does, he will be banned in death from joining his Jewish ancestors and immediate family members in the shared burial grounds. Perhaps you have experienced this dilemma yourself.

Although this consideration may be outdated for a lot of not-especially religious Jews, especially in light of the fact that something like 30 to 50 percent of the general population have them now, the rumor still circulates, at least among those of us who are not incredibly familiar with the Jewish religious customs.

According to Rabbi Chani Benjaminson, the Torah prohibits Jews from tattooing their bodies. However, there is no general rule against burying those who have tattoos that applies to all Jewish cemeteries. The forbidding of tattooed bodies in Jewish funeral grounds depends on the laws of each individual burial society. Because every sector has the right to decide who can and cannot be buried on their lands, sometimes—though rarely—a tattooed person will be denied because they had in life defied the Jewish Law. But there is no law that itself applies to burying people with tattoos in any Jewish plot.

The Rabbi at Amy Winehouse's funeral, deemed "progressive" by CNN's Richard Allan Greene, claims there isn't even an absolute Jewish law that specifically forbids its people to get tattoos. He says there is no direct evidence of this rule, but that the misperception may have stemmed from instructions in the Biblical book of Leviticus, which prohibits the marking of one's skin. However, Rabbi Mark Goldsmith also confirms that as these instructions were part of a series of "Canaanite cultic practices" that Israelites were not meant to follow, they should not be considered.

Either way, young people of all faiths and heritages with strict parents but rebellious feelings have an equal chance of getting shunned from the families for breaking traditions.

Sources: Chani Benjaminson, *Chadbad.org*, "Ask The Rabbi," "Can a Person with a Tattoo be Buried in a Jewish Cemetery?" Richard Allen Greene, "Winehouse Burial Raises Jewish Questions about Tattoos, Cremation," CNN, 2011.

CENTRIFUGAL FORCE VS. CENTRIPETAL FORCE

Some people claim when a person says centrifugal force, what they are really referring to is centripetal force. Nevertheless, centrifugal is the term used far more often in popular culture. While the distinction between the two is certainly not black and white, especially for non-physics experts, both terms and phenomena do separately exist.

As centripetal force is the more substantial and universally valid force, we will define that one first. Centripetal force, put relatively simply, is the force that pulls a rotating object toward the center of what it is rotating around. For instance, as the moon rotates around the earth, the centripetal force is supplied by gravity that keeps pulling the moon toward the center of the earth. If this force did not exist, the moon would break away and move in a straight line at a constant speed (according to Newton's first law of motion). More applicably, if you had a tennis ball tied to the end of a string and spun it in circles around you, the centripetal force is supplied by your hand holding onto the string so the ball doesn't fly away.

The primary difference between centripetal and centrifugal force is that they occur in different frames of reference. This basically means different viewpoints to measure from. For instance, if a person is standing on the street and throws a ball down the street and it goes 40 feet away from you, you would say the street is the frame of reference used to measure the distance. Also, if you are moving at a constant speed in a straight line and throw a ball, you measure from the distance in which you threw the ball from.

In general, if you are either standing still or moving at a constant speed in a straight line, you are using an inertial frame of reference. There is also, not surprisingly but definitely more complicated, a non-inertial frame of reference. These frames of references occur when a force accelerates in some way that we can't see or don't control, due to a change in direction or change in speed that we don't expect. As an example, a person on a merry go round experiences a non-inertial force/frame of reference. A person watching someone from the ground on a merry-go-round sees that the person on the ride is rotating in a circle around the center on a fake plastic horse. However, the person on the horse looking straight ahead cannot really see that they are moving, but rather only feels the force rotating them. They feel a force pulling them (centrifugal force) away from the center of the merry-go-round while they are actually being pulled toward it.

> Centrifugal force and centripetal force are the same thing, but they occur in opposite directions because they are seen from different points of reference. So while both of these forces exist, centripetal force is the one that we can more easily measure, and centrifugal force is the one we commonly talk about because it's the one we "feel."
>
> **Sources:** Andy Ganse, "The Difference Between 'Centripetal' and 'Centrifugal' Force," Applied Physics Laboratory, University of Washington, 2006; *Merriam-Webster*, compared definitions of "Centripetal" and "Centrifugal."

THE YEAR ENDING DECEMBER 31, 2000 IS THE FIRST YEAR OF A **CENTURY**

The year beginning January 1, 2000 and ending on December 31, 2000 is the last year of the 20th century, not the first year of the 21st. The reason is that the Christian calendar dates from January 1 of the year 1, not the year 0.

CARNEADES ON THE FALLACY OF **CERTITUDE**

Carneades of Cyrene (c. 214-c. 129 B.C.) was the founder of the so-called Third or New Academy. With the Stoic Diogenes of Babylon and the Peripatetic Critolaus he was a member of the celebrated Athenian delegation of philosophers sent to Rome in 156-155. Though none of his writings survives, his lectures in Rome were famous in their time for their dialectical and rhetorical power as well as for their fearless moral independence, and are recorded in the Cato Maior of Plutarch and in the Lucullus and other works of Cicero.

He is the greatest systematic figure in classical skepticism, like Arcesilaus denying all possibility of certitude. His arguments lead to the withholding of judgment; he nevertheless admitted different stages of clarity in human perception, and the perception which carries conviction he entitled a "convincing or probable presentation" (pithanè phantasiá; see Sextus Empiricus, Pros mathematikoús ("Against the schoolmasters,") vii, 184 f.). The positive aspect of Carneades' skepticism was his theory of probability, but his negative criticism of the metaphysicians' failure to find rationality in religious beliefs made a great impression in his day. He repudiated all dogmatic doctrines such as Stoicism, and did not even spare the Epicureans as previous skeptics had done. He denied the immortality of the gods, their allegedly superhuman qualities, pantheism, fatalism, and providence. He refused to accept any moral values as absolute, while indicating the necessity of learning how to conduct one's life by combining wise thought with wise action. The quotation below is based on hearsay and is further diluted by translation; yet it still seems to echo the quiet voice of a moderate thinker born on the green hills of Cyrene.

"There is absolutely no criterion for truth," said Carneades. "For reason, senses, ideas, or whatever else may exist are all deceptive, Even if such a criterion were available, it could not be separated from the feelings produced by sense impressions. It is the faculty of feeling that distinguishes the living creature from inanimate things. By means of that feeling, the living creature becomes perceptive both of itself and of the external world. There is no sensation or perception of anything unless the sense is irritated, agitated, or perturbed. When an object is indicated, then the senses become irritated and somewhat disturbed. It is impossible that there be an unperturbed presentation of external things.

The subject is more or less persuaded by the image it perceives. The strength of that persuasion depends on the disposition of the subject and on the degree of irritation produced by the image. It is not the distinctness of the image that constitutes its credibility.

The only way we can ever obtain certitude is by the difficult process of examination. We cannot be satisfied with evidence that is incomplete and only probable. Our certitude is always a precarious one. Science must rely on probabilities therefore, not on certitude."

The witty bent of Carneades' mind can be judged from his retort to the master from whom he learnt logic, Diogenes: "If I reason correctly, then I am satisfied; if wrong, give me back my mina," the fee for the lectures.

Sources include: *The Oxford Classical Dictionary* (Oxford, 1949); and Dagobert D. Runes (ed.), *Treasury of philosophy* (New York, 1955).

CHAMELEONS MATCH THEIR BACKGROUND

Most people would swear that this is the case, though few of them have seen a chameleon. In fact, though experiments have proved that many of these lizards can indeed change color rapidly, there is no evidence that the color of their background has any but a marginal importance, the main factors influencing color change being light, temperature, and the chameleon's health and feelings.

Those keeping a chameleon are advised not to take too seriously the fallacy perpetuated by Shakespeare in *Hamlet* (HI, ii, 98) that the reptile lives on air.

"CHAMOIS"-LEATHER DERIVES FROM THE CHAMOIS

Not any more. Nowadays, defying the Trades Description Act, "chamois" has nothing to do with the Alpine creature, but derives from the flesh side of sheepskin, reduced to an even thickness with a pumicestone and soaked in lime-water and a solution of sulphuric acid.

THE NECESSITY OF **CHANCE**

In *Chance and necessity* (London, 1972), Jacques Monod of the Institut Pasteur commits the "Only One" or "Nothing But" fallacy observed in the case of TEILHARD DE CHARDIN.

Strange to say, however, where Teilhard's evolutionary theories admit only design, Monod's beliefs admit only chance. "Chance alone is at the source of every innovation, of all creation in the biosphere ... This central concept of modern biology is no longer one among other possible or even conceivable hypotheses. It is today," writes Professor Monod with absolute finality, "the sole conceivable hypothesis, the only one that squares with observed and tested fact. And nothing warrants the supposition—or the hope—that on this score our position is ever likely to be revised."

Now, it is not possible to accept both Monod's position and Teilhard's. The remaining alternatives are (a) that one of them is wholly correct and the other wholly incorrect, which is highly unlikely to be the case, since each case is so thoroughly argued; and (b) that both of them are wrong, which is highly likely, since each argues that his position is wholly correct and admits of no reconsideration. In scientific thought, dogmas as opposed to proofs are quite frequently found to be wanting. (Sir Isaac Newton persuaded millions of the absolute reality of space and time, which cannot be wholly correct if Einstein's theories of relativity are wholly correct. Again it seems likely that while Newton was in grave error, Einstein appears not to have been wholly correct).

CHARMS

It is a fallacy to assume that the wearing of any charm (see also AMULETS) can bring good fortune to the wearer, though this compound of fear and ignorance has never shown any sign of dying out in any society or in any age. The best that can be said of the error is that it bestows a spurious confidence on the superstitious owner of the charm (which can turn to panic more readily if the charm can be seen not to be "working") and the owner then attributes success to the wearing of the charm rather than to the confidence he induced in himself by wearing it. The mundane proof of the fallacy is that, in any given baseball or football match of importance, many players on both sides wear charms, though it is evident that both teams cannot win (especially in the event of a draw).

ROBERT **CHARROUX** AND THE MYSTERIOUS UNKNOWN

For those with an unconquerable aversion to historical and archaeological facts, Robert Charroux's books will be required reading. *The mysterious unknown* (London, 1972), for example, comprises twenty-two chapters teetering on the brink between the obvious on the one hand (the well-known Moebius Strip is adduced as a mystery!) and baseless speculation on the other. If you don't believe me (and please don't!), here are the chapter-titles and a specimen example from each: Unsolved enigmas (St. Brendan's Isle), Fantastic science (the Moebius Strip), Ancient sciences (a plant to make granite malleable), Memory chromosomes (Dolmens, cathedrals and rugby matches on other planets), Tradition and the mystery of the megaliths (Carnac and the Trojan War), Celtic civilization (Were the Incas Celts?), Vanished civilization (Denis Saurat's giants), Atlantis (The Hebrews, were they Bretons?), Other sites for Atlantis (The Caspian, Heligoland, the Mediterranean, Mongolia), Hyperborea and Egypt (Was Apollo an Extra-Terrestrial Being?), Barbarian civilizations (The Celts of San Agustín), The Mystery of the Pyramids (The Curse of the Dead), The Mystery of Phantasms (How to see flying saucers), Words, Apes and Dolphins (The Yeti, is it Hanuman?), The Water of Life (The power of rain water), Ancient mysteries (The mystery of Delos), The Mystery of Agartha and of Shamballah (The luminous race), The Universe (Who created it?), Oddments and oddities (Napoleon, Breton or Charentais?), Prediction and the end of the world (Electronic astrology), Sorcery (Never eat beans), and Extra-terrestrials and the journey to Bâavi (Life on Mars).

As if this were not enough, M. Charroux's revelations in another book, *Masters of the world*, include a fallacious proof that a universal deluge (with waves of 6,000 feet!) did indeed occur; the allegedly "secret" powers of jade, which are presumably no longer secrets and are certainly not powers; and an erroneous exposition of the inscriptions on Tibetan stone discs, which the author claims prove that spacecraft visited Earth in the remote past.

In 100,000 years of man's unknown history (New York, 1971), M. Charroux asks us to believe that superior ancestors brought on a worldwide nuclear disaster, and that the tragically impaired survivors gradually climbed back up the scale of evolution to restructure the human race! It is not clear as to how our ancestors came to a state of knowledge analogous to our own as regards atomic physics in the absence of any proof, neither is there any indication in the fossil record to support these wild theories.

Ridicule of his ideas did nothing whatsoever to daunt M. Charroux, however, whose Legacy of the gods (New York, 1974) merely amplifies his previous theories. He has answered the following "enigmas" to his own satisfaction by using the atomic explosion theory:

1. Probability of a civilization on a fracture line naturally favorably to development.
2. Likelihood of an atomic cataclysm.
3. Valleys of death and vitrified cities.
4. A natural cataclysm responsible for the Earth's inclination of 23°27."

5. Exodus of the ancient Mexicans [according to one of the Charroux theories, one nuclear explosion occurred near present-day Las Vegas, and the other in the Gobi Desert].
6. Reasons for the disappearance of the horse from the land where it originated.
7. Taboo on North America and men's refusal to live there.
8. Civilization in the United States before Sumer.
9. Stories of a land of "white ancestors" and quests for the Happy Isles, Brazil Island, Hyperborea, and Thule.
10. Light came from the west.

If it is not a colossal hoax, Legacy of the gods must rank as one of the strangest compendia of unintentional mistakes ever crammed between the covers of one book, yet it has sold tens of thousands of copies. Let us look at some of the ideas scattered forth without benefit of illustrations, index, source material, or reference to previous theorists (apart from a complete acceptance of Velikovsky!). There was a Venusian expedition to Armenia. The Russian politician Molotov benefited from secret powers bestowed on him by the leader of the lamas of Central Asia. The Master of the World is alive and well in the People's Republic of Mongolia: his name is Jebtsung (or, if you believe the back cover of the British paperback, Jebstung). "In the vast area now studded with such cities as Las Vegas, Los Angeles, Salt Lake City, Kansas City, Saint Louis, Memphis, Little Rock, Dallas, New Orleans, and Houston, there were once the proud cities of superior ancestors who had achieved space travel, cybernetics, television, and atomic fission." Prehistoric men dressed in hats, jackets, trousers, and shoes, and lived in a kind of golden age whose resources were numerous, inexhaustible, and easy to exploit. [Why did they not then use some of our fossil fuel supplies?] There was an atomic war between Atlantis and Mu, in which both were destroyed. In 1962, a Brazilian called Rivelino de Manfra da Silva was kidnapped, and seventeen chickens, six pigs and two cows were stolen "by the crew of a craft presumed to be extraterrestrial."

Some of the above is too comic for comment; much of it shows an ignorance of geology, astronomy, and history which is breathtaking; most of it is material for nightmares.

M. Charroux makes the world infinitely more terrifying to immature minds than it really is: we must trust parents, teachers, and librarians to offset such nonsense with excellent popular history, such as the *History of mankind* issued under the auspices of Unesco, beginning with Prehistory and the beginnings of civilization by Jacquetta Hawkes and Sir Leonard Woolley (London, 1963); and with excellent popular science, such as Isaac Asimov's *Guide to science* (2 vols., New York, 1972). The extra knowledge gained is worth all the extra effort involved.

FALLACIES IN **CHEMISTRY**

As Charles A. Browne has explained, "the history of chemistry is largely an account of the mistakes that man has made in his effort to arrive at a satisfactory explanation of the constitution, properties, and transformations of matter . . . The chemical texts of a hundred years ago are now rejected because of certain errors of statement. A century hence the chemistry books of our time will meet with a similar rejection."

When, then, did chemistry begin? Was it with the applied chemistry of prehistoric man, who learnt to tan hides, to dye wool, and to smelt ores? Was it with the first unified principle or law of the Ionic nature philosophers, who reduced all chemical operations to the action or interaction of the "four elementary principles": earth, air, water and fire? Was it with the first experiments of the Chinese (not later than the 7th century), the Indians (not later than the 8th century), the Arabs, or the later Europeans? Was it with Boyle in the 17th century, or with Lavoisier in the 18th?

All these answers are relatively true or false, depending upon one's point of view. What is certain is that progress was steadily made (by Francis Bacon, van Helmont and others) when experiments began to prove old ideas wrong, and when subsequent experiments with better equipment and better theories displaced the old.

Thales (640-546 B.C.) sought to reduce the world around him to a single principle, and believed that this principle was water. Jan Baptista van Helmont (1577-1644), one of the founders of modern experimental chemistry, demonstrated to his own satisfaction that Thales was correct in this assumption! The Ionic philosopher Anaximenes suggested that the original element from which the universe was created was air. Heraelitus stated it to be fire. Empedocles (c. 455-395) was more influential than any other early Greek scientist in claiming that there are four elements: air, fire, water and earth. The Empedoclean world view continued to find adherents in England as late as the 18th century, and some occultists even now have been unable to rid themselves of this acutely over simplified account of the universe. The later scientist Democritus (c. 400-357 B.C.) is the father of modern chemistry on account of his atomic theory, but his idea that there is no design or purpose in the universe was repugnant to his contemporaries, to later cultures dominated by religion, and to occultists and Teilhard supporters today. Democritus argued, against Aristotle, that the same substance may exist in different states. The Aristotelean world view was more sympathetic to the prejudices of later thinkers than was the doctrine of Democritus: it was against tremendous opposition that Bacon, Galileo, Gassendi, Boyle and Newton propagated the atomic conception of Democritus, with the ideas it entailed.

Fallacious a priori reasoning led to the gigantic error of alchemy, and to such mistakes as those of Philo of Byzantium and Hero of Alexandria (both of the 2nd century B.C.) on the question of combustion. Early scientists tended to accept a false system of enquiry, and then to devise experiments to illustrate the truth of such preconceptions rather than to test the validity of the preconceptions. Charles A. Browne summarizes the chemical accomplishments of the Greeks by saying that "their work was distinguished on the one hand by many brilliant conceptions, some of which had a great influence on the future history of the science, and that it was characterized on the other by a great lack of experimental ability, such as was needed for subjecting their speculations to practical tests. They failed to make proper use of such experimental knowledge as they already possessed, for had they applied the densimetric method of Archimedes (287-212 B.C.) to testing the gold and silver that they thought to obtain by the transmutation of base metals, they would have demonstrated the fallacy of alchemy at the outset and thus saved the world from one of the greatest illusions of the human mind."

Paracelsus (1493-1541) asserted that "the object of chemistry is not to make gold but to prepare medicines." But he was still a firm believer in transmutation, citing the apparent conversion of iron into copper by placing a nail in a solution of blue vitriol. Paracelsus also gave much wider currency to the fallacy of the "three principles." Some alchemists, including the Arab Abu Musa Ja'afar as-Sufi, known as al-Jabr (and more frequently in the West as "Geber"), propagated the fallacy that all metals consist of sulphur and mercury. Christian alchemists were not keen on dualism, however, and in order to make a trinity, added a third "principle," which was salt. The theory was that the skill of transmutation lay in the theory and practice of combining more or fewer of the three ingredients. The fact that alchemists could not actually find the hypothetical components in laboratory tests was explained away by quoting Aristotle's distinction between actual and potential properties.

It was left to Robert Boyle, in his *Skeptical Chymist* (London, 1661, and available in (an Everyman edition), to demolish the alchemical doctrines of the four elements, and the iatrochemical doctrines of the three principles.

Sources include: Charles A. Browne, "Error in chemistry" in Joseph Jastrow (ed.), *The story of human error* (New York, 1936); and J. R. Partington, *History of chemistry* (4 vols., London, 1961-70).

ADULT CHICKEN POX

Some parents and even probably some schools condone exposing children to chicken pox as early as possible, assuming it is better to let the pox come and pass while one is still young. When one sibling gets chicken pox, the parents often want their other children to get it at the same time. Despite general convenience

(Continued)

factors for the parents, there is also the idea that it's important to get chicken pox when you're young because once you get older, getting the pox is much more severe.

It is true that chicken pox in adults can become more complicated than in children. These complications are caused by a bacterial infection, leading sometimes to pneumonia, bone or skin infections or in worse cases, brain inflammation or hepatitis. And although chicken pox is quite common because it is so highly contagious, it still can be life threatening in rare cases, particularly without vaccination. Before vaccination was implemented in 1995, four million cases of chicken pox annually were reported, and between 100 to 150 deaths occurred per year. But since immunization became widespread, only about ten people die from chicken pox a year.

But adults are not necessarily those with the highest risk for death or serious consequences from getting chicken pox. Like many other diseases including the common cold, newborns, pregnant women, and those with weak immune systems have a higher likelihood of fatality after catching a case of the pox than healthy, fully grown people.

Along the same lines, there is a somewhat popular misconception that adults who get chicken pox are more likely to develop shingles. Actually, the exact opposite, in a sense, is true.

As we have already mentioned, the chicken pox virus is extremely contagious and will most likely be contracted at an early age with fairly minimal exposure to others with the virus. In addition, it is possible for people to contract chicken pox through direct exposure to a shingles rash if they have not received immunization or if they have not had chicken pox before. This only happens through physical contact, and only when the rash is active (the cysts have not dried up yet).

Thus, a person can never develop the shingles virus itself through physical, or any other (airborne) contact from another person who has the shingles virus. Shingles can only occur from the reactivation of the "varicella-zoster" virus in someone who has had chicken pox already, which typically only happens as a result of aging, being HIV positive, or getting cancer.

Sadly to say, higher risk for health complications most likely has a lot less to do with chicken pox itself than the fact that adults have weaker immune systems (and maybe less willpower and definitely a faded sense of invincibility) than children.

Sources: Directors of Health Promotion and Education, "Chickenpox;" MedTV, "Adult Chicken pox"; Kristen A. Bechtel, MD, "Pediatric Chicken pox," *Medscape* Reference page; *New York Times*, Health Guide, "Shingles."

CHOCOLATE IS UNHEALTHY

When asked to picture gluttony, what might come to mind is an overweight and balding office employee shoveling too much chocolate cake into his or her mouth when no one is looking at a holiday party. When we think of vice, we might imagine a middle-aged woman outside a cupcake shop debating whether or not she can manage the guilt of treating herself to a chocolate dessert on a Tuesday afternoon, having no particular occasion to celebrate.

But as of late, the stereotypical health risks associated with chocolate, such as too much sugar and fat, have been countered by an abundance of potential benefits in the age-old and beloved dessert. According to studies at Harvard University, *European Journal of Nutrition*, and other sources, chocolate has the potential to boost blood flow, decrease platelet stickiness (possibly meaning less risk of heart disease), and to even out high cholesterol levels. These positive effects are thanks to antioxidant chemicals in cocoa called "flavonoids," which are said to help prevent cell damage and inflammation.

What's important to note, though, is that not all chocolate is this good for you. In fact, it's really only a moderate dose of dark chocolate on a daily or weekly basis that will benefit health. Because a lot of chocolate is processed (such as most brand name candy bars, which generally contain milk chocolate), they lose a lot of their flavonoids in the process. It's better to stick with dark chocolate or cocoa powder, though not enough calorie-wise to counteract those healthy and hardy foods that are supposed to make up the majority of your daily nutrition intake.

On another note, a recent study reported in the BBC news claims that eating chocolate is more of an aphrodisiac than a prolonged kiss. When subjects had their heart rates and brain activity monitored during both activities, it was found that chocolate left a longer lasting and overall more intense "high" than kissing did. Perhaps in some cases, the effects of chocolate on the body and brain lasted four times longer. Somewhat surprisingly considering the stereotype that chocolate is only a turn-on for women (and/or solace during their menstrual cycles), the stimulating properties of chocolate proved to be equal in its effects on women and men.

This may, arguably, be because chocolate contains some caffeine, which is an actual chemical stimulant. But if a drug is as

(Continued)

tasty and comforting as chocolate seems to be for most, why not try it for a healthy boost of emotional and physical well-being?

Sources: Majorie Ingall, "Chocolate can do good things for your heart, skin, and brain," CNN, 2006; "Heart-Health Benefits of Chocolate Unveiled," Cleveland Clinic, 2011; "Chocolate 'Better Than Kissing,' " BBC News, 2007.

CIGAR FALLACIES

Sydney Brooks, while visiting the cigar factories in Cuba early in the 20th century, discussed erroneous beliefs held by laymen on the subject of cigars:

"The average smoker believes that a dark wrapper means a strong cigar and a light wrapper a mild one; and he is absolutely wrong. There is no connection whatever between color and strength. Squeezing cigars and smelling them are equally fallacious as tests of quality. So, too, is the color and firmness of the ash; the notion that the whiter the ash and the longer it stays on, the better the cigar, is altogether erroneous. The best Havanas burn with a clear steel-grey ash, and its duration and length are determined mainly by the size of the pieces used in the fillers.

Then, again, the men in Havana, heedless of the club reputations they are shattering, insist that a spotted cigar means less than nothing so far as quality, whether good or bad, is concerned; that the barometer affects cigars far more than the thermometer; that the silky-looking wrapper is as much to be avoided as the veiny one or the one that is oily in patches; that cigars should be neither so soft as to yield readily to the pressure of the fingers nor so dry as to crackle; that most of the talk about "condition" is pure ignorance, the Americans being right in preferring a moist cigar, and the English equally right in preferring a drier one—the vital point in each case being the proper period of recovery from the seasickness that cigars contract as easily as their smokers, a period that varies with the length of the voyage; that except for the expert, who has given his whole life to the business, there are virtually no outward indications that can be relied upon in choosing a cigar; and that for the average man, anxious to find out whether a given Havana is of good quality throughout and will burn well, the only real test is to smoke it."

Sources: *The London Daily Mail*, 19 April 1911.

SMOKING **CIGARETTES** HELPS YOU LOSE WEIGHT

You remember those girls who you drove by outside the cafeteria during lunch break, waiting outside smoking a cigarette, too skinny and probably not enjoying it all that much?

High-schoolers who struggle with eating disorders, models, and perhaps those who turn to smoking as an easier way to lose weight than working out or dieting should be aware that smoking does not actually help you get skinnier.

Appropriately, according to a survey of over one thousand Montreal teens ages twelve to seventeen, there was no difference found between smokers and nonsmokers in terms of average body weight.

Additionally, although nicotine is a mild stimulant, and therefore temporarily suppresses appetite, it does not actually cause one to lose weight. For some, the reason cigarette smoking may be appealing to kids (or may have been appealing in the past) is a result of celebrities who smoke, and are also portrayed as skinny and attractive, giving teens the idea that smoking leads to weight loss and attractive figures, and/or being badass. In addition, as cigarette smoking keeps one's mouth busy, it can serve as a substitute for putting food in one's mouth.

Other studies have shown that there is only a slight difference in heart rate and pulse in nonsmokers and smokers, and that upon cessation, metabolism rate does not slow down in any significant way. So, it seems, although tobacco might be a natural diuretic, and blood pressure and heart rate is slightly increased upon smoking, direct weight loss from cigarette smoking is not notable in biological terms.

But in terms of psychological impact, smoking after meals does probably prevent people from eating more, because it serves as a kind of stopping point. The risk of weight gain after quitting because of an inability to control one's eating is just another reason why picking up smoking was probably not the best method to use for sustaining a healthy body image in the first place.

Sources: Carrie Paulus, "Nicotine as a Means for Weight Control: Advantage or Disadvantage?" Vanderbilt University Psychology Department; CBS News, Health, "Smoking Won't Help Teens Lose Weight, May Stunt Growth: Study," 2008.

CINDERELLA WORE GLASS SLIPPERS

Of the three hundred or so early versions of this popular fairy tale (including a Chinese story of the 9th century), not one described Cinderella's slippers as made of glass, because they weren't. The medieval French version used by Perrault (1628-1703), author of the Cinderella we know today, described the slippers as "pantoufles en vair," or slippers of white ermine, Ferrault remembered the word as "verre," or glass, and thus it has erroneously been ever since.

SCOTTISH HIGHLAND CLANS COMPRISED A CHIEF AND HIS FOLLOWERS, WHO ALL BORE HIS NAME AND WERE RELATED TO HIM BY TIES OF BLOOD

This fallacy has been refuted by a study of rentals and similar documents such as Exchequer Rolls and Forfeited Estates Papers.

It can be proved that there could not have been any blood tie between the first chief of such clans as the Bissets, Chisholms, Grants and Frasers, whose chiefs were originally Norman. In fact, however, the same is true in the case of clan chiefs of purely Scottish origin. A Highland rental of 1505 (for Kintyre) shows a large number of surnames borne by long-term tenants on the estates of Macdonald, the clan chief. Similar pictures are presented by estates such as Lochiel and Clanranald which were forfeited after Culloden. Gregory, in *Collectanea de rebus albanicis* (published by the Iona Club), showed that these tenants were representatives of families which had been on the lands in question from long before, under a succession of different, and unrelated, chiefs. "They were not, nor did they claim to be, of the blood of the individual whom they acknowledged to be their chief. They appear to have formed the bulk of the population of the Highlands." Gregory amplifies the point by citing the case of the Stewart followers, sixty-nine of whom were killed at Culloden, and a further forty of whom were wounded. Between them, these followers bore eighteen different surnames, none of them Stewart.

The word "clan" has been understood in three different senses: the narrowest indicates the family of the chief himself; the next circle consists of families descended from that of the chief; the widest sense include followers lacking any kinship with the chief and his family. The third class has been called "septs," but it is now clear that the term "septs" (roughly "divisions") ought to be applied instead to the second class, and the term "followers" or "tenants" would more helpfully describe the third class. Sources include: Gordon Donaldson (ed.), *Common errors in Scottish history* (London, 1956).

CLEOPATRA WAS AN EGYPTIAN

Cleopatra (68-30 B.C.) was the eldest daughter of Ptolemy XI, the illegitimate son of Ptolemy VIII, son of Ptolemy VII. The Ptolemies were a Greek dynasty, and Cleopatra was Greek.

The granite obelisks known as Cleopatra's Needles have nothing whatsoever to do with her, but were erected at Heliopolis by Thothmes III about 1600 B.C. The "Cleopatra's Needle" on the Embankment in London was brought to England in 1878.

COCA COLA CAN DISSOLVE HUMAN TEETH

In America, people are extremely concerned about their dental hygiene, and moreover, how clean, white, straight, and intact their teeth appear. Doctors and dentists often say that consuming diets containing too much acid is a very damaging thing to do to our precious dentures, which is just one of the many reasons there are negative stigmas attached to drinking too much coffee, alcohol, and/or soda.

Luckily for us, it has been tested and proven that teeth do not deteriorate in coke at all. This is because calcium hydroxyl apatite, the name for that which coats the outer part of human teeth, is indeed sensitive to acids, but the acids in Coca Cola (carbonic, phosphoric, and citric) are not nearly strong enough to alter the average healthy tooth at any greater extent than turning them somewhat brown.

However, as the experiment consisted of immersing a tooth in coke for twenty-six hours straight, one would probably have to be gargling soda on a multi-daily basis in order to even achieve this discoloring.

Sources: "Do teeth dissolve in coke?" *Psapce.org*, Creative Commons Attribution-Noncommerical-Share Alike, 2010.

COCKERELS SING "COCK A DOODLE DO"

They do if they sing English, but we are assured that English-singing cockerels are in a minority. French cockerels sing "coco-rico" and German and Italian cockerels sing "kikiriki." Virtually every language has a different way of representing animal and bird noises, and it is a fallacy that they can or should all be represented in an identical fashion.

ONE PERSON CAN BE A **COHORT**

The American novelist Mary McCarthy has written, in *The groves of Academe:* "The old poet had left, accompanied by two of his cohorts." Now it is an author's privilege to coin neologisms, and to redeploy archaicisms in the interests of a dense, vital vocabulary. But if recognized dictionary-meanings are to be changed, then some warning ought to be given if the common reader is not to be confused. In Roman times, a "cohort" was a body of infantry forming one tenth of a legion. The term was applied also to a body of auxiliaries of roughly the same strength (300 to 600 men), and later also to a body of cavalry. A later meaning acceptable to many, cited in the *Oxford English Dictionary*, is the figurative use as "a company, band; especially of persons united in defence of a common cause": that is, "cohort" has become a collective noun, but not yet a singular. An old poet accompanied by two of his cohorts—if the last word were to be used correctly—would find himself pursued by up to twelve hundred people.

COINCIDENCES ARE AMAZING

"In the eternal search for verification of the supernaturalism which engrosses so much of popular 'philosophy,' nothing passes for more cogent evidence than coincidence. The marvelling over unexpected juxtapositions is at once the mark and the diversion of banal minds, and most of them do not require very remarkable happenings to constitute coincidences. Those who for lack of knowledge or imagination expect nothing out of the ordinary are always encountering the unexpected. One of the commonest of 'coincidences,' as Professor Jastrow has pointed out, is the crossing of letters in the mail. It happens a thousand times a day yet thousands of men and women whip themselves into amazement every time it happens. As far as they are concerned, it is complete and final proof of the supernatural, whether it be telepathy or Divine guidance or merely soul calling to soul. There it is, sealed, stamped, and delivered. Yet of all human happenings, what is more likely than that lovers or relatives should simultaneously decide to write to each other?" Thus Bergen Evans, in *The natural history of nonsense* (London, 1947).

But one can scarcely condemn Arthur Koestler's mind as "banal" and he too is a believer in some magical properties of coincidence, or "synchronicity" as he prefers to call it, following Jung, in his anecdotal *The roots of coincidence* (London, 1972). Jung kept a diary of coincidences, as did Paul Kammerer, whose faking of scientific evidence is recorded in Arthur Koestler's *Case of the midwife toad* (London, 1971). Kammerer's pathetic notebook of coincidences, as cited by Koestler in his work defending the notion of "synchronicity" as a supernatural phenomenon within the field of "extra-sensory perception," includes such trivia as the fact that on November 4, 1910 his brother-in-law went to a concert where he had seat no. 9 and cloakroom ticket no. 9. Kammerer's *Das Gesetz der Serie* (Stuttgart, 1919) proposes that there is a law of series in the same way that gamblers maintain that (until they lose) they are on a "lucky streak." He concludes that seriality is "ubiquitous and continuous in life, nature and cosmos. It is the umbilical cord that connects thought, feeling, science and art with the womb of the universe which gave birth to them." This theory leads Kammerer (and Koestler with him) to conclude that there is a reason for believing in telepathy, though no such cases have been proved experimentally. As an example of the credulity surrounding allegedly "telepathic" coincidence it is sufficient to quote Renée Haynes, an ardent believer in extra-sensory perception, who quotes in her postscript to *The roots of coincidence* an article by W. J. Tarver in the *New Scientist* (October 24, 1968).

Tarver, then Chairman of the Veterinarians' Union, suggested that "a gifted 10%" of dogs in boarding kennels "after being settled for a week or two become wildly excited at almost the exact moment when their owners begin the return journey from their holiday." This assumes (a) that the wildly excited dogs are gifted; (b) that all kennels take an exact note of the time at which all their dogs become wildly excited; (c) all dog-owners take an exact note of the time at which they return from their holiday (when they pack their bags? board an aircraft?); (d) that dogs in kennels only become wildly excited at the thought of their owners; etc. But more damaging to the case of Tarver, Haynes and Koestler is the simple figure of 90 percent of cases which do not fit any kind of assumed pattern; one might well be justified in asking a percentage nearer to 30 before any kind of statistical inference could reasonably be made, with a negative percentage of around 70. One's attitude to the coincidental and the serial must depend upon one's attitude to Koestler's rider intended to dull the skeptical intelligence: "The type of stringent controls applied to ESP experiments, and the presence of skeptical observers, would certainly not facilitate their occurrence." Koestler is thus in fact arguing: "I say this; therefore, though I cannot prove this because this is unprovable, you should believe me." This is the fallacy of authority, claiming something to be true merely because of the status of the claimant. Bergen Evans has dealt with the fallacy as follows: "Whereas the trained mind accords belief to plausible evidence only and grants a possibility solely on the basis of a sound inference from established facts, the untrained mind insists that a proposition must be true if it cannot be disproved. 'You can't prove it *isn't* so!' is as good as Q.E.D. in folk logic—as though it were necessary to submit a piece of the moon to chemical analysis before you could be sure that it was not made of green cheese."

It is also worth analyzing a "coincidental" phenomenon that appears to be magical to all except those who have ever given a moment's thought to probability. The example comes from George Gamow's One two three infinity, and can be played as a party conjuring trick by anyone without facility at sleight-of-hand. The fact is that, of any twenty-four people selected at random, it is probable that two or more will have the same birthday. There are indeed 27 chances out of 50 that two of twenty-four will have the same birthday. The probability that the birthday of any two people will fall on the same day is 364/365. The probability that a third person's birthday will differ from those of the other two is 363/365, and so on, until the 24th person in the series involves odds of 342/365. Now, the series of 23 fractions must be multiplied together to reach the probability that all 24 will be different. The final product is a fraction reducing to 23/50. Therefore, on average, you would lose 23 times out of 50, and win your bet 27 times out of 50. On a technicality, one ignores February 29th, which lowers the probability, and the fact that birth dates tend to cluster at certain times of year, which increases the probability.

Interestingly, a coincidence of 2 birthdays is almost certain in a group of 40, and in a crowd of 100, you would be safe in taking odds of 3.3 million to 1! (It is, of course, already a mathematical certainty in a crowd of 366).

I verified Gamow's hypothesis in *Who's Who 1979* (London, 1979). If you take the first 24 names, you will find that two have birthdays on November 6. If you take the first 24 names with full birth-dates in the International Who's Who 1978-9 (London, 1978), you will find that two have birthdays on May 29. And so on.

Sources: Bergen Evans, *The natural history of nonsense* (London, 1941) and Arthur Koestler, *The roots of coincidence* (London, 1972).

COMMON **COLD** FALLACIES

1. Being Cold Causes Cold

There exists an age-old but persistent myth that leaving the house without a jacket in cold weather makes one more likely to catch a cold. Despite how frequently colds occur in children and adults in the U.S. (average of eight times per year), this old wives' tale as to how this virus is transmitted is unfounded.

In reality, you can only really catch a cold when your system becomes infected with the virus through your nose. Supposedly, when a nasal cell gets infected with a cold virus, parts of the immune system in your body are activated. The cold symptoms are triggered by something called natural inflammatory mediators of the immune system. When these mediators are activated by a cold virus, they cause sneezing/cough reflexes, leakage of blood vessels, mucus secretion, and the other seasonal annoyances we all know and love as cold symptoms.

So, keeping a safe distance from all your peers is the best way to avoid getting a cold. And much better and practical to carry hand sanitizer and Vitamin C in your bag instead of an extra sweater.

2. It's Possible to Sweat Out a Cold (or Hangover)
In both of these cases, you feel like crap—sluggish, tired, achy, and the works. So what can you do to feel better and make it through the day? Other than popping twice the usual amount of Advil every couple hours or trying to sleep it off, you could try and sweat it out, can't you?

Let's focus on the cold first. You have tried rest and eating healthy and lots of fluids, but it's now day three on the couch watching daytime T.V. and you are sick of feeling, well, sick. Some people believe it's possible to get rid of a common cold by sweating it out. In order to do so, you would basically cover yourself in excessive amounts of clothing, heating pads, and fleece blankets in order to overheat yourself, causing your body to perspire accordingly. In this way, you would be sending off the virus out with your sweat.

Unfortunately, this is not the case. And realistically speaking, there still is no sure fire way to cure the common cold. The cold contains something like 200 viruses, and they all need to travel through your system in due course before you can fully recover. Therefore, you can't force these viral infections out before they are ready to go. But on the bright side, after day three, cold symptoms generally begin to subside after running their course.

Now, we will discuss the cure for a self-inflicted illness: the hangover. It is debatably an ever more widely believed notion that in order to fight off a hangover, you need to sweat out the toxins that are still lingering in the bloodstream from the night before. Sure enough, this strategy is a bust.

As hangovers are primarily caused by dehydration via consuming a vast amount of alcohol in a short period of time, it is not a good idea to try and overheat your already hydration depleted body. Laying out in the noonday sun at the beach or going to a sauna, therefore, can actually be quite harmful in the

(Continued)

event of a hangover. Extreme heat from the sun or from a heavy duty source like a sauna can cause dangerous blood vessel and flow pattern changes in the body. Additionally, this kind of heat to an already overheated body can, in severe cases, lead to serious blood pressure drops and abnormal heart beats.

Some claim that a bit of nonstrenuous exercise can be helpful for recharging the body and moving along the hangover, but it is not recommended to break much of a sweat.

So, if you have a cold, take it easy. If you have a hangover, take your sweater off.

3. Going Outside With Wet Hair Causes Cold

Similar to the myth that being cold causes cold, going outside with wet hair is also typically (and falsely) warned against. Apparently, this idea dates all the way back to the 1st century, when Celsus wrote in his classical medical work that the season winter in and of itself causes headaches, coughs, and all other infections that attack the chest and lungs.

Luckily, winter itself is not the culprit for the noted period of time we call "cold season." Again, the idea that wet hair causes cold most likely comes from the fact that going outside in freezing temperature with your hair wet makes you feel colder. Even if going outside in the cold with wet hair does lower body temperature, it does not mean that your immune system is being weakened and therefore you are more likely to catch a cold. As mentioned earlier, colds can only be caught through germs. Your body temperature is entirely irrelevant, aside from personal comfort.

4. Airplanes Induce Sickness (colds)

For a number of reasons both psychological and purely mythical, people are afraid of flying, and in a more mild sense, afraid of airplanes. Not surprisingly, people are more convinced that they will get sick while travelling in an airplane than in other forms of public transportation like buses, cars, boats, and trains. Perhaps because being in an airplane really makes us feel like there is no escaping other germs, as there are no open windows, and no access to the outside world as we know it (nowhere in sight throughout the flight).

Some people even preemptively feel cold symptoms coming on before they board a flight, perhaps as a manifestation of fear of getting sick, and all other anxieties that come with putting one's life in the hands of a stranger controlling a multi-thousand pound machine through mile stretches of sky.

Whatever the cause of this quite common fear of catching illness on planes, the reality is quite different. A number of news sources have cited a range of in-flight passengers saying they are convinced that they always get a chest cold or flu symptoms after flying, based on the bad air circulation, spread of germs through seats, blankets, bathrooms, etc.

In terms of the air quality, it is an illusion (or delusion) that it is unregulated. The reason people may believe this is because of the low humidity on planes. The fact that they get dehydrated may make them feel that they are breathing in stuffy air, and therefore breathing in germs. However, modern airplanes generally take 50 percent of the air existing inside the airplane and then mix it with new air from outside that becomes heated by engines, and filtered by HEPA filters to sterilize it before it comes back into the cabin.

There are reasons why people may feel that they are getting sick on an airplane, such as dehydration, nausea from turbulence, air pressure changes, heat, etc. But in general, the likelihood of catching a cold or becoming seriously ill post-flight from being trapped in a mini-germ city for seven hours cross country is not higher than that of getting sick from your coworkers in your office.

So next time you fly, reconsider the bottles of Nyquil and hand sanitizer in your carry-on before unnecessarily provoking all your fellow pissed off and paranoid fliers in the already endless security line.

Sources: Common Cold (*commoncold.org*), Jack M. Gwaltney, MD, Frederick G. Hayden, 1999-2007; Kids Health on Common Cold, 1995-2011; CNN health, "10 Hangover Remedies: What Works?" Anne Harding, 2010; ABC news, "10 Myths about the Common Flu and Cold," Joseph Brownstein, 2008; Vanderbilt University Health Psychology Home Page, "Can You Really Catch a Cold From Going Outside with Wet Hair?" Emily Motayed, 2008; MSNBC Today, "Germs on a Plane: Can you Get Sick Flying?" Dr. Judith Reichman, 2006; ABC News, "Myth: Airplane Air Makes you Sick," 2005.

COLD FALLACIES

1. Feed a Cold and Starve a Fever
The implication of this ancient, universal saw is that patients with colds must be given a great deal to eat, and those with fevers very little. This is nonsense.

The original meaning might have been more intelligible as "if you give too much food to a patient with a cold, he will then contract a fever, during which he will not desire to eat." That is, that one must not give patients with colds a great deal to eat. This too is nonsense, for there is no known correlation between cold cure and the consumption of food. Those with a bad cold often have a fever too.

Patients with a cold normally require no more food than when they are in normal health, and no less. Patients in the early stages of fever will have little desire to eat, and in the later stages they will require extra food to make up their previous loss.

2. Colds Can Be Prevented by Building Up Resistance
Apart from the obvious fact that a normally healthy person will be less likely to take cold than someone less healthy, there are no grounds for hoping that one could build up resistance against the common cold by such activities as strenuous exercise or "toughening the body" by sleeping out of doors. Noah D. Fabricant indicates the absurdity of trying to stave off the cold in *The common cold* (Chicago, 1945). A Gallup poll of 1945 showed that, as a group, farmers have slightly more colds than other groups in the population.

Nobody yet knows what causes the common cold.

Source: Bergen Evans, *The natural history of nonsense* (London, 1947).

COLD-BLOODED ANIMALS
Some animals are warm-blooded and some are cold, so we are taught as young children. Warm-blooded animals are mammals, while cold-blooded are reptiles, insects, and other less human and therefore less important creatures. While this distinction is more or less true, some clarification needs to be given for the oversimplification of these two different genres of those with blood pulsing through their veins.

Warm-blooded animals include all mammals plus birds, who keep their body temperatures between 97 degrees and 104 degrees Fahrenheit. They are also called Homoiotherms, and basically are distinguished from cold-blooded animals because they have the ability to heat their own bodies (without external factors, such as, namely, the sun).

The name "cold-blooded" for the other animals is less scientific than their formal name, Poikiotherms, but also less accurate in a literal sense. These non-mammalian animals do not always have to keep their blood cold the way "warm-blooded" animals need to sustain a fairly high body temperature at all times to survive. Instead, the temperature of the former types of species' blood depends on their climate. So, for instance, if a reptile swims and lives primarily in fifty degree waters, its blood and body temperature will stay at the same level. If their body temperatures get too low, they must migrate to a climate or location where they can absorb the sun in order to reheat their bodies and resume their lives accordingly.

Sources: "Warm- and Cold-Blooded Animals," Texas Parks and Wildlife.

THE THREE PRIMARY **COLORS** ARE BLUE, RED AND YELLOW

The primary colors are actually blue, red and green, though artists often use red, yellow, and blue together.

BEING **COLOR-BLIND** MEANS NOT BEING ABLE TO SEE COLORS

The very label, "color-blind" suggests that those with this condition are literally blind of color, and therefore only see in black and white, or some kind of gray. Fortunately, this is far from the case.

According to Dictionary.com, color-blindness is defined as the "inability to distinguish one or several chromatic colors, independent of the capacity for distinguishing light and shade."

Sources with studies on the statistics involved in color-blindness note several basic facts: about 8 percent of males are colorblind in some way, while only 0.5 percent of females are affected. Put another way, men are roughly 100 times more frequently color-blind than women.

More importantly, however, the most common form of color-blindness by far is called "Deutanomaly," which basically means that people with this condition are less able to distinguish red and green color hues, while they are for the most part still adept at recognizing other colors the way anyone else would.

THE **COLOR-BLIND** CAN SEE ONLY GREY

This is undoubtedly true of the most extreme cases, but much more frequently the blindness applies to only one color or two. Most color-blindness seems to apply to green, and less to red, while some of those who are color-blind confuse green and red. The color-blind are otherwise good at matching colors and tend to have normal vision in all else. About one man in twenty-five is color-blind, but only about one woman in 250.

Source: F. W. Edridge-Green, *Color-blindness and color-perception* (London, 1891).

THEO GIMBEL AND THE **COLÓR-TREATMENT** OF SHOCK

At the Hygeia Studios, near Tetbury, Gloucestershire, Theo Gimbel claims to treat shock and other forms of mental illness successfully by the use of such devices as a "Color Therapy Instrument" and a "Color Wall." In a leaflet on the latter, it is stated that the "instrument has the effect of altering the rate and depth of respiration to some extent, and may, by deepening the respirations, prevent a state of shock from developing . . . Some preliminary research carried out on volunteer asthma sufferers suggests that relief is obtained for some of these patients when "treated" with the Color Wall . . . The instrument consists basically of two important forms: the outer one which is subjected to the dim level of light within the treatment area and the inner form which is lit by the arrangement of lights which have the task of illuminating the vertical and horizontal relief forms.

By the way of the special arrangement of lights the horizontal forms are stressed by the fading in of the blue lights, the vertical by the fading in of the red lights and both forms have been carefully designed so as to be noncompelling to the onlooker.

The texture of the forms is left so that the eye can see the material without being mystified. The outer form is blue and has an anticlockwise movement. There are deep psychological reactions to both these factors. The inner shape is white so as to reflect the true color of the lights. The size is also significant in relationship to the average length of the human spine." The Color Wall costs £750.

There is no experimental proof, in a statistically meaningful sense, that such a color system has any of the healing properties attributed to it (doubtless in good faith), and clearly any patient suffering from mental distress would gain more from the Cotswold ambience of serenity than from looking at any combination of color patterns.

The Hygeia Studios also offer a "Color Level Lamp" with the advice that one should switch to yellow "for obtaining feeling of detachment" or to orange "for happy, relaxed but aware atmosphere."

Or you could invest in a "three Dimensional Cross," advertised as follows: "As more and more churches are becoming aware of the rays of power and healing which radiate from the Altar—and indeed—from the very vestments worn by the Celebrant, the increase in spiritual power given by a Cross which points in all directions will be appreciated." But surely every sculptural cross ever made has been in three dimensions?

COLORFUL FOODS ARE HEALTHIER FOR YOU

You've probably heard of the phrase, "coloring your plate." College cafeterias, kids TV programs, and consumer health magazines alike promote the cause. As cheese, bread, and greasy carbs are generally bland in color, it's important to throw some greens and even better yet, blues, purples, and oranges into the mix at any or every meal.

Although it is true that part of being healthy means not overdoing any one food group, and trying to include an equal variety of protein, carbohydrates, and fruits and veggies into your diet, the idea that color is always better is not 100 percent accurate.

Obviously, when we say "color" we don't mean the dyes that come from artificial flavoring in sweets such as popsicles, ice cream, frosting, and a good variety of other sugary desserts. What we actually mean is natural coloring in fruits and vegetables.

In simple terms, pigments in given foods carry some of their nutrients, but by no means do all nutrients come from their color source. While nutrients that come with color are generally limited to flavonoids, melanins, carotenoids, and porphyrins (think, carrots), nonpigment nutrients span a much larger field. For example, the onion, which is one of the whitest vegetables out there, is a great source of vitamin C, B6, chromium, phosphorous, manganese, copper, and houses a variety of unique and beneficial to health sulfur molecules.

Another example of this discrepancy is the prominence of green lettuce as the healthiest lettuce. White cabbage is actually better for you, despite its unpopularity. White lettuce has a huge amount of vitamins, including vitamin K, C, A, and B, calcium, iron, and fiber: a well rounded meal in and of itself, we may venture to propose. White beans are just as nutritious and hardy as red or pink pinto beans, with equal amounts of fiber and protein.

Even celery, which so often gets talked down for its blandness and association with eating disorders (because it supposedly takes more effort to eat than it does to provide any nourishment), is actually quite full of nutrients. It contains some calcium, vitamins A, C, and K, and most surprisingly, protein. So, though your eyes might shun the foods that don't match your colorful and

(Continued)

zesty personality, be sure to tell your stomach that there may be something to gain inside those with off-white exteriors as well.

Sources: Cathy Erway, "Food, Glorious Food Myths," subcategory: "Packed with Nutrients, Despite their Color," *New York Times*, 2009; "Do Darker colored fruits and vegetables have more nutrients than lighter colored ones?" *World's Healthiest Foods.org*.

FALLACIES ON **COMETS**

It is peculiar that the *Encyclopedia of superstitions* (2nd ed., London, 1961) by E. and M. A. Radford contains no index reference to comets, for superstitious fears of comets and what they are supposed to mean have bedevilled human life for several thousand years, and in many societies still do.

1) Comets Are Portents

A typical example of such fears can be found in a book by the astrologer John Gadbury (1627-1704): De cometis: or a discourse of the natures and effects of comets, as they are philosophically, historically, and astrologically considered. With a brief (yet full) account of the HI late comets, or blazing stars, visible to all Europe. And what (in a natural way of judicature) they portend. Together with some observations on the nativity of the Grand Seignior (London, 1665). There is of course no possible relationship between the appearance of comets and the course of earthly events.

2) Volcanoes Are Comets

I am indebted to the erudite Augustus de Morgan's hilarious *Budget of paradoxes* (London, 1872) for a reference to an anonymous work, published in London about 1856, which I fear I have not seen. I content myself with its title, and de Morgan's riposte. Comets considered as volcanoes, and the cause of their velocity and other phenomena thereby explained, "The title explains the book better than the book explains the title."

COMMON SENSE

The most persistent of all fallacies is that which credits the man-in-the-street with enough intelligence and knowledge to see through the propaganda, lies, and deceitful advertisements both commercial and noncommercial that assail him every day. One way to check this is to visit your local bookshop or public library and see how many books on superstitions and pseudo-science fill the shelves in comparison with the number of titles that discuss and analyse those cults objectively.

Another way is to read sociological surveys of any group beliefs (prisoners in a jail; adolescents on a housing estate: parents at a school) such as the Lynds' Middletown (1925), which was based on the "typical" small American town of Muncie, Indiana. In the daily newspaper they found that 37 display advertisements of a total of 68 were devoted to "remedies" such as salves and soaps (see pp. 437-8). Muncie residents confessed to beliefs that a little bag of asafetida worn about the neck would prevent a child catching contagious diseases; that a worn leather shoestring around the same unfortunate child's neck would keep away croup (or cure croup if caught); that secret incantations could cure erisypelas; and that wrapping old hatbands round the mother's breast at childbirth would prevent breast infections and diseases . . . We laugh at the Wise Men of Gotham, but Gotham is our home town.

CONSPIRACY THEORIES OF HISTORY

Numerous fallacies have been connected with the theory that one or other group has secretly manipulated world politics for their own ends undetected until the author's own exposé was triumphantly published. The most notorious of such theories is that persistently suggesting that the world is in the hands of the Jews. The Russian tract The secret of the Jews (possibly drawn up by the Russian secret agent and occultist Yuliana Glinka) formed the basis for the Protocols of the Elders of Zion which purported to be documents proving the existence of such a conspiracy, all totally fabricated. Norman Cohn and Léon Poliakov have shown that the Nazi use of the conspiracy theory owed a great deal to anti-Jewish and anti-masonic propaganda of certain Roman Catholic writers at the turn of the century.

Johannes Rogalla von Bieberstein, in Die These von der Verschwörung, 1776-1945 (Berne, 1977), traces a powerful conspiracy theory to a reaction against the activities in the 1770s of the Illuminati, a Bavarian secret society; to its exploitation by royalist propagandists after the French Revolution; and thence to the Roman Catholics who turned the rumor against liberals and socialists, as well as against their more familiar targets, the freemasons and Jews.

More dangerously, conspiracy theories have been utilized by most political leaders at most times to justify the existence of secret agents whose principal purpose is to stifle opposition to the leaders; whereas it is the very existence of the repressive state police/army that stimulates opposition.

THE CONTINENTAL LAND MASSES HAVE ALWAYS BEEN FIXED

Despite the fact that Alfred Wegener showed how the hypothesis of Continental Drift could explain features of zoological and botanical distribution, for example, as early as 1912, it was only about 1960 that the mounting evidence in favor of Wegener's hypothesis finally disposed of the fallacy that the Earth's continents were always disposed as they are now. The large-scale error brought with it such fantastic fallacies as the "land bridges" which were once thought (and until very recently) to have sunk without trace into the depths of the South Atlantic Ocean. Wegener pointed to corroborative evidence such as the occurrence of similar geological formations in West Africa and North-East Brazil that might once have been joined.

John Ziman observes that this important fallacy was held very widely in a mature and sophisticated field of science for more than half a century after it had been confuted. "Throughout this period," he notes, "the basic facts and hypotheses were well known, and there was no serious attempt to suppress publication of "uncomfortable" truths by either side. The scientific system was working quite normally; individual scientists conscientiously carried out their research, which was communicated according to the "norms" of our model. [See Ziman, pp. 4-5]. Unfortunately, in this case the "knowledge" produced by "science" was not as reliable as we usually assume, and the "map" of Earth history in the archive was hopelessly misleading.

"It is instructive, also, to note that the main arguments against continental drift came from mathematical physicists, who could easily show that the tidal mechanisms that Wegener had suggested were quite insufficient to bring about such large effects. But they failed to realize that this did not rule out some other mechanism which nobody had yet thought of. The epistemological irony is that the geologists—supreme experts in the observation and interpretation of visual patterns—rejected first-rate evidence from fossils, rocks and landscapes because they thought it was in conflict with quantitative mathematical reasoning which few of them really understood. This episode shows that pattern recognition is every bit as reliable as a source of consensible knowledge and as a means of arriving at a scientific consensus, as discourse in the logico-mathematical mode."

Sources: A. Hallam, *A revolution in the earth sciences* (Oxford, 1973); H. Takeuchi and others, *Debate about the Earth* (San Francisco, 1967); and John Ziman, *Reliable knowledge* (Cambridge, 1978).

THE LAW OF **CONTRADICTION**

"Nothing is both A and Not-A," states Aristotle's Third Law which was taken to be axiomatic until the 19th century. But it is fallacious, as the following example will show.

It is "obvious" that in the infinite sequence 1, 2, 3, 4, 5, etc. there are "more" numbers than there are in the sequence 2, 4, 6, 8, etc., each being continued indefinitely; for the first contains all the evens

2, 4, 6, 8, . . . that broke up the second, and in addition all the odds 1, 3, 5, 7, etc., none of which occurs in the second.

But look at this:

1, 2, 3, 4, 5, 6, 7, . . .
2, 4, 6, 8, 10, 12, 14, . . .

The numbers are paired off, one-to-one, no matter how far out we go. Therefore, if we keep on going, and never stop pairing numbers, each number in the bottom row will have a unique mate in the top, for the numbers in the bottom row are got by doubling three in the top. But these rows are the sequences with which we started. The argument about the paired rows shows that there are just as many numbers in the bottom infinite row as in the top. Therefore there are just as many even numbers as there are numbers altogether, odds and evens. But we saw how obvious it was that there are fewer evens than numbers altogether. So Aristotle's Third Law is defied by the first sequences of numbers which we come across.

Two contradictory statements may both be true, according to Anicius Manlius Torquatos Severinus Boethius (c. 455-c. 524) in his *Introductio ad syllogismos categoricos* which was edited by J.-P. Migne in Patrologiae cursus, vol. 64 (Paris, 1860), cols. 761-832.

Boethius, better known for De consolatione philosophiae, argues that opposition between pairs of statements may sometimes be apparent rather than real, as in the following cases:

1. Equivocation
"Cato is not strong" and "Cato is strong" may be equally correct if referring in one instance to mental and in the other to physical powers. Similarly, "Cato killed himself at Utica" and "Cato did not kill himself at Utica" are both true if the two historical Catos are recalled; one committed suicide at Utica, and the other did not.

2. Univocation
"Man walks" and "Man does not walk" fail to contradict each other if "man" refers in one case to mankind and in the other to a particular individual. This fallacy is more common in languages like Latin or Bahasa Indonesia which have no definite article.

3. Different Parts
"The eye is white" and "the eye is not white" may be equally correct even if there is only one eye in question, since one statement may refer to the pupil and the other to an eyeball: two different parts.

4. Different Relations
"Socrates is on the left" and "Socrates is on the right" will both be true if one stands in the appropriate relation to Socrates.

5. Different Times
"Socrates is sitting down" and "Socrates is not sitting down" will both be correct at different times.

6. Different Modalities
"The egg is an animal" and "the egg is not an animal" are both correct if one proposition refers to a potentiality and the other to an actuality.

Sources include: E. Temple Bell, *The search for truth* (London, 1935) and Charles Hamblin, Fallacies (London, 1970).

COPROLITES ARE THE DUNG OF DINOSAURS
Buckland, the geologist who first analysed coprolite, had already found in 1829 many types of dinosaur remains in the Lias at Lyme Regis (Devonshire, England), where coprolite material was also discovered. Jukes-Browne correctly called Buckland's association of the two finds "an erroneous conclusion" (in Quarterly *Journal of the Geological Society*, 1875), but the damage had been done, and another common fallacy was on its way to the storehouse of folk "knowledge."

Coprolite is the name given commercially to phosphatic nodules, which were mined extensively in Cambridgeshire in the second half of the 19th century.

Source: Richard Grove, *The Cambridgeshire coprolite mining rush* (Cambridge, 1976), pp. 3-4.

CORRELATABLE DATA ARE THEREBY CAUSAL
A common cause of belief in fallacies in the belief that correlatable data show some kind of causal connection.

Harold A. Larrabee, in *Reliable knowledge* (Boston, 1954, p. 368), points to a near-perfect correlation between the death-rate in Hyderabad from 1911 to 1919 and fluctuations in the membership of the International Association of Machinists during the same period. The fact that nobody seriously takes such a correlation to imply causality does not prevent economists, politicians, and even trained historians from discovering causal connections in data which may simply be coincidental correlation.

To say that A caused B, one must first show that A_1 occurred before B_1; second, that there is in fact a correlation between A and B; third, one must find a presumptive agency connecting A and B. Thus, there is fairly good statistical evidence that smoking causes lung cancer; there is a proved correlation; the temporal connection exists; and the agency is presumed to be the inhalation of smoke and the deposit of carcinogens in the lung. Though the precise nature of the agency is not completely understood, the fact of its existence seems clear enough to the independent and unbiased observer.

CENTRE OF **COSMIC BROTHERHOOD STUDIES**

When next you are in Switzerland, you might care to look in at no. 15 Avenue E. Pittard, Geneva. Not only is the Centre "directed by extraterrestrials and their Vicars on Earth" (Spokesman Adoniesis—job-title Extraterrestrial Scientist), but they have the cure for cancer (found by an Italian veterinarian, one Dottore Bonifazio).

I wonder if the cancer was brought by extraterrestrial visitors in the first place.

THE HUSBAND OF A **COUNTESS** IS A **COUNT**

In French, a comtesse is the wife of a comte, and in Italian, a contessa is the wife of a conte. But in English, a countess is the wife not of a count, but of an earl, from the Anglo-Saxon *eorl* (a warrior). The word "count" (originally Lat. comes, Acc. comitem meant "companion") eventually became a military title, as in Comes littoris Saxonici (Count of the Saxon Coast), the Roman general responsible for the southeastern coastline of Britain.

COURTS OF LOVE EXISTED AND PRONOUNCED VERDICTS IN THE MIDDLE AGES

Books published as recently as 1937 perpetuated the error that medieval Courts of Love existed. Alfred Jeanroy, in *La poésie lyrique des troubadours* (2 vols., Toulouse, 1934) states that "the existence of these alleged Courts of Love must be relegated to the rank of those legends which, however attractive they may be, should none the less be banished from literary history." The legend was started by the 16th-century writer Jean de Nostredame, based on a misreading of poems by the troubadours. Gatherings of knights and their ladies frequently turned their conversation, as might be expected, to the finer points of love and courtship, but Nostredame is quite mistaken when imagining that tribunals of great ladies sat in judgment on cases involving distracted lovers. The term "court," as understood in medieval France, referred to social gatherings and not to official enquiries of any kind.

A **CRAB** IS A RED FISH THAT WALKS BACKWARDS

The Académie Francaise read out this draft definition to the great French naturalist Cuvier, who gravely replied, "Perfect, gentlemen. But if you will give me leave, I will make one small observation in natural history. The crab is not a fish, it is not red, and it does not walk backwards. With these exceptions your definition is excellent."

The edible crab of the United States is blue, while the common crab found in Britain is brown; they are crustaceans, not fish; and they are capable of moving in any direction when on land or the sea-bed, but more usually move sideways.

One is only provoked to remark that, if intelligent men can make so many errors on a common observable phenomenon, how is it possible to put any trust in the opinions of theologians, philosophers, or economists whose currency is the untestable theory?

CRANIOLOGY

Dr. Horst Bettelheim writes from Lübeck that one should give attention to Johann Kaspar Spurzheim (1776-1832), whose theories of craniology, or phrenology, seemed to reinforce those of Gall, though in fact they were merely similar.

Common sense was always a virtue of the essayist William Hazlitt, and he never showed it to better advantage than in *The plain speaker: opinions on books, men and things* (2 vols., London, 1826), in Essay XIV, "On Dr. Spurzheim's theory." Spurzheim, in Hazlitt's skeptical view, "is the Baron Munchausen [sic] of marvellous metaphysics. His object is to astonish the reader into belief, as jugglers make clowns gape and swallow whatever they please. He fabricates wonders with easy assurance, and deals in men 'whose heads do grow beneath their shoulders, and the anthropophagi, that each other eat.' He readily admits whatever suits his purpose, and magisterially doubts whatever makes against it. He has a cant of credulity mixed up with the cant of skepticism—things not easily reconciled, except by a very deliberate effort indeed." Hazlitt selects the following as a specimen of Spurzheim's peculiar reasoning:

"The doctrine, that every thing is provided with its own properties, was from time to time checked by metaphysicians and scholastic divines; but by degrees it gained ground, and the maxim that matter is inert was entirely refuted. Natural philosophers discovered corporeal properties, the laws of attraction and repulsion, of chemical affinity, of fermentation, and even of organization. They considered the phenomena of vegetables as the production of material qualities—as properties of matter. Glisson attributed to matter a particular activity, and to the animal fibre a specific irritability. De Gorter acknowledge in vegetable life something more than pure mechanism. Winter and Zups proved that the phenomena of vegetable life ought to be ascribed only to irritability. Of this, several phenomena of flowers and leaves indicate a great degree. The hop and French-bean twine round rods which are planted near them. The tendrils of vines curl round poles or the branches of neighboring trees. The ivy climbs the oak, and adheres to its sides, &c. Now it would be absurd to pretend that the organization of animals is entirely destitute of properties: therefore Frederick Hoffman took it for the basis of his system, that the human body, like all other bodies, is endowed with material properties."

Hazlitt, as open-mouthed at all of this as any twentieth-century reader, comments: "here be truths," but "dashed and brewed with lies" or doubtful points. Yet they all pass together without discrimination or selection. There is a simplicity in many of the propositions, amounting to a sort of bonhomie. There is an over-measure of candor and plainness. A man who gravely informs you, as an important philosophical discovery, that "the tendrils of vines curl round poles," and that "the human body is endowed with material properties" may escape without the imputation of intending to delude the unwary. But these kind of innocent pretences are like shoeing-horns to draw on the hardest consequences. By the serious offer of this meat for babes, you are prepared to swallow a horse-drench of parboiled paradoxes."

But Hazlitt's sparkling skepticism did not convince everybody. Sir Arthur Conan Doyle, whose belief in fairies and spirit photographs was as total as his mastery of the detective story, makes the great Sherlock Holmes deduce from a large hat that its wearer was "highly intellectual." How many readers would recognize in this inference a flattering allusion to a phrenological dogma of the time?

Walt Whitman's belief in phrenology was heightened by the discovery that he was well developed in all faculties, and he dotted Leaves of grass with craniological exhortations of the type "0 adhesiveness—0 pulse of my life," adhesiveness being an imagined phrenological faculty concerned with mutual attraction.

As early as 1807 a commission set up in France to investigate phrenology found no evidence to support the theories whatsoever, and in 1901 it was definitively proved that brain lesions cause disorders totally unconnected with the map of the skull drawn up by competing phrenologists.

THOMAS **CRAPPER** INVENTED THE TOILET

Thomas Crapper, a plumber from the late 1800s, did not invent the flush toilet, contrary to popular belief. However, some things which may have perpetuated this rumor could be the fact that he did invent the "ballcock," which is a device used in flush toilets. *Merriam-Webster* defines the ballcock as "An automatic valve whose opening and closing are controlled by a hollow float at the end of a lever."

(Continued)

Instead of Crapper, a man named Sir John Harrington was actually the one who designed the first toilets and then had them installed in the Queen's quarters back in 1596 (Crapper wasn't even born until 1836). The first patented flush toilet was in 1778, also in England.

Whether or not Mr. Crapper was the sole inventor of the ballcock is still up for debate, and why not? We the people sometimes really love believing in the validity of a good joke.

Sources: Merriam-webster.com; Dr. William L. Krinsky, *New York Times*, "Of Facts and Artifacts," 1999.

THE FALLACY OF **CREATIVE THINKING**

The author of the above title (there is no book—just the title) is the American hoaxer Alan Abel, of Zanesville, Ohio.

Abel gave a spoof lecture to advertising executives on the inefficiency involved in thinking up new ideas when one can simply steal them from other people. He was astonished to receive urgent requests for his "book" from the president of a large advertising agency.

This is hardly surprising, however, for it took three years for the American public to discover that Abel's Society for Indecency to Naked Animals (despite the obvious legpull in its name) was merely a parody of the various leagues to inculcate puritanical behavior. Something of the sort induced Abel to announce as visitors from France the Topless String Quartet, and the 1971 Sex Olympics, or the International Sex Bowl. He really did get asked for tickets, interviews, and the film rights. The "Sex Olympics" apparently fooled the American columnist Harriet Van Home, and the London *News of the World*, among others.

REPORTS OF **CRIME** AND VIOLENCE IN THE MASS MEDIA DO NOT CAUSE VIOLENCE

Among the cases which refute this fallacy are:

1. As soon as a popular newspaper reported in 1872 that children were being abandoned in France, eight children were abandoned in Marseilles in a single day.
2. There were several murders by children after the Jack-the-Ripper atrocities in London.
3. The murderer Haigh copied the acid-bath methods formerly employed by George Sarrett in France, which were widely reported in the press.

4. In 1857 in New York, when a woman killed her husband, three other women did the same a few days later.

At the same time it is clear that not all violence is caused by the viewing of violent films, television program, or reading violent comic strips or books. It is simply that "a few abnormal minds are seriously affected by what they see and read. In 1960 a youth committed a murder while holding-up a bank on the day that another youth was hanged at Wandsworth." And such cases of blind imitation are probably so infrequent that it would be a ludicrous over-reaction to attempt to ban completely all violence in the mass media. The editors should beware of giving too much publicity to unsavory people and doings.

Source: Christopher Hibbert, *The roots of evil* (London, 1963).

COW TIPPING

Cow Tipping is depicted in many cultural contexts as a common and exhilarating rural American pastime, such as in the cult favorite film, *Heathers*. As cow tipping comes up primarily in over the top comedies where the line between fiction and reality is obvious, a skeptic might ask: do people really believe cow tipping is something others do for fun? According to one frustrated country-dwelling Harvard College student (and to us), this is a very highly believed fallacy.

In his article in the *Harvard Crimson*, John Larew insists that since he arrived at college, every time he has told someone (especially someone from the city) where he grew up (deep in the country), they inevitably ask what he does for fun, and whether or not he's been cow tipping. Before he can answer with the negative, the inquirer goes on to brag about his own adventures going cow tipping, though generally it is revealed that he himself has never seen it done, but he has loads of friends who have.

This author also points out that even Susan Orlean, whose book *The Orchid Thief* was the inspiration for the popular movie *Adaptation* makes the mistake of depicting cow tipping as a real pastime in her investigative book, *Saturday Night*. Notably, the *New York Times,* in a 1990 review of the book, does indeed perpetuate the mistake when the editor writes: "Saturday night is associated with pleasure and abandon, with toppling cows in rural Pennsylvania, or with taking your dog to the vet to have its teeth cleaned."

Despite these many misconceptions, Larew along with a number of scientists, academics and farmers, has proven the impossibility

(Continued)

of cow tipping in practice. First of all, cows sleep standing up, thus, tipping a cow over in sleep is impossible because said cow would not have been standing up in the first place.

According to a professor of dairy science at the Virginia Polytechnic Institute and State University, the average weight of a full grown dairy cow is between 1,250 and 1,300 pounds. Thus, hypothetically, if someone did happen to find an upright cow who wasn't bothered by the fact that it is being forcibly pressured to lose its balance and fall over, it would take at least two, if not more, humans to accomplish the task.

Source: John L. Larew, "Cow Tipping is a Load of Bull," the *Harvard Crimson*, 1990.

THE BABY **CUCKOO** INTENTIONALLY KILLS ITS RIVAL YOUNG IN THE HOST NEST

No. During the first few days of its existence, the young cuckoo "possesses closely-packed tactile organs on its back and sides, far in excess of the usual quantity. Experiments have shown that when this spot is touched the young bird reacts as if it had been pricked with red-hot needles." Thus, on touching the foster-parents' young, it becomes sensitive, burrows into the nest and arches its back rigidly to escape the painful pressure of the other young birds, thus unknowingly forcing them out of the nest. Being the largest of the young, with the largest beak and most vigorous movement to attract attention, the cuckoo would probably have survived at the expense of its foster-brethren in any case.

Source: Johann A. Loeser, *Animal behaviour* (London, 1940, p. 128).

CURSE OF THE PHARAOHS

Lord Carnarvon, who financed the excavation of the Tomb of Tut-Ankh-Amun in Egypt, died of a mosquito bite six weeks after his visit to the tomb. Howard Carter, who discovered the tomb also died—seventeen years later. The joke about the "Curse of the Pharaohs" which took in so many people in 1922, when the tomb was first opened, was started by the Egyptologist Arthur Weigall as a hoax. It is not at all remarkable that ten people connected in some way with the Tut-Ankh-Amun expedition died within ten years. Richard Adamson, a survivor, expressed his disbelief in the curse on television in 1971.

This hoax became a fallacy because it was so tenacious in the popular mind that when a director of the Cairo Museum, Dr. Mehrez, died in the early 1970s, his death was connected with the "curse."

HISTORY IS CYCLICAL

1. Phases of History

Giambattista Vico (1668-1744) is only one of the millions of people, learned and lay alike, whose concept of the world they live in has been hopelessly confused by the fallacy that "this kind of thing happens every hundred years." Vico made a false analogy between the life of a human being and the course of a civilization. He argued that a man or woman, in the course of a lifetime, passes through phases of feeling, imagination and thinking. In the same way, a civilization passes through ages of gods, heroes, and humanity. A purely bestial phase passes into a primitive period, then to an intellectual and spiritual period, and finally to an era of humanity. The "energies" of the civilization then fade and die away, to be followed by another primitive phase. The problem with this world-view is that it is entirely fallacious as a principle, even if it can be made into a Procrustean bed that certain civilizations can be stretched to fit. In what sense, for instance, does the great and enduring civilization of China correspond in phases to the civilizations of the Congo pygmies or the Indians of the Canadian plains? Similar cyclical theories, attractive in their simplicity but wholly useless as tools for the understanding of the course of human societies, have been propagated by Oswald Spengler and Arnold Toynbee, but their principles are no more scientific than those of Vico's Principi di una scienza nuova intorno alla natura delle nazioni (Naples, 1725).

The fallacy that "knowledge proceeds by the removal of one error at a time and its replacement by a truth' was never more amply demonstrated, two and a half centuries after Vico, than by Edward R. Dewey, in his silly book *Cycles: mysterious forces that trigger events* (New York, 1971). If you have—as I am afraid you do have (in Pittsburgh)—a Foundation for the Study of Cycles, then, friends, what you will get is a series of studies of cycles. Even if the cycles aren't there.

John Sladek has examined Dewey and the Cycles thoroughly in *The new apocrypha* (London, 1974), exposing the fallacies inherent in the theories of cyclical effect in weather, high finance, and the abundance of tent caterpillars in New Jersey. He notes the existence of two types of fallacy: cycles which exist and are not mysterious, though claimed to be so by Dewey; and cycles which do not exist, but are claimed by Dewey to be real. An example of the first type is that the abundance of fox, lynx, wolf, marten, mink, coyote, hawk and owl reaches a maximum every 9.6 to 9.7 years, and then falls again. To Dewey, this is mysterious. John Sladek looks for a natural explanation instead, and finds one. "We're also told," he writes, "that the incidence of a certain disease in North American humans follows the same cycle. The disease is tuleremia, or rabbit fever. Hm. Sure enough, the rabbit abundance follows the same cycle. Obvious cause-effect relationships between rabbits, rabbit-connected disease, and rabbit predators come to mind."

The second type of fallacy (the cycles which are alleged to exist but are in fact imaginary) is provided by Professor Raymond H. Wheeler, once of the University of Kansas, who has attempted to relate history to weather. Both, he states, run in 400-year cycles of four phases, each of a century (though no rational explanation is offered for such a bizarre theory). The first period has cold and dry weather, corresponding to anarchy and weak governments; the second is warm and dry, with stronger governments; the third is cold and wet, with dictatorships; the fourth is warm and wet, with dissolving states. It would be a remarkable contribution to knowledge if such a scheme could be applied to each civilization at every period, for it would then be possible to work out where a particular civilization stood, and how it was likely to proceed in terms of strength and stability.

The problem with cycles is that they don't fit, if they can be found. But generally they resemble the Emperor's new clothes. They just aren't there at all.

2. Civilizations Have One Life-Cycle and One Creative Cycle

This idea was propounded by Nikolai Yakovlevich Danilevsky (1822-1885) in Russia and Europe: a viewpoint on the political relations between the Slavic and Germano-Romanic Worlds (1871), Oswald Spengler (1880-1936) in Der Untergang des Abendlandes (Decline of the West, 1918), and Arnold Joseph Toynbee (1889-1975) in *A study of history* (11 vols., 1934-1959).

The fallacy is of course that of giving objective shape and pattern to an essentially chaotic phenomenon such as world or even national history in which events are uncontrollable, even by totalitarian methods.

Pitirim A. Sorokin, in his closely-argued Modern historical and social philosophies (New York, 1963), states that "the central idea of Danilevsky, Spengler, and Toynbee that each great culture or civilization has only one life-cycle and one cycle of creativity (with a minor "Indian Summer" and "second religiosity") is entirely untenable so far as real cultural systems are concerned. Even in regard to social groups it is tenable only for a small fraction of them. It is not at all tenable as applied to all social systems . . . Great cultural systems have many quantitative and qualitative ups and downs in their virtually indefinitely long life-span. Even big social systems like the Chinese or the Egyptian or the Hindu states and nations have had several ups and downs in their political and social history. So also have many families, religious or economic bodies, political parties and other social groups. In their "success," "creativity," "wealth," "membership" and "power," most of them have several ups and downs in their life-history instead of just one life-cycle and one period of creativity."

Sorokin supplies tables which conclusively demonstrate the fallacy of a specificity of cultural creativeness of each "civilization" or "nation" or "country" and prove that the field of creativity shifts in the course of time from religion or the fine arts to science or philosophy.

Examples of creative periods are provided from Ancient Egypt, Greece, and France. From India the examples are as follows:

Religion	c. 1000 B.C., c. 600—400 B.C., c. 272—232 B.C., c. 1—100 A.D., c. 788—860
The State (native, not foreign) and (to some extent) Economics	c. 321—186 B.C., 78—96 A.D., 320—500, c. 606—647, 1350—1600
Philosophy	600—400 B.C., 100—500, 600—1000
Science	700—500 B.C., 400—1150 (climax c. 500—625)
Literature	400 B.C.—100 A.D., 350—750 [but note the various periods of creativity in each different language. Ph.W.]
Sculpture	c. 150 B.C., 400—725 A.D.
Architecture	1489—1706
Music	1600—1771
Painting	450—750, 1615—1800

3. History Repeats Itself

This is quite impossible, despite the protestations of thousands of amateur (and even a few professional) historians to the contrary. The passage of time changes a nation and its places; change to places and people affects all factors taken singly or collectively (from government to sanitation), and nothing can be repeated identically. John Duncan Mackie was guilty of perpetrating this fallacy in *A history of Scotland* (2nd ed., Baltimore, 1966, p. 141): "history had repeated itself exactly . . . the year 1286 was come again [in 1542]" and G. A. Williamson, editing Eusebius' *The history of the Church from Christ to Constantine* (Harmondsworth, 1965, p. 10) falsely claimed that "No one can read Eusebius's account of how the cathedral of Tyre, with all its elaborate symbolism, rose from the ashes, without thinking of Coventry. Truly that generation and this are one." Not only is it unlikely that the inhabitants of Sur (ancient Tyre) in Lebanon and Coventry are even aware of each others' existence; it is an affront to intelligent readers to ask them to believe that all the surrounding circumstances of early Christianity and mid-20th century bomb warfare have any but the remotest resemblance.

D

"Defend me, therefore, common sense, say I,
From reveries so airy, from the toil
Of dropping buckets into empty wells,
And growing old in drawing nothing up."
—WILLIAM COWPER, *The Task* (Book III)

"A doubt that doubted everything would not be a doubt."
—LUDWIG WITTGENSTEIN,
Uber Gewissheit: On certainty (Oxford, 1969)

THE "DAME TROT" OF CHILDREN'S LITERATURE ONCE EXISTED

Children's literature is filled with references to, and stories about, a shadowy figure called Dame Trot, related by some to the go-between Urraca (known as "Trotaconventos" or "Trot-the-Convents") in Juan Ruiz's 14th-century *Libro de buen amor*. She appears in English in such works for children as *Old Dame Trot and her comical cat* (London, 1803) and its *Continuation . . .* (London, 1806).

Perhaps the mythical Dame can be traced back to the medical school which flourished at Salerno, in southern Italy, from the eleventh century to the fourteenth. A gynecological textbook produced at Salerno, *De passionibus mulierum,* was long attributed to a woman professor named Trotula. However, someone interested more in truth than in legend discovered that the famous "Trotula" was in fact a Salemitan male doctor called "Trottus."

DANTE CALLED HIS COMEDY "DIVINE"

Dante Alighieri wrote his great trilogy as *La Commedia* (as opposed to a "tragedy") in the early 14th century, but it was not printed until 1472, at Foligno. The Botticelli drawings probably commissioned by Lorenzo de' Medici inspired a remarkable series of engravings by Baldini first published in 1481. The epithet "divina" was coined neither by Dante himself nor by any of his contemporaries, but appeared first on the title-page of Lodovico Dolci's edition of the great poem dated 1555.

111

DEAD BODIES CAUSE PESTILENCE

The French Government, during World War I, found it necessary to issue an official communiqué stating that pestilence is not caused by dead bodies on a battlefield.

NO LIFE EXISTS IN THE DEAD SEA

But it does. Micro-organisms were reported to exist in the Dead Sea in *Nature,* September 12, 1936, p. 467. The old tale that "birds will not fly over the Dead Sea" has also been exploded by eye-witnesses.

Additionally, J.B. Salgues *(Des erreurs et des préjugés répandus dans la société* (3rd ed., Paris, 1818, vol.1, pp. 262 ff.) confutes several more Dead Sea Fallacies: that its waters can support iron and bricks, and that its vapors kill fish, birds, and plants.

The major source of Dead Sea fallacies is, however, Andrew D. White's *A history of the warfare of science with theology in Christendom* (London, 1955, 2 vols. in 1, vol. 2, pp. 209 ff.). Dr White deals with the curious fallacy of Lot's wife turned into a pillar of salt (there are analogous false explanations for curious natural phenomena in all other religions and mythologies); the foul smells of the area attributed to supernatural causes (actually caused by sulphur in mineral springs); the error that "the very beautiful apples" that grow there will "burn and are reduced to ashes and smoke as if they are still burning"; the notion that the Dead Sea is the mouth of Hell (due to the hot springs in the area); and the hoary errors repeated in Sir John Mandeville's *Travels* that "if a man cast iron therein, it will float above. And if men cast a feather therein, it will sink to the bottom, and these be things against kind."

Source: William G. Duncalf, *The Guinness book of plant facts and feats* (Enfield, 1976).

FALLACIES CONCERNING DEAFNESS AND THE DEAF

Fallacies concerning the deaf (1883), an anonymous publication reprinted in New York in 1976, should be supplemented by Harry Best's *Deafness and the deaf in the United States* (New York, 1943), and especially ch. XVIII, "Popular conceptions regarding deaf, pp. 327-338.

Mary Plackett, Chief Librarian of the Royal National Institute for the Deaf, London, writes: "Deafness—which has been described as "the least understood and most misunderstood of disabilities"—is an area full of fallacies. Those we most commonly encounter are:

1. "Deaf and Dumb" (a term now frowned upon because it is so open to misinterpretation)
"Dumb" does *not* imply "unable to speak"; a profoundly deaf child is physically capable of speech but cannot learn to speak in the normal

way, which is by imitating what he hears said. This may seem like common-sense, but the link between hearing and speech needs explanation as few, if any, people realize it intuitively. Also, "speech" means "language" as well as articulation; learning how to use words is equally dependent on imitation, which is why the reaction "Well, at least they can read and write" shows a lack of understanding of the situation.

Nor does "dumb" mean "stupid"; a child may be multi-handicapped, both deaf and mentally handicapped, but deafness *per se* is not an intellectual handicap. From this, it is apparent that the results of deafness in infancy and early childhood are totally different from those of deafness acquired in adulthood, and the two groups have little in common.

2. Lip-reading

It is only in popular fiction that it is possible to lip-read a bearded stranger side-view across a smoke-filled cafe! Lip-reading is in fact *very difficult,* even in ideal conditions, and relies largely on guess-work, as many sounds look alike on the lips; it is effective only in a one-to-one conversation.

3. Hearing Aids

These do *not* restore normal hearing in the same way that spectacles restore normal vision. Deafness is more often a problem of discrimination than lowered volume, so amplifying sound, which is what a hearing aid basically does, may be helpful but does not solve the problem.

4. Sign Language

This is *not* universal, but differs from country to country and is in fact far more regionally varied than spoken language because it has not been subjected to the standardising influence of the mass media. It is not merely a pantomimic representation of spoken language, but a language in its own right, with a grammatical structure which does not correspond to spoken English, for example." (Personal communication, December 17, 1979). Harry Best points out that, because of ignorance, the general public may treat the deaf as "extraordinary, exceptional, or odd—out of the way, out of place and out of tune with, divergent from, at variance to, the general population. The deaf are liable to be looked upon as "queer" or abnormal, and at times as even surly, or uncivil, or rude, or brutish; they may be regarded as morose or moody—perhaps without capacity to laugh; they are to be approached . . . with a degree of caution; they may even be shunned or rebuffed." The famous philosopher Herbert Spencer fell into this trap in his *Principles of sociology* (London, 1897, p. 827), where he writes in error: "A brute thinks only of things that can be touched, seen, heard, tasted, etc.; and the like is true of the untaught child, the deaf-mute, and the lowest savage." [Since the passage is reprinted from *The Nineteenth Century* (Vol.15, 1884), it is strange that neither Spencer nor his editor noted that, however few a deaf-mute's capacities may be, hearing can hardly be one of them!]

In scientific terminology, more harm than good is often done by grouping the deaf with the "defective classes" as is so often done. But the differences separating each such group from another are often greater than the differences between each group and the rest of the population. Thus, in some American legal works (including the *Corpus Juris*), the deaf have been classed under the heading "insane" in connection with wills, and the witnessing of documents. In special U.S. census reports before 1900, the deaf and blind were included in the "Dependent, Defective and Delinquent" classes.

"Another serious misapprehension respecting the deaf, notes Harry Best, "arises from the impression not infrequently current, and apparently encouraged at times in the proceedings of a scientific body, to the effect that a large proportion of the deaf are so either because of a similar condition in their parents or because of the existence in the parents of some physical disease." There are no grounds for this common fallacy. Nevertheless, we find in the handbook of the Child Welfare Exhibit in New York in 1911 (on page 38): "Mating of the Unfit. "The Law." Marriage of cousins, insane or feebleminded, alcoholic, syphilitic parents and effects. The cost—7,369 blind infants, 89,287 deaf and dumb, 18,476 feebleminded."

Other fallacies concerning the deaf are those which consider them in some way homogeneous as a group, though they are in fact as representative of the whole of society as those who happen to bump their knees on a wall; that they are wholly dependent, which in fact is seldom the case; and that, as a group of people, they are unhappy and wholly to be pitied, when many of the deaf lead a full and happy life and indeed, in the words of Harry Best, "all things considered, cheerfulness may be said to be an attribute of the larger number of the deaf."

THE CHRISTIAN MARRIAGE SERVICE ORIGINALLY INCLUDED THE WORDS "TILL **DEATH US DO PART**"

The longer that you think about it, the stranger the phrase appears. In fact, it was not originally "Till death us *do* part" or even "Till death us *does* part" but "Till death us *depart*" until 1662, when the verb "depart" was still also transitive. It meant "divide" or "separate," and was used by Barrow in 1667, for example: "The closest union here cannot last longer than till death us depart."

It was in 1662 that "depart" was changed in the marriage service to "do part," grammatically also in the subjunctive mood and hence equally correct.

THE **DEATH-WATCH BEETLE'S TICKING** PRESAGES DEATH

The natural noise made by the genus of wood-boring beetles Anobium is a kind of click. Many nervous children and even adults have been taught in misnamed "fairy" stories that Death personified comes knocking at your door and, when you hear a knocking without anyone apparently near, the hour of your death is nigh.

An illogical connection is made between two events or ideas causally unrelated and, among those susceptible to heart trouble, it is quite true that death by shock might ensue. All the more reason for destroying at its root the baseless, ignorant belief in the menacing power of the Anobium beetle. It is also of course true that if you ignore a death-watch beetle long enough, thinking it to be patient Death, your walls and ceilings will eventually crumble and the prophecy will be fulfilled in a different way!

DE BONO'S FIVE WAYS TO BE WRONG

"Some characteristic mistakes are a natural part of the thinking process," writes Edward de Bono in his *Practical thinking* (London, 1971). "These mistakes cannot be avoided because they arise directly from the way the mind works." However, one must always be able to recognize the kinds of common mistake made in everyday thinking:

1. The Monorail Mistake
This involves going from one idea to another without taking into account factors extrinsic to those ideas. Such mistakes are of the type "Chinese Communism is a good thing for China, so it must be a good thing for Spain."

2. The Magnitude Mistake
This is the mistake of the type "If you don't wash the dishes, you can't love me like Jessie loves her husband," which ignores the great love that might have been displayed by the wife's working for 40 hours as a secretary while her househusband looked after the baby and cooked the meals.

3. The Misfit Mistake
This is the mistake of the type "You sound just like Gwilym on the "phone and because you have a Welsh accent you must be Gwilym."

4. The Must-be Mistake
Arrogance is responsible for the closed mind which resists examining alternative explanations which remain within the bounds of credibility. This mistake is of the type "dinosaurs all died out within a relatively short period, so someone must have shot the dinosaurs, so we must find out who it was."

5. The Miss-out Mistake

This involves selecting a solution which covers part of a problem, but not the whole of it. A propaganda film may show a magnificent new hospital in a poor country as evidence of progress, while missing out the pictures of children in the next street suffering from disease and malnutrition.

Edward de Bono is quick to point out that these mistakes are not confined to the stupid, careless, or ignorant: "Even the most intelligent and highly educated people make exactly the same kind of mistake. They may be dealing with ideas like political stability rather than the building of a garden shed but the type of mistake is the same." One can recognize these mistakes in the arch-patriot, in the racist club, in the religious cult, in the political terrorist, and in the next-door neighbor who won't speak to you because of something you once said about a friend of his that he did not like.

Our author sadly reflects that you can probably remember "things you were taught at school about geography (valleys, river deltas, rice-growing countries, etc.) and about history (dates of battles, names of kings, etc.) But can you remember what you were taught about thinking?"

TO "**DECIMATE**" AN ARMY IS TO DESTROY ALL BUT A TENTH

The Latin *decern* ("ten") is the root of the verb "to decimate" which writers regularly use to mean "slaughtered to such an extent that only one-tenth survived," in a military context.

But a decimated army is reduced *by* a tenth, not *to* a tenth, so that in fact nine-tenths survive, and a decimated army of a hundred can be restored to its former strength by the recruitment of 10 percent of its reduced numbers plus one soldier.

THE AMERICAN "DECLARATION OF INDEPENDENCE" WAS SIGNED AND PROCLAIMED ON JULY 4, 1776

Montagu and Darling carefully demolish these fallacies (for there are three of them) in their *Ignorance of certainty* (New York, 1970).

"It is a fact that members of the Second Continental Congress did *not* sign the document known to fame as the Declaration of Independence on July 4, 1776. American independence was *not* proclaimed to the world—as so often asserted—on that date. The official name of the document was *not* "the Declaration of Independence."

Firstly, independence was resolved—and the signing took place—on July 2, 1776. Secondly, it was on July 3 when the document was first published in two Pennsylvanian papers, the *Gazette* and the *Journal*. Congress voted on the Declaration on July 4, but it was not until

July 8 that the document was proclaimed by being read publicly from the balcony of Independence Hall. Thirdly, the official title of the document is "The Unanimous Declaration of the Thirteen United States of America," the word "Independence" occurring nowhere in the title.

STEBBING ON THE **DEFINITION** OF FALLACIES

"The word 'fallacy' has unfortunately often been used in different senses," writes L. Susan Stebbing in *Thinking to some purpose* (Harmondsworth, 1939, pp. 156-7). "It is used sometimes as a synonym for error of fact," as in the statement: "It is a fallacy to suppose that aeroplanes can be built by mass-production." This is, in my opinion, a plainly erroneous use of the word. The speaker meant that aeroplanes cannot, in fact, be produced by methods suitable to the production of, say, motor-cars. I shall assume, without further discussion that the speaker, in using "fallacy" in this sense, was simply showing his ignorance of the correct usage of the word. There remains to be noticed an ambiguity that is more important for our present purpose. If we say: "He is guilty of a fallacy," we sometimes mean to imply that he is guilty of a deception. The *Shorter Oxford English Dictionary* gives as a meaning of "fallacy," now obsolete, "deception," "trickery."" This obsolete meaning does, I think, influence our modern usage. It would certainly be an advantage if we recognized that to accuse a person of having committed a fallacy is not to accuse him of intent to deceive. A fallacy is a violation of a logical principle; "to fall into a fallacy" is to slip into "an unsound form of argument," that is, to make a mistake *in reasoning,* not in what is *reasoned about.* If we mistakenly suppose that we have premises adequate to establish our conclusion, then we are reasoning illogically and thus committing a fallacy.

If we think of a fallacy as a deception, we are too likely to take it for granted that we need to be cautious in looking out for fallacies only when other people are arguing with us. We come to suppose that a fallacy is a trick and, thus, as involving deliberate dishonesty. Thinking along these lines, we are apt to assume that where there is no dispute, and so no disputant, there is no danger of fallacies, so that honesty of intention will suffice to keep our reasoning sound. This is a profound mistake."

MACKAY ON **DELUSIONS**

Charles Mackay's engrossing compilation, *Extraordinary popular delusions and the madness of crowds* (London, 1852; expanded from *Memoirs of extraordinary popular delusions,* London, 1841) includes not only common fallacies such as haunted houses, alchemy, astrology, necromancy, augury, divination and omens; but also the mania for tulips (in the year 1800, the normal price in England was fifteen guineas for a single bulb); the disproportionate attention paid to the hair and the

117

beard in political, religious, and social history (at the end of the 11th century the Pope decreed excommunication for longhaired men during their life and denial of prayer for them after death); the curious belief that slow poisoning was less offensive (especially in the 18th century in Europe, and above all in Italy); and the popular admiration of certain criminals, such as Jonathan Wild, Jack the Ripper, Vidocq, Schubry of Hungary, Schinderhannes of Germany, and Rob Roy of Scotland. In recent times one might cite the train robber Biggs and the vicious Kray brothers, exalted into mighty folk-heroes by the mass media.

Mackay, who wrote *Forty years' recollections* (1876) in autobiographical vein, observed in his preface to the 1852 edition of his book on delusions, "In reading the history of nations, we find that, like individuals, they have their whims and their peculiarities; their seasons of excitement and recklessness, when they care not what they do. We find that whole communities suddenly fix their minds upon one object, and go mad in its pursuit; that millions of people become simultaneously impressed with one delusion, and run after it, till their attention is caught by some new folly more captivating than the first. We see one nation suddenly seized, from its highest to its lowest members, with a fierce desire of military glory; another as suddenly becoming crazed upon a religious scruple; and neither of them recovering its senses until it has shed rivers of blood and sowed a harvest of groans and tears, to be reaped by its posterity. At an early age in the annals of Europe its population lost their wits about the sepulchre of Jesus, and crowded in frenzied multitudes to the Holy Land; another age went mad for fear of the devil, and offered up hundreds of thousands of victims to the delusion of witchcraft. At another time, the many became crazed on the subject of the philosopher's stone, and committed follies till then unheard of in their pursuit of it."

DENTAL FALLACIES

"Clean teeth never decay" is a fallacy promulgated by at least one manufacturer of toothpaste. A clean surface is desirable, but impossible to obtain, owing to the perennial omnipresence of bacteria. However, the truism that toothpaste, dental floss, and brushing must all fail in various ways to prevent decay (they can only at best reduce the *speed* of decay) should not be taken by any youngster as an excuse to avoid brushing the teeth to remove as much as possible of accretions caused by eating and drinking. One's *general* health is a factor as important as frequent brushing in dental health.

It is frequently believed that "primitive" peoples suffer less from tooth decay than do more "civilized" peoples. This ignores the sugar-chewing Jamaicans, whose teeth decayed long before the white man arrived, and the Neanderthaloid "Rhodesian" man of about 30,000 years ago was found to have decay in nearly every tooth of the upper jaw. The generalization is, however, true in the case of metropolitan white men vis-à-vis Zulus: according to V. Suk (*American Journal of Physical Anthropology,* vol. 2, 1919, pp. 351-88), at the age of 18, only 10-15 percent of the former have, "perfect" teeth, while the figure among the latter is 85-94 percent.

An interesting fallacy, recurring in 1976 (*The Penguin medical encyclopedia,* 2nd ed., p. 433), is the old notion that "human jaws have receded in the course of evolution, and there is now barely room for the full set of permanent teeth." But there never was. Adolph H. Schutz, writing in *Current Anthropology* (vol. 7, 1966, p. 356), states that "unequivocal crowding of teeth is quite common among recent wild monkeys and apes. I have never failed to encounter cases with displaced, twisted, or impacted single or several large teeth in collections of primate skulls, and often such manifestations of unmistakable maladjustment in the size of the teeth and the jaws, resulting in crowding, are much more pronounced than in the two or three instances found in the Australo-pithecines."

Human teeth constitute irrefragable evidence, according to some, that Man is essentially a meat-eater, with the natural ability to rend animal flesh. Nothing could be more absurd: comparative anatomy proves the frugivorous and *not* the carnivorous origin of Man.

Cuvier states that "the natural food of man, judging from Ms structure, appears to consist principally of the fruits, roots, and other succulent parts of vegetables." Linnaeus, Gassendi and later commentators corroborate this view. Sir Henry Thompson wrote in his *Food and feeding:* "The characters of his teeth and digestive organs indicate that during his long history of development [Man] has lived mainly on roots, seeds, nuts and fruits; in other words, he has been a vegetable feeder." A. S. E. Ackermann, in his *Popular fallacies* (4th ed., London, 1950), adds: "The assertion so often made that alcohol and animals are "sent" as food is absurd. The mere fact that we have been accustomed to eat flesh-food no more proves that animals were created for this purpose than the existence of cannibalism proves that missionaries are "sent" to the South Sea Islanders solely as an article of food, or the former existence of slavery that black men were "sent" to be slaves of the white."

Even a number of otherwise intelligent people still believe the hoary fallacy that an aching tooth should not be extracted until the "swelling" has gone down. While modern dentistry can usually avoid extraction in many circumstances, there are occasions when extraction is called for. Swelling indicates an abscess at the root of the tooth. Pus must always be evacuated and the best manner of achieving this in the case of a tooth is its removal. Unless this is done, the abscess may open and discharge, or it may break into the cellular tissue, causing general septic poisoning.

On the invention of dental "crowns" and "bridges," C. E. Wallis wrote in the *British Dental Journal* of March 15, 1915: "Many people have thought that the making of dental crowns and "bridges" was introduced to mankind by our American cousins, but in various museums of ancient Greece and Rome are to be seen excellent examples of gold bridges and artificial teeth, such as were probably used by the plutocracy, if not by the aristocracy of those early days."

The best ancient dentists were the Etruscans, who made partial dentures, with gold bridge work, as early as 700 B.C. The art was lost during the Middle Ages, and Queen Elizabeth I, concerned to conceal the sinking of her face due to the loss of her front teeth, appeared in public with her mouth stuffed with fine cloth. It is not until the end of the 17th century that dentures were available to the rich again.

Sources include: M. F. Ashley Montagu and Edward Darling, *The prevalence of nonsense* (New York, 1967); and Edward de Bono *(ed.), Eureka!* (London, 1974).

NOBODY BELIEVES IN THE **DEVIL** ANY MORE

The Christian notion of the Devil, or Satan, derives from the post-exilic Hebrew concept, itself influenced by Babylonian and Assyrian traits, though the Hebrew notion was originally that of an "opponent." Solomon is said, in his message to Hiram, King of Tyre, to have congratulated himself on having no "Satans," and was thus enabled to build the Temple, which his warlike father David had not been able to accomplish. In later Judaism, the idea of Satan is colored by Persian dualism, and Samael, highest of the angels, merges with Satan into a single entity.

The New Testament Satan reproduces the later characteristics of his Hebrew prototype. In Matthew he becomes "Prince of Demons," and in Ephesians we find the Devil ruling over a world of evil beings who dwell in the lower heavens.

In the Middle Ages, belief in Satan, satanic powers and witchcraft grew to epidemic proportions; both torture and burning threatened those who fell foul of the authorities suspicious of heresy, and Protestantism was as virulent in its seeking-out of the "devil-haunted" as the Roman Catholicism from which it derived fear and irrational loathing of an imaginary evil "being." In fact, belief in the devil is not decreasing.

Dr. Clyde Z. Nunn, of the Center for Policy Research in the United States, has shown that belief in the existence of the Devil *rose from 37 percent to 48 percent* in the period from 1964 to 1973. Dr. Nunn ascribes the growing belief to "uncertainty and stress" at a time "when things seem to be falling apart and resources seem limited for coping with it."

Sources include: *Tucson Daily Citizen,* April 4, 1974.

DIAMOND FALLACIES

1) Diamonds Can't Be Split By a Hammer on an Anvil

Diamond is graded 15 on the 15-point Mohs Hardness Scale, and is thus the *hardest* substance known, but it is relatively *brittle*. Yet Pliny the Elder convinced antiquity (and the belief persisted until the 19th century in diamond-rich South Africa) that "these stones are tested upon the anvil, and will resist the blow to such an extent as to make the iron rebound and the very anvil split asunder." There are so many errors in Pliny that one is tempted to wonder whether he was writing, delightedly, with tongue in cheek to discover whether he could indeed fool all of the people all of the time.

In 1476, Swiss mercenaries found diamonds belonging to Charles the Bold, Duke of Burgundy, after the Battle of Morat, and struck them to test for genuineness. They powdered—so they were!

The clever French jeweller Jean-Baptiste Tavernier (1605-89), who visited the Indian diamond mines in the 17th century, found that some merchants knew the true facts, but persuaded simple miners that their diamonds were not real by breaking them with a hammer. They proceeded to make away with the pieces after the disappointed miners had left.

2) Mossian Produced Diamonds from Graphite in 1893

In 1893, the French chemist Ferdinand Moissan claimed that he had produced diamonds after dissolving graphite in molten cast iron. Most of the objects found were black and impure, but one object was colorless and almost a millimetre long. Moissan was therefore credited with the production of synthetic diamonds. However, his results were never repeated, and it is believed that they were falsified by one of Moissan's assistants, who had wearied of the fruitless experiments, and decided to end them by secretly introducing a real diamond of little worth into the molten cast iron.

In 1962, with a pressure of 200,000 atmospheres and a temperature of 5,000°C (conditions not available to Moissan), graphite was turned to diamond without the use of a catalyst.

Sources: Isaac Asimov, *Guide to science* (2 vols., New York, 1972); Eric Bruton, *Diamond* (2nd ed., London, 1978).

"WHAT THE DICKENS!" DERIVES FROM CHARLES DICKENS

The common expression has nothing to do with *any* member of the Dickens family at all, but is simply a euphemism (via "Dick-son") for "What the Devil!" coined in a more squeamish age than our own.

Source: Eric Partridge, *Name into word* (London, 1949).

DIGESTION FALLACIES

1. Cocktails Aid Digestion
This fallacy is so common that no amount of proof seems to have any effect. In Health for everyman (1937), R. Cove-Smith categorically states that "the habit of cocktail-drinking is quite defenceless; cocktails irritate the stomach, cause a fictitious appetite and delay digestion."

2. Green Apples Will Give You Indigestion
Anything will give you indigestion if eaten too quickly. The fallacy about eating unripe apples probably arose from the greed of little boys who stole the apples before they were mature, straight from the tree, and gobbled them down quickly because they were afraid of being caught and, since it was not yet the apple season, they were avid for apples.

The real cause of their indigestion was the haste with which the food was eaten. Dr. August A. Thomen assures us, in *Doctors don't believe it: why should you?* (New York, 1935), "If an apple is eaten slowly, and sufficiently chewed, the stomach cannot distinguish between a ripe and an unripe one."

3. Slapping the Stomach Is a Cure for Indigestion
"Several years ago a medical man in New York attained so high a reputation for the cure of dyspepsia that he had no difficulty in obtaining a fee of five hundred dollars for each case he undertook, payable in advance. His patients were bound by solemn oath not to reveal his mode of treatment; but after his death scores of them considered themselves freed from the obligation and published the secret, which mainly consisted in slapping the stomach," etc.

The symptoms of dyspepsia can be relieved by a wide range of drugs, but *not* by slapping the stomach.

Sources: George Black, *The doctor at home* (p. 441), quoted in L. P. Jacks, *Among the idolmakers* (London, 1912, p. 127).

DIOGENES OF SINOPE LIVED IN A TUB
No reference to this legend is made in the authoritative article by K. von Fritz in the 2nd ed. of the *Oxford classical dictionary* (1970). His main principles were that happiness is attained by satisfying only one's natural needs and by satisfying them in the cheapest and easiest way. What is natural cannot be dishonorable or in-decent and therefore can and should be done in public. Conventions which are contrary to these principles are unnatural and should not be observed.

Diogenes' biographer, Seneca, wrote over three hundred years after the death of Diogenes that "a man so crabbed ought to have lived in a tub like a dog." E.Cobham Brewer, in *A dictionary of phrase and fable,* corrupts this to "Diogenes. A noted Greek cynic philosopher (about 412-323 B.C.), who, according to Seneca, lived in a tub. . . ." A textbook example, perhaps, of the rise of a common fallacy.

MEN DON'T ASK FOR **DIRECTIONS** BECAUSE THEY ARE BETTER NAVIGATORS THAN WOMEN

This stereotype is depicted in Hollywood movies and more than likely, carried out in typical family road trips by the father and/or father figure. Even when a man is clearly lost, he will drive around in circles a dozen times with a car full of frustrated passengers before pulling over to ask for directions.

Despite the clearly apparent fact that not all men are instinctively good at directions, there is also some interesting research that shows the different ways in which men and women navigate their general surroundings.

In an experiment conducted by psychology and linguistics professor, Dr. Thomas Bever, it was found that in both rats and humans, there were notable differences in the way each gender thinks about and experiences sense of direction.

It is suggested that there are two primary ways in which animals and humans navigate directionally. The first, and decidedly more male way of using directions, is based on time and distance perception. In other words, a man keeps track of where they are and where they are going based on how much time has passed and at what speed, relative to the point they started. The second, more "feminine" directional strategy is to measure where they are based on familiar visual landmarks.

Bever's findings determined that when landmarks, or objects in the path he constructed were removed, women had a harder time re-identifying the path they had just taken on a digital map. On the other hand, when the geometric shape of the maze was altered, men were more disoriented than women. Men overall were better at choosing drawings that represented the maze than women. However, when all the students were asked to identify intersections in a series of twenty photographs of their university's underground tunnel system, the women were more correct in their identification, and in arranging the photographs sequentially.

Overall, it was determined that women appear to be much more visually oriented, noticing subtle differences in surroundings in order to find their way around, while men's navigation tactics depend more often on spatial motion memory.

(Continued)

A *Times* article that reported these findings suggests that maybe men are better at reading maps because it is easier for them to transfer drawings into spatial movement than through looking at a series of random landmarks. But this doesn't necessarily show why women would be more inclined to ask for directions. Perhaps it's because the person who gives you directions on the side of the road is likely to tell you to turn left at the next stoplight or McDonalds rather than to draw you a simple map of the route you need to follow.

Either way, there are no wrong answers here. The two strategies of navigation are separate but equally efficient. So, you'd think having a male and female in the front of a car using these two and only ways humans figure out where they are going would be enough to get that family of four to their destination. Then again, two people turning the steering wheel in opposing directions might not be the key to moving forward, according to physics.

Sources: Sandra Blakeslee, "Why Don't Men Ask for Directions? They Don't Feel Lost," *New York Times*, 1992.

DOCTORS TAKE AN OATH WHEN THEY QUALIFY

In some countries this is true, but not in all. British doctors take no oath, though an unwritten code of ethics is taken for granted. The Hippocratic Oath, taken on admission to the medical school and guild on the Greek island of Cos, was sworn by "Apollo the physician, and by Asklepios, Hygeia, and Panacea and all the gods and goddesses." Hippocrates was born about 460 B.C. and lived to be about 100: he wrote some, though not all, of the books attributed to him, and even now represents the ideal of the medical doctor, free from magic and superstition: a humane observer and servant of the sick irrespective of their wealth or social position.

DOGS HAVE EXTRASENSORY PERCEPTION

Nobody and nothing has yet been proved to have extrasensory perception, despite a great propensity on the part of many enthusiasts to prove just that. But the literature on dogs' strange abilities, every one of them based on a misunderstanding of the dog's brain so far as it has been studied so far, is almost as voluminous as that on extrasensory abilities among human beings.

The *Odyssey* (Book XVI) was one of the first texts to invent canine clairvoyance: the dogs of the swineherd Eumaeus "with a low whine shrank cowering to the far side of the steading" in the presence of the goddess Athene, though Telemachus couldn't see her, and Virgil and Lucan agree that dogs have this special power. They can also find their way back home by an unexplained power. Or, according to Stefansson *(The friendly Arctic,* New York, 1924), not: a lost dog "rarely finds its way back." His Eskimo hunter Emiu nearly lost his life in a blizzard through foolishly trusting his dogs to find their way back to camp. He had picked up this notion from white men! Eskimoes have their own irrational beliefs, but they have enough practical experience of dogs' weaknesses to doubt the white man's blind faith in their powers, Dickens perpetuated the fallacy in *Little Dorrit,* where the dog "recognizes" Rigaud's villainy despite the gullibility of his master.

DOG FALLACIES

1. A Dog's Mouth Is Cleaner Than a Human's

We'll go ahead and state the obvious: people love their dogs. Perhaps in some cases more than they love their friends, family members, or dare I say, their own children. There are roughly 78.2 million dogs owned by people in the United States alone. Not to mention, the close relationship between dogs and humans has existed since early centuries when dogs helped us with survival via hunting.

So, yes, dogs are beloved creatures for us, perhaps representing a bond between human and animal that can't be replicated between us and any other mammals (sorry, cat lovers). Dogs are therapeutic. Your dog will love you no matter what. And he will generally protect you from what he perceives as a threat. And in return, all you have to do is feed him, walk him, and pet him (Not including grooming and vet costs . . . But did you know that dog grooming is actually one of the few industries that is essentially recession proof?).

Given all this history between us and our dogs, plus the fact that they are so adorable, might we even go so far as to say giving them the occasional kiss is actually quite sanitary, as their mouths are cleaner than the mouths of humans? Some of us certainly would, as this myth about the hygiene of a K9's mouth being more immaculate than even those cleaned bi-annually by modern dentistry still very much exists.

So, does this myth have any reasonable backing? Apparently, the belief that dogs' mouths are cleaner than ours came from the observation that dogs lick their wounds in order to heal them.

(Continued)

And in fact, their wounds do heal on their own generally speaking. But this is not because their mouths are exceptionally clean or sanitary, but rather because they use their tongues to wipe away dead tissue. In addition, the licking stimulates circulation, helping the healing process along as well.

But when it comes to whether their mouths are actually more sanitary than ours, it is not true. Logically speaking, a dog eats garbage, raw meat, and in some cases, dead mice and other rodents. None of these things are considered appetizing or edible to the human palette.

Having said this, there are some experts who claim that despite the fact that humans have cleaner mouths than most animals,' it's still more likely that one would get sick from kissing another human than kissing his or her dog. This is because diseases are species specific, so most illnesses that your dog may be carrying in his mouth would not spread to human immune systems.

So go ahead and kiss your dog goodnight. But if you're fantasizing about a lady and the tramp spaghetti dinner for two with little Fido, you might want to reconsider.

2. Dogs See in Black and White
Contrary to how the vision of dogs is depicted in some movies and television programs, such as the dog, Spike, in Nickelodeon's former kids program, *Rugrats*, dogs actually can see some color and not just in black and white and gray. Their vision defects are actually relatively equivalent to the most common type of color blindness in humans, which is called deuteranopia. Deuteranopia is categorized as a difficulty distinguishing green and red. So, in a sense, as this type of color blindness exists in some form or another in about 8 percent of the American population (as I mentioned in previous topic), technically dogs can see just as well as about 10 million American humans! This may as well be considered yet another reason why dogs are man's best friend.

Of course, dogs still lack crucial modes of seeing that humans possess. Mainly, (as the many articles justify), dogs can see better at night because they more "rods" than humans, but they don't have as many "cones" as us, and therefore don't have the sharp visual details that we naturally have during the day. So, even all the color blind people out there can still look on the "bright" side!

Sources: "Myth: Dogs Have Cleaner Mouths Than Humans," ABC News, 2005; The Humane Society of the U.S., "U.S. Pet

Ownership Statistics," 2011; Don Glass, "Dog Mouth vs. Human Mouth," *Moment of Science* section, Indiana Public Media, 2003; Lauren Johnston, "Is the Pet Industry Recession-Proof? So far, New Yorkers Still Spending on Pets," *NY Daily News*, 2009.

DOUBLE **DIPPING**

Double dipping is the practice of taking a bite of your carrot then sticking the bitten end back into the communal ranch bowl before finishing it off. Hearing "no double dips" is common with little kids who don't want to give away too much of their precious Dunkaroos frosting to their friends with not-so-lax-about-lunch parents. Doubling dipping thus always seemed (at least to us) more along the lines of "no give backs," with health on its side. In other words, the warnings against double dipping are nothing more than playful whines and protests of kids against sharing their treats with their friends.

Professionals have proven, lo and behold, that the kids were right, and greediness takes the cake again. In one study published in the *British Medical Journal*, scientists compared bacteria in dip and the mouths of volunteers eating it, plus, bitten crackers versus "clean" crackers. In the findings, three to six double dips transferred roughly 10,000 bacteria from mouths of those who bit crackers to the dip.

Another little fascinating tidbit related to this study is that between cheese dip, chocolate syrup, salsa, and water, our favorite Mexican dipping sauce was found to pick up the most bacteria from the saliva of double dippers. Looks like we should all start keeping our dip in zip lock bags, and don't forget a straw to ensure only your own spit will be transmitted from point A to point B.

Sources: Tara Parker-Pope, "11 Health Myths that May Surprise You," New York Times, 2009; Dr. Aaron E. Carroll and Dr. Rachel C. Vreeman, *Don't Swallow Your Gum!: Myths, Half-Truths, and Outright Lies About Your Body and Health*, 2009.

SOME PEOPLE ARE **DOUBLE-JOINTED**

No: there are no recorded cases of this. People commonly said to be "double-jointed" have ligaments holding the end of the two articulating bones slightly looser than customary, thus permitting greater freedom in the relative movements of their parts.

DRAGONFLIES STING

The dragonfly (*Libellula*) belongs to the order *Neuroptera:* none of the *Neuroptera* stings. The dragonfly lives on flies and other insects captured on the wing, and if you are lucky enough to entice a wandering dragonfly into a room infested with mosquitoes, you will soon have an insect-free environment and a well-contented dragonfly.

Source: John Phin, *Seven follies of science* (New York, 1912, p. 210).

DRAGONS SURVIVE IN INDONESIA

David Attenborough's excellent BBC television program "Zoo quest for a dragon" showed the "dragon" of Komodo, an island in Eastern Indonesia, being trapped, but as Attenborough was careful to point out during the program itself, the "dragon" is technically just a monitor lizard: a carnivorous amphibian. A good description and illustrations can be found in David Atten borough's own book *Zoo quest for a dragon* (London, 1957).

AN ABSOLUTE DROUGHT IS A PERIOD WHEN NO RAIN HAS FALLEN

No. Rain can fall in Britain to the point of 0.01 inches without affecting the term"absolute drought." The British definition (not accepted internationally) covers a period of fifteen days, *none* of which has received as much as 0.01 inches.

A "partial drought" is a period of at least twenty-nine consecutive days, during which the mean daily rainfall does not exceed 0.01 inches. This definition, again, is British in origin and is not accepted internationally,

Source: W. G. Moore, *A dictionary of geography* (3rd ed., Harmondsworth, 1963).

THE DRUIDS

We know very little about the ancient druids, and what we do know is wrong. A.L. Owen's useful book *The famous Druids* (Oxford, 1962) is a mine of information on fallacies connected with the Druids.

It has been stated, for example, by no less a person than the founder of Gonville & Caius College, Cambridge, John Caius himself, that Cambridge University was founded by the Druids. Owen also puts us all in his debt by noting the allegation (pp. 35-47) that the ancient Druids wore galoshes. The ancient Druids mentioned by Caesar are not to be confused with the United Ancient Order of Druids, the secret society founded in London in 1781 whose members may indeed have, from time to time, worn galoshes. Readers may like to be warned off Rowland Jones' *The origin of language and nations hieroglyfically . . . , defined and fixed* (London, 1764; *A postscript,* London, [1768?]), a work which sets out to show that the Druidical religion was the original religion of all mankind (though the word *Druidai* is regrettably a Greek plural long antecedent to the Old Celtic stem *druid-,* and the word is traceable back as far as Sanskrit); that the Druids had used *English* (though Old English is known to have borrowed the root from the Celtic family); and thus that English was the original language of all mankind.

The whole story is so marvellously consistent. And absolutely wrong in every detail.

FALLACIES ON HOW TO COUNTERACT DRUNKENNESS

There are a number of strategies that people (especially young people) believe (or would like to believe) will help them get sober in the event that they find themselves drunk in the wrong place and/or at the wrong time. Here are a few favorites:

1) Drinking Coffee

As alcohol is a natural depressant, what could be a more natural reaction to counter the lows with the highs than with a cup o'joe? Had a couple drinks and need to drive home? Since you're basically just as tired now at this party than you are in the morning driving to school, a cup of coffee should do the trick in perking you up just enough to get to your destination, right?

All signs point to no. Aside from the fact that nothing will actually get you sober faster besides time, drinking coffee is in some ways a more negative attempt to counter the effects of alcohol, as both beverages are acidic. And most likely, come morning, you will experience no relief from unhappiness and nausea.

2) Energy Drinks

Recently, there has been a widespread trend in caffeinated alcoholic beverages, which have hit the stores marketing to sleep-deprived and overworked teens, people trying to party, and those still young at heart across the US. These drinks, though they have been outlawed in many states or no longer contain caffeine, included Sparks, the orange, sweet-tart flavored liquid in a can, Joose, and Four Loko (a whopping 12 percent alcohol in a 24 oz. can).

According to the FDA, roughly 25 percent of college students consume these energy drinks, regardless of how short lived, or non-existent, their effects may be. In many cases, they are still consumed by optimistic students even after they no longer contain caffeine in the hopes that other ingredients such as Taurine will give them the same kind of sociability boost.

(Continued)

129

However convincing caffeine may be in its initial stimulating character, drinking it simultaneously with alcohol will ultimately have the adverse effect. According to a study conducted by the Department of Physiology and Pharmacology at Wake Forest University (though also perhaps clear to the common man upon realizing that alcohol and coffee are not simultaneous in their mind altering properties), caffeine lessens the sedative effects of alcohol but not its effects on cognitive functioning abilities; including motor coordination, awareness of physical ailments like dehydration, visual reaction time, and so on.

Basically, caffeine will never be able to sharpen the sloppiness that comes along with the loss of basic brain functioning abilities whilst heavily drinking to any degree even remotely close to something resembling sobriety. As your ability to remember this helpful word of advice halfway through your second Loko may falter, it's probably best to soak it all in now.

3) Water

Whether it be splashing cold water on your face or drinking several bottles of Poland Spring after drinking all night, you cannot become sober faster. If you continuously drink water throughout the night in addition to alcohol, you may end up being less intoxicated, but this is more a result of the glass of water in between drinks leaving time for the alcohol to leave your system than any kind of guard against ethanol's strength.

Also, if you drink water, you do have less chances of being hungover the next day, as you will be slightly more hydrated going to bed than you would be passing out having consumed nothing but alcohol. But even so, there are no guarantees that you won't still feel like crap in the morning regardless of how much water you drank the night before.

In addition to these few beverages that have been deemed immunities against intoxication, neither power naps nor cocaine have a chance against humanity's favorite elixir of life, alcohol.

Sources: Amanda Gardner, "Caffeine Doesn't Sober You Up," *U.S. News*, Health, 2009; Wiley Online Library, "Effects of Energy Drink Ingestion on Alcohol Intoxication," 2006; Red Watch Band Post of Stonybrook, "Fact or Fiction: Will Coffee Help Sober You Up?"; Total DUI, "The Myths of 'Sobering Up'"; Larry Greenemeier, "Why Are Caffeinated Alcoholic Energy Drinks Dangerous?" *Scientific American,* 2010; FDA News Release, 2010, http://www.fda.gov/NewsEvents/Newsroom/PressAnnouncements/ucm234109.htm.

A LITTLE DUTCH BOY PUT HIS FINGER IN A **DYKE** HOLE TO SAVE THE CITY OF HAARLEM

The Dutch have ridiculed since 1873, when the story was apparently first invented by an American, the legend that a brave urchin sacrificed his life to save his native Haarlem from being flooded. He is alleged to have kept his finger in the hole in the dyke wall, though it did not occur to the readers that the amount of water that might trickle through a hole small enough to be stuffed by a little boy's finger might not in fact be quite so lethal, after all. Better, perhaps, if he had simply run to warn the inhabitants of Haarlem.

But the picturesque will usually drive out common sense when the two are in conflict, and the Netherlands Tourist Association has bowed to the weight of error by erecting a bronze statue to the invented lad.

E

"Every day of my life makes me feel more and more how seldom a fact is accurately stated; how almost invariably when a story has passed through the mind of a third person it becomes very little better than a falsehood, and this, too, though the narrator may be the most truth-seeking person in existence."

—NATHANIEL HAWTHORNE (in a notebook)

"Es ist nichts schrecklicher als eine tatige Unwissenheit."
(There is nothing more terrible than active ignorance)

—JOHANN WOLFGANG VON GOETHE,
Sprüche in Prosa, III

EARTHQUAKE FALLACIES

1) Earthquakes (and/or Natural Disasters) Can Be Predicted
Though institutes have been established with the primary or secondary purpose of predicting the time and place of earthquakes, there is no method yet available for doing so.

"Owing to the complexity of the processes involved, . . . it is by no means clear that such research is bound to lead to satisfactory methods of earthquake prediction. The Earth's rotation is affected not only by processes in the crust and mantle, where earthquakes occur, but also by the circulation of the atmosphere and by motions in the liquid metallic core, where the Earth's magnetism originates."

There are so many earthquakes in Japan and the related zones that no skill is required to anticipate further disasters of the same type. The type of prophecy which is irrational is that based on no knowledge of natural phenomena.

A recent example that comes to mind is that of the Australian house-painter John Nash. His first prediction was that Adelaide would be destroyed by an earthquake and engulfed by a tidal wave on January 19, 1976. The only result of the prophecy was that thousands irrationally abandoned their homes. When nothing happened, Nash decided to leave Adelaide and settle in Warwick, Queensland. His second prophecy was that Warwick would be the safest place in Australia. Unluckily for Nash, within a few days Warwick—like much of eastern Australia (but not Adelaide!) was hit by the severest floods ever known in that region.

2) Earthquakes Can Be Prevented

P. Norcott, in his booklet *Bigger and better earthquakes* (Broad-stairs, Kent, 1971), suggests three methods of preventing earthquakes. One is to erect huge flywheels at the Poles and start them whirling; this will keep kicking the Earth round, to keep the rate of axial spin fairly constant. Another is to build huge dams to stop the ocean waters sloshing about from one sea-basin into another; this will reduce tidal friction and thus reduce the rate at which the Earth's rotation is slowed down by the Moon's tidal influence. A third method of preventing earthquakes, states Mr. Norcott, is to split the Moon in half, towing one hemisphere round to the other side of the Earth so that gravitational forces will cancel each other out.

Source: Professor R. Hide, letter to *The Times,* September 8, 1976.

EARTHQUAKE FALLACIES

1) A Doorway Is the Safest Place to Stand During an Earthquake

For those of us who grew up in places where earthquakes were commonplace, we may not need this myth to be debunked. But for everyone else who didn't receive earthquake emergency lessons, this may be helpful to know. In the event of an earthquake, of all places to take shelter inside a house or building, the door frame is not the safest bet.

The reason this mistake is so common is because back in the days where adobe homes (in the West, the place that gets the most earthquakes) were prevalent, the doorway was the most stable place to stand while the rest of the clay house lost its balance. Now that we have much sturdier buildings (presumably), a better chance of survival during an earthquake would be underneath a table, or some other piece of heavy duty furniture.

2) Hot and Dry Climates Are More Prone to Earthquakes

It is definitely a common misconception that earthquakes occur more often in certain temperatures and climates. For instance, earthquakes are a lot more common in California and the west coast than on the east coast or Midwest. This is mistakenly attributed to the weather being drier, without humidity, less seasonal change, etc.

However, earthquakes originate many, many miles below the surface, underneath the region of our earth that is affected

(Continued)

by surface weather patterns. Earthquakes are due to rocks, or plates, moving up against each other and creating friction miles under the ground. When enough stress builds up, energy is sometimes suddenly released. Waves move up through the rocks and shaking the earth from below. For instance, earthquakes in California occur because the Pacific plate is moving northwest, scraping horizontally past the North American plates at a rate of about two inches per year. This occurs more here than in other places because of a "fault" in the layout of the area. The rupture begins at one site of the fault plane called the hypocenter (deep down in fault region), and ends at the epicenter, which is the point directly above the hypocenter but on the surface (on land).

The fault line, to clarify, is the boundary between the alternating motions of two kinds of plates (i.e., the Pacific vs. the North American). The fault can extend from under the ocean onto land like the West Coast of the United States. San Andreas is the part of the fault on land in California.

So, basically, this has nothing to do with temperature outside, but rather, occurs way beneath us.

3) An Earthquake Will Cause California to Break Off and Drift Into the Ocean

Californians certainly do not want to believe this will ever happen. However, for the rest of the country, predicting that California will ultimately be sent off on its way to start its own country like it's always wanted to be has been not only a long standing joke, but also a reality.

But the Southern California Earthquake center informs us otherwise. Despite the very real possibility of a huge earthquake causing serious destruction to Californians across the coast and endangering innocent lives at a moment's notice, the Golden State is going to be staying put, in one "state" or another.

As discussed above, earthquakes are caused by two plates rubbing up against one another because they are naturally moving towards one another in opposite directions. When the friction cannot be contained, energy is released and earthquakes occur. Because the Pacific and North American plates are moving against one another underwater, the more northern and southern parts of California may begin to move apart in different directions also.

But, for one, in this case, the state would not break off as a whole from the rest of the country, but more likely, would split itself into two, perhaps including chunks of other more Western parts of the U.S. as well. Also, even if a massive quake causes a massive shift in plate direction, plates travel at a super short distance at a time (a matter of feet at most). Thus, for an entire mass of land to actually break up and shift to a noticeable degree, it would take millions of years.

So, maybe California will eventually be underwater. But by that point, the human race might have been extinct for years already and universal life as we know it will be operating out of Mars. C'est la vie.

Sources: Southern California Earthquake Center, "Earthquake Myths" and "Putting Down Roots in Earthquake Country"; Discovery, *How Stuff Works*, "Is it true that Scientists are Predicting a Really Big Earthquake will Sink Western California?"

EARWIGS ARE SO CALLED BECAUSE THEY HIDE IN HUMAN AND ANIMAL EARS

It seems that they were so called (in most languages, not only in English: cf. *auricularia, gusano del oido, perce-oreitte, Ohrwurm*, etc.) because the rear wings suggest the shape of a human ear, and that this name then induced the folk-belief that they hid in human ears. That they do not in fact do so seems commonly accepted by entomologists. One reason is that the human ear contains bitter wax as a repellent against such invasions, and another is that earwigs eat vegetable matter and would have no interest in the perils of inhabiting human or animal ears.

LOOKING INTO A TOTAL SOLAR ECLIPSE CAUSES *TOTAL* BLINDNESS

While, yes, there is some danger in looking into an eclipse, the idea that one might accidentally glance upwards at the exact moment an eclipse is occurring and become eternally blind is an exaggeration.

For one, a total eclipse, where the moon is entirely blocking the sun, is totally safe to look at. It is actually the lesser known phases of a solar eclipse that can be potentially damaging to eyes. These phases include annular, hybrid, and partial eclipse, and they can occur at given times without actually going into a total eclipse. Eclipses can happen 2-5 times a year, and considering

(Continued)

their relative frequency, there are extremely few cases reported of people going blind annually from looking into them. Here is one specific instance reported of a partial solar eclipse leading to blindness in military troops stationed in Hawaii in 1962:

> There was still enough energy in the exposed sliver of Sun to burn out the centers of their retinas. Over the next few days, many of the soldiers had trouble in shooting accurately on the rifle range. Their vision had dropped from 20/20 to 20/200 . . . Some had permanent loss of visual sharpness.

Though this is quite unfortunate, only a minority of them did not recover their normal eyesight from this incident, and those who did not, though "legally blind," (20/200) did not end up completely losing their vision. Additionally, it is not possible for even a partial eclipse to cause eye damage unless one stares directly into it. The ABC Science article explains how damage occurs via heat energy, in that the energy from the sun is concentrated into the central part of the retina in the eye, a main factor of vision. Looking at the sun means the heat rays are going straight to your central retina, causing, perhaps, more damage than if you were not starring directly into the sun.

So basically, staring at a partial eclipse is indeed dangerous, just as staring at the sun is dangerous, because the sun is not meant to be stared into by the human eye, even if you are wearing UV ray-blocking sunglasses.

Humorously, NASA severely warns its readers not to look into an eclipse without extensive protection, and probably not to watch it in real life at all but rather on a projector after recording the live version. Yet, the last two sentences of the article enthusiastically read: "In spite of these precautions, the total phase of an eclipse can and should be viewed without any filters whatsoever. The naked eye view of totality is completely safe and is overwhelmingly awe-inspiring!"

Sources: ABC Science, "Eclipse Blindness," Karl S. Kruszelnicki, 2004; http://eclipse.gsfc.nasa.gov, "Eye Safety During Solar Eclipses," Fred Espenak.

ECONOMIC FALLACIES

There are three main categories of error in economics.

1. Time

Many economic propositions which are governed by a time factor do not explicitly state it. Thus, in modern dynamic economics, it is often asserted that elements in the economic system will grow at an equilibrium rate, but all that can be stated is that the rate will *tend* to move towards equilibrium.

2. Composition
Terms are used collectively in one part of an argument and individually elsewhere. For instance, it is frequently declared that what is prudent behavior for an individual or a single firm must be prudent for the country as a whole, but if all citizens of a nation try to save more (spend less), it does *not* follow that the total level of savings will rise: it may fall. Those who favor customs unions or free trade areas are guilty of this fallacy by ignoring the distinction between the interest of a particular country or regional grouping and that of the world as a whole.

3. Variables
Mistakes are often made by treating variable quantities as fixed, for example the former "Iron Law" that wages tend to sink to the level of bare subsistence. Alfred Marshall (1842-1924) did much to explode this type of fallacy, anticipating the work of the computer by introducing into economic theory a new sense of the way in which different factors are mutually dependent.

Source: Arthur Seldon and F. G. Pennance, *Everyman's dictionary of economics* (London, 1965).

ECSTASY CREATES HOLES IN THE BRAIN THE SIZE OF ICE CREAM SCOOPS

In 1998, a study was published in the prestigious journal, *Science*, which for the first time revealed hard evidence of ecstasy's damaging effects on the human brain. This study, funded by the National Institute on Drug Abuse, allowed scientists to use PET scans to visually compare the brains of users and nonusers of ecstasy. The scans showed those who had used MDMA had noticeably less serotonin transports in their brains than those who had never taken it.

According to the *New York Times*, the man in charge of this study, Dr. George A. Ricarte, a neurologist at Johns Hopkins University, was considered the best-known Ecstasy expert of the war of drugs movement for nearly twenty years. Between 1988 and 2003, he was given at least $10 million from the National Institute on Drug Abuse for his research and promotion of the cause.

Following the 1998 study, Ricarte was met with accusations regarding the validity of his control subjects; the fourteen people who he tested for a deficiency in serotonin synapses and fibers were not required to be tested beforehand through urine or saliva

(Continued)

samples in order to determine which drugs they were currently using or whether they were clean at the time of the testing or not.

However, the real blow for Ricarte and the government's anti-ecstasy movement came in 2002, after a study they had published in *Science* was renounced for its faulty proof that ecstasy was able to cause permanent brain damage in a single night. In this $1.3 million study, Ricarte based his conclusions on the fact that after he had given ecstasy to primate subjects, two of them died. It turns out, what he had dosed them with turned out to not even be ecstasy. Instead, they were injected with heavy levels of methamphetamine. He claimed that the labels on the two vials had been accidentally switched.

While Johns Hopkins defended Ricarte, other doctors and professionals in brain-related research fields have openly criticized his ethics. Dr. Julie Holland, a professor of psychiatry at NYU, claimed that Dr. Ricarte had a tendency to manipulate his data to make drugs look bad, in order to win over more federal grants. Others agreed.

Over the span of twenty years or so, Dr. Ricarte published many studies with findings that linked ecstasy and other amphetamines with Parkinsons related tremors, depression, memory loss, and sleep deprivation. Even ten years since this *Times* article was written, there is still no specific evidence has been found to prove that recreational Ecstasy use leads to permanent brain damage.

Ricarte's reputation was not the only one to suffer as a result of his mistake. Ten years after the primate scandal, a study led by Professor John Halpern of Harvard Medical School re-asserting that ecstasy does not cause brain damage was published in the journal *Addiction* in 2011. It was funded by the U.S. National Institute on Drug Abuse, as a continuous effort to compensate for their multi-decade long demonization of the drug.

The common fallacy you may have heard about ecstasy taking ice cream scoop-sized holes out of your brain comes from Ricarte's research, and was used as part of an anti-ecstasy government campaign. Needless to say, it will not.

Sources: Donald G. McNeil Jr., "Research on Ecstasy is Clouded By Errors," *The New York Times*, 2003; Robin McKie, "Ecstasy Does Not Wreck the Mind, Study Claims," *The Guardian*, 2011; Johns Hopkins University, Office of Communications and Public Affairs, "Hopkins Study Shows Brain Damage Evidence in 'Ecstasy' Users," 1998; "Ecstasy on the Brain," *New Scientist*, RBI Limited via *Media Awareness Project*, 2002.

ECTOPLASM

A visible "emanation" from the body of a spiritualistic medium. One of a number of conjuring tricks performed by the so-called "physical" mediums to convince the credulous of their powers. The mediums claim that levitation, bumps, knocks, the movement of distant objects and the production of "ectoplasm" are due to the activity of discarnate spirits. All such "experiments" are carried out in varying degrees of darkness and none has yet been proved genuine by disinterested investigators.

D. H. Rawcliffe, in *Illusions and delusions of the supernatural and the occult* (New York, 1959), shows that the "spirit-substances" are seemingly "white doughy streams issuing from the mouth (sometimes regurgitated cheese-cloth), the nose and even the genitals of female mediums . . . One enterprising medium even hid her "ectoplasm" in a hollow comb which searches previous to the séances for a long time failed to reveal."

Michael Faraday, wearying of the endless series of fraudulent "spiritualists" and their like whom he had in a rash moment offered to test, deserves for his patience the last word:

"What a weak, credulous, incredulous, unbelieving, superstitious, bold, frightened, what a ridiculous world ours is, as far as concerns the mind of man. How full of inconsistencies, contradictions and absurdities it is."

Sources include: Michael Faraday, *Life and letters,* vol. 2 (London, 1870, p. 307).

BROWN **EGGS** ARE MORE NUTRITIOUS THAN WHITE

Not so. British mothers are taught so by their grandmothers and so do not question the belief. Similarly, American mothers are told by their grandmothers that white eggs are purer than brown. The color is simply laid on by the bird for its own purposes long after the contents of the shell, and even the shell itself, are completed. The chemical composition in all eggs of the same species of bird appears to be the same.

KEEPING **ELECTRONICS** ON IN A PLANE DURING TAKE-OFF POSES SAFETY RISKS

Since the beginning of the new millennium, it has become standard for airlines to require all passengers on any given flight to turn off all electronic devices before taking off. While this seems like a reasonable request, the actual reasoning behind it remains somewhat hazy. Many people simply accept the idea that having

(Continued)

electronics on during take-off may cause "interference" with the flight. Fair enough, why risk it?

But what exactly does interference mean? And is that really the primary reason why we are asked to turn off our cell phones for the duration of the flight?

Well, ladies and gentlemen, here are three official reasons why we are required by the FAA (Federal Aviation Agency) to turn off electronics during flights:

1. to "make sure" passengers listen to safety instructions
2. to lessen the "presence of loose objects getting in the way" in the event of an emergency.
3. to ensure that there is no possibility of electronics interfering with the airline's "avionics."

While these are all debatably self-explanatory protocol, the third point is a little more daunting, as it acknowledges the power of technology without actually identifying (or seemingly, knowing) the level of power it has in this instance. Despite the fact that technological interference with airline communications from passenger cell phones during takeoff has never been proven in a particular instance, the hypothetical "interference" is still very much feared. This is the case perhaps because no one actually knows whether or not there could be some destructive uncontrollable interactions between two types of technology that humans can't control, thus putting them in danger.

However, while the FAA prohibits the use of electronics during take-off due to potential safety issues in the air, the FCC states that their reasoning for this ban is due to "potential interference with wireless networks on the ground." When there was an attempt to lift this ban in 2004, the FCC overruled it because there was not sufficient "technical evidence" provided by "interested parties" to prove that there is no potential for harm in using wireless electronics on board. But, just to clarify, there is also just as little evidence (evidence being zero) that there is any danger in using cell phones on planes.

While it seems the airlines may be worried for the safety of their passengers and the depths and grandiosity of the technological age, they also might just be worried about liabilities from mobile network users going about their days. But much more strikingly to note, this ban really is essentially based in a governmentally regulated potentially totally irrational fear.

Sources: *fcc.gov / guides / wireless-devices-airplanes; faa.gov.*

LOVETT AND **ELECTRICAL PHILOSOPHY**

Richard Lovett (1692-1780), a well-known Worcester fraud, advertised in 1758 that he could effect marvellous cures (of sore throats, for instance) by means of electricity.

His *Electrical philosopher: containing a new system of physics founded upon the principle of a universal plenum of elementary fire* (Worcester, 1774) used the concept of electricity without deducing any single phenomenon from our knowledge of electrical principles. His works show an ignorance of electricity remarkable even in a lay clerk of Worcester Cathedral during the 18th century.

Sources: Augustus de Morgan, *A budget of paradoxes* (2nd ed., Chicago, 1915).

ELEPHANT FALLACIES

1) **Elephants Are Afraid of Mice**
Cartoonists and others have often shown an elephant cowering away from a mouse. Those who work in elephants' stalls either in zoos or in circuses have from time to time seen mice running about not far from the elephant but, far from panicking, it seems that the elephants—mainly due to their relatively poor vision—cannot even see the mice.

2) **Elephants Live to an Age of 100 Years or More**
It has been reported at secondhand, even by some biologists, that elephants are frequently longer-lived than men, though the longest-lived human being reliably known is the 113-year-old Delina Filkins (New York), born in 1815 and deceased in 1928.

By contrast, the oldest known elephant, Kyaw Thee (Burma) died at seventy in 1965, though Modoc (died in 1975 at Irvine, California) *may* have been as old as the seventy-eight years claimed at death.

Sources: Keepers at Schönbrunn Zoo and London Zoo.

THE **ELEVATOR** DOOR CLOSE BUTTON ACTUALLY CLOSES THE DOOR FASTER

When tardy, no one wants a party in the elevator. In other words, most of us have probably had the experience where we are running late to work, an interview, or class in a large building and we simply do not want to hold the elevator for our peers in any of the floors in between ground and destination. On the flipside, most of us would probably prefer to cruise right up to the top in a solo elevator, psyching up or calming down before entering

(Continued)

professional territory flustered and late. Presumably, that's just the kind of scenario the "close" button is for.

Unfortunately, in most elevators, the close buttons are just placebo. Almost all modern elevators built after the early nineties have close buttons that perform their functions instantaneously only during "emergency situations" with a key "held by an authority." And even in older elevators, close buttons reportedly only work about 10 percent of the time. The other 90 percent of the attempts to get the doors to shut by pressing the close button, even repeatedly, is proven ineffective.

There are a number of theories that attempt to explain this inconvenient deceit, some more sinister than others. One idea is the simple illusion of control that gives people the impression that they are more in charge of their everyday existences than they are. Others are borderline conspiracy theories, including one that models itself on Darwinism.

A blog called, *Design with Intent* presents the idea that elevator buttons are just one of many potential "deliberate false affordances" installed strategically to weed the weak out; for instance, in a scenario where people inside the elevator start pushing the close button repeatedly while another person is running to catch it, the button's existence is designed especially to intimidate said runner into taking the stairs. Similarly, the *Design with Intent* blog cites another explanation for the button placebo, the "extinction burst" theory. Here's the example:

"Imagine you live on the tenth floor and you take the elevator up there. One day it stops working, but for a couple of weeks you enter the elevator, hit the button, wait a minute, and only then take the stairs. After a while, you'll stop bothering to check whether the elevator's working again—you'll go straight for the stairs. That's called extinction.

Here's the thing. Just before you give up entirely, you'll go through an extinction burst. You'll walk into the elevator and mash all the buttons, hold them down, press them harder or repeatedly, just anything to see whether it works. If it doesn't work, hey, you're not going to try the elevator again.

But if it does work! If it does work then bang, you're conditioned for life. That behavior is burnt in."

More straightforwardly, The *Straight Dope* mentions one of its several reasons for why the elevator buttons don't close on command: elevator doors are programmed with a set "time delay," such as ones you see in crosswalks (the countdown timer for

(*Continued*)

pedestrians to walk). So, if elevator doors are meant to close in three seconds, pressing the button maniacally won't cut those three seconds in half. If anything, it more likely will probably make three seconds seem a lot more like sixty.

Sources: The Straight Dope; *Gizmodo*, Elevators, "Things You Don't Know About Modern Elevators"; Dan Lockton, *Design with Intent* Blog, "Placebo Buttons, False Affordances, and Habit-Forming," 2008.

ELIXIR OF LIFE

A supposed drug or essence with the capability of prolonging life indefinitely or forever. Also known as the Philosopher's Stone. Like the vain attempts to transmute base metals into gold, this idea may have originated in India (before 1000 B.C.). Elixirs were also thought to heighten sexual powers. The fact that arsenical poisoning inhibits putrefaction in its victims reinforced belief, paradoxically enough, in the efficacy of the elixirs.

For the Chinese, gold was not a form of currency, but an imperishable substance, so the emphasis in China was always on the making of gold as a substance to confer longevity or even immortality on the human body. The intention was to change cinnabar (the most highly reputed of substances rich in *yang,* the active or male principle) into lead, lead into silver, and silver into gold. This too is impossible, as is the belief that artificial gold is a substance of such potency that the eating of food from vessels made of it would be conducive to longevity. The human body is subject to laws of decay and decomposition well-known to medical science, and no drug or essence can alter those laws. Plastic surgery and the transplantation of organs are of course different matters, completely foreign to alchemical tradition.

Sources include: F. Sherwood Taylor, *The alchemists* (London, 1952).

FOREIGN **EMBASSIES** ARE "ON FOREIGN SOIL"

It is popular wisdom that embassies and consulates are, in effect, part of their own national territory. British police, for example, never enter an embassy in London without the ambassador's prior permission. Similarly, Russian police have tried to prevent would-be defectors from entering the British Embassy in Moscow, but have never crossed the threshold in pursuit. The Vienna Convention of 1961, which set the present code of practice on diplomatic immunity, says that diplomatic premises are inviolable, and the host state has a "special duty" to protect them. But the ruling is unclear on people held against their will, or seeking political asylum in an embassy, as in the famous case of Cardinal Mindszenty, who lived for years in the American Embassy in Budapest.

But foreign embassies in Britain are on English soil, not foreign, according to a ruling of Mr. Justice Cumming-Bruce in the High Court on May 11, 1972. The matter arose in a case involving the attempt to validate a Talak divorce obtained by a husband in a ceremony at the United Arab Republic (now the Arab Republic of Egypt) Consulate. Mr. Justice Cumming-Bruce ruled against the Egyptian-born Mr. Jan Pierre Radwan, who had claimed that his Talak divorce (in which he said of his wife "I divorce thee" thrice) was valid in English law.

Mr. Justice Cumming-Bruce was "satisfied that the term "extra territoriality" has been used to describe, in a compendium phrase, that bundle of immunities and privileges which are accorded by receiving States to envoys sent by foreign States.

The building occupied by a foreign embassy and the land upon which it stands are part of the territory of the receiving State and are therefore under the jurisdiction of the receiving State though members occupying it are primarily under the jurisdiction of the Sending State."

Regarding marriages in embassies, the judge stated that an ambassador was entitled to perform them only if the law of the country in which they were situated permitted them.

Source: *Daily Telegraph,* May 12, 1972.

EMBER DAYS ARE SO-CALLED FROM THE ASHES OF REPENTANCE IN WHICH PENITENTS SIT

The four periods of fasting and prayer in the Christian Church (one in each season) are called Ember Days from the Old English *eymbryne* from their regular recurrence (ymb-round; ryne-running) and have nothing to do with ashes or "embers."

Source: *Oxford English Dictionary.*

A PENNY THROWN OFF THE EMPIRE STATE BUILDING WILL INSTANTLY KILL THE PERSON IT LANDS ON

We've all heard it, but where this myth came from beats us. Perhaps New Yorkers constantly want to remind themselves just how tall the Empire state building really is. Tall enough for something as small and insignificant as a penny to become a weapon of death on its way down from the top and drive six feet into the pavement?

Not quite. A penny, even falling from New York's tallest sky-scraper would not kill anyone. There is absolutely no threat of pennies endangering any ground level passersby, first and fore-most because it only weighs about a gram. Also, a penny would not fall straight down but rather it would "tumble," creating more air resistance and not gaining much speed before hitting "terminal velocity" (only reaching around 100 mph and carrying a maximum weight of one foot when it hits the ground).

So, it might hurt a little if a penny hit you on the head, but mostly it would just probably be startling.

Sources: Marshall Brain, Discovery's *How Stuff Works*, "What if I threw a penny off the Empire State Building?"

ALWAYS CONSULT THE LATEST EDITION OF ENCYCLOPEDIAS

The layman always looks at the date of *publication* of an encyclope-dia, while the professional librarian looks to the date of the *latest source quoted* in the articles' bibliographies, and the specialist scholar (who has in any case little personal need of a general reference book for his own scholarly purposes) looks to the article's ability to take into account the *latest research,* its thoroughness, and balance.

Technical articles are usually the weak part of a general ency-clopedia, since they have gone partly out of date while the multi-volume work has been going through the press. For the humanities and social sciences, it is by no means certain that later editions of an encyclopedia should be preferred. Increasing costs of printing, bind-ing and overheads constrain editors to reduce the length of articles and the quantity of illustrations from one edition to the next. In the case of the *Encyclopaedia Britannica,* for instance, the 11th ed. (29 vols., 1910-11), takes 12½ pages to discuss Indian Law while the 14th ed. takes 8½ pages, and the 1974 ed. takes up less than half a page in the *Micropaedia* (p. 332 of vol. V). Always consult an *earlier* edition for an article in the humanities, to check what has been omit-ted from the later edition you consulted first.

The myth of the Britannica (New York, 1964) was a valuable cor-rective by Harvey Einbinder to the expensive advertisements pro-moting that encyclopedia. However, since Einbinder wrote, listing 666 articles in the 1963 which he found faulty, out-of-date, or inaccu-rate, the *Britannica* has been forced to pack in even more fashionable new topics, and their standards have declined again. Other general encyclopedias are even less comprehensive.

THERE IS MORE **ENERGY** IN 100 GRAMS OF FRIED BEEFSTEAK THAN IN THE EQUIVALENT WEIGHT OF WHITE SUGAR, WHOLE WHEAT FLOUR, RAW RICE OR CHEDDAR CHEESE

Quite wrong. And there is nearly *three* times as much energy in 100 grams of butter! R. A. McCance and E. M. Widdowson, in their standard work *The composition of foods* (3rd rev. ed., 1960), list the energy-properties of selected food and drink as follows (per 100 grams in each case):

Whole wheat flour	339 kcal.	raw potatoes	70
white bread	243	canned peas	86
raw rice	361	boiled cabbage	9
whole fresh milk	66	orange with peel	27
butter	793	apple	47
cheddar cheese	425	white sugar	394
fried beefsteak	273	bitter beer (100 ml)	31
fried haddock	175	spirits (gin, whiskey 70 proof, 100 ml)	222

"EPICUREANISM" IS SYNONYMOUS WITH GLUTTONY

The word "epicure" has come to be applied to anyone devoted to the pleasures of the table. Epicurus (341-270 B.C.) on the contrary held that philosophy consisted in the wise conduct of life, to be attained by reliance on the evidence of the senses, and by the elimination of superstition and of the belief in supernatural intervention. His ethics teach that pleasure is the only good, but by this he intimated that a perfect harmony of body and mind is to be sought in plain living, and in virtue.

Source: Sir Paul Harvey, *Oxford Companion to Classical Literature* (Oxford, 1937, entry "Epicurus").

ESKIMOES LIVE IN IGLOOS

A Denver, Colorado, newspaper once erected an imitation snow house near where they kept some reindeer (at the municipal buildings) and hired an Eskimo, who had never seen that type of dwelling except in the movies, to explain to visitors that he and other reindeer herders of Alaska dwelt in that kind of house when they were at home.

By a census of the 1920s, fewer than 300 of over 14,000 Eskimoes in Greenland had ever seen an igloo!

Source: Vilhjalmur Stefansson, *The standardisation of error* (London, 1928, pp. 49, 84).

ETYMOLOGICAL FALLACIES

In the words of A. Smythe Palmer—and every philologist would quickly endorse them—"there are a multitude of words which have been either altered from their true form or perverted from their proper meaning owing to popular mistakes or misunderstandings as to their derivation or kinship to other words." The *Oxford English Dictionary,* Skeat's *Etymological dictionary* and Partridge's *Origins* (4th ed., 1966) are primary reference tools, though perhaps too voluminous for those interested primarily in errors of etymology. For the latter study one might commend *Folk etymology* (1882) and *The folk and their word-lore* (1904) by A. Smythe Palmer, as regards the English language. He considers the erroneous metamorphosis of foreign words, verbal corruptions, mistaken analogies, and misinterpretations.

Etymology is a science based on the laws of language and demands a historical and comparative knowledge not only of the particular language studied, but also of those related in any relevant manner.

Fanciful sources for names are almost as widespread as they were before etymological dictionaries made them indefensible. Thus, one can still find countrymen who derive the word "partridge" from the birds' habit of lying between the furrows of ploughed land, and so they part ridges *(Gentlemans Magazine,* February 1892). De Traun, in his *Livre des créatures,* claimed that the same bird was called "perdix" because it loses *(pert, per-du)* its brood. Eric Partridge, who ought to know, honestly admits that he doesn't. He merely quotes Hofmann's opinion that the Latin *perdix,* adopted from Greek, might echo the whirring wings of the rising bird.

My own favorite etymological fallacy is connected with the fallacy of the Tower of Babel, and can be found in the *Opera* (Antwerp, 1580) of the 16th-century Flemish scholar Johannes Goropius. On finding that the word "sack" is similar in many of the languages we have since learned belong to the Indo-European linguistic group *(sakkos* in Greek, *saccus* in Latin, *sacco* in Italian, and *saco* in Spanish, etc.), Goropius concluded that, at the moment of the confusion of language, every single laborer working in the Tower of Babel remembered to carry away his sack.

THE EXCEPTION PROVES THE RULE

Five "senses" of this nonsense are cited by Margaret Nicholson in *A dictionary of American-English usage* (New York, 1957), which is avowedly very heavily dependent on Fowler's *Modern English usage.*

1. The original simple legal sense;
2. The secondary, rather complicated, scientific sense;
3. The loose, rhetorical sense;
4. The jocular nonsense;
5. The serious nonsense.

But even the first of these is undermined if we return to the origin of the Latin phrase: *exceptio probat regulam,* which does not mean what it appears to mean at all, but "the exception *tests* the rule." That is, the apparent exception affords the opportunity of testing the universality of the rule, since if the apparent exception is genuine, the rule is false, whereas if the exception is not genuine, at least we have discovered that the "exception" is false, In his *Etymological dictionary* (1921), Weekley suggests that the phrase is an abbreviation of a phrase *exceptio probat regulam in casibus non exceptis,* meaning "the exception proves the rule in cases not excepted."

EXPERTS ARE INVARIABLY CORRECT

"Experts," a modern term for those professionally acknowledged to be competent in their field(s), are usually reliable about what they have empirically found to be the case. Where they are often completely unreliable is in the prophecy of what is feasible. Sir Humphry Davy, despite his eminence, laughed at the suggestion that London might some day be lit by gas. Learned men categorically denied Stephenson's claim that a railway locomotive could travel as fast as 12 miles an hour. In *Der Neue Geisterglaube* (1882, p. 261), W. Schneider reported a case in which a scholar asserted the impossibility of a steamship's ever being able to cross the Atlantic Ocean.

Connoisseurs will love to hear the oracular statement by Lord Rutherford, as reported in the *Evening News* of September 11, 1933: "The energy produced by the breaking down of the atom is a very poor kind of thing. Anyone who expects a source of power from the transformation of these atoms is talking moonshine, but it is enormously interesting to scientists." See also *Nature* for September 16, 1933, p. 433.

EXTRAPOLATION FROM MISLEADING DATA

All data is misleading when extrapolated in a certain way, without due regard to common sense or research into variable factors involved. Mark Twain loved to deflate pompous nonsense, as the following passage from *Life on the Mississippi* (New York, 1917, pp. 155-6) demonstrates.

"The Mississippi between Cairo and New Orleans was twelve hundred and fifteen miles long 176 years ago. It was eleven hundred and eighty after the cut-off of 1722. It was one thousand and forty after the American Bend cut-off. It has lost sixty-seven miles since. Consequently, its length is only nine hundred and seventy-three miles at present.

"Now, if I wanted to be one of those ponderous scientific people, and 'let on,' to prove what had occurred in the remote past by what had occurred in late years, what an opportunity is here! Geology never had such a chance, nor such exact data *to* argue from! Nor 'development of species,' either!

"Glacial epochs are great things, but they are vague-vague. Please observe: In the space of one hundred and seventy-six years the lower Mississippi has shortened itself two hundred and forty-two miles. That is an average of a trifle over one mile and a third per year. Therefore, any calm person, who is not blind or idiotic, can see that in the Old Oölitic Silurian period, just one million years ago next November, the lower Mississippi River was upward of one million three hundred thousand miles long, and stuck out over the Gulf of Mexico like a fishing-rod. And by the same token any person can see that seven hundred and forty-two years from now the Lower Mississippi will be only a mile and three-quarters long, and Cairo and New Orleans will have joined their streets together, and be plodding comfortably along under a single mayor and mutual board of aldermen."

Mark Twain's gibe at "science" is as fallacious as his conclusions, of course, but the joke at the expense of those who exploit statistical data for their own ends is as true today as it was when his book first appeared in 1883.

THE **EYE** CAN BE REMOVED BY SURGEONS, WASHED, AND REPLACED

In a letter to *The Daily Telegraph* (June 26, 1911), Sir E. Ray Lankester found it necessary to repudiate this fantastic notion, which continues apparently to be widely believed. "The eyeball cannot (as many people erroneously believe) without destruction, be moved forward or 'laid on the cheek,' since such a movement would tear the muscles attached to it, and also the optic nerve."

The Daily Mail (April 7, 1927) was again compelled to devote an article to this fallacy; "The popular myth that ophthalmic surgeons remove eyes, scrape or treat them, and replace them was exploded yesterday when the Royal Westminster Ophthalmic Hospital gave a demonstration of its methods and apparatus. Although frequently spoken of, and although people can always be met who believe they have been the subject of such an operation, it never has been done, said one of the hospital's leading surgeons."

Eye transplants are, of course, another matter.

READING IN THE DARK CAN RUIN OR DAMAGE **EYE SIGHT**

Even though it is the twenty-first century and people (ahem, kids today) just simply don't read as often as they used to, there are

(Continued)

some of us who still get to say "I told you so" to our parents for unnecessarily switching on the glaring light in our faces every time we were just winding down to an 18th century classic novel and sleepy-time tea in the twilight hours.

Ophthalmologists (fancy word for eye doctors) say that reading in the dark might make those reading more prone to squinting, which might lead to headaches or tiredness. But this temporarily condition will have no effect on long term vision functionalities.

While some researchers and doctors take extra precautions by warning young people against reading in the dark too often, their findings are based on population studies that may not take economic factors into consideration. According to the *New York Times*, population studies in the U.S. have shown rates of myopia (nearsightedness) are more frequent in people with higher education and in those with jobs that require a lot of reading, such as lawyers, editors, and doctors.

However, it is quite possible that the rest of the population develops nearsightedness just as often and at the relative same age ranges, and that these statistics are due to the fact that most people don't have jobs as lawyers or doctors, don't have the resources to get their eye sight checked out, or simply, wait till old age when they are really nearly blind rather than simply slightly inconvenienced in proper sight abilities mid-age.

So, read in the dark all you want; though it might cause fatigue, sleepiness may just be the very medicine for sleep that those who open a book in bed with the lights dimmed were hoping for.

And hey, this isn't just for classic hardback readers. If you have an iPod or a Kindle with all your favorite novels on them, feel free to turn the back light all the way down to zero. It won't hurt your eyes, and it certainly won't hurt your battery life on your commute to work tomorrow.

Sources: Anahad O'Connor, *Really?* Blog, "The Claim: Reading in the Dark Will Damage your Eyes," *New York Times*, 2006.

EYES ARE RUINED BY FINE NEEDLEWORK

A number of common errors are connected with allegedly excessive use of the eyes, whether in needlework, microscopic study or watchmending, J. D. Rolleston, in the *British Journal of Ophthalmology* (November 1942) drew attention to the fallacies that operation for cataract should be delayed until the moment is judged correct; that eyes should be bandaged in acute inflammatory conditions; and that the loss of one eye necessarily involves impairment of the other's visual ability.

FLIMSY **EYEBALL** FALLACIES

1. If You "Go Cross-eyed" Too Much, Your Eyeballs Will Get Stuck That Way

Going cross-eyed, or more politely, "developing strabismus," is not caused by looking at your nose. This oddly sadistic challenge children pose to their peers (to try it out and see if they do actually go cross-eyed), is pretty sensibly disproven by most people's experience, such as the commonality of normal eyesight into adulthood despite the popularity of this childhood activity.

The worst that would happen if you kept your eyes in one position for more than ten minutes or so is that you would experience muscle strain, fatigue, and maybe a few eye spasms, but not to worry, as they would return to normal in an hour or less!

Furthermore, going cross-eyed is not usually caused by muscle movements, but rather from a problem with the control center of the brain (neurons, rather than muscle injuries). One might argue that this is not something that people believe into adulthood, because it can easily be written off as an irrational childhood fear. But if we asked you to stare at your nose right now and hold it there for two minutes without looking away, would a vague feeling of discomfort telling you that this is indeed a very unnatural way to focus your eyes not come over you, even if it never materialized into an actual thought?

2. Your Eyes Will Pop Out of Their Sockets if You Sneeze With Them Open

Another common childhood myth underestimating the stability of your eyes is the one that says you have to sneeze with your eyes closed. Not because it is a natural reaction, but rather, because if you keep them open during a sneeze, the force of it will knock your eyeballs right out of their sockets.

Again, this is not so. We can even provide you with an explanation as to how eyeballs are firmly attached to the head, in order to prove that it is impossible for a sneeze to send them flying out. Eyeballs are attached to the eyes by muscles (specifically, the medial and lateral rectus, superior and inferior oblique . . . you get the idea) which hold them steady and allow them to move from right to left, up and down and even diagonally towards your nose and back again.

Some people assume the reason you close your eyes when you sneeze is to keep the bacteria and particles out that caused you to sneeze in the first place. This is also not the case. Actually,

(Continued)

151

there is absolutely no functional explanation for why your eyes close at all. It is just a bodily reflex, as random as when your leg pops up when the doctor hits your knee with a rubber mallet and tells you everything is going according to plan.

Sources: Discovery Health, "What if I Crossed My Eyes for 10 Minutes?" Marshall Brain and "If you Sneeze With Your Eyes Open, Will Your Eyes Pop Out of Your Skull?" Amy Hunter; Optometrists Network, "Strabismus."

F

"The faintest of all human passions is the love of truth."
—A. E. HOUSMAN

"For 'ignorance is the mother of devotion,' as all the world knows."
—ROBERT BURTON, *The Anatomy of melancholy*

FAIRIES AND FAIRY RINGS

Fairy rings, to dispose first of them, are caused by a circular-seeding fungus which, by its annual decay, renders the soil unfit for a new crop of fungus but increases the fertility of the ground. There consequently appears a gradually increasing circle of grass which is greener than the surrounding turf. The traditional explanation, harmless enough to those who don't mind misleading ignorant children into a lifetime of superstitition by the primrose path of faery, is that such rings spring up where fairies habitually dance, or grow above a subterranean fairy village. E. and M. A. Radford's *Encyclopedia of superstitions* (London, 1961) observes that if anyone ran nine times round such a ring on the night of the full moon, he would hear the fairies laughing and talking below. Walter P. Wright, in *An illustrated encyclopedia of gardening* (London, 1932) advocates not running round the ring but destroying it "by syringing with a pound of sulphate of iron dissolved in three gallons of water." It is not recorded what the fairies thought of Walter Wright.

European and other folklores are saturated in fairy myths, from the "men of peace" or *daoine sithe* of the Scottish Highlands to the Greek woodland spirits and the Scandinavian elves. The industrious Puck of Shakespeare's *A midsummer night's dream* is only one of the most famous fairies of English lore. A belief in fairies is as old as the hills themselves, for it dates to animist days long before Christianity overtook country "wisdom." It seems that the earliest stage of a religious system has been ignorant awe of the elements and natural phenomena such as trees and animals. Much or all of nature is believed to possess individual spirits capable of feeling, reason and volition. The animists (35 percent of an intensively missionaried province of South Sulawesi remain animists according to Darby Greenfield, *Indonesia: Bali and the East,* New York, 1976) believe in the existence of spirits in streams, the wind, wood and iron, and carve fetishes to retain their

153

magic power. This nature worship entered European romanticism as pantheism, and retains an integral if embarrassing hold on many people who would otherwise claim to be above such primitive beliefs, despite the absence of the slightest shred of evidence that spirits of any fairy kind exist.

Joseph Jastrow, in *Wish and wisdom* (New York, 1935), retells the belief of Sir Arthur Conan Doyle in fairies; this the inventor of Sherlock and Mycroft Holmes justified by "fairy photographs" showing two girls with "fairies." Elsie, age sixteen, and Frances, age ten, were taken back to the scene of their alleged fairy encounter four years later under test conditions, which proved completely negative. Conan Doyle also believed in "spirit photographs" in which "extra" faces appear "in a cloud of ectoplasm." Dr. W. F. Prince, Research Officer for the American Society for Psychical Research, patiently explained time and again the detailed methods by which these photographs had been fraudulently manipulated. Conan Doyle, who published a *History of spiritualism* in 1926, refused to accept the evidence, having founded a Society for the Study of Supernormal Photographs.

"FALL" IS THE AMERICAN WORD FOR "AUTUMN"

There is nothing American about the use of "Fall" for the third season of the year other than its current use in the United States; both "Fall" and "Autumn" have a long European ancestry: the latter from the Latin "autumnus" (possibly from Etruscan?), and the former from the Old English "feallan," akin to the Old Frisian "falla."

"Fall" in this sense can be found in the works of Raleigh, Drayton, and other writers of the Elizabethan period. Source: Eric Partridge, *Origins* (4th ed., London, 1966).

FAMINE IS LOGICALLY BOUND TO OCCUR

William and Paul Paddock, in their *Famine 1975!* (Boston, 1967), carefully demonstrated the inevitability of widespread famine in or before the year 1975. How they did this was by taking singly all the devices and tactics proposed to forestall famine (agricultural innovations, land reform, government bounties and controls, population-control devices such as the IUD, sterilization and the pill) and by proving that each panacea individually is quite inadequate to solve the problem, and consequently famine was bound to occur. One does not need hindsight (similar presagers of doom have cropped up every decade since the 18th century) to see that they were guilty of assuming that famine was *logically bound to occur,* simply because *logically it could occur.* Since most of the measures were applied, at roughly the same time, famine was averted, and human intelligence (with rapidly increasing technological capability) can be relied upon to minimize most of the threats that do and will threaten modern man.

FASCISM IS DEAD IN ITALY

Following the death of Benito Mussolini, and particularly in view of the gathering strength of the Communist Party since World War II, it is tempting to believe those who dismiss the neo-fascists in Italy as of no account.

The following table, drawn from official statistics, shows the voting strength of the Italian fascist party (MSI) in post war general elections:

Year	Votes for the MSI	% of total vote
1948	526,670	2%
1953	1,580,293	5.8%
1958	1,407,718	4.8%
1963	1,569,815	5.1%
1968	1,414,764	4.4%

FASCISM IS DEAD IN WEST GERMANY

According to the Bundesamt für Verfassungsschütz's official figures up to October 1, 1966, only 22% of the age-group in the Nationaldemokratische Partei Deutschlands (NPD) was over 60 (compared with that age-group's total percentage 20% in the Federal Republic), whereas 29% was aged 46-60 (27% of the total population were in that age-group), 27% aged 31-45 (25%), and 22% aged 16-30 (28%). In 1966, therefore, nearly half of the fascist party's total membership consisted of people under the age of 46. In round figures, actual party membership in 1966 stood at the 25,000 mark, and was rising quickly.

As regards the voting strength of the neo-fascists, the 1965 elections in West Germany brought the fascist party 664,193 votes, equivalent to 2% of the votes cast; this strength was more than doubled in 1969, when the party polled 1,422,010 votes (4.3% of the total), but drastically reduced in 1972 (last figures available) to 207,465 votes (0.6% of the total).

Sources include: Heinrich Fraenkel, *Neo-Nazism—cause or effect?* in *The Humanist,* February 1967 and official statistics.

THE **FAUST** STORY IN EUROPEAN LITERATURE IS BASED ON LEGEND

An absurd concoction of implausible tales on a figure called Johann Faust was published under the title of *Historia von D. Joh. Fausten* (Frankfurt, 1575) by the printer Johann Spiess. The sensational booklet, containing a direful warning against theological heresies, among them necromancy, was reprinted, translated, and rewritten for popular consumption all over Europe in succeeding centuries, until Christopher Marlowe created the *Tragicall history of Dr Faustus* in 1588-9 (entered in the Stationers' Register in 1604 but apparently not published in 1604).

From England the tragedy returned to Germany, where Gotthold Ephraim Lessing made the heretic into an altruistic lover of knowledge who deserved salvation in fragments of a play, *Faust* (1759). It was left to the great Goethe to produce the most lasting works on the story of Faust (complete edition, 1834), which completely transform the medieval story. Faust is saved in Goethe's epic drama. Other treatments of the story include the operas *Faust* by Gounod and *Mefistofele* by Boïto, Paul Valéry's *Mon Faust,* and Thomas Mann's *Doctor Faustus.*

Johann Faust was, however, a real man—a travelling magician and mountebank who lived in Germany from the 1480s to about 1540. He is mentioned by Trithemius (b. 1462) in a letter dated 1507, and by several other contemporaries, including the demonologist Wierus, who states that Faustus was a drunkard who had studied magic at Cracow and was eventually strangled by Satan after his house had been shaken by a tremendous din.

Sources include: H. G. Meek, *Johann Faust* (1930); and Lewis Spence, *An encyclopaedia of occultism* (New York, 1960).

STRONG ALE FOR **FERTILITY**

Eighteenth-century England was a haven for quacks of all descriptions, as *The Compleat Housewife* (London, 1753) comprehensively proves. A "Mixture to Promote Breeding" from this household manual consisted of three pints of strong ale in which the childless wife boiled three "ox-backs" (the spinal marrow of the ox), catmint and other herbs, stoned raisins, dates, nutmegs "prick'd full of holes" and "the syrup of stinking orris." To ensure fertility, the mixture was to be imbibed each night, out of the husband's sight.

There is no recorded instance of the mixture having achieved the desired result, and no published refutation known before the one you are reading now.

IDENTIFICATION BY **FINGERPRINTS**

In the *Medical bibliography* (London, 1970), ed. by L.T. Morton, it is stated that it was J.E. Purkinje who first suggested the use of fingerprints for identification purposes in a paper contributed to the Transactions of the University of Breslau. However, Purkinje drew attention only to the patterns discernible on fingerprints. The first published suggestion that prints should be used for identification seems, to have occurred in a letter from Sir Henry Faulds to *Nature,* October 28, 1880, "On the skin-furrows of the hand." W. J. Herschel, in *Nature,* November 25, 1880, claimed that he had used the system on contracts in India as early as 1858.

Sources include: Francis Galton, *Finger prints* (London, 1892).

FISH FALLACIES

1) Fish and Plant Life in the World's Seas Are Dying

The well-known underwater diver and author Jacques-Yves Cousteau has claimed more than once that "the vitality of the seas, in terms of fish and plant life, has declined some 50 percent in the past twenty years."

However, in 1970 the U.N. Food and Agriculture Organization reported an *increase* in the world fish catch of 10 percent.

2) Fish Can Fly

Not one of the hundred or so species of "flying fish" can actually fly in the commonly accepted sense. They do, however, have enlarged pectoral fins which enable them to glide just above the sea's surface at a maximum of ten miles an hour for a maximum of two hundred yards. They usually glide to escape predators such as dolphins.

3) Fishes Drink

The popular saying, sometimes uttered in admiration and sometimes in scorn, "he/she drinks like a fish," relies on the fallacy that fish drink. It may look as though water passes to their stomach when you see their mouths open, but actually their gullets are very tightly constricted, and hardly any water gets as far as the stomach.

4) Fishes Cannot Drown

Fish breathe by taking oxygen from the water just as animals breathe by taking oxygen from the air. So it follows that if oxygen is withdrawn from water, they must either obtain oxygen from some other source, or drown. Causes of the diminution or disappearance of the oxygen supply include the decay of a great deal of vegetation, or increased animal respiration at the bottom of certain lakes. If fish do not choose to move from areas of lakes poor in oxygen to areas richer in oxygen they perish. This happens quite frequently and regularly.

5) Fish Are Especially Good for the Brain

This fallacy, propagated in dozens of Bertie Wooster stories and novels by P. G. Wodehouse (on whom otherwise be blessing), appears ultimately to derive from the views of the German philosopher Friedrich Büchner (1824-1899), that "without phosphorus there is no thought"; of the French chemist Jean Dumas (1800-1884) that "fish are a rich source of phosphorus"; and finally of the Swiss naturalist Jean Louis Agassiz (1807-1873) that "fish are good for the brain."

This assumption ignores the fact that phosphorus occurs in many foods other than fish, and the further fact that other foods are equally good for the brain.

"There is no foundation whatever for this view," stated Sir Henry Thompson in *Food and feeding,* and Dr. Charles Hill ("The Radio Doctor") declared that "as for brain food, there are no foods for the brain except work."

Source: *The Times,* January 3, 1972, p. 17.

FIVE-SECOND RULE

We've all wanted to believe in this myth at one time or another. For instance, when you drop your slice of pizza on the dirty sidewalks of New York City, or your cotton candy at the Carnival slips out of your hands just as you were about to put it into your mouth and satisfy your hunger with the perfect sugary treat. Really, there is not much that is more disappointing than watching your meal fall to the ground. Along the same lines, there is really nothing logical that justifies being able to still eat that meal you dropped on the ground, except, when we cue in: the five-second rule.

The five-second rule asserts that even if you drop an item of food on the floor, it is still safe to eat it as long as it has not been there for more than five seconds. If the edible item is rescued in less than five seconds, it means there was not enough time for germs from the floor to be transferred into it. Following this logic, it's alright to put said morsel into your mouth and ingest into your system immediately after wiping it off a little, yeah? Not quite.

The origin of this myth, aside from wishful thinking, is more or less unknown. But according to one source, Genghis Khan first declared that anywhere between twelve to twenty hours was an acceptable amount of time for food to remain on the ground, however contaminated, to still be consumed risk free.

Sadly, this old Mongol warrior may have been a little off here. Several studies have tested the five second rule theory, sprinkling the floor with both E-coli and Salmonella bacteria. In both cases, the bacteria spread instantaneously into the food dropped onto the sprayed surface.

There is a small hint of truth to this myth: the longer a piece of food remains on the floor and/or ground, the more bacteria it will pick up. But any contact at all your cookie, candy, sandwich or peanut has with the ground still may warrant up to one hundred bacteria transfers. So even if you are foaming at the mouth thinking about how badly you wanted that snack, it is probably worth the extra dollars, time and/or effort to invest in a new one instead of, so to speak, eating dirt.

Sources: Mary Schroeder, M.S., R.D. and Pat Kendall, Ph D., R.D., "The Five Second Rule: Myth or Fact?" Colorado State University, Safe Food Rapid Response Network, 2004; Sue Anne Zollinger, "The 5 Second Rule: Truth or Myth?" Indiana Public Media, Moment of Science section, 2010.

WILHELM **FLIESS** AND THE NUMBERS 23 AND 28

In his monumental biography *Sigmund Freud: life and work* (3 vols., London, 1953-7), Ernest Jones devotes chapter 14 of volume 1 to "The Fliess Period (1887-1902)," a time during which Freud enjoyed a "really passionate relationship of dependence" on Wilhelm Fliess, a man whom Jones describes as "intellectually his inferior." Fliess and Freud exchanged hundreds of letters, but Freud destroyed those he had received and we know the correspondence only from the 284 written by Freud, and sold by Fliess's widow to a Berlin bookseller.

In 1897 Fliess published *Die Beziehungen zwischen Nase und weibliche Geschlechtsorganen in ihrer biologischen Bedeutungen dargestellt* ('The relationships between the nose and the female sex organs from the biological viewpoint").

Fliess argued that neuroses and sexual problems could be treated by applying cocaine to alleged "genital spots" inside the nose. He stated that cases had occurred in which miscarriages were produced by anesthetising the nose, and special treatment of the nose could help menstrual pains. He operated on Freud's nose on two different occasions.

Furthermore, Fliess considered the numbers 23 and 28 the key to sexuality (and to much else). The normal male has a cycle of 23 days, and the normal female has a cycle of 28 days. If a patient asked in all humility why he or she did not experience such a cycle (not to be confused with the menstrual cycle, though the two are related by evolutionary origin), then Fliess would simply point out that one was not a normal male or female! This was easy for him to say, because he considered *everybody* to be really bisexual. The cycles of 23 or 28 days respectively continue throughout life, and even determine one's date of death! Freud endorsed all of Fliess's early work, and at one time suspected that sexual pleasure was a release of 23-day energy, and sexual apathy a release of 28-day energy. Freud expected to die at the age of 51, because it was the sum of 23 and 28, and besides,

Fliess had told him that the year would be critical. In fact, Freud lived from 1856 to 1939, so he lived to be 83. If he had managed to survive until May 6, 1940, he would have been 84, which would have been three times 28, but numerology ignores the near misses. As Ernest Jones writes: "There is much obscure evidence indicating some periodicity in life—the most obvious being the fluctuations in sexual desire—but the difficulty has always been to discover any regularity in it. Needless to say, Fliess was mistaken in thinking he had solved the problem. The mystical features in his writing, and the fantastic arbitrariness with which he juggled with numbers—he was a numerologist *par excellence*—have led later critics to consign most of his work to the realm of psychopathology."

Of few books could this sweeping statement be made with more feeling than of Fliess's 584-page tome *Der Ablauf des Lebens: Grundlegung zur Exakten Biologie* ("The rhythm of life: foundations of exact biology," Leipzig, 1906; 2nd ed., Vienna, 1923) which has been described with candor by Martin Gardner as "a masterpiece of Teutonic crackpottery. Fliess's basic formula can be written $23x + 28y$, where x and y are positive or negative integers."

Freud was convinced—for a time—but he also admitted that he was deficient in any mathematical skill. Fliess knew a little arithmetic, but that is all. He did not understand, to the end of his life, that if any two positive integers without a common divisor are substituted for the 23 and 28 in his basic formula, it is possible to express any positive integer. Roland Sprague has shown, in a recent puzzle book, that even if the negative values of x and y are excluded, it is *still* possible to express all positive integers greater than a certain integer. The work of Fliess has been definitively demolished by J. Aelby, but the cult is still alive today, for "biorhythms" were also postulated by a professor of psychology at the University of Vienna, Hermann Swoboda (1873-1963). His 576-page volume *Das Siebenjahr* ('The year of seven," 1917) contains useless mathematical analyses of the alleged rhythmical repetition of births through generations. Swoboda designed a slide-rule to determine the so-called critical days of biological rhythms which is as meaningful as belomancy.

Neither doctors nor mathematicians can see any worth in the theory of biorhythms, but that does not stop the books pouring from the presses: *Biorhythm* (New York, 1961) by Hans J. Wernli; *Is this your day?* (New York, 1973) by George S. Thommen; *Body time: physiological rhythms and social stress* (London, 1974) by Gay Gaer Luce; *Biorhythms and human reproduction* (New York, 1974) by Ed Ferin; and *Biorhythms: a personal science* (London, 1976) by Bernard Gittelson. The Fliess and Swoboda notions have reached an enthusiastic audience in Japan, following the publication of *Biorhythms for health design* by Kichinousuke Tatai.

In *The encyclopaedia of reality* (London, 1979), Katinka Matson compounds the fallacy. "It has been determined," she asserts without justification, "that there are three different kinds of biorhythms: physical rhythm [23-day cycle]; sensitivity rhythm [28-day cycle]; and intellectual rhythm." The last, according to Katinka Matson, is a 33-day cycle discovered by Alfred Teltscher in Switzerland during the 1920s as a result of his work with students in high school and college. The unsubstantiated theory is that during the first 16½ days of this cycle you think clearly and creatively, while in the second period of 16½ days you think less clearly and less creatively. Since nobody can prove this one way or the other, however, the theory is valueless. So is the so-called Orcadian rhythm connected with physical changes by day and night. Katinka Matson alleges—but without any proof—that the behavior of circadian rhythms can be measured in man by checking protein metabolism, urine flow, body temperature, and sensory changes. Reactions to stress, pain, drugs, and disease "are partially determined by circadian rhythms." Or then again, perhaps not.

FLU FALLACIES

1) Swine Flu Is Worse Than Normal Flu

There are some main distinguishing features between swine flu and regular influenza, such as the fact that swine flu is originally transmitted from animal to human (properly called "zoonosis"), the influenza virus itself is really not all that different than the regular seasonal flu.

Although some sources report that swine flu symptoms can become more severe than those of the normal flu, including vomiting, nausea, and diarrhea in more severe cases, generally the symptoms are reported to be the same in most cases: fever, cough, sore throat, body aches, headache, chills, fatigue, etc. Also, swine flu (H1N1 in 2009), is spread just like normal flu: by coughing or sneezing near someone. The recent outbreak of swine flu was not a pandemic, and like in cases of seasonal flu, vaccines were available to prevent it from becoming too widespread and too severe. Perhaps the surgeon's masks they gave out at health services in colleges were a little over the top.

The death toll seems to not have even been particularly severe, especially in comparison to all the hype the swine flu caused. Studies show that there were only fifty cases of swine flu reported since 1958 (and recorded in medical literature), and only six reported deaths. The deaths included one person who was pregnant, one had

(Continued)

leukemia, and one who had Hodgkin's lymphoma, meaning, half of them were in risky medical conditions anyway.

Those in risk for contracting swine flu were essentially the same as they are for susceptibility to normal seasonal flu, studies show, people over sixty-five, younger than five, and pregnant women. Although there were indeed a high number of deaths reported in Mexico from the swine flu virus (159 people as of 2009), overdramatic and overprescribed America was ready with vaccinations and antiviral medications to combat the "pandemic" and then some.

Essentially, it seems the reason people were so afraid of the swine flu outbreak was because it was a virus we weren't prepared for, and moreover, due to the exaggerated connotations of the word "swine," aka a foreign animal infection getting into our bloodstreams and destroying us all like in popular modern zombie movies.

2) Flu Shot Gives You the Flu

If you ask a crowd of friends whether or not they've gotten their annual flu shot yet, you will most likely get mixed responses. Besides the obvious "yes" or "no, not yet," answers, there will also be a good number of people who have not and will not get the shot because they don't trust it and/or have heard that there is risk of contracting the flu rather than preventing it, upon receiving the vaccination.

The reason this fairly common skepticism exists (aside from general distrust of modern Western medicinal techniques) is generally because in every vaccination, the virus it is preventing must be contained in the vaccine. However, in the case of the seasonal flu shot, the influenza virus is inactive. The way in which these viruses are deactivated is typically through heat or formaldehyde. Meaning, the virus particles can no longer replicate when released into the system, but they are intact enough to be recognized by the immune system, evoking a response. Supposedly, the vaccines are tested a number of times before general public administration to make sure they are safe.

Some people do still get sick after getting a flu shot. This may be because they are actually just coming down with a bad cold or sinus infection that appears to be as severe as the flu would be. Also, as the flu virus differs slightly every year/season, it is possible that the vaccination administered will not protect everyone from still contracting the flu, particularly in those who or older, under six, or with weak immune systems. Also, as the immunization takes two weeks to take effect in the body after the shot, it is possible that someone can get the flu in the two week intermit period.

While some forms of immunization may have vaccines with viruses that are still active to a small degree, in which case there would be reason to avoid them, the flu shot really cannot make your chances of getting the flu any worse than they are without it. So, principles in this case really have no place.

Sources: U.S. Department of Health and Human Resources, *Flu. gov*, "Misconceptions about the Flu Shots"; *Harvard Health Publications*, Harvard Medical School, "10 Flu Myths"; *National Geographic News*, "U.S. Swine Flu No Worse than Seasonal Flu, Experts Say," Christine Dell'Amore, 2009; Centers for Disease Control and Prevention (CDC), "2009 H1N1 Flu ('Swine Flu') and You," 2010.

FLYING SAUCER FALLACIES

1) Flying Saucers Are Common

Of those observed in the U.S.A., many things we have called flying saucers are really skyhook balloons used for cosmic-ray research, whereas an unfortunate crank literature early arose to identify them with vehicles sent from outer space. Frank Scully, in *Behind the flying saucers* (Chicago, 1951) categorically stated that the saucers were piloted by inhabitants of Venus who were exact duplicates of earthmen except that they were three feet tall. But then at least Scully confessed (in *True* magazine, September 1952) that his book had been a hoax from beginning to end.

After Orson Welles' notorious broadcast of H. G. Wells' *The war of the worlds* in 1938, which was mistaken for a genuine report of invasion from outer space, dozens of Americans frantically telephoned news that they had not only seen the Martians, but some had even felt the heat-rays.

The first reports of flying saucers occurred in 1947, when Arnold, a Boise (Idaho) pilot flying over the Cascade Mountains of Washington, reported nine circular objects in diagonal chain formation moving at high speed and slightly smaller than a DC-4 which happened to be in the sky at the same time. Then the usual flood of similar "sightings," some of them probably hoaxing or imaginary, filled the U.S. newspapers, until in 1951 the Office of Naval Research published a report showing how their balloons, in effect giant plastic bags a hundred feet in diameter, could reach a height of 100,000 feet and travel with jetstream winds at more than 200 miles an hour. Furthermore, at a distance the balloon takes on the appearance of a saucer.

After the publication of the official report, sightings of "flying saucers" decreased, but a mass hysteria movement based on fear and ignorance makes good news, and the media were reluctant to let this story alone.

Arnold himself persisted with his assertions in a blaze of publicity, including an article "I *did* see the Flying Disks" in Raymond Palmer's magazine *Fate* (Spring, 1948), and a fifty-cent pamphlet entitled *The flying saucer as I saw it*. The magazine *Life* (April 7, 1952) printed an argument in favor of the extra terrestrial origin of flying saucers after the official report, and large numbers of crank books prove the durability of human folly against all the available evidence. One such is by the mystic, scholar, and novelist Gerald Heard: *Is another world watching?* (New York, 1951), in which the intruders are said to come to Earth from Mars. They are super-bees about two inches long with an intelligence much higher than Man's.

George Adamski is one of the most celebrated flying-saucer writers, having published *Flying saucers have landed* (with D. Leslie, London, 1953), *Inside the flying saucers* (New York, 1955), and *Flying saucers farewell* (New York, 1961). Several years before the Moon was visited by men, he was able to state authoritatively that vegetation, trees, animals and human beings lived on the Moon, just out of sight of the Earth, in the temperate section. He obtained this information from an inhabitant of Saturn whom he had met in a café and who subsequently (in 1955) took him for a ride in a flying saucer which was able to hover only a few thousand miles from the Moon.

With Earthmen like these, who needs enemies from outer space?

Sources include: Martin Gardner, *Fads and fallacies in the name of science* (New York, 1957), pp. 55-68.

2) There Is Statistical Proof for Flying Saucers

There are hundreds of thousands of reports of Unidentified Flying Objects on file all round the world and so, the UFOlogists conclude, there must be growing evidence for the existence of extraterrestrial visitors in UFOs. In fact, as Ian Ridpath explains in *New Scientist* (July 14, 1977), statistics prove just the opposite.

"There are simply too many UFOs being seen to support the extraterrestrial hypothesis. Imagine, for a moment, that there are one million other civilisations in the Galaxy, all sending out starships. Since there must be something like 10 billion interesting places to visit (one tenth of all the stars in the Galaxy), then each civilisation must launch 10,000 spaceships annually for only one to reach here every year. If each civilisation launches the more reasonable number of one starship annually, then we would expect to be visited once every 10,000 years. Alternatively, the higher number of reported UFOs might be taken as indicating that we are something special. If so, then life cannot be a very common phenomenon in the Galaxy—and thus there would be fewer civilisations to send out starships, and we would expect a smaller number of UFOs."

Ian Ridpath concludes: "Despite 30 years of study, the field of UFOlogy has failed to produce *one* concrete example of alien visitation, from any dimension. Most scientists would draw their own conclusion from such an abject lack of results, but they do not have the indefatigable optimism of committed UFOlogists for whom the Perfect Case, like the Second Coming, is an article of faith."

But what if a panicky schoolboy or housewife tells you: "I've just seen a flying saucer?" and you have no reason to suspect a hoax? Patrick Moore, in a program devoted to UFOs in the series *The Sky at Night* (B.B.C. Television, December 11, 1979), discussed some of the hundreds of explanations possible to account for unusual sightings of objects in the air, from frisbees to pollen drifting a few feet above his fifteen-inch telescope. Weather-balloons and other balloons account for many of the reported UFO sightings: also responsible are car headlights, the Moon seen low on the horizon or through dense mist or cloud, flocks of migrating birds, satellite debris, lenticular clouds, meteors and meteorites, radar reflections (not necessarily from solid objects), flares from jet aircraft, aircraft reflections, ball lightning or similar meterological phenomena, and ice clouds.

Patrick Moore hoaxed the public by alleging, quite falsely, that he had seen a UFO near East Grinstead in the mid-1950s: over twenty people wrote to the newspaper to confirm his hoax report! There is also conclusive proof that the film of "UFOs" taken from a New Zealand airplane late in 1978 was in fact a film of the planet Venus, and the appearance of swift movement caused not by Venus but by the airplane!

Sources include: Ian Ridpath, "Flying saucers thirty years on," in *New Scientist,* July 14, 1977; and Patrick Moore, *The Sky at Night,* December 11, 1979.

3) Flying Saucers at Socorro, New Mexico
A mass of new data seems to endanger the Flying Saucer Myth, graphically described by the late Donald Menzel as "the greatest nonsense of the 20th century."

One of the best sources for the erosion of belief is the now declassified material in the official U.S. documents Project Sign (begun in 1948), Project Grudge (1949) and Project Blue Book (1952), the last-named closing in 1969. None of these authorities, nor the independent Rand Corporation investigation for the U.S.A.F., was believed respectable by the UFO Establishment, who claimed that the armed forces and security forces were combining in a cover-up operation.

The declassification of saucer-sighting records proves that studies were discounted when they were not to hush up the dangers to our planet, but to save time and money. All the reports were probably misinterpretations or fabrications dreamt up for fame or riches, and there are probably no extra terrestrial vehicles among us, either now or in the past.

The problem is that sightings make headlines, and exposures rate only one-line apologies, if that. Readers are recommended to keep by their bedside—in case of "sightings" through the bedroom window—a copy of *UFOs explained* (New York, 1974) by Philip Klass. Klass has gone to great trouble to find out the truth behind the celebrated saucer landing at Socorro, New Mexico, in 1964. It was apparently a publicity stunt by the local mayor, who owned the land on which the UFO in question made its alleged impression.

LONDON **FOG**

What was first referred to somewhat endearingly as the London fog, or "Pea Soup Fog," due to its thick yellow hue, actually turned out to be the result of post-industrialization and its pollution. For the most part at least, the fog of London that is romantically depicted or described in certain art forms, such as in Sherlock Holmes books and movies, is not weather related.

The dramatic shots in Holmes' movies make the city of London and its inhabitants look like they are engulfed in much more than your average fog. This is because when the fog did roll in heavy to the city of London, those were the times that the effects of the pollution from smoke chimneys and general poor air qualities were most strongly felt and most widespread amongst civilians.

According to etymology online, the term "London fog" first came to use in 1830. The more specific "London smog" was supposedly coined in 1905 by a member of the London Coal Smoke Abatement Society, Henry Antoine des Voeux. The word smog is, in a basic sense, a combination of smoke and fog.

Although the deadly London smog of 1952 was indeed deadly, and triggered in part by "natural fog" turning the air colder and denser, the majority of the smog was caused by years of accumulating pollution from coal fires, heavy smoking, and other various acids and chemicals in the air.

Additionally, as air temperatures are generally higher in the center of London than in the suburbs and areas immediately surrounding it, and the city has less vegetation, there is typically less wet fog in London proper. In modern times, there is, happily, less lung and air-blackening smoke circulating the London skies as well.

Sources: John Nielsen, "The Killer Fog of '52," NPR, 2002; Gaia Piazzesi, Dissertation on "The Catalytic Hydrolysis of Isocyanic Acid (HNCO) in the Urea-SCR Process," Swiss Federal Institute of Technology Zurich, 2006; R.E. Waller, "London Fog," *Science New Series* vol. 161, 1968.

FOOD FROM A DENTED OR OPENED CAN SHOULD NOT BE EATEN

Food in damaged cans will only be contaminated if germs have entered through a split in the tin. Otherwise, food from opened tins is no more susceptible to infection than is fresh food. The cans themselves cannot cause poisoning.

THE LIFE OF **FOOD-GATHERERS** IS HARSH AND RELENTLESS

It depends what your standards are. Presumably Australian aborigines would consider the traffic in Sydney harsh and relentless compared with their quiet and happily communal existence. If one is judging by the hours of work that one has to work, the contrast is even more obvious. The Bushmen of the Kalahari Desert in southern Africa work a twelve to nineteen hour week to gather food for their subsistence, and spend the rest of the time in leisure activities, while the Hadza people of Tanzania spend less than two hours a day in their search for adequate food.

BIRD-TRACK **FOSSILS** HAVE BEEN DISCOVERED IN MASSACHUSETTS

Professor Edward Hitchcock (1793-1864) of Amherst College stunned scientists in 1836 with his reports of species of Ornithichnites (bird-track fossils) which he claimed to have discovered in Massachusetts. A further five years of research and classification brought his list of species up to twenty-seven, as described in the *Final Report on the Geology of Massachusetts* (1840).

For the proof that Hitchcock's "bird-track" fossils were in fact fossilized prints of dinosaurs and other reptiles, see *American Journal of Science,* 2nd ser., vol. 29, 1860, pp. 361-3.

FOX-HUNTING HAS BEEN POPULAR IN BRITAIN SINCE MEDIEVAL TIMES

Not at all. British fox-hunting as a popular field sport dates from the latter part of the eighteenth century. The first reference to hunting the fox occurs as early as 1278, but the most popular field sports in Britain until medieval times were hunting the boar, the deer, and the hare.

FRANCHISE AND CHAIN ARE SYNONYMOUS TERMS

In many of our minds, a franchise is just a fancy name for a not so fancy chain restaurant. Originally, in the 13th century, "franchising" meant freedom, exemption, right, and privilege. Perhaps not quite the words we think of upon inching our cars up to a McDonald's drive through with cranky restless kids in the backseat.

The term took an essentially strictly legal turn when "to franchise" became a company's permission to another to sell its products and services in 1959.

A franchise, as a noun, is basically just a subset of a chain store, such as a restaurant, hotel, or small business. When chains take the franchised form, the entrepreneur licenses the chain's "business concept," which means the franchise has the right to use the enterprise's brand name, marketing strategies, organizational norms, and operating manuals. In return for these rights, the franchise (or, franchisee), has to pay the franchiser a start fee and then continuous fees for these rights as well, which are known as royalties. But, it is also able to keep its own establishment's earnings.

There are different forms of franchises, mainly based on the level of dependence they have on their franchisers. There are even more various forms of chains. But on a basic level, chains seem to have slightly less freedom, in that the products they sell or prices cannot vary at all depending on the individual store/location and are generally operating directly under the policies/control of a single corporation.

It's hard to decipher the variation between franchise and chains. For instance, McDonalds is a franchise, while Starbucks is a chain. From a glance, it may be somewhat surprising to learn that Starbucks is not a franchise. Andrew Harrer of *Bloomberg News* cites Starbucks rather tastefully as an "international chain of coffeehouses." Maybe it's the success of Starbucks as a corporation without relying on the franchising technique that startle people so much, or because the word "chain" evokes a long line of American disillusionment.

Sources: *Etymology Online*; Olav Sorenson, Jesper B. Sorensen, "Finding the Right Mix: Franchising, Organizational Learning, and Chain Performance," *Strategic Management Journal* Review, 2001; Eric Scott, *Chron.com*, "Chain Vs. Franchise," Hearst Communications, Inc.; Business Day, *New York Times*, "Starbucks Corporation," 2011.

"FRANKENSTEIN" WAS A MONSTER

By analogy, possibly, with Bram Stoker's fictional Count Dracula, Mary Wollstonecraft Shelley's *Frankenstein* (1818) is often believed to be a story of an eponymous monster, but Frankenstein was an imaginary student of medicine in Geneva who learned the secret of imparting life to inanimate matter and, after constructing the semblance of a human being from bones gathered in charnel-houses, gives it life. The creature inspires all who view it with fear and loathing, and it comes to feel only hatred for its creator. It kills Frankenstein's brother, his bride, Frankenstein and finally itself.

FRECKLES CAN BE REMOVED BY LEMON JUICE

"Nothing will remove freckles," write Ashley Montagu and Edward Darling in *The prevalence of nonsense* (New York, 1967). "At least, nothing will remove freckles *only*. There are preparations which will remove the skin, if that's what you want. Then the freckles disappear."

Freckles are a series of small areas of pigmentation usually evoked by exposure to the chemically active ultraviolet rays of the sun, but since most of these pigment cells do not reach the dead surface layer forming the outermost portion of the skin, no substance applied to the surface of the skin can have any effect on those cells which lie deeper.

Preparations sold to remove freckles are, so far, all believed fraudulent and can cause injury to the skin.

WARM WATER FREEZES SOONER THAN COLD

A fallacy which even caught out the illustrious Francis Bacon *(Novum organum,* 1620). The reverse is the case.

There is an interesting exception which is not widely appreciated. Water which has been boiled and then cooled to the same temperature as the cold fresh water will freeze just ahead of the other, probably because the boiling process drives off the carbonic acid gas and air, and deposits any calcium carbonate previously in solution.

I suppose that, as boys, many of us remember pouring boiling water on a snowy hillside to make a slide, but the true purpose of that is to make for a smooth surface once the snow has frozen again.

ALL FORMS OF INSECT LIFE CAN BE KILLED BY FREEZING THEM

Micro-organisms cannot be killed by the intensest natural cold, so the old fallacy that if you put meat in a refrigerator or freezer you will thereby kill off any bacteria present should be scotched at once. What you have done is merely to freeze them: once they are thawed out they are free to infect you again. Daddy-long-legs' grubs frozen experimentally at Kew Gardens survived on thawing.

Interestingly, some fish die before freezing temperature is reached, while others can be frozen yet survive. Instances are recorded of dogs swallowing frozen fish whole, only to experience intense discomfort when the fish were thawed by the warmth of the dogs' stomach. Fish swallowed in this way are usually regurgitated.

The Alaskan blackfish remains frozen for several months in the winter, and seems none the worse when thawed out by the warmth of spring.

THE **FRESHMAN** FIFTEEN

Leaving home to go to college for the first time is emotional, and many students are unsure as to how to channel their nervous energy, as well as how they will feel when they are transitioning to a new environment. That being said, the cure for all eighteen year olds' homesickness is certainly not gaining fifteen pounds in (arguably, laxative sprinkled) cafeteria food.

According to studies, although some weight gain is common in college freshmen, fifteen pounds is a gross exaggeration. For example, in a survey of Northeastern College freshmen, the average weight gain for males was 3.7 pounds, while the average for women was 1.7. Other surveys done on the same topic have found similar results, though sometimes men have slightly less weight gain than women. Overall, average weight gain for college freshmen was found to be an uneventful 2.7 pounds.

Clinically speaking, the "sophomore slump" is more likely to be a reality amongst lethargic and emotionally confused second years than excessive weight gain is for the self-image obsessed first year.

Sources: Nicole L. Mihalopoulos, MD, MPH, Peggy Auinger, MS, and Jonathan D. Klein, MD, "The Freshman 15: Is It Real?" *Journal of American College Health*, 2008.

IT TAKES MANY MORE MUSCLES TO **FROWN** THAN IT DOES TO SMILE

It's fairly clear where this fallacy spawned from: nobody likes looking at a pouty, sour face, especially not on adults. So, all the more reason to feed kids this myth when they're young. Better yet, tell them their faces might get stuck in that expression (eyebrows slanted down toward the nose, nose slightly wrinkled, mouth curved down) if they frown too often.

According to legend, it takes something like thirty-five muscles to frown, where as it only takes six facial muscles to smile. So, why not smile when you disapprove? It's easier.

But according to the plastic surgeon, Dr. David Song of the University of Chicago Hospitals, when you count up all the muscles in the face that can be utilized for emotional expressions, there are eleven that are used for frowning and twelve for smiling. While the amount of energy produced by individual muscle movement has not been compared between the two, Song believes that smiling still actually takes less effort than frowning, as people smile more often and thus the muscles have been more adequately exercised.

Either way, there are in reality very few muscles in the face (roughly fifty-four), and most of them are not used for smiling or frowning. And in any event, the vast difference in muscles used between the two gestures is undoubtedly over exaggerated in most cases, in order to get people to smile more.

Still, keeping in mind what Dr. Song said, instead of hitting the gym tomorrow morning, why not just spend an extra fifteen minutes grinning at yourself in the bathroom mirror to ensure that your mouth stays camera ready?

Sources: Straight Dope interview with David H. Song, 2004.

FROZEN FOOD FALLACIES

Among the many errors concerning food freezers capable of storing food in bulk are:

1. That Housekeeping Bills Are Necessarily Cut
This assumes (which is not always the case) that long-term savings on bulk buying will offset a probable increase in consumption and the initial capital cost of the freezer and the increased energy bills paid to keep the freezer working. It often happens that food is wasted, or menus are repetitive to "use up" what is left in the freezer. "Bulk cooking," writes Carol Macartney, "is a chore unless one has sufficiently large pots and pans, and bulk buying needs to be carefully thought out."

2. All Food Freezes Well
No: as Carol Macartney indicates, "Hard-boiled eggs go rubbery; salad ingredients, like lettuce and chicory, go limp and mushy; milk and single cream separate out." A bottle of fizzy drink might once be placed in the freezer to keep it cool, but never again, after the liquid and gas expand while freezing and the bottle explodes.

3. Freezing Is "Unnatural"

"Nothing could be farther from the truth," observes Carol Macartney. Freezing something alters it very little, if at all, and when the food is thawed out, the natural life cycle resumes. The exceptions are vegetables, which may discolor or develop off-flavors unless some of the enzymes are destroyed before freezing. vegetables should be blanched before freezing; if not, most should be eaten within six weeks of freezing.

4. Frozen Food Must Go Bad After a Certain Time

Not unless there is a power failure. Theoretically, there is no limit to the time during which food may be kept frozen. In practice, however, most home frozen foods will suffer a slight loss of eating quality after a period varying between three and six months. Fatty foods and bread should not be kept longer than a month, ideally, while sauces and commercially frozen foods should be used within three months. Pork should be eaten within six months, but poultry will keep well for up to a year.

5. Freezing Destroys the Flavor of Food

This observation is faulty. Most commercial frozen foods are on the bland side because they are created for the mass market, so it is easy to see how the idea arose that frozen foods have less flavor. But the flavor has not been destroyed in freezing: it was never present in the first place.

Sources: The Royal Society for the Promotion of Health, *Frozen food in the home* (London, 1977, pp. 5-6: "Myths and misconceptions" by Carol Macartney); and Gwen Conacher, *Food freezing at home,* published by the Electricity Council.

THE "FUNNY BONE" IS FUNNY AND/OR A BONE

Those of us who have experienced the tingling sensation that occurs after hitting the sensitive spot near our elbows on a piece of furniture unexpectedly know that there is not much that is funny about it. It feels unusual and somewhat unnerving, sort of like the transition between numbness and pins and needles that happens when a hand or foot falls asleep.

Speaking of unnerved, the funny bone is not only not funny, but it is also not a bone. It is, go figure, a nerve called the ulnar nerve. The ulnar nerve extends down the arm, across the elbow, and into the fingers (fourth and fifth fingers primarily). Because it comes up so close to the skin just above the elbow, it is more sensitive, and more likely to be triggered when banging an elbow on a coffee table or the like.

Typically, nerves run very deep into muscles, but the ulnar nerve comes close to the skin near the elbow, as most people have very little skin and muscle in that exact location on their bodies. As the electrical impulse which is sent to the brain from the nerve being pinched upon its being slammed on something hard is technically and experientially painful, we still might ask why it is called a funny bone. One fairly prominent theory is that "funny bone" is a pun on the Latin word, *Humerus*, which refers to the area between the shoulder and the elbow.

For those of us who didn't catch the joke the first time, we could also leave it at "funny" meaning funny in a strange and suspicious way, not funny in a laugh out loud kind of way.

Sources: Louise Chang, MD and Heather Hatfield, "Medical Mysteries, She Wrote," Web MD; *Merriam-Webster Dictionary*, "Funny Bone."

G

"Great truths find no resting place in the heart of the people so, all mankind living in error, how may I teach them even if I know the way myself? If I know that I cannot instruct successfully, the attempt will be another error. It is consequently better to desist from the attempt. But, if I make no effort, who then will do it?"

—CHUANG TZU

"The goal for all is the same. Different names are given to the goal only to suit the process preliminary to reaching the goal."

—SRI RAMAN MAHARSHI (1879-1950),
Talks (Tiruvannamalai, India, 1955)

IN ENGLISH PLACE-NAMES, "**GATE**" IMPLIES THE PRESENCE OF A GATE

This hoary fallacy is repeated incessantly, and indeed many who have never studied etymology quite rightly proclaim that the Anglo-Saxon *geat* does indeed mean "gate."

But, in those parts of England (notably the East) which saw invasion and occupation by the Danes, the Danish "gata" means "road" or "way" or "street," so that as H. F. Tebbs correctly states in *Peterborough: a History* (Cambridge, 1979), the "Cumbergate" of Peterborough is the "street of the woolcombers." However, the "Westgate" of Peterborough is not the "West street" but the "street of the weavers, or websters." Folk etymology is often downright wrong, and where correct it is frequently misleading!

ROMAN "**GAUL**" WAS MODERN FRANCE

It was in fact much more extensive, including the Low Countries, Switzerland, and parts of northern Italy, in addition to continental France. Allcroft and Plaistowe, in their edition of Caesar's *Gallic War*, Book I, write: "In the time of Caesar the Gauls occupied roughly the whole of that part of Europe which lies west of the Rhine and north of the Pyrenees, together with much of Switzerland, and that part of the Italian peninsula which lies to the north of the rivers Rubicon and Macra (thence called Gallia Cisalpina). They had once overrun the land as far as the Tiber, and had routed the Etruscans and settled in the Po Valley; but in the year 218 B.C. the Romans had planted the colonies of Placentia and Cremona as the symbol and safeguard of the final reduction or expulsion of these Cisalpine Gauls."

GAUTAMA'S LIST OF FALLACIES

The *Nyāyasūtras* of Gautama, a 2nd-century Indian writer also called Aksapāda, have been edited, and translated from the Sanskrit, by Gangānātha Jhā (2 vols., Poona, 1939).

His list of five types of fallacy, usually accompanied by the commentary of Vātsyāyana (who is perhaps better known as the 5th-6th century author of the *Kama Sūtra)* formed the basis of subsequent Indian lists, much as Aristotle's list (see also LOGICAL FALLACIES) formed the basis of Western lists.

1. The erratic or inconclusive reason. Thus, "Sound is eternal because it is intangible," whereas some intangible things are eternal while others are not.
2. The contradictory reason. Thus, Yoga doctrine states both that "The world ceases from manifestation, because it is non-eternal" and that "The world continues to exist, because it cannot be utterly destroyed." These cannot both be unacceptable, because they are mutually exclusive; if one is right (which is not certain), then the other must be wrong.
3. The neutralized reason. Instead of leading to a decision about an argument, a reason may lead to an inconclusive answer, or be repetitious of the thesis itself. Thus, "Sound is non-eternal because we do not find in it the properties of the eternal thing" is a statement that offers no conclusion.
4. The unknown or unproven reason. Thus, "Shadow is a substance, because it has motion" is guilty of this fallacy because it is not known whether a shadow has motion.
5. The inopportune reason. Thus, if thesis and reason refer to *different* times, a paradox will arise not unlike that of Achilles and the tortoise, wherein it is argued that Achilles will never catch up a yard on the tortoise because before he can catch up a yard he must catch up 35 inches then 34 inches, and so on *ad infinitum*. [In a variant, Boethius argues that "Socrates is sitting down" and "Socrates is not sitting down" may both be true but at different times.]

GELLER, URI

A phenomenon of mass gullibility of the 1970s, the Israeli conjuror Uri Geller is widely believed to possess certain "extrasensory" perceptions which enable him to bend metal spoons, break metal forks, stop watches, and draw facsimiles of sealed drawings. Otherwise intelligent television viewers are persuaded that he possesses "psychokinetic abilities," "supranormal faculties of the mind" or "paranormal magnetic power."

The various fallacies have been patiently exposed by another conjuror, James Randi, who has travelled the world behind Geller doing the same tricks by means of his training in "magic," and has written a famous exposé, *The magic of Uri Geller* (London, 1976) to contradict claims made in Uri Geller's *My story* (London, 1976).

As early as the December 1973 issue of the International Brotherhood of Magicians (British Ring's) magazine *The Budget,* conjurors were debating the two classic dilemmas arising from performances such as those by Geller: *(a)* is he morally justified in prolonging the hoaxing of the mass media and the general public? and *(b)* does the conjurors' ethical code demand that conjurors keep silent?

The consensus was that he should be backed up. As one conjuror wrote, "I address those of our membership who might find themselves tempted to prove or disprove the various theories which abound at this time. Remember the ethics expected of us—it is so easy to fall into the ever-open trap."

Naturally, failure on the part of those members of society most immediately able to refute Geller's allegedly paranormal powers to do so has only permitted the fallacy of "extrasensory perception" to gain a deeper hold on the receptive human imagination.

Sources: Barbara Smoker's article in *New Humanist* (February, 1974) and Christopher Evans' article in the same journal (July/August 1976).

YOU CAN PREDICT YOUR BABY'S **GENDER** BASED ON PREGNANCY SYMPTOMS

Even though it is now quite possible using modern technology to determine your unborn baby's gender with almost 100 percent accuracy, some people still insist on abiding by old school methods of guessing whether themselves or their pregnant friends and relatives will be pushing out a boy or a girl come springtime.

There are several old wives' tales that people swear by. For instance, it is often said that the severity of morning sickness is an indicator: if you are having a girl it is worse than if you are having a boy. However, I happen to know that my own mother prides herself on suffering very little from morning sickness, which she accredits to having two girls and zero boys.

Another popular myth, which has supposedly been around since the times of old English folklore, is that babies who are carried high in the womb are going to be girls, versus those who appear to be lower in the abdomen, who will be boys. According to this legend, the positioning of the fetus is symbolic of the gender roles to be: boys sit lower in the womb because they are more independent, while girls need to be carried higher up because they need more protection. But, again, there are other sources that insist the positioning is reversed.

In order to investigate whether these myths held any weight (puns), experts and researchers have conducted relevant studies. For example, researchers from Johns Hopkins University assessed 104 pregnant women who had no knowledge of the gender of their babies-to-be. The findings proved that the positioning of fetus in a woman's stomach, severity of morning sickness, and comparing the current pregnancy to a previous one were all ineffective ways to predict gender.

Other more bizarre myths involve judging whether you have more of a sweet tooth or a taste for sour things (the former meaning you'll have a boy and the latter a girl is on the way). Also, you can simply take a sample of your urine, mix it around in a cup of Draino, and consider yourself the proud mother of a new baby boy if the liquid turns to green. In the former scenario, cravings that pregnant women have are fairly arbitrary and depend on individuals, the only truth to it is that women's hormones shift during pregnancy, creating heightening repulsions and desires for certain scents and tastes.

In the case of the Drano gender test, if you still had some reason to believe in its reliability, you can consult the findings of the researchers at the University of Washington, which dates back to the 1980s. In other words, if you are a curious pregnant woman reading this right now, we ask that you please have the sense not to try this at home.

Sources: Krisha McCoy, MS, "True or False: You Can Predict Your Baby's Gender by How You Carry the Pregnancy," Beth Israel Deaconess Medical Center at Harvard Medical School; Stephanie Watson, "Can You Guess Your Baby's Sex?" Web MD, *Health and Pregnancy*.

GENERALIZATION AS A FALLACY

A dangerous type of generalization, which is alas all too common, is the stereotyping of national characteristics, often even by eminent historians. This is Henry Steele Commager, in *The American mind* (New Haven, 1950), falsely attributing to all Americans a single set of ideas or tendencies:

"The American was incurably optimistic . . . He had little sense of the past . . . He preached the gospel of hard work . . . The sense of equality permeated the American's life and thought . . . The American was good natured, generous, hospitable, and sociable . . . Carelessness was perhaps the most pervasive and persistent quality in the American . . . The American was at once intelligent and conservative, independent and reliable . . . The American was romantic and sentimental . . ."

Commager is strictly incorrect in all of these opinions, since they are postulated of "the American" instead of "an American." The former is a figure of speech of the kind condemned by G. K. Chesterton in *Heretics* (London, 1905): "the universal modern talk about young nations and new nations; about America being young, about New Zealand being new. The whole thing is a trick of words . . . Of course we may use the metaphor of youth about America or the colonies, if we use it strictly as implying recent origin. But if we use it (as we do use it) as implying vigor or vivacity, or crudity, or inexperience, or hope, or a long life before them, or any of the romantic attributes of youth, then it is surely as clear as daylight that we are duped by a stale figure of speech."

MEN OF **GENIUS** ARE ALWAYS SMALL

Cesare Lombroso, in his *The man of genius* (London, 1891) affirms that the greatest conquerors, generals, artists, theologians, lawyers and politicians have all been small men. The only exceptions, according to Lombroso, are Volta, Petrarch, Helmholtz, D'Azeglio, Foscolo, Monti, Mirabeau, Bismarck, the Dumas, Schopenhauer, Lamartine, Voltaire, Peter the Great, Carlyle, Washington, Flaubert, Turgenev, Kropotkin, Tennyson, Whitman . . .

[And as many more as you need to list in order to prove Lombroso's confident assertion a fallacy].

GEOMANCY

The *Shorter Oxford English Dictionary* defines this term as "The art of divination by means of lines and figures, formed originally by throwing earth on some surface, and later by jotting down on paper dots at random."

Emile Grillot de Givry, in his *Picture museum of sorcery, magic and alchemy* (New York, 1963, p. 301), offers a slightly different definition: "Geomancy is divination by earth; it was also known as the Art of the Little Dots, which was formerly confused with cartomancy [divination by playing cards. Ph.W.]. It consisted in throwing a handful of earth on the ground and examining the figure thereby formed, or even in marking dots at random on a sheet of paper and interpreting their position." The origin of this fallacy was the more general error that each of the four "elements" (actually the notion of these elements has been proved wrong) had its own mode of divination, or foretelling the future. Pyromancy was divination by fire (if pounded peas caught fire quickly the augury was in some obscure manner considered "good"); hydro-mancy was divination by water; and aeromancy was divination by examining the variations and different phenomena of the air in a manner not easily grasped.

This all seems harmless enough until one realizes how much "geomancy" and similar activities are being pursued at this very minute. The Institute of Geomantic Research was recently founded in the Cambridge area and counts among its publications a quarterly journal (vol. 1, no. 1, 1976) and the so-called "Nuthampstead Zodiac," a map of parts of Herts., Essex, and Cambridgeshire which claims that signs of the zodiac have been built by man, a claim made also for the Pendle area of Lancashire and the Glastonbury area. The Institute, operating from 142 Pheasant Rise, Bar Hill, Cambridge, obtained sixty members during its first year; within its scope are terrestrial geometry, aligned sites, ley-lines, and the geometry of sacred buildings. Their *Geomancy of Cambridge* is claimed to include "startling information" about King's College Chapel and other sacred sites in the city.

Belief in the mystic powers of the zodiac and all related fallacies are held because the believer has been unable to make the mental leap from the superstition of astrology to the science of astronomy. It would be a pity for the young to be deluded into thinking that there were some truth in geomancy.

Additionally, Chen Li-fu, of the Council of the Chinese Cultural Renaissance in Taipei, has contributed a summary of the Chinese concept of geomancy which, though equally fallacious, is very different.

"The Confucians advocated administration by talent, and hoped that a ruler could appoint talented people to government positions. Mencius said that a ruler should "put the talented and able in government jobs." But the decision as to who was talented and who was able was made by a ruler, who had the authority to appoint anyone, with or without qualifications. Law had no force on a ruler, and talent meant nothing to him. The ruler was unrestricted, so neither the Confucians nor the Legalists could realize their hopes.

In a time when democracy was unknown, scholars had no way to break this obstacle but placed their hopes on heaven, or God. This is the reason why theories of geomancy became popular during the later Han dynasty.

The theories of geomancy had existed in China for a long time. But the theories of *yin* (female), *yang* (male), *shun* (prosperity) and *ni* (adversity) were considered as having to do with natural phenomena, not with either personal affairs or with government administration.

A legend is told of the Chou dynasty that, when it was reported that six *yih* (sea birds) were seen flying over the capital of the Sung state in the interior, an imperial officer said, "This is a matter of *yin* and *yang,* which indicates neither good luck nor bad luck to us. Our good or bad luck is decided by ourselves."

In the *Book of Changes,* there were statements such as: "When the heaven shows some phenomena they indicate good or bad luck." This is the first recorded Chinese opinion that human affairs can be affected by natural phenomena. The first Chinese philosopher of geomancy, Tsou Yen, lived in the period of the Warring States, but his writings have been lost. After the foundation of the Han dynasty, and the expansion of centralized power, the authority of the Emperor became unlimited. To curb his excessive power, scholars turned to geomancy, hoping that the fear of heaven's punishment might induce the emperor to act for the benefit of the people.

Tung Chung-shu, in his book *Chun Chiu Fan Lu,* used a mixture of Confucianism and geomancy to interpret historical events in the periods of Spring and Autumn and the Warring States; His theory was that the air of heaven and earth are combined, finding their two extremes in the *yin* and the *yang.* With the coming into existence of these extremes, the four seasons and the five elements were produced. According to Tung, "Heaven and people are one. Those who obey the mandate of heaven will prosper, and those who defy it will perish." Tung said; "When Confucius wrote the *Annals of the State of Lu,* he described human affairs as well as natural phenomena. Every time there was a great mistake on the part of human beings, there followed a natural disaster."

Tung's theory was adopted in the later Han dynasty, to the point that the three *Kung* (chief of the general staff, prime minister, and imperial censor) were dismissed by the emperor whenever a natural disaster occurred. Chen Chung condemned this practice, saying "The three *Kung* were not the persons who should have been held responsible. We know they had no power but only titles. The man who should be responsible was the *Shang Shu* (the emperor's secretary-general), because he had the power and handled national affairs. Therefore, to blame the three *Kung* and not the *Shang Shu* for natural disasters was unfair."

Professor Chen concludes his study of ancient geomantic philosophy: "This unreasonable system based on superstition, however, lasted for a long time. It was only after the later Han dynasty ended, and in the Period of the Three Kingdoms (220-265), that the practice was stopped by Emperor Wen of the Wei state."

Sources: Dan Jackson, article "The zealous hunters of the zodiac" in *Cambridge Evening News,* December 10, 1976, p. 15.

DISEASE CAUSES **GERMS**

It has been proved experimentally time without number that germs cause disease. However, if you happen to believe the opposite you are in good company: that of as many naturopaths as you can find condemning drugs as somehow "less natural" than "natural remedies," and that of George Bernard Shaw.

I wonder how many playgoers who enjoy the satire and paradox of *The Doctor's Dilemma* also bother to read the extensive preface that Shaw wrote for his play? Or the papers, collected as vol. 13 of the standard edition of Shaw's Works, which he entitled *Doctors' Delusions?* Or chapter XXVII, "The Collective Biologist," of his *Everybody's political what's what?* The great GBS, compulsive talker and opinionated wit, proved yet again that the general public often prefer to believe an interesting falsehood rather than a plain and simple fact.

The preface to *The Doctor's Dilemma* being notorious, it may be more useful to take the lesser-known passage from *Everybody's political what's what?* (London, 1944, p. 240):

"Now diseases spread beyond the class in which they begin. A German monk named Oken discovered in 1808-11 that our bodies are made up of living cells, which he was intelligent enough to call Transmutations of the Holy Ghost, which is the Christian name of the Life Force. The smallest of these cells, invisible even through the electron microscope, may swarm in the blood. When the Life Force goes wrong, how or why nobody knows, they change their shapes and divide into armies with distinctive uniforms, in which they fight and eat one another, whilst their human host suffers discomfort, pain, disablement, disorder of normal functions and their organs: in short, disease or illness. When the lungs go wrong a uniform peculiar to them is assumed by the cells, another and different one when the bowels go wrong and produces involuntary contractions that may kill the patient, and so on. These specialized cells, called germs, microbes, bacilli, spirochetes, leucocytes, phagocytes, and what not, can escape into the air by the breath, the spittle, the handkerchief, the excretions, the clothes, and can convey the disease to anyone unlucky enough to come in contact with them while in a negative state of defence, and thus unable to prevent them from multiplying millionsfold by splitting in two."

Bernard Shaw concludes: "When the physiologists discovered these curious incidents of disease, their first crude conclusion was that the microbes not only operated and spread the diseases but were actually the diseases themselves, and that if you could kill the microbes you could abolish the diseases. Like all crude first conclusions this was easily and eagerly swallowed, and at once became popular and persistent, as it is at present."

Shaw therefore advocated the abolition of handkerchiefs in favor of spitting and blowing one's nose on the ground; and the abolition of drains in favor of discharging waste direct from sewers into open streams and rivers, where sunlight—he claimed—would kill the germs in a matter of seconds.

As a public health adviser, Shaw was an entertaining dramatist.

THE **GETTYSBURG ADDRESS** WAS FIRST PUBLISHED BY BAKER & GOODWIN IN NEW YORK

Until recently, it was almost universally assumed that Abraham Lincoln's Gettysburg Address first appeared in book form in 1863 in a 48-page booklet published by Baker and Goodwin in New York.

We now know, however, that this edition was preceded by one virtually hidden on page 16 of Edward Everett's much longer oration, published on November 22, 1863 by the *Washington Chronicle,* and totally forgotten, while the immortal words of Lincoln on democratic government ring as gloriously as ever.

GHOSTS

The perpetuation of fear in succeeding generations of the young in most human societies derives partly from the fear and ignorance of the adults, and partly from the universal adult need to control the young by all means at their disposal,

Most tales of apparitions in psychical research history date from the period before 1900, when superstition and belief in the supernatural were stronger than they are now. Those unusually nervous (such as children, or lonely women) had only to think about ghosts for an unusual sound or sight to induce the belief that spectres were at hand. Romantic literature of the 19th century throughout Europe encouraged a belief in magic and ghosts which was an exacerbation of the fears of hell-fire nurtured by priests and parsons in the Middle Ages, before, and after.

The simple mind is capable of great illusion. Suggestion and autosuggestion are always stronger than skepticism among the young, the rural, and the otherwise impressionable. The works which have enjoyed the longest and greatest repute among those interested in reports of ghosts (which are connected with the fallacy of life beyond death, a self-evident impossibility) are *Phantasms of the living* (2 vols., London, 1886), by E. Gurney, F. W. H. Myers, and Frank Podmore; and Myers' *Human personality and its survival of bodily death* (2 vols., London, 1903). These works, written from a viewpoint of total commitment to both the idea of bodily survival after death and the existence of ghosts, were nevertheless unable to admit more than a small number of "fairly conclusive cases," repudiating the vast majority as spurious.

Yet neither book publishes any contemporary written evidence, and E. Parish, analyzing them both in *Hallucinations and illusions* (London, 1897, p. 104), concluded that a large percentage of reported cases contained unmistakable evidence of a dream state of consciousness. D. H. Rawcliffe, in *Illusions and delusions of the supernatural and the occult* (New York, 1959), declares that "a purported telepathic, clairvoyant or prophetic experience must more or less correspond to some external event to render it veridical ; and the only admissible evidence in such cases is an account of the experience written down, or otherwise recorded—*before* the external event takes place—in a diary, a letter, or other document," Needless to say, there are no cases which obey the minimal scientific requirement of proof.

The sighting of new phantoms continues unabated in the world of sensational journalism.

John G. Fuller, whose writings we have already examined under the entry ARIGÓ, is the author of *The ghost of Flight 401* (New York, 1976), which purports to prove that ghosts have survived the crash of an Eastern Airlines flight from New York to Miami on December 29, 1972.

Throughout the whole book there is not a single statement that has been proved or verified experimentally under test conditions, and the onus is entirely on John G. Fuller to supply such proof before his stories can be credited, since they contradict what we know of the body's death. No spiritual survival has yet been proved.

R. A. Nagler observes, reviewing the book in the New York *Library Journal* (October 15, 1976), how "Fuller's leaps of faith that pass for documentation mar his credibility."

For the benefit of those still frightened of the dark, of "inexplicable" noises, and of shapes and shadows, *there is no such thing as a ghost!*

Sources: *Phantasms of the living* (2 vols., London, 1886), by E. Gurney, F. W. H. Myers, and Frank Podmore; and Myers' *Human personality and its survival of bodily death* (2 vols., London, 1903).

GINGER ALE CURES NAUSEA

Most of us are probably familiar with the notion that ginger is an age old, homeopathic, and effective cure for nausea, indigestion, and upset stomachs. Greek physicians dating back to the earliest centuries are reported to have claimed that eating ginger root helps alleviate stomach problems, or is good for the stomach. It is also a common remedy for various medical ailments which has been used in countries such as India, Arabia, and China for up to 4,000 years.

(Continued)

Ginger is considered by most modern physicians and medical practitioners a valuable treatment for illnesses ranging from mild nausea or menstrual cramps to osteoporosis and cancer with chemotherapy (as a pain reliever).

Ginger itself is a type of root or stem from underground (rhizome) of the plant, Zinger Officinale. The active ingredients, or, compounds, in ginger root are volatile oils and pungent phenol compounds, such as gingerols and shogaols.

While some studies prove no definite improvement in health or reduction of painful symptoms in patients undergoing chemotherapy, especially as compared to other drugs given to them, others have proven otherwise. One trial found that ginger powder was just as effective as the drug metoclopramide in controlling or lessening nausea and vomiting in chemo-therapy patients. Likewise, a series of studies compiled and explored by expert, Borrelli and his team, who drew from over thirty sources, also found that ginger was four times better than placebo in curing symptoms of nausea and vomiting in pregnant women.

Although the effectiveness of ginger is still not consensually agreed upon as a cure for all ranges of illnesses in severity, it is definitely a fall back plan or supplemental resource for those suffering temporarily from an upset stomach, motion sickness, or digestive problems.

That being said, the effects of ginger ale on nausea are not at all on an equal plane with those of ginger in its purer form. Though ginger ale may have once contained ginger extract as an active or predominant ingredient, it no longer does, especially in the United States. So-called ginger beverages made by companies like Shweppes or Canada Dry are as illegitimate in their ginger content as they are in their taste. They mostly just contain fructose corn syrup, like many other sodas, as a substitute (albeit an unconvincing one) for ginger.

Other beverages that contain real ginger extract, such as in ginger sodas like Reed's ginger brews or authentically made ginger cookies, are obviously more likely to be helpful in curing nausea. Whether the alcoholic drink, ginger beer, is more likely to improve nausea than fake ginger ale, however, probably depends more on how much of either product you consume.

Sources: Chau Che, MD., "Myths and Realities: Ginger Ale in Treating Nausea and Vomiting," *Clinical Correlations*, The NYU Langone Internal Medicine Blog, 2009; *Reed's Inc.*, "Reed's Ginger Brews"; University of Maryland Medical Center, "Ginger," Medical Reference.

GIRAFFES

1) The Giraffe Has More Cervical Vertebrae Than Any Other Mammal

Because of its long neck, the giraffe is the subject of this observation by most visitors to zoos or wildlife parks. So just check on your next visit to a science museum: like man, the whale, and all other mammals, the giraffe has seven cervical vertebrae.

2) Lysenkoism

Trofim D. Lysenko was the Soviet Union's leading authority on heredity and evolution. With Lamarck, the pre-Darwinian French scientist, Lysenko believed that evolution worked through the inheritance of traits which organisms acquired in response to their surroundings, as in the case of the giraffe's long neck. Giraffes stretched their neck to eat leaves which were beyond the reach of lesser animals, and because this trait was effective, giraffes with longer and longer necks were born, Darwin accepted this fact, but suggested that it was more important that the giraffes with shorter necks died out, thus proving the survival of the fittest. Evolution theory has now rejected Lamarckianism, but it was official party policy in the USSR and in two articles on Lysenkoism for the Saturday Review (December 4 and 11, 1948), the Nobel Prize-winning geneticist H. J. Muller described what had happened to Lysenko's opponents: "In 1933 or thereabouts, the geneticists Chetverikoff, Ferry, and Ephroimson were all, on separate occasions, banished to Siberia, and Levitsky to a labor camp in the European Arctic . . . from 1936 on Soviet geneticists of all ranks lived a life of terror . . . Ironically, the great majority of the geneticists who have been purged were thoroughly loyal politically; many were even ardent crusaders for the Soviet system and leadership as the writer well knows through personal contact with them."

Muller continues to explain that the Lysenkoist view "implies a mystical Aristotelian "perfecting principle," a kind of foresight, in the basic make-up of living things, despite the fact that it claims in the same breath not to be "idealistic" at all."

The fallacy of regarding Lamarckianism as a kind of dogma inherently sound and not to be tested experimentally and discarded if found wanting is compounded by the fallacy of elevating a scientific hypothesis to the status of a political truism, when the two ideas are entirely distinct. Racist dogmas were similarly at the back of German fascism.

GLASS IS A LIQUID

Judging by appearances, we probably don't think about glass as being liquid at all. But glass icicles *can* be a handy substitute for

(*Continued*)

the real temperature-sensitive thing while holiday decorating. Also, some solids *do* take liquid form.

Glass, however, is not a super cooled liquid, as has been popularly claimed at various times on the Internet and elsewhere in the past couple of decades. Proponents of this belief often point to centuries-old glass in the cathedrals of Europe that is noticeably thicker at the bottom than at the top as evidence that glass "flows" like a liquid, albeit very, very slowly.

The reason this mistake is made is because normally when a liquid is cooled to below its melting point, it turns to crystallized solid. Some liquids become super cooled and never become fully solid even when they are cooled below their melting point, due to viscosity. Some argue glass is just an amorphous solid, or super cooled liquid. There is only a subtle distinction proving that this is not the case: there is still a second phase that needs to take place in the transition between a super cooled liquid and glass, but it is, interestingly, less drastic than the change from liquid to solid crystallization.

In other words, glass is technically less of a "solid" than average liquids become when they are cooled to below their melting point, but it is also not a liquid. And those old glass windows? They're thicker at the bottom simply because of how glass panes were made at that time, and were set with the thicker side on the bottom because that end was heavier. Not the result of flowing glass.

Source: Philip Gibbs, "Is Glass Liquid or Solid?" *Math.ucr.edu*, 1996.

BLUE **GLASS**

Between 1870 and 1880 America and Europe were engulfed in a wave of enthusiasm for blue glass and blue light. Blue and violet rays were thought to be especially good for certain ailments. In 1861 General A. J. Pleasonton experimented with blue rays in a grapery, which was covered and encased by sashes of glass of which every eighth row of panes was, as he supposed, violet in color. He had good results, reported in *Blue and sun-lights, their influence upon life, disease, etc.,* a paper read in 1871 to the Philadelphia Society for Promoting Agriculture. "I investigated the matter, and found that the glass was a dark mazarin blue—owing its color to a preparation of cobalt which had been fused with the material composing the glass," Pleasonton's ideas on blue glass were eagerly taken up, and a wealthy Baltimorean suffering from chronic rheumatism was to be seen on sunny days, driving in a phaeton of which the cover was a canopy of blue glass.

Dr. Seth Dancoast of Philadelphia published a work called *Blue and red light; or light and its rays as medicine* "not only to prove that the gentle Blue ray has curative properties for some disorders, and the strong, Red ray for others, but to demonstrate just why they, and not the Green or the Yellow, must be employed, and how they act, and then explain the best methods of employing them."

VENETIAN GLASS IS MADE IN VENICE

The particular sand needed for Venetian glass is not found in Venice, but in Murano—an island in the lagoon easily accessible by regular *vaporetto*—and that is where "Venetian" glass has always been made. The glassblowers are still active on Murano, and a visit to them, with the fine early church on neighboring Torcello, is an integral part of any holiday in the Veneto.

GOLD FALLACIES

1) Gold Can Be Grown

In his *Relationes curiosae* (Hamburg, 1683), E. W. Happel fell prey to the ancient fallacy that gold can be grown, an idea nearly as prevalent in the Middle Ages as the fallacy concerning the possibility of transmuting base metals into gold.

The growable gold, "aurum vegetabile," has been claimed in legend from Poland, Hungary, Germany, and France, Of course there is not a word of truth in it. No metal can be said in any meaningful way to "grow" unless you find more of it, or expand it. Our precious metals are not being depleted in the same wasteful way as are our fossil fuels (such as coal or oil or natural gas), but few significant gold mines are left. The cliche "he's found a gold-mine" was always an exaggeration, for the immense labor of mining sufficient gold for profitability has seldom been rewarded in a more spectacular manner than, say, coal mines or tin mines.

2) Base Metals Can Be Transmuted Into Gold

In his magisterial *Science and civilisation in China* (vol. 5, part II, Cambridge, 1976), Dr Joseph Needham (writing with Lu Gwei-Djen) has proposed the terms "aurifaction" to denote the idea of transmuting base metals into gold, which was known to be impossible at least a thousand years before the composition of the Hellenistic works which influenced first Islamic and then Christian "adepts"; and "aurifiction" to describe the well-known recipes for faking gold known as early as the Hellenistic technical papyri. Needham suggests that earlier historians P. E. M. Berthelot and E. O. von Lippmann were mistaken in thinking that metalworkers practising aurifiction finally duped themselves into believing that aurifaction was possible.

Needham thinks that the social barriers which ruled out contacts between the metalworkers and scholars perpetuated the myth of transmutation, for the metalworkers knew that their fakes could not pass the cupellation test, while the scholars bypassed the cupellation test because they were ignorant of its existence or because their definitions of gold assigned the metal and its imitations to a single class.

Thousands of years have passed since the first "alchemists" attempted the impossible achievements of transmuting base metals into gold and mixing an elixir of eternal life (see also ELIXIR OF LIFE), and as neither task has been fulfilled, we must put another two toman aspirations into the category of common fallacies.

It is usual to consider alchemy an essential rang on the ladder which leads up to modern chemistry, and while there is no doubt that scholars and craftsmen were led to discover more of the chemical world in their lust for gold, knowledge, and eternal youth than they would otherwise have done, this half-truth conceals the important question of the scientific attitude, which so sharply divides the scientist from the mere adventurer. As P. M. Rattansi observed in *The Times Literary Supplement* (November 12, 1976), alchemy "is a difficult study because the adepts wrapped up their wonted secrets in obscure symbols to conceal them from the uninitiated. Robert Boyle in the seventeenth century pointed out that such mystification had robbed the "chymists" of the gain in scientific understanding which a vast knowledge of materials, chemical reactions, and laboratory reactions had brought within their reach."

3) Gold Paint Is Made of Gold
There is no more gold in "gold" paint than there is in mosaic "gold." The glittering in both is due to stannic sulphide, a golden-yellow crystalline compound of one atom of tin combined with two atoms of sulphur. It is obtained by heating tin amalgam, sulphur, and ammonium chloride in a retort.

Sources: F. Sherwood Taylor, *The alchemists* (London, 1952).

GOOSEBUMPS (SERVE A PRACTICAL PURPOSE FOR HUMANS)
We are not referring to the popular book series by R. L. Stine. And had his fright inducing stories not been so popular amongst kids and young adults, the name itself would probably seem much sillier than it does sinister.

There is a lot that is strange about goosebumps. Although there does not seem to be a definite consensus on when the term "goosebumps" came about, it was preceded by "goose pimples," and before that, the even more crude "goose skin." The word "goosebumps" first came to its usage in 1919, while "goose skin" dates back to the 1700s. Some sources claim that this original term, used to describe the sensation of human skin suddenly becoming infested with bumps due to contracting muscles at the base of hair follicles followed by papillae erection, has been around since the Middle Ages.

Although the term's origin date is disputed, the reason for why goosebumps are called "goosebumps" is generally agreed upon by those interested in the topic. Put simply, goose skin is called "goose skin" because it resembles just that: the texture of a goose's skin after its feathers have been plucked.

The biological practicality of goosebumps in humans, however, is moot. We humans adopted this mechanism from our animal ancestors but it no longer has any helpful function for us. In animals, the rising of hair that comes with the bumps that form with tensing of muscles serves to keep them warm, as it provides insulation. But while our muscles also contract when we are cold, our hair standing up doesn't make us any warmer.

Additionally, we, like other animals, get goosebumps when we experience fear. Again, this mechanism is completely unnecessary for humans. However, when an animal senses fear, its fur standing on end has a much more visually striking effect. This image of a dog or cat appearing bigger than it really is a useful device that helps them scare off predators or other natural threats.

As more emotionally intelligent and responsive than other animals, humans also get goosebumps from their reactions to feelings. Who hasn't embarrassingly gotten goosebumps after reading the ending of a psychological thriller, becoming sexually aroused, or hearing a beautiful singing voice? This physical reaction to emotional triggers is due to the subconscious release of a stress hormone, commonly known as adrenaline. In addition to goosebumps, other bodily responses to emotions like anxiety or passion, such as sweaty palms, increased heart beat, and butterflies in the stomach, are caused by the stimulation of adrenaline or in popular terms, "an adrenaline rush."

Sources: *Etymolonline.com*, "Goosebumps;" "Goosebump," *WordNet*, Princeton University; George A. Bubenik, "Why Do Humans Get 'Goosebumps' When They are Cold, or Under other Circumstances?" *Scientific American*, 2003.

A **GRANGERIZED** BOOK IS ONE PUBLISHED WITH PROFUSE ILLUSTRATIONS FROM OTHER BOOKS

The common error repeated yet again in Josefa Heifetz Byrne's *Dictionary of unusual, obscure, and preposterous words* (London, 1979) concerning "grangerized" books is that, in Mrs. Byrne's words, James Granger's *Biographical history of England* (3 vols., 1769-74 and later editions) was "richly illustrated" with "pictures and designs from the books of others."

No: the whole, and original, idea of Granger's book was to print some blank leaves on which owners could paste their own illustrations, whether drawn by themselves, or removed from other works. The notion quickly caught on, and other books were published with a view to being "grangerized."

GRAPES CAN CURE STOMACH ULCERS AND ALCOHOLISM

John Camp reports an announcement in the magazine *Prevention* to the effect that a diet of grapes will be of value in the treatment and cure of arthritis, rheumatism, alcoholism, mental instability, migraine, kidney ailments and stomach ulcers. He adds: "With the 'nature cure' industry geared either to the relief of symptoms or to protecting the reader from illnesses that he is probably never likely to suffer from, it is no surprise that business is booming. Thousands of people who claim to distrust doctors and begrudge the cost of medical insurance cheerfully spend their hard-earned money on products of unspecified content, products which promise only to 'revitalize the bloodstream, give sparkle to the eye, color to the lips and spring to the step.' Curiously enough, few people who swallow either these tonics or their descriptions seem to prove their efficacy."

Source: John Camp, *Magic, myth and medicine* (London, 1973).

"PATIENCE, YOUNG **GRASSHOPPER**" IS A QUOTE FROM *THE KARATE KID*

When you type this quote into Google, there are a good amount of sources that mistakenly claim it is taken from the movie, *The Karate Kid*. Even sources such as NPR and the *Huffington Post* have made this error. However, neither the original 1984 nor the 2010 remake of *The Karate Kid* were the first to coin the, for some reason, very famous quote, "Patience, Young Grasshopper."

In reality, it is first popularized in the 1972 TV series *Kung Fu*. So, even if there was some cheesy use of the term Grasshopper, as an endearing name for the young kung fu master in training (Jaden Smith) in the new *Karate Kid* movie, the phrase is not part of its legacy.

GRAVITY IS A FORCE PULLING OBJECTS BACK TO EARTH

The Gravity Research Foundation was founded in 1948 with the specific purpose of discovering a type of "gravity screen" which will "cut off gravity" in the same way that a sheet of steel cuts off a light beam. However, Einstein showed that gravity is not a "force" as had been imagined earlier, but a warping of the space-time continuum. One of the Foundation's mistaken endeavors is to measure the effect of changing relations of the sun and moon on human beings; another belief is that weight (i.e., gravity) has a greater effect on temperament than body-type has, so that the discovery of a gravity screen could change a person's weight and thus alter his temperament.

When theories like these are offered, serious scientists are yet again in danger of losing their gravity.

Source: Martin Gardner, *Fads and fallacies in the name of science* (New York, 1957, pp. 80-100).

THE **GREAT** DANE IS A BREED OF DANISH DOG

The Great Dane, the largest breed within the European mastiff family, is not connected with Denmark in any way so far historically recorded.

In the sixteenth century, Great Danes were most frequently known as "English Dogges," and about 1680 they were bred in great numbers at the princely courts in Germany. The largest and best of the breed were called "Chamber Dogs" *(Kammerhunde)* and wore gilded collars, while the lesser animals were known as "Life Dogs" *(Leibhunde)* and wore collars with a silver finish. At the first German dog show, held at Hamburg in 1863, "some very grave-looking Doggen took part in the event." Of these, eight were said to be "Danish Doggen" and seven announced as "Ulmer Doggen." "The truth is," confides *The new complete Great Dane* (New York, 1974), "that of all these dogs not one had ever seen Denmark, nor had any of them even been born there, as their papers indicated." At the 1876 show, the judges called the Great Dane the "Deutsche Dogge," as it had been called for centuries.

THE **GREATEST** ACHIEVEMENT OF GREEK ART IN THE FIFTH CENTURY B.C. WAS IN SCULPTURE

Charles Seltman, in his *Approach to Greek art* (New York, 1960), argues very convincingly that the major mode of classical Greek art was not that of the sculptor, but that of the engraver. "Exciting as are the marbles of the Parthenon and certain sensitive tombstones of Attic work, it is not among such things that the finest art of the fifth century is *to* be sought. The most admired artists among the Greeks themselves were not the masons, nor even the modellers, casters, and finishers of fine bronzes, but the *celators* [or engravers]."

"For more than four centuries men have been instructed that the very best things which the Greeks ever made were of marble, and that is why you may read in a book on Greek art written little more than a score of years ago that "sculpture was in many ways the most characteristic art of Greece; . . . it achieved the highest attainments." Such has been the usual approach to Greek art. The prize must go to sculpture in stone, with which large works cast in bronze were often associated; next came painting, which is now represented mainly by drawings made on the surface of ancient vases; third came the so-called "minor arts," under which label were grouped with condescension and convenience the work of die-cutters, gem-engravers, jewellers, and celators (or metalchasers). But does such "classing" in any way correspond with the ideas which the Greeks themselves held about artists and art? It is certain that they had very different views. Even in the distant age of bronze the inhabitants of Greece and the islands held the skilled worker in metal in very high regard. His art was both a mystery and a delight, and he was thought to owe his gifts to supernatural beings around whom many legends grew."

Although a subject of this nature is not amenable to clear-cut, final objective judgments, there is no doubt that the exquisite vases and metalwork of the Greeks have been consistently under-rated.

CLASSICAL **GREEK CIVILIZATION** MADE LIFE COMFORTABLE FOR ITS CITIZENS

E. B. Castle, in *Ancient education and today* (Harmondsworth, 1961), has emphasized that the material life of the Athenian civilisation, which we take as the paradigm of classical Greek city-states, was characterized by extreme poverty. "Almost every tool and gadget which make our lives bearable were unknown to the Greeks. The homes of the men who built the Parthenon would have shocked the dwellers in a modern council house."

In *The Greek Commonwealth* (Oxford, 1911), Alfred Zimmern stressed that Herodotus did not exaggerate when writing that poverty and impossibility were the constant companions of the Athenians. "It is easy to think away railways and telegraphs and gasworks and tea and advertizements and bananas. But we must peel off more than this. We must imagine houses without drains, beds without sheets or springs, rooms as cold, or as hot, as the open air, only draughtier, meals that began and ended with pudding, and cities that could boast neither gentry nor millionaires. We must learn to tell the time without watches, to cross rivers, without bridges, and seas without a compass, to fasten our clothes (or rather our two pieces of cloth) with two pins instead of a row of buttons, to wear our shoes or sandals without stockings, to warm ourselves over a pot of ashes, to judge open-air plays or law-suits on a cold winter's morning, to study poetry without books, geography without maps, and politics without newspapers. In a word we must learn how to be civilized without being comfortable."

THE INTERIOR OF **GREENLAND** IS ICE-FREE

Adolf Erik Nordenskibld (1832-1901), who achieved great celebrity by leading the *Vega* expedition through the Northwest Passage, was a distinguished scientist reputed to be the greatest expert on the Arctic of his period.

The purpose of his expedition to Greenland in 1883 was to prove "wholly unjustified" the widely-held belief that Greenland's interior is covered with ice. "On the contrary," explained Nordenskibld, "the following considerations seem to indicate that on the whole it is a *physical impossibility* that the interior of an extensive continent should be completely shrouded in ice under the climatic conditions that obtain south of 80° North latitude on our globe." First, if a glacier is to be formed, more snow must fall than can be melted in the summer, a condition which must be fulfilled at the source regions of all the glaciers, including those which come down to the sea along the shores of Greenland. But where are the glacier-sources: in the high centre, or in narrow mountain chains surrounding a lower interior? In the former case, air that comes in from the sea will descend from the coastal mountains and be warmed as it descends. If the air descends to the same elevation it had before the water-vapor in it was condensed out as snow, it will in fact be warmer than before its ascent, for it will contain the "latent" heat released whenever water is condensed. Nordenskiöld believed that the interior of Greenland lies lower than the surrounding mountain chain, and will have no ice cover, for winds reaching the interior are relatively warm and too dry to contribute enough snow to maintain such a cover. Why may not Greenland have a high centre, with a permanent ice cover, as observers (including Nordenskiöld himself) might have deduced from coastal inspection? The analogical argument is that, if one does not know from experience what the interior is like, one judges what it must be like from the geomorphology of lands which are already known. "We do not find such a form in any of the continents of the globe whose relief is known," stated Nordenskiöld, "and one can therefore with the utmost probability assume that Greenland does not possess it. On the contrary, the geologic character of Greenland, which in many respects resembles that of Scandinavia, indicates a relief much like that of our country, consisting of mountain ranges and peaks alternating with deep valleys and plains."

Nordenskiöld *might* have been right by analogy. In fact he was wrong, in the same way that an Egyptian oasis-dweller of Siwa or Fayyum would be wrong if he assumed—without having been there—that oases in the east of Egypt (on or near the Nile) would be as arid as his own.

In 1883 Nordenskiöld made the expedition destined to answer once and for all the question of the ice-free interior of Greenland. He found only the monotonous ice-sheet that later expeditions have found. Even then, however, Nordenskiöld was not convinced, until Nansen's crossing of 1888.

Sources include: John Leighly, "Error in geography," in Joseph Jastrow, *The story of human error* (New York, 1936, pp. 114-9).

THE WORD "GREMLIN" WAS INVENTED DURING WORLD WAR II

On the radio program *Desert island discs* (British Broadcasting Corporation, October 27, 1979), the writer Roald Dahl claimed to have invented the word "gremlin" during the Second World War.

B. J. Watson of Hull, in a letter to *Radio Times* (December 1-7, 1979), claimed however that the word was already familiar to readers of *The Aeroplane,* where it occurs three times in a poem published on April 10, 1929. Gremlins are "mischievous imps which inhabited aircraft and were held responsible for all the unaccountable failures, both mechanical and human, which occurred. They were particularly active during the War when there were, of course, many more unexplainable incidents."

The earliest published evidence for "gremlin" in the 1972 Supplement to *The Oxford English Dictionary* is dated 1941, but Dr. R. E. Allen, Senior Editor of the Oxford dictionaries, writes: "The only additional information we have in our files is an unverified reference to *Newsweek* of September 7, 1942, which is said to trace the word back to 1923" [personal communication, 1979].

Can any reader offer an instance of the use of "gremlin" before 1923?

"GREY OWL" WAS A NORTH AMERICAN INDIAN

Many authors use pen-names, for a variety of reasons, but do not claim a whole new identity in the process to mislead the public. Where an attempt is made to deceive the public, the imposture must be revealed.

Such is the case of "Grey Owl," who emerged from the Canadian wilds in the 1930s claiming to be Wa-Sha-Quon-Asin (meaning "Grey Owl"), son of an Apache mother and a Scottish-born Indian scout, born in Mexico.

But he was really Archibald Belaney, an Englishman raised by two maiden aunts in the seaside resort of Hastings. In 1906 he left England for Canada, where he lived for a time with the Ojibway Indians, and married an Ojibway girl. In 1915 he joined the Canadian Army and served in Flanders, where he was wounded. Invalided out, Belaney spent some time in a military hospital near Hastings, and married a childhood sweetheart, Florence Holmes. However, he returned to Canada alone late in 1917, where he took up again with his Ojibway wife and began writing the sequence of excellent wild life books which seemed so authentic that his publishers were easily hoaxed into assuming that he was a true Indian. *The men of the last frontier* was enthusiastically reviewed, and Lovat Dickson, in his autobiographical *House of words* (London, 1963), explains how he was induced to publish *Pilgrims of the wild* and *Tales of an empty cabin,* which he did in all good faith.

"Grey Owl" died in 1938, at the age of fifty-one, following his second triumphant British tour, during which he greeted King George VI in Ojibway and English with "I come in peace, brother." Belaney's maiden aunts were soon traced, and frankly gave the show away.

Sources include: Norman Moss, *The pleasures of deception* (London, 1977, pp. 167-175).

ALL CHILDREN SUFFER FROM **GROWING** PAINS

There is nothing normal about growing pains, though I always understood there was as a child. These pains are not an inevitable concomitant of growing up, but are caused (usually in the legs and back) by physical strain or exhaustion, disease of the bones, or a manifestation of rheumatism. Growing pains are not often serious, but they should not be dismissed if they persist.

Source: J. A. C. Brown, *Pears medical encyclopaedia* (London, 1967).

THE **GRYPHON**

Lewis Carroll, who wrote a great deal on logic and mathematics, peopled Alice's Wonderland with both real and imaginary animals, so that children who know Bill the Lizard and the White Rabbit find no difficulty in accepting the objective reality of the gryphon. After all, one might argue, if the luckless dodo once existed, might not the gryphon have done so too?

Certainly the Greeks believed the fabulous beasts to inhabit Scythia, where they guarded Scythian gold. But by the 17th century, the belief was falling gradually into desuetude. As Sir Thomas Browne writes: "That there are Griffons in Nature, that is a mixt and dubious animall, in the fore-part resembling an Eagle, and behinde the shape of Lion, with erected eares, fore feet, and a long taile, many affirme, and most I perceive deny not; the same is averred by Aelian, Solinus, Mela, and Herodotus, countenanced by the name sometimes found in Scripture, and was an Hieroglyphick of the Egyptians.

"Notwithstanding wee finde most diligent enquirers to be of a contrary assertion; for beside that Albertus and Pliny have disallowed it, the learned Aldrovand hath in a large discourse rejected it; Mathias Michovius who write of those Northerne parts wherein men place these Griffins, hath positively concluded against it, and if examined by the doctrine of animals, the invention is monstrous, nor much inferior unto the figment of Sphynx, Chimaera, and Harpies: for though some species there be of a middle and participating natures, that is, of bird and beast, as we finde the Bat to be, yet are their parts so conformed and set together that we cannot define the beginning or end of either, there being a commixtion of both in the whole, rather then an adaptation, or cement of the one unto the other."

Gryphons don't exist.

DR. GUILLOTIN INVENTED THE **GUILLOTINE**

An understandable mistake, but he merely encouraged the machine's use in the interest of a painless death. It was invented by a German mechanic called Schmidt under the direction of Dr. Antonio Louise, and was thus known first as a "Louison" or "Louisette."

Neither was Guillotin the first victim of the machine—that was the highwayman Pelletier (April 25, 1792). Guillotin outlived the Revolution by twenty years, dying at the age of seventy-six on May 26, 1814.

SWALLOWED **GUM** GETS STUCK IN YOUR SYSTEM FOR SEVEN YEARS

Maybe it's because our mothers' mothers viewed chewing gum as a habit that was far from classy, or maybe because teachers didn't want to find gum stuck to the bottom of their students' desks (or, moreover, didn't want to get blamed for janitor complaints about too much gum in one particular classroom). Regardless, the rumor about gum being nearly impossible to digest has prevailed for as long as chewing gum has been around, or at least, since it's been considered by teen pop culture as fun and more importantly, cool.

The practice of gum chewing has indeed been around for much longer than we can probably imagine. Recent research has found that DNA from primitive gum chewers of quid, balls of plant material, from a southwestern American tribe of Native Americans dates back to 2,000 years ago! Perhaps for a soothing affect along the lines of a more do-it-yourself nicotine gum?

Reportedly, during colonoscopy and capsule endoscopy procedures, gum is hardly ever encountered in the tract, unless it is only a maximum of a week or so old. Additionally, nothing (including foreign, nonperishable objects) would remain that long in the digestive tract unless it were bigger than a quarter.

Of course, gulping down gum instead of spitting it out on a regular basis is not condoned. But, if the juicy fruit flavor has been gone for hours, your jaw is sore, and you still can't find a trashcan, don't worry about it not coming back out the other end in a matter of days.

Sources: John Matson, *Scientific American*, "Fact or Fiction?: Chewing Gum Takes Seven Years to Digest," 2007.

H

"He who has heard the same thing told by 12,000 eye-witnesses has only 12,000 probabilities, which are equal to one strong probability, which is far from certainty."
—VOLTAIRE

"How rarely reason guides the stubborn choice, Rules the bold hand, or prompts the suppliant voice."
—SAMUEL JOHNSON, *The vanity of human wishes*

TEMPERATURE AND **HABITABILITY** ARE CONNECTED WITH LATITUDE

The assumptions of the ancient Greeks, both right and wrong, were frequently inherited by the Romans and—unless they clashed with Church dogma—subsequently found their way into medieval encyclopedias, and even—as in the case of astrology or belief in ghosts—into the modern *Weltanschauung*. Such is the case with ideas about the habitability of the Earth, and its range of temperature.

The Greeks were familiar with the harsh continental winters of Scythia, near the Euxine (our Black Sea) and with the heat and desolation of the North African and Arabian deserts. Their experience led them to believe that Athens, Corinth, Thebes, and the islands represented the centre of the habitable world, with ideal temperatures. The farther one roved from the shores of the Mediterranean, they taught, the less habitable the world became.

Later studies of climatology and demography have led to very different conclusions. Moreover, human types have evolved regionally to cope adequately with local conditions: Eskimoes and Australian aborigines might soon die if confronted with each other's conditions, or with those of Greece. Latitude is only one of many determining factors. The fallacy of the Greeks was to assume that specific conditions applied generally: this corresponds to the error of an experimenter with rats who assumes that lessons learnt from rats will be applicable to human beings.

HADES IS A PLACE

Hades is not a place. It is not even an imaginary, legendary, or mythical place. It is the name of a god—Pluto. In Greek mythology, he is the god of the underworld, a gloomy, sunless kingdom barred by the rivers Styx, Acheron, Phlegethon, and Cocytus.

The "kingdom of Hades," that is Pluto's kingdom, gradually came to be misunderstood by contraction as "Hades," so that Hades became a place-name. However, out of deference to Greek mythology, it is appropriate if we return to the usage of "the kingdom of Hades," and keep "Hades" for the god Pluto himself. If you believe that the Roman poets thought the kingdom of Hades a horrible region, it is worth recollecting that Virgil places the blessed dead in Elysium, itself situated within the kingdom of Hades.

HAIR CAN TURN WHITE NATURALLY OVERNIGHT

Normally through fear, horror, or terror, goes the well-authenticated story in the cases reported by *Time:* March 2, 1942 (C. Yates McDaniel, after witnessing "the collapse of Singapore at close hand";) May 31, 1943 (Ernie Pyle, whose hair merely turned grey during the African campaign); August 14, 1944 (Air Marshal Coningham); and September 4, 1944 (Jimmie Hines, but over a period of three years, in Sing Sing).

However, this is ridiculous in the light of due natural processes, and all recorded eases of "overnight" bleaching are either exaggerated, or due to bleaching or the sudden removal of artificial color. In their *Diseases of the skin,* R. L. Sutton and R. L. Sutton, Jr. write, "Sudden, overnight blanching, reliably reported, is doubtless the result of the removal of cosmetic coloration or the application of a bleach. Physiological and anatomical facts are incompatible with the possibility of actual, nonartificial, instant blanching."

HAIR ON MEN'S BODIES IS A SIGN OF STRENGTH

This curious fallacy probably derives from the Biblical story of Samson and his hair. Ordinary daily observation by doctors shows no correlation whatsoever between the amount of hair on a man's body and his actual or potential strength.

A man with hair on his chest is commonly thought to be uncommonly strong, "like a gorilla." The gorilla has hair on his belly, his back, his shoulders, arms and legs, but none on his chest.

Source: R. M. Yerkes and Ada W. Yerkes, *The great apes* (New Haven, Conn., 1929).

THE HAMBURGER WAS INVENTED IN HAMBURG, GERMANY

The issue of where the Hamburger was invented and who invented it is quite a riveting one. Americans fight over which
(Continued)

state, or even which city or town can claim the bragging rights as to the invention of the modern hamburger. But, according to sources, it seems reasonable to conclude that the Hamburger was not invented by Americans at all. Most likely, it first came about in its most primitive form in the life and times of the Mongols.

There are a number of reasons why it makes (some) sense that the Mongols were the Hamburger creators. First of all, they were clearly resourceful. They were an unstoppable killing force conquering village after village throughout and around modern day Russia. As they were mostly busy trying to take over the known world, they would stash raw meat in their saddles or strapped to their backs so they wouldn't have to stop frequently for more nourishment. The meat would eventually become grounded, having been crushed underneath their saddles during massacres for a while, so it would be warm and tender enough for these brave warriors to enjoy on the go!

Thus, when Ghengis Khan and the rest of his gang took over the feeble beginnings of other Russian clans, they brought the pulverized meat with them, which the Russians later renamed "Steak Tartare," after the Tartars (their name for the Mongols).

It is speculated that the reason "hamburger" got its name is because in the 1500s, Germany began trading with Russia through the Hamburg port. From there, the so called "Hamburg Steak" (which arose as a term in 1884) was brought back to the West, where we put it between bread and called it a Hamburger. It is unclear as to who actually coined the term Hamburger, though it is thought to be, not illogically, named after the city of Hamburg.

But, the Hamburger in its most early stages was not invented in Hamburg by Germans or by Americans. Who knew that such a classic American staple really came from Eastern Europe?

Sources: John Berman, Drew Millhon, "A Major Beef! Who Invented the Hamburger?" ABC News, 2007; *Etymonline.com.*

HAY FEVER

The following fallacies are discussed by August Astor Thomen in *Doctors don't believe it* (New York, 1935, pp. 155-160):

1. That hay fever is contagious
2. That it is caused by goldenrod
3. That it occurs chiefly in so-called nervous people
4. That it is a disease of the eyes or nose

5. That there is such an ailment as "nose cold"
6. That the term "hay fever" is an accurate one
7. That it is a trivial matter
8. That it is spontaneously cured after seven years
9. That it is contracted as a result of the patient having lived in, or visited, a certain place
10. That it occurs most often in educated people; that diet is a factor in its causation
11. That it is caused by proximity to weeds, grasses, and trees when they are in bloom
12. That all are equally susceptible to it; that it cannot be cured
13. That it can be cured by a nasal operation.

THE HUMAN **HEART** IS SITUATED ON THE LEFT OF THE THORAX

The heart is situated in the *center,* immediately behind the breastbone and between the lungs; only the point is directed towards the left. If a line were to be drawn down the center of the chest to divide the heart into two parts, the slightly larger part would be found on the right side. This may dispose of a few strip cartoons or Hollywood movies which show the bullet "to the heart" oozing blood only on the left. Or it may not.

PITY MY BROKEN **HEART**

From about 1175 and from Chaucer's "Yet wole I telle it, though myn herte breste" (from *Troilus and Criseyde,* Book I) to the most banal pop song six hundred years later, hearts have been breaking, cracking ("My old heart is crack'd, is crack'd!" cried Lear), and wilting under the strain.

Which is odd, for the Elizabethans and Jacobeans regularly used the Greco-Roman notion of loving with the liver familiar since Homer. In *The merry wives of Windsor,* when Pistol is asked whether he loves Ford's wife, he replies: "With liver burning hot." But it's all in the mind, you know. When stimulated, the liver secretes bile, the heart pumps blood, and the brain "secretes" thoughts including those of love. It is a fallacy so longstanding as to be incapable of eradication that the heart can be tough, loyal, can be eaten or—best of all—that the woman who no longer seeks you out either "has no heart" or "has given it to somebody else." To say that nobody believes all this non-sense *literally* is beside the point: such errors and ambiguities lead to other woolly, uncritical thoughts, and then to grosser errors, such as a "patriotic" appeal to declare war, or to victimize racial minorities.

Heartburn is a pain totally unconnected with the heart, inciden-tally. It is caused by excess acid in the stomach, and can be relieved by taking in moderation an alkali such as bicarbonate of soda.

90 PERCENT OF BODY **HEAT** ESCAPES FROM YOUR HEAD

In addition to the common cold-related fallacies we have already discussed (see also COMMON COLD FALLACIES), there remains the widely held belief that wearing a hat and a scarf in cold weather is particularly crucial because, as we can all recite to ourselves in unison, "Most of your body heat escapes from your head."

However, like countless other phrases and conditions we are repeatedly exposed to all our lives and therefore inadvertently accept as fact, the truth here is in fact a lie. This former "truth" we speak of had been circulating untouched for at least half a century, until 2008, when a study published in the *British Medical Journal* proved all of us wrong: you do not actually lose more of your natural internal heat by having one part of your body exposed to cold weather conditions, instead of another.

When you think about it, it does seem somewhat arbitrary that the head would be the chosen exit from which heat flees the corporal vessel. The logic behind it has never really been explained, at least as far as we know. Perhaps it's because we humans have brains. These brains make us not only egotistical, but also (sometimes as a result of our egos), irrational. Maybe someone at some point thought: our brains are where we store all our information, and therefore they require more energy and more heat. So, when our heads are nakedly exposed to the cold, a lot more of our overall body heat is at jeopardy than it would be had we been walking around barefoot. Of course, this is only our personal stab at rationalizing the behavior and thinking of our fellow species.

The scientists of the above mentioned study figured out not why this theory makes sense, but at least were able to trace back to the origins of where it came from. Supposedly, the assertion that people first and foremost must wear hats in order to protect themselves from a hypothermic like state came from a US army manual survival guide in the 1970s. According to the guide, 40 to 45 percent of body heat escapes from your head. This information is thought to have come from a misdirected scientific experiment conducted by our fine military in the 1950s, in which subjects were put into "survival suits" and exposed to Arctic-like temperatures. As their heads were the only body parts left uncovered, the most heat was said to have escaped from that region.

In addition to the recent scientific studies proving that this is indeed not true, it is also worth noting in simple terms that had these subjects not been wearing gloves in arctic climates, the results probably would have shown the same amount of body heat escaping from their hands.

Also, the face, chest, and head are the most sensitive areas of the body, and therefore feel colder than other limbs when the harsh winter morning wind strikes them unshielded. But our degree of physical comfort is not always parallel with our inner biological workings and realities.

So, the next time that notorious all season, fashionable scarf wearer you know gets on a high horse about the utmost practicality of his or her extravagant neck accessories, go ahead and knock 'em back down with the cold hard facts.

Sources: Ian Sample, "Scientists Debunk the Myth that you Lose most Heat through your Head," *The Guardian*, 2008.

AS **HEAVY** AS LEAD

It is frequently believed, following the saying that something is "as heavy as lead," that lead must be the heaviest element. In fact, "heavy" is the wrong adjective to use in this context: the correct word is "dense." The densest element known, since its discovery in 1804, is in fact osmium (22-59 grams per cubic centimetre), so one should more accurately be saying "as dense as osmium."

Platinum, uranium and tungsten are also all "heavier than lead"!

HELEN OF TROY WAS ABDUCTED BY PARIS

"Everyone knows" that Helen, wife of Menelaus, was abducted by Paris. Andromache curses Helen with the words: "The beauty of your glance has brought/This rich and noble country to a shameful end."

In Euripides' *Trojan women* (lines 368 ff.), Cassandra states that the war was caused by the folly [a euphemism for the imperialistic zeal] of the Greeks, and Helen herself freely admits (1. 946) that she eloped with Paris of her own accord.

Vellacott sums up the situation thus: "Euripides shows how the precise interest of an intellectual theory, and the helpless anguish of a human being, both contribute to that Greek propensity for fixing the blame on some convenient scapegoat, which demonstrated itself in innumerable cruelties throughout Greek history and, as Thucydides observed, reached a new level of atrocity in the Peloponnesian War."

Source: Philip Vellacott, *Ironic drama: a study of Euripides' method and meaning* (Cambridge, 1975, pp. 136-46).

HICCUP CURES

Hiccups are a strange phenomenon. Less clear as to the functional purpose than burping, and even more mysterious as to what brings it on than sneezing, hiccups are one of a kind.

Hiccups seem to be as randomly brought on as they are eliminated. They are very difficult to have control over either. Although there is pretty much no scientifically sound way to get rid of the casual hiccup (rather than the actually more serious malignant/persistent hiccups following major operations), here is list of moderate to completely bizarre at home remedies people continue to stand by:

1. Stimulating the Nasopharynx

Basically, this is the part of the pharynx that is most connected to nasal cavities. These methods include: forcible tongue traction, gargling water, quickly swallowing sugar and/or ice cubes whole, and drinking liquid from the side of the glass further away from your mouth.

By doing any of these things, you supposedly have a chance of disrupting part of the "hiccup reflex arc." However, the source in which we are obtaining this obscure information from claims, the likelihood of any of these things actually curing hiccups is not high at all. This makes sense, as attempting to consume water in a way which will ensure that your beverage will "go down the wrong pipe" and/or gagging on an ice cube until it makes its way uncomfortably down your throat are not so much remedies as they are other problems that distract from the problem at hand. In other words, if your back hurts and you want it to go away, slapping yourself in the face is only going to move the pain elsewhere, in the hopes that once the secondary pain subsides, the original one will subside along with it.

2. Forced Constriction

Some other interesting techniques you can try to get rid of a pesky case of the hiccups consist of massaging or pressing on certain pressure points, nerves, and other unsuspecting regions of the body, such as the temples. Also, you can try popping your ears, as you would on an airplane when your sinuses begin to feel clogged. Moreover, you can press on your eyes until you see stars and hope you can still see properly when you open your eyes again.

How trying to make yourself pass out in one form or another is a healthy or effective way to cure hiccups we have no idea, and would have been utterly convinced the author of this article was pulling these out of his (excuse the profanity) ass, had he or she not provided an extensive list of credible sources listed for the information.

3. Digital Rectal Massage (Really? Really)
A personal favorite. Apparently, following a case report of a forty-year-old man finding relief in this remedy, select doctors who wrote up the report in an issue of *Canadian Family Physician* truly advocated that a good way to get rid of the hiccups is to, yes, massage your inner anus with your fingers (or with a catheter).

No witty comment necessary.

4. Ejaculation
We are still not joking. This may, along the lines of being "scared" out of the hiccups, interrupt the hiccup reflex by unexpectedly shocking the nervous system (pleasure and/or panic).

5. Holding your Breath or Breathing into a Paper Bag
This may lead to mild respiratory acidosis (or, getting high and delirious on your own carbon dioxide), but hey, if it'll make your hiccups go away so you don't sound like a drunken idiot while you're trying to hit on that pretty girl at the bar, all these tricks sound totally worth it to us.

Sources: NYU Medical Blog, *Clinical Correlations*, "Myths and Realities: Does Holding Your Breath Really Cure Hiccups?" Cindy Mui M.D., 2009; *The American Journal of Nursing*, "Hiccups," John J. Calabro; Medscape, Reference page; *Dictionary.com* for many of these clinical terms. Peleg R, Peleg A., "Case Report: Sexual intercourse as potential treatment for intractable hiccups," *Canadian Family Physician*, 2000.

HIBERNATION IS THE SAME FOR ALL ANIMALS
When we think of hibernation, we may equate it with certain animals going to sleep and staying asleep throughout the winter. When we see squirrels stocking up on acorns, or if we just simply see acorns scattered throughout the streets during the autumn months, we assume it is the season for these critters to prepare themselves for hibernation mode. They are going to stock up and eat all their food so they get fat enough to sleep through the winter without waking up. Similarly, whether we want to believe it or not, most of us tune into the news (or find out from friends who listened to the news) on Groundhog's Day to see whether the groundhog saw his shadow. If he does, we will not only have at least six more weeks of winter to

(Continued)

endure, but the groundhog will also go back into hibernation for the time being. Or at least that's what's implicit, right?

However, hibernation is different for certain animals. True, there are certain animals that do more or less lay down in the fall and don't emerge until the spring, for instance, the raccoon, skunk, chipmunk, hamster, and hedgehog. Also, certain bears have the blessing of hibernation worked into their yearly schedules.

But the animal whose hibernation tactics have as of late been proven to be slightly more complex than those of other animals is the black bear. Unlike other animals that go into hibernation, the black bear is able to survive for up to 100 days without eating, drinking, urinating, or exercising. Also, it can sleep for months with a body temperature of up to 88 degrees. This is notable because in most other animals, such as rodents, body temperatures can drop to anywhere from 40 to 32 degrees Fahrenheit during hibernation. Also, these smaller animals then must wake up every few days from their deep slumber in order to raise their body temperatures, eat the food they have stored, and empty their bowels.

A good amount of research is being conducted into how humans can benefit from the black bear's hibernation strategies. For instance, bears during hibernation are able to gain all the nutrients they need for survival from within their own bodies via fat cells breaking down to provide sufficient water and calories per day. Muscle and organ tissues provide protein. Human bodies react similarly in a situation where they are forced to survive without anything going into their bodies. However, our bodies cannot supply their own proteins from within.

If we figure out some way to imitate this, or apparently, to preserve organs for long enough that they are able to develop these functions, we may someday be able to hibernate too. So maybe next time you don't want to get out of bed to go to Jury Duty in the dead, dark of winter, channel the black bear.

Sources: Peter Tyson, "Bear Essentials of Hibernation," Peter Tyson, PBS Nova, 2000; Brian M. Barnes, "Freeze Avoidance in a Mammal: Body Temperatures Below 0 degrees Celsius in an Arctic Hibernator," *Science Magazine*, 1989.

A **HIGH BROW** IS THE SIGN OF INTELLIGENCE AND NOBLE BIRTH

The descriptions "highbrow" and "lowbrow" have recently been joined by "middlebrow" to indicate various levels of intellectual calibre: a "highbrow" journal, a "lowbrow" newspaper, a "middlebrow" radio program. The implication is that a low forehead is reminiscent of our remote apelike ancestor. Like all such assertions, it can be proved wrong only by testing. Karl Pearson and many others since have proved it wrong by testing. In his pioneering paper "Relationship of intelligence to size and shape of the head and other mental and physical characters" (*Biometrika,* 1906), Pearson reported the examination of head form in 1,010 students of the University of Cambridge, a further 2,200 schoolboys aged 12, and 2,100 other schoolboys. Having ascertained their intellectual levels from their teachers and scholastic records, he found no correlation whatsoever between head form and intelligence. Subsequent tests have supported Pearson. It is worth pointing out that the data collected by Pearson may not have been totally reliable individually, but *en masse* it is likely that variations and errors would have cancelled each other out.

HIPPOPOTAMI SWEAT BLOOD

From Biblical times to at least the nineteenth century (and who knows, beyond?), it has been popularly believed that the hippopotamus sweats blood. The view has been encouraged by popular magazines and by circus exhibitors.

What actually happens is that the hippo's skin secretes a reddish, oily liquid in warm weather. This makes the skin more resistant to water and possibly protects it from the air. This liquid is not blood, even if it looks like blood from a (safe) distance.

Source: Osmond P. Breland, *Animal facts and fallacies* (London, 1950).

HISTORICAL FALLACIES

These are numerous, and have been divided into three main types: fallacies of *inquiry,* including fallacies of question-framing, of factual verification, and of factual significance; fallacies of *explanation,* including those of generalization, narration, causation, motivation, composition, and false analogy; and fallacies of *argument,* including those of semantic distortion and substantive distraction. As David Hume ruefully asked, "When we run over libraries persuaded of these principles, what havoc must we make?"

D. H. Fischer has also identified five main types of fallacist's fallacy:

1. An argument which is structurally fallacious in some respect is therefore structurally false in all respects.

2. An argument which is structurally false in some respect, or even in every respect, is therefore substantively false in its conclusion.

3. The appearance of a fallacy in an argument is an external sign of its author's depravity.

4. Sound thinking is merely thinking which is not fallacious.

5. Fallacies exist independent of particular purposes and assumptions.

Source: David Hackett Fischer, *Historians' fallacies: toward a logic of historical thought* (New York, 1970).

HOCK IS A WINE FROM THE RHINE

Hock as a name for a German wine is an abbreviation for "hockamore," a garbled anglicism for Hochheimer, and otherwise known in Shakespeare as "Rhenish."

Hochheim, its place of origin, is actually on the river Main, however, and the growth of "Rhenish' to describe all the wines from Hochhein as well as from the Rhine valley is a common error.

Source: Ivor Brown, *I give you my word* (London, 1945).

HOLIST FALLACIES

The holist fallacy is the mistaken idea that a historian should select significant details from a sense of the whole thing. Though plausible at first glance, this would prevent a historian from knowing anything until he knows everything, which is both absurd and impossible.

The weakness of holism is best exemplified by the attack on Hegel's *Philosophy of history* in Bertrand Russell's *History of western philosophy* (London, 1945), pp. 743 and 745.

"The view of Hegel and of many other philosophers," writes Russell, is that the character of any portion of the universe is so profoundly affected by its relations to the other parts and to the whole, that no true statement can be made about any part except to assign its place in the whole. Thus there can be only one true statement; there is no truth except the whole truth . . . Now this is all very well, but it is open to an initial objection. If the above argument were sound, how could knowledge ever begin? I know numbers of propositions of the form "A is the father of B," but I do not know the whole universe. If all knowledge were knowledge of the universe as a whole there would be no knowledge. This is enough to make us suspect a mistake somewhere."

Hegel's work is so riddled with fallacies that D. H. Fischer, author of *Historians' fallacies* (New York, 1970), states that most of the fallacies in his book could be illustrated by [Hegel's] arguments. "All metahistorians, by definition, are guilty of this mistake—Toynbee, Spengler, Sorokin, Marx, Comte, Kant, Condorcet, Vico—and others who have tried to discover *the* "meaning" of *the* "past."

HITLER AND **HOLOCAUST** FALLACIES

1. Hitler Was in Love with a Jewish Woman Who Broke his Heart

There are, clearly, a great many theories as to why Hitler was the way he was and how he could have possibly committed the crimes against humanity that he did. Aside from psychological studies on his character that try to explain his anti-Semitism as a result of him being underappreciated as an artist, beaten by his father, or ostracized in school, there is another somewhat farfetched, though interesting, theory that Hitler's heart was broken in his youth by a Jewish woman whom he never got over. Supposedly, this served as a catalyst for his hatred of Jews.

Although this theory, like the others, can easily be disproved with the logic that the root of Hitler's problem was too deeply embedded in his character and neurological make-up to be ascribed to one external source or cause, there is something to be said for attempts at rationale.

According to a childhood friend of his, August Kubizek, Hitler in his youth had a teenage infatuation with a girl named Stefanie Isak. Kubizek does admit that Hitler's fixation on Stefanie was nothing serious, particularly as Hitler never actually spoke to her but only watched her from afar, interacting with the members of the bourgeoisie society he resented.

Turns out, Stefanie was not actually Jewish. The reason for the misperception likely comes from the fact that the name Isaac is of Hebrew origin. So, with this hard evidence at hand, we can all see why Kubizek decided to write an entire book under the assumption that Stephanie Isak was Jewish, right?

Nonetheless, this rumor is a bust, leaving the most valuable thing to take from the story a confirmation of how mentally unstable Hitler really was, in all areas of his life (he expressed elaborate fantasies about kidnapping the girl and committing suicide together, which he actually ended up doing in real life with his mistress Eva). To say his failed romances were the trigger for his behavior as leader of the Third Reich is to trivialize Nazi atrocities.

2. Hitler's Grandfather Was Jewish

This rumor is relatively widespread.

Adolf Hitler's father, Alois, was an illegitimate child, giving rise to the notion that Alois's father may have been Jewish. Hitler's paternal grandmother, Maria Schicklgruber, gave birth to Alois in 1837 without revealing the identity of the father. Five years later, she married a man named Johann Georg Hiedler,

(Continued)

209

and while a baptismal certificate was later issued declaring that this man was Hitler's real father, few historians believe this to be the truth. The certificate wasn't issued until 1873, when both Maria and Johann Hiedler were already dead, and it is most likely that Alois was behind this, in order to get an inheritance.

The rumors about Adolf's real paternal grandfather being Jewish really began in 1930, when, according to Hitler's former lawyer, Hans Frank, a relative of Hitler's threatened to black-mail him with evidence of his Jewish heritage. Frank investigated, and found that Maria (his maternal grandmother) had been working as a cook for a wealthy Jewish family named Frankenberger at the time of Alois's birth. This family had a 19 year old son, who possibly could have gotten Maria pregnant.

However, there is no evidence proving that Maria Schicklgruber ever lived in Graz, where she was said to have worked for this family. Hans Frank got his information about Hitler's Jewish heritage from a distant relative of Hitler's, who had claimed to have proof of a correspondence between Maria and the Frankenberger family. However, no concrete documentation of these exchanges ever emerged, making it fair to conclude that the identity of Hitler's maternal grandfather will forever remain a mystery, and that anyone who claims to be Hitler's distant relative is probably either evil or insane.

3. Hitler's Mother Was Killed by a Jewish Doctor

Yet another theory as to where Hitler developed his warped worldview is based on the notion that his mother was killed by a Jewish doctor. Though the family did have a Jewish doctor while in Austria, Dr. Eduard Bloch, who treated Klara Hitler for breast cancer (of which she died in 1907), Bloch testified that Hitler had no resentful feelings for the doctor at all despite his closeness with his mother.

In fact, Hitler seemed to consider Bloch as a kind of exception. Hitler sent Bloch postcards, his artwork as gifts, holiday wishes, as a token of his gratitude for all he had done for his mother. In 1937, Hitler called Bloch an *Eleljude*, "noble Jew" and he said if all Jews were like him, there would be no "Jewish question."

The yellow star was removed from Dr. Bloch's home and he was allowed to remain there until 1938, when his family was also allowed the privilege to leave Austria. Although they were not allowed to keep their life savings, they were clearly not treated in the cruel and inhumane manner that other Jewish families and individuals were under Hitler's rule.

So, even though Hitler's mother died while under Bloch's care, Hitler decidedly did not harbor any resentful feelings towards the faithful family doctor.

4. The Germans Made Soap from Jewish Bodies

Rumors circulated throughout concentration camps and elsewhere in central Europe that the Nazis were taking fat bodies of murdered Jewish people in order to produce soap bars.

The rumors suggesting that Germans manufactured soap from humans is traced back at least to French anti-German propaganda in the early stages of World War I. The rumor related specifically to the use of the bodies of Jewish people for this likely spread by word of mouth to concentration camps in the early 1940s. However, there is no evidence in the form of old shipping bills, receipts for economic transactions, or physical remains in manufacturing plants, as there was to prove that gold teeth and hair was taken from Jewish bodies and sold. Additionally, there is documentation of Heinrich Himmler (*Reichsführer* of the SS, military commander, and top member of the Nazi party) sending word to the head of the Gestapo, Heinrich Muller, stating that Jewish bodies must be burned or buried at the camps and that nothing else should be done with the deceased, as Americans were becoming suspicious that the soap rumor was true.

Furthermore, despite the fact that holocaust survivors and some other researchers have claimed that the blue bar soap presented at camps, stamped with the letters RIF for Reich Industry Fat or PJF for Pure Jewish Fat, DNA tests run on the soap flakes have found no trace of human fat or other body parts in the products.

5. Germans Used Jewish Bones to Pave the *Autobahn*

This one is patently false. While the Germans did in two specific instances crush bones of Jewish people who had been killed during the holocaust, neither instance was for the purpose of paving the *Autobahn*.

The two instances were as such: first, in the operation Reinhard death camps of Belzec, Sobibor, and Treblinka in Poland. Second, bone crushing took place in the former Soviet blocs, Latvia, Estonia, Ukraine, Belarus, and Lithuania, where German police detachments called *Einsatzgruppen* shot thousands of Jews and buried them in shared massive graves. As the Germans began to realize that they might not be able to win the war in the East against Russia, they began hiding evidence of the Holocaust. Thus, exhumation crews were sent to these territories to dig up the graves, burn bodies and crush bones in order to erase all

(Continued)

physical evidence of the crimes. A specialized machine was used to crush the bones down into fine powder, after which the debris, along with the ashes, were re-buried.

That said, there is still no evidence that these remains were ever used in the making of the Autobahn, the highway system planned by Hitler to span throughout Germany. The building of the Autobahn began in the 1930s, but was stopped during the war period, only to be resumed in the 1950s.

Sources: "Holocaust Misconceptions," Illinois Holocaust Museum and Education Center; August Kubizek, *The Young Hitler I Knew*, 2006, London; Andrew Roberts, "Hitler's Secret Jewish Girlfriend," Daily Mail UK News, 2006; "Was Hitler Part Jewish?" *The Straight Dope*.

"HOME, SWEET HOME" IS A BRITISH SONG

The words are by the American John Howard Payne, and the music by Sir Henry Bishop taken from a Sicilian air. The song was first heard in the opera *The maid of Milan,* first produced at Covent Garden in 1823.

HOMEOPATHIC REMEDIES FOR ILLNESS

1. Aromatherapy

The fact that sulphur has a smell generally considered unpleasant, and roses have a smell-range generally considered pleasant must not lead one to the arbitrary conclusion that one's health or temperament can be changed by exposure to a particular smell.

Benjamin Walker, in his Encyclopedia of metaphysical medicine (London, 1978), does however draw this conclusion. For Mr. Walker, eau-de-cologne creates a mood of purity, musk a mood of sensuality, cloves a mood of suspicion and slander, and bergamot a mood of meditation and piety.

A moment's reflection will show that no amount of bergamot will affect a burlesque show on Broadway, and no amount of eau-de-cologne will change the course of an adulterous affair.

2. Electric Homoepathy

Less than a century ago, the name of Count Cesare Mattei was celebrated in the field of European medicine. The journalist W. T. Stead tirelessly promoted Mattel's activities, as did Commissioner Booth-Tucker of the Salvation Army, and Lady Paget, in an organ as reputable as the *National Review*. Mattei was praised by all but orthodox doctors for his new methods, which he claimed were a direct advance on the homoeopathic remedies of S. C. F. Hahnemann.

Mattei clinics were established in France and Britain. His *Nouveau guide pratique de l'électro-homoeopathie* (Nice, 1881) was followed by the equally influential *Médecine électro-homéopathique* (Nice, 1883), which I have read with growing incomprehension. The book purports to be a kind of user's manual to a series of herbal concoctions. Much of it is in the form of a dictionary of ailments, each of which (from infertility to bronchitis) can be cured by the internal or external application of a combination of remedies. There are 31 from which to permutate, five liquids *(liquides électriques)* and 26 in the form of pills.

The pages at the end of Mattel's manual are crammed with lists of successful treatments, just like advertisements in the crank naturopathy magazines today. Thus, Signora Gualdi, a Roman, was said to have been cured of breast cancer (4 April 1869–6 June 1870); one Signora Zoboli was cured of cancer of the uterus by C pills; and the Bolognese Signora Bagnoli was also cured of cancer of the uterus.

Mattel's "treatments" were eventually proved worthless. The herbal remedies were discarded, and the all-purpose "electricity" silently vanished from much of the homoeopathic literature. "We no longer believe," as J. A. C. Brown observes in the *Pears medical encyclopaedia* (London, 1965), "that electricity has some magic effect upon neurasthenia or insomnia, nor is it usually accepted that electric shocks applied to a paralysed nerve speed its recovery—although it may prevent the muscles supplied by the nerve from wasting while healing is taking place spontaneously."

3. Floritherapy

Flowers are the "quintessence of nature," according to Edward Bach in *Heal thyself* (London, 1931). From this meaningless aphorism, Bach drew the fallacious conclusion that it is possible to work out a system relating flowers to human moods, unwilling to recognize the fact that every human being is an individual.

Furthermore, according to Bach, there is practically no disease that cannot be cured by flowers and no mood that cannot be evoked by them. He is thus not only a bad logician but also a quack doctor.

Here in alphabetical order are some of the flowers recommended by Edward Bach, together with the properties that he assigns to them. There have been, and still are, other floritherapists, but there is no full agreement as to the flower required to treat ailments or to evoke moods. According to Bach, anemones provoke small worries, the azalea induces fickleness, clematis inspires courage, the cornflower produces staidness and sobriety, dandelions (and marigolds) provoke jealousy, the hyacinth suspicion, the iris indifference, the lilac trouble, and the pansy flightiness. The petunia arouses anger, the sunflower aids falseness, and the sweet pea inspires conservative attitudes, so beware of the trade unionist who specializes in sweet peas, petunias and sunflowers.

Madeleine Kingsley's hilarious article on Mrs Kaye McInnes, making "Exultation of Flowers" in the Scottish Highlands, appeared in *Radio Times,* July 30–August 5, 1977. Since the death of her husband in 1975 Mrs McInnes has been the sole distiller, packager and supplier of the "100 per cent water without herbal or chemical ingredients" to 28,000 customers "from Israel to Alaska." Not only does Mrs McInnes attempt to coax from plants in her garden "electrical impulses in stable suspension," but she sells them *in water* at "a price that just keeps the operation ticking over." "Her claim is that "at least 38 different flower radiations' concentrates go into each bottle: sunflowers, periwinkle, white clover, potentilla, Star of Bethlehem . . . Every creature on earth, you see, gives out its own unique cosmic radiations, invisible wavelengths if you like."

Elizabeth Bellhouse, a Somerset lady, produces a healing water and ointment of a type similar to that of Mrs McInnes. Her "Vita Florum" is alleged to heal all ills, from lassitude in canaries to gangrene in human beings and, in her words, "takes precedence over all the presently known and acknowledged laws of chemistry, physics and biology." Unlike Mrs McInnes, Miss Bellhouse does not glean her ingredients from her own garden, but travels around Europe under "the divine guidance of the Virgin Mary," with whom she is apparently in quite frequent touch.

4. Homeopathy

A cult purporting to be of medical significance. It was invented by Samuel Christian Hahnemann and first adumbrated in his *The Organon* (1810). The name of the cult is contrasted with *allopathy,* a term coined by Hahnemann to describe the treatment of disease by drugs having effects opposite to the symptoms, in other words, orthodox medicine.

Homoeopathy depends on the inaccurate belief that an overdose of quinine (for the treatment of malaria) causes symptoms like those of malaria. He therefore argued that small doses of a drug cure symptoms like those that larger doses would cause. Homoeopathic drugs are diluted by trituration with milk sugar. A 1:10 mixture is finely ground and a fresh 1:10 mixture with sugar is made of the resultant powder. At the 30th such dilution or "potency" there is one part of drug to 10^{30} parts of milk sugar, so that it is only by something like a miracle if the patient gets even a single molecule of the drug. Hahnemann's other teachings included the statement that seven-eighths of all chronic diseases are variations of psora, commonly known as the itch.

The cult spread rapidly across Europe in the 1820s, reached England and America in the 1840s, when it was the subject of Oliver Wendell Holmes' *Homeopathy and kindred delusions* (1842) and by 1900 there were twenty-two homoeopathic "colleges" in the United States. Now there are no specifically homoeopathic colleges though New York Medical College and the Hahnemann Medical College in Philadelphia still offer graduate courses in the subject. Misleadingly, some excellent doctors call themselves "homoeopathic" to indicate their lack of faith in all drugs; this attitude is healthily skeptical, but rare. The cult's leading journal is *The Journal of the American Institute of Homeopathy*.

5. Honey Is a Powerful Curative

Honey is a compound of about 76.5 percent sugar and about 23 percent water, with traces of minerals and vitamins but in insignificant quantities. That fact does not prevent cranks from claiming honey as a curative for all kinds of illness and disease, as well as an aphrodisiac. Benjamin Walker, in his *Encyclopedia of metaphysical medicine* (London, 1978), affirms that "Honey, from the honey bee, used both as a food and drink, is regarded as a superlative sex invigorator, especially if mixed with pepper," despite a total absence of evidence for the absurd fallacy.

But those with honey bees in their bonnet will fly straight for a book which will apparently make solid their wildest fantasies. Cecil Tonsley's *Honey for health* (London, 1969) goes so far as to report without irony an allegation that a gangrened foot had been cured by tying it inside a bag of honey. No medical explanation is offered for the purported miracle. Needless to say.

6. Naturopathy

A medical cult not to be confused with the simplicity of diet and regular exercise which it recommends in common with orthodox medicine. Naturopaths believe that the body will keep naturally healthy instead of having to cope with unnatural foods, customs, and medicines. They object to food grown with the aid of artificial fertilizers, yet it is farming (the systematic interference with nature to provide food) together with similar methods of adapting environment to needs which has enabled man to survive in competition with creatures that possess wings, claws, power, bulk or speed. As to avoiding medicines, the chemists have yet to produce anything as lethal as the "natural" poisons of some medicinal plants. All chemicals (to which naturopaths illogically object) are made from naturally-occurring raw materials.

Naturopathy had no single founder, but grew up as an anti-scientific reaction to the gradual development of drugs in eighteenth- and nineteenth-century Europe. An early U.S. pioneer was the Seventh Day Adventist John H. Kellogg, and even now Adventism stresses nature therapy.

Though numerous books and magazines testify to the extremism of most naturopaths, nothing has yet equalled the great five-volume *Encyclopaedia of physical culture* (1912), by Bernarr Macfadden, with its injunctions against the internal use of drugs and medicine and against consulting orthodox doctors. Most suggested cures involve diets, exercises, and water therapy; cancer for instance should be treated by fasting, exercises, and a "vitality building regimen." Macfadden subsequently recanted his views on cancer (he now believes that it can be cured by a diet consisting solely of grapes).

Sources: Peter Wingate, *The Penguin medical encyclopedia* (2nd ed., Harmondsworth, 1976); and Martin Gardner, *Fads and fallacies in the name of science* (New York, 1957); Martin Gardner, *Fads and fallacies in the name of science* (New York, 1957); and Peter Wingate, *The Penguin medical encyclopedia* (2nd ed., Harmondsworth, 1976).

HONG-KONG IS A CITY IN CHINA

Hong-Kong is not quite a city in China, nor is it a separate country. It is somewhere in between: most basically, a city-state.

The island of Hong-Kong was colonized by the British during the First Opium War in the late 1830s/early 1840s, and extended into other surrounding territories throughout the remainder of the century. Though briefly occupied by Japan after WWII, the British regained control over Hong-Kong commons until 1997 when sovereignty was given to China. Hong-Kong was then made a special administrative region (SAR) of the People's Republic of China.

Hong-Kong, unlike the different countries of the EU and different states in the US, has a different currency than China. It is allowed a separate constitution called Basic Law and it is able to have a separate governing body. Both SARs in China (Hong-Kong and Macau) are responsible for all of their own issues except for issues like national defense.

This degree of independence while still remaining "part" of China was designed somewhat uniquely for the two SARs in China, under the theory "one country, two systems."

HORSE FALLACIES

1) Human Life Is Impossible Without the Horse

"Without the horse, there could have been no culture; our cities would have remained unpaved; there could have been no civilisation, even life would have been impossible." This theory commits the fallacy of exaggeration.

2) A Galloping Horse Always Has At Least One Hoof on the Ground

It is astounding that the fallacy should have survived the demonstration of about 1878 by the photographer Eadweard Muybridge (1830-1904, an Englishman who emigrated to the U.S.A. in 1852) which actually culminated in a book, called *Animal locomotion* (11 vols., Philadelphia, 1887). Every so often the newspapers publish photographs which again demonstrate this well-known fact. The difficulty is that the tiny fraction of a second when all four feet are off the ground cannot be detected by the human eye unaided.

Source: Peter Pollack, *The picture history of photography* (London, 1963, p. 225.); Urbain Gohier, *Pour être sages* (Paris, 1914).

DRINKING **HOT TEA** COOLS THE BODY

A very widespread fallacy, which was exploded by Dr Leonard Williams, in the London *Evening Standard* of May 25, 1922, among others. It derives from the relative coolness we feel shortly after *raising* the temperature by drinking hot tea. The drinking of hot tea during a heat wave might in fact cause heat stroke if one were already very near to heat stroke. Drink cold water (but not too much or too quickly) in a heat wave. Cold water absorbs heat as we drink it, as its temperature has to be raised in our system from say 60°F to 98.5°F, our blood temperature. Thus, the drinking of a half a pint of cold water at 60°F absorbs 24 British thermal units, a usefully large amount of heat.

IN BRITAIN **HUMAN RIGHTS** BEGIN AT BIRTH

The Congenital Disabilities Act 1976 invested the human foetus with sufficient status in law to sue if it is born alive but damaged.

This is quite a significant piece of legislation, because it is estimated that around a thousand children are born handicapped in the "U.K. each week. The causes include radiation, drugs, diseases during pregnancy, pollution, and the genetic shortcomings of the parents. Parents will now take greater care, it is hoped, of the unborn child.

APPRECIATING THE **HUMANITIES** NECESSARILY MAKES ONE MORE HUMANE

The traditional defense of the humanities in schools, colleges, and universities is that they widen and deepen our sympathies. The late F. R. Leavis of Cambridge passionately advocated English studies as the core of any syllabus in order to strengthen these sympathies and Henry Sidgwick saw the function of literary study as the apprehension of "noble, subtle and profound thoughts, refined and lofty feelings," seeing in literature the "source and essence of a truly humanizing culture." The argument runs that we shall be more humane after we have absorbed Dostoevsky's *Crime and punishment* and Goethe's *Faust*. Matthew Arnold's idea of poetry as a vital substitute for religious dogma found its 20th-century parallel in Leavis's view of the study of English literature as the "central humanity."

In some instances this may be so, but George Steiner is only one of many skeptics: "The simple yet appalling fact is that we have very little solid evidence that literary studies do very much to enrich or stabilize moral perception, that they *humanize*. We have little proof that a tradition of literary studies in fact makes a man more humane. What is worse—a certain body of evidence points the other way. When barbarism came to twentieth-century Europe, the arts faculties in more than one university offered very little moral resistance, and this is not a trivial or local accident. In a disturbing number of cases the literary imagination gave servile or ecstatic welcome to political bestiality. That bestiality was at times enforced and refined by individuals educated in the culture of traditional humanism. Knowledge of Goethe, a delight in the poetry of Rilke, seemed no bar to personal and institutionalized sadism."

Sources include: George Steiner, *Language and silence* (London, 1967).

THE **HUNDRED YEARS' WAR** LASTED FOR A HUNDRED YEARS

It might seem obvious to call a war by the length of time from beginning to end, but the Hundred Years' War between England and France lasted from 1337, in the reign of Edward III (the first action being a naval battle off Sluys), until 1453, in the reign of Henry VI (the last action being the battle of Castillon). The cause of the "war," which was really an interrupted sequence of shorter wars, was the claim by England to the crown of France. The result was that the English were expelled from the whole of France except Calais.

"HUSBAND" ORIGINALLY MEANT A MARRIED MAN

When Sir John Paston wrote to his mother, in 1475, that "I purpose to leeffe alle heer, and come home to you and be your hosbonde and balyff," he was merely using the term "husband" in its true sense of a man who managed a household, as its head. *Hus* is the Anglo-Saxon for "house" and "bondi" the Old Norse for "freeholder" or "yeoman."

We retain the original sense of the word in the verb "to husband" (*sc.* one's resources) and the abstract noun "husbandry." A husband need not be married at all.

I

"If our aim is never to succumb to falsehood, it would be prudent for us to abstain from using language altogether. Our behavior might still be hesitant or misguided but it is only with the use of language that truth and error, certainty and uncertainty, come fully upon the scene."
—A. J. AYER, *The problem of knowledge*
(Harmondsworth, 1956, p. 52)

"If one understands principle clearly, one will be happy to follow it. One's first task, then, is to investigate principle to the utmost. It does not matter whether one does it through study, reading books, investigating history, or handling human affairs, and it does not matter whether one studies one thing deductively or many things inductively." When enough effort has been made, one will achieve a thorough understanding. When that is done, one will see the distinction between right and wrong and abandon all superstitious beliefs in spiritual beings and immortals."
—*Reflections on things at hand: the neo-Confucian anthology* (New York, 1967)

ICING ALWAYS HELPS HEAL INJURIES

No, we're not talking about putting a Smirnoff Ice in your glove compartment so that your buddy in the passenger seat will have to find some way to get down on one knee and chug it on the way to an event he should probably be sober for.

That being acknowledged, when you bump your lip on something and it swells up, or when you fall down and scrape your knee, the solution, if not a band-aid or a hospital run, is too often to put ice on it. Likewise, during sports injuries, where lots of swelling in a specific area occurs right away, icepacks are the number one go to.

Is icing always the best solution? In most cases, yes. Icing helps prevent rapid blood flow into surrounding vessels at the site of injury. This prevents the injury from getting worse, and probably reduces pain as well.

But not always. According to one study by Cleveland neuro-inflammation researchers, icing after injuries may actually hinder the healing process of swollen sites on bodies. The findings indicate that in some major physical traumas such as muscle injuries after chemical infection, freezing, and taking certain medications, inflammation is necessary for improvement.

The inflamed cells were found to produce high levels of a hormone called an IGF-1 (insulin-like growth factor), which notably increases the rate of muscle regeneration after injury. Therefore, logically speaking, too much reduction of swelling via ice or other anti-inflammatory methods may slow down the natural recovery process.

All in all, icing is probably the best method to use in typical sports injuries, such as a sprained ankle or bruised bone, but not so much in the case of chemical spills or muscle trauma that has been inflamed and moreover, problematic, for more than just one game out of the season. In the latter case, at least you will have an excuse to put a Smirnoff ice in your friend's shower before the early morning ski trip you're going to miss out on.

Sources: "Swelling Turned on Its Head: Why Putting Ice on an Injury may Prevent Healing," *Daily Mail Newspaper,* UK, 2010; Courtney Humphries, "When to Ice and Heat an Acute Injury," *Boston Globe,* 2010.

THE WORD **"IDIOT"** ORIGINALLY MEANT "MENTALLY DEFECTIVE"

The Greek *idiótes* denotes a private person, as opposed to someone fulfilling a public office. But, in ancient Greece, it was considered indispensable for the individual to obtain experience of public life, as part of his education. Those unqualified to take part in public life, whether mentally incapable, or simply untaught, were known as "idiots."

English writers understood the word in its original sense right up until the seventeenth century, Jeremy Taylor (1613-67), who was at Caius College, Cambridge, wrote for example: "It is clear, by Bellarmine's confession, that S. Austin [*sc.* Augustine] affirmed that the plain places of Scripture are sufficient to all laics, and all *idiots* or private persons" *(A dissuasive from Popery).*

FRANCIS BACON'S **IDOLA**

Bacon dealt with fallacies in many of his works, not always consistently. The definitive statement of his views is to be found in the

Novum organon as edited (with notes) by T. Fowler (Oxford, 1878), an editor who usefully compares the *idola* of Francis Bacon with the *offendicula* of Roger Bacon.

The *eidolon* in Plato is the transient image of a real thing (*Republic,* vii, 516A) and Bacon uses the word to denote the false notion of a thing, or an erroneous manner of regarding it. Bacon identifies four types of *eidolon* or *idolon,* two ineradicable from the human mind, a third creeping almost undetectably into the mind, and a fourth imposed from outside the mind.

The first category consists of *idola tribus,* or "idols of the tribe," that is to say those fallacies which are accepted by the whole of humanity or at any rate by a large segment of it.

Bacon illustrates this tendency with the following errors: that of assuming a greater order, purpose or regularity in nature than there actually is; the tendency to generalize from a small number of cases; the belief that man is the measure of the universe; and the tendency to support an assumption by quoting affirmative instances and omitting all negative instances.

The *idola specus,* or "idols of the cave," are errors incidental to the peculiar mental or bodily constitution of each individual, so that his view of things is distorted by his individual circumstances. Errors of this type include the disposition to regard as perfect only what is new or only what is old. Bacon warns every student of nature to "take this as a rule, that whatever his mind seizes and dwells upon with particular satisfaction is to be held in suspicion."

Idola fori, or "idols of the market-place," are the fallacies arising from the influence exercised over mind by mere words. Some words are names for non-existent things which are supposed to exist because they possess a name. Others are names abstracted from a few objects and applied recklessly to all that has the faintest connection or analogy with these objects, thereby causing widespread and lasting confusion.

Idola theatri, or "idols of the theatre," are fallacious modes of thinking which result from received systems of philosophy and from erroneous methods of demonstration. Bacon takes as an example the "sophistical" philosophy of Aristotle which forces nature into abstract schemata and explains by definitions; the "empirical" philosophers whom he attacks for jumping to conclusions from experiments which are too few in number and too limited in extent; and the "superstitious" philosophers who corrupt philosophy by the introduction of theological and poetic notions.

SULLY ON **ILLUSIONS**

In *Illusions: a psychological study* (London, 1881), James Sully devotes twelve chapters to: the study of illusions; the classification of illusions; illusions of perception (four chapters); dreams; illusions of introspection; other quasi-presentative illusions: errors of insight; illusions of memory; illusions of belief; results. On the connection between fallacy and illusion, Sully states: "No sharp line can be drawn between much of what, on the surface, looks like immediate knowledge, and consciously derived or inferred knowledge. On its objective side, reasoning may be roughly defined as a conscious transition of mind from certain facts or relations of facts to other facts or relations recognized as similar. According to this definition a fallacy would be a hasty, unwarranted transition to new cases not identical with the old ... Illusion becomes identified at bottom with fallacious inference."

THE HUMAN SOUL IS **IMMORTAL**

Nothing that we know is *immortal;* some things just last longer than others, but there is no guarantee at all that the universe itself is immortal. One of the most fallacious "proofs" of the immortality of the human soul was made by the British physicists Balfour Stewart and Peter Guthrie Tait. The following paraphrase of a characteristic extract from their *The unseen universe* (1875), a bestseller of popular science in the late 1870s and 1880s, has been made by E. Temple Bell.

"Matter is made up of molecules (size A), which are vortex-rings composed of luminiferous ether. The luminiferous ether itself is made up of much smaller molecules (size B), which are vortex-rings in a second or sub-ether. Call these smaller molecules and the sub-ether in which they are embedded the Unseen Universe.

The human soul exists in the Unseen Universe. It is made up of the smaller molecules (size B). In life it permeates the body like a subtile gas. The thoughts we think in life are accompanied by vibrating motions of the molecules (size A) of the brain. These motions undulate through the material universe. But, by the conservation of energy, part of these motions will be absorbed by the molecules (size B) of the soul. Therefore the soul has memory. On the dissolution of the body the soul with its memory intact becomes a free agent in the sub-ether. The physical possibility of the immortality of the soul is thus demonstrated."

As E. Temple Bell writes, in *The search for truth* (London, 1935): "Had these daring theorizers taken the trouble to doubt their *assumptions* about the atoms they might have proceeded with less enthusiasm to their truly remarkable *proof... Pick the assumptions to pieces till the stuff they are made of is exposed to plain view* —this is the cardinal rule for understanding the basis of our beliefs."

IT IS ILLEGAL TO **IMPERSONATE** A LIVING MEMBER OF THE ROYAL FAMILY ON THE BRITISH STAGE

Oddly enough this idea persists years after the restrictions were lifted (1968). Queen Elizabeth the Queen Mother was legally impersonated by Amanda Reiss in Royce Ryton's *Crown matrimonial* which opened at London's Haymarket Theatre on 19 October 1972.

INDIAN INK COMES FROM INDIA

The *Oxford English Dictionary* defines "India ink" or "Indian ink" as "a black pigment made in China and Japan sold in sticks; understood to consist of lampblack made into a paste with a solution of gum and dried. More accurately called *China ink.*"

It is not clear how the designation "Indian" arose, but Pepys used it in his diary entry for November 5, 1665: "Mr Evelyn, who . . . showed me most excellent painting in little, in distemper, India incke, water colors."

THE POPE OF THE ROMAN CATHOLIC CHURCH CLAIMS TO BE **INFALLIBLE**

Roman Catholics weary of repeating that this has never been the case. The statement of infallibility was first made at the Vatican Council of 1870, but refers only to occasions when the Pope speaks *ex cathedra,* that is from the Chair of St. Peter (metaphorically, of course; the chair on which he sits is several centuries later). In fact, there has so far been no occasion when he has proclaimed *ex cathedra,* so there has been no case in which the claim has been reasserted since 1870. Another fallacy is that infallibility began to operate only in 1870: it was predated to St. Peter himself. Laymen who point to the corruption and wickedness of certain popes are guilty of another fallacy: the Pope does not claim to be *impeccable.* Source: Catholic Truth Society, London.

INFLUENZA IS A NEW DISEASE

The pandemic of 1918-9 killed some twenty million, most of them as a result of pneumonia or other complications, and it was perhaps the scale of that pandemic that persuaded most people that the disease is a product of the 20th century. Influenza (Italian, "influence") was given its present name in 1741, but had been known earlier under other names, such as *grippe.*

As early as 1797, in *Medical and vulgar errors refuted,* John Jones ridiculed the fallacy that "the influenze . . . is a very dangerous distemper, and a new one; never known in this country till a few years ago." "It is neither a new nor a dangerous distemper," snorted the good Dr. Jones.

Source: Charles Creighton, *History of epidemics in Britain* (vol. 2, Cambridge, 1894, p. 304).

ASSOCIATION WITH THE INSANE LEADS TO **INSANITY**

"Another popular fallacy, often confidently asserted in the press, is the pernicious effect of association with the insane. According to this theory, those who nurse and attend the alienated must in time become unbalanced. There is no evidence for this belief. Doctors and nurses attached to mental hospitals are specially trained, and their insight into the abnormal mind is, if anything, a protection against contagion."

Source: Dr. George Somerville, in *New Health* (October 1929).

COUNTING SHEEP IS AN EFFECTIVE WAY TO FIGHT **INSOMNIA**

Who hasn't, in the midst of some sleepless night, tried to picture sheep leaping over a fence one by one, convinced that it would eventually put your mind right to rest? What a better way to dull all anxious, unsettled feelings and thoughts from the day before or in anticipation of days to come than to focus on imaginary farm animals in single file instead? That's the idea, or, lack thereof.

Sadly, this falling asleep method hardly ever seems to work. Why? Precisely because trying to stay engaged in this closed-eye sheep scenario while also possessing a regularly functioning, active mind, is simply too boring. According to a survey conducted by Oxford University scientists on this topic, it is actually most ineffective to attempt to count sheep while falling asleep. Instead, insomniac subjects, when asked to imagine scenes like waterfalls and beaches, fell asleep roughly twenty minutes before their usual sleep time.

These scientists concluded that a good explanation for these findings is that while counting sheep is boring and thus difficult to focus on, the "tranquil" landscape scenes are more engaging. Another theory suggests that counting sheep takes too little brain power, while conjuring up a whole elaborate environment might take more energy, and thus produce fatigue and sleep sooner.

So, in a sense, it seems as though creativity matters even when falling asleep. So stop regurgitating the same conversations you had with your boss or your boyfriend that day, and start building your own indoor city.

Sources: Anahad O'Connor, "The Claim: Counting Sheep Helps you Fall Asleep," *Really?* Blog, *The New York Times*, 2010; "Counting Sheep Keeps you up," BBC News, 2002.

C. G. JUNG AND **INTROVERT** AND EXTRAVERT

Frieda Fordham, in *An introduction to Jung's psychology* (Harmondsworth, 1956), describes how "Jung's division of people into extraverts and introverts has already come to be widely known, if not fully understood." But this division did not originate with Jung at all. In *Sense and nonsense in psychology* (Harmondsworth, 1958), H. J. Eysenck is at pains to state: "It would be wrong to credit Jung with the discovery of this personality dimension. The very terms extraversion and introversion can be found as far back as the sixteenth century, and in more modern times the English psychologist Jordan and the Austrian psychiatrist Gross both anticipated Jung in putting forward theories very similar to his." Eysenck's list of typical introverts includes Hamlet, Sherlock Holmes, Robespierre, Savonarola, Spinoza, Cassius, John Stuart Mill, the March Hare, Sir Stafford Cripps, Faust, Cato the Elder, Don Quixote, and Kant. Examples of extraverts are Mr. Pickwick, Bulldog Drummond, Boswell, Mr. Punch, Caliban, Dumas, Donald Duck, Churchill, Pepys, Cicero, Falstaff, and Toad of Toad Hall.

It is only fair to Jung to stress that he also postulated the existence of a continuum from extraversion to introversion on which all human beings could be placed. The extravert is a person valuing the outer world in its material and immaterial aspects (wealth and the goods it can buy; power and the influence it can bring), who makes friends easily, and who tends to trust others. The introvert tends to distrust his fellow-man, makes friends only with great difficulty, and spends much of his energy in mental and intellectual exercise.

IRIDOLOGY

This fallacy, also known as iridiagnosis, is still widely practiced, despite the availability of such expository texts as Henry Lindlahr's *Iridiagnosis and other diagnostic methods* (1917) and Bernard Jensen's equally intriguing *Science and practice of iridology* published from the Hidden Valley Health Ranch, Escondido, California, in 1952.

Iridology was founded by a Budapest doctor called Ignaz Peczely, who published a book in 1880. Lindlahr's account is that Peczely founded the science of iridology at the age of ten when he broke an owl's foot. "Gazing straight into the owl's large, bright eyes," explains Lindlahr in presumably hushed tones, "he noticed at the moment when the bone snapped, the appearance of a black spot in the lower central region of the iris, which area he later found to correspond to the location of the broken leg." One will not insult the reader's intelligence by asking searching questions of this hearsay testimony of a ten-year-old's opinion of an owl's broken foot. But it is worth asking, as Martin Gardner feels obliged to ask, in *Fads and fallacies in the name of science* (2nd ed., New York, 1957), why J. Haskell Kritzer, in his *Textbook of iridiagnosis* (5th ed., 1921), feels it necessary to explain how to recognize artificial eyes, so that long diagnoses of these cause no embarrassment!

Iridology is based on the fallacy that the iris is divided into some forty "zones" running clockwise in one eye and anticlockwise in the other, and that these zones are connected by nerve filaments to various parts of the body. These filaments are, however, not detectable by anatomists. Iridiagnosticians claim to be able to diagnose disease by looking at spots on the eyes, called for some reason "lesions."

A fashionable word in current iridology is "sanpaku," immortalized in Sakurasawa Nyoti's *You are all sanpaku* (New York, 1970). The feeling is that, if you check the state of your iris in time, you may be able to convert your diet to MACROBIOTICS and thus prevent premature decease. "Sanpaku" is a condition in which the white of the eye is visible between the lower lid and the pupil, denoting serious physical and/or spiritual illness. "Sanpaku" sufferers sleep badly, have difficulty in thinking, bad memories, and sexual impotence.

THE AURORA **ISLANDS** LIE SOUTHEAST OF THE FALKLAND ISLANDS

The islands, first discovered by the *Aurora* in 1762, reported again by the *Princess,* Captain Manuel de Oyarvido, in 1790, and by other vessels at various dates including the Spanish surveying vessel *Atrevida* in 1794, and recorded on all charts of the South Atlantic until the 19th century, do not exist.

Neither do Saxemberg Island, 600 miles NW of Tristan da Cunha; the Belcher Islands "in Hudson Bay"; S. Brandan's Isle to the west of the Azores; or Mayda, shown in the middle of the Bay of Biscay on a map published in Chicago as recently as 1906.

It is by no means a simple case of an island's temporarily rising above the surface of the sea and then returning below, or a vast ice floe such as that recorded by the Norwegian whaler *Odd I* in 1927 off the South Shetlands. These are pure inventions, repeated uncritically by succeeding generations. Admiralty charts still mark some islands "E.D." (existence doubtful) or "P.D." (position doubtful).

Source: Rupert T. Gould, *Oddities* (2nd ed., London, 1944).

ITALIAN IS THE FIRST LANGUAGE OF ITALIANS

"Italian" is actually Tuscan, which has spread since the time of Dante (1265-1321) to become the *lingua franca* of the whole of Italy, of newspapers, radio, television and books. But, to quote *Romagnol; Language and Literature* (New York, 1972) by D. B. Gregor: "Italians are bilingual, and Italian is their second language. Each man's mother-tongue is the speech of the region in which he was born; and how big that region is, and what its frontiers are, depends on historical events and geographical features . . . Romagna is one such region, and Romagnol one such *patois* elevated to literary dialect." If the criterion of a language is that it should have produced important works of literature, then Romagnol for example again has to be taken into consideration for *Pulon Matt* (Cambridge, 1976), translated with facing text by D. B. Gregor from a burlesque 16th-century epic on the scale of Ariosto's *Orlando furioso*. Sardinian, Friulan, Neapolitan, and Sicilian are other major Italian regional languages with important literatures.

J

"J'ai tant médit de la vie que, souhaitant enfin lui rendre justice, je ne tombe sur aucun mot qui ne sonne faux" (I have meditated on life so long that, hoping to do it justice at last, I encounter not one word that does not ring false).
—EMIL CIORAN, *Le mauvais démiurge* (Paris, 1969)

"The Judgement of man is fallible."
—PUBLIUS OVIDIUS NASO, *Fasti,* Book V

"JACK" IS SHORT FOR "JOHN"

"Jack" is on the contrary short for "Jacobus" (Latin for "James") through the Old French "Jaques" (modern French "Jacques"). It has curiously enough come to be the commonest pet form of "John," though the correct pet form "Johnny" has its periods of ascendancy over the wrong word.

STEVE **JOBS** AND APPLE, INC. FALLACIES

1) The Bite Out of an Apple Logo for Apple Inc. Is a Tribute to Alan Turing

Since the rise in popularity of apple products in the 2000s, and perhaps maybe before as well, the company has developed an immense cult-like following (Take, for instance, the melodramatic stories about Steve Jobs' resignation all over the media). Or more seriously, the way in which Jobs' death has seemed to touch so many on a personal level being the ultimate evidence as to how effective his strategy was of personalizing his product and vision.

On a more symbolic level, high school students and the middle-aged tech savvy alike have gotten the infamous apple logo tattooed on all types of areas of their bodies. There are tons of stories that have been concocted and spread through the grapevine about the origin of the logo we know today. Among the most interesting is the popular misconception that the Apple logo is a tribute to Alan Turing, the famous mathematician who notably committed suicide by biting into a cyanide-laced apple. Sadly, this was far from the creator's intention.

(Continued)

In reality, Steve Jobs designed the logo himself to be a sketch of Isaac Newton sitting under a tree with an apple falling on his head, representing gravity. But the apple logo with a bite out of it has even less great significance. The man Jobs hired for the new logo design, Rob Janoff, stated in various interviews that despite the common myths about the origins of the logo, his creation was not even intended to represent knowledge. He says he just made it with a bite "for scale" (or, so people would know what fruit it was. In hindsight, he claims, he probably made the logo simple and recognizable in this way because it is easily accessible to people "across cultures."

However, it appears much more likely that the logo was only designed solely for what the man who designed it was hired for: to make a simple and attractive logo that will sell.

2) Steve Jobs Made $1 a Year at Apple

Technically, Steve Jobs did receive an annual salary of only one dollar from Apple as its CEO, from 1997 until his resignation in 2011. However, to believe that Steve did not receive any personal compensation from Apple at all and made all his money through investments is also misleading. For instance, Jobs in 2010 received a whopping $248,000 for use of a private plane (for business purposes, of course). Also, the former CEO of America's proudest creation owned 5.5 million dollars in Apple's stock and was the company's single largest shareowner. In 2010, Apple's stocks closed at over $300, giving Jobs a personal earning of nearly 2 billion dollars. And this was only in one year, with only one new version of the iPhone and iPod (plus the iPad, but who's counting).

3) Mac Computers and Windows Computers are Incompatible

Although Windows laptops and desktops definitely do not have the glossy connotations nor the backing of the tool bar that has coined simplicity, the two types of computer are really not all that different. Because of the popularity and initially much more easy to use macbooks, the idea of the PC seems foreign, clunky, slow, and foreign to Apple loyalists everywhere.

Although the "rivals" do run on different operating systems, pretty much all common computer software is created for both Mac and PC computers. This includes both Microsoft and all its variations (Excel, Word, Powerpoint), Internet browsers like Safari and Firefox, and even Photoshop and Apple's own baby, iTunes.

The main difference between the two is really the appearance of the desktop and the way the menus are organized. Macs have an application menu at the top of the screen, separated from the running applications below. PCs tend to combine them. Macs are simpler by design, but you also have to make sure to click "Quit Application" when you exit iTunes or Firefox in addition to just ex-ing out, which apparently is not the case with PCs.

However, there are many advantages to having a Mac as well, namely, good aesthetics, and moreover, the convenience of your phone, music, and computer all being compatible, and knowing that if something goes wrong with all three of them, only one trip to the Apple store and a good old chat with a friendly genius bar employee will do the Job (pun intended).

4) Steve Jobs Had a Personal Barcode on His Car Instead of License Plates

There was a popular rumor that exploded a while back when a blogger posted a photo of Steve Jobs' silver Mercedes parked in the Apple parking lot. There were no official license plates on the car, but rather, a mere scannable barcode inside the frame of the space the plates should have been. If Jobs' overwhelming success in personalizing the iPod and other otherwise unassuming products that came out of his multibillion dollar corporation wasn't enough, he as a person having his own barcode was really the icing on the cake.

Luckily, Jobs still maintained some traces of humanity amidst all the public fame. Though Jobs was notably private about his personal life throughout his career, police sirens did not need to sound every time he cruised through downtown Palo Alto to pick up some frozen lasagna for family dinner at the grocery store.

5) Jobs Had a Special Permit that Freed Him from License Plates and Standard Vehicle Laws

On the same topic, there were rumors, even from Steve Wozniak, saying that Jobs obtained a special permit in order to drive around without a license plate. However, this has been proven not to have been the case by the author of Jobs' biography, Walter Isaacson, and the CTO of Entrust (who had worked with Apple on security projects in the past).

In reality, the reason Jobs was able to always drive his Mercedes around without plates was because he had discovered a loophole in the California state vehicle laws. Apparently, in California, when someone purchases a car they have a six-month period before they need to get number plates installed. Jobs essentially

(Continued)

just made a deal with his car leasing company that he would always change cars within six months of his lease, exchanging his current silver Mercedes SL55 AMG for another identical model.

Supposedly, the car company was okay with this not only because it was technically legal, but also because it was easy enough to use the fact that Steve Jobs had leased a car for just six months as a selling point for potential buyers.

Isaacson notes that he had pointed out to Jobs that driving around without license plates was actually a lot more conspicuous than with them, a comment to which Jobs just shrugged his shoulders, and at other times, claimed it was a little game he liked to play to avoid parking tickets. At the end of the day, Jobs was just thinking differently; words which he certainly lived by.

6) Alternative Medicine Killed Steve Jobs

As most of us know, Jobs struggled with pancreatic cancer for years before his recent death in October 2011. In more depth, Jobs also used solely alternative medical remedies to try and fight off his illness for roughly nine months or so before he switched over to standard medical treatment. In light of this, some claim that this insistence on Jobs' part to use only alternative treatment for cancer was a choice that ultimately killed him.

Interestingly, David Gorski of Science Based Medicine argues against this claim. Although he says he is open to the possibility that alternative medicine may have played a role in leading to Jobs' untimely death, he asserts strongly that there is as yet no definite proof to believe this is by any means certain.

In response to the argument that if Jobs had not waited nine months to undergo surgery to remove the tumor in his pancreas, it would not have spread to the tissues aligning the organ, Gorski argues that it is unclear whether it was the original tumor that was seen on imaging before the operation or whether it was already the microscopic tumor deposits outside of the pancreas. And thus, it's questionable whether the tumor had actually spread, and if it had spread, whether the doctors had correctly identified it on imaging in its early stages. It is also debatable, given the secrecy of Jobs' illness and the characteristics of this specific kind of pancreatic tumor (insulinoma) to be relatively painless and under the radar, whether the tumor would have been found to have spread to his tissues already even if the surgery was undergone immediately.

Although it seems in a sense Gorski is playing the devil's advocate here, he is right when he says it is very possible that seeking alternative medicine practices in response to his cancer contributed to the worsening of his condition, which is very different from and much more likely than arguing that alternative medicine is what killed him.

Sources: *Time Magazine*, Techland, "Steve Jobs Still Makes A $1 Salary," Michelle Castillo, 2011; Discovery Company, *How Stuff Works*, "Top 5 Myths about Apple" and "Top 5 Myths about Steve Jobs," Jonathan Strickland and Susan L. Nasr; David Gorski, "Steve Jobs' Medical Reality Distortion Field," *Sciencebasedmedicine.org;* David Heath, "The truth about Steve Jobs' number plate," itWire, 2011; Josh Rosenthall, "The story behind Steve Jobs' Mercedes Benz and its missing license plate," *Edible Apple* blog, 2011.

JOSEPH WORE A COAT OF MANY COLORS

Much more picturesque than the truth, but the *Cambridge Bible* editors kindly divest us of yet another appalling mistranslation. Joseph, according to the original Hebrew, wore "a long garment with sleeves." But as there is no reliable support for the tales of Joseph, regrettably even that emendation seems to do little service.

Source: *Cambridge Bible* (*Genesis,* p. 351, n.3).

A JUGGERNAUT IS A HUGE VEHICLE, SUCH AS AN ARTICULATED LORRY

"Juggernaut" is merely the anglicized form of Jagannath, (Hindi, "Lord of the World") an idol of Krishna at Orissa in India. The English sense stems from the entirely erroneous belief that devotees of Krishna threw themselves beneath the wheels of the idol as it was carried in procession at the annual festival on a huge carriage.

Source: Eric Partridge, *Origins* (4th ed., London, 1966).

BUTCHERS ARE EXEMPT FROM JURY SERVICE

Jane Green, contributing to *Notes and Queries* (January 29, 1938), explored this ancient fallacy, which was believed by Fuller, Locke, Butler, Swift, Lamb, and Hazlitt. She described it as "quite mythical," at any period of English law. It may have arisen from the fact that physicians or surgeons actually practising are exempt, and from the opinion that butchers can be grouped with them on the analogy that, since they are so accustomed to seeing animal flesh cut, they are hence devoid of human feelings!

K

"Knowledge being to be had only of visible and certain truth, error is not a fault of our knowledge, but a mistake of our judgment, giving assent to that which is not true."
—JOHN LOCKE, *Essay concerning human understanding* (1690), Book IV, Ch. XX

"Knowledge is the only fountain, both of the love and the principles of human liberty."
—DANIEL WEBSTER, *Address delivered on Bunker Hill,* 1843

KARMA

One of the Hindu scriptures states: "As the dweller in the body experiences in the body childhood, youth, and old age, so he passes on to another body. The steadfast one grieves not thereat."

In Christianity this fallacy is known as REINCARNATION. In Islamic mysticism (Sufism), there is a saying "I died from the mineral and became a plant. I died from the plant and became an animal. I died from the animal and became a man. Wherefore then should I fear? When did I grow less by dying?"

The difficulty in accepting any of these yearnings for immortality, new life, or even godhead in the case of al-Hallaj, the mystic who claimed "Anā 'j-haqq" ("I am the Truth") and was judicially executed for blasphemy, is that no scientist in the relevant fields of medicine, genetics, or biology will agree that in any meaningful sense one body can die and the "spirit" (in fact the life) can pass to another body, whether that of the same species, or a different species.

THE **KEELY** MOTOR

Perpetual motion is a mirage that many inventors have seen but never reached. The confidence trickster John E. W. Keely defrauded the public with an essay on the perpetual motion machine which he called "a vibratory generator with a hydropneumatic pulsating engine," which is nonsense for a machine allegedly able to run on air, water and a motor to produce a "vaporic substance . . . having an elastic energy of

10,000 pounds to the square inch . . . It is lighter than hydrogen and more powerful than steam or any explosives known . . . I once drove an engine 800 revolutions a minute of forty horse power with less than a thimbleful of water and kept it running fifteen days with the same water."

This prodigious machine was first demonstrated in Philadelphia in 1874, and quickly attracted admirers (among whom were the leading theosophist Mme. Helena Blavatsky [see THE ODIC FORCE]), and investors. The spiritualists claimed that it ran on aetheric force (the *Vril* invented by Edward Bulwer-Lytton in his novel *The Coming Race,* 1871). Tests were always carried out in Keely's home, and involved such feats as requiring the motor to tear ropes asunder, and twist iron bars. The apparent source of energy to fuel the motor was one pint of water. Scientists were not allowed to inspect the motor, which is really just as well for Keely and the spiritualists, for after Keely's death in 1898 it was discovered that the fraudulent "inventor" was powering his motor from compressed air equipment in his cellar.

Despite Keely's exposure, so many people believed in his miraculous machine that Frank Edwards could write as late as 1959: "The secret of Keely's mystery motor died with him. Scientists could never agree on how it had operated"!

Sources include: Frank Edwards, *Stranger than science* (London, 1959); Charles Fort, *Wild talents* (New York, 1975); Daniel Webster Hering, *Foibles and fallacies of science* (London, 1924); and Curtis D. MacDougall, *Hoaxes* (New York, 1958).

HELEN **KELLER** WAS BORN BLIND, DEAF, AND DUMB

There is a widespread belief that the blind deaf mute Helen Adams Keller (1880-1968) was born with all her disabilities, but in fact she was born entirely normal.

It was in 1881 that the infant was struck by what may have been scarlet fever, from which she recovered with so many faculties tragically impaired. The gradual acquisition of her independence, with the loving aid of Anne Sullivan Macy, Polly Thompson, and Winifred Corbally, is one of the most inspiring examples of the power of the human spirit to transcend physical handicaps. Mark Twain remarked: "The two most interesting people of the last one hundred years are Helen Keller and the Emperor Napoleon Bonaparte."

Sources include: Helen Keller, *The story of my life* (New York, 1954); and Richard Harrity and Ralph G. Martin, *The three lives of Helen Keller* (New York, 1962).

INFINITE **KNOWLEDGE** IS POSSIBLE

1) **We Can Know Everything**

Ernest Renan wrote in 1863 to Berthelot: "Who knows but that man may succeed in learning the last word about matter, the laws of life, the laws of the atom? . . . He who shall possess such science will verily be the master of the universe . . ."

The contrary has since proved to be the case: that discoveries constantly upset previously-held "certitudes" so that less and less is truly *known* about more and more.

2) **There Is an Ultimate Explanation for Everything**

Jacob Bronowski said in July 1973: "One aim of the physical sciences has been to give an exact picture of the material world. One achievement of physics in the 20th century has been to prove that this is impossible . . . There is no absolute knowledge. And those who claim it, whether they are scientists or dogmatists, open the door to tragedy."

Alan McGlashan's exhilarating, witty examination of intellectual errors, *Gravity and levity* (London, 1976) comes to the same conclusion. The more we learn, the less we can be sure of absolute explanations of even the simplest scientific or religious statement. "This tireless quest for the Ultimate Explanation," observes McGlashan, "time after time proved mistaken, survives every exposure, springing up in new forms with each generation of men." One of his examples is taken from contemporary French thought. "Even today, when leading scientists and thinkers are at last beginning to catch sight of the paradoxical nature of reality, there is this flourishing French school of structural philosophy, headed by such distinguished figures as Lévi-Strauss, Foucault, and Lacan, which carries the quest for a single and final explanation of everything to a point which approaches the psychotic. Structuralism claims to have already revealed "the few primary hidden codes" that determine all human thought and behavior, and is now seeking the master-code behind all codes, "the system," to use Foucault's words, "underlying all systems." Such arrogant claims recall those of Nietzsche and Freud in earlier generations.

Freud is recorded to have made this outburst to Carl Gustav Jung: "Promise me never to abandon the sexual theory. That is the most essential thing of all. You see, we must make a dogma of it, an unshakeable bulwark." With Jung we must ask: " A bulwark against what?"

While each of us has the potential to extend knowledge and understanding beyond those of the last generation, we must equally accept with perfect humility the potential of the next generation to understand and know more than we do ourselves. There is a dreadful warning in the statement made by the French chemist Berthelot in 1887: "From now on there is no mystery about the Universe."

3) Scudder Klyce and the Unification of All Knowledge

Announced as "a verifiable solution of the 'Riddle of the Universe,' Scudder Klyce's first book, modestly entitled *Universe,* was rejected by eighteen publishers, and produced in a mercifully limited edition of a thousand copies by the author, a retired naval lieutenant, in Winchester, Mass.

Allowing Klyce, as an engineer, recognition as an "experienced scientist" and his strange theories the collective recognition of "parascientism," we can listen to the words of John Ziman: "Parascientism is a dangerous disorder for the experienced scientist, tending to lower his skeptical guard, and often bringing out an extraordinary capacity for credulity and self-deception. To those who are afflicted by it, the only answer of the scientific community must be: come with reliable consensible evidence, come with sound argument, and we will be ready to be convinced—but until that day you must not expect us to put much faith in your claims, nor to give much support to a cause in which we do not really believe" (*Reliable knowledge,* Cambridge, 1978, p. 148).

Universe, as if to bolster faulty arguments with sound authority, boasts introductions by the philosopher John Dewey (whom Klyce was later to pillory in the distasteful *Dewey's suppressed psychology,* Winchester, Mass., 1928), the eminent writer David Starr Jordan, Chancellor Emeritus, Stanford University, and the engineer Morris Llewellyn Cooke.

The attempt to unify all knowledge is a task so hopelessly grandiose as to muffle praise at the author's audacity: even in the 16th century the scope of science was far too wide to admit of mastery by any one individual, as Leonardo da Vinci had attempted in vain during the Renaissance.

Specialization had become essential by the 19th century, and in the 20th century even journalists and science correspondents, bound by the nature of their function to attempt superficial coverage of many scientific topics, were relying to a great extent on secondary sources.

The reader will be able to judge the aims of Klyce in *Universe* from the claims he makes. "Some of the particular things the book does are: Establishes a sound logic. The logic used by the ordinary man is right; that used by Aristotle and nearly all books is wrong. Removes the fundamental error from mathematics, and makes mathematics simple; proves Euclid's 'axiom' about parallels, and intelligibly solves the various problems of non-Euclidian and n-dimension space. Revises and unifies the equations of physics—about a dozen,—and makes a somewhat new one that is easier:—vortex whirls. Shows how gravity works. Shows what is wrong with Newton's law of gravity, and why. Makes Einstein's theory actually intelligible—showing that it is one sort of possible language out of an infinite number of possible valid languages or logics. The book shows that everyday language (Euclid's and Newton's and Christ's) is valid, and the most economical and practical—and uses it. Shows intelligibly what electricity, light, matter, energy, etc., are. Gives birth, life, death of solar system. Shows how to get energy out of atoms, etc. That simple and easy physics is used in the last third of the book to solve qualitatively the more complicated human problems—those of age, growth, death, life, birth, sex, medicine, immortality, good and evil, freedom of will, religious experiences and ethics in general, money, taxes, business principles, value, etc. Proves that the Constitution is right, and shows what democracy is, and proves that it is right and that all other forms of government and 'legal' law are wrong. Proves (verifiably, of course) the doctrines of Christ; disproves the essential ones of Paul and theologians."

Most of us would be interested to feel convinced of a selection from any five of Klyce's dogmas, but we probably own up to enough ignorance to repudiate claims to so much conviction on any one day of the year.

Klyce was upset when his proofs fell on stony ground: even the one about making the Earth fly out of its present orbit round the sun. His suggestion was to make the Earth field difference surface relatively stronger, making gravity relatively weaker, then "we have in some humanly controlled degree harnessed the solar whirl field to the Earth, and can work ourselves out of the present orbit"

This *magnum opus* was succeeded by *Sins of science* (London, 1925), which spent most of its time berating the scientific establishment for ignoring the findings of Scudder Klyce, born in Friendship, Tennessee, in 1879, and the most misunderstood of men. Of *Sins of science* the author wrote: "This book is unavoidably novel in several ways: 1. It states the answer to the bottom riddle of the universe— states what essential truth or religion really is. 2. It shows that the commonsense man practically knows the answer—and always has, since there have been men. 3. It shows that the real difficulty about essential truth is that the professional teachers of it, the so-called experts, have been tangled up in words. Hence, the book, surprisingly, needs only to show what we common men already know practically:—how words work. 4. Because nearly all our leaders have held the riddle of the universe to be impossible of solution,

I have become so interested in stating it clearly that I shan't be able (and won't try) to avoid displaying my interest hereafter. And such love of one's job is unfashionable, and hence novel, in this day of scientific detachment, disinterestedness and cold-blooded neutrality or 'objectiveness.' 5. Finally, our intellectuals are teaching basic error, and (refusing to concern themselves with the whole truth) are leading trusting laymen, especially unprotected children, towards destruction. And I am so strongly desirous of showing that error clearly, so that we can avoid its perverted teachers and protect our children."

Perhaps you can protect your children from some of Scudder Klyce's errors, while I am explaining to them that "disinterestedness" does *not* mean lack of interest in one's job or in anything else, but lack of bias, prejudice, or advantage to one's self.

Readers who have come so far through a morass of empty assertions may feel let down to be told that the bottom riddle of the universe (to use the Klycean phrase) is "That the common man is ordinarily right and sound—that the voice of the people is the voice of God. The final sum of truth is that God, or perfection, or infinite beauty, goodness, justice or happiness exists."

Or, to put it rather more succinctly, *Vox populi, vox dei*. But the hilarious fallacy in Klyce's ponderous conclusion—that he is restating the wisdom of the ages which has always trusted that "the voice of the people is the voice of God"—is that what Alcuin actually *meant* when he wrote the Latin phrase *ca.* 800 in his *Admonitio ad Carolum Magnum* (Epistle 127) was "[We should not listen to those who are wont to say that] the voice of the people is the voice of God [for the voice of the people is bordering on madness]."

It would be grossly unfair to the memory of Scudder Klyce if readers thought that only he had claimed to possess the secret of unifying all knowledge into a single system. Most literatures and cultures possess similar examples. One of the most curious, beyond the sacred scriptures of religious groups which tend to be regarded by adherents as all-sufficient and all-true, is one Bronislaw Trentowski, whose *Grundlage der universellen Philosophie* (Karlsruhe, 1837) was put forward as a complete and ultimate system of knowledge. And nobody should forget the case of "The Little Red Book" consisting of quotations from the sayings and writings of Mao Zedong (to use the officially-approved *pinyin* romanisation) which seemingly lost some of their magic powers after the death of Mao.

Sir Hermann Bondi, writing on "The lure of completeness," in *The encyclopaedia of ignorance* ed. by Ronald Duncan and Miranda Weston-Smith (Oxford, 1977), observes that "no understanding whatever is needed of anatomy, physiology, or the properties of leather to establish that one cannot pull oneself up by one's bootstraps. Indeed one can argue that science is possible only because one can say *something* without knowing *everything*. To aim for completeness of knowledge can thus be essentially unsound. It is far more productive to make the best of what one knows, adding to it as means become available. Yet in some sense the lure of completeness seems to have got hold of some of the greatest minds in physics: Einstein, Eddington, Schrödinger and most recently Heisenberg have aimed for 'world equations' giving a complete description of all forces in the form perhaps of a 'unified field theory.' A vast number of hours and indeed years of the time of these towering intellects have been spent on this enterprise, with the end result (measured as one should measure science, by the lasting influence on others) of precisely zero."

4. Francisco Sanchez and the Difficulty of Attaining Knowledge
A Jewish doctor who taught and practiced medicine successively in Montpellier, Rome and Toulouse, Sanchez (1552-1632) is best known for a Latin *Tractatus de multum nobili et prima universali scientia, quod nihil scitur* (Lyons, 1581), which has been translated into Spanish by Marcelino Menéndez y Pelayo as *Que nada se sabe* (Madrid, 1923?), the title signifying "That nothing is known."

Like his predecessor (and distant relative) Michel de Montaigne, Sánchez valued Aristotle's teaching in the field of natural science, but in philosophic and scientific thought he repudiated the unquestioning obedience given to Aristotelian authority, and concluded that "nothing is known" for certain except by experiment and observation. Sanchez taught that knowledge cannot be attained through the long-held syllogistic mode of reasoning of the scholastic philosophers, who attached arbitrary definitions to words. Perfect knowledge is denied to men, who can only gradually and by painstaking trial and error approach a state of imperfect knowledge. Sanchez opposed superstitions, such as astrology and prophecy, which are still held vigorously today in certain countries and in certain sections of the population. His works have apparently never become available in English.

Sources include: Philip Ward, *The Oxford Companion to Spanish Literature* (Oxford, 1978).

CRACKING **KNUCKLES** CAUSES ARTHRITIS AND/OR OSTEOPOROSIS

As obnoxious as the sound of knuckles cracking is for the silent bystander during an exam, or in any other location in which this noise is audible, negative survey results between joint cracking and bone and joint disease have been proven to let knuckle-crackers around the world let out a big sigh of relief.

A study recorded in *Journal of the American Board of Family Medicine* found that subjects who identified as current or former knuckle crackers were no more or less likely than non-crackers to have hand arthritis or osteoporosis (roughly 18 percent versus 20 percent).

Medical professionals agree that while knuckle-cracking doesn't prove to give anyone arthritis, one who has the misfortune to possess this vice might as well quit now as nothing good can come from it (healthwise), and it's also really damn annoying.

Sources: Providence Medical Group, "Ask an Expert: Knuckle Cracking and Arthritis," 2004; Kevin deWeber, MD, Mariusz Olszewski, MD, Rebecca Ortolano, MD, "Knuckle Cracking and Hand Osteoarthritis," *Journal of the American Board of Family Medicine*, 2011.

KOALAS ARE BEARS

They look like bears, some of their habits are bear-like, and they are certainly as large and as adorable as many bears are. And despite the misleading "koala bear" name that this animal is given in children's story books galore, the koala is not technically a bear.

The koala is actually a marsupial, which is a species categorized primarily by the fact that they have a pounch in which they carry their young, like our friends, the kangaroo! Interestingly, koalas are tree dwelling and strictly plant eating. The quite common mistake people tend to make, of classifying koalas into the bear category arose back when Europeans first arrived in Australia. These settlers believed (rightfully so) that Koalas resembled bears and thus began to call them koala bears. It is likely that these native Europeans had never seen a marsupial before, so their ignorance dictated this false label.

(Continued)

In fact, the koala is most closely related to the wombat, as both species originally had an external tail, as is indicative in the koala's skeletal structure. However, the koalas no longer have use for a tail, as they have evolved in a way that allows them to become tree dwellers.

So, there you have it. Koalas are not bears, and calling them so is both inconsiderate and incorrect.

Sources: Australian Koala Foundation, "Interesting Facts About Koalas" and "Frequently Asked Questions."

L

"A lie travels round the world while Truth is putting on her boots."

—CHARLES HADDON SPURGEON, Saltcellars (1885)

"Learning without thought is lost; thought without learning is dangerous."

—CONFUCIUS, Analects

SPICY FOOD BRINGS PREGNANT WOMEN INTO **LABOR**

For those who have never been pregnant, nor been the soon to be father of a nine-month pregnant woman's unborn child, this idea may seem a bit farfetched. But then again, it makes sense that these women at the end of their ropes (at the tail end of pregnancy) are pretty eager to book it as quickly as possible to the finish line.

Therefore, many theories about how to speed up the onset of labor have been researched by professionals, and more impressively, experimented upon by pregnant women themselves. In addition to spicy food, sex, walking, and laxatives have been tested as ways to trigger labor. According to a notable survey done by Jonathan Shaffir of Ohio State University, a high number of women who had just given birth reported to have tried at least one, if not multiple, of the above mentioned do-it-yourself methods of bringing about labor.

He gave them a questionnaire that listed options: walking, sexual intercourse, nipple stimulation, exercise, masturbation, eating spicy food, laxatives, herbs, acupuncture, and starvation. A vast majority of women who responded had tried walking, about half had tried sex, and about a fourth ate spicy food, followed closely behind by nipple stimulation. Thankfully, none tried starvation: a technique which is said to starve the baby into leaving the uterus.

Interestingly, the homeopathic labor technique which was the least commonly used by pregnant woman, nipple stimulation, is

(Continued)

243

apparently the only method that actually has some professional backing. Upon stimulation of the nipples, a hormone called oxytocin is triggered, which can physiologically lead to uterine contractions. The rest of these methods, more or less, are either potentially unsafe (like in the case of laxatives) or not scientifically proven to bring about real results.

But maybe if you are at the brink of labor and not feeling especially sexual, nor do you want to take laxatives, ordering extra hot sauce on those enchiladas may just bring about the perfect amount of intestinal (or psychological) activity to get things moving.

Sources: Emily Caldwell, "Walking, Sex, and Spicy Food are Favored Unprescribed Methods to Bring on Labor," Research News, Ohio State University.

BEING **LACTOSE** INTOLERANT IS UNCOMMON

How many people do you know who are lactose intolerant? Probably not many, at least to the extent where they truly can't enjoy the occasional ice cream cone or half and half in their cappuccinos.

Not much about lactose intolerance had been studied until fairly recently, when the discovery that the majority of the adult population on a worldwide scale is unable to easily digest lactose in milk and other dairy products was made.

The ability to digest lactose, a sugar/carbohydrate in milk (professionally called "lactase persistence") is found to be common in those of European dissent, in addition to some African, Middle Eastern, and Southern Asian peoples, but it is very much absent in all other parts of the global population. This trait has been developed over time, in the Old World, through human evolution and adaptation.

It is predicted that about 65 percent of the human adult population down-regulate (or deregulate) the production of intestinal lactase post-weaning. In other words, in most cases, human bodies stop producing lactase after they no longer are breast feeding. As lactase is needed in order to digest lactose (the main carbohydrate in milk), without it, drinking milk leads to bloating, flatulence, cramps, and nausea.

The specific reasons as to why this trait exists in some types of people as opposed to others are still being debated by experts.

There is speculation that there was some kind of survival of the fittest element to it in the ancient times, depending on demography, but nothing certain has been concluded.

In any event, America was not part of the Old World, so whether our genes are compatible with lactose tolerance is irrelevant. Those of us from European descent are less likely to be lactose intolerant, though there may be a fair amount of your friends who have to take Imodium or other antidiarrheic pills postdessert.

Sources: Yuval Itan, "A Worldwide Correlation of Lactase Persistence Phenotype and Genotypes," BioMed Central, *Evolutionary Biology*, 2010.

A **LADYBUG**'S NUMBER OF SPOTS CORRESPONDS WITH ITS AGE

Sadly, this is very much a myth. Its falseness is proven mainly by the fact that the average lifespan for ladybugs is confirmed by experts at one to two years.

However, spots come in a number of different colors, and are important because they serve a variety of functions in a ladybug's life. For one, the number of spots on a ladybug's wings determines what type of ladybug it is. For example, the nine-spotted ladybug can be distinguished from the two-spotted ladybug by counting its spots. Also, there is a ladybug called the "spotless ladybug" . . .

For those who do have spots, ladybugs use them as a warning against predators, communicating to bigger animals and bugs that the ladybug tastes bad, and in some cases might be poisonous to the predator. This visual warning is the predecessor for the ladybug's "best defense," a "yellow, foul-smelling liquid," that they release from their antennae when they feel threatened or uncomfortable about an encroaching insect or animal. Ladybugs are apparently poisonous to lizards and birds, but luckily, not to humans!

Sources: *South Jersey News*, "Brainstorm: Ladybugs," Courier News, 2004.

CHARLES **LAMB'S** FALLACIES

One of the *Last essays of Elia* (London, 1833) is on popular fallacies, which Charles Lamb lists as follows: that a bully is always a coward; that ill-gotten gain never prospers; that a man must not laugh at Ms. own jest; that such a one shows his breeding—that it is easy to perceive he is no gentleman; that the poor copy the vices of the rich; that enough is as good as a feast; that of two disputants the warmer is generally in the wrong; that verbal allusions are not wit, because they will not bear a translation; that the worst puns are the best; that handsome is as handsome does; that we must not look a gift-horse in the mouth; that home is home though it is never so homely; that you must love me and love my dog; that we should rise with the lark; that we should lie down with the lamb; and, that a sulky temper is a misfortune.

THE NUMEROUS **LANGUAGES** OF WEST AFRICA HAD A MINUTE RANGE AND WERE UNRELATED TO EACH OTHER

The full extract from Arnold Toynbee's *Mankind and mother Earth* (Oxford, 1976) is: "In the tropical forests of West Africa, before these were opened up by invaders from outside the region, there used to be numerous languages, apparently unrelated to each other, in close juxtaposition. The range of each of these languages was minute. The inhabitants of two villages that were separated from each other by only a few miles of forest might be unable to communicate with each other by word of mouth. Their lingua franca was dumb-show. The vocal languages that are now widely current in West Africa have come in from outside . . ."

Thomas Hodgkin, in the *Times Literary Supplement* (November 19, 1976), describes the extract as "A mist of ancient errors. The forest was not 'opened up by invaders from outside the region.' If we follow Greenberg, there are three main language families in West Africa of which one, Niger-Congo, is the most important and widespread. Though there has been some linguistic fragmentation, here as elsewhere in the world, the major language groups count their members in millions. Travellers' tales about dumb-show communication have been shown to be largely legend. All, or almost all, West African languages—major and minor—have developed within the region."

If one of the most respected historians of our time can concoct such a tissue of errors and legends, what chance has even the best-read layman to understand the sequence of selected events presented in the textbooks as "history"? Hodgkin concludes his review by observing that: "Absorbed in his dialectic of civilizations, [Toynbee] forgot, or perhaps never sufficiently considered, Marx's useful maxim (though having a 'high respect for Marx and Engels's intellectual powers' he confessed to being 'ill-read in them') in The Holy Family: History does nothing; it possesses no immense wealth; it wages no battles. It is man, real living man who does all that, who possesses and fights. 'History' is not, as it were, a person apart, using man as a means to achieve its own aims; history is nothing but the activity of man pursuing his aims."

To which one might also reasonably add, "History, as it is normally understood, might more accurately be termed 'human history' to put into perspective its insignificant span of time compared with geological history and, in particular, astronomical time."

LASERS ARE ANTIGRAVITY DEVICES

Light amplification by stimulated emission of radiation (LASER in acronym form) makes light appear to be made up of long stretches of waves of even amplitude and frequency (coherent light) because the photons are of the same size and move in the same direction, so the wave packets are all of the same frequency and "lined up" in such a way as to "melt together."

But not if you believe John Fenn Smith. According to his book *The laser* (London, 1971), what lasers really are, are antigravity devices. They prove that time does not exist. John Fenn Smith goes on to define gravity as the respiration of energy particles normally hidden inside atoms. Since the first successful laser was constructed only as recently as 1960 (by the American physicist Theodore Maiman), it can be seen that fallacies are multiplying in correlation with the speed of invention and discovery.

LAWSONOMY

"The knowledge of Life and everything pertaining thereto" is the definition given to this allegedly parallel system of world knowledge by Alfred William Lawson, Supreme Head and First Knowledgian of the University of Lawsonomy, Des Moines, Iowa. Lawson's doctrines appear in the self-published *Lawsonomy* (3 vols., 1935-9), Manlife (1923), and Penetrability (1939) and over fifty other publications.

The fallacy that applies to all such claimants to universal knowledge and understanding is simply that after a lifetime of study, meditation, learning and thought one is still very far from grasping the principles of a wide range of arts and sciences. Such humility is foreign to Lawson's nature. He wrote anonymously in the "blurb" of Manlife, "In comparison to Lawson's Law of Penetrability and Zig-Zag-and-Swirl movement, Newton's law of gravitation is but a primer lesson, and the lessons of Copernicus and Galileo are but infinitesimal grains of knowledge." A certain Cy Q. Faunce ('sycophancy' = flattery?), whose name has not yet been established as pseudonymous, called Lawson "the greatest tree of wisdom ever nurtured by the human race."

It is not sufficient to draw up a map of human knowledge; it is first necessary in all modesty to indicate the deficiencies of the map of knowledge painstakingly acquired by civilization over the millennia. This Lawson does not trouble to do, saying "The basic principles of physics were unknown until established by Lawson." Those who have troubled to examine Lawson's books do not deny that there may be elements of truth in most of them dotted about if one is clever or imaginative enough to disentangle them in the welter of neologisms and vague assertions which are often unsupported by experimental data. What is denied is that, as a system, Lawsonomy has any validity in the light of traditional physics. Lawson repudiates the concept of "energy," hypothesizing a cosmos with neither energy nor empty space but substances of varying density. Substances of heavy density move towards sub-stances of lighter density through the operation of suction and pressure, two key oft-recurring terms in Lawsonomy. Another common term is zig-zag-and swirl, defined as "movement in which any formation moves in a multiple direction according to the movements of many increasingly greater formations, each depending upon the greater formation for direction and upon varying changes caused by counteracting influences of suction and pressure of different proportions." This is a complicated way of saying that no object in the universe moves in a simple straight line or simple curve because it partakes of a number of motions which end up by causing it to follow an uneven path, though not of course necessarily either zig-zag or swirl. Among his many odd theories are the idea that the North Pole has an opening which sucks into the Earth substances supplied by the sun and by gases from meteors; and another that the South Pole is the Earth's anus, discharging gases. In the human brain there are mental organizers ("menorgs") or tiny living creatures building and operating the mental instruments within the cells of the mental system, and these strange creatures are Good. They are opposed by the mental disorganizers ("disorgs") which are vermin that destroy the cells and instruments carefully built by the menorgs. This fantasy makes good science fiction, but nobody should be required to believe it.

His Direct Credits Society was founded after the Great Crash in the interests of economic reform. In his book Direct credits for everybody (1931) he proposed to abolish the gold standard and to issue valueless money and interest on debts. This aspect of his system attracted tens of thousands of followers at the height of America's financial insecurity. Lawson sold his University in 1954 after an investigation for tax-dodging, and it is now a shopping center.

The power of the man to attract adherents to one facet of his system or another can be assessed by the illustrations in such books as Fifty speeches (1941) and Lawson's mighty sermons (1948). In A new species (1944) he predicts the gradual evolution of a super race developing from mankind capable of communicating by telepathy which he explains, another example of the universal principle of suction and pressure.

Sources include: Lawson's own books and Martin Gardner, Fads and fallacies in the name of science (New York, 1957, pp. 69-79).

"GREAT **LEADERS** ALWAYS KNOW WHERE THEY ARE GOING"

One of the great fallacies in historiography is to assume that because events occurred in a certain manner and at a certain time, they were bound to do so. Historical determinism is as fallacious as every other kind of determinism, yet many historians seem incapable of avoiding it in their own work.

J. L. I. Fennell's Ivan the Great of Moscow (New York, 1962) includes the following passage: "Ivan III, more clearly than any of his predecessors or followers on the grand princely throne of Moscow, knew precisely where he was going. He knew his goal, the means at his disposal, the obstacles to be encountered. He never over-estimated his own strength or underestimated that of his enemies. His cold reasoning told him just how far he could abuse the freedom of his subjects and tamper with the sanctity of religious institutions. He never fought a war for the sake of fighting, sought a friendship from altruism, or disgraced a subject through spite. All the deeds of this dedicated, hard-headed ruler and shrewd diplomat were directed toward one goal only."

Yet 336 pages later Fennell confesses: "Almost nothing is known of his personal qualities or of his private life" and one suspects that Ivan (1440-1505) had no great idea what he was going to do or how he could achieve his aims but, like most rulers before or since, simply did the best he could to retain maximum power for as long as possible.

LEAD PENCILS CONTAIN LEAD

The "lead" in pencils is a compound of graphite and clay or occasionally plumbago. The name was given to it in the sixteenth century when the contents were commonly believed to be lead, but were not even then.

THE **LEANING** TOWER OF PISA WAS DELIBERATELY BUILT TO LEAN

It is a bell-tower, begun in 1174, which was built on too small a base and too shallow a foundation and subsided in one direction. It continues to stand because a vertical line drawn through its centre of gravity passes through the base. The fact that the tower leans testifies not to the ingenuity of a designer or builder, but to the builder's incompetence.

LEFTHANDEDNESS IS UNNATURAL

A fallacy in the categories "those who do not do as I do must be wrong" and "the majority must be right because the majority is always right." The former fallacy presumably needs no explanation, for it is observed daily in all walks of life by most people whose guiding first principle is not tolerance of others. The latter is exemplified by the mutually contradictory "facts" that "Hinduism must be the true religion because it is held by a majority of Indians" and "Hinduism cannot be the true religion because it is not held by a majority of the human race."

Lefthandedness is in fact as natural to lefthanded people as righthandedness is natural to righthanded people. Those anxious to derive the derogatory meaning of English "sinister" directly form the original meaning of the Latin "sinister" ("left," "lefthanded"), are wrong according to the Oxford English Dictionary. The English word derived first from the transferred meaning ("inauspicious," "unfavorable"), and acquired the meaning "left" only later, and less commonly.

Sources include: Martin Gardner, The ambidextrous universe (London, 1967).

LEMMINGS COMMIT SUICIDE

The lemming, a small rodent inhabiting the central mountain chain of Norway and Sweden, is popularly believed (if one can call the Encyclopedia Britannica, 14th ed., vol. 13, p. 905, a source and distillation of popular belief) to "descend . . . in countless multitudes and proceed in a straight line until they reach the sea, into which they plunge and are drowned." The reason for this lunacy is stated to be that their march "is a survival from the old times when there was dry land over the Baltic and North Seas."

But lemmings have more sense than those who write on their communal suicide for of course it has never happened. They do breed in larger numbers in certain years, and then if the food supply in the mountains is low, they do descend in varying numbers. They can and do swim streams, and it is probable that some reach the ocean and imagine that it is another smal stream, get out of their depth, and drown. But the cosmic death wish is a fallacy, as is the regularity with which they are said to emerge from the mountains, as is their multiplicity. Most lemmings stay in the mountains. Not one has been known to commit suicide. John Masefield (in The Lemmings) declared that the fatal urge comes on them once in a hundred years, whereas Breland, in Animal facts and fallacies (London, 1950, pp. 62-3), claims that their feeding grounds become overpopulated roughly every three or four years.

LEMURIA

"Lemuria" is a hypothetical landmass invented by a zoologist, P. L. Sclater, in the 19th century to account for the geographical distribution of the lemur, which he placed in the Indian Ocean. The theosophists, who had taken up the popular myth of Atlantis from Plato's Critias and Timaeus, now supported the myth of Lemuria, Madame H. P. Blavatsky, founder of Theosophy, decided that five "root races" have so far appeared on Earth, and two more are to come. Each root race has seven "sub-races" and each sub-race has seven "branch-races." Such speculations have of course more to do with numerology than with anthropology.

"Lemurians" were the third root race. They were ape-like giants who gradually evolved into something like modern man, but Lemuria was engulfed in a great convulsion shortly after a sub-race had migrated to Atlantis, where they began the fourth root race.

Rudolf Steiner asserts in Atlantis and Lemuria (1913) that the Lemurians were unable to reason or calculate, living chiefly by instinct and communicating by telepathy. They lifted enormous weights by exercising great will power.

The British, who gave the world Jabberwocky and The Lord of the Rings, also gave the world James Churchward, who attained the rank of colonel with the Bengal Lancers and, while in India, claimed to have been permitted by a temple priest to see (and with the priest's help, to decipher) a collection of Lemurian tablets which Churchward then published and described in four hilarious "Mu" books which are so full of geological and archaeological howlers and anachronisms that even fellow Lemurian "scholars" have regarded them as a deliberate hoax. Lemuria, or "Mu" as Churchward called the island, was the original Garden of Eden where man was created 200 thousand years ago. However, Churchward's particular Lemuria was situated in the Pacific Ocean, not the Indian (tallying with Madame Blavatsky's opinion), and its level of civilization was not that of the cave-dwellers of Steiner or the giants of Blavatsky, but highly superior to all existing societies. All human races come from Mu, whose most powerful colony lies buried below the Gobi Desert. The Aryans are the closest (though still degenerate) descendants of the mighty men of Mu, which Churchward saw as the first and leading instance of the way in which Aryans dominate colored races. Churchward began to write in 1870, at the time of the great occult revival, but his books were not published until much later: *The lost continent of Mu* (New York, 1926), *The children of Mu* (New York, 1931), *The sacred symbols of Mu* (New York, 1933), *and Cosmic forces of Mu* (New York, 1934). The reader's skepticism concerning the "lost language" of Mu, called "Naacal" by Churchward, may be heightened by the fact that his tablets were never published, nobody ever saw them, and he failed even to identify the monastery or temple where he "found" them.

Yet in 1936 a Lemurian Fellowship was founded in Chicago to promote the study of Mu. The writings, by a "reincarnated Lemurian," were published by Lemurian Book Industries in Milwaukee, and promised new "super-cities" to be built in Southern California.

Sources: L. Sprague de Camp, *Lost continents* (New York, 1970).

LICE PREFER CLEAN HAIR

Unfortunately for grade school teachers and parents, there is no real statistical evidence to show whether lice prefer clean or dirty hair. They will attach themselves to any available human head, regardless of personal hygiene, and the likeliness of contracting lice is almost entirely dependent on the level of contact one person's head has with another.

It has been found, however, that girls are two to four times more frequently infested with lice than boys, and children between the ages of three and ten (or between ages four and fourteen according to another source) are more often found with lice in their hair than any other age group.

According to the NYC government and word of mouth, lice prefer clean hair but the number of lice inhabiting the human scalp increases when there is a subsequent lack of hygiene/combing in that particular head of hair. On the other hand, according to Professor of Medicine Rick Speare, there is no evidence to show that lice prefer clean hair, though they do prefer longer hair, or at least occur more often in longer hair.

It is possible that the rumor of lice being inclined to inhabit cleaner hair more often than dirty came from the '50s and earlier generations as a social means to keep up appearances, when parents tried to counter the negative social stigma that lice means lack of hygiene. This latter seems to be the most reasonable explanation, as it definitely still occurs in suburban communities today.

Sources: *NYC.gov*; ABC *Health & Wellbeing* blog, "Do Lice Only Like Clean Hair?"

TO BE **LICKED** INTO SHAPE

It was a common error throughout much of human history that kittens, puppies, fox-cubs, bear-cubs and indeed all young are born formless, and the mother's first task is to "lick them into shape."

It is only comparatively recently that the general public has come to be persuaded that the infant has its limbs, body, and head in miniature, and that the licking process is a combination of washing and sheer maternal affective contact.

ONE CANNOT **LIE** AND TELL THE TRUTH SIMULTANEOUSLY

The lie or falsehood is a particular sensitive area of fallacy-theory, by which I refer to the importance of paradox in such statements as the demonstration that a man may lie and tell the truth at the same time by asserting that he is lying (in the 3rd-century *Lives of eminent philosophers* by Diogenes Laertius, translated by R. D. Hicks for the Loeb Classical Library, London, 1925). If the reader still thinks that an argument cannot be valid if the conclusion contradicts a premiss, ponder this example from *Charles Hamblin's Fallacies* (London, 1970):

Epimenides was telling the truth when he said "I am lying."

Therefore, Epimenides was lying when he said "I am lying."

If this is still not sufficiently sophisticated to convince you, consider this apparently correct paradox:

No class is a member of itself.

Therefore (since it follows that the class of classes that are not members of themselves is not a member of itself, and from this that the class of classes that are not members of themselves is a member of itself), at least one class is a member of itself.

LIFE WAS CARRIED TO EARTH BY METEORITES

Anyone who greatly enjoyed David Attenborough's BBC Television series *Life on Earth* and the book based on it will be puzzled by *Lifecloud* (London, 1978) a book by Fred Hoyle and N. C. Wickramasinghe.

The eminent authors argue that life did not begin here on Earth at all, but a primitive biological system evolved in interstellar space and was carried to Earth, and probably to other planets, by meteorites.

A symposium entitled "Life-forms in meteorites" appeared in *Nature* for March 24, 1962, but generally scientists—while keeping an open mind—have not been impressed by claims for this particular theory of the origin of life. In the late 19th century, the German Otto Hahn examined a number of meteorites and claimed that they contained tiny fossilized organisms. Though his findings were challenged, in late 1961 several carbonaceous chondrites were examined by Professor Nagy and Dr. Claus of New York, who reported a very large number of microscopic fossils in two meteorites. Confirmation of the Nagy and Claus findings has been disputed; there is also the problem that all organic-containing rocks are notorious for containing mineral structures that resemble fossils but are not in fact fossils.

Professor Harold Urey has suggested that the carbonaceous chondrites are fragments of the black region of Moon's surface that have been knocked off by collision with other meteorites, such as siderites. Professor Urey further suggests that these black regions are the remains of organic matter carried to the Moon by gigantic splashes from Earth's primitive seas—again caused by the collisions of meteorites!

Soviet scientists have proposed that the impact of the Siberian meteorite was a crashed space-ship.

Dr. M. M. Agrest, writing in the Moscow Literaturnaya Gazeta in 1959, declared his belief that the Biblical description of the destruction of Sodom and Gomorrah is actually a description of a nuclear explosion, while a rocky platform in Lebanon is not a natural outcrop, but a launching-pad for alien spaceships!

The fallacy is that of proposing far-fetched theories as fully substantiated scientific hypotheses. One must assume that—unless convincing proof is shown by obtaining new life from a meteor at some time or another—the Lifecloud thesis of Hoyle and Wickramasinghe is very far from proven, and needs experimental verification.

Sources include: Michael H. Briggs, "Life on other planets," in *The Humanist*, July 1962.

LIGHTNING NEVER STRIKES TWICE
IN THE SAME SPOT

The fear of lightning felt by primitive peoples, animals, and children has led, like the fear of the unknown that has encouraged the spread of religion, to a whole host of mistaken notions which lie more in the realms of folklore and superstition than in the field of the popular fallacy. Perhaps the commonest fallacy is that lightning never strikes twice in the same place. However, the mast on the top of the Empire State Building was struck sixty-eight times in the first ten years of its existence. Human beings are not very good conductors, but are struck roughly ten times as frequently as the laws of chance would indicate for the space they occupy.

Lightning is not a zig-zag in shape. The many photographs now available show that the old theory is wrong, and that lightning is most frequently in the form of a river, with tributaries; ball lightning, recorded but rare, is attested in *Nature* (June 1919, p. 284).

Among the fallacies exposed by Sir H. Spencer Jones, the then Astronomer Royal, in the *Daily Mail* of September 16, 1936, were the notions that if mirrors, scissors, knives or other bright objects, are covered (or curtains are drawn) the risk of lightning's striking is reduced.

LIGHTNING FALLACIES

While the original edition of *The Book of Common Fallacies* already covered the most popular lightning safety myth, which is that lightning never strikes the same place twice, we are going to go ahead and add a few more.

There are a good amount of misconceptions about what to do in order to avoid being struck by lightning. Lightning is a strange phenomenon, and really who gets struck and who does not is kind of arbitrary, and almost always circumstantial.

So here begins the debunking of safety measures countless families swore by:

1. Metal Attracts Lightning, Rubber Resists It

First of all, metal does not attract lightning. It does not repel it either. Where lightning will strike depends on how high up a structure is, its shape (more pointed objects tend to get struck more often), and its proximity to other objects (if your house is the only object for miles on every side, it is more likely to get struck).

However, metal does conduct lightning. So, it's best to stay away from structures made entirely of metal during a lightning and thunder storm. For example, it's wise not to lean on telephone towers, metal fences, railings, or motorcycles in the presence of lightning.

Somewhat confusingly, metal can, in a sense, protect you, if you are inside a car when lightning strikes. The safety you may

(Continued)

experience while in a vehicle during a storm is not due to the rubber tires repelling the lightning. Instead, think of it this way: you are inside a car, the lightning strikes the car, and as metal is a conductor of lightning, it will serve as a middle man between you and the ground which the lightning bolt will ultimately retreat to.

2. You Are Always Safe from Lightning Indoors
Essentially, the roof above you is struck before your head is because the lightning hits that first on its way down. This is not to say that you are 100 percent safe from lightning indoors. You should, reasonably, avoid touching electrical appliances such as telephone cords, TV cables, computers, iPads, electrical sockets . . . and pretty much anything that will most likely be useless once power is long gone (in this hypothetical situation where the lightning and thunder storm is so severe that being indoors, on lock down mode is still not safe enough).

Some people still argue that lightning can come in through cracks in closed windows, but if your house was built or renovated anytime past 1750, the coast is probably clear.

3. If You Are Stuck Outside When Lightning Strikes, Lie Flat on the Ground
Lightning is not fire. You are not dodging a bullet. No camouflage is necessary in this war.

Instead of dropping to the ground and laying on your stomach in the event of a lightning and thunder storm, you should do what's in right now: the "lightning crouch." This protective maneuver involves putting your feet together, crouching down in a low squat, tucking your head, and covering your ears.

While laying flat on the ground does in fact have its benefits, such as getting low enough to decrease your chances of being the tallest and therefore most likely structure for electrical currents to become attracted to, the lightning crouch is your best bet. This way, you can get as low to the ground as possible, with the least bodily exposure to the ground (which can carry electrical currents that are deadly even from 100 feet away).

However, being inside during a lightning storm is always the safest option, as long as you aren't taking a bubble bath near an open window, talking on your home phone with your laptop on the toilet seat next to you.

Sources: National Weather Service, Lightning Safety, "Lightning Safety Myths and Truths"; Lightning Safety Group, "Top-10 Myths of Lightning Safety," 2002.

LINGUISTICS FALLACIES

1. Words Cannot Mean Their Opposite

For the student of words from the careful listing of Roget to the subtle imagination of Lewis Carroll, nothing is more enchanting than words in any language which mean their own opposite, something which is regularly believed by the unwary to be impossible.

Let formerly meant to prevent, as when Hamlet, intent on following his father's ghost, shouts at those who would stop him, "Unhand me, gentlemen. By heaven, I'll make a ghost of him that lets me!" Nowadays, he would say that he would make a ghost of anyone who would *not* let him follow his father's spectre.

Scan means to scrutinize with great care; or to glance so briefly that one takes in the headlines or main points only. For instance, "The bibliographer scanned the first edition carefully to ensure that it was perfect in every detail," and "The traveller barely scanned the front page before handing the magazine to his wife."

Shame and *shameless* are virtually the same thing; so are *valuable* and *valuable*. *Nice* in medieval usage meant "foolish, dull, strange, or stupid." I can *distract* (entertain) a reader without, I hope, *distracting* him (sending him out of his wits).

2. A Phrase or a Sentence Means Only What It Says

Linguistic philosophers have done much in the 20th century to clear away some of the confusion attaching to such problems as single, dual and multiple meanings. However, it is still common to read or hear statements to the effect that *absolute* clarity is possible in normal usage. Ambiguity lurks in most phrases, clauses, and sentences, and we only discern their real meaning in the way that we hear our partner's conversation at a noisy party: by shutting out the alternatives. For instance, how many meanings can you find at first sight in the phrase "pretty little girls" camp? The obvious three are "a pretty camp for little girls," "a pretty and little camp for girls" and "a camp for girls who are both pretty and little."

But if you take the word "pretty" in its colloquial sense of "quite," "fairly," or "rather," there are two more interpretations: "a quite little camp for girls" or "a camp for rather little girls."

Source: Willard van Orman Quine, *Elementary logic* (Boston, 1941, pp. 30-31).

LIONS ARE NOT SCAVENGERS

The popular picture is that of the patient lion, spending hours in pursuit of prey, while hyenas and jackals scavenge the scanty remains of the victim. In fact it is the lioness who usually does the hunting, the kill is often slow and painful (by strangulation in many cases), and the lioness is not above scavenging herself. Both lion and lioness are recorded as having eaten their own cubs, and both occasionally kill indiscriminately, and not only for immediate food.

Source: George Beals Schaller, *The Serengeti lion: a study of predator-prey relations* (Chicago, 1972).

LOCH NESS MONSTERS

Since the discovery of the coelacanth, a "fossil" still alive, I have been guilty of a bias towards the existence of a "Loch Ness Monster." However, the awesome kraken turned out to be a giant squid, and the continued failure decade after decade since 1933 to find physical evidence for such a monster's existence has been discouraging to "believers." Since 1961 the systematic scientific work performed by the Loch Ness Phenomenon Investigation Bureau has produced insufficient evidence to warrant a revision of Maurice Burton's *The elusive monster* (London, 1961).

Now comes a persuasive argument against the existence of a monster or monsters from Dr. T. E. Thompson of the Department of Zoology, University of Bristol. In a recent personal communication he has written: "Unless "Nessie" is presumed to be immortal, we should expect to find a breeding population of these monsters in the Loch. Such a population must consist of a sizeable number of individuals if it is to be stable; after all, ecologists express legitimate concern for large vertebrates such as rhinoceroses when their numbers fall below a hundred. It is impossible to believe that substantial numbers of large reptiles (as Nessie is usually claimed to be) could exist in the Loch without fairly frequent sightings. This objection is made the more cogent by the fact that reptiles (especially large reptiles) must breathe air at the surface. Finally, one must remember that the Loch must have been frozen during the recent geological past, and so Nessie's ancestors must have entered the Loch after the subsequent thaw. By what route? There cannot be underground channels connecting the Loch with the sea, because the Loch would drain down to sea level if there were. There is no freshwater connexion to the sea ample enough to submerge even a small monster. And an overland route would be impossible for an aquatic vertebrate of the size and specialisation claimed."

Dr. Thompson concludes: "The Loch Ness monster is based on superstitious nonsense. That the myth is perpetuated is largely the fault of opportunistic journalists, but it is regrettable that reputable scientists can occasionally be just as naughty. This is a pity because the general public already has difficulty in disentangling science fiction from science fact."

LOGICAL FALLACIES

Until recently it has been usual to classify fallacies with Aristotle into the thirteen types listed in his Peri ton sophistikon elenchon, known in Latin as *De sophisticis elenchis*, and in English as *Sophistical refutations*. A few of the more independent thinkers have challenged Aristotle, among them Pierre de la Ramée in *Aristotelicae animadversiones* (Paris, 1543; facsimile ed. with introduction by W. Risse, Stuttgart, 1964), who refused to consider fallacies as a proper subject for logic on the ground that the study of correct reasoning is enough to clarify fallacies, but one of Ramée's own disciples, Heizo Buscher, published a work on fallacies: *De ratione solvendi sophismata solide et perspicue ex P. Rami logica deducta et explicata, libri duo* (3rd ed., Wittenberg, 1594).

Both Bacon and Locke produced rivals to the Aristotelian theory of fallacies, but the succeeding centuries managed to confuse the later theories with the earlier and thus made little progress. Mathematical logicians such as Boole took no interest in the realm of fallacies, and the only major book on the subject which does not merely regurgitate Aristotle, or at least use him as the basis for belief or reaction is *Fallacies* (London, 1970), by C. L. Hamblin, Professor of Philosophy in the University of New South Wales.

Because the kinds of error that men may fall into are unlimited, it has been argued that there can be no exhaustive classification of fallacies. As H. W. B. Joseph writes in his *Introduction to logic* (1906): "Truth may have its norms, but error is infinite in its aberrations, and they cannot be digested in any classification." M. R. Cohen and Ernest Nagel, in their *An introduction to logic and scientific method* (London, 1934) agree that "it would be impossible to enumerate all the abuses of logical principles occurring in the diverse matters in which men are interested."

Nevertheless, there is a relatively small number of commonly found fallacy-types, which Aristotle divided into two major categories : those dependent on language and those outside language.

Fallacies Dependent on Language

1. Equivocation, or ambiguity of terms. J. A. Oesterle's example in his *Logic: the art of defining and reasoning* (Englewood Cliffs, N.J., 1952; 2nd ed., 1963) is: "Whatever is immaterial is unimportant; whatever is spiritual is immaterial; therefore, whatever is spiritual is unimportant,." This is fallacious because of the punning use of "immaterial."

2. Amphiboly, or the ambiguity of grammatical structure. Examples are frequent, due to carelessness or haste in composition, or to poetic cunning, as in "The Duke yet lives that Henry shall depose" (Shakespeare, *King Henry VI*, Part II, Act I, sc. iv).

3. Composition, and its contrary, Division. It is a fallacy of composition to argue that because each footballer selected for a national team can play well, the team will therefore play well as a whole. It is a fallacy of division to argue that because the Italians are a demonstrative people, every individual Italian is a demonstrative person.

4. Accent, or the perversion of meaning in a phrase or sentence by false emphasis in speaking or writing. Originally, as the name "accent" shows, the fallacy arose simply through mistaken Greek pronunciation (though Greek had no written accents when Aristotle wrote). A slightly garbled example in Latin cited by Pope John XX or XXI, also known as Petrus Hispanus (1210/20-77) is "Omnis populus est arbor; gens est populus; ergo gens est arbor," which depends on the word "populus" meaning both "poplar" and "people": "Every poplar is a tree; a nation is a people; therefore a nation is a tree."

5. Figure of speech, or the confusion of two words apparently of the same grammatical type or origin, but actually different. The classic instance is John Stuart Mill's figura dictionis in his Utilitarianism (ch. 4, p. 32), where he writes: "The only proof capable of being given that an object is visible, is that people actually see it. The only proof that a sound is audible, is that people hear it; and so of the other sources of our experience. In like manner, I apprehend, the sole evidence it is possible to produce that anything is desirable, is that people do actually desire it." Mill's error is to think that the ending "-able" in "desirable" is to be equated with the "-ible" in "visible," but this is wrong, since something "visible" is something that can be seen, whereas in the common acceptance something "desirable" is something worthy of desire, not something that can be desired.

Fallacies Dependent on Thought (not on language)

1. Accident, or the confusion of an essential difference or resemblance with inessentials. It consists in applying a general rule to a particular case whose "accidental" circumstances render the rule inapplicable.

An instance of the fallacy of accident might be: Nehru is different from Gandhi; Nehru is a man; therefore, Gandhi is different from man.

2. A dicto secundum quid ad dictum simpliciter, and its converse, which are really a variant of the fallacy of accident. Arguing from the universal to the particular, one might say (fallaciously) that what is bought in the market is eaten; raw meat is bought in the market; therefore raw meat is eaten. Arguing from the particular to the universal, one might say (equally fallaciously) that taking drugs to ease pain is beneficial, therefore taking drugs is always beneficial.

3. Petitio principii, or "begging the question" is the fallacy of reasoning in a circle, or assuming that which is to be proved. Thus, early astronomers stated that the sun must be moving because the Earth was standing still. J. S. Mill pointed out that all valid reasoning is bound to commit this fallacy, since all proof ultimately rests on assumptions which are not derived from others but are justified by the set of consequences which are deduced from them. (But then Hume and others argued that every argument a dicto secundum quid must be fallacious, since it is impossible to enumerate all conceivable particular cases one intends to govern by a general rule).

4. Consequens, or the fallacy of assuming that because a conclusion is reached by invalid arguments it is necessarily false, Thus, if the weather is foggy, the flight will be delayed; the flight is delayed; therefore, the weather is foggy. Or, if the weather is not foggy, the flight will not be delayed.

5. Many questions, a fallacy depending on receiving an answer "yes" or "no" to a question which is more complex than the answer could reveal. Thus, the simple answer cannot be given to the question "Have you stopped beating your wife?"

6. Ignoratio elenchi, or ignoring the conclusion to be proved or disproved. This is the fallacy of offering a misleading or irrelevant conclusion. One such fallacy is that of the person making an assertion who places the burden of disproof on his opponent, whereas it is incumbent on the former to offer proof. Thus, in a court of law the trial is opened by the case for the prosecution, and the evidence for the charge or claim must be proved before a conviction can be obtained. If the charge implies the defendant's presence at a given place and time, the defendant may then prove the negative (as in the case of an alibi) by showing that he was actually somewhere else at the time.

This is a most significant fallacy, for it includes various devices used by the unscrupulous to back up worthless arguments. Some of these devices are the argumentum ad hominem (which attacks a case by defaming those who hold it); ad populum (which excites the feelings of one's listeners to prevent them from forming a balanced judgment); ad ignorantiam (which trades on the ignorance of those addressed, often by using high-flown words); and ad verecundiam (which appeals to authority and usage, rather than to reason).

7. Non causa pro causa, or the reductio ad absurdum. This fallacy derives from the wilful use of absurd but unstated arguments from an innocuous statement to an absurd conclusion. One should guard against it by ensuring that all propositions in one's premises are stated and not merely inferred. A common type of non causa fallacy is

the superstition: "the captain of the winning team at Wembley wore a rabbit's foot, therefore rabbit's feet are lucky," since it is usual that all twenty-two players will have some superstition or other, but that the losers will not blame their defeat on inefficacious talismans.

The logical fallacies were described in the 19th century by, among others, Jeremy Bentham, whose *Book of fallacies* (London, 1824) has been revised and edited by Harold A. Larrabee (Baltimore, 1952). Sydney Smith (1771-1845) reviewed the book wittily by giving an example of each fallacy in turn in his celebrated Noodle's oration (Edinburgh Review, vol. 42, 1825, pp. 367-89).

Sources include: Charles Leonard Hamblin, *Fallacies* (London, 1970).

THE **LOOFAH**, LIKE THE SPONGE, IS A SEA PRODUCT

The loofah looks like a member of the sponge family, but is totally unrelated. It is in fact the fibrous part of the fruit of one or two species of Luffa aegyptiaca, to give it the scientific name by which one can note that it is native to Egypt. It belongs to the order Cucurbitaceae. That is, it is related to the gourd and the cucumber.

It is still found as a bath-sponge, but in the West Indies it has also been used as a type of dish-cloth, and has been worked up into baskets.

"TO **LOOSEN**" IS THE OPPOSITE OF "TO UNLOOSE"

The two words mean approximately the same. To loose something is to set it completely free; to loosen it is to make it more loose than it was but not completely free; and to unloose is, to use the *Oxford English Dictionary* definitions: "to relax, slacken the tension or firmness of (some part of the body, one's grasp or hold, etc.); to set free from bonds, harness, etc.; to release from confinement; to set free for action; to bring into play; to undo, untie, unfasten (a knot, belt, band, bundle, etc.); to detach, so as to get rid of or remove; to become loose or unfastened."

The paradoxical result is that "to tighten" is the opposite of "to loosen," but "to untighten" is the same as "to unloose."

LUNATICS ARE AFFECTED BY CHANGES IN THE MOON (LATIN: LUNA)

We recall Othello (Act V, scene ii):
> *"It is the very error of the Moon;*
> *She comes more nearer Earth than she was wont,*
> *And makes men mad"*

But it was already a common error among the Greeks that there was a connection between the changing moon and the periodically insane, that is to say, those who enjoy lucid intervals. Plutarch should not, therefore, have been puzzled by aristocratic Roman matrons who carried moon-amulets on their shoes to attract the lunacy-bearing moon-spirit so that it might enter the crescent charm and not its wearer.

Simple observation has helped to diminish the effect of this fallacy, though as always those who choose not to observe, and then to correlate their data with their assumptions, will continue to cherish the latter rather than the former.

M

"The man who wishes to educate himself must first learn how to doubt, for it is the doubting mind that will arrive at the truth."

—ARISTOTLE

"A man may live long, and die at last in ignorance of many truths, which his mind was capable of knowing, and that with certainty"

—JOHN LOCKE, *Essay concerning human understanding* (1690), Book I, Ch. II

MACBETH'S MURDER OF DUNCAN WAS UNPRECEDENTED IN SCOTTISH MONARCHICAL HISTORY

The Macbeth familiar to us all from Shakespeare's tragedy bears little or no resemblance to the figure known to historians from the documentary record. Every playwright has a duty first and foremost to write a good *play:* it is the audience's duty to avoid connecting dramatic form and function with the facts and theories of reputable historians who have access to records unknown to Holinshed, on whose compilation Shakespeare based *Macbeth.*

Macbeth ruled from 1040-57, a good span for a Scottish king in the Middle Ages. He was not regarded as a usurper, as is proved by the fact that he is buried on Iona, the resting-place of legitimate kings.

There were probably at least two attempts to deprive Macbeth of the throne, including those in 1046 and 1054 led by Siward of Northumbria. In 1054, Malcolm was apparently given possession of part of southern Scotland, and this may be the reason why some chroniclers believe Macbeth to have been killed in 1054. Macbeth was actually killed by Malcolm III in 1057, near Lumphanan in Mar and not in his own castle.

Neither did Macbeth kill Duncan in his own castle (Act II. iii. 11, *Lady Macbeth:* "Woe, alas! what, in our house?"). It was at "the Smith's House" near Elgin.

Inevitably, most controversy centers on the bloodiness of the deed, and the connivance of Lady Macbeth, whose part in the plot gave Dmitri Shostakovich the idea for his opera *Lady Macbeth of Mtsensk,* later retitled after the "heroine" *Katerina Ismailova.* Not only was there no bloody Lady Macbeth in Mtsensk: there was probably no guilty Lady Macbeth of Scotland, either. Macbeth alone should be blamed, but for what?

Macbeth was probably Malcolm II's nephew, writes E. L. G. Stones in *Common errors in Scottish history* (London, 1956, p. 6), and "may well have considered his claim to the throne to be as good as, and probably better than, that of Duncan I." This is substantiated by A. O. Anderson's "Macbeth's relationship to Malcolm II" in *Scottish Historical Review*, vol. 25, p. 377). Under the earlier system of collateral succession, Macbeth had a double claim to the throne: through his wife, Gruoch, almost certainly a granddaughter of King Kenneth III (997-1005); and through his mother, probably a daughter of King Kenneth II (971-995).

Macbeth's murder of Duncan I was not an isolated act of butchery, but part of a traditional pattern, according to which a king was murdered by a successor of the alternate line. Thus, Dr. Stones tells us, "Constantine (995-7) succeeded by the killing of Kenneth II, and was killed by his successor Kenneth III." Kenneth III was murdered by his successor, Malcolm II (1005-1034), Duncan's grandfather. Macbeth's murder of Duncan I, which has been so enormous in the public imagination, was neither more nor less savage than Malcolm III's murder of Macbeth.

Sources include: William Shakespeare, *Macbeth,* ed. by J. Dover Wilson (Cambridge, 1947).

MACHIAVELLI TAUGHT EVIL AND MACHIAVELLIANISM IS AN EVIL DOCTRINE

Lord Macaulay, taking as a pretext for an attack on the erroneous views about Nieeolò Machiavelli the 1825 translation of the complete works into French by J. V. Périer, published in the *Edinburgh Review* of March 1827 a delightfully written and scholarly refutation of many such mistakes.

"We doubt whether any name in literary history be so generally odious as that of the man whose character and writings we now propose to consider. The terms in which he is commonly described would seem to import that he was the Tempter, the Evil Principle, the discoverer of ambition and revenge, the original inventor of perjury, and that, before the publication of his fatal Prince, there had never been a hypocrite, a tyrant, or a traitor, a simulated virtue, or a convenient crime. One writer gravely assures us that Maurice of Saxony learned all his fraudulent policy from that execrable volume. Another remarks that since it was translated into Turkish, the Sultans have been more addicted than formerly to the custom of strangling their brothers. Lord Lyttelton charges the poor Florentine with the manifold treasons of the house of Guise, and with the Massacre of St. Bartholomew. Several authors have hinted that the Gunpowder Plot is to be primarily attributed to his doctrines, and seem to think that his effigy ought to be substituted for that of Guy Faux, in those processions by which the ingenuous youth of England annually commemorate the preservation of the Three Estates. The Church of Rome has pronounced his works accursed things. Nor have our own countrymen been backward in testifying their opinion of his merits. Out of his surname they have coined an epithet for a knave and out of his Christian name a synonym for the Devil."

Later in the same essay, having discoursed further in a similar vein, Lord Macaulay exonerates Machiavelli from the charges made against him by a close examination of what Machiavelli actually wrote in the context of his homeland and of the period in which he lived. "It may seem ridiculous to say," Macaulay continues, "that we are acquainted with few writings which exhibit so much elevation of sentiment, so pure and warm a zeal for the public good, or so just a view of the duties and rights of citizens, as those of Machiavelli. Yet so it is."

In his brilliant essay "The originality of Machiavelli," to be found collected in the volume *Against the current* (London, 1979), Isaiah Berlin examines the paradox of the Italian political thinker whose style is, by universal consent, as intelligible as it is concise. For scholars and other readers are so totally in disagreement as to Machiavelli's real meaning that Sir Isaiah finds no difficulty in listing no fewer than 22 distinct, well-documented interpretations.

And the Berlin conclusion? His view is that Machiavelli stated or implied a view contrary to the whole tradition of European thought: he has no apparent interest in the compatibility of a course of action recommended in *Il Principe* with either Christian or pagan ethics. Nor does Machiavelli think—again in Sir Isaiah's reading—that Christian or pagan ethics are necessarily false or true. He merely thinks that, as a statesman or a politician, one must give up the practice of morality.

MACROBIOTIC COOKING

Michel Abehsera is only one of many authors who have contributed to the mania for Zen macrobiotics over the last twenty years. Where Aristotle had to deal with those who believed in armomancy (a method by which his contemporaries deduced from a person's shoulders whether he or she was a fit sacrifice for the gods), we have to deal with cranks who try to convince everybody that one's diet should be balanced between *yin* and *yang* foods. It turns out that it is almost impossible to apply this meaningless principle beyond a fixed diet of whole grain cereal, and it becomes increasingly difficult to convince oneself that whole grain cereal and nothing but the grain cereal is a balanced diet.

Abehsera has inflicted upon an ever-credulous public a book entitled *Zen macrobiotic cooking* (1968). Its only virtues are negative: it sensibly suggests that overeating is bad for you, and that a high fat diet is to be discouraged. On the positive side there is little here that a good textbook on nutrition does not explain better. For a balanced diet, ignore the "balanced diet" fiends.

George Ohsawa runs his own foundation, the Ohsawa Foundation, to propagate the doctrine embodied in his book *Zen macrobiotics* (Los Angeles, 1965). He states that a diet of 100 percent whole grain cereal and "sips of liquid" will cure cancer and adds: "this also applies to mental diseases and heart trouble" and he adds for good measure haemophilia, though doctors have long known that this is a hereditary disease.

"**MAD** AS A HATTER" REFERS TO MADNESS OR HATTERS

Lewis Carroll with his penchant for linguistic games presumably knew perfectly well that his "Mad Hatter" meant "a venomous adder," but since his readers may have been misled by Tenniel's drawings, it should be pointed out that "mad" meant "venomous" and "hatter" is a corruption of "adder," or viper, so that the phrase "mad as an atter" originally meant "as venomous as a viper."

AUSTRALIAN ABORIGINE HEALERS USE A **MAGIC** SNAKE

Ronald Rose's *Living magic* (New York, 1956) includes a number of instructive exposures of "magic" claims based on conjuring tricks. The conjuring tricks in these cases, however, are fraudulent because they claim to be more than they are: they claim in some cases to heal.

Some Australian aboriginal healers are supposedly masters of a "magic snake" to assist the working of miraculous cures. Rose cites the following experience, as described by an aborigine who had been taken in, on one plane at least.

The healer "lay on his back. His body gave a shiver and his mouth opened. From his mouth the boys saw a thing come forth, a live thing that was not a snake, nor was it a cord. But it looked like a cord and moved like a snake. Slowly it issued from the gaping, quivering jaws, the length of a man's finger but not so thick. It moved about on the man's face and became longer, almost as long as man's arm. It left his mouth and crawled in the grass. Then it returned to the man's body."

In fact, Ronald Rose discovered that the "magic snake" is a freshwater worm, which the aboriginal conjuror hides in his mouth, allowing it to emerge when he chooses. Experts on the natural history of Australia realize that the worm in question passes its early life in the body of other water denizens, emerging fully grown to the amazement of the aborigines, who—all except the "healer"—are easily persuaded that any "snake" born as an adult must be magical.

DOGS HATE THE **MAILMAN**

This is all too true from the point of view of postal service employees, particularly ex-dog lovers like the writer of the blog, *All the Dogs want to Kill Me*. Ryan Bradford, a recently employed mail man, was featured in a *USA Today* article for his blog and his conviction that dogs really do hate him now that he is a mailman, where as before, dogs always loved him. His blog features disposable photos of dogs barking at him as he approaches to deliver the mail.

Although Bradford seems to take the canine hostility as a personal vendetta, it has been proven by dog experts that dogs don't act aggressively towards the mailman due to his uniform or his appearance. Instead, the barking·of dogs at mailmen is triggered by the actions the latter makes in relation to the dog's perception of his territory and role.

According to several dog training websites and information from dog behavior professionals, a dog initially barks at the mailman because said man is an unfamiliar person entering the dog's territory; dogs tend to consider strangers unwelcome. The dog barks because he feels he and his territory are being intruded upon. Generally, a new visitor arriving at the house where a dog lives will get welcomed inside and make peace with the canine. Old Fido will then settle down, realizing the visitor is no longer a threat.

However, in the case of the mailmen and other delivery people, they come once a day to deliver something, oftentimes entering the yard but never coming into the house. The dog barks at the mailman, either from inside the house or in the yard and watches as the intruder turns around and leaves "submissively" after putting the mail in the box. The dog takes the mailman's retreat from the house as being a result of his barking and warnings. He then continues to bark at the mailman every day, perhaps even getting more aggressive because he believes this visitor is unwelcome and intrusive.

Therefore, the unfriendly relationship between dogs and mailmen is really due to the fact that the dog experiences recurring

> success and feels entitled to bark to its heart's content, perhaps a more exhilarating and natural feeling for a domestic animal than most of its interactions with humans allow for.

MALARIA IS CAUSED BY BAD AIR

The origin of the word is Italian, "mal aria" meaning "bad air," since it was observed that those exposed to night air in certain lowlying parts of Italy were liable to contract the disease.

Shakespeare propagated the fallacy in *The Tempest* (II, ii, 1-3)

*"All the infections that the sun sucks up
From bogs, fens, flats, on Prosper fall, and make him
by inch-meal a disease!"*

It was Sir Ronald Ross who first identified the cause of malaria as micro-organisms injected into human blood by the bite of the anopheles mosquito. This type of mosquito breeds in stagnant water, which should be filled in wherever possible; where this is not possible, the body should be covered up as far as possible by clothes during the day and by mosquito nets round the bed at night, as well as by the use of fine wire-gauze over windows and extra doors.

Source: Sir Ronald Ross, *Memoirs: with a full account of the great malaria problem* (1923) and review (by W. G. King) in *Nature*, 7 July 1923.

MALTHUS ADVOCATED BIRTH CONTROL TO LIMIT THE GROWTH OF POPULATION

Those who have not read *An essay on the principle of population* (London, 1798) often believe that Thomas Robert Malthus (1766-1834) taught birth control as a method to curb the fast, disastrous rise in population that he predicted.

Malthus, Professor of Modern History and Political Economy at the East India Company College, Haileybury, suggested that population increases geometrically while food production can increase only arithmetically. He claimed that the cause of the increase in Britain's population during his lifetime was an increase in the birth rate, whereas we now know that there was a *fall* in the *death rate*. But Malthus never advocated birth control: his recommended measures were late marriage and strict sexual continence. He was also wrong (we realize) in asserting that food supplies can only be increased arithmetically.

Source: Alexander Gray, *The development of economic doctrine* (London, 1931).

"MANDARIN" IS A WORD OF CHINESE ORIGIN

A mandarin is thought of as a high-ranking Chinese official, but the Chinese name for such an official is *kuan* and the word "mandarin" derives ultimately from the Indo-European *man* (mind), giving *mantra* (counsel), *mantrin* (counsellor, minister) in Sanskrit, the Malay *mantri* and the Portuguese *mandarim* (the official) and *mandarino* (the language) from *mandar* (to command).

THE **MANDRAKE** SHRIEKS WHEN PULLED OUT OF THE GROUND

According to Benjamin Walker, "Human semen, the vital essence of the male, has been recognized in all occult lore as a highly charged liquid, replete with magical substances and sinful to waste. Fresh human semen was said to be eagerly sought by vampires, witches and succubae, who would extract it during *congressus subtilis*. In Europe, the semen ejaculated by a man at the moment of his hanging was believed to be particularly powerful, and was sometimes collected straight after emission, to be used as an ingredient in magical potions. If it fell to the ground it was said to produce the mandrake plant."

We must give Benjamin Walker the benefit of the doubt—given his guarded use of reported speech—that he believes the tissue of fallacies above, and the extra fallacy occurring on page 14 of his *Encyclopedia of metaphysical medicine* (London, 1978) that the mandrake plant can be used as an aphrodisiac. The plant is found in Genesis 30, 14-17, where the childless Rachel asks Leah for it. (The delivery of Joseph is, however, attributed to God, not to the mandrake, so our errors are truly tangled hereabouts.) In some countries the mandrake was believed to glow at night but, in most places where it grew, the legend spread that the plant would shriek when pulled up. There seems to be not the slightest foundation for this belief.

THE PRINTED BOOK IN FIFTEENTH-CENTURY EUROPE SUPERSEDED **MANUSCRIPTS** ENTIRELY

The spread of printing from moveable types in 15th-century Europe did *not* mean the extinction of the scribe-class. As Curt Buhler enquired in *The Fifteenth-century book* (Philadelphia, 1960): "what happened to the various categories of writers of literary works, who practiced their trade prior to 1450, once the printing press was established? The professionals previously employed by the large scriptoria seem to have done no more than to change their titles and thereupon became calligraphers; in any event, they went right on doing what had been their task for centuries . . .

"Some scribes joined forces with the enemy and became printers themselves—though some of those upon whom Fortune did not smile later forsook the press and returned to their former occupation. This is rather strong evidence for the belief that a scribe, in the closing years of the fifteenth century, could still make a living for himself with his pen."

MARES ARE IMPREGNATED BY THE WEST WIND

Pliny tells us in Book VIII (chapter 42) of the *Historia naturalis:* "It is well known that in Portugal, in the district of Lisbon and the Tagus, the mares turn away from the west wind and are fertilized by it. The foals born of such a union are extremely fast but do not live longer than three years." Pliny's share of common sense can be judged from the fact that he died while *observing* the eruption of Vesuvius in AD 79 that destroyed Pompeii and Herculaneum.

His predecessor, Virgil, oddly enough believed the same story (and may indeed have been a source for Pliny's nonsense) which he told in Book III of the *Georgics.* Varro, Solinus, and Columella also give credit to the fallacy.

It does indeed go back to Homer *(Iliad,* xvi, 150) and to Aristotle *(Hist. Anim.* vi, 18) and forward to the times of the so-called skeptic Pierre Bayle (1647-1706), who compiled the great *Dictionnaire historique et critique* (Paris, 1697).

The tale may have originated from accounts by Phoenician sailors, those accomplished merchants, who praised the fertility of the Portuguese soil, the soft ocean breezes of the summer off Portugal, and the fine horses bred along the Portuguese coastline who were as swift as the wind. A garbled version of these factors may easily have led Roman writers to amplify the legend vaguely known from Homer and Aristotle. Or not. We just don't know how grown men come to believe such fallacies in the first place, or how they can presume on the equal ignorance of their readers to accept it all: hook, line, and sinker.

MARGARINE IS THE GLYCERIDE OF MARGARIC ACID

Michel Chevreul, the 19th-century French chemist, identified three fatty acids: the oleic, the stearic, and the margaric (the last-name from its pearly lustre: Gk. *margarites* = pearl). But "margaric acid" is really a simple combination of oleic and stearic acids, as was demonstrated by a later chemist: there is no such thing as a "margaric" acid. But by that time the error was deeply embedded in the popular and expert mind alike, *Margarin* having been applied to the glyceride of the imagined fatty acid and this, through a misapplication of the chemical term, was transferred to the butter substitute we know today. In French the "g" is hard and it should properly be so in English pronunciation—after all, we don't say Marge-aret or Marge-ot or Marge-uerite.

Sources: Bergen Evans, *Comfortable words* (London, 1963).

MARIE-ANTOINETTE SAID "IF THE PEASANTS HAVE NO BREAD, LET THEM EAT CAKE"

The quotation from the *Confessions* of Jean-Jacques Rousseau runs: "Enfin je me rappelai le pis-aller d'une grande princesse à qui l' on disait que les paysans n'avaient pas de pain, et qui répondit: "Qu'ils mangent de la brioche." (I finally recalled the thoughtless aphorism of a great princess, to whom someone said that the peasants had no bread to eat, who replied "Then let them eat cake.")

It has always been assumed that it was Marie-Antoinette whom Rousseau pilloried in this manner, but that cannot be the case, for she arrived in France in 1770, some two years after Rousseau wrote the passage in question.

MARIJUANA FALLACIES

The positive and negative effects of smoking marijuana have long been debated by the public, in politics, and by medical experts alike. And while there is still really no definite answer as to whether the drug is a good or bad drug overall, there are definite health-related benefits it provides to those who are ill.

1) Marijuana is only a Recreational Drug

The fact that marijuana has been branded as such a recreational drug due to its link in popular culture to the '70s hippie movement seems to have for many overshadowed the drug's legitimate medicinal benefits.

There is significant scientific evidence to show that marijuana improves symptoms in those with multiple sclerosis, Lou Gehrig's disease, and for pain and discomfort in people with AIDS. Also, it is shown to help improve appetite in cancer patients undergoing chemotherapy.

On a certain level, the FDA doesn't want to fund the testing of marijuana's health pros and cons because there is also no reason to believe there are more positive than negative effects of the drug, or enough to warrant legalizing it (kind of like the government reasoning for making people turn off cell phones on planes).

The FDA asks, more or less, what is the point in legalizing marijuana itself (to be smoked), when they are more than willing to provide unlimited amounts of marijuana for manufacturers to extract the main active ingredient to use for the drug Marinol? Yet, doctors and patients report that smoking marijuana itself is more effective in relieving symptoms in certain illnesses than the Marinol drug. Dr. Eric Braverman of a multispecialty medical clinic in Manhattan supports the FDA's stance when he says if marijuana itself were legalized on a federal level, our society would be more or less, ruined.

2) Marijuana Causes Long Term Memory Loss

In regards to memory, the only real findings have been that short-term memory loss is notable in subjects right after they smoke weed, when they are currently "high" on marijuana. The mechanism for how exactly short-term memory is altered is still unknown. At the same time, according to a study by the University of Kentucky College of Medicine, it was found that the ability to access long-term memory was not influenced by smoking.

3) Marijuana Causes Lung Cancer

For a fairly long time, a debate has been going on in which people are constantly trying to prove either that marijuana does or does not definitively lead to lung cancer. While we know smoking cigarettes does increase risk of lung cancer, the effects of marijuana smoke on lungs are much less clear cut.

According a study by the National Institutes of Health's National Institute on Drug Abuse, even in the heaviest marijuana smokers of those surveyed, there was no increase in incidence in patients with lung, head, or neck cancer.

While some surveys have also been conducted which do show some parallel between marijuana users and lung cancer development, such as one by the Medical Research Institute in New Zealand, there are many others, such as research done by Harvard University, that indicates that marijuana not only does not lead to lung cancer, but also plays a part in preventing it. To brief the latter claim, these researchers have found reason to believe that the active ingredient in marijuana, THC, actually blocks EGF induced tumor growth and spread in the lungs and lung tissues.

Clearly there are some negative aspects to smoking pot, such as paranoia, potential for mental health problems, and social isolation. And if you smoke it incessantly, chances are you will probably experience times where you forget something simple, such as where you placed your shoes. However, you probably forgot where your shoes are because you were high when you took them off, not because you quit smoking weed forty years ago and you are still feeling the effects of short term memory loss.

Sources: Gardiner Harris, "Researchers Find Study of Medical Marijuana Discouraged," *New York Times* Health, 2010; Marc

(Continued)

Kaufman, "Study Finds No Cancer-Marijuana Connection," Washington Post, 2005; Science Daily, "Marijuana Cuts Lung Cancer Tumor Growth in Half, Study Shows," 2007; Richard Beasley, "Cannabis use and risk of lung cancer: a case-control study," *European Respiratory Journal*, 2007; Loren L. Miller, "Marijuana and memory impairment: Effect on free recall and recognition memory," *Pharmacology Biochemistry and Behavior*, 2002.

"MARMALADE" DERIVES ITS NAME FROM MARY QUEEN OF SCOTS

A correspondent to the London *Sunday Times* has stated that marmalade was first made by a French chef to Mary, Queen of Scots, during her imprisonment in Fotheringhay Castle, to cheer her up during an illness, "marmalade" being a corruption of "Marie est malade."

This is completely wrong. The Old French *mermelade* means "made of quinces," marmalade having originally been made from quince (Portuguese, *marmelo*). Sources include: T. C. Skeat (grandson of the great etymologist), personal communication, November 23, 1978.

A **MARTYR** IS ONE WHO DIES FOR A BELIEF

This idea is very commonly believed, but it is only partly true. The Greek *martyr* means "witness," and Skeat's definition is "one who suffers for a belief: death is not a necessary part of the definition, though in religion a "martyr" is generally taken to denote someone who died a heroic death rather than renounce a belief.

The Tolpuddle Martyrs, six Dorset labourers who suffered for their belief in trade unionism in the 1830s, were not executed but merely transported to Australia in 1834 and permitted to return before their seven-years sentence was up.

MATCHES ARE PRIMITIVE

If we're counting the basic mechanism of creating fire, which involves rubbing two sticks together then perhaps the "match" came first, back in the 1500s or perhaps before. However, the modern match was technically invented, and importantly commercialized to the public shortly after the lighter.

The first lighter, which granted was a lot different than what we now think of as lighters (Bic pocket lighters in fun colors), was invented by Döbereiner, a German chemist, in 1823. He noticed that when platinum metal reacted to hydrogen, the platinum glowed, "red to white hot" and then when more hydrogen was added, it burst into a hot "nearly colorless" flame. Dobereiner turned this discovery into a lighter within days, using his new chemical equation plus a glass cylinder inside a bottle, inside a lamp. He created a controlled flame that could be turned on and off using a stopcock.

Shortly after, in 1825, the first friction match was invented by English chemist John Walker. According to documentation, Walker did not think his invention was important enough to patent, as he essentially invented the match by accident, when he figured out that sulphide of antimony and chlorate of potash made a mixture that ignited with friction. A writer in *Notes and Quieres* notes that he remembers buying a box of matches called "friction lights," in which a piece of sandpaper was included with a box of matches for lighting, from Walker for one shilling and four pence in 1826.

Several years later (1832) another man, Isaac Holden, discovered the same mechanism and brought it to public attention as the "Lucifer match." Commercial manufacturing of the creation began in 1833. Walker was never given official credit for his invention, and it's really quite admirable and (in our opinion) badass that he was so nonchalant about inventing the first modern match. "What do you mean patent it? You mean patent fire? Come on, people, making fire in the palm of our hands is really nothing new," we can hear him saying now . . .

Sources: *American Scientist*, "Dobereiner's Lighter," Ronald Hoffman, 1998; *Archaeologia Aeliana*, or, Miscellaneous Tracts Related to Antiquity, "Annual Report of The Society of Antiquaries: Curator's Report for 1909."

MATHEMATICAL FALLACIES

1. Maxwell on Mathematics Fallacies

Dr. E. A. Maxwell of Queens' College, Cambridge, has written a useful (if brief) introduction: *Fallacies in mathematics* (Cambridge, 1959) in which he explains that a mathematical fallacy "leads by guile to a wrong but plausible conclusion," whereas a mistake is an error of little consequence and a howler denotes an error which leads innocently to a correct result. Dr. Maxwell devotes his final chapter to howlers, no space at all to mistakes, and ten chapters to fallacies. Among the geometrical fallacies are: "To prove that every triangle is isosceles"; "To prove that every angle is a right angle"; "To prove that, if ABCD is a quadrilateral in which AB=CD, then AD is necessarily parallel to BC"; and "To prove that every point inside a circle lies on its circumference."

The algebraic and trigonometrical fallacies include: "That $4 = 0$"; "That $+1 = -1$"; "That all lengths are equal"; and "That the sum of the squares on two sides of a triangle is never less than the square on the third."

Dr. Maxwell also disposes of the fallacies that $0 = 1$; that $2 = 1$; that m $= 0$; that a cycloid has arches of zero length; and some "limit" fallacies.

2. Mathematical Truths Can Be Completely Proved Within the System

Kurt Gödel, in an epoch-making paper published in 1931, showed that the deductive system of A. N. Whitehead and Bertrand Russell's *Principia mathematica* (Cambridge, 1910-13), and also related systems such as standard set theory, contain "undecidable" statements, which may be defined as statements that *are* true within the system but cannot be proved to be true *within* the system. More precisely, Gödel demonstrates that if a system (like that of *Principia mathematica*) satisfies certain reasonable conditions such as consistency (defined as "freedom from contradiction"), then it allows the formation of sentences that are undecidable. Gödel also shows that, if such a system is consistent, there is no way to prove that consistency within the system. In a certain sense, therefore, mathematical truth cannot be completely proved.

However, as E. Nagel and J. R. Newman stress in their *Gödel's proof* (London, 1959, p. 101), "Gödel's proof should not be construed as an invitation to despair or as an excuse for mystery-mongering. The discovery that there are arithmetical truths which cannot be demonstrated formally does not mean that there are truths which are forever incapable of becoming known, or that a "mystic" intuition (radically different in kind and authority from what is generally operative in intellectual advances) must replace cogent proof. It does not mean, as a recent writer claims, that there are "ineluctable limits to human reason." It does mean that the resources of the human intellect have not been, and cannot be, fully formalized, and the new principles of demonstration forever await invention and discovery."

3. Everything is Number

The profound teaching of Pythagoras (c. 588-500 B.C., if he ever lived at all: Greek *python,* a soothsayer), included the above saying. By "numbers," he meant the common whole numbers and the fractions obtained by dividing one whole number by another, such as 3/4, 11/5, 6/25 and so on. These together are the "rational numbers." It followed that both a side and a diagonal of any square would be measurable by (rational) numbers. But if a side of a square is measured by a (rational) number, a diagonal of the same square is *not* measurable by any (rational) number. So not everything is "number," even in mathematics. The square root of two is an irrational number.

Plato followed Pythagoras in the irrational worship of number, and John Dee (1527-1608) wrote in his preface to the first English translation of Euclid's *Elements:* "All things (which from the very first original being of things, have been framed and made) do appear to be formed by reason of numbers. For this was the principal example or pattern in the mind of the Creator" [spelling modernized].

The fallacy was perpetuated in 1935 by Sir Arthur Eddington, and is still a commonplace.

4. Any Angle Can Be Trisected

Several thousand mathematicians—most of them amateur—have proved to their own satisfaction (though they have rarely convinced anyone else) that any angle can be trisected. After all, it is simple to bisect an angle, and to divide a line segment into any number of equal parts. It is easy to trisect a right angle of 180°, and—by bisecting the 30° angle—the 45° angle. Many special angles can be trisected, but a general method which can be applied to any angle is impossible. The rigorous proof was first supplied by P. L. Wantzel in 1837, and is expounded for the curious non-mathematician by Richard Courant and Herbert Robbins in their What is mathematics? The impossibility of trisecting an angle has not stopped a small army from wasting their time: one thinks of William Upton's Geometry versus algebra; or the trisection of an angle geometrically solved (The Author, Bath, c. 1849); James Sabben's A method to trisect a series of angles having relation to each other; also another to trisect any given angle (2 pages, 1848); the Very Reverend Jeremiah Joseph Callahan's The trisection of the angle (Pittsburgh, 1931); and of Maurice Kidjel of Honolulu, whose book—written with K. W. K. Young—called The two hours that shook the world claimed not only to trisect the angle but also to square the circle and to duplicate the cube!

5. Squaring the Circle

Montucla's Histoire des récherches sur la quadrature du cercle (Paris, 1754: 2nd ed., 1831) and Augustus de Morgan's Budget of paradoxes (London, 1872) are full of accounts of pseudo-mathematicians who have obtained by illegitimate means a Euclidean construction for the quadrature of the circle, or a finitely expressible value for n, and proceeded to use faulty reasoning and/or defective mathematics to establish their assertions.

When the squaring of the circle is spoken of, it is assumed that the restrictions of Euclidean geometry apply. The problem is so ancient, and has been tackled by so many leading mathematicians of every generation, that every claim to have solved it must, tentatively at least, be considered fallacious.

6. Pi Is Equal to Three and One-eighth Exactly

Despite the fairly widely-acknowledged fact that *pi,* the ratio of the circumference to the diameter of a circle, is equal to roughly 3,14159265 . . . , James Smith (1805-1872) of the Mersey Harbour Board wrote extensively to prove that *pi* was equal to exactly 3 1/8. For those curious to learn Smith's reasons for his monomania, his books include *The ratio between diameter and circumference in a circle demonstrated by angles, and Euclid's theorem, Prop. 32, Book 1, proved to be fallacious* (Liverpool, 1870) and *The quadrature and geometry of the circle demonstrated* (Liverpool, 1872).

Sources: Eric Temple Bell, *The magic of numbers* (New York, 1946, p. 111). Robert Carl Yates, *The trisection problem* (National Council of Teachers of Mathematics, 1971); and Martin Gardner, *Mathematical carnival* (New York, 1975, Chapter 19); Augustus de Morgan, *A budget of paradoxes* (2nd ed., 2 vols., Chicago, 1915, vol. 2, pp. 103–). Incidentally, de Morgan's great collection of popular and scholarly errors contains many other references to *pi.*

ADVANCES IN **MEDICINE** ARE OFTEN MADE BY DOCTORS

A detailed refutation of this idea was made by W. Bulloch of the London Hospital in a lecture to the Hospital Officers' Association on January 18, 1918. The research, discovery and experimental work are mainly due to pathologists, bacteriologists, botanists, anatomists, and others working in laboratories, and the consequent advances were made in the overwhelming majority of cases *not* by doctors, and *not* at the patients' bedside. The diagnosis of diseases is done mainly by pathologists and none of the following are the work of practising doctors or nurses: diphtheria serum, X-rays, anti-typhoid inoculation, the use of penicillin, and insulin.

Source: A. S. E. Ackermann, *Popular fallacies* (London, 1950, p. 172).

ANIMAL PARTS AS **MEDICINE**

A medical fallacy resting on some such analogical argument as "foxes are thought to possess unusual respiratory powers, therefore foxes' lungs should be prescribed for asthma" or "bears have hairy coats, therefore bear's grease should be rubbed on the head as a cure for baldness."

Fallacies of this type have led telepathists to confuse their alleged powers with those of radio waves, for example. The error lies in inferring a further (unwarranted) degree of resemblance from a known or observable degree.

MEMOIR VS. AUTOBIOGRAPHY

We hear the term all the time, but can anyone actually really describe exactly what constitutes a Memoir? If you're writing about your life, why not call it an autobiography? If you want to exaggerate or dramatize your life a little, why not call it fiction? Better yet, a novel that is based on a true story? All the same, it seems there are always memoirs on best-seller lists nowadays. It could be because we are living in an era where advertising your work as a novel has a negative stigma, I mean, we know what the classic novels are.

But what about "autobiography"? Technically, the term, "autobiography" is a much newer term than "memoir." But, aside from sounding quite dry as an artistic genre, James Frey is a prime example of what happens when you exaggerate events in your life that are claimed to be autobiographical, because the term implies that the story you are telling is 100 percent true.

But can anyone's own account of their entire life ever be completely honest? My high school journalism teacher would reply, "had he just called it a memoir, none of this would have happened."

In reality, there is really technically very little difference in definition between a memoir and an autobiography. Wikipedia categorizes the memoir as a literary genre, "forming a subclass of autobiography, even though the terms are almost interchangeable." In the Random House dictionary, an autobiography is defined as "a history of a person's life written or told by that person." This term originated in the late 1700s. The memoir, however, has been around since the 1500s. According to *Etymology Online*, its original meaning was: "a note, memorandum, something written to be kept in mind." The more modern definition, as "an account of one's personal life and experiences" came about in the 1670s from the plural form of memoir: *memoria*, or, memory.

Memoir is distinguished from an autobiography primarily in that it places stronger emphasis in outside events. Authors of

(Continued)

autobiographies focus on themselves as the center of the work and their own personal life's events, where as a memoir includes events the writer took part in or observed closely firsthand. A few examples cited only in the *Encyclopedia Britannica* include memoirs written in the 17th century about the English Civil Wars and various French memoirists who give insight into both one's own character and the French court. Traditionally, memoirs were really only written by politicians and members of court society, and shortly after by military leaders and businessmen, dealing exclusively with writer's careers and public lives rather than private life.

In modern times, the gap has closed considerably between the personal and external in memoir writing. Memoir writing sometimes seems to take the form of self-help books or inspirational stories post-independent struggle with family, substance abuse, or existential crises. Maybe this means we have begun to find our wars and current government systems less relevant to our own lives. Or maybe it's solely a personal question.

Sources: Dictionary.com. *Dictionary.com Unabridged.* Random House, Inc., dictionary.reference.com/browse/autobiography; *Etymonline.com*; *Encyclopedia Britannica.*

MENSTRUATION FALLACIES

The dread of blood which is common throughout human societies seems to be responsible for most of the irrational fears connected with the perfectly natural process of menstruation. The loss of blood is often exaggerated: it is in fact no more than an average of two fluid ounces a month, according to John Camp in *Magic, myth and medicine* (London, 1973, p. 181), Other errors are: that intercourse with a menstruating woman will make a man sick, and produce feeble-minded children if the union is fertile; that women should not eat cold (especially frozen) food, or bathe, during menstruation; that women are in some way "unclean" at that time; and that they will contaminate a temple (in Hindu Bali).

Pliny reports that at the approach of a menstruating woman, seeds become sterile, plants become parched, and fruit drops from the trees. Lest we laugh at Pliny, remember that nowadays it is still widely believed that a girl cannot bear a child until she begins to menstruate; that the process is controlled by the moon; and that only human females menstruate (females of all apes and monkeys menstruate: see S. Zuckerman, *Functional affinities of man, monkeys, and apes,* London, 1933, p. 40).

BEARS ARE MORE LIKELY TO ATTACK MENSTRUATING WOMEN

There are a fair amount of myths that say that certain external factors, such as full moons, can directly effect women's menstrual cycles, or vice versa. We know that women's sexual attractiveness to men may increase while they are menstruating, and/or that their biological and emotional feelings may be more sensitive at that time of the month. But when it comes to a non human species (our furry but deadly friends, bears) suddenly becoming irresistibly attracted to women mid-cycle, it seems a little harder to believe.

But never fear, this belief stops here. In a detailed and informative report by Bear Management Biologist Kerry Gunther on bear attacks spanning the past few decades, he found that there is little to no correlation between bear attacks and women being on their periods. In his findings by type of bear, polar bears were the only group who had any parallels between smell and menstrual blood, and besides, they were only attracted to used tampons. Luckily the majority of us won't be going camping in the Arctic.

According to the Yellowstone data on bear attacks, between 1980 and 2005, there were 37 bear-related injuries in human visitors. Of these 37, the majority of them were male (29 versus 8). Of these eight women victims, only one was actively pulled out of her tent in the night by a bear and killed. As she was not on her period at the time, we can safely say that this was not an act of passion on the animal's behalf, but rather a tragic case of being in the wrong place at the wrong time.

Source: Kerry A. Gunther, "Bears and Menstruating Women," Yellowstone National Park, Bear Management Office, 2006.

MERMAIDS EXIST

The basis of this fanciful invention of love-starved seamen is the sea-cow family: the manatees found along the coast of Latin America and as far north as Florida; and the dugong found in the Indian Ocean, the Indonesian island chains, and as far as Australia. When they surface, these mammals project their rounded heads above the water in a manner not unlike that of a drowning human being, and at a distance could certainly be mistaken for a human.

Sources include: Osmond P. Breland, *Animal facts and fallacies* (London, 1950, pp. 40-1).

THE HUMAN EYE CAN **MESMERIZE** WILD ANIMALS

By building up a relationship with certain animals, particularly the dog, human beings can affect their actions. They have no power at all over wild animals, or even over those domestic animals which choose not to obey, as cat-lovers will agree with alacrity. Francis Galton, in *Inquiries into human faculty and its development* (London, 1883), states that man "has no natural power at all over many other creatures. Who, for instance, ever succeeded in frowning away a mosquito, or in pacifying an angry wasp by a smile?"

METAPHYSICAL MEDICINE

"Metaphysical medicine" is defined by Benjamin Walker, in his *Encyclopaedia* of the subject (London, 1978), as "applied to the causes and treatment of disease believed to arise from pathologies of what is known in occultism as the second body, or the non-material substratum of the human organism."

"No doubt," writes Maurice Richardson in *The Times Literary Supplement* (March 17, 1978), "the esoteric brigade will be queueing up for this at the occult bookshops in Paranoia Row where, in addition to the works of Madame Blavatsky and the mahatmas, you can buy a Kilner auroscope and a radiesthetic pendulum for home diagnosis . . . There are various inaccuracies, some blatant like the statement that "there are over thirty women to every male in English mental asylums." And the article on *Asylums* makes all the very worst abuses and backwardnesses typical of the modern mental hospital in Britain and America. Among minor errors, it was not Baudelaire but Gerard de Nerval who led a lobster on a chain. And it is news to me that Milton suffered from congenital syphilis; that Swift was attacked by it; and that Shakespeare was an epileptic."

There is no proof that Walker's "second body" exists, therefore there can be no proof that any of the remedies put forward to treat diseases of the "second body" can be used with advantage. The whole encyclopedia is a curiosity of useless learning.

"**MIDDLE-AGED** SPREAD" IS INEVITABLE

There is nothing inevitable about a young man's acquiring a paunch or other indications of incipient obesity. This can be prevented by increasing the amount of exercise taken and reducing the amount of calories consumed.

THE **MIDDLE CLASS** IN ENGLAND ROSE DURING THE TUDOR PERIOD

Louis B. Wright's *Middle-class culture in Elizabethan England* (Chapel Hill, North Carolina, 1935) identified a close interactive causal connection between the rise of the middle classes and the rise of the Tudors, an allegedly "bourgeois" dynasty, whatever that term might mean.

J. H. Hexter's closely argued analysis of Wright's argument exposes the tautology: everyone who is rising is admitted to the middle class. Hexter finds that "there is little evidence, then, that the Tudor period saw any extraordinary development in the middle class of group consciousness, group pride, or will to power," and no proof of the proposition that Tudor monarchs favored commerce in any special way, or that they manifested "middle-class characteristics in any intelligible sense."

More significant than all this is the common desire of certain modern European historiographers to discover the "rise of the middle class" in every period from the 12th century to the 20th.

THE LONGEST DAY IS ALWAYS THE SAME AS **MIDSUMMER'S** DAY

In the northern hemisphere, Midsummer Day is always June 24. Midsummer as a time of year is the week around the summer solstice (June 21), and the longest day is variable. If a solstice happens to fall late in the day on June 21, by Greenwich time, that will be the longest day of the year at Greenwich, even if it is only by a fraction of a second, but the longest day that year in Japan will be June 22 (local time) and the same applies to other eastern longitudes. If a solstice occurs late on June 21 in one year, it will be nearly six hours later next year, that is to say early on June 22. In the year 2000, the summer solstice reaches its earliest date for a hundred years: two hours into June 21.

Astronomically, summer begins about June 21. The season is normally understood to include the months of June, July and August in North America, but May is normally included as a summer month in Britain.

Source: *Whitaker's almanack for the year of Our Lord 1980* (London, 1979).

MIGRAINE AND HEADACHES ARE MORE COMMON AMONG THE HIGHLY INTELLIGENT, AND ARE CAUSED BY HIGH BLOOD PRESSURE

It certainly flatters the migraine sufferer (like the present writer) to be told that his affliction proves high intelligence, but a team from Britain's Medical Research Council has emphatically denied any such relationship.

The same team repudiated the widely held view that headaches are a symptom of high blood pressure. More than four hundred patients subject to headaches were tested, and their blood pressure was on average neither higher nor lower than average. John Camp writes: "Neither of these findings was agreed with much enthusiasm by the public, and patients with chronic headache will continue to think their doctor neglectful if he does not test their blood pressure at the first opportunity." Source: John Camp, *Magic, "myth and medicine* (London, 1973).

A **MILDLY INFECTIOUS** PERSON CAN TRANSMIT ONLY A MILD INFECTION

The fact that this fallacy has been so widely held shows how dangerous common fallacies can be! How "mild" an attack becomes depends entirely upon the ability of our system to withstand the attack: the infection itself has nothing to do with the case. An infected person will consequently transmit the disease to another seriously, if the latter is weakened, or mildly, if the latter is strong.

Source: A. S. E. Ackermann, *Popular fallacies,* 4th ed. (London, 1950, p. 145).

MILK TURNS SOUR DURING A THUNDERSTORM

One of the many fallacies connecting two events together, when a third event is the cause of both.

Hot, humid weather favors *both* the occurrence of thunderstorms *and* rapid development of bacterial changes in milk producing the lactic acid which, at a certain point, turns milk sour. There is no necessary connection between the two phenomena which may be caused by sultry weather.

MILK FALLACIES

1. Drinking Milk Makes Mucus

When you wake up with dry crusted clots of snot blocking your breathing passages, followed by endless watery mucus flowing out of your nose all day, you probably aren't in the mood for dairy. Likewise, when we're sick, we're encouraged to eat spicy foods, soup, protein, and drink a lot of water. Although the above mentioned ingredients may seem to make up a more healthy diet for the victims of influenza, milk and dairy products do not actually hinder the healing process.

In a poll of people with the common cold, no significant increase in mucus production was found (an average of only 1.1 grams per day) after subjects drank 11 glasses of milk per day for 10 days.

However, it was also discovered that those who had believed beforehand in the fallacy that milk made colds worse were much more likely than those who didn't to report a cough and increased congestion levels after the experiment, while their quantitative results still showed no higher nasal secretion levels than they had had going into it.

This belief may indeed die hard, as apparently, drinking milk does create the illusion of extra mucus production. Moreover, all kinds of milk, but whole milk in particular, coats the tongue and mouth, somewhat imitating what most humans would consider to be the effects and texture of mucus. So although the mucus and milk relation is proven to be a myth, it remains one stubborn placebo.

2. Two Percent Milk

It would seem that because the two types of milk that fall in between skim and whole are labeled as one and two percent, being one percentage apart, that they should be fairly similar in nutritional value and contents.

In actuality, two percent milk contains a lot more than two percent of the calories from fat. The percentages for both one and two percent milk refer to the milk to fat percentage by weight.

Roughly speaking, two percent milk has about 130 calories and five grams of fat. These two figures add up to inform us that there are approximately 35 (some sources say 45) percent calories from fat in two percent milk. By comparison, one percent milk has only about 27 percent calories from fat, if not less. In addition, one percent milk is said to be closer to skim milk, in that both of these grades of milk derive less fat from the vitamins A and D. Whole milk contains about 50 percent calories from fat. So, depending on the source, two percent milk is closer in its fat calorie content to whole milk than to its misleading counterpart, one percent.

One percent milk can be placed in the same category as skim milk, in that both of these types share the "good" nutritional ingredients with two and whole percent milk such as calcium, vitamin D (though the former two need to be fortified with this vitamin), and potassium, but they do not contain as much fat, so therefore they are healthier for anyone above the age of two.

The point of this all being, if you are standing in the dairy section at a supermarket, debating between one and two percent milk, knowing that the choice is hardly different than deciding between skim and whole milk may make the decision process easier. Or if you prefer the old "ignorance is bliss" state of mind

(Continued)

while grocery shopping, then feel free to disregard this explanation entirely.

Sources: Densie Webb, "The Lowdown on Low-Fat and Low-Calorie Claims," Denise Webb, Chicago Tribune, 1993; Editors of the Berkeley Wellness Letter, "The New Wellness Encyclopedia," University of California Berkeley, 1995; Joy Bauer, "Skim, Soy, More: Which Milk is Best?" MSNBC Today Health, 2010. Carole B. Pinnock, *American Journal of Respiratory and Critical Care Medicine,* "Relationship Between Milk Intake and Mucus Production in Adult Volunteers Challenged with Rhinovirus-2," American Thoracic Society, 1990; Patricia Queen Samour, Kathy King Helm, "Milk and Mucus," *Handbook of Pediatric Nutrition,* 2005.

WHITEHEAD'S FALLACY OF **MISPLACED** CONCRETENESS

Alfred North Whitehead (1861-1947) argued that men have mistakenly ascribed a concrete nature to essentially abstract notions in an attempt to understand the world in which he finds himself.

Thus, poverty, love, and angels are merely verbal signs which are too often given a concrete form or are discussed as though they had identical meanings for different people at different times in different places. Whitehead's belief was that such notions are in fact always derived from actual human experience, and the abstract notions are invented and secondary. It is dangerous to treat the abstract ideas as concrete. Whitehead's rejection of reductionism, known as the "fallacy of misplaced concreteness" is based on his denial that what we have so far discovered (e.g., as regards atoms) is the *whole* of what is contained in the reality independent of ourselves.

Sources: Conrad Hal Waddington, *Tools for thought* (London, 1977, pp. 24-5).

CLARK ON **MISTAKES**

Although not all mistakes are fallacies, all fallacies are mistakes. In *The mistakes we make* (London, 1898), C. E. Clark included a large number of popular errors under the following headings: Things that we call by their wrong names; mistakes we make about places and their names; mistakes we make about plants and their names; mistakes we make about animals; some literary stumbling-blocks;

common errors in speech and writing; words, phrases, and things that are misunderstood; misstatements by famous authors and others; common mistakes of many kinds; historical mistakes; mistakes we make in connection with religious history; and, mistakes we make in connection with ancient history.

Clark's sequel, *More mistakes we make* (London, 1901), covered: Orthographical vagaries; murdered traditions; murdered quotations; the patriotic ill-treatment of foreign words; an arabesque of confusion; on natural history; pictorial mistakes; and a miscellaneous assortment.

MOLEOSOPHY

A fallacious technique purporting to foretell or diagnose character by interpreting the moles on the human body. A mole on the right hand implies success in business; on the left hand, possession of an artistic temperament; on the right knee, a happy marriage; on the left knee, possession of a bad temper.

But anyone foolish enough to be taken in by such nonsense will presumably not have had the intellectual curiosity to read so far.

Source: P. Showers, *Fortune telling for fun and popularity* (Philadelphia, 1945).

ENGLISH MONASTERIES, BEFORE THE SUPPRESSION, WERE SCHOOLS, INNS, AND POOR LAW INSTITUTIONS

School textbooks seem to take centuries, rather than decades, to catch up with historical facts. One fallacy which is repeated from textbook to examination answer, and eventually back again, is the part played by English medieval monasteries in lay education.

It was neither the practice nor the duty of monks to educate the general public, and it was only after the Council of Trent (1543-63) that the "teaching congregations" (the Jesuits and Oratorians, for example), were established on the Continent of Europe. It was the *secular* clergy and the parochial or diocesan foundations—*not* the monks and monasteries—which provided schools and schoolmasters, in accordance with papal ordinances, particularly that of Innocent III of 1215. Some wealthy monks did provide some grammar schools (Abbot Samson's at Bury St Edmunds in Suffolk is a case in point) but they did so as private benefactors, and the school house was outside the monastery precinct. In some houses, the senior monks acted as trustees for school lands (as at Worcester or Canterbury), and the Dissolution involved simply a change of trustees, and had no connection with the day-to-day running of the school. It was the Chantries Act of 1547 which hit the grammar schools, despoiling the parochial foundations (including ecclesiastical gilds and colleges) with which the schools are closely bound up. "The drowning of youth in ignorance" was the work of Somerset, not of King Henry VIII.

Similarly, the use of monasteries as inns in southern England was a rare occurrence (though commoner in the north), and southern abbeys had in most cases built inns for visitors well before 1536.

Finally, the place of almsgiving and help for the poor generally in monasteries has been greatly exaggerated. Monks generally enjoyed two servants each on average, and it has been argued that the employment of servants in this way was a form of poor relief, but many of these were able-bodied workers who assisted on farms and in vegetable gardens. It was commonly alleged in 15th-century visitations that monastery dogs were given leftovers ("broken vittles") that were intended for the poor. Yet many monasteries and abbeys were housed in extremely remote areas (Tintern and Rievaulx, for instance), where only a few paupers existed.

And the dispossessed monks did not swell the ranks of Tudor beggars. They were offered good pensions, and many secured comfortable benefices, as can be shown by extant pension-lists. Many complained that their pensions were not received regularly, but then this was equally true of salaries in the Tudor Civil Service.

Sources: G. Baskerville, *English monks and the suppression of the monasteries* (London, 1937); and Historical Association, *Common errors in history* (London, 1951).

A SNAKE CANNOT KILL A **MONGOOSE**

There is a theory that the mongoose is protected against snakebite by eating a certain plant, thus obtaining a preventative antidote. This is not true. A mongoose can easily be killed by a snake if it does not immediately seize the snake behind the head to render it powerless and then break its backbone by biting it or cracking it like a whip. If the mongoose makes a mistake in this process, it can easily be bitten to death, an occurrence seen frequently in India.

FULL **MOON** FALLACIES

Myths about the moon have been around for centuries, possibly arising even earlier than we have written records for. Quite clearly, the most specific and culturally significant legend about the full moon's effect on sanity is the emergence of the werewolf. But it seems unfair to our readers to assume that with the degree to which the werewolf myth has been spoofed in movies and TV that anyone really believes they exist during full moons, or ever.

Yet certain studies and common people still insist that there are definite parallels between certain phases of the earth's moon's cycle and deviant behavior in humans. A *Scientific American* article cites a survey of college students, almost half of which (45 percent) said they believe "moonstruck" people are more likely to engage in unusual activity or behavior during a full moon. Here are a few more specific notions:

1) A Full Moon Makes People Act Crazier

A "lunar effect" or "Transylvania effect," originated in simpler times as the idea that people would go crazy and, therefore, turn into Werewolves during full moons. This myth has evolved into the vaguer idea that bad or strange activity is triggered in people during full moons. Supposedly, Aristotle and ancient scholars believed that the moon caused people to act crazy because as the brain is mostly "moist," it must be the most susceptible to the moon's influence, just as the tides corresponded to the effect of full moons. Some modern psychiatrists tried to follow up on studies to prove this theory to be true, as the brain is 80 percent water and therefore the moon may indeed change neurological patterns more easily within the brain, as the theory went. Although the topic is pretty much considered a "pseudoscientific theory" now, there apparently is some scientific evidence to support the claim, however, more so in the behavior of animals than humans, which doesn't help much.

2) Full Moon Affects Mental Illness

Some studies support the possibility of lunacy relating to mental illnesses, primarily schizophrenia and epilepsy. According to a study in the *Journal of Psychological Nursing and Mental Health Service*, schizophrenic patients do sometimes show signs of deterioration in quality of life and "mental well-being" during a full moon. Also, epileptic seizures are supposed by some researchers to be somewhat triggered by full-moon times.

Additionally, according to a collection of surveys and studies cited and listed on an educational website, there is generally no relation at all between full moons and psychiatric hospital admissions. In fact, in at least two studies, it was found that mental hospital admissions were higher during the new moon or quarter moon and lower during the full moon.

Thus, we think it's safe to say that schizophrenic and epileptic patients are likely to experience signs of deterioration in mental well-being at random, completely independent of the lunar phase.

(Continued)

So, unfortunately it's not realistic to blame your car getting towed, almost hitting that deer that walked in front of your car suddenly, or drunk dialing your mother on the full moon that night.

3) Crime Rate Goes Up During a Full Moon

Like the relation between mental illness and the full moon is believed by some professionals in the field (a 1995 study found as many as 81 percent of them), the correlation between crime rate and the moon is suggested by police, and accepted in police culture. But again, there are no reliable statistics at all to prove that this is true aside from "personal" experience, or the occasional "evidence" where the correlation exists but crucial factors like controls were not placed on the experience. Therefore cannot be proven to be a cause and effect relationship between the moon and the crime rate and/or mental breakdown.

While there are perhaps one or two articles that claim that aggression is more common during arrests when there is a full moon, the vast majority of studies and statistics find no relation between serious crimes like stabbing, gunshot wounds, prison violence and the phase of the moon.

As many sources assert, the reason people like police officers continue to believe in these myths is because they see what they want to see. The superstitious can tell themselves crime rate increases on full moons, but crime rate may just increase on a day where the moon happens to be full, or be perceived to be full by the observer, and it is simply a matter of coincidence.

According to a couple of Wisconsin psychiatrists, these people are falling prey to "illusory correlation," (believing in in patterns that don't really exist). This is because, the article explains, we tend to remember events more than we remember "non-events." In one event, a nurse who believed in the lunacy in full moons would take more notes on her patients' behavior during full moons. However, when no correspondence is found between a full moon and expected behavior, the "non-event" is erased from our memories. This is because, obviously, we want real life events to match up with our preconceived beliefs. Nobody wants to be wrong, to put it plain and simply. Not even the superstitious.

4) Full Moon Corresponds to Menstrual Cycle

It seems logical to some, and it has been around since, well, tales from ancient days and lands: women's menstruation cycles must be linked with the cycle of the moon. As both periods and full moons come out about every 28 days, once a month, they must come out at the same time each month.

On a basic level, this correlation between the two cycles could not stay intact forever, if only for the mere fact that women get their periods only roughly every 28 days, but it varies depending on the person, the environment, weight gain and loss, and in some cases, birth control. (Think: pregnancy scares.) On the other hand, the full moon occurs exactly on schedule every 29.53 days.

In a similar realm, there are also rumors that more births happen on full moons. However, there have been a good number of studies done to show that there is no higher concentration in number of births and the full moon than in any other phase of the lunar cycle.

There are also ancient myths that say women used to get their periods based on the effect that the light from the moon had on their body's fertility cycles. With the rise of modern electric lighting and even fire, however, it has been a long time since women had significant and direct enough exposure to the moon light and the moon light alone to have it be the sole regulator of their period cycles. Some argue that because there is not even a real proven correlation between menstruation in animals and the moon, it is unlikely that primitive humans were any different.

Interestingly, one psychiatrist is cited in an article on the lunacy effect proposing that the moon light did have some effect on our people in past centuries, especially those who slept outside. Following this theory, the people who got too much exposure to moon light when they were trying to sleep experienced frequent sleep deprivation, and therefore were more likely to develop aggressive behavior, irritability, depression, and bipolar disorder.

Fascinating as it is to feel this human connection to our primitive ancestors, it still seems like a stretch. Having been a college student with roommates who kept the lights on while I was trying to sleep or nap, I would argue strongly that putting a piece of reasonably thick cloth over your face will most likely suffice in preserving your mental sanity.

Sources: *Scientific American*, "Lunacy and the Full Moon," Scott O. Lilienfeld, Hal Arkowitz, 2009; University of Washington, *Neuroscience for Kids*, "Moonstruck! Does the Full Moon Influence Behavior?" ABC News Law and Justice Unit, "Bad Moon Rising: The Myth of the Full Moon," Chris Francescani, 2008; *The Skeptics Dictionary*, "Full Moon and Lunar Effects."

HAVING TWO FULL **MOONS** IN A MONTH MEANS WET WEATHER

No. We know that there is absolutely no connection between changes of the moon and changes in the weather, since various scientists have taken the trouble to check the erroneousness of such superstitions. Horsley found that the weather tables of 1774, published by the Royal Society, showed that only ten changes of weather out of a total of forty-six occurred on days of lunar influence, only two of them being at the new moon, and none at all at the full. . .

Sources: Richard Inwards, *Weather fallacies,* in *Nature,* August 15, 1895.

MOSQUITOES BITE INDISCRIMINATELY

Yes, in the season where mosquitoes are rampant (summer), we're all a little more likely to get bitten than not if we spend all day outdoors in a meadow with bare feet and no insect repellent. But the idea that mosquitoes don't have preferences in whom they bite and why is lacking in credit.

Scientific mosquito studies in the last decade or so have revealed that mosquitoes rely a great deal on their sense of smell for survival (and for scoping out human blood). Research into mosquito prevention strategies has shown that in order for female mosquitoes to find the nourishment they need for their eggs in human blood, they use olfactory receptors on their antennas to respond to chemicals in human perspiration. More specifically, studies have been conducted which have found that at least twenty-seven of mosquitoes' seventy-two receptors are programmed, so to speak, to detect these human sweat chemicals. Some of these chemicals—sweet, musky, and/or aromatic—for instance, can be more desirable to certain mosquitoes than others.

According to the International Anopheles Genome Project (a consortium in Paris conducting research on mosquito bites and disease in humans), some mosquitoes, such as the *An. Gambiae* species prefer indoor environments and sleeping humans for their primary blood sources.

Scientists are still looking into particular new ways to keep mosquito bites in humans down by inventing prevention strategies, such as chemicals to put on humans, which would effectively block the mosquito olfactory senses that draw them to us. In the meantime, remembering to apply plenty of unscented deodorant every day may help those of us with excessively pungent body odor to keep the hungry bugs away.

Sources: *Sunday Times*, "Sweat and Blood: Why Mosquitoes Pick and Choose Between Humans," Hannah Devin, 2010; *Environmental Health Perspectives Journal*, "Outsmarting Olfaction . . . ," Charles W. Schmidt, 2005.

MOSS IS A DRUG

Usnea, an official drug in the pharmacopeia until the 19th century, was recommended as a curative in the first edition of the *Encyclopedia Britannica* (3 vols., Edinburgh, 1771). Many testimonials to its efficacy were available, having been provided by grateful patients ostensibly cured of wasting or nervous diseases.

This is odd, because usnea was moss. Not the moss that one finds on damp ground or stone, but moss scraped from the skull of criminals who had been hanged in chains! For external applications, the corresponding prescription was a piece of the rope with which the criminal had been hanged, used to stroke on affected skin.

Source: Howard W. Haggard, *Devils, drugs, and doctors* (London, 1929).

MOTHS EAT CLOTHES

Not quite so simple. What actually happens is that clothes-moths lay eggs on cloth, and these eggs develop into larvae which then eat tiny particles of cloth. The larvae change into pupae, each forming a tiny cocoon, and after a time the fully grown moths emerge from the cocoons. The adult moths do not eat cloth.

HITTING STICKS TOGETHER IS THE BEST WAY TO WARD OFF MOUNTAIN LIONS

Mountain lion encounters are somewhat rare, especially, obviously, if you aren't in the wilderness. But if you do come across one, and it unmistakably sees you, there are a number of things you could and should do to try and save yourself. There are also some things you should never do if you want to stay alive.

While you do generally want to make a good deal of noise and commotion to try and threaten the lion and let him know you are not his prey, banging sticks together is not the sure fire way to send this message. According to general safety types on mountain lion encounters, it is probably a better option to carry

(Continued)

a sturdy walking stick in order to fight or ward off a lion than to stand there creating not particularly loud or threatening clamor with two percussion-sized sticks. If the lion attacks, your best bet is to attack back with whatever instruments you have available. Basically, the noise you create is secondary to the necessity of posing a physical threat and staying on the defense.

Importantly, you don't, under any circumstances, want to bend over when in contact with a lion, as you instead want to do all you can to exert your presence, standing up tall, opening up your jacket, extending and waving your arms, speaking in a firm deep voice, and even throwing heavy objects if needed. Bending over to gather up some sticks on the ground is more likely to give the lion the impression that you are an animal, and thus less threatening and more appealing to eat for dinner.

Sources: "Mountain Lion Safety Tips," UCSC, California police department of Fish and Game; "If You Encounter a Mountain Lion," Missouri Conservation Department.

BLACK IS THE COLOR OF **MOURNING**

White is the prevalent color of mourning, particularly in the Far East, Ancient Rome, and Sparta. In England mourners wore white up until the Middle Ages, and Henry VIII is recorded as having worn it for Anne Boleyn (who wore *yellow* for Catherine of Aragon). Yellow is worn in Egypt and Burma. Deep blue was worn during the Republican Roman period. Greyish-brown is the traditional colour of mourning in Ethiopia and pale brown in Iran. Among the Celts and Gypsies the prevalent color of mourning is red.

A **MULE** IS THE OFFSPRING OF A SHE-ASS AND A STALLION

Not technically, no. A mule is the offspring of a he-ass and a mare. The correct name for the off-spring of a she-ass and a stallion is a hinny. Everyone asserts that a mule is incapable of giving birth, but the operative word is "ordinarily," for cases have been known. And as for the legend of its stubbornness, let the *Oxford English Dictionary* defend the animal: "With no good grounds, the mule is a proverbial type of obstinacy."

MURDER WILL OUT

"Truth will come to light; murder cannot be hid long; a man's son may; but at the length, truth will out," is a dramatic point made by

Shakespeare in *The Merchant of Venice* (II, ii, 75) but though many believe that both truth and murder do eventually emerge, nothing is less axiomatic. Truth will only emerge if someone has the wit, courage and energy to compel it to do so, for it will not emerge of its own accord. So with murder.

William F. Kessler and Paul B. Weston, in *The detection of murder* (New York, 1961), open their book by declaring that "nowhere in the world is the investigation of unexplained or unexpected death so casual and haphazard as it is in the United States. Of the close to 300,000 deaths in the United States each year from suspicious or violent causes, only a little more than 10,000 are officially recognized as murders."

One in thirty detected as *murders*? And few of those with a conviction in the case? It looks as though neither in the U.S. nor elsewhere will "truth" or "murder" out.

N

"The narrower the range of man's knowledge of physical causes, the wider is the field which he has to fill up with hypothetical causes of a metaphysical or supernatural character."

—ANDREW LANG, in *Myth, ritual and religion*
(London, 1899)

"Nemo solus satis sapit" (Nobody is wise enough by himself)
—PLAUTUS, *Miles Gloriosus*

FALLACIES ON NAPOLEON

1) The Origin of Napoleon Bonaparte

All we know for certain is that he was a pure Semite (Eugene Gellion-Danglar, *Les sémites et Ie sémitisme,* 1882); of Germanic origin, to be traced back to Conrad and his wife Ermengarde (Wencker Wildberg, *Commentaires sur les Mémoires de Napoléon);* Greek, "Bonaparte" being a translation of Calomeros (Princess Luden Murat, *Les errants de lagloire,* 1933); the son of an Italian bandit (pamphlet of 1814 cited in Jean Tulard, *L'Anti-Napoléon,* 1965); a descendant of Totila, king of the Ostrogoths (*Mémoires curieux,* 1821); a descendant of Tedix of Cadolingi, Count of Pistoia in Italy *(Annuaire générale héraldique universe!,* 1901); a descendant of Corsican hussars *(Bonaparte démasqué,* 1814); and a Florentine named William, who took the surname of Bonaparte in 1261 (Hubert N. B. Richardson, *A dictionary of Napoleon and his times,* London, 1920).

2) Napoleon I Was the First to Call England "A Nation of Shopkeepers"

He merely quoted Adam Smith's *Wealth of nations* (London, 1776), having it first from Barère, who publicly used it of England in the French Convention of June 11, 1794, in allusion to Howe's battle of June 1: "Let Pitt, then, boast of his victory to his nation of shopkeepers."

Adam Smith actually wrote, "To found a great empire for the sole purpose of raising up a people of customers, may at first sight appear a project fit only for a nation of shopkeepers. It is, however, a project altogether unfit for a nation of shopkeepers; but extremely fit for a nation that is governed by shopkeepers."

Napoleon's actual words were, "L'Angleterre est ime nation de boutiquiers."

NAPOLEON WAS SHORT

We're all familiar with the term, "Napoleonic complex," as it refers to a small man with an overexerted ego, presumably to cover up his insecurities about his unintimidating physical appearance.

In fact, Napoleon was not actually particularly short. He was five foot seven, the average height for a male for the time period. The perception of old Bonaparte being much shorter and smaller than his actual height originally came from popular depictions of him in the British Toy press. Additionally, in the decades following Napoleon's existence and power, confusion in the differences between the British inch (2.54 cm) and the French *pounce* (2.71) contributed to this misconception.

Napoleon was thus used as a main go-to reference in order to illustrate behavior associated with the 20th-century psychological diagnosis of the "inferiority complex."

NATURE HAS "LAWS"

The "laws of nature" are observed and recorded by men, and thus as clearly man-made as penal or commercial laws. They, like penal or commercial laws, must also be modified in the light of changing circumstances to conform to new facts.

Julian Huxley wrote in his *Essays of a biologist* (1923): "A law of Nature is not [and I wonder how often this fallacy has been exploded, only to reappear next day]—a law of Nature is not something revealed, not something absolute, nor something imposed on phenomena from without or from above; it is no more and no less than a summing-up in generalized form, of our own observations of phenomena; it is an epitome of fact, from which we can draw general conclusions."

I would add only this: where agreed "laws of nature" are attacked explicitly or implicitly by those writers whose ideas are generically termed "fallacies" throughout this book, the onus is clearly upon them to prove that the "laws of nature" have been changed (and to show where and how). The onus is not upon those who accept the current but perennially-mutating "laws of nature" to show why they do so.

NATUROPATHY

A medical cult not to be confused with the simplicity of diet and regular exercise which it recommends in common with orthodox medicine. Naturopaths believe that the body will keep naturally healthy instead of having to cope with unnatural foods, customs, and medicines. They object to food grown with the aid of artificial fertilizers, yet it is farming (the systematic interference with nature to provide food) together with similar methods of adapting environment to needs which has enabled man to survive in competition with creatures that possess wings, claws, power, bulk or speed. As to avoiding medicines, the chemists have yet to produce anything as lethal as the "natural" poisons of some medicinal plants. All chemicals (to which naturopaths illogically object) are made from naturally occurring raw materials.

Naturopathy had no single founder, but grew up as an anti-scientific reaction to the gradual development of drugs in 18th- and 19th-century Europe. An early U.S. pioneer was the Seventh Day Adventist John H. Kellogg, and even now Adventism stresses nature therapy.

Though numerous books and magazines testify to the extremism of most naturopaths, nothing has yet equalled the great five-volume *Encyclopaedia of physical culture* (1912), by Bernarr Macfadden, with its injunctions against the internal use of drugs and medicine and against consulting orthodox doctors. Most suggested cures involve diets, exercises, and water therapy; cancer for instance should be treated by fasting, exercises, and a "vitality building regimen." Macfadden subsequently recanted his views on cancer (he now believes that it can be cured by a diet consisting solely of grapes).

Sources: Martin Gardner, *Fads and fallacies in the name of science* (New York, 1957); and Peter Wingate, *The Penguin medical encyclopedia* (2nd ed., Harmondsworth, 1976).

ADAM, EVE, AND THE **NAVEL** DISPUTE

Adam and Eve are mythical ancestors in some Eastern religions: the question of whether they had a navel is therefore pointless to debate. That has not prevented those with nothing better to do from debating it. Sir Thomas Browne, the eminent Norwich physician, decided in the middle of the 17th century that Adam and Eve had no navel. Sir Thomas, disapproving of the way in which earlier artists had depicted the primal pair, did not stop short of criticising Michelangelo Buonarroti and Raphael for their "unrealistic" inclusion of navels. "This is observable," notes Browne in Book V, chapter V of the *Pseudodoxia epidemica* (London, 1646), "not only in ordinary and stayned peeces, but in the Authenticke draughts of Urbin, Angelo, and others; which notwithstanding cannot be allowed, except we impute that unto the first cause, which we impose not on the second, or what we deny unto nature, we impute unto Naturity it selfe; that is, that in the first and most accomplished peece, the Creator affected super-fluities, or ordained parts without all use or office . . . Now the Navell or vessells whereof it is constituted, being a part precedent, and not subservient unto generation, nativity, or parturition, it cannot be well imagined at the creation or extraordinary formation of Adam, who immediately issued from the Artifice of God; nor also that of Eve, who was not solemnly begotten, but suddenly framed, and anomalously proceeded from Adam."

Nevertheless, great artists continued to paint Adam, Eve, and even God, with a navel. A Hamburg physician called Christian Tobias Ephraim Reinhard sprang at them again, in the middle of the 18th century, with his *Untersuchung der Frage: ob unsere erstern Urdltern, Adam und Eva, einen Nabel gehabt* (Hamburg, 1752). Dissertations are still—let it be remarked—being written on matters as intrinsi-cally insignificant, not to say foolish.

Reinhard justified the Biblical account of the Creation of man and woman (and of everything else) in all particulars and in general. "And whoever doubts this," he added, "is declared an unworthy mem-ber of the Church and is hereby handed to the Devil."

So now you know.

NERO FIDDLED WHILE ROME BURNED

The violin was not invented until the 16th century, so that story must surely die soon. Was the instrument a lyre or lute-type then found in Rome? It is known that he played an instrument and also that he wrote poetry (Suetonius records having seen his notebooks with his own era-sures), but he was at Antium when the fire that ruined half of Rome broke out in AD 64. The rumor that he had had the fire started began to circulate when he took the opportunity to build on the ashes his own colossal Domus Aurea. Nero himself put the blame on Christians, who were no more likely to have started the fire than he was.

Source: *Oxford Classical Dictionary* (Oxford, 1949).

COMINALE REFUTES ALL NEWTON

Antinewtonianismi pars prima (Naples, 1754) and *pars secunda* (Naples, 1756) is a detailed, largely fallacious refutation of everything that Newton wrote, by Celestino Cominale, Professor of Medicine at Naples.

Augustus de Morgan, in *A budget of paradoxes* (2nd ed., Chicago, 1915, vol.1, p. 162), observes of the work: "The first volume upsets the theory of light; the second vacuum, *vis inertiae*, gravitation, and traction. I confess I never attempted these big Latin volumes, numbering 450 closely-printed quarto pages. The man who slays Newton in a pamphlet is the man for me. But I will lend them to anybody who will give security, himself in £500, and two sureties in £250 each, that he will read them through, and give a full abstract; and I will not exact security for their return. I have never seen any mention of this book: it has a printer, but not a publisher, as happens with so many unrecorded books."

NIGHT AIR IS BAD FOR YOU

We have the authority of Shakespeare, in Act II of *Julius Caesar,* for the statement.

"And will he steal out of his wholesome bed, To dare the vile contagion of the night And tempt the rheumy and unpurged air To add unto his sickness?" Night air is colder than day air, so that anyone failing to take the precaution to add a blanket or two may feel cold, or aggravate influenza.

Florence Nightingale, no less, in her *Notes on nursing* (1860) scoffed at "the dread of night-air. What air can we breathe at night but night-air? The choice is between pure night-air from without and foul night-air from within. Most prefer the latter. An unaccountable choice."

In cities, night air may contain less carbonic acid, since fewer fires are burning, but central heating has done away with much of the air pollution which troubled our ancestors, and the terrible "pea-souper" fogs of London associated with Victorian times are fortunately a thing of the past.

On balance, night air may be marginally better for you than day air.

NIGHTINGALES SING ONLY AT NIGHT

No known species of nightingale sings only by night, though both *Daulias luscinia* and *Dautias vera* (common in Britain) are more usually heard at night.

Source: A. S. E. Ackermann, *Popular fallacies* (4th ed., London, 1950).

NIGHTMARES ARE CONNECTED WITH MARES

The Old English *maere* (incubus, a demon descending on you while you sleep, in the popular fancy) is the source of the second syllable in our familiar word for a bad dream, "nightmare." Related to the word "maere" are the Polish *zmora,* the Czech *mura* (both meaning "nightmare") and the first syllable of the Old Irish *Morrigain,* denoting the Queen of the Little People.

The modern English *mare* is derived by contrast from the Old English *mearh* meaning "horse," and has no connection with "maere" at all.

Sources: C. T. Onions, *The Oxford dictionary of English etymology* (Oxford, 1966).

NOBEL INSTITUTED SIX PRIZES IN 1901

When the Nobel Prizes were first awarded, in 1901, there were five different categories in which the prizes could be awarded: Chemistry, Literature, Medicine and Physiology, Peace, and Physics. Economics, the sixth prize awarded nowadays, was instituted as recently as 1969.

Incidentally, the Swedish chemist and engineer Alfred Nobel (1833-96) set up the Nobel Foundation in 1866, thirty-five years before the first prize was awarded.

A "NORMAL" PERSON HAS ONE BOWEL MOVEMENT PER DAY

Although it is a bit of a faux pas to discuss so openly, we believe this is all the more reason to give people some clarification on this point. Despite what one may consider "normal" according to what their parents or physicians told him or her growing up regarding bowel movements, it is equally as regular to go several days without getting the urge to empty one's bowels as it is to expect a bathroom trip after each meal of the day.

Medical experts unanimously agree that the typical range of what's considered regular and healthy for the average person to empty their bowels can go from three times a day to three times a week.

Furthermore, if your regularity has changed a little over time, don't fret, as both constipation and healthy bowel activity are relative, and forgiving!

Sources: familydoctor.org; about.com.

THERE ARE NUTS IN MAY

On this fallacy depends the popular children's song "Here we go gathering nuts in May." As Brewer states in *A dictionary of phrase and fable*, the phrase is a perversion of "Here we go gathering *knots of may*," referring to the old custom of gathering knots of flowers on May Day, or, to use the ordinary phrase, "to go a-maying." Of course there are no nuts to be gathered in May.

PROSPER RENE BLONDLOT AND **N-RAYS**

Blondlot, Professor at the University of Nancy, and a distinguished physicist, could by no stretch of the term be considered a pseudo-scientist, yet he was responsible for one of the most notorious fallacies adopted—though for only two years or so—by the European scientific establishment in the 20th century.

At the beginning of 1903, Blondlot was devoting a great deal of study to the X-rays then recently discovered by the German physicist Röntgen, and thought he had found new rays quite distinct from X-rays, one of their differences being that the new "N-rays" (N for Nancy) could be polarized. Blondlot believed that N-rays could travel through metals and many other substances normally opaque to spectral radiation, and published his preliminary findings in the Proceedings of the Académie des Sciences on March 23, 1903. Not only did Blondlot manage to list all the properties of his N-rays (which we now know did not exist), but he measured their wavelengths. Other scientists reportedly repeated his experiments and made additional observations of an effect which we are sure was a figment of their imagination. Lucien Cuénot has suggested that the discovery of (and further interest in) the N-rays might have been begun and fostered by a laboratory assistant at Nancy, though it is certainly remarkable that such eminent figures as Becquerel, Bordier, Broca, Ballet and Zimmern should have endorsed the existence of the rays. Rostand points to the urge to make discoveries common among most scientists, a weakness for preconceptions, and autosuggestion, all elements which feature strongly in occultism and parascience generally.

The two-year history of N-rays can be summarized briefly. Blondlot first "discovered" them in the radiation emanating from an X-ray tube; later he detected them in the radiation emitted by incandescent burners, and even from ordinary sources of heat and light. When they struck a small spark or flame, they increased the brightness. They also increased the phosphorescence of chemical compounds such as calcium sulphide. The sun was found to be a source of N-rays, which could be stored and re-emitted as secondary radiation by certain substances such as carbon sulphide, quartz, limestone, and eventually impure water, the last a unique example of "phosphorescence in a liquid body."

Blondlot now theorized that, if N-rays actually intensify the brightness of a given source, then surely other rays, the so-called inhibitors, must have an opposite effect. The postulate was swiftly confirmed, and the inhibitors were named N_1-rays.

Other scientists moved into the field: Macé de Lépinay proved that sound vibrations give rise to the emission of N-rays in the vicinity of the antinodes; Bichat found them emerging from liquefied gases and Lambert from soluble ferments. Bugard recorded the rotation of the plane of N-rays' polarization under the influence of a magnetic field. Charpentier found them emerging from ozone, and observed that N-rays were conducted by a copper wire. Pabre reported the emission of N-rays through contractions of the uterus during labor, the intensity of the emission being proportional to the force of the contractions.

It is worth repeating that N-rays do not exist and never have. "No less extraordinary," writes Jean Rostand, "is the *degree-of consistency, and of apparent logic that pervaded the whole of this collective delusion;* all the results were consistent, and agreed within fairly narrow limits." Lucien Cuénot concludes: "All critics (and all investigators have to be their own critics first and foremost) must be skeptical of everything—of their desire to make new discoveries and above all of the right-hand men: assistants are not usually given to a scrupulous love of truth, and have little aversion to rigging experiments; they are quite ready to flatter their superiors by presenting them with results that agree with their *a priori* notions. Alternatively, they often get malicious pleasure out of deceiving their superiors, thus driving them to commit errors—envy and ingratitude often go hand in hand."

Sources include: Jean Rostand, *Error and deception in science* (London, 1960, pp. 12-29).

"One of the first duties of man is not to be duped."
—CARL BECKER

"Order and disorder are purely human inventions ... If I
should throw down a thousand beans at random upon a
table, I could doubtless, by eliminating a sufficient number
of them, leave the rest in almost any geometrical pattern
you might propose to me, and you might then say that that
pattern was the thing prefigured beforehand, and that the
other beans were mere irrelevance and packing material.
Our dealings with Nature are just like this. She is a vast
plenum in which our attention draws capricious lines in
innumerable directions. We count and name whatever lies
upon the special lines we trace, whilst the other things and
the untraced lines are neither named or counted."
—WILLIAM JAMES, *Varieties of religious experience.*
(Connoisseurs of the fallacious will note the personification—
even the sexual identification—of "Nature")

THE PRINCIPLE OF **OCCAM'S RAZOR** IS THAT
THE SIMPLEST EXPLANATION IS BEST

William of Occam (or Ockham), who died about 1349, defended evan-
gelical poverty as a Franciscan against Pope John XXII, and spent
some time in prison at Avignon on a charge of heresy in 1328. In
the popular mind, he is unfairly remembered for his enunciation of
the principle of parsimony, or Occam's Razor, by which "entities must
not be unnecessarily multiplied." The simplest explanation is the
best provided but *only if* it covers all the known facts. Instead of reasoning from universal premises passed down from a higher authority, we should generalize from natural observations, a doctrine later
espoused by Francis Bacon, Hobbes, and indeed all empiricists.

Occam's epistemology rejected any relation between knowledge of
the universe and knowledge of God, and denied any possible human
knowledge of divine psychology. He equally rejected Thomist ontol-
ogy and St. Augustine's belief in eternal ideas which constitute the
archetypes of the universe in the depth of divine essence, and Occam

denied the usefulness and truth of the speculations of all the great Doctors of the Church.

Occam was one of the main agents for the dissolution of the medieval synthesis of religion and philosophy which culminated in the rise of modern science and technology in the face of opposition from monotheistic religions.

Sources include: Dagobert D. Runes, *Treasury of philosophy* (New York, 1955).

THE WORLD HAS A DIFFERENT, "OCCULT," HISTORY

The Irish journalist and hypnotist J. H. Brennan has written *An occult history of the world*. Volume 1 (London, 1976) offers a refreshingly eccentric view of world history, which takes into account the theosophical works of Madame Blavatsky, bizarre Stonehenge theories, several disparate explanations of the Pyramids of Gizah, and the myth of Atlantis, together with a resume of the main points from Erich von Däniken.

Mr. Brennan summarises his esoteric history of the world as follows:

1. A knowledge of the evolutionary process existed many thousands of years before Darwin published his *Origin of species.*
2. "Blind" evolution, such as Darwin postulates, actually began on this planet, in the oceans, something more than 2,000 million years ago, and over a period of 300 million years produced relatively complex sea creatures. [This view tallies to some extent with orthodoxy]
3. An extra-terrestrial race—or races—existed in our solar system and may have inhabited the Moon.
4. These aliens were far from any life form that we should recognize as such. They were not a product of any animal or vegetable evolution, but consisted of energy patterns and may, in some sense, have "fed" off the Sun.
5. A pressing concern of this race was the establishment of intelligent, physical life on Earth. [But for which conceivable motive?] With such a project in view, an invasion of our planet was mounted by the extra-terrestrials about 2,000 million years ago.
6. Examination of native life forms convinced the aliens that such forms were unsuited to the evolution of intelligence. They were consequently destroyed. [But how?]
7. At the time the planet was "disinfected," vast geological upheavals, either natural or provoked, produced areas of dry land on the surface of the Earth. [If natural, how could one explain the breathtaking coincidence? If provoked, how to explain the method of provocation?]

8. A limited number of the aliens undertook the first step towards the creation of a new terrestrial race in a variety of selected environments.
9. The prototypes of this new race were actually drawn, or projected, out of the essence of the aliens themselves.
10. As such, the prototypes were non-material. They consisted of energy-patterns probably not so very different from those of the original aliens. They had, at this stage, neither self-consciousness nor intelligence and were looked on as incomplete. To offer alternatives to existing theories or facts or systems, it is first of all necessary to indicate in which ways the existing patterns of knowledge are inconsistent, and to show that the improved patterns are consistent. Mr. Brennan has failed in the former objective as signally as in the latter, and we shall have to continue to modify our views of cosmology, astronomy, geology, and prehistory from the corpus of what scientists can already generally agree on. The rejection of findings, by thousands of scientists all over the world, which are mutually consistent, must be regarded as an exercise in science-fiction rather than as a viable new theory.

AN **OCTOPUS** CAN STRANGLE A MAN

Pure fantasy. It has been reported rarely that a swimmer has been held by one of the eight suckers of an octopus, but no harm has ever resulted, at least to the swimmer. Octopuses are also alleged to have bitten human beings with their beaklike mouths and to have injected venom, but no consequence has ever been more serious than a slight and temporary swelling.

THE **ODIC FORCE**

In 1845, the *Researches* of the physicist Karl von Reichenbach appeared as a special volume of the respected *Annalen der Chemie und Physik.* For twenty years, he argued the existence of a physical force which could be felt or seen only by "sensitives." Despite the increasing skepticism of scientists who questioned his assumption that *any* given force can be perceived *only* by sensitives, Reichenbach managed to obtain a hearing in Berlin in 1862 before a commission of seven experts. He complained bitterly that odic reception was worse in Berlin than in his native Vienna, and blamed the climate. Whatever the reason, when an independent expert brought his own magnets to make the current reversible and obtain a degree of control, Reichenbach's sensitives (mostly neurotic young women) failed to tell positive from negative, or even whether the current was on or off.

The independent commission found: "That the demonstrations of Baron von Reichenbach have in no way established what they were intended to show, and give no proof of a new natural force."

Joseph Jastrow's verdict on "Od" and the "Odic Force" is as follows: "The diagnosis of the "case of *Od*" turns upon three data: first and dominant is the conviction that there is an undiscovered force; second is the rationalized search for it, its properties to be determined by physical and chemical research; third is the reliance upon peculiarly constituted sensitives to demonstrate it. The first is pure assumption; the second is the approved procedure, *if* rightly carried out; the third is a fateful error."

It is curious in this connection to note the science-fiction novel *The Coming Race* (London, 1871), by Edward Bulwer-Lytton (1803-73), about a subterranean race which has achieved a high degree of creativity and civilization through using *Vril,* an energy embodying all the natural forces, and reminiscent (in the claims made for it) of *Od.* Connoisseurs of fallacies will cherish the fact that, having been told about *Vril,* the extraordinary Mme. H. P. Blavatsky (the theosophist) assumed that it was real, and not only claimed that it was employed by the lost Atlanteans, but that it was the energy used in the Keely motor!

Sources: Joseph Jastrow, *Wish and wisdom* (New York, 1935).

ROGER BACON ON **OFFENDICULA**

Roger Bacon (c. 1214-1294) recognized four categories of *offendicula,* which might be translated "impediments to thought." These are "excessive reliance on authority," "slavery to custom," "subjection to the weight of popular opinion," and the "concealment of ignorance by pretending knowledge."

Source: Roger Bacon, *Sumule dialectices* (written about 1245) in Bacon's *Opera hactenus inedita,* ed. by Robert Steele (fasc. 15, Oxford, 1909).

OMENS

Primitive people (in all civilizations) have always, in lieu of seeking actual experimental knowledge which requires the acquisition of books, the art of reading and writing, leisure for study, diligence, and native ability, tried to master their unmanageable lives by "finding out what to do" themselves or by resorting to those who claim to be able to foretell the future. It is still commonplace to hear an otherwise intelligent person declare, "that's a good omen."

Fallacies involving telling the future include aeromancy (divination from cloud-formations in the air), alectryomancy (from cockerels), alphitomancy (from grains of wheat), alveromancy (from barley), amniomancy (from the amniotic membrane occasionally enveloping the head of the newborn), axinomancy (from an axe and hatchet), clidomancy (from keys), cromniomancy (from onions) . . . And that is a selection from only the first three letters of the English alphabet!

The credulity of men can be estimated in direct contrast to their willingness and ability to learn.

THE "ALL MEN ARE DRIVEN BY ONLY ONE THING" FALLACY

In *Leviathan* (London, 1651), Thomas Hobbes the English philosopher declared: "In the first place, I put for a general implication of all mankind, a perpetual and restless desire of power after power, that ceaseth only in death." And his book is based solely on that supposition.

Robert Ardrey, in his *Territorial imperative* (New York, 1966), argues that man's territorial attitude is the key to much of his activity, for good and ill.

Gordon Rattray Taylor, in his *Sex in history* (New York, 1954) seeks to demonstrate not merely "how closely attitudes to sexual matters interlock with other social attitudes" but also how they "dictate them." For him, as for countless other writers past and present, all men are driven by only one thing. They only differ in their opinion as to what that is. Let the reader, young and old, beware of the writer who simplifies phenomena essentially complex. Some men may be driven by the urge for power, or territory, or sex. But not all. One might as well say that all men are driven by the urge to collect stamps or learn Danish. Evelyn Underbill deserved the last word for a generalization of this type which will be prized by every collector of human fallacies: "There is a sense in which we may think of the whole life of the Universe," she wrote in *Worship* (New York, 1936), "seen and unseen, conscious and unconscious, as an act of worship, glorifying its Origin, Sustainer, and End."

THE FIRST CHINESE WAR OF 1839-42 IS CORRECTLY CALLED THE OPIUM WAR

Opium may have been one of the pretexts, but the "Opium War" was really caused by a concatenation of circumstances related to the British right to trade in Kwangtung (then known as Canton).

The Emperors of China were always reluctant to deal with foreign merchants, who were limited to the port of Kwangtung and could communicate with local officials only through a Chinese mercantile association. However, local merchants and government officials derived great profits from the opium trade before the importation of opium was prohibited by an Imperial Edict of 1800 and, illicitly, also after 1800. Opium smuggling was a thriving trade, with the connivance of both merchants and corrupt officials. In March 1839, the Chinese had demanded that all opium held by the British in Kwangtung and in depot ships offshore should be surrendered.

The British Superintendent of Trade, Captain Elliot, complied with this demand, handing over opium then valued at more than £2 million. But the Chinese then demanded that foreign merchants should sign a bond agreeing that, if any opium were found on board a British vessel thenceforward, the guilty would be executed and ship confiscated, and it was this additional demand which made the crisis deteriorate to sparking point. War was declared when the Chinese demanded that a British subject be punished for killing a Chinese in a brawl on July 7, 1839. Great Britain did not in fact ask to import opium after the war was over, neither was any such request incorporated in the Treaty of Nanking of 1842.

Sources include: W. C. Costin, *Great Britain and China,* 1833-1860 (Oxford, 1937); and Historical Association, *Common errors in history* (London, 1951).

THE **ORANGUTAN** BELONGS TO THE HUMAN SPECIES

The *orangutan* (properly *orang hutan,* Malay = "man of the forest"), is an anthropoid ape, that is a member of the ape family. The popular American writer on animals, Ivan T. Sanderson, wrote in *Animal treasure* (1937) that both the orangutan and the gorilla:

"I can only regard . . . as a retrograde form of human . . . life."

There is perhaps more excuse for the Scottish judge Lord Monboddo (1714-1799), who described in *Of the origin and progress of language* (6 vols., 1773-92) and *Antient metaphysics* (6 vols., 1779-99) his pet orangutan as an example of "the infantine state of oar species" who could play the flute but "never learned to speak." Thomas Love Peacock (1785-1866), with de Quincey the most underrated English writer of the early 19th century, wrote a hilarious conversation-piece on the unfortunate Monboddo: *Melincourt, or Sir Oran Haut-ton* (1817), Mr. Sylvan Forester, a wealthy young philosopher, has trained an orangutan in everything but speech, and bought him a baronetcy and a seat in Parliament. The amiable, chivalrous Sir Oran plays the flute to perfection and enchants the company.

Source: C. B. Tinker, *Nature's simple plan* (Princeton, N.J., 1922).

ORGONOMY

Wilhelm Reich (1897-1957) was a psychoanalyst under Freud and held a number of important teaching and administrative posts in Viennese psychoanalytical organizations. A Marxist, he published an extraordinary book, partly inspired by the anthropologist Malinowski, called *The function of the orgasm* (1927) in which he stated his theory that the sexual frustration of the proletariat caused a thwarting of its political consciousness, and it was only through uninhibited release of the sexual urge that the working class could realize its historic mission. The Marxist authorities were unimpressed, labelling his book "un-Marxist rubbish" and he soon parted too from Freud, being formally expelled from the International Psychoanalytical Association in 1934.

In the 1930s Reich seems to have lost his mental balance, and in 1939 he became obsessed with "orgone energy," inventing the term "orgonomy" to describe the science of this new type of energy. He issued the *International Journal of Sex-Economy and Orgone Research,* later renamed the *Orgone Energy Bulletin: The Annals of the Orgone Institute;* and numerous books and pamphlets to try to demonstrate that he had discovered the biological basis that Freud had been seeking for his theory of the libido, or sexual energy.

Orgone energy, according to Reich, is a nonelectromagnetic force permeating all nature. It is the life force of Bergson made accessible and usable by means of a therapeutic box called an Orgone Energy Accumulator. According to a former translator, Dr. Theodore P. Wolfe, this box is the "most important single discovery in the history of medicine, bar none." It consists of a short phone-box type of structure made of sheet iron on the inside, and an organic material (such as celotex or wood) on the outside. Orgone energy is allegedly attracted by the organic substance on the outside, and is passed to the metal which then radiates it inward. The metal reflects orgone, so the box soon acquires a high concentration of the energy. Reich's anonymous booklet *The Orgone Energy Accumulator* (1951) advertised it as a cure for hay fever, anemia, cancer in early stages, acute colds, chronic ulcers, and any kind of lesion or abrasion,

(Incidentally, Reich also invented a rainmaking device called C.OR.E. or Cosmic ORgone Engineering which does not spray the clouds. As Irwin Ross reported in the *New York Post* (*Sunday Magazine*) for September 5, 1954, it merely draws orgone out of them, weakening their cohesive power and causing them to break up.)

Legal action to prevent "orgone energy accumulators" being shipped interstate and to prohibit the distribution of publicity matter mentioning orgone energy was taken by the U.S. Food and Drug Administration in 1954. They estimated that a thousand of the orgone boxes had been sold. After a series of careful tests, FDA official scientists concluded that "there is no such energy as orgone and that Orgone Energy Accumulators are worthless in the treatment of any disease or disease condition of man. Irreparable harm may result to persons who abandon or postpone rational medical treatment while pinning their faith on worthless devices such as these."

After being diagnosed by a psychiatrist as a paranoid, he became intensely religious and started to pray. He identified himself with Christ in his book *The Murder of Christ* (which I suppose is one step more logical than identifying Christ with *amanita muscaria* as John Allegro has done in his book *The sacred mushroom)* but he made a number of valuable contributions, including *The sexual revolution* (1930), reissued in 1969.

Sources: *Humanist,* February 1970 (pp. 46-7), and Martin Gardner, *Fads and fallacies in the name of science,* 2nd ed. (New York, 1957, chapter 21).

AN **ORPHAN** IS PARENTLESS

It is often stated that an orphan is one who has lost both father and mother, but the *Shorter Oxford Dictionary* defines "orphan" as "one deprived by death of father or mother," so that a child with one parent still living should properly be referred to as an orphan.

OSTEOPATHY

A theory invented by Andrew Taylor Still (a man with no identifiable medical training) in 1874 which states that diseases are caused by a malfunctioning of the nerves or blood supply, which is due chiefly to the dislocation of small bones in the spine. These dislocations, or "subluxations of the vertebrae," press on nerves and blood vessels and prevent the body from manufacturing its own curative agents. Still's eccentric autobiography (shown by investigation to be full of invention and fraudulent claims) records that by his system of spinal rubbing, he grew three inches of hair in a week on a head completely bald, and that by his methods of spinal manipulation he "cured" malaria, yellow fever, diphtheria, diabetes, dandruff, obesity, piles and constipation.

There are 11,000-odd practitioners of osteopathy in the United States today. As Martin Gardner quietly points out, "the back rub feels pleasant—especially for patients with repressed sexual longings."

Osteopathy should not be confused with reputable manipulative surgery. As Sir Herbert Barker wrote in *The Daily Telegraph* of February 7, 1935: "My correspondence, the lay and professional press, and my friends, all make it very apparent that practically the entire public believes that osteopathy and manipulative surgery are one and the same thing . . . Bone-setting, or manipulative surgery—a British and very much older system of therapeutics—deals only with injuries, and derangements of the joints, ligaments, muscles and tendons, and some acquired deformities."

Sources include: Martin Gardner, *Fads and fallacies in the name of science* (New York, 1957).

OSTRICH FALLACIES

1. Ostrich Wings Are Useless, as the Bird Cannot Fly
The ostrich cannot fly, but uses its wings to turn sharply when eluding a hunter. Ostriches can both jump and swim.

2. Ostriches Bury Their Heads in the Sand
This curious fallacy probably arose from the observation that, when sighting danger from afar, they occasionally drop to the ground with their necks parallel to the ground and watch intently. Then, if danger approaches, they do what every other animal with strong legs is likely to do: they run like hell.

President Woodrow Wilson is only one of a thousand politicians and orators who have used the picturesque figure of speech, obviously thinking it a fact and not a fallacy. In a speech on February 1, 1916 he declared: "America cannot be an ostrich with its head in the sand." To which one is tempted to add "neither can an ostrich," for it would quickly suffocate.

3. Ostriches Can Digest Coins and Keys
Metallic and other hard substances are taken into the gizzard by ostriches, much as common fowl take small sharp pebbles, but they are not digested, despite Shakespeare:

"Ah, villain, thou wilt betray me, amd get a thousand crowns of the king by carrying my head to him; but I'll make thee eat iron like an ostrich, and swallow my sword like a great pin, ere thou and I part" (Jack Cade to Alexander Iden)—*King Henry VI,* Part 2 (IV, x).

But the fallacy that such metal objects are actually digested by ostriches was repudiated by Sir Thomas Browne in *Pseudodoxia epidemica* (London, 1646), Book III, chapter 22: "The common opinion of the Ostrich, Struthiocamelus, or Sparrow Camel, conceives that it digesteth iron, and this is confirmed by the affirmations of many: besides swarms of others, Rhodiginus in his prelections taketh it for granted, Johannes Langius in his epistles pleadeth experiment for it; the common picture also confirmeth it, which usually describeth this animal with an horseshoe in its mouth. Notwithstanding, upon inquiry we find it very questionable, and the negative seems most reasonably entertained ..."

Ostriches eat vegetables and grass in the wild; in captivity according to the London Regent's Park Zoo they will eat almost anything, from meat to keys and coins, but of course they cannot *digest* these latter. Cuvier shall have the last word: "The powers of digestion in this bird are certainly very great, but their operation is confined to matters of an alimentary character."

THE **OUIJA** BOARD CONNECTS THOSE PRESENT WITH DISTANT EVENTS OR PERSONS

The "ouija" board (combining the French and German words for "yes") is a flat piece of polished wood with the letters of the alphabet in a line, semi-circle or circle along one side. On this a small board, mounted on casters, slides about when participants place their hands on it and may spell out words and sentences by the pointing of an arrow. In other cases an upturned wine glass slides towards a letter which the participants allege is chosen by spirits directing them.

Michael Faraday investigated the ouija board phenomena and came to the following conclusion: "It is with me a clear point that the table moves when the parties, though they strongly wish it, do not intend, and do not believe that they move it by ordinary mechanical power. They say the table draws their hands; it moves first and they have to follow it." After testing various substances with different electrical properties, Faraday found that "No form of experiment or mode of observation that I could devise gave me the slightest indication of any peculiar natural force—nothing but mere mechanical pressure exerted inadvertently by the turner."

The ouija board is a method of autonography midway between table-turning and automatic writing.

Sources include: D. H. Rawcliffe, *Illusions and delusions of the supernatural and the occult* (New York, 1952) and Richard Cavendish, ed., *Encyclopedia of the unexplained* (London, 1974).

AN **OVATION** IS A MAJOR TRIUMPH

The popular press frequently refers to an ovation accorded to a figure deserving of every reward. But the Latin *ovatio* is, to quote Cassell's *Latin dictionary* (1948 printing) merely "a kind of lesser triumph in which the victorious general proceeded to the Capitol on horseback or on foot." An ovation is thus a secondary triumph.

OXFORD BELLS ARE MAGICAL

Louis Pauwels and Jacques Bergier, in *The dawn of magic* (London, 1963), claim to "have studied certain reports of the occult section of the German Intelligence Service—notably a lengthy report on the magical properties of the bells in the belfries of Oxford which were thought to have prevented bombs from falling on the town."

With breathtaking understatement the authors add: "it is undeniable that there is an element of aberration here; but the fact that it affected supposedly intelligent and responsible men, thereby illuminating certain aspects of both visible and invisible history, is equally undeniable."

OZONE AT THE SEASIDE IS GOOD FOR YOU

There is no ozone at the seaside, for the simple reason that the ozone layer is roughly fifty kilometers above sea level. The *University Correspondent* (July 1, 1914) reported that "The existence of ozone in air has always been doubtful, the chemical evidence for its presence being quite unsatisfactory . . . The smell attributed to it at the seaside really arises from decaying seaweed."

Sir Edwin Ray Lankester, a valuable popularizer of science, explained to readers of *The Daily Telegraph* (February 26, 1912) "that the presence of ozone . . . in respired air in even very minute quantities acts as an irritant to the air passages and is highly injurious. It produces no effect whatever on the respiratory processes which go on in the lungs, but it is not altogether negligible from the point of view of fresh air and ventilation."

"Concentrations of even one part in the million are too irritative, and quickly depress the metabolism and lower the temperature of rats, and are unpleasant to man . . . ," reported Dr. Leonard Hill and Dr. Martin Flack in their paper *The influence of ozone in ventilation* to the Royal Society of Arts (February 7, 1912).

P

Populus vult decipi. ("The people want to be deceived.")

—ANCIENT ROMAN SAYING

"El prudente saca fruto de los ajenos errores." (The prudent profit from the mistakes that others make)

—JOAQUÍN SETANTI

THE BIGGER THE FEET, THE BIGGER THE "PACKAGE"

It's about time we got to this one. Like many of these other fallacies, the size-tells-all myth is probably most common among preteens, more specifically, preteen girls who have not yet had the pleasure of making the acquaintance of the male genitalia in "person." The imagination needs a basis. In this case, the standard of measurement is foot, or rather, shoe size.

There are a few variations of this hot topic. The first is in the form of a popular, though definitely played out, joke. Let's set up a familiar scenario: A male and a female are sitting on a couch at a party. Out of desperation and in a semi-drunken stupor, the boy might say something smooth like, "I like your shoes. But unfortunately, I don't think they'd fit on me." The girl might reply, "Yeah, your feet are pretty big," while the boy responds happily, "You know what they say about big feet?" The answer being either a coy "big socks" or the more obvious downward glance.

The doctors and authors of a recent book on common myths about bodies and health make the interesting suggestion that the prevalence of the shoe-size comparison is due to the basic human desire to want to find patterns in everything. More generally, we like to be able to have explanations for things and to put them in familiar categories (social networking, anyone?). Regardless of this instinct, cold hard facts prove us wrong here.

Several studies have been conducted, where 100 plus men were asked to put their masculinity on the line against their foot size. In every instance, there was found to be no "hard" correlation between the two respective male body parts.

(Continued)

Another rumor often heard in ladies' locker rooms is that manhood size is not just equal to *the* man's shoe size, but more humbly, it is half the shoe size plus one inch. We have not yet been able to find specific research on this claim. For now we can leave it an alluring mystery, unless we have any brave volunteers?

Sources: J. Shah, N. Christopher, "Can Shoe Size Predict Penile Length?" *Urology Journal*, BJU International, 2002; Dr. Aaron E. Carroll and Dr. Rachel C. Vreeman, *Don't Swallow Your Gum!: Myths, Half-Truths, and Outright Lies About Your Body and Health*, 2009.

THE **PANAMA HAT** COMES FROM THE CENTRAL AMERICAN STATE OF PANAMA

A Panama hat is one made from the undeveloped leaves of the stemless screw-pine (*Carloduvica palmata*) and has nothing to do with the nation of Panama.

PARAMNESIA

A common psychological phenomenon defined as "distortion or falsification of memory or recognition," so that one is wrongly conscious that "all of this has happened before" or "I can guess what will happen next" or "I was here in a former (or later) existence." This illusion is also known as "déjà vu" (French, "already seen"). The significance of this fallacy is that Plato's firm belief in extrapolation from past experience induced him to use it as an argument for his belief in a previous existence.

Source: James Drever, *A dictionary of psychology,* revised by Harvey Wallerstein (Harmondsworth, 1964).

PARROTS CAN LIVE TO BE A HUNDRED

Not so far as the experts have been able to obtain reliable records, "Hundred-year-old parrots certainly belong in the realm of the fable; nevertheless a raven in captivity reached an age of 69 years."

Source: Grzimek, *Animal life encyclopaedia,* vol. 7 (New York, 1972, p. 73).

THE **PATHETIC** FALLACY

An error of "imaginatively endowing inanimate objects with life," according to Toynbee (in *A study of history,* London, 1935, vol. I, p. 18).

It permeated Greek religion as both anthropomorphism (human forms) and anthropopathism (human feelings), and can be found throughout such masterpieces as the *Iliad*, the *Odyssey*, and the *Oresteia* of Aeschylus. The fallacy was attacked as early as the sixth century B.C. by Xenophanes of Colophon, but it persists to this day in such various guises as the "Statue of Liberty" or the "two faces of Communism." Theodore Roosevelt even went to the absurd length, in a drafted speech, of comparing nations of the world to specific animals, including monkeys, hyenas and hippopotami. Max Lerner (in *America as a civilization,* 2 vols., New York, 1961, vol. 1, p. 28) wrote of a national compensation in the United States for "the sacrificial slaying of the European father." The psychoanalytic approach to history is fraught with such fallacies, and is invariably simplistic to the point of absurdity.

PATRIOTIC FALLACY

A nationalistic extension of the fallacy of egoism, the fallacy of patriotism is to assume that one's own country or region is superior to that of other men. The fallacy is still held almost universally, though not officially, even at the United Nations and other international organizations.

Antoine de Rivarol, in *De l'universalité de la langue française* (Paris, 1784), claimed that "English literature is not worth a second glance," and much worse judgments, private and public, have led beyond fights and duels to full-scale wars completely based on prejudice. "The West," stated Gobineau in his absurd *Essai sur l'inégalité des races humaines* (1853-1855), "has always been the center of the world." Think about it.

A **PEAL OF BELLS** IS THE NAME OF THE EIGHT BELLS IN THE BELFRY

An appeal (or summons) of bells was early corrupted to "a peal" and in campanology refers to 5,040 changes, or the varying of the order in which the bells come down as they are being rung. The bells peal, but are not in themselves a peal.

PEANUT BUTTER IS THE BEST TOOL FOR GETTING GUM OUT OF HAIR

While there is no real way to prove this with statistics, or otherwise than word of mouth, it seems worthy to dismiss this fallacy, abiding by majority vote. Although peanut butter typically trumps ice and combing in its effectiveness in removing chewing gum

(Continued)

from hair, it seems that there is another non-blade related method which is considered slightly more reliable. This product is oil.

Because peanut butter generally contains a good amount of oil, this is probably why it is so often used or recommended as the top choice for gum removal. But in this case, why not use olive oil? The consensus on a variety of online forums, particularly Youtube videos, is that the two products are equally effective in removing gum from hair at best. At worst, scissors are your only option.

THE **PEARL HARBOR** DISASTER COULD NOT HAVE BEEN WORSE

Military historians teach that victories are not always as sweeping as they might have been, and that defeats are not always tragedies: they might well have been worse. This is in fact precisely the case with Pearl Harbor, though few Americans can be persuaded to see it that way.

Briefly, the Japanese attacked the Pacific Fleet while the latter was still in harbour on December 7, 1941, and inflicted a defeat. However, as Leo Rosten showed in *World* magazine (August 1, 1972), after strategists had already made the point in more scholarly publications, the loss to American ships would almost certainly have been far greater if the fleet had been at sea. In harbor, many ships were repaired after attack. At sea, many more lives and ships would have been lost. The Japanese boats were faster than the American boats, and the Japanese had six aircraft carriers against one on the American side.

A **PEDAGOGUE** ORIGINALLY MEANT A TEACHER

The Greek *paidagogos* was "a slave who led a boy to school, *hence* [my italics], a tutor, instructor," and not originally the boy's teacher. It was in Latin that *paedagogus* came to mean "a preceptor," and this usage passed into French and other modern languages with its changed meaning.

Source: Walter W. Skeat, *An etymological dictionary of the English language* (Oxford, 1888).

PERPETUAL MOTION CAN BE ACHIEVED BY AN "OVERBALANCING WHEEL" MECHANISM

This idea has been "discovered" time and again by inventors the world over. Henry Dircks, for instance, illustrates in his *Perpetuum mobile* (London, 1861; second series, 1870), machines of this type by the Marquis of Worcester and Dircks himself. The weight of each smaller ball and its attached rod slightly exceeds that of the larger ball; in consequence, it extends or contracts the lazy-tongs when the rod is vertical (in other positions the rod is prevented from sliding by stops inside the hub). In spite of the fact that the larger balls on one side of the wheel are much farther from the center than those on the other, the wheel has no tendency to rotate.

If ingeniously made, the mechanism *wastes* very little power, but cannot generate any.

Source: Rupert T. Gould, *Oddities,* 2nd ed. (London, 1944), for the chapter *Orffyreus' wheel,* pp. 89-116.

A LIT CIGARETTE WILL IGNITE **PETROL**

The signs on filling-stations exhorting one to extinguish cigarettes always impressed me (as a nonsmoker), but when I perhaps foolishly tried to ignite petrol from a lighter with a friend's cigarette, I failed. When the glowing tobacco was dipped into the petrol it was extinguished. (This is not a recommendation for anyone to smoke at filling-stations, or indeed at all.) And petrol vapor and oxygen are of course very dangerous near a lit cigarette or any form of fire.

COLOR OF **PHLEGM** INDICATES SEVERITY OF ILLNESS

You could be coughing up mucus left and right, swallowing and salivating in alternating rhythms all day. As long as what you're bringing up is still colorless, there's nothing to worry about, and the symptoms will pass in due time.

But if you wake up, hack up an especially unpleasant amount of phlegm into your bathroom sink, only to realize that it is yellow or green in hue, you're in trouble. You should probably schedule a doctor's appointment immediately, cancel all your obligations for the day, and call up all your friends and family members so that they realize that you are more or less bedridden. So the myth goes (at least for those of us who have moderate hypochondriac tendencies).

Generally, having yellow or greenish mucus is not an indication of a severe infection that needs immediate medical attention and/or antibiotics, but it is rather a natural part of the body's reaction to viruses that are no worse than the common cold.

Many of us also use antibiotics as a go-to guaranteed instant relief remedy for Upper Respiratory Infections (URIs) can come in the form of any type of virus in the head or chest that affects your throat, nose, sinuses, and/or ears. This classification is essentially just a broader way to categorize the common cold virus and the complications that may come along with it. However, these illnesses only last about a week, and don't require prescription medication,

(Continued)

medical attention, or anything really aside from over-the-counter pills to relieve symptoms, rest, water, and waiting for the virus to run its course.

In the first few days of URI infection, you will typically experience a thin and clear layer of mucus secreting from the nose or in the back of the throat. After the third day or so, mucus may become thicker and darker in color (yellow and/or greenish tint). This process is quite normal and is simply a way in which the body reacts when immune cells fights back against infection. The change in color of phlegm also can be a sign that the bacteria in the nose is growing back.

According to this explanation, mucus coloration is actually more of a sign of your body getting rid of the virus than it is a warning that the virus is too powerful for you to fight off sans-professional help. Other sources, such as Dr. Schaffner of the Dept. of Preventative Medicine at Vanderbilt University, says the shade of your mucus secretions has nothing to do with what sickness you have.

Unless you find blood in your sink after your morning phlegm exorcisms, don't panic.

Sources: Lesley Alderman, "Patient Money; When the Sniffles Start, Think Before you Buy," *New York Times*, 2010; Arizona University Health, "Yellow-Green Phlegm and Other Myths"; Dartmouth College Health Service, "Care for Upper Respiratory Infections," Department of Health and Human Services; *Centers for Disease Control and Prevention*, "A Guide for Parents Questions and Answers: Runny Nose (with green or yellow mucus)."

THERE IS A REAL DANGER IN CELL **PHONES** EMITTING SPARKS

Only in the past decade or two, cell phones have become an immensely essential part of our lives. It seems only yesterday we had all our friends' home phone numbers memorized, while now it's hardly necessary or even common for households to have a land line.

Cell phones make our lives easier in many ways. The most obvious: we carry them with us, so we are able to be reached and presumably, to reach others, at all times of the day and night. Also, with text messaging, we can communicate with people to make plans for later even at otherwise inconvenient times, such as in a loud environment or during class or work. In more dire situations, such as if our cars break down in the middle of a deserted rural street (or in the middle of a five-lane highway), you know help is only as far away as a quick dial on your hand-held touch screen.

But along with the benefits of this revolutionary communication device come downsides, side effects, and downright paranoia. For an example of the last instance, we give you the cell phone explosion at gas stations myth. Like turning off your cell phones on airplanes (except more over the top), turning off your cell phone at gas stations is not only encouraged by the common man in common speech, but there are also warning signs at gas pumps, informing careless car drivers of the risk of their mobile phone catching spark and setting off a life-threatening explosion.

Shockingly, this myth has absolutely no basis in reality whatsoever. The rumor about the risks of cell phone explosion originated, ironically enough, back in 1999 on the world wide web! The first source to report this liability was the *China Post*, which told the tale of an Indonesian man who caught on fire while getting his tank filled by an attendant. Said man was using his cell phone, and the accident was said to have occurred because the petrol vapor was ignited through the static electricity from his phone, leading to flames and explosion. Thereafter, many other stories of this type cropped up worldwide.

The duality of the power of modern technology devices is demonstrated by what the Federal Communications Commission has to say about gas stations and cell phones. While they acknowledge that there are no documented incidents where cell phones have ignited fires at gas stations and that the risk of this ever occurring is purely theoretical, they still must alert the public against engaging in this kind of potentially dangerous activity. The FCC stresses that although the threat of using cell phones at gas stations is very remote, they still insist there is good reason to follow the instructions on gas station pumps advising against it (potential ignition sources being listed as "automobiles" and "static electricity"). Seeing as, of course, the only time you would be using your cell phone in the proximity of cars and electrical energy is at a gas station, this informative piece of governmental evidence is solid as a rock.

Sources: Federal Communications Commission, "Wireless Phones at Gas Stations"; Cameron, Keith, "Mobile Phone Sparks New Call for Ban," *South China Morning Press*, 1993 via *Snopes*.

PHRENOLOGY AND PHRENOMAGNETISM

A pseudo-science founded by the otherwise able Viennese anatomist Franz Josef Gall on the intrinsically unlikely notion that the outward shape of the skull, when analyzed, can reveal the owner's character. The shape of the brain has no influence on the shape of the skull: phrenology has therefore no basis in fact at all, but it is still widely held to be scientific by cranks and the ignorant, despite the fact that a majority of its own members voted to put the British Phrenological Society into voluntary liquidation in 1967, when most of its important library was divided between University College London and Cambridge University.

The Scottish surgeon James Braid (1795-1850) thought that a valid medical technique (also called phrenomesmerism) consisted of passing an operator's fingers over the scalp of a hypnotized patient. The patient then feels the sensation or emotion associated with the phrenological organ so touched, although Braid's physiological explanation (to use Lewis Spence's understatement in the *Encyclopaedia of occultism* (New York, 1960) "is a somewhat inadequate one." It can be read—if anyone feels the desire to do so—in *Neurypnology* (London, 1843; 2nd ed, *On hypnotism: Neurypnology,* London, 1899).

Sources: J. A. C. Brown, *Pears medical encyclopedia* (London, 1967) and David de Giustino, *Conquest of mind* (London, 1975), the latter on the British phrenologist George Combe (1787-1852); *Neurypnology* (London, 1843; 2nd ed, *On hypnotism: Neurypnology,* London, 1899).

PHYSIOGNOMY

The doctrine of a mystical connection between the human body and the universe. The Rosicrucian Robert Fludd attempted in 1619 to demonstrate the link between the microcosm (man) and the macrocosm (universe). This is illusory, but even more so is the supposed indication of destiny by an interpretation of "the mystery of the human head" which Fludd purported to unravel by dividing the face into three "worlds." The "divine world" is the forehead, the "physical world" comprises the nose and eyes, and the "material world" comprises the inverted triangle based on the jaw and chin.

Lavater defined physiognomy as "the knowledge and realization of the link between the exterior and the interior, the visible surface to the invisibility which it covers."

THE "PICTS" OF SCOTLAND HAVE A KNOWN ORIGIN

T. F. O'Rahilly, in his *Early Irish history and mythology* (Dublin, 1946) refers to the wild speculations of "archaeologists," some of them professional, historians and linguists on the question of the race and origin of the *Picti,* "the painted people" (unfortunately for identification, all the *Britanni* tribes were painted). Bede began the wild goose-chase with a theory that the Picti came from Scythia, an Irish tradition. Modern writers have described them as "Goedels," as "Brythons," as Celts who spoke a Gallo-Brythonic dialect allied to both Gaulish and Brythonic, and as a pre-Celtic people of non-Indo-European origin. They arrived in Britain in the Early Bronze Age, the Middle Bronze Age, the Late Bronze Age, and in various phases of the early Iron Age, depending on the "expert" that you happen to read. Affinities have been found for them among the Eskimoes, the Finns, and the Illyrians. The Pictish question has been "settled," but seldom to the satisfaction of more than the writer, by H. M. Chadwick, V. Gordon Childe, T. Rice Holmes, Henri Hubert, Joseph Loth, R. A. S. Macalister, Eoin MacNeill, Adolf Mahr, O'Rahilly himself, Julius Pokorny, Joseph Raftery, and W. J. Watson. F. T. Wainwright has said that in some of these explanations "the element of fiction, even fantasy, is so pronounced that Bede's story of Scythia appears (by comparison only) to be a model of scientific sobriety."

Insufficient evidence is available at present for the "Picts" to be identified either by race or origin.

Source: F. T. Wainwright (*editor*), *The problem of the Picts* (London, 1955).

THERE WAS A **PIED PIPER** OF HAMELIN

Well, if there was a Pied Piper of Hamelin, (the German place-name is really Hameln) there was also a Pied Piper of Lorch, a Pied Piper of Brandenburg, and pied pipers with the gift of spiriting away children in Far East and Middle East legend.

In other words, there was no historical pied piper at all.

Sabine Baring-Gould, in *Curious myths of the Middle Ages* (2nd ser., 1868) found the piper tradition in Greek myth as Apollo (but he must have meant Pan), and in Sanskrit myth before that. He took the myth to refer to the wind in the reeds and thus to be as universal as the wind itself. The story has been attributed to the bubonic plague ("pied" meaning "spotted"), carried by the rats to the children and then away, "over the hills." Robert Browning's poem lent credence to popular views of the legend's historicity. Some writers believe that the story derives from an actual case of child abduction, and others that it derives from the historical "Children's Crusade" (1212), in the course of which children from France and West Germany marched to the Mediterranean shore with the intention of sailing to the Holy Land after the disastrous failure of the Fourth Christian Crusade (1202-4). The Children's Crusade is a genuine historical fact (though the Crusade never really began in any but a propagandistic sense), and has been described by G. Gray in *The Children's Crusade* (New York, 1870) and elsewhere.

Sources include: E. Cobham Brewer, *A dictionary of phrase and fable* (Rev. ed., New York, 1964); and *The Oxford dictionary of the Christian Church* (London, 1957, *sub voc.* "Children's Crusade").

HOMING **PIGEONS** HAVE AN UNERRING INSTINCT FOR RETURNING TO THEIR POINT OF ORIGIN OVER HUNDREDS OF MILES

Common knowledge, indeed. But not to anyone who has had to train' a homing pigeon, beginning from ten feet. Rewards are given to the pigeon for each success, and not for each failure. A homing pigeon cannot be taken completely out of sight of any known landmark and expected to return, so its "Instinct" is in fact simply the use of a visual memory. This is assisted by careful breeding of the birds with the best proven memories. As for the ability of *carrier pigeons,* the U.S. Army Signal Corps (the largest breeder and trainer of carrier pigeons) does not expect its best birds to return over a distance exceeding twenty-five miles, and then only after repeated training flights over the same territory.

Sources: William Rowan, *The riddle of migration* (Baltimore, 1931, p. 81) and *New York Times Magazine,* April 27, 1941, pp. 14, 19.

IN ARCHITECTURE, THE TERMS **"PILLAR"** AND "COLUMN" ARE INTERCHANGEABLE

How many popular writers on travel and famous buildings can tell the difference between a column and a pillar? A column is always cylindrical in plan. A pillar, on the other hand, need not be cylindrical in plan. The two words are used interchangeably in hundreds of major reference works, including for example Arnold Whittick's *Symbols* (2nd ed., London, 1971).

Source: John Fleming and others, *The Penguin dictionary of architecture* (Harmondsworth, 1966).

PILTDOWN MAN IS THE "MISSING LINK" BETWEEN APES AND MEN

The "head" of a prehistoric man "found" at Piltdown in England in 1912 was hailed and published as the vital "missing link" between apes and men.

The forgery was exposed by J. S. Weiner, K. P. Oakley and W. E. Le Gros Clark in *Bull. Brit. Mus. (Nat. Hist.) Geol.,* vol. 2, no. 3, 1953, pp. 139-46. The solution began with relative dating techniques, and was concluded by the chronometric method of radiocarbon. Bowie and Davidson's radiometric assay of the Piltdown specimens agreed with results from fluorine analysis, showing that the cranium is post-Pleistocene, and the animal remains are derived from varied geological sources. The jawbone and tooth are modern specimens faked to match fossilized human skull bones.

It is still not quite clear to whom we owe this intriguingly well-planned fraud, though J. S. Weiner (*The Piltdown forgery,* London, 1955) claims it is to Charles Dawson.

Sources include: Ronald Millar, *The Piltdown men* (London, 1972); and Don Brothwell and Eric Higgs (eds.), *Science in archaeology* (2nd ed., London, 1969, pp. 39-42).

RAY'S ORIGINAL **PIZZA**

New York is known for its great pizza. Apparently, so is the name Ray. But despite the multi-decade long debate over who owned the first Ray's pizza shop, the great irony is that there really is no original Ray.

The *New York Times* has covered this topic twice, once back in 1991 shortly after the investigations in New York into who was the original Ray, and again in September 2011. The first Ray's was opened in 1959 on 27 Prince Street by Ralph "Ray" Cuomo where it had remained, despite constant legal struggles, until October 30, 2011. Cuomo told the *Times* in 1991 that the reason he chose Ray instead of Ralph for the restaurant was because the latter name would have sounded "Maybe too feminine."

Cuomo wanted to focus on solely his personal, family-style restaurant. So, after briefly opening an uptown Ray's, he sold the rights to a Sicilian immigrant, Rosolino Mangano in 1964. This is when the drama began. Mangano claimed even to the *NYT* in 1991 that he was the reason for the success of Ray's. Despite the fact that he never technically went by Ray, he decided he should take credit for Ray's Original everywhere because no one had heard of Ralph Cuomo, but they knew *him* as Ray.

Regardless, in the '80s, another man named Gary was sold a Ray's by Mangano and became curious about the origin of Ray's. He decided to join forces with Ralph Cuomo upon discovering who he was, and they fought a legal battle against Mangano and his franchise for five years until they all finally became one universal "Ray's Original" (complete with the signature coat of arms with tomatoes, cows, and wheat).

(Continued)

The popularity of the name Ray's and its pizza doesn't end there. In 1973, another Sicilian immigrant, Joe Bari, bought Ray's Pizza on 76th and 3rd Ave. from Mangano. Thereafter, he opened and renamed five more Ray's in Manhattan and Long Island, which he renamed "Ray Bari Pizza." According to the *Times* article, Bari also said that his restaurants were really the original Ray's, as he made them famous. He first wanted to stake legal claim to the name Ray's but then he decided to give Mangano and Cuomo the rights to trademark on a federal level Famous Ray's and Original Ray's. Why "original" and "famous" seem to be considered synonymous by all these self-proclaimed Rays is beyond us.

Humorously, Mangano, right after he agreed to join the franchise, supposedly rode around in a black limo around New York and New Jersey and told all the illegitimate Ray's they had to use his logo and ingredients if they didn't want to be sued. Bari's sauces were accused of being too watery, and thus he didn't quite make the cut. Additionally, despite Cuomo's family-style, authentic Italian food intentions in his Little Italy location, he also spent a fair amount of time in jail for mob-related activities.

So, what is original about Ray's? New Yorkers and people from all over the U.S. can argue endlessly about which place is the original Ray's, just as the original Ray himself has endlessly popped up in the flesh.

"RING AROUND THE ROSIE" REFERS TO THE **PLAGUE**

The popular nursery rhyme in which children join hands in a circle, chant uncomfortably somber lyrics, spin around, and fall down at the end, is rumored to have been inspired by the outbreak of the bubonic plague, and/or "black death." The reason for this perception is obvious. The song goes: "Ring around the rosie, pocket full of posies, ashes, ashes (or hush, hush, hush), we all fall down." The ring around the "rosie" is meant to be the rash forming on skin, herbs and spices that were used as a way to try and ward off catching the plague and spreading it around public places are the pocket full of "posies . . ." and the rest is self-explanatory (death in mass).

However, there is no way evidence proving that the song is literally written about the plague. The Ring Around the Rosie "lyrics" were not published until 1881, in *Mother Goose*, a collection of nursery rhymes by Kate Greenaway. Although there are recordings of the game being played by children in slightly earlier texts, such as Ann S. Stephens' novel set in New York in 1855, *The Old Homestead*, the plague occurred significantly earlier than that, in the 1340s. Thus, it doesn't make much sense that the tune and rhyme would have been a reaction to an epidemic that happened centuries earlier.

One might argue, the Great Plague was rampant in 1665, so it's possible that "Ring Around the Rosie" could have cropped up in childhood games as a response to it around the same time, and that it just wasn't recorded for another hundred years or so. However, the refuting evidence that is most frequently cited is by the trusted childhood folklorists, Iona and Peter Opie. According to them, the plague theory did not begin to circulate until the 1950s, and therefore it was only in hindsight that people intended to give an innocent child's verse a dark historical association.

Sources: The Phrase Finder (phrases.org.uk). "The Meaning and Origin of the Expression: Ring a ring o'roses, a pocketful of posies . . ." 1996-2010; Project Gutenberg's Mother Goose or the Old Nursery Rhymes, Anne Storer and *The Online Distributed*.

IF THE WORLD'S **PLANKTON** ARE POISONED THE MAJOR SOURCE OF OXYGEN WILL BE DESTROYED AND ALL LIFE ON EARTH WILL PERISH

J. Piccard wrote in *Time* (November 8, 1971) that "Phytoplankton generate most of the Earth's oxygen. All you need do is knock out the surface phytoplankton and the entire marine life cycle is disrupted." Other writers took up the theme, and the newspapers ran "scare" stories prophesying the end of the world, which always makes a good story. It is always possible, but not by destroying plankton. L. C. Allen had already quietly pointed out (in *Nature,* July 25, 1970, p. 373) that only 0.0001 percent of our oxygen comes from living plants. Most of the rest is the accumulation of 2,000 million years of photosynthesis. Atmospheric carbon dioxide has probably grown by some 11 percent since 1890, but carbon dioxide still constitutes less than 0.033 percent of our air.

PLANTS GROW BY THE FORCE OF LOVE

This fallacy derives from the fact that people who love plants spend more time and money, and usually have more accurate and profound knowledge of plants, than people who do not love them so much. But then this applies to all other fields of endeavour, too, so there can be no reasonable grounds for asserting that plants respond in some "psychic" or supernatural way to careful, knowledgeable attention. They respond naturally to good treatment in the same way that dogs kept by knowledgeable owners are better fed, groomed, and trained than dogs owned by the ignorant or uncaring.

The Findhorn Community's *The Findhorn Garden* (1975) claims not only that their plants grow better than elsewhere—which might well be true, given the loving attention described above. The book also claims that fairies live at the bottom of the Findhorn garden in a very literal, though spiritual, sense. One might justifiably ask for evidence more concrete than capital carrots or better broccoli before one submits atavistically to the childhood fascination with faery.

But why spoil such a fantasy world? Does it matter if Eileen Caddy called herself "Elixir" and claimed divine guidance for establishing a community at Findhorn, and for co-operating with plant-devas or fairies in the Findhorn Garden? Are there not worse ways to live?

Most of those subject to recurrent hallucinations are placed under medical supervision of some kind, and most of those believing in fairies are subject to mild ridicule. It seems that Findhorn and its community are immune to criticism, and this must be disturbing at a time when orthodox Christianity is under increasing pressure, and millions are seeking "new age" religions to assuage some kind of hunger. Having identified beliefs as fallacious, it is undesirable to foster them actively or passively to watch while others do so. It must be possible to pursue the wholly admirable ecological aims of the Findhorn Community without a silly theology.

It is important to realize that every age has its believers in the soul of plant life. Perhaps the most eminent of all was Gustav Fechner (1801-1887), a professor of physics at Leipzig whose theories were attractive at exactly that moment (1848) when the first wave of spiritualism broke out (as a result of the self-confessed fraudulent Fox sisters.

Fechner's *The soul life of plants* (1848) expresses the well-known concept that consciousness permeates the whole of creation, not merely those beings we happen to call "sentient." The idea was old with Plato, and infiltrates most works of mysticism and crypto-science if they go on long enough.

Elementary psychophysics (New York, 1960) keeps the works of Fechner in print and accessible to the next generation of cruel vegetarians.

PLATINUM IS WORTH MORE THAN GOLD

We all know, at least symbolically, that silver is worth more than bronze but worth less than gold. (As to whether old or new friends are gold, we still aren't sure.) If you finished in first place, you won. And when you win, you're golden. But what about gold in comparison to the less commonly mentioned during relay races element, platinum?

Metaphorically, (or commercially), it would seem that platinum is the more prestigious fine metal. After all, you only get free access into the first class lounges in airports if you are a platinum member of American Express; mere gold card holders must still sit with all the plebeians. Additionally, if a record sells more than one million copies in the United States, it is officially said to have "gone platinum." Gold is lower on the ranks (while diamond is the highest, but we'll save the question of where that rock falls into place on the spectrum of literal and figurative wealth for a rainy day).

But how valuable is platinum really?

Apparently, platinum is indeed quite rare, perhaps even more rare than gold is. However, gold is much more frequently sought out for human usage than platinum, and has been throughout years and years of our existence. While the uses of platinum are more varied (including vehicle emissions control devices, electronics, chemical industry, electrodes, anticancer drugs, etc.), the large majority of gold is used for jewelry (50 percent) and investments (40 percent).

In addition, platinum is said by some sources to actually be more valuable in the jewelry world, as it is less likely to tarnish or fade out than gold is over time. Likewise, it is said to be rarer, so, more expensive, right?

It may be true that some jewelers will try to jack up prices of a gold piece that is coated in platinum (or platinum gold), but when it comes to the market (and arguably, psychological) value, gold still definitely takes the cake.

We've seen what happens during economic crisis and uncertainty: people invest in gold. Gold has historical, religious, and historical significance for us humans. Therefore, despite the fact that gold has no seriously practical value to us, when regular currency looks bad, we're in debt, and/or there's no cash in our wallets, we turn to the items of gold we've stashed away, which may be old coming-of-age gifts, inherited heirlooms, and the like. Pawn shop brokers around every corner proudly hold up signs in

(Continued)

red reading, "Will Buy Gold for Cash." This is what the recession looks like.

Not surprisingly, in times of economic stability, gold is not held as something so valuable in the market place. In fact, platinum is said to out-value gold in times of economic growth. Overall, the price of platinum fluctuates more, perhaps not so coincidentally, in correspondence with the market and therefore, with the human need to believe that gold is something to worship and hold above all other precious and rare metals, after religion and the economy have failed them.

Sources: "Platinum versus Gold/Considerable Slack," *The Speculative Investor*, 2002; Andy Soos, "Gold Mining Boom Increasing Mercury Pollution Risk," *Environmental News Network*, 2011; Michael George, "2006 Minerals Yearbook: Platinum-Group Metals," U.S. Department of the Interior, 2007; "A Platinum Premier," Diamond Cutters International.

"**PLAY** IT AGAIN, SAM"

One of the most evocative lines from any film, quoted above from Humphrey Bogart's famous scene in the 1943 film *Casablanca,* directed by Michael Curtiz, refers to the song "As Time Goes By," by M. K. Jerome and Jack Scholl.

The trouble is that Bogart never said it. I awaited the line with bated breath on a recent showing of the movie, and can confirm that the line really runs, "Play it, Sam."

Source: Liz-Anne Bawden, *The Oxford companion to film* (London, 1976).

MARCO **POLO** WROTE A HISTORY OF HIS TRAVELS TO THE EAST

Only in the figurative sense; the man who actually *wrote* Marco Polo's narrative of his adventures was a certain Rustichiello or Rusticiano of Pisa, who was in jail with Polo in 1298-9 after the victory of the Genoese over the Venetians in Curzola Bay. The original text as dictated seems to have been in *French,* however, not in the Venetian dialect, and the first printed edition appeared in *German* in 1477.

Source: *The Book of Ser Marco Polo,* trans. and ed. by Sir H. Yule. With a supplement by H. Cordier. (2 vols., London, 1920).

POINSETTIAS ARE POISONOUS

Aside from the two names sounding misleadingly similar, there is nothing particularly poisonous about poinsettias.

The myth apparently originated in the United States in the 1900s, when the two year old child of an army officer was said to have eaten a poinsettia and died of poisoning. In reality, the plant is not more lethal for human consumption than most other festive plants used by families during the holidays.

However, while the poinsettia plant itself is not toxic, the genus to which the Poinsettia plant belongs does indeed contain some potentially fatal-when-eaten plants. But according to our friends at Poisonex, a company which specializes on deeming whether things in our world are truly poisonous or not, poinsettias do not make the cut. According to their data, a child who weighed fifty pounds would have to consume over 500 poinsettia plants in order to even reach a moderately life threatening level of toxicity in their bodies.

The symptoms that result from accidentally ingesting a poinsettia plant include nothing more than diarrhea, vomiting, and/or moderate discomfort in the gastrointestinal tract. So, the body's elimination of a non edible flower can be likened to bad hangover symptoms after a wild night out of drinking. Or, in the case of children, accidentally eating dish soap or detergent. Nature over nurture?

Sources: ASPCA, "Poinsettia;" Melissa Conrad Stopper, MD, "Are Poinsettia Plants Poisonous? Fact or Fiction?" *Medicine Net.*

BRITAIN IS A SOCIETY WITH LESS **POLICE** SURVEILLANCE THAN ANY OTHER

Not according to the *Police Review,* discussing in a 1976 editorial the Police National Computer-Unit based in Hendon, whose experts predict that by 1979 this unit will have on file more than 36 million names and entries, "It is to be far more comprehensive than any other computerized intelligence service in the world." The police claim that the computer contains data only on stolen vehicles and convicted criminals, but the size and structure of the installation is such that it must contain information about innocent members of the public which could then be used against them by friendly or unfriendly governments who obtained licit or illicit access to the computer,

After U.S. Pentagon intelligence officials disclosed that dossiers had been compiled on 25 million innocent American citizens, the U.S. Government ordered most of the dossiers to be destroyed. The U.K. National Health Service computers contain secret and personal details about many millions of people. The patient has no right to see his own medical record, but those who happen to obtain access to the computer can check on it at any time for whatever purpose can be justified. The British M.P. Brian Walden, a member of the Franks Committee to examine the Official Secrets Act in 1971, concludes that "Some of the activities of the state security services are grossly intrusive and some of the consequences of their actions are very unfair to individuals."

SODA + **POP ROCKS** = DEATH

Perhaps no mature and well-informed adult believes this myth. However, only a matter of years following pop rocks—the carbonated candy that "pops" in your mouth—was first released to the public in 1975, rumors were already widely circulating that mixing this candy with a carbonated soda or beverage could cause one's stomach to, literally, explode.

Due to the extensiveness of this rumor that was likely invented by the restless imaginations of kids, the creators of this product, General Foods, had to write letters to parents and schools explaining and proving that the amount of gas contained in the candy is not remotely enough to cause stomach explosion or damage.

The candy was discontinued in 1983, but has since returned with a new manufacturer and supposedly, slightly new ingredients. We can only hope that the ingredients are a little less lethal this time.

Source: Dr. Marvin J. Rudolph, "Pop Rocks The Inside Story of America's Revolutionary Candy," 2006.

POLTERGEISTS

From the German "Polter" (noise) + "Geist" (spirit), an alleged "ghost" capable of making its presence known by noises; often extended to the phenomena of "throwing spirits." There is of course no such thing as a poltergeist in Germany or anywhere else, despite works such as Nandor Fodor and Hereward Carrington's *The story of the poltergeist down the centuries* (London, 1953).

Literally thousands of cases have been reported by the gullible public to the cynical media over the centuries. In France, there was the case of St. Jean Marie Baptiste Vianney (1786-1859), Curé d'Ars. In his book *The Curé d'Ars* (London, 1927), Abbé Francis Trochu says of the villagers and Vianney, "The name of M. Vianney got into their low songs; anonymous letters, full of the basest insinuations, were sent to him, broadsheets of a like nature were placarded on the door of the presbytery, and at night a wild hubbub took place under his windows . . . His front door was splashed with dirt, and for a space of eighteen months a miserable creature stood, night after night, under his windows, insulting and reproaching him as if he had been guilty of leading a disorderly life."

Despite these known natural phenomena, it was apparently necessary to attribute to the Devil and to poltergeists subsequent phenomena such as blows "struck against doors" and shouts "heard in the yard in front of the presbytery." Just as Vianney was able to fall asleep, "he would start up, awakened by shouts, mournful cries, and formidable blows. It seemed as if the front door were being battered in with a sledgehammer. Suddenly, without a latch having been moved, the Curé d'Ars perceived with horror that the Devil was close to him." But of course, it was merely the villagers' further vindictive attempts to get rid of him.

A similar case of a "poltergeist" at Epworth Rectory in North Lincolnshire was recorded during December 1716 and January 1717, by Samuel Wesley's wife and daughters. Many studies have been devoted to the story, one at book length in Dudley Wright's *The Epworth phenomena* (London, 1917). Frank Podmore, in *Modern spiritualism* (vol. 1, London, 1902, pp. 38-39) attributes the phenomena to Wesley's daughter Hetty, a suggestion scorned by G. W. Lambert as "ridiculous." Lambert, in vol. 38 (June 1955) of the *Journal* of the Society for Psychical Research, blames the tidal river Trent (actually four miles from Epworth). The likeliest explanation, as offered by Trevor H. Hall in *The Rationalist Annual* (vol. 83, 1966, pp. 3-14), is the same as the most reasonable explanation of the Curé d'Ars affair, that is to say that the noises were caused by vindictive neighbors and parishioners who wanted to get rid of a clergyman they hated. This is all the more likely when one realizes, in the words of W. H. Fitchett *(Wesley and his century,* London, 1906), that "The stubborn fen-men did not take kindly to those who, like the Wesleys, were not of their stock, ... They stabbed the little rector's cows, maimed his sheep, broke the dams at night to flood his little fields. They harried him for his debts, [and] tried, not unsuccessfully, to burn his parsonage over his head. Then they accused him of having set fire to it himself."

But poltergeist traditions occur all over the world, and once a timid mind has been tamed with threats of an inimical spirit, it soon grows to fear any falling object or strange noise. "Spontaneous" throwing or falling is invariably attributed to one person in the family, and spiritualists explain this by suggesting that that person is "psychic" and attracts the poltergeist. In fact, the person (usually an adolescent boy or girl) is solely responsible for the phenomena, and maladjusted children, often bored, seek to draw attention to themselves by causing the phenomena—many cases are documented in the literature of psychical research. As Lyall Watson writes in the otherwise credulous best-seller *Super Nature* (New York, 1973), poltergeist phenomena are "produced unconsciously by someone in the vicinity suffering from a frustration of pent-up aggression."

Tinnitus is a recognized complaint which consists of hallucinatory noises, usually singing, caused by inflammation of the middle ear. Some tactile hallucinations are due to the early stages of psychosis, while the reports of elderly people that they are being pricked or nudged by poltergeists are attributable to neurotic delusions. The delusions are real enough, but there are no poltergeists!

WAS THERE A "POPE JOAN"?

A scandalous story, still widely believed, alleges that in 855, between the pontificates of Leo IV and Benedict III, a woman was unanimously elected Pope. The philosopher Leibniz lent his support to the following absurd tale. A young Englishwoman called Joan, born at Ingelheim near Mainz, travelled in a monk's habit from Fulda to Athens, and later in Rome so delighted churchmen by her learning that, still in male attire, she became known as "the Roman wonder." After being elected pope, she had an affair with her valet, which came to light when, in the course of a procession from the Colosseum to the church of S. Clemente, she gave birth to a child and died. Friedrich Gontard, who writes of Pope Joan in *Die Päpste* (Munich, 1959), suggests that "the fable probably originated in the tenth century when, over a period of sixty-seven years, each pope was more sinister, more worthless, and more dangerous than the one before him." The story continued to obtain credence until the 16th century, for the tradition says that every Pope up to Leo X (1513-21) had to undergo a sex test. At the enthronement ceremony an antique chair with an open seat (the *sella stercoraria)* was occupied by the newly elected Pope; after due examination a deacon called out *Habet!* "He has"), whereupon the people of Roman chorussed *Deo gratias!* (Thanks be to God!).

A papal bust of "John VIII, a woman from England" in Siena Cathedral was renamed "Pope Zachary" by Pope Clement VIII (1592-1605). See also Lawrence Durrell's amusing novel on the nonexistent woman, *Pope Joan,* which of course merely had the effect of reawakening the popular fallacy that such a pope had once existed.

EATING FOODS WITH **POPPY** SEEDS WILL MAKE YOU FAIL A DRUG TEST

Opiates such as heroin and morphine are made from poppy flowers and seeds. In light of this, there are rumors warning students and young and old professionals alike not to eat any foods with poppy seeds before a drug test, as the test does not discriminate between heroin users and innocent, hardy breakfast eaters.

Although there have been cases reported where people have tested positive for drug use when they really only ate a poppy seed bagel or hamburger bun, this faulty correlation is not by any means guaranteed. First off, this mistake only really occurs when the method of drug testing is through urine samples, not when blood is drawn.

Also, studies reported by drug testing company, *Med Review*, show that although poppy seeds in baked goods do come up positive for opiate use (mainly codeine and morphine), the levels are fairly low. Additionally, the Department of Health and Human Services (DHHS) states that it doesn't consider opiate usage legitimate when it comes up as lower than 300 ng/ml, and in some cases, 3000 ng/ml on drug tests. In one case reported, a subject tested 487 ng/ml after eating two "doses" of poppy earlier that morning (specifically, two bagels from the cafeteria plus a Burger King hamburger the night before).

So, in order for a person to be considered as an opiate user in standard procedure drug testing, he or she would have to eat approximately six bagels within a more or less six hour period before coming in for a drug test. Anyone up for the challenge?

Sources: Fox News, "Foods and Failed Drug Tests," 2010; hhs.gov/asl/testify/t980723f.html; *Poppies.org, The Opium Poppy FAQ, "Can Eating a Poppy Seed Bagel Cause You to Fail a Drug Test?"*

PROPER **POSTURE** CORRECTS ALL ILLS

Many naturopaths eventually arrive at a conclusion similar to those of Mabel E. Todd *(The thinking body,* 1937) and Bess M. Mensendieck *(The Mensendieck system of functional exercises,* 1937): that good posture is better than bad posture. This is not news: good spinach is after all preferable to bad spinach. The fallacy arises when the advocate of good posture exaggerates beyond all reasonable likelihood the beneficial effects which will accrue from good posture.

The self-educated Australian Frederick Matthias Alexander (d. 1955) established a school in London in 1904, and made many distinguished converts to the Alexander Regeneration Technique taught there, among them G. B. Shaw, the philosopher John Dewey, and Aldous Huxley. After spending the war years in Stow, Massachusetts, Alexander moved back to England, establishing a new base at Bexley, in Kent. An Association of Alexander Teachers was set up at 3 Albert Court, Kensington Gore, London S.W.7.

Therapeutic successes have been claimed for the Alexander Technique in cases of migraine, fibrositis, slipped discs, sciatica, footache, and heart trouble: all by an improvement in posture. Three basic assertions are made:

1. People must keep still and let the natural reaction to any kind of situation and stimulus occur of its own accord.
2. Man is One, and there is a localized seat of this psychophysical integration—a steering wheel for *all* functions of the organism, a "central control." This "central control," announced by Rudolph Magnus of Utrecht in his work on posture entitled *Körperstellung,* is the region where the head joins the neck. From this point, according to Magnus, the entire muscular system of animals is controlled.
3. Every living organism from plant to man is subject to two opposing lines of power running through it: gravity pulls it down—the antigravity-force of the organism bears it up. Correct balance of the head on the spine allows the antigravity-force to flow through us freely, counterbalancing gravity. (Any more of this and readers will be in danger of losing their antigravity.)

Professor J. H. Robinson of Columbia University has written that Alexander's Technique could "free people from ill health and depression, remodel the aged, and teach people how to work with the maximum generation of vital energy and the minimum expenditure of their resources." It could also free the human system from "stagnant eddies in which toxins can accumulate." Needless to say, there is not a shred of experimental evidence to justify any one of the wilder claims made for the Alexander Regeneration Technique or for any similar medical cult, yet such fantastic cure-alls continue to attract hundreds of new adherents every year, and one—Ruth Borchard—even managed to publish an article on Alexander, "A way to spontaneous living" in *The Humanist* for June 1963.

Sources: Wilfred Barlow, *The Alexander Principle* (London, 1973) (Wholly pro-Alexander).

POWDERED GLASS IS POISONOUS

Oddly enough, there is quite a literature refuting this fallacy, topped by Dr. Richard Mead, physician to King George II, who offered, if someone gave him two large diamonds, to crush one to a powder and eat even that!

It is alleged, without documentary proof yet known to me, that oriental monarchs were poisoned by drinking powdered glass in coffee. If the glass were so coarsely powdered as to produce mechanical injury to the alimentary canal (which would not be *poisoning* at all), it would presumably be noticed by the drinker; if on the contrary it were finely powdered, it would cause no injury of any kind. Details of experiments proving this were made available in Pierre Jean George Cabanis' *Les curiosités de la méde-cine*. The same error has been dealt with by Sir Thomas Browne in Book II, chapter V, section 2 of his *Pseudodoxia epidemica* (London, 1646) and by John Phin in his *Seven follies of science* (New York, 1912, p. 211).

PREFORMATION

A group of 17th-century zoologists claimed to discern all the necessary parts of an adult being preformed in the individual egg. Charles Bonnet suggested about 1750 that every female contains the germs of all her descendants, enclosed one within another. He actually did see a new generation forming within and emerging from the body of the plant-louse and felt justified in formulating his idea as a general principle. He did however combat the erroneous scientific explanation of the vitalistic philosophy by pointing out that the bodily functions work on mechanistic principles and that the use of the "soul" as an explanation is merely a facile begging of the question.

Source: Howard M. Parshley, *Error in zoology,* in Joseph Jastrow, *The story of human error* (New York, 1936).

DRINKING MOUNTAIN DEW CAN PREVENT PREGNANCY

However bizarre this fallacy may seem, it is still sadly believed—and perhaps even practiced—by ignorant, but eager, newly sexually active teens. Let's explore.

Although consuming the Pepsi-owned greenish-yellow beverage Mountain Dew, before intercourse to ensure infertility is equally as absurd for males and females, the logic seems to stem from the idea that the ingredients in Mountain Dew help lower sperm count. Various sources claim the specific ingredient said to have this sperm-reducing effect is the food coloring in the soda, Yellow 5. Therefore, if a boy downs a few Dews before engaging in the act, he won't have enough sperm to pass along to the female that is usually necessary to cause risk of pregnancy.

Lo and behold, there is no grain of truth to this myth. This idea that soda or caffeine of any kind will lower sperm count is also as far as we know, totally unfounded. Yet even if this was true at all, and sperm count does actually decrease after drinking some wildly unhealthy amount of Mountain Dew before sex, be sure, kids, that this method is no substitute for using a condom.

Sources: *Stayteen.org*, "Myth vs. Fact"; *Toptenz.net*, "Top 10 Conception Myths."

IT IS BAD GRAMMAR TO END A SENTENCE WITH A **PREPOSITION**

It would instead be accurate to state that "if it is possible to end a sentence less awkwardly than with a preposition, the preposition should be avoided." But it would sometimes be much more awkward to avoid the preposition. What about this sentence, culled from a war-time *Reader's Digest?*

"Little Tommy, ill upstairs, complained to his mother as she sat down to read to him: 'What did you bring that book I didn't want to be read to out of up for?'"

"It is a good rule to go by" is a better sentence than the clumsy "It is a good rule by which to go."

SIR ROBERT WALPOLE SAID "EVERY MAN HAS HIS **PRICE**"

The first reference to this well-known "saying" by Walpole apparently occurs in a report of a speech in November or December 1734 according to A. F. Robbins in the *Gentleman's Magazine* (no. IV, pp. 589-92 and 641-4), but the report was roundly denied by Horace Walpole as a fabrication.

Morley wrote in chapter 6 of his *Life of Sir Robert Walpole* (London, 1889): "Walpole has no doubt suffered much in the opinion of posterity as the supposed author of the shallow and cynical apophthegm that every man has his price. People who know nothing else about Walpole believe and repeat this about him. Yet the story is a pure piece of misrepresentation."

He never delivered himself of that famous slander on mankind. One day, mocking the flowery and declamatory professions of some of the patriots in Opposition, he insisted on finding self-interest or family interest at the bottom of their fine things. "All these men," he said "have their price." If Morley's quotation is correct, then the "Every man has his price" saying commits the fallacy of mistaking the part for the whole.

THE EAGLE ON THE SEAL OF THE **PRESIDENT** OF THE U.S. CHANGES DIRECTIONS DURING WAR AND PEACE

Lurking in the word of mouths and in American popular culture alike is the misconception that the U.S. Presidential seal changes directions, facing either the arrows or the olive branch depending on whether the United States is presently at war or peace.

For those of you who didn't know, the official seal of the President of the United States is actually different than the Great Seal of the United States itself. However, while the two seals are otherwise identical, the Great Seal eagle's head is pointed to the right, while the President's eagle is pointed to the left, indeed, facing the talon in which it holds the arrows of war.

According to the official Heraldry site of the U.S. government, no one really knows why the President's seal was originally designed with wartime symbolism in 1880, more than 100 years after the U.S. Great Seal was created. Some theories say that the eagle is facing left (which is not the norm in traditional heraldic composition) simply because it was intended to be the main distinguishing factor between the two seals. Others say the design was simply an error.

The origin of the misperception that the eagle changes direction depending on war and peace time was most likely when the head of the eagle was officially changed from left to right in 1945, which was meant to be a symbol of peace at the time. But it has remained the same since, while world peace has not.

In typical American fashion, this myth was nonetheless perpetuated in the media. For instance, on an episode of *West Wing* a character explains that the official seal of the eagle is replaced during war times where it is facing the arrows instead of the olive branch. This is, shockingly, inaccurate. Regardless, we, as spectators, have the reassuring option to believe that mentally and morally, all America really wants is permanent peace time for all of us.

Sources: Official Heraldry of the United States, "Presidential Seal"; The Internet Movie Database (IMDB), "What Kind of Day Has it Been," Factual Errors.

PRIDE GOES BEFORE A FALL

"Pride goeth before a raise," wrote Ogden Nash, and his sly aphorism at the expense of the Old Testament (Proverbs, xvi, 18) was as mistaken as the supposed original, "Pride goeth (or goes) before a fall." The Latin version of the Hebrew original familiar since the Middle Ages runs "Contritionem praecedit superbia: et ante ruinam exaltatur spiritus," which might be rendered "Pride goes before contrition, and hauteur before destruction." The popular misreading eliminates the crucial fourth, fifth, sixth and seventh words of the above translation.

PRINTING FROM MOVEABLE TYPE WAS INVENTED BY GUTENBERG

In the *Novum Organon,* Francis Bacon attributed the invention of printing, gunpowder and the magnet to "the moderns," by implication Europeans. J. B. Bury, in his *Idea of progress* (London, 1920), writing three centuries later than Bacon, awards the "Moderns" the palm over the "Ancients" precisely for those three inventions.

"Yet nowhere in his book," complains Joseph Needham, "is there even a footnote pointing out that none of the three was of European origin." Printing, gunpowder, and the magnet, were all invented by the Chinese.

As late as 1952, writing in *The Times,* the then Keeper of Oriental Books and Manuscripts in the British Museum stated that, while block-printing was known and used in 8th-century China, it was left to Europeans to devise printing with moveable types.

"This is of course nonsense," observes Dr. Needham. The first known user of moveable types was "Pi Sheng (*fl. c.* A.D. 1060), who used porcelain or earthenware, while the Koreans were doing a good deal of printing with copper or bronze founts at the end of the fourteenth century, i.e. well before the time of Gutenberg. Yet the Museum of Printing at Mainz contains no reference to the Chinese inventions, and organizers of commemorative exhibitions in our own country have generally been loth to acknowledge them."

Sources include: Joseph Needham, *Within the four seas: the dialogue of East and West* (London, 1969)

PRIVATE MEANINGS FOR PUBLIC WORDS

One commits a grievous fallacy when discussing matters with words of commonly agreed meanings yet with a private significance. In the B.B.C. Brains Trust programs during and just after World War II, Professor C. E. M. Joad earned a remarkable notoriety for his refusal to be bamboozled by such ambiguities: "it depends what you mean by . . ." was his method of clarifying any given points to be debated.

He would have been rightly impatient with the 19th-century lady who complained that she did not like a house because it was "very romantic." Sir Lewis Namier, in his essay "History and political culture" in the symposium *Varieties of history,* ed. by Fritz Stern (New York, 1956), records that when her puzzled correspondent asked her why she should not have wished it to be "very romantic," the lady replied, "When I said *romantic* I meant *damp.*"

PROPHECY

If one out of every hundred predictions comes true, as seems more than reasonable according to statistical probability, that hundredth prediction is greeted by the gullible as a prodigy, when it is of course a mere coincidence. Nobody has ever bothered to count up all the predictions that went wrong: it is much more exciting to tot up the right ones. "The End of the World" is, however, one of the frequent prophecies that seems to be honored more in the breach than the observance, but thousands of others can be read in world journalism. Take for instance the "tidal wave" that was to destroy Weymouth at 3:53 P.M. on May 29, 1928.

THE **PROPORTIONS** OF THE HUMAN BODY WERE DISCOVERED BY ITALIAN RENAISSANCE ARTISTS

A large number of fallacies concerned with "inventions" or "discoveries" derive from the loss of knowledge through inadequate libraries and missing links in the chain of scholarship. Rediscoveries and reinvented methods or techniques are often claimed to be new, and while fraud may sometimes be involved, plain human ignorance and failure to do basic research are the normal reasons for a false claim to originality.

The proportions of the human body were investigated four thousand years before the Italian Renaissance by Egyptian artists. A human hand measured one square of a grid, and by the same grid-measure a man's height was determined at eighteen squares.

Source: British Museum Egyptian Gallery, Case J: Scribes and Artists, 1976.

PROSTITUTES CAN BECOME STERILE BECAUSE THEY DEVELOP ANTIBODIES WHICH DESTROY HUMAN SPERMATOZOA

This hoary notion is based principally on moral grounds and cannot stand up to examination. It has been repeated as recently as 1977 by Dr. J. Cohen in his *Reproduction:* "Some prostitutes . . . have been shown to have a high of anti-sperm antibodies of unusual kinds, and it is possible that in such cases all sperms are prevented from reaching the site of fertilization."

Dr. T. E. Thompson, Reader in Zoology in the University of Bristol, has kindly supplied the following refutation of this fallacy: "While some studies have identified anti-sperm antibodies in the blood of prostitutes, others, no less reliable, have found comparable antibodies in blood from "ordinary" infertile women. The figures given by the Kolodny team (1971, details given in Cockett and Urry's *Male infertility, workup, treatment and research,* New York, 1977), show anti-sperm antibodies to be detectable in 17 percent of prostitutes tested, 14 percent of non-prostitutes who were infertile, and 4 percent of nuns. These results plainly show, in Cockett and Urry's collective wording, that "exposure to spermatozoa was not the only reason for antibody formation. Positive results were associated with the laboratory doing the testing, unknown factors, and possible cross-reacting antibodies."

Dr. Thompson further observes (personal communication, June 5, 1978): "There are other fallacious elements in this highly moral proposition. First, there is no evidence that blood-borne antibodies can affect sperm-success in the short time between semen ejaculation and egg penetration. Second, the assumption is made that prostitutes copulate more frequently and receive more semen thereby than might be the case in other women, hence eliciting a greater risk of the production of circulating antibodies against spermatozoa; neither the assumption nor the conclusion is much more than a guess.

"Prostitutes do run a considerable risk of contracting a venereal disease, which in turn may lead to sterility, but that is another story."

PROVIDENCE

"Providence" may be defined as "obtaining one's just reward in the future by the simultaneous or successive occurrence of preordained events," and is—at least thus defined—a very prevalent fallacy.

The absorbing *Curiosities of literature* (3 vols., 1791-1823) by Isaac D'Israeli (1766-1848; it was his son Benjamin, 1st Earl of Beaconsfield, who changed his style to "Disraeli") has a chapter "Of a history of events which have not happened" (see also PROPHECY). It begins with an indictment of the fallacious notion of Providence. "Some mortals have recently written history, and 'Lectures on history,' who presume to explain the great scene of human affairs, affecting the same familiarity with the designs of Providence as with the events which they compile from human authorities. Every party discovers in the events which at first were adverse to their own cause but finally terminate in their own favor, that Providence had used a peculiar and particular interference; this is a source of human error and intolerant prejudice. The Jesuit Mariana, exulting over the destruction of the Goths in Spain, observed that 'It was by a particular providence that out of their ashes might rise a new and holy Spain, to be the bulwark of the catholic religion'; and unquestionably he would have adduced as proofs of this 'holy Spain' the establishment of the Inquisition, and the dark idolatrous bigotry of that hoodwinked people. But a protestant will not sympathise with the feelings of the Jesuit; yet the protestants, too, will discover particular providences, and magnify human events into supernatural ones."

Livy was guilty of this fallacy when speculating idly on the consequences which might have resulted had Alexander the Great invaded Italy.

"PRUNEY" TOES AND FINGERS COME FROM PROLONGED WATER ABSORPTION

Your mother always used to tell you not to stay in the bath too long, unless you want to get pruney fingers and toes. Though nobody really wants to feel like part of their bodies are becoming soggy, we have always assumed there was no explanation for the fact that they did become that way, aside from a physical indicator that you are overstaying your body's welcome in the pool or the bath.

As of recently, there has emerged a potentially logical or even biological reason to explain why our fingers and toes react the way they do to extended exposure to water. According to evolutionary neurobiologist Mark Changizi, the reason these water-induced wrinkles occur is to serve a purpose much like treads do on tires: to keep water draining out. Wrinkles act as channels that diverge further from one another as they get further away from the tips of fingers, making it easier for water to drain through them when we put our digits to wet surfaces, and thereby, giving us a more effective and stronger grips on slippery ground or objects around us.

You may ask, "Why do these tracts only occur when you are in the water for a long period of time?" Interestingly (though less concrete as a scientific finding), Changizi suggests it would be impractical for fingers and toes to get wrinkly every time they were exposed to water, such as when you are rinsing hands off, caught in the rain, or when you accidentally spill water on yourself.

Additionally, scientists discovered in the 1930s that these wrinkles do not form on fingers that have been partially severed. Therefore, perhaps, the pruning process is a neurological one rather than just a mechanism of our skin absorbing water from the outside.

Why our bodies may have adopted the proper tools to prepare us for life underwater, however, is fascinating, unsettling, and altogether quite mysterious.

Sources: Anahad O'Connor, *Really?* Blog, "The Claim: Fingers wrinkle because of water absorption," *New York Times*, 2011; Eyder Peralta, *The Two-Way news* blog, "Why Do Fingers Wrinkle When they Get Wet?" NPR, 2011.

PSYCHIC FALLACIES

1. John Taylor and the Psychic Children

Professor John Taylor, in *Superminds* (London, 1975) and on television, has repeatedly asserted that spoon-bending of the Uri Geller type, now carefully discredited by James Randi in *The magic of Uri*

Geller (London, 1976), is accomplished by a series of "psychic" children. A believer in the paranormal, but an intelligent critic of many charlatans, Stan Gooch has described in his book *The Paranormal* (London, 1978, pp. 63-4) how Taylor showed a beautiful model of a dog made entirely of paper clips to a conference as proof of a child's "psychic" powers. Taylor explained that the boy told him that he had put paper clips loose in a box, shaken it, and produced the model by this process of shaking. The boy's mother is an artist and Professor Taylor suggested to Stan Gooch that the boy had inherited his mother's talent. Gooch writes: "I must say that quite another explanation occurred to me, as perhaps it will to the reader—that the boy's mother, or the boy himself, had made the model in a perfectly normal way. I am of course not saying that either of them actually *did*."

However, in the *New Scientist* for July 14, 1977, Professor Taylor intimated that the "powers" of the children investigated have diminished in direct relation to the tightening of test conditions, and that he is no longer convinced that there *is* a metal-bending effect. Yet the damage is done: for every reader of the *New Scientist* aware of Professor Taylor's retraction of his original assertions, a hundred thousand will have been impressed by the television claims—and will continue to be impressed.

2. Psychic Photography

Due to the impressive advances in photography and cinematography in the last twenty years, much attention has been given to the question of recording events supernatural or inexplicable by natural causes on to film.

It would be so (literally) wonderful to discover that thoughts can be filmed that many thousands of events have been arranged with a view to producing such an occurrence. The best-publicized are the "psychic photography" sittings arranged between leading parapsychologists and a Chicago hotel-worker named Ted Serios in the 1960s. Dr. J. Eisenbud, then associate clinical professor of psychiatry at the Medical School of the University of Colorado, was finally persuaded by Serios in 1964 to test the "thoughtography" by which Serios claimed to be able to transfer his thoughts on to film under laboratory conditions. Eisenbud's book *The world of Ted Serios* (New York, 1967) tried to prove that Serios could impress a mental image on to polaroid film by the effort of mental concentration. Serios was filmed during four sessions of roughly three hours each by Dr. Ian Stevenson and Dr. J. G. Pratt of the University of Virginia in 1968 and, as one might expect, the doctors (of the Department of Psychiatry) took a great many shots of a sweating, anxious face. The failure rate was alarmingly high, but there were a few apparent successes, none of which excluded the possibility of fraud by conjuring or other means. Furthermore, Serios was in the habit of holding a tube of rolled-up film paper in his right hand.

The Stevenson-Pratt trials were never finished, the conclusion of the scientists being remarkably restrained in the circumstances: "We remain fully aware that we have not been able to describe conditions and results which should remove all doubt that the Serios phenomenon is paranormal. But weighing the various features we have discussed, and considering again our failure to detect anything the least suspicious of conjuring, we think that our findings increase the importance of further research with Ted."

Dealing with the Serios case, Dr. Christopher Evans has written in *Cults of unreason* (London, 1973, p. 190): "Apart from such obvious tricks as tampering with the negative in the development stage or allowing the light to enter the camera through one or other of its sides, it is not at all difficult to mark photographic film with radioactive energy. In this latter case the trickster would merely have to arrange for a small piece of radioactive material to be near the camera—he could, for example, conceal it in a finger ring, and real, if rather diffuse, images would appear on film which had never been exposed to ordinary light. These and many other tricks have been used and, no doubt, will be used again in the production of thoughtographs of one kind or another."

One is reminded of the sensational reports in the 1920s concerning the "psychic photographer" William Hope, whose "wonderful abilities" Sir Oliver Lodge had consulted and praised. In 1922, the investigator Harry Price spent some time with Hope, the leading light of the Crewe Circle of spiritualism. Unknown to Hope, however, Price made sure that his plates could not be switched by using plates which had been X-rayed with a photographic company's trademark. In fact, of course, Hope *did* switch the plates, and produced a photograph of Harry Price with "a beautiful female 'extra' swathed in cheesecloth." The X-rayed trademark was missing from the plate, so Hope—like all other self-professed psychic photographers so far studied under test conditions—was proved a fraud by Price in his article "Cold light on spiritualistic phenomena" *(Journal of the London Society for Psychical Research,* May 1922).

3. Philippine Psychic Surgery

Members of the Union Espiritista Cristiana de Filipinas claim to cure serious illness by psychic methods, the most advanced psychic healers becoming the best surgeons. In her uncritical *Mindpower* (London, 1976), Nona Coxhead states that a healer, having acquired the "gift of the spirit," "approaches the patient in a trance-like state, focusing his mind-energy on what he is to accomplish and 'attuning' to the energy of the patient, on which he also draws." Nona Coxhead refers specifically to the Rev. Tony Agpaoa, "whose fame as one of the Philippine healers has spread over the globe." Agpaoa "has said that he could open the body of a patient without a drop of blood, but that his people would find it harder to believe in *bloodless* psychic surgery than they do seeing the gore, tissue and organs."

Two well-researched television documentaries, both shown before the publication of *Mindpower,* effectively demolished the case for the Philippine psychic surgeons. The first program showed the healers' point of view. This removed any suspicion of prejudice. The case rested on the actual changes in condition shown by British patients after treatment in the Philippines. The panel consisted of the patients' own doctors, who were asked to note any improvement. Not only did the doctors observe no improvement—they might after all be considered partial: they observed no change whatsoever, as demonstrated in the second of Mike Scott's documentaries, shown on Granada Television in February 1975.

Psychic "surgeons" almost invariably "operate" on the stomach or other soft areas of the body, producing handfuls of "tumors" later discovered, on analysis, to be animal tissue palmed in by the "healer." A close-up camera picture showed a healer with his fingers doubled under to fake entry into the body, after which the camera team was asked to withdraw.

The surgeons claim to be able to operate by instructions from the world beyond. However, the present world offers at least the favored few delights of this world that include limousines and well-equipped homes. Many poor "healers" working by a combination of luck and autosuggestion are undoubtedly sincere, though misguided. The reader may describe the remainder in any terms he feels appropriate. See also THE "MIRACULOUS CURES" OF ZE ARIGO.

Sources: I. Stevenson and J. G. Pratt, "Explanatory investigations of the psychic photography of Ted Serios," in *Journal of the American Society for Psychical Research,* vol. 62, 1968, pp. 104-129.

THE FOUNDATIONS OF FREUDIAN **PSYCHOANALYSIS** ARE LOGICALLY UNASSAILABLE

The successful error: a critical study of Freudian psychoanalysis (London, 1941) is by Rudolf Allers, Professor of Psychology at the Catholic University of America. Professor Allers, writing as a Catholic for a Catholic publisher, has nevertheless tried to put aside his personal prejudices against psychoanalysis, and his critique should be read by all those with an ever-open mind. The conclusion reached by Allers is "that psychoanalysis rests on several gross logical fallacies, all of which are of the kind known to logic as *petitio principii.*

"Psychoanalysis, in fact more than once, takes for granted what it claims to prove and surreptitiously introduces its preconceived ideas into its reasonings so as to give the impression that these ideas have resulted from facts and evident principles."

The first fallacy is termed by Allers "the fallacy of resistance." In Freudian theory, the term "resistance" is more than a mere description of the objective finding, but actually implies many of the theoretical views characteristic of the Freudian system. "The observed phenomena—namely the interruptions occurring in the chain of free associations and the so-called efforts to be made by the person analyzed and the analyst—are viewed as a kind of ocular demonstration of resistance. Resistance itself, not the mere objective facts enumerated above, is what is 'observed' according to the psychoanalysts. But all that they are observing is that no association occurs to the patient." Allers goes on to remark that the belief of the participants that they are actually observing resistance is founded merely on their earlier acceptance of Freudian doctrine, and not on any objective fact.

The second fallacy described by Rudolf Allers is the alleged causal connection between the conscious mental phenomena (idea, feeling, dream, symptom, misspelling or others) and the "unconscious" material brought forth in the course of analysis. Such a causal relation can be proved only in the case of abnormal symptoms which disappear after the unconscious phenomena have been made conscious; there can be no objective proof in a case involving no abnormal symptoms to begin with. "Because the psychoanalyst, before he even starts an analysis, is previously convinced that all relations he will eventually be able to establish are of the nature of causation," writes Allers, "he discovers only such relations." There are of course other relations, such as sense or meaning.

In a science, words may be used to denote only one idea or thing, such as the unique words and things "hydrogen," "field vole," or "differential calculus." But, in Freudian psychoanalysis, "determination" has at least four meanings: (a) a connection pertaining to logic and semantics, or signification; (b) a connection between two terms due to association; (c) causal determination, e.g., the rise of mercury in a thermometer is "determined" by the caloric state of the surrounding medium; (d) emotional states are "determined" by certain contents of consciousness, another word used in this context being "association."

The third fallacy is the use of interpretation in Freudian theory and practice. There is no logical reason for connecting a memory arising from the unconscious with a mental fact of consciousness, *unless* the revival of the memory can be proved to cause the disappearance of the symptom. "Sometimes," writes Allers, "—seldom enough—the assent of the analyzed person may replace the criterion of therapy.

This assent is not only very often not given, but even after analysis has been pushed back to the deepest layers of the unconscious, and after resistance has been very much reduced, such an assent is utterly without value, when the unconscious material refers, e.g., to the prenatal phase of life." It goes without saying that such absorbing and fascinating studies as that of Freud on Leonardo da Vinci lack all scientific value when the analyst is dealing with symptoms that cannot disappear. He cannot prove that he is correct, but any truly scientific hypothesis *must* be testable.

Dr. H. J. Eysenck attacks Freudian psychoanalysis *as a science* in *Uses and abuses of psychology* (Harmondsworth, 1954) and in its sequel *Sense and nonsense in psychology* (Harmondsworth, 1957). He argues that psychoanalysis is a religion rather than a science. The analyst frames his theories not as clear-cut hypotheses testable by experiment but as vague *obiter dicta* almost totally resistant to refutation, since they can always be reinterpreted. Like a religious apologist, the Freudian claims that there can be no valid criticism of his doctrines from outside Freudianism. "Every psychoanalyst must pass through a training analysis in which all his actions, dreams, and fantasies are interpreted in Freudian terms, and in which he forms strong emotional bonds with his teacher, bonds which predispose him to accept such interpretations as correct, and which will make it impossible for him to make objective, unbiased judgments about the true relevance of analytic concepts."

It is claimed that two-thirds of the analyst's patients recover, on average. Dr. Eysenck, however, shows that so do two-thirds of neurotic cases receiving no treatment at all.

PSYCHOLOGICAL FALLACIES

One of the most exhaustive treatments of fallacies in psychology also ranges much farther afield. Joseph Jastrow's *Fact and fable in psychology* (London, 1901) appeared before the boom in parapsychological studies and similar attempts to make spiritualism respectable before a critical modern audience. The eleven chapters cover: The modern occult (theosophy, spiritualism, alchemy, astrology); The problem of psychical research; The logic of mental telegraphy (now known as telepathy); The psychology of deception; Hypnotism and its antecedents; The natural history of analogy; The mind's eye; Mental prepossession and inertia; A study of involuntary movements; and, The dreams of the blind.

Readers are referred to Jastrow's compendium for detailed illumination of fallacies in this field.

PSYCHOMETRY

Psychometry, also known as "object-reading," will be treated here as a fallacy since the burden of proof for the existence of psychometric

phenomena contradicting or supplementing currently accepted verifiable phenomena lies on those who wish to prove the case but have
so far failed to do so. It is a branch of extrasensory perception and
is subject to the same criticisms which are frequently applied to
other branches: that is to say that there is no evidence yet universally acceptable to the objective investigator despite the great mass
of reporting which has been done.

W. G. Roll has advocated belief in psychometry in an article on
Gustav Pagenstecher (1855-1942), a German doctor working in
Mexico, in the *Journal of the American Society for Psychical Research*
(no. 61, 1967). Pagenstecher worked with only one person, the "sensitive" Maria Zierold, whom he "tested" by giving her an object which
was then used as the center of object associations. The principle is
that if a piece of string is detached from an identification plate used
by a German soldier during World War I and shown to Mrs. Zierold,
she could connect it with its original associations. An ability to do
this is considered virtually proven if a likely association results in
one or more tests, but cases of failure are seldom or never recorded
and it is impossible to double-check original results.

The controversial Dr. J. B. Rhine stated his belief in psychometry in *New worlds of the mind (New* York, 1953), defining it as
clairvoyant "free association" in connection with a token object.
Psychometric archaeology has been defended by John Foster Forbes
in such strange works as *The unchronicled past* (London, 1938) and
object association is common in radiesthesia and other pseudo-medical practices. Belief in the healing powers of sacred relics is also a
form of psychometrical belief. Dowsers and other mediums claim to
detect oil-bearing or water-bearing strata and spirits of the dead
respectively by object association, though there is so far no evidence
that success has been other than accidental or of more than average
frequency.

The revival of fascination with the occult characteristic of western
civilization in the 1970s might be exemplified by an attractively produced pictorial book by Janet and Colin Bord called *Mysterious Britain*
(London, 1972), which attaches equal and uncritical significance to
prehistoric circles, holy wells, mazes, leys and tracks, and King Arthur.
A photograph of stone walls of herringbone design in Cornwall is cap-
tioned with the suggestion that these walls "show Cretan influence,
this design being common in the walls on the island of Crete."

Mr. and Mrs. Bord repeat as factual evidence the results of a visit
to Glastonbury Tor of John Foster Forbes and the psychometrist
Iris Campbell in 1945, Forbes had already written two works which
propounded the value of psychometry to archaeological research, so
he can hardly be considered an objective investigator. He and Miss
Campbell visited Glastonbury Tor specifically to record impressions

that Miss Campbell received with a view to "throwing more light on its early history." The Bords relate that the rites practiced on the Tor "were designed to restore bird and flower life forms to a more complete condition, [having] become greatly impaired due to the succession of natural calamities that had befallen the earth. The ritual involved a dance of circular motion, moving sunwise and upwards round the spiral path, A tremendous vortex of power was produced which, on an etheric level, created a canopy of a 'glazed substance.' This could act as a receiving centre for the absorption and refraction of regenerative forces to which the bird and flower life could respond."

It is not clear what this means, if anything, but its connection with verifiable archaeological evidence is inexistent, and it would be a service if commentators were to say so. John Foster Forbes' applications of psychometry to archaeology can be read in *The unchronicled past* (London, 1938), *Ages not so dark* (1939), and *Giants of Britain* (1945).

PUBERTY FALLACIES

1) Having Baby Teeth Means You're Still a Baby

If only due to the name alone, still having "baby teeth" during pre-teen or adolescent years is sometimes mistaken as being a sign of immaturity or underdevelopment. However, dental maturity is not as strong an indicator of maturity as a number of other physical changes that occur in an adolescent's development. In terms of the effectiveness of deciphering the true onset of maturity in an adolescent, it is best to stick to strictly skeletal, somatic, and sexual indications. These may manifest in the physical through an adolescent's changing bone structure (the jutting jaw-line in boys), the emerging child-bearing hips in girls, pubic hair growth and voice changes. To sum up, no, having baby teeth does not mean you are still a baby, because baby teeth are easier to conceal. It is easier to feel like an outcast when you look less developed physically than when you have some baby molars hidden away. How many teeth you have doesn't seem to be as important, particularly because they all fall out eventually and baby teeth molars don't look that different from permanent ones. Plus, it's cool to have braces in middle school, right?

2) Having Pubic Hair Means Puberty Has Started

Somewhat surprisingly, the appearance of pubic hair can occur much earlier than any other symptoms of puberty onset, and at very tender ages. Visible pubic hair does not, however, necessarily mean that puberty has begun in the child who receives it. Getting just pubic hair and body odor indicate an increasing adrenal secretion of weak androgens, also called "adrenarche," if they are not accompanied by breast or testicular enlargement. This is different than "true puberty," which is characterized by the activation of the hypothalamic-pituitary-gonadal unit.

Before 1997, it was said that adrenarche (basically just developing pubic hair) was premature in girls at age eight and in boys at age nine. However, now they have reassessed the situation and realized pubic hair development can be normal in girls as young as seven or even six, especially in the case of African Americans.

3) Drinking Milk Causes Early Puberty

Supposedly, girls are hitting puberty slightly earlier in age than they used to be in the United States. Although not everyone is in consensus over this trend's legitimacy, some of those who support it attribute it to obesity, while others blame . . . milk. Milk contains calcium, and obviously we've all heard about the benefits of drinking as much milk as possible when we're young and our bones are still growing. But is there a limit to how much we should drink? Are our bones growing a little too quickly upon excessive milk consumption, triggering the onset of puberty in girls who are too young to understand why they suddenly have tender breasts and inexplicable feelings of angst?

According to one proponent of milk who dismisses these concerns, there are several main arguments as to why milk is not causing this trend in increasingly early puberty onset in girls in America.

Statistics show that kids who consume milk frequently (more often than others) actually on average tend to have lower body weights than those who don't. This suggests that milk does not lead to obesity, nor does its consumption correlate with kids who have more "mature" body types and, thus, body weight.

Secondly, girls today drink less milk overall than their mothers did in earlier generations, meaning the trend in earlier puberty is one that stands apart from overall milk intake.

Finally, milk has always contained a natural bovine growth hormone, BST, in very small amounts. Some dairy producers also inject a synthetic version of this hormone (rBST) in cows in order to increase milk production. Supposedly, milk from both treated and untreated cows is the same by FDA standards. 90 percent of the hormones are destroyed during pasteurization and supposedly do not affect the human body, because they are

(Continued)

cow specific. Therefore, hormones from milk cannot be explained to be the cause of hormonal development in humans.

Sources: Dairy Council of California, "Myth Buster: There is No Scientific Evidence that Drinking Milk Causes Early Puberty"; *Western Journal of Medicine*, "Myths and Variations in Normal Pubertal Development," Jon M Nakamoto, 2000; Robert M. Malina, Claude Bouchard, *Growth, Maturity, and Physical Activity*, Second Edition, 2004.

THE **PURITANS** OF NEW ENGLAND PRACTICED RELIGIOUS TOLERATION

It was for many years held almost as a dogmatic truth that "the Puritan settlers in New England established religious freedom there.

"They have left unstained what there they found—Freedom to worship God."

This may almost be described as the reverse of the truth, according to the Historical Association. In the Plymouth (Mass.) and Connecticut settlements, political rights were enjoyed exclusively by church members—that is to say, by the Puritan congregations. It was the terrible intolerance of the Massachusetts government (including flogging, deporting, and even executing their opponents) which led to the withdrawal of settlers under Roger Williams to Rhode Island, where for the first time religious toleration was permitted. It was this attitude which was despised by other New Englanders, who excluded Rhode Island from the New England Confederation.

Probably the most bitter persecutions in New England were directed against the Mormons: the prophet of the Latter-Day Saints was attacked by mobs and was shot at several times, being lucky to escape westward with his life.

Sources include: *Cambridge History of the British Empire* (vol. 1, Cambridge, 1929, ch. V).

PYRAMIDS OF EGYPT

The best-known pyramids of Egypt have occupied the imagination of cranks of many countries for several centuries, and no attempt is made here to summarize the numerous occult and pseudo-scientific interpretations of these funerary monuments. All known pyramids contain or have once contained sarcophagi, and most bear the names of the kings buried within them. The pyramid of Cheops was *not* an astronomical observatory-cum-table of measurement which can be interpreted as a chronological guide to the principal events of past and future history. The methods of planning and construction are known in outline, if not in full detail, and are adequately published in I. E. S. Edwards' *The Pyramids of Egypt* (1947), though it was W. M. Flinders Petrie, in *The Pyramids and Temples of Gizeh* (London, 1883), who first proved that all the pyramids were intended and used as tombs.

One important fallacy still prevalent was first propounded by Richard Lepsius, who suggested that their size corresponded to the length of their owner's reign: this is known as the "accretion theory." It is odd that it should have been suggested at all, since all one needs to refute it is a chronology of Pharaonic Egypt together with a tape measure. Thus, the pyramid of Pepi II (who reigned for ninety-four years) should have become several times as large as that of Mykerinos, who reigned for about eighteen years. In fact, the considerations involved were probably the ruler's inclination, power, and religious beliefs.

Leonard Cottrell, an excellent popularizer of Egyptology, has an absorbing chapter in *The mountains of Pharaoh* (London, 1956) entitled "The great Pyramidiot" devoted to a handful of those cranks whose "prophecies have often been proved wrong, their calculations inaccurate, their theories unacceptable by any unprejudiced mind." Yet Cottrell rightly complains that these theorists still have their followers, especially since one of them, Charles Piazzi Smyth, was not only Astronomer-Royal for Scotland but a brilliant mathematician and a fluent, engaging writer. His absurd, fantastic works included *Life and work at the Great Pyramid . . .* (3 vols., Edinburgh, 1867); *Our inheritance in the Great Pyramid* (London, 1864); and an undignified attack, *The Great Pyramid and the Royal Society* (London, 1874), when the Society rightly rejected a paper on his interpretation of the design of the Great Pyramid.

Smyth was of course not an Egyptologist at all, and denied that the Ancient Egyptians designed the Great Pyramid, though he admits that they may have labored on it. It was not a tomb, but a mysterious laboratory interpretable by mathematical calculations based on the dimensions, capacities and proportions of its outer structure and inner galleries and chambers. He was inspired by another crank study: *The Great Pyramid. Why was it built? And who built it?* (London, 1859) by a publisher, John Taylor. A clue to his methods can be obtained from the fact that the Pyramid's measurements were not exactly round numbers in any known system of mensuration, so Smyth invented the "Pyramid inch," corresponding to .999 of a British inch. He then measures the base line of the Pyramid (inaccurately, according to Flinders Petrie) and after dividing it by 366 (which is not exactly the number of days in a natural year), he finds that the resultant length (roughly 24 British inches) is "a length approaching nearly one ten-millionth of the earth's semi-axis of rotation." From this meaningless figure, Smyth feels able to deduce that the architect of the Great Pyramid had "laid out the size of the Great Pyramid's base with a measuring rod 25 inches long in his hand; and in his head, the number of days and parts of a day in a year, coupled with the intention to represent that number of days in terms of that rod on each base side of the building."

The Rev. John Davidson and Edgar Stewart are others of that legion of pyramidologists whose motive was less to understand and appreciate the civilization of Pharaonic Egypt than to demonstrate to the world their own ingenuity.

Moralizing over the Great Pyramid with not the slightest idea of its purpose, Samuel Johnson wrote in *Rasselas* (1759): "No reason has ever been given adequate to the cost and labor of the work. The narrowness of the chambers proves that it could afford no retreat from enemies, and treasures might have been reposited, at far less expense, with equal security. It seems to have been erected only in compliance with that hunger of imagination, which preys incessantly upon life, and must always be appeased by some employment. Those who have already all that they can enjoy, must enlarge their desires. He that has built for use, till use is supplied, must begin to build for vanity, and extend his plan to the utmost power of human performance, that he may not be soon reduced to form another wish. I consider this mighty structure, as a monument of the insufficiency of human enjoyments." I consider this judgment a piece of pompous drivel which sheds more light on the preoccupations of the author of *The vanity of human wishes* than on the subject of his digression.

Q

Quell: What you say often seems negative—without a principle to follow.

Finger
(pleased): That's it. So many people pretending to have the whole truth, the citizens we need are those who know they haven't the whole truth: call them "the enquirers." They're the men who decide on a provisional solution in a particular context.

—PHILIP WARD,
The Quell-Finger Dialogues
(North Harrow, 1965)

"Quo magis cogito, magis dubito." (The more I think, the more I doubt)

—FRANCISCO SANCHEZ

QUICKLIME DESTROYS A CORPSE

Some writers of detective stories still labor under the odd delusion that quicklime will "eat" a dead body, and it helped to convict the multiple murderess Mrs. Belle Gunness of La Porte, Indiana, whose fourteen victims were excellently preserved in the tell-tale substance.

Source: Stewart Holbrook, *Murder out yonder* (New York, 1941, p. 141).

QUICKSANDS SUCK IN HUMAN BEINGS

So do rivers, come to that, but quicksands (a mixture of sand and water) will support the human body much more easily than water unmixed with sand. A sucking sound that panicking victims fear is made only when a large object or person is pulled *out* of a quicksand. The force creating the suction is in the puller, not in the quicksand or bog, or whatever the quagmire may be. The danger lies simply in exhausting oneself by struggling; those who do not struggle seldom sink below the armpits.

So don't panic. If you sense you are getting into a quicksand, lie down and *roll* across it. If it should be too soft to roll on, lie on your back with your mouth as high as possible. The quicksand is denser than your body, and so your body cannot sink completely into it.

Source: Lawrence Perez, in *Science News Letter,* April 12, 1941, p. 232.

R

"Reasons are not like garments, the worse for wearing."
—THE EARL OF ESSEX to Lord Willoughby,
January 4, 1599

"Religion is still parasitic in the interstices of our knowledge which have not yet been filled. Like bedbugs in the cracks of walls and furniture, miracles lurk in the lacunae of science."
—J. B. S. HALDANE, *Science and life* (London, 1968)

A **RABBIT** SHOULD BE PICKED UP BY THE EARS

Merely because a rabbit's ears are relatively large, it does not follow that rabbits should be picked up by their ears, as the popular theory goes. They should be picked up by the skin behind the shoulders, as guinea-pigs should. Cats should be lifted below the front part of the body, with the back legs resting on your arm. Geese or swans should be picked up by the wings just behind the back, never by the delicate legs. Small cage-birds such as canaries should be enclosed in the hand from the back, taking care not to grip them too tightly.

RABIES

Fallacies connected with hydrophobia or rabies include the following:

1. That it can be cured by the use of a madstone.
2. That it can be prevented if the dog that has bitten a person is immediately killed.
3. That mad dogs foam at the mouth and are always greatly excited.
4. That it can be prevented by applying to the wound some of the hair of the dog that did the biting. [This nonsense was attributed by Athenaios in his *Deipnosophisiai*, or "Banquet of the Learned" in the 3rd century A.D. to the Greek comedian Aristophanes (448-380 B.C.)]

Source: A. A. Thomen, *Doctors don't believe it* (New York, 1935, pp. 321-8).

RAILWAYS WERE BUILT FOR TRAINS

A virtually ubiquitous fallacy. The steam locomotive had not been invented when the first wooden railways were laid. Their purpose was to run trucks of coal from the pithead to the harbor for transportation.

Such railways were first used in 1602 at Newcastle-upon-Tyne, England, It was not until 1820 that iron was used for train-tracks, and not until 1857 that iron was replaced by steel.

RAIN FALLACIES

1. Gunfire Produces Rain

While so-called "primitive" tribes enact rainmaking rituals in most parts of the world as they have always done, fallacies about the subject are still prevalent among the world's intelligentsia. Many otherwise intelligent people declare that atomic or nuclear tests have upset the world's climate, though they can adduce no shred of evidence for this. Heavy gunfire as a source of rain has always been criticized. British farmers petitioned the Admiralty in 1910 to postpone the Navy's gunnery exercises, fearing that the explosions would precipitate unwanted rainfall. Coincidental rainfall at the Battle of Waterloo was immediately attributed to cannonfire. Japanese rice-growers use a cannonade to make rain, while French *vignerons* let off their rockets near harvest to stave off impending showers!

Aircraft are used to induce rain to fall from large cumulus clouds at least fifteen degrees below freezing point, but it is quite fallacious to argue that these highly localized experiments can ever have a long-term or global effect. Or that any two groups of citizens would ever agree on a common rainfall policy!

2. "Rain at Seven, Fine at Eleven"

A popular fallacy based upon the error that rain does not last for more than four hours at a time. It might be observed that, having no clock, the rain does not know when (or where) it is seven o'clock, any more than it can recognize eleven.

Similar nonsense includes such sayings as "Fine on Friday, fine on Sunday," which depend for their usage on the general lack of interest in checking dubious generalizations about the weather against the facts. The rain doesn't know about Fridays; neither does the Sun.

See also WEATHER.

3. Rain on St. Swithin's Day Means Rain on the Following Forty Days

No amount of facts will change opinions held firmly enough, and this is one of those persistent tales it would be derogatory to attribute to old wives because old husbands also believe it. The French go one better. "If it rains on S. Médard's Day (June 8), it will rain for forty days" and "If it rains on S. Gervais's Day (June 19), it will rain for forty days."

Bishop Swithun (838-62) of Winchester was canonized in 912, at which time his remains were translated from a grave outside the

Cathedral ("where the sweet rain of heaven might fall upon his grave") to a shrine within, whereupon he showed his grave displeasure by making rain for forty days.

Unfortunately for all such "miracles," the act of verification proves the fallacy. The Greenwich Observatory carefully collated records in 1861 for the preceding twenty years, when it appeared from the average of those years that the greatest number of rainy days after St. Swithin's Day occurred when July 15 (St. Swithin's Day) was dry. On six occasions St. Swithin's Day was wet, and the average number of rainy days (up to August 24) which followed was 18 1/2. In the other fourteen years, when St. Swithin's Day was dry, the average number of rainy days which followed was 19 1/4 . In not one single case did it rain for every one of the forty days: the maximum was 31 days, and that occurred in 1848, when St. Swithin's day was dry!

Sources: David Gunston, *Scientific rainmaking encounters serious limits* in *Humanist,* January 1968, pp. 22-23; *Public Opinion,* July 20, 1894.

RANDOMNESS FALLACIES

As the species on this planet with the highest level of intelligence and little grasp on how to most effectively utilize this quality, we, as individuals, look for explanations and patterns in everyday life. We are always making associations; a song reminds you of a memory, a street reminds you of a person, a firm handshake means business, and so on.

We find explanations for why we came down with the common cold. Likewise, you might list all the potential reasons the person you are waiting for is taking so long, (i.e., "she's probably still looking in the mirror" or "he's probably still in the front of the T.V.") because you have seen him or her behave that way before. Thus, your past experiences with this person become "knowledge" that is much more reassuring to you than uncertainty. We try to find common trends in people we have dated ("having a type"), we hope that our resumes will indicate some kind of pattern in jobs we've had, and we spout out explanations for why or how we possibly could have left that credit card at the bar again after having learned what a pain it is to replace it in the past.

On a more straightforward level, people also often make the mistake of believing they can find a pattern in random systems, which is part of the reason why gambling is so popular and so addicting. Call it fate, luck, skill, or lucky guessing, but here are some instances in which getting it "right" is completely random:

(Continued)

1) Heads or Tails

So you're having an argument with your friend over who is going to be the one to tell a third friend of yours the bad news (left up to the imagination and/or prior experience). You decide rock-paper-scissors takes too long, and "Eeny, meeny, miny, moe" is unfair. So, you flip a coin. After arguing over who is going to be the one to flip the coin, and thereafter, whether or not it counts more when the quarter lands in the palm or when you flip it over onto the top of the non-catching hand, you call tails and it's heads. You play two out of three, then best out of five. You've called tails twice and both times it's been heads. So, you reason, if you call heads on the next round, odds are with you.

Well, this is not really true.

You could toss the coin twenty-five times and every time it could still land on heads.

There is skepticism by critics and mathematicians who claim that flipping a coin is not a 100 percent 50/50 chance because it is done by human hand, and one can train themselves to flip in a way that the coin will land in their favor.

However, this still does not mean that there is any statistical basis for one outcome affecting another. And the rationale behind the idea that just because one side has appeared frequently, the other will need to appear soon to even it out, is totally irrational.

2) The Shuffle Mode on Your MP3 Player Is Biased

Steve Jobs had it all figured out. He even knew how to create the perfect shuffle mode—one in which the songs that come up appear random, yet every song that comes up tends to be the exact one you wanted to hear. Or some of the more cynical of us may think we were the ones who figured it out. It's not actually random—the iPod plays certain songs more than once before playing every song in random order once.

It does seem sensible—computer programming systems are certainly advanced enough nowadays to bring up things (songs, sites, words) more often when you play, search, or use them frequently enough. And let's face it, the play count on iTunes is a dead giveaway.

But the iPod shuffle mode bias is a perfect example of the way in which people want to prove that true randomness doesn't exist. In actuality, putting your songs on random is and always will remain completely random (unless you select the setting in which you can prioritize your shuffle mode to play only favorite songs, or play them in order from favorite to least favorite).

According to Stanford mathematician Keith Devlin, randomness is particularly hard to recognize because true random sequences often inevitably form certain patterns. But the fact that the particular numbers and patterns that are formed are essentially unpredictable in their outcome makes these sequences random. So, he says, true random systems will repeat certain songs and neglect others, such as, presumably, in the iPod shuffle mode.

I would wager that the reason you might think shuffle mode tends to bring up songs you really like or that you play frequently is probably because the majority of songs you have on your iPod are probably ones that you enjoy. So from that angle, odds are certainly in your favor.

3) The Lottery

In one form or another, the lottery has existed in society for centuries. In practice, objectivity is questionable. In theory, lottery winners are supposed to be picked totally randomly. In a typical 6-from-49 lotto, a player chooses six different numbers from one to forty-nine to write in any order on a sheet. Then six numbers are drawn totally randomly out of a hat (or in most places, rotating ping pong balls with numbers written on them are pulled from a machine), and if the number sequence matches the numbers on a player's sheet, that player wins.

Even in the fairly small scale lottery scenario described above, the chances of winning are slim. In the American Mega Millions lottery, a similar technique is used, but one that further decreases the probability of winning. Players still pick six different numbers, but they are split into two separate pools. Players first choose five different numbers from one to fifty-six. The sixth number, however, is chosen from an entirely separate pool of numbers (from one to forty-six). This basically means that although the selection is just as random, the probability of winning the Mega Millions lottery is substantially lower because two different sets of random number samples are being used. You may have a winning first five-number set, but unless you match the "Mega Ball," you don't win the jackpot, and the Mega number cannot be used for matching a one of the first five numbers, or vice versa.

So you have two pools of randomly chosen numbers. But is this really random? Let's go back to the iPod shuffle question for a minute.

While some might argue that the iPod shuffle mode is not truly random because it plays every song on your iPod only once, that is not for lack of randomness, but rather for an alteration in probability. In other words, although every song is only being

(Continued)

chosen once, each time a song is chosen from a pool of however many songs you have, the selection of which song will be played is equally as random every time, despite the fact that the pool gets smaller after more songs have already been played. So, when a playlist of thirty songs begins, it might seem like which song will play first is more of a toss up than when there are only two songs left unplayed it is only that you have the memory of the twenty-eight songs prior to the remaining two that makes the outcome seem more limited, while in actuality it is no less random than flipping a coin (50/50) and the result is no more certain.

Though there was a recent rumor that a geological statistician named Strivastava "cracked" the American lottery, he only really just figured out a simple way to "probably" win the tic-tac-toe lottery card. Meaning, he figured out a pattern in the layout of the cards which got him the right answer about 90 percent of the time. But the scratch-off lottery cards are really worth hardly anything, awarding in some cases less prize money than the cards themselves had cost to purchase. Professional mathematicians are not paid to come up with a flawless design for these cheap lotto cards, and therefore, the occasional winning pattern is more likely to come up than in a lotto system that is truly random. Plus, Strivastava calculated the time he would have to invest and money he would be spending versus what he would earn, and the probability of winning, and found easily that he could not reasonably support himself financially by winning the tic-tac-toe lottery as a profession.

The truth of the matter is that sometimes there is no explanation, no order, no rhyme, and no reason behind an occurrence. An accident might just be an accident, a formula might be a random pattern, and we might just need more than one bad experience to learn to avoid similar situations in the future. Maybe there are patterns in our lives in hindsight, but in future events, randomness creates the pockets of order for us to pick out within the general chaos.

Sources: Susan Stamberg, "Doing the iPod Shuffle," NPR, 2008; CBS News, "Coin Toss Not Random: UBC Researchers," 2009; John Lehrer, "Cracking the Scratch Lottery Code," *Wired*, 2011.

RAUDIVE VOICES

Just as Ted Serios has claimed to be able in some manner to impress thought onto film, so Konstantin Raudive (1909-74) claimed to be able to record extraterrestrial voices on to tape. His book on the subject, *Breakthrough: an amazing experiment in electronic communication with the dead* (Gerrards Cross, 1971) is an exercise in credulity so bizarre as to become an object-lesson. Briefly, it is alleged that sounds of human voices heard either faintly or in garbled fashion are in fact those of spirits of dead persons of terrestrial origin, or alternatively the audible proof of visitors from outer space. In fact, of course, the phenomenon dates from the recent improvements in the quality of tape itself, and tape recorders, and from the rapid increase in the amount of broadcast and telecast information, often by satellite.

The naive frequently misunderstand broadcasts in languages other than their own, ascribing to them an origin from outer space!

"Raudive" voices were in fact noted as early as 1959, when such voices were reported by the Swede Friedrich Jürgenson. He believed that these voices were not only extra terrestrial, but that they were speaking directly to him. All of this material can be read in Jürgenson's Swedish-language *Rösterna fru°n rymden* (Stockholm, 1964) and the German-language *Sprechfunk mit Verstorbenen* (Freiburg, 1967), but there is really no need for speculation, after the exhaustive essay on the subject by D. J. Ellis, "Listening to the Raudive voices," in *Journal of the Society for Psychical Research,* no. 48, pp. 763, 1975, pp. 31-42. Mr. Ellis not only rejects all the supernatural claims by Jürgenson and Raudive: he offers simple, direct explanations of the phenomena concerned which render alternative discussions totally unnecessary. He concludes: "None of the voices examined in these tests appeared— from the reports of the listeners—to be inconsistent with having originated, in the case of microphone recordings, from odd sounds or uncontrolled utterances by persons present, or, in the case of the radio recordings, from normal radio transmissions."

"RE" IS AN ABBREVIATION OF "REFERRING TO" OR "REGARDING"

A commercial letter might begin: "Re. your communication of yesterday's date. . . ." This is often taken to mean "Regarding your communication. . . ." hence the full stop after re. But *re* is not an abbreviation, and should be italicized (or underlined) as a foreign word. It is the ablative form of the Latin word *res,* meaning "matter," "thing," or "affair," and in business means "in the matter of. . . ."

RED-HAIRED WOMEN ARE INCLINED TO ANGER

I imagine that this is only true if you are foolish enough to tell an inoffensive lady who happens to have red hair that she is inclined to anger! An old tradition, just as worthless, says that red-headed persons are deceitful and unreliable because Judas Iscariot had red hair! It is extremely unlikely that Judas had red hair (it was more likely black) but even if he had, the color of his hair would not consequently damn all others with red hair. "Girls with particularly red hair are good or especially evil," says the *Manuel du physionomiste des dames* (Paris, 1843).

An old English rhyme has a different fallacy: a man with black hair but a red beard is the worst man of all. "A red beard and a black head. Catch him with a good trick and take him dead."

"RED" SQUARE IN MOSCOW WAS SO CALLED AFTER THE RUSSIAN REVOLUTION

The name *krasniy* ("red," "beautiful") was applied to Moscow's Red Square long before the Bolshevik October Revolution of 1917 and has therefore nothing to do with the "East is Red" slogan or the "Red Flag" motif.

Incidentally, it is another common fallacy that there was only one revolution. There had been dozens of Russian revolutions prior to the Bolshevik victory, one of the most notable being the 1905 Revolution, which began with the Bloody Sunday massacre of January 9, (or January 22, the Old-Style Russian Calendar being thirteen days behind the Gregorian Calendar of the West up to February 1918). Another error is to believe that St. Petersburg changed its name to Leningrad. In fact, St. Petersburg changed its name in 1914 to Petrograd, and only from 1924 became Leningrad.

REINCARNATION

A fallacy known to the Greeks as metempsychosis and part of many religions' dogmas. It was known to the Ancient Egyptians, the American Indians, and still forms an integral part of Hindu and Buddhist beliefs.

Reincarnation became big business when a Colorado businessman named Morey Bernstein published *The search for Bridey Murphy* (1956). The author hypnotized a housewife, Virginia Tighe, who began to recollect an earlier existence as an Irish girl, "Bridey Murphy." The United States audience, conditioned to a belief in reincarnation by the medical diagnosis of Edgar Cayce, made the book a best-seller, and millions who read Bernstein's book never learned of the sequel.

Mrs. Tighe had in fact been brought up in a house very similar to that of "Bridey Murphy," one of her neighbors had been a woman called Bridie Murphy, and Mrs. Tighe had been in love with Bridie's son. The events claimed by Mrs. Tighe to have happened to "Bridey Murphy" had in fact happened to her.

We are indebted to the *Chicago American* for its brilliant exposé of this particular example of "reincarnation."

Sources: *Journal American* (New York City), June 10 to June 18, 1956, *Time,* June 18,1956 and *Life*, June 25,1956.

THE EFFICACY OF SACRED **RELICS**

A Duchess of Alba made her son, who was ill in Paris, drink pulverized relics and wash in them. To the great astonishment of his mother, the child nevertheless died.

Source: Pierre Antoine de La Place, *Pièces intèressantes* (Paris, 1790).

FALSE **REPUTATIONS**

Historical judgements are frequently wrong, and almost invariably depend not so much on the actual deeds and saying and writings of the famous, as on the historian's bias, and on the reader's prejudices. Thus, it is inconceivable that an American view of Mao Zedong (to use the new *pinyin* romanization) will coincide with a Chinese view past, present or future. Examples of errors due to such prejudices can be found in the present volume under Aethelred and Bligh, but all historical biography should be read as skeptically as one would read current journalism, for many "considered judgments" appearing in books are merely fossilized "off-the-cuff opinions" originally written in haste for a newspaper or magazine deadline.

There are not as many reconsiderations of reputation in print as we need. Historical critics should update biased views of well-known figures every decade, perhaps on the lines adopted by the Calvinist Jacques Barthélemy Salgues. His *Préjugés des reputations* (Paris, 1830) dealt with the then current reputations of Mme. de Genlis, Robert d'Arbrisselles, Mme. de Maintenon, the Prophet Muhammad, Martin Luther, Cardinal Richelieu, Urbain Grandier, M. de Bonald, St. Dominic, Comte de Maistre, St. Thomas Becket, the Abbe Lamennais, St. Bernard, the Abbe Frayssinous, the King of Prussia, Mme. de Staël, Metternich, Wellington, and Talleyrand.

THE "WHITE" **RHINOCEROS** IS WHITE

Both "black" and "white" rhinoceroses are grey-brown in color. The term "white" is a corruption of the Afrikaans word *wijd*, which means "wide," and refers to the animal's lips. The "black" rhinoceros's is distinguishable by its pointed upper lip, used for browsing on thorny bushes, while the white rhinoceros feeds on grass. The rhinoceros's horn does not have a bony core, despite the common assumption: it consists of keratin, the material of which human fingernails are composed.

Source: Zoological Society of London, *London Zoo guide* (London, 1977, p. 27).

RICE-PAPER IS MADE FROM RICE

Rice-paper is not made from rice, but derives from the pith of the so-called rice-paper plant whose scientific name is *Aralia* or *Fatsia Papyrifera*.

RICKETS CAN BE CURED BY BAGS HUNG 'ROUND THE NECK

Rickets is a disease due to the deficiency of vitamin D found mainly in fats.

Common fallacious treatments in the past have been as varied as the quacks have been ingenious. A typical advertisement for curing rickets, found in *The Intelligencer* dated October 16, 1664, runs:

"SMALL BAGGS to hang about Children's necks, which are excellent both for the *prevention* and *cure* of the Rickets, and to ease children in breeding of Teeth, are prepared by Mr. Edmund Buckworth, and constantly to be had at Mr. Philip Clark's, Keeper of the Library in the Fleet, and nowhere else, at 5 shillings a bagge."

There was apparently no harsher treatment for such frauds then than there is for more sophisticated pseudo-medical deceivers nowadays.

EARTH'S RING

Some traditional astronomers may still not know that the Planet Earth once had a ring like that which Saturn proudly possesses to this day. Isaac Newton Vail (1840-1912) of Barnesville, Ohio, described in *Waters above the firmament* (1886) how each planet passed through a phase in which it had a ring like Saturn's. Vail took the example of the Earth's "ring" to be the source of the flood waters recorded in *Genesis*.

Naturally, if planets other than Saturn had had such a ring, it would have caused related phenomena which are—however—in fact missing. Yet this simple datum of astronomy is ignored by members of the Annular World Association, which courageously promulgates the theories of Vail to a hostile or uncaring world from its headquarters in Azusa, California.

Sources: Martin Gardner, *Fads and fallacies in the name of science* (New York, 1957, p. 128).

ALL ROCKS ARE DEPOSITIONS FORMED IN SUCCESSION FROM WATER PREVIOUSLY COVERING THE GLOBE

Abraham Gottlob Werner (1749-1817) propounded the above theory, arguing that the minerals (included in his time within the general designation "fossils") "which constitute the beds and strata of mountains were dissolved in this universal water and were precipitated from it."

Werner and his followers were known as "Neptunists" as opposed to the "Plutonists" led by James Hutton (1726-1797) of Edinburgh. The plutonic theory explained granite and similar rocks as the result of a crystallization of molten material far below the earth's surface and far removed from water in its nature. Basalt is formed from lava flows and could not be a precipitation from the sea. Rudolf Raspe (author of *The adventures of Baron Münchhausen)* did much to sink the Neptunist fallacy into oblivion.

Source: A. G. Werner, *New theory of the formation of veins,* translated by Charles Anderson (Edinburgh, 1809).

INDIAN **ROPE-TRICK**

The "Indian rope-trick" is claimed to be a conjuring performance in which a small boy climbs a rope in full view of an audience *in the open air* and then disappears. The feat has been replicated on stage easily enough by means of ladders, mirrors, special lighting, and/or light-absorbing material for the boy's clothes. Other variants are the use of a "rope" consisting of jointed bamboo rods, or the substitution of a monkey dressed in turban and *dhoti* for the boy.

But no Western (or indeed Eastern) conjuror has been able to repeat the stage feat in the open air, as has so often been claimed by the gullible. Lord Northbrook, Viceroy of India, offered £10,000 in 1875 to anyone who would demonstrate the Indian rope-trick. Though the offer was widely advertised, no claimant came forward.

Source: D. H. Rawcliffe, *Illusions and delusions of the supernatural and the occult* (New York, 1959, pp. 297-301).

THE **ROUND** TABLE IN WINCHESTER CASTLE DATES BACK TO THE TIME OF KING ARTHUR

The round table which has hung on the wall of Winchester Castle for over 600 years has been the subject of much ill-informed speculation, though Norman Wymer in *The story of Winchester* (London, 1955) has stated that "any suggestion that it may be the authentic 'Round table' is clearly ridiculous."

"The Mystery of King Arthur and his Round Table" was a BBC 2 television program produced by Robin Bootle and shown on December 20, 1976; the program notes in *Radio Times* asked "Did the Knights of the Round Table sit here?," but the team of scientists answered in a resounding negative. The radiocarbon dating gave a period of 1270-1390 (the median date being 1330), the tree-ring evidence showed a date of 1336, and the carpentry typology suggested a date between 1250 and 1350. This conclusive evidence proves that the table dates to about 1336, and was therefore probably made by Edward III in connection with his abortive project for an Order of the Knights of the Round Table.

Source: Personal communication from Robin Bootle, January 11, 1977.

"RIGHTY TIGHTY, LEFTY LOOSEY"
IS AN ABSOLUTE **RULE**

Generally, this is the rule of thumb for unscrewing most jars and bottle caps, unlocking doors with keys, and screwing on bulbs, nuts into bolts, and other types of hardware and household practices.

Apparently there are, nonetheless, some rare and fascinating exceptions. According to public forums on home improvement and modes of pipe maintenance, these outliers consist namely of old propane (gas) cylinders as well as some other specialized pipe fittings. Additionally, one source suggests that really, in reference to changing pipes, "righty tighty and lefty loosey" could very well be switched depending on which side of the pipe you are standing on and/or changing it from.

Also, utilities such as pipes, saws, or tank valves that are left-hand threaded are programmed in an opposite manner (clockwise to open, counterclockwise to close).

So, if you find yourself spending hours trying to screw a propane tank in by turning it to the right and it just simply won't fit, maybe try switching to the left!

S

"A substantial and severe collection of the heteroclites or irregulars of Nature, well examined and described, I find not: especially not with due rejection of fables and popular errors: for as things now are, if an untruth in Nature be once on foot, what by reason of neglect of examination, and countenance of antiquity, and what by reason of the use of the opinion in similitudes, and ornaments of speech, it is never called down."
— FRANCIS BACON, *The advancement of learning* (1605)

"She forms and expresses an immense variety of opinions on an immense variety of subjects."
MR. WITITTERLY OF MRS. WITITTERLY,
IN CHARLES DICKENS,
Nicholas Nickleby

THE **SAHARA** REGION OF NORTHERN AFRICA IS PERENNIALLY DRY

Though the North African desert is, outside the Polar Regions, the least-populated area of the globe, with fewer than two million inhabitants, there is archaeological and even more abundant geological evidence that the "desert" was once more fertile and even now possesses seven major water regions of underground water reservoirs totalling an estimated 15,000,000 cubic meters of groundwater. This figure is increasing by some 4,000 million cubic meters a year by the acquisition of rainwater running underground from the desert's fringe areas towards the central rock-bound aquifers.

Source: UN Food and Agriculture Organization, Rome.

SALAD DAYS ARE THE HAPPIEST DAYS OF ONE'S YOUTH

Not so! Despite the nostalgic musical play by Sandy Wilson "salad days" are the gauche, anxious, lonely days recalled by Cleopatra in Shakespeare's *Anthony and Cleopatra* (I,v), when she remembers that her youthful days were "salad" days because she loved badly, like a salad, green and cold. The implication is entirely pejorative: "salad days" look forward to a maturity which is expected to be far more enjoyable.

SALIVA IS A DISINFECTANT

Retiring after a bloody conflict, the combatants are often said to "lick their wounds," with the meaning that they are disinfecting open wounds by the application of their own saliva. Sir Alexander Fleming discovered lysozyme in human saliva, and lysozyme is an antiseptic, but it is not seriously recommended by a doctor as a remedy for open wounds. Shakespeare wrote (lines 915-6) in *Venus and Adonis:* "And there another licking of wound, "Gainst venomed sores the only sovereign plaster," and there is the tradition of Jesus' curing a blind man with His spittle as evidence of the antiquity of the fallacy that saliva can cure blindness. Like blood, the saliva is considered by primitive peoples in many countries to possess a kind of spiritual power. Thus, in *The discovery of witchcraft* (London, 1665), Reginald Scot recommends against the efficacy of evil spells that one should spit into one's right shoe before putting it on in the morning, or alternatively that one should spit into one's own urine.

Ritual spitting for good luck is still practiced by those about to undertake a physical contest or a physical feat of some kind: as well as the forgotten superstitious benefit, it serves as a boost for confidence in the same way as the ritual "war-dance" boosts the confidence of New Zealand "All-Black" rugby union teams.

Saliva is not a useful or recommended disinfectant where any effective alternative is readily available.

SANDWICHES WERE INVENTED BY THE FOURTH EARL OF SANDWICH (1718-1792)

No! The compulsive English gambler certainly ate cooked meat between two slices of bread at the tables rather than leave them for an elaborate cooked meal, but the Romans had introduced the idea throughout their Empire seventeen centuries earlier.

SAP RISES

In the spring it is believed in the folklore that sap "rises," and likewise in the autumn that it "falls." But in fact sap moves from the center of the tree to the bark and back—never up or down.

NORTH AMERICAN INDIANS INTRODUCED SCALPING

Writing as "C. W. Ceram," the archaeologist Kurt Marek has produced an excellent account of North American archaeology in *The first American* (New York, 1971). I wonder how many readers were as surprised as I to learn the truth about the practice of scalping from pp. 295-6.

Marek indicates that the tragedy of the invasion of "Indian" territory by the Whites began in earnest with the California gold rush of 1849. "The deeds and misdeeds of those years have undergone a romantic transfiguration," in the author's words, "they have become legendary. Later it was said that they showed the American character at its best and at its worst. The groups that suffered the most during that time were the Indians.

"The aboriginals were driven back step by step. When they defended themselves with their few poor weapons, when in their hunger they attacked wagon trains or plundered ranches, frightful reprisal campaigns were waged against them. Early in the [1860s] panic swept the country east of Sacramento when Indians, probably Yahi, killed five white children. But in the years 1862-67 the whites had killed between 3,000 and 4,000 Indians. One detail alone suggests the senseless cruelty of the times: *the whites introduced scalping,* which was unknown to the Californian tribes."

Thomas T. Waterman relates: "On good authority I can report the case of an old prospector-pioneer-miner-trapper of this region, who had on his bed even in recent years a blanket lined with Indian scalps. These had been taken years before. He had never been a government scout, soldier, or officer of the law. The Indians he had killed purely on his own account. No reckoning was at any time demanded of him."

An American "Indian" is of course only by idiotic convention so called. Columbus thought he had landed in India, so he called the inhabitants "Red" to distinguish them from the "Brown" or "Black" Indians he was expecting. "Indian" denotes a citizen of India, of whatever color, race, or religion, but there is absolutely no connection between the racial types native to the Indian sub-continent and the American continent.

TO SCAN A PAGE IS TO GLANCE THROUGH IT PERFUNCTORILY

Nowadays we often hear of someone who had not enough time to read a book properly: he confesses that he merely *scanned* it. To the extent that it is a widespread meaning, it must be correct, for the English language recognizes no academy or official dictionary (despite the high status generally accorded to the *Oxford English Dictionary*). But if one remembers that a gunner *scans* the horizon for any sign of the enemy even now, then we must recall the original meaning, which was to scrutinize carefully, to examine point by point, to look at all parts intently.

SCHIZOPHRENIA IS CHARACTERIZED BY HAVING SPLIT PERSONALITIES

Schizophrenia has been commonly misunderstood by the public, and to some degree, by professionals, up until just a few decades ago. Calling someone a "schizoid," or associating someone who is schizophrenic with obvious outward shifts in personality, is a widespread notion (or up until recently, was) but it is really and sadly quite inaccurate.

It is simply not true that schizophrenics are mostly identifiable as having split personalities. This primary symptom is categorized under a very different disorder, Dissociative Identity Disorder (formerly known as Multiple Personality Disorder). The misperceptions most likely come from the fact that the Greek root of the word schizophrenia informs words such as "split" and "mind." However, the word itself does not refer to split personalities or multiple identities.

The development of symptoms of schizophrenia in patients, and nonetheless, to their observers, is actually quite subtle. Schizophrenic symptoms typically come on slowly and vaguely, but are eventually categorized by moderate to severe delusions, hallucinations, and lessening of one's ability to organize thoughts or words coherently. While people with schizophrenia might feel that they are victims of an otherwise unrealistic conspiracy and/or will feel that an external source is actively taking control of their own thoughts and mind, they do not shift between one or more significantly different personalities at random like those with multiple personality disorder do.

Findings generally show that patients with schizophrenia have many more negative symptoms than split personality disorder patients do, as well as notably less severe positive symptoms. Negative symptoms in both cases include anxiety and depression, and in schizophrenia also includes social isolation. The rates of psychosis in DID subjects are much higher than in schizophrenics as well.

Schizophrenic tendencies are actually closer to those of manic depressives, or people with Bipolar I Disorder. Both bipolar and schizophrenic patients tend to experience extremes: euphoric highs and depressive lows.

Despite the fact that schizophrenia affects something like 24 million people worldwide, there is still a negative social stigma associated with the disorder and those who have it. According to a survey from 1966, people still believed that schizophrenics were violent, unable to manage money, and generally incapable of living on their own. Although it can certainly be true that people with schizophrenia may need assistance from others while they are trying to cope with the worst of their symptoms, that they are still often placed in the same category as alcoholics, drug users, and those with much more severe psychotic disorders is strikingly misinformed.

We are now over a decade into the 2000s. We know that "schizophrenia" is not a synonym for "psycho killer." However, it is serious, and too often goes undetected in its early stages. We need to take steps in understanding schizophrenia instead of pushing it away, so that people who begin to develop symptoms of this disorder don't wait until its too late to seek out help.

Sources: Colin A. Ross, MD, "Dissociative Identity Disorder," *Metapress.com*, 2006; Steven R. Hirsch, "Schizophrenia," 2003; Jo C. Phelan, Bruce G. Link, JStor Article, "Public Misconceptions of Mental Illness in 1950 and 1996: What is Mental Illness and Is it to be Feared?" *Journal of Health and Social Behavior*, Vol. 41, 2000.

THE **SCIENTIFIC METHOD** IS APPLICABLE ONLY BY SCIENTISTS

We all need to apply the scientific method every day in at least one way or another. The fact is, however, that "it is at least as rare to come across a scientist who consistently applies the true scientific method as it is to find a writer with an impeccably lucid prose style," as C. H. Waddington writes in *Tools for thought* (London, 1977).

John R. Platt, in *The step to man* (New York, 1966), has even gone so far as to suggest that "the scientific method" is found so rarely that one should rename the true "scientific method," calling it "the method of strong inference." The method was developed during the Renaissance (to confine ourselves to Europe, though it was familiar in China much earlier), and is classically described in Francis Bacon's *Novum organon* (1620).

The method involves making a series of hypotheses as to how things may be working, and then to design an experiment which will show whether these hypotheses are false.

John R. Platt describes the procedure in more detail, and although he refers solely to problems in science, notes that one can reverse the definition so that science may be defined as all those problems which this method is capable of solving. This is what he writes: "Strong inference consists of applying the following steps to a problem in science, formally and explicitly and regularly: (1) devising alternative hypotheses; (2) devising a crucial experiment (or several of them) with alternative possible outcomes, each of which will, as nearly as possible, exclude one or more of the hypotheses; (3) carrying out the experiment so as to get a clean result; and recycling the procedure, making subhypotheses or sequential hypotheses to define the possibilities that remain; and so on."

Francis Bacon stated that the scientific method "must analyse nature by proper rejection and exclusions; and then, after a sufficient number of negatives, come to a conclusion on the affirmative instances," and to put his view into historical perspective it is important to remember that the deductions being made in Bacon's period were from Pliny, Aristotle, and the Bible, for example, empirical and rational science having scarcely begun. "The first necessity under such circumstances," writes Waddington, "was indeed to debunk the unfounded myths which formed the greater part of accepted wisdom about the nature of the subjects which science had to investigate. Emphasis on rejections and exclusions of the conventional wisdom of the dominant group was very right and proper."

SCIENTOLOGY

The wittiest exposé of this modern psychological and religious phenomenon is *The mind benders* (London, 1971), by the former scientologist Cyril Vosper. Chris Evans writes in the *New Humanist* (September 1972, p. 196): "Vosper's attack is focussed principally upon the aspects of the cult that, as a one-time senior administrator within it, he knows most about—the inefficient, amateurish administration, the ludicrous self-importance of its officials, the ruthless "ethics" orders which guide and control the social behavior of followers and the hefty fees charged for arguably valueless training."

Vosper's central argument does not prove the tenets of scientology fallacious. This is the conclusion of the report, *Enquiry into the practice and effects of Scientology* (London, 1971), issued by a commission headed by Sir John G. Foster and published by Her Majesty's Stationery Office. Lord Windlesham, in an official letter from the Home Office, declared scientology "to be harmful and contrary to the public interest," though the movement's founder, L. Ron Hubbard, was the only scientologist precluded (on August 13, 1970) from entering the United Kingdom whatever the purpose of his visit.

The then Minister of Health, Kenneth Robinson, replied on December 5, 1966 to a question in Parliament, "I do not think that any further enquiry is necessary to establish that the activities of this organisation [the Church of Scientology] are potentially harmful, I have no doubt that Scientology is totally valueless in promoting health and in particular, that people seeking help with problems of mental health can gain nothing from the attentions of this organization."

Source: *Hansard,* vol. 737, col. 183.

"GREAT SCOTT!" DERIVES FROM
SIR WALTER SCOTT

The exclamation "Great Scott!" derived from the United States General Winfield Scott (1786-1866), a notoriously fussy candidate for the presidency in 1852. Scott failed in his bid, but he has a greater—if unwanted—significance as the origin of a popular phrase.

Source: Eric Partridge, *Name into word* (London, 1949).

GREEK AND ROMAN **SCULPTURE**
WAS MONOCHROME

Almost all excavated examples of classical sculpture reveal traces of color, so that the white or cream figures now shown in museums all over Europe, and especially in Greece and Italy, give no idea at all of the polychrome magnificence of the originals. Judging by holes in some of the Elgin Marbles in the British Museum, to give but one instance, real bridles and reins were attached to figures of horses, while humans' sandal-straps were of real leather and stone hands grasped actual weapons.

Gisela Richter writes in *A handbook of Greek art* (London, 1959, p. 46): "All stone sculpture, whether of limestone or marble, was painted, either wholly or in part. Though much of the original color has disappeared, enough traces remain to make its general use certain, as indeed it had been in Egypt (even for colored stone) and as was desirable in the brilliant light of Greece. Another general Greek practice was the addition of accessories in different materials. Eyes were sometimes inlaid in colored stone, glass or ivory; metal curls, diadems and wreaths were added, and even earrings and necklaces; likewise metal spears, swords, and the reins and bridles of horses. Only the holes for attachment now generally remain."

One is mystified. As curators of museums are trained nowadays to provide display facilities to encourage a more imaginative approach on the part of their visitors, and a keener awareness of what life and art were actually like in earlier times, why is it almost unheard of for curators to reconstruct Greek and Roman sculptures in their original colors and with their original trappings? The cost would be very slight and the clues from ancient writers and traces of color are abundant.

SCURVY CAN BE AVOIDED BY MOVING THE BODY

D. M. Occomore, writing in *The East Anglian Magazine,* December 1976 (p. 79), on Essex step-dancing, states that "The idea was that if a man moved his body he was less likely to contract that curse of seamen's ills, scurvy. The Admiralty insisted that the men dance the hornpipe. Whether this was the origin of the step-dance adopted by landsmen can only be guessed at."

The sole cause of scurvy is a vitamin C deficiency, and the disease was common in naval campaigns when fresh food was difficult to obtain. The remedy for scurvy is a diet including fresh vegetables, most fresh fruit, or lime and lemon juice. The British Navy introduced a regulation issue of lime juice in 1795, and this measure virtually eliminated scurvy; the British Board of Trade introduced a similar measure for the mercantile navy in 1865.

The association of dancing and scurvy is wholly fallacious.

SEALING-WAX IS MADE OF WAX

At one time, it is true, sealing-wax was made with beeswax. However, beeswax was replaced centuries ago by a harder, more durable compound of rosin, shellac, and turpentine. The sealing-wax you buy today has no wax in it at all.

ASIMOV'S SECURITY BELIEFS

During a lifetime as a professional writer of popular (but carefully researched) science and science fiction, Isaac Asimov has drawn up a list of fallacies which in his view sustain the majority of mankind and prevent their accepting truth, reason, and responsibility:

1. There exist supernatural forces that can be cajoled or forced into protecting mankind.
2. There is no such thing, really, as death,
3. There is some purpose to the universe.
4. Individuals have special powers that will enable them to get something for nothing.
5. Yon are better than the next fellow.
6. If anything goes wrong, it's not your fault.

IT IS LEGAL TO SELL YOUR WIFE, IF DONE IN PUBLIC

The *Annual Record* for 1832 describes the sale of a farmer's wife in Carlisle. The husband placed her in a chair with a straw halter round her neck and offered her for sale. She went for twenty shillings and a Newfoundland dog. The usual causes for such a sale, recorded on many occasions particularly in England in the 18th and 19th centuries, were the inability of a husband to maintain his wife, or her shrewish tongue or idle nature.

In 1881 a woman at a London County Court produced a stamped receipt to prove that she was not living in adultery with her second "husband," since her first spouse had sold her for twenty-five shillings some years before. A. R. Wright's *English folklore* (1928) mentions several sales occurring between World War I and World War II, but it is of course nonsense to imagine that wife-selling was ever sanctioned under English *law* at any period.

THERE IS NO DIFFERENCE BETWEEN CLUB SODA AND **SELTZER**

For the majority of people who do not count on the brilliant carbonated water mixture to cure hangovers and stomach aches, there is probably very little apparent difference between drinking club soda and drinking seltzer. Most waiters at restaurants don't even seem to recognize or acknowledge the difference.

Although there really is very little distinction between the two forms of water with bubbles (gas), there is some variation. When the terms are defined side by side, the main difference between them is that club soda (to add even more confusion, it is also called "soda water") contains some sodium bicarbonate. Both drinks, however, are considered effervescent water beverages with carbon dioxide.

Technically, seltzer is closer in its makeup to mineral water (also goes by the name of "sparkling water"), whereas club soda is essentially soda without any flavoring, corn syrup, or caffeine (soda water!). In plain terms, seltzer is slightly more natural, but club soda is better for indigestion.

Sources: *Merriam-Webster Dictionary*, "Club Soda" and "Seltzer."

SEXUAL ATTRACTION IS CAUSED BY GRAVITY

A widely-distributed broadsheet distributed by Gulam Rasul of Sahiwal, Pakistan, and bearing the rubber-stamped message "Give me the old time Religious Pamphlets," offers several fallacies in a small area. Family planning is the chief pursuit of Mr. Rasul, whose "hints" begin:

1. Why there is a sex attraction between a male and a female; should there have been none what could have happened since God knew to create from clot/clay. (Vibrations of speaker due to distance between magnet and disc.)
2. Sex attraction is a gravity attraction. To go against gravity like a rocket (for mysticism-sublimation) requires sound sex valves not punctured. (Sexual power = Force = Pressure/Puncture = Waste of energy = Loss of work) [My copy has the rubber-stamped addendum (Leads to corruption).]

Further "hints" from Sahiwal include: "Students do curse the examiners; After success these students when act examiners are being cursed by other students. Or, leave the poor to die. They are breeding like mosquitoes and flies. Poverty is the punishment for disobeying the contents of Quran in Surat Al-Nur, para. 33; which reads "Those can't afford to get married should stay decently and wait until they earn sufficient wealth by God's grace for this option."

Sources: Broadsheet received from author, January 1980.

SEXUAL FALLACIES ACCORDING TO BRIGGS

Michael H. Briggs has listed the following fantasies surrounding the problems of sex, birth, and pregnancy:

1. "Aphrodisiacs" increase sexual desire, as stated by "Pilaff Bey" in *Venus in the kitchen* (London, 1952), from a reputable publisher. See also WATER IS AN APHRODISIAC.
2. Strict dieting during pregnancy will limit the size of the child, in the erroneous view of many mothers.
3. Intercourse, sneezing, and the mother's bumping into objects will affect the development of the child, in the view of L. Ron Hubbard, founder of Scientology. All gynaecologists know that the baby is protected by amniotic fluids from even severe blows on the mother's body.
4. Numerous births are genuine. A certain Countess Margaret of Henneberg is reputed to have given birth in Easter week 1276 to 365 children the size of mice. 182 were boys christened "John" by the Bishop of Utrecht, and 182 girls were christened "Elizabeth." The odd one out was hermaphroditic. This fantasy is to be found in *Pepysian garland* (London, 1922), edited by H. Rollins.
5. A child's month of birth is significant in later life, according to at least one child psychologist, who claims that Spring children are more successful than those born in Autumn and Winter. This belief was tested in 1933 (see Pintner and Forlando in *Journal of Educational Psychology,* vol. 24, p. 561) by analyzing the distribution of birth months among 25,166 eminent Americans. The differences from month to month were as negligible as would have been required to prove an absence of positive evidence, though as a matter of interest the "top month" was marginally October!
6. The view that male children are carried on the left and females on the right has been mistakenly believed since the 5th century B.C. Greek philosopher Parmenides of Elea.
7. The age of females at marriage is thought to vary widely around the world. But it depends what you mean by "marriage," for the Indian ceremony (which took place generally between the ages of 13 and 14 during the 1930s in India) is more akin to the western practice of engagement, or formal betrothal, and the average age at which Indian mothers (in Bombay and Madras) had their first baby at that time was 18-19.
8. Many people still think that only females menstruate, but many members of the monkey family do also. D. L. Gunn and others exploded the fallacy connecting menstruation (whose cycle averages 28 days) with the lunar cycle (averaging 29 1/2 days) by

surveying large groups of women and finding no detectable relationship (*Journal of Obstetrics and Gynaecology,* vol. 44, 1937).
9. Writings by Wilhelm Reich involving his fantastic "orgone energy"
are not to be taken seriously because this alleged energy has not
been detected by unbiased observers. Reich compares earthquakes
with a sexual embrace preceding coition.
10. Sexual elixirs have been second only to elixirs of life as a trap for
the unwary and the gullible. One John R. Brinkley sold one such
elixir which, on analysis, proved to be 99.9 percent water with a
trace of hydrochloric acid for flavor and methylene blue for coloring.

Source: Michael H. Briggs, "Popular fantasies about sex" in *The
Humanist,* October 1962, pp. 306-9.

SEXUAL FALLACIES

Just to name a few more:

1) Men Think About Sex Every Seven Seconds

Unfortunately, we have not yet invented a way to read people's
thoughts (properly, at least). Thus, this statistic cannot be proved.
However, according to the Kinsey Institute, an organization frequently referenced for sex stats, the majority of men do think
about sex at least once a day (54 percent); they do not literally
think about sex close to six different times per minute.

2) Men Think About Sex More Frequently Than Women

Again, an age-old stereotype is that men are much more sexual
than women, as they think about sex more often and act on sex
more often. In other words, they have a lot more trouble keeping it in their pants. A survey of men and women between 18
and 25 on their sexual thoughts presents the findings in a more
complex way. While men were reported to think about sex once
an hour and women only once every two hours, the ranges varied greatly in both genders. Regardless of gender, this cohort of
subjects reported thinking about sleep and food as often as they
think about sex.

The researchers also found that the more uncomfortable a
woman feels about her own sexuality, the less likely she is to
report it (not shockingly). Additionally, the gender stereotype
that has been perpetuated for ages, that men are supposed to be
more interested in sex than women, has made women less likely
to report frequent sexual thoughts, researchers found.

Therefore, they say, basically, that their own statistics are
undermined by the fact that women are not being totally honest

(Continued)

with how often they truly think about sex. And considering the fact that both men and women think about eating and sleeping (also basic human desires) the same amount, it could reasonably be predicted that if women were more comfortable admitting how often a sexual thought really does cross their minds each day, the frequency would match that of men's.

3) Sexual Fantasies Are Unhealthy

One author of an article in *The Sunday Times* article speculates whether or not men's sexual thoughts are more sinister than women's. But again, this cannot really be proven.

Supposedly, 35 percent of men have admitted to having sexual thoughts or fantasies about rape. But there is no known correlation between men who have these thoughts (or admit to them) and people who actually commit sex crimes, nor can scientists, police, or psychologists draw a definitive line between men (or women) who actively and frequently engage in rape role play and known sex offenders.

According to the Kinsey findings, there are no significant patterns between people who have diagnosed mental disorders such as depression, anxiety, psychopathology, and psychological sadism/masochism and those who practice BDSM (Bondage, Discipline, Domination/Submission, Sadism/Masochism). Logically enough, sex offenders likely have more deep-seated psychological problems than couples who want to spice up their sex lives.

Finally, the survey finds sexual fantasies to be positive, as the couples or people with the most "healthy" (and expressed least dissatisfaction in) sex lives had thoughts related to sex more frequently.

4) Looking at Porn Is Uncommon in Sexually Active People

Looking at porn is apparently very far from uncommon for people of all walks of life. Not even taking into consideration old school forms of pornography such as magazines, photographs, videos, etc., the frequency of porn users on the Internet is truly quite remarkable.

Statistically, literally over half of all activity on the Internet is found to be related to sex. Furthermore, U.S. revenues from the porn industry alone exceed those brought in from huge companies like CBS, ABC, and NBC combined.

Although men do tend to report visiting pornography websites on a regular basis much more frequently on a monthly basis than women (25 percent versus 4 percent), judging from the intensely high profits that these sites are bringing in on a national scale, it seems more than certain that women are also visiting these sites, and that many more men than have admitted doing so are as well. As we no longer have to take the trouble of stuffing a naked *Playboy* girl photograph under our pillows when mom walks in, and sneaking off to watch adult films when your wife isn't around no longer has to be delegated to business trips in the hotel room, it makes sense that pornography has become such a common and not to mention, profitable, part of the American life.

After all, if anything has stayed consistent over the years, it's sex. And sex sells.

Sources: *iub.edu / ~kinsey*; Paul Joannides, *As You Like It* blog, "Do Men REALLY Think About Sex More than Women?" *Psychology Today*, 2011.

PEELING LABELS OFF BEER BOTTLES MEANS YOU'RE **SEXUALLY FRUSTRATED**

If you've ever been a college student, caught at a particularly fidgety moment, or alone at a bar full of men (or women) who approach you with an all too overt pick-up line, you have probably heard that ripping labels off your bottles is a sign of sexual frustration.

There is, however, absolutely no evidence whatsoever to prove that there is any truth to this myth. According to word of mouth, ripping labels off bottles could mean anything from boredom, symptoms of recently quitting smoking, general or circumstantial nervousness, or just purely habit. The most concrete evidence against the sexual frustration fallacy is that fidgeting is often a trait of people with ADHD. Or, shockingly, anxiety.

Most people who comment on various forums on this topic deny that there is any link between sexual frustration and bar scene fidgeting, as, in their personal experience, they have found themselves absentmindedly ripping labels off their beers even in a time of abundant sexual activity. Others say they have never heard of the connection.

But, considering there are two Facebook groups with close to 1,000 members perpetuating this myth (i.e., "I rip beer bottle labels so I must be sexually frustrated"), people don't seem to question its legitimacy much. Maybe that's because in people young (or cheap) enough to still be drinking beer out of bottles on a regular basis, sexual frustration is the norm.

Sources: *Facebook, Snopes, The Straight Dope.*

SHAKESPEARE FALLACIES

1. Shakespeare's Plays Were Written by Bacon, Rutland, Oxford, Stanley, Marlowe, Dyer ...

The theory that Francis Bacon, Viscount St. Albans, wrote the plays previously attributed to William Shakespeare appears first to have been suggested by Herbert Lawrence in *The life and adventures of common sense* (1769) but was not to surface again until J. C. Hart's *The romance of yachting* (New York, 1848). Since then the supporters of Bacon have been the chief opposition party to the Stratfordian party which remains in power.

Edward de Vere, 17th Earl of Oxford, was first suggested as a candidate for the authorship by J. T. Looney, ably supported by Percy Allen, William Kent, and others. William Stanley has been suggested since 1890, notably by A. W. Titherley and A. J. Evans. Two of the more recent figures nominated are Sir Edward Dyer (1545-1607), proposed by Alden Brooks and Christopher Marlowe, according to Calvin Hoffman in *The man who was Shakespeare* (London, 1955). But Marlowe was killed in 1593 and Mr. Hoffman is forced to suggest a theory that the inquest was a frame-up, and that Marlowe was not killed, but smuggled to the Continent by his patron, Sir Thomas Walsingham, who had arranged for another man to be killed and identified as Marlowe. The real Marlowe survived and passed off his plays as Shakespeare's. They never met (though they were both in London in 1592 and as there were only two theatres there at the time it would have been extremely difficult to avoid meeting) and never influenced each other.

It seems to be fairly probable that Shakespeare is after all the author, if only because other candidates arrived so curiously late on the scene, long after Shakespeare's quality had been identified and widely studied and performed. The insuperable problem is that if *one* of the above factions is correct, as is likely, then all the other factions are presumably completely wrong (though the ingenious J. M. Robertson went so far as to consider the plays a scissors-and-paste compilation!).

The testimony of Ben Jonson seems to be conclusive for the authenticity of Shakespeare's authorship of the plays: he "loved the man, and did honor his memory (on this side Idolatry) as much as any." Again according to Jonson, Shakespeare "was not of an age, but for all time."

2. William Shakespeare Used a Vocabulary Much Greater Than That Useable Today

Quite the contrary. The English language has grown enormously since Elizabethan times. Webster's unabridged dictionary of 1934 listed over 600,000 words, while the 3rd ed. of 1961 cut the "unabridged" [sic] to a mere 450,000. It is reckoned that more than a million words in present-day English have not yet become obsolete, whereas, according to Irving J. Lee (in *Language habits in human affairs,* New York, 1941), Shakespeare used fewer "than twenty thousand different words in his plays." The average vocabulary of the contemporary English-speaker is certainly lower than that of Shakespeare, but writers and others of high literacy can make use of a lexicon far in excess of that useable by our greatest playwright.

SHARKS FREQUENTLY ATTACK AND EAT MEN

Human cowardice must be responsible, together with the usual barrel-load of scientific ignorance and refusal to shake off old prejudices, for this fallacy, recently revitalized by the best-selling novel and film *Jaws.* Actual cases of men being attacked by sharks are so rare that the U.S. Navy's Bureau of Aeronautics thought it worth stating in the pamphlet *Shark sense* (1944) that "there is practically no danger that an unwounded man floating in a life-jacket will be attacked by a shark." A foremost expert, Captain William E. Young, wrote in *Shark! Shark!* (New York, 1933) that he had never known of a shark attacking a living man, though he thought it might happen. Bergen Evans concludes his remarks on this fallacy in *The natural history of nonsense* (London, 1947, p. 81): "Of the several hundred varieties of sharks only half a dozen have the denture necessary for man-eating, and of these not all have the disposition. Of those that have, few get the opporunity, and of those, few make the most of it."

FALLACIES ON SHARK ATTACKS

To add to Philip Ward's discussion in the section above, we will also explore the reasons for human obsession with and fear of sharks. As land dwelling human beings in a world dominated by bodies of water, we are naturally afraid of what we are not masters of. While some of us are born to be swimmers, divers, surfers, sailors, destined to be one with the sea, a lot of us are quite intimidated by it.

There are many terrifying things about the sea. For one, there is so much of it in such great depths that the extent of what dwells miles and miles beneath sea level is perhaps still one of our greatest mysteries. In addition, the ocean houses one of the world's oldest and therefore arguably, scariest, predators: sharks. The shark is as fascinating as it is horrifying to humans, as we can see through the overwhelming popularity of the creature in the media: take, for instance, news sensationalizing of real

(Continued)

events, the television program *Shark Week*, movies like *Jaws* and documentaries such as *Open Water*.

Even if some of these media outlets do address fallacies about sharks, such as in episodes of *Shark Week*, the general hype surrounding sharks and shark attacks gives off false perceptions and exaggerations about the commonality of shark attacks and the dangers of sharks in general. Here are some of the most common misconceptions about our ancient sea dwelling foes:

1) Human Death by Shark Attack Is Common

With all the attention the press and media gives instances of shark attacks, it really does seem like they occur quite frequently. Actually, shark attacks (and moreover, fatalities due to shark attacks) are so rare that when they do occur, we can count on our beloved American media sources to overdramatize the tragedy to no end.

Worldwide in the past ten years, there has been an average of 77 reported shark attacks per year, only 3-4 of which end in death. Official statics compare the number of shark attacks per year to deaths by other types of uncommon disasters, proving how uncommon shark attacks really are. For instance, death by lightning strikes are well over 10 times more common than by shark attacks (37.9 vs. 0.05 overall averages from years 1959-2010). Dog attack, tornado, and even collapsing sand hole (quick sand) fatalities are more common.

2) All Sharks Are Dangerous/Attack Humans

There are many sharks that are too small to do any serious damage to humans, let alone take bites out of them. The great white does indeed attack the most often. The tiger and bull shark also have fairly high levels of attacks recorded. However, the Florida Museum of Natural History warns the reader to keep in mind that those who are attacked by a shark often times mislabel the type of shark. As the great white is the most commonly known to humans, it is quite possible that the victim may insist he or she was bitten by a great white, when really it could have been a shark less commonly known but about the same in size: the requiem shark.

Although the Great White, Tiger, and Bull shark remain the "big three" in the levels of threat in the shark attack realm, the reason there are more fatalities recorded with these three is because their jaws are larger and their teeth are sharper, meaning they are much more likely to do damage than their smaller, duller dental friends.

3) Sharks Have Poor Eye Sight

Although they do have empty, soulless eyes, these are not factors that affect their ability to see. Apparently, sharks do see quite well and in color, in fact. One expert claims sharks are able to see (from underwater) bright objects such as buoys, paddles, and bright colored boats from up to seventy feet beneath the surface of the ocean.

4) Sharks Attack Humans Because They Mistake Them for Seals

The understanding as to why human shark attacks occur at all tends to be that they mistake us for their normal prey. Why? Perhaps because they have poor vision, and therefore mistake our flailing limbs near the surface of the water with fish flapping around their natural habitat. As we know now, sharks do not have poor vision. So, we can cross this explanation off the list.

Additionally, an expert shark researcher, R. Aidan Martin, tells *National Geographic* that the way in which sharks attack humans is also quite different in terms of their tactics and their purpose than it is when they attack seals and other prey. He has personally witnessed countless sharks attack their prey, observing that they would always shoot up from the water to the surface and "pulverize" their prey with great force. By contrast, human shark attacks usually consist of just one casual bite.

Sharks, he insists, are curious animals. They use their teeth much like the way we use our hands: to approach something unfamiliar and get a feel for what it is by touching it. Once they've tossed it around in their mouths for a while and have gotten a sufficient feel for the texture and consistency, they'll spit your piece of flesh and/or limb right back out and be on their way. Unless you're one of those unlucky 0.5 percent who blend in a little too well with aquatic life.

Sources: Florida Museum of Natural History, "Ichthyology," Category: "Shark Attacks"; Jennifer Hile, "Great White Shark Attacks: Defanging the Myths," *National Geographic*, 2004.

SHAVING MAKES HAIR GROW BACK THICKER

Young girls—and perhaps boys as well, but for the opposite reason—often hold strong to the belief that once you shave an area of your body, there's no turning back. Hair will be thicker and darker on your legs, armpits, or face once you take a razor to said area for the first time. This is perhaps why, among many other reasons, girls do not shave off the hair that naturally grows in the moustache area or the stray hairs under the chin, but instead they wax

(Continued)

or bleach them. Boys on the other hand, may begin shaving their faces before Mother Nature intended in hopes that the peach fuzz will grow back into something resembling the initial phases of a beard. Luckily, or unluckily, depending on gender and/or genetics, this is only a myth. The reason hair may seem thicker or more "stubbly" after it has been shaved off is because it is shorter and looks less natural in its growing back stage. According to experts, how thick and dark hair follicles are depends on hormones and genetics, as well as its location on the body. Most people have thicker hair under their arms and on legs and in the pubic region, especially after hitting puberty.

Another explanation for the misperception about hair growing back thicker after shaving might be that girls are likely to begin shaving upon the first physical signs of puberty. Thus, when they shave their armpits for the first time and see it growing back thick and dark, they may remember back to when they did not have armpit hair to begin with, which presumably was not long before. In comparison, the stubble that appears under the arm within hours after shaving might be alarming.

There are obvious benefits to waxing instead of shaving, such as length of time one has to wait until the next time hair removal (approximately one month vs. one week). But if you thought waxing was a way to avoid unsightly prickly hair from reappearing, now is the time to realize that beauty really is a pain.

Sources: Dr. Lawrence E. Gibson, "Adult Health," *Mayo Clinic*; Teen Girls' Health, "Shaving Tips for Teen Girls," Web MD, 2010.

IF AN ATTACK OF **SHINGLES** SUCCEEDS IN ENCIRCLING THE BODY, THE PATIENT WILL DIE

Pliny the Elder collected this theory and believed it in the first century A.D.: "It kills if it encircles." Two thousand years or so later, J. B. Harrison found himself repudiating the same notion in *Chambers' Edinburgh Journal* (1850, p. 389): "There is a vulgar error, that if the eruption completes the circle, it is fatal . . . fortunately this is not the case, but the complaint *does* seldom get quite round."

The last word belongs to F. W. Morton Palmer, in *Notes and Queries* (April 20, 1940, p. 285), who explains that the popular fallacy is based on "the synthesis of two facts. An attack of shingles is *never* fatal . . . Also shingles *never* meets round the body . . ."

SILHOUETTES WERE INVENTED BY ÉTIENNE DE SILHOUETTE

E. F. Carter, in his *Dictionary of inventions and discoveries* (2nd ed., London, 1974), dates the invention of the silhouette to 1759 and attributes it, and most people still do, to the Controller-General of France, Étienne de Silhouette (1709-1767), but the *Encyclopaedia Britannica* is perfectly right in rejecting this explanation. The shadow outline of an object, usually a profile, obtained by projecting the shadow on to a sheet of white paper, tracing in the outline, and afterwards filling in with a dark color, most usually black, was familiar in the first half of the 18th century.

Silhouette was named Controller-General through the influence of the Marquise de Pompadour in 1759, but before the year was out Silhouette was removed for proposing a land-tax on the estates of nobles and the reduction of pensions. In allusion to the sacrifices which he demanded of the nobles (including the conversion of their tableware into coinage), "silhouette" came to refer to any figure reduced to its simplest outline.

"SIRLOIN" WAS ORIGINALLY SO CALLED BY KING JAMES I

In a 1978 television program, the owner of a certain British stately home claimed proudly that it was in his home that James I had jokingly dubbed an excellent helping of beef "Sir Loin."

Actually "surloin" (the preferred, though less common spelling) comes from the 14th-century French word *surlonge* (the upper part of a loin of beef), and it occurs as "surloyn" as early as the reign of Henry VI in the accounts of the Ironmongers' Company. Sources include: W. W. Skeat, *An etymological dictionary of the English language* (Oxford, 1888).

SECONDHAND CIGARETTE SMOKE IS WORSE FOR HEALTH THAN WOOD BURNING SMOKE

How could something that conjures up such a wholesome image (of Laura Ingalls Wilder and her family gathered 'round the fireplace listening to Pa tell stories during a blizzard, of course) be called sinister or harmful? True, wood burning fires have been around, well, since the dawn of mankind roughly. But apparently, very recent research has begun to prove that in fact, this very smoke is quite unhealthy to inhale.

According to the Environment and Human Health organization, the effects of wood smoke and cigarette smoke are actually

(Continued)

THE BOOK OF COMMON FALLACIES

quite similar, as they both contain carcinogens. Wood smoke has properties and chemicals that can potentially scar the lungs, such as carbon monoxide, sulfur dioxide, and formaldehyde. Additionally, both cigarettes and wood smoke have polycyclic aromatic hydrocarbons (PAHs) and dioxin. PAHs are said to contain carcinogens (a type of chemical).

According to the Environmental Protection Agency (EPA), one single fireplace burning ten pounds of wood for an hour emits 4,300 times more PAHs than thirty cigarettes. Although smokers themselves shouldn't use this as a personal justification to smoke more often or to continue smoking, it is somewhat groundbreaking that suddenly researchers have reason to speculate whether spending the evening at a house party filled with thirty smokers is actually more dangerous than opening presents on Christmas morning by the fireside in a closed living room.

Sources:*ehhi.org / woodsmoke; epa.gov / woodstoves / healtheffects .html*

SNAKE FALLACIES

Dr. Heitor Coutinho writes from Sao Paulo to contribute many more snake fallacies to my original collection. A selection of his will appear below, with my grateful acknowledgments:

1. Snakes deliberately commit suicide

This fallacy derives from the observation that occasionally a captured snake will bite itself in the heart when stuffed by a collector into a bag. But no snake has proved to have taken its own life intentionally.

2. Venomous snakes will die if they swallow their own venom

They will not. Their poison is aimed at securing prey, not mainly at killing enemies.

3. The American puff adder is venomous

It is not, unlike the dreaded African puff adder. The American puff adder has to use its puff to frighten enemies and hypnotize prey.

4. Cobras can be "charmed" by a snake-charmer

Snakes sense vibrations on the ground rather than "hear" as human beings can hear, for they have no ears. It may look as though the cobra is being charmed by a flute's sound, but in fact the cobra is merely swaying in tune with the flute to get into a striking position! The charmer has sufficient skill to keep out of striking distance, or he never lives to see another day.

5. Snakes swallow their young to protect them from danger

This fallacy derives from false deduction; if one observes a large snake swallowing a smaller snake, it is because the larger snake is exceptionally hungry, and will cannibalize its own kind rather than starve.

6. St. Patrick drove the snakes out of Ireland

There are quite a number of islands without snakes, but one does not have to allocate a saint to each in order to account for that fact!

7. Rattlesnakes always rattle before they strike

No: Dr. A.I. Ortenburger of the University of Oklahoma studied this habit among Arizona rattlesnakes, and found that only 4 percent of those he collected did in fact rattle before they struck.

8. Rattlesnakes lay eggs

They do not—indeed, many snakes do not lay eggs.

9. Rattlesnakes add one rattle each year, so their age can be determined by counting their rattles

You're mixing them up with rings on a tree. A rattle is added each time the snake sheds its skin, but the frequency of shedding skin depends not on the calendar but on the amount of food it eats. It may shed its skin less frequently than annually, or four or five times in a year: the average is two or three times. But even if you know how well the snake has eaten, you might still guess wrongly, because rattles frequently break off.

10. Snakes coil round a tree

Painters and cartoonists often depict this scene, but it is entirely fallacious. A snake climbs a tree with its whole body extended in a straight line, gripping the trunk or branch with its expanded ribs and clinging with the concave rows of pointed scales as it presses against the bark. At rest, too, it clings to the upper surface of a branch, and does not coil round.

11. The blind-worm is a kind of snake

The blind-worm is a member of the lizard family without visible legs. Neither is it blind. Neither is it venomous.

SAYING "GOD BLESS YOU" AFTER A SNEEZE ORIGINATED WITH THE RISE OF THE PLAGUE

Many people believe that the custom of blessing someone after a sneeze began in the era of Pope Gregory's ascendance to the Papacy, right as the black plague picked up, around AD 540-600. You might be thinking, "that seems reasonable, AD 540 was a pretty long time ago." We agree. Yet, this apparently was not the first known instance in history of death's association with sneezing.

(Continued)

According to a number of references, namely *The Scientific Monthly* article by Dr. Wilson Wallis, sending a blessing to someone after they sneeze arose from superstitions predating the 14th century, and from all over the world, beginning with ancient Greece. It spans a great variety of countries and religions, both differing in theories about the symbolism of sneezing. A lot of early sneezing practices were actually associated with good luck. For instance, in ancient Greece, when a bridegroom sneezed, the typical response, apparently, was "Some good spirit sneezed out on thee a blessing." A bit of a drawn out (and perhaps more genuine) way to say, "God Bless You," it would seem.

Some of these superstitions are, however, somewhat contradictory. In Hindu, a sneeze can mean either that the spirit is leaving or entering a person through the nose. Regardless, the person who observes the sneeze must say either "Live!" to which the sneezer replies "Same to you," and then the bystander has to say "God Bless You." In Persian tradition, the evil spirit or "fiend" already lives in the body before the sneeze occurs. The sneeze originates as an instinct, which is a fire in the body. The instinct alone arises in the body and wages war with the evil spirit and then sneezing symbolizes the victory over the fiend. What these various reactions to sneezes have in common generally is that the blessing or "God Bless You" is necessary in addition to the sneeze itself, in order to fully ensure that the spirits that took possession of one's soul/body are completely cleared out. In other words, you're in the clear.

It is also noted that "God Bless You" was popular in the Renaissance era, following the belief that when someone sneezes, their heart stops for a few seconds. Fortunately, this is not the case.

SNEEZING IS CONNECTED WITH CONTRACTS

Michael Scot, a 13th-century astrologer, claimed that it is possible to foretell the business future by an accurate interpretation of sneezes. After a contract has been drawn up, if you sneeze once the contract will be kept, but if you sneeze three times it will be broken. To make your business venture successful, sneeze twice or four times, then stand up and walk about.

Scot also pointed out, from his presumably extensive knowledge of sneezing, that a double sneeze in the night for three successive nights will foretell a death in the house.

These irrational and wholly unsubstantiated opinions which were stated as facts are due to the usual astrologer's fallacious view that the universe has a great design, and the pitifully tiny Earth is the center of the universe.

Source: L. Thorndike, *A history of magic and experimental science* (8 vols., London, 1923-58, vol. 2, p. 330).

SNOW FREQUENTLY FALLS AT CHRISTMAS

Snow never falls in Australia at Christmas of course, for Christmas is in the summer there, but even in England snow at Christmas is a rarity. Countless stories, novels, cards and paintings have kept the fallacy alive. Writing in *Nature* (June 1938, p. 938), Sir Richard Gregory states that "even frost at Christmas, at any rate in the London district, is a relatively rare occurrence. Over a period of eighty-three years snow fell only twice on Christmas Eve, and only six times on Christmas Day."

SOCIAL FALLLACIES

A short compendium of some social myths was written by Barrows Dunham; *Man against myth* (London, 1948). These fallacious ideas include:

1. That you can't change human nature.
2. That the rich are fit and the poor unfit.
3. That there are superior and inferior races.
4. That there are two sides to every question.
5. That thinking makes it so.
6. That you cannot mix art and politics.
7. That you have to look after yourself.
8. That all problems are merely verbal.
9. That words will never hurt me.
10. That you cannot be free and safe.

SOMATOGRAPHY

Defined as the "mapping out of the soul," somatography is described by the founder of the Company of Somatographers, Mr. Bryn Jones (a Welsh businessman), as a form of healing incorporating "both hard and soft tissue massage, exercise and natural remedy."

According to *The many ways of being* (London, 1976), edited by Stephen Annett, Bryn Jones became interested in healing in the 1960s, when "he received a series of visionary experiences. These instructed him in an understanding of how to heal through the subtle bodies, and this was the beginning of somatography." Mr. Jones claims that "traumatic experiences from the distant past linger in our subtle bodies and obstruct our future growth." Mr. Jones has introduced into his massage of auras some radionic equipment designed by the American Mark Gallot. Treatment may also consist of change of diet, exercise, natural remedies, and meditation. Somatography aims to help in the treatment and cure of mental illness, loss of vitality, and physical complaints.

Maintenance of an open mind requires that we do not rule out the possible existence of an aura of some kind; it is, however, fallacious to claim that we know what it is, what ailments it may have, or how to cure them.

THE SKILL OF THE **SOPHISTS**

Socrates, a mouthpiece of Plato, mocks the sophists at Athens who can make any fallacy appear true by smooth but erroneous "reasoning." Such sophists are at work, however, in all countries and at all times (each of us is our own sophist, and to some extent the sophist against others and a victim of others) and it is necessary to see the following translation as universally applicable.

In the *Euthydemus*, Socrates describes to Crito the astonishing sophistry of Euthydemus, and remarks: "So great is their skill that they can refute any proposition whether true or false." Dionysodorus, another sophist, attempted to prove to a certain Ctessipus that the father of Ctessipus is a dog. The result is that what seems to have been logically proved is logically fallacious and must be re examined carefully to discover the source of the fallacy. Dionysodorus: You say you have a dog?

Ctessipus: Yes, a villain of a dog.
     D.:   And has he puppies?
     C.:   Yes, and they are very like him.
     D.:   And the dog is their father?
     C.:   Certainly, for I saw him mate with the mother of the puppies.
     D.:   But is he not yours?
     C.:   He certainly is.
     D.:   Then as he is a father, and as he is yours, therefore he is your father and the puppies are your brothers.

The fallacy in logic is here as clear as the fallacy in common sense.

SORTES PRAENESTINAE

The "Prenestine Lots" of ancient Rome consisted of an urn containing the letters of the Latin alphabet which was turned over, after having been shaken. Any resulting words which fell on the ground were taken to be omens.

Nowadays, we call it Scrabble, and few people, if any, believe in omens from the fall of the letters. But in classical antiquity omens were regularly drawn, fallaciously, from a very wide variety of sources.

YOU CAN MAKE UP FOR LOST HOURS OF **SLEEP** ONE NIGHT BY DOUBLING THEM THE NEXT

You may have told yourself more than once, if you pull an all-nighter to finish this paper tonight, then you can make up for the sleep you lost by sleeping through the day and into the night beginning the following afternoon. Whether or not you truly believed this was possible or you were just trying to make yourself feel justified in leaving your work to the last minute, we're here to inform you that it doesn't work that way.

Scientists agree that the average American needs eight hours of sleep a night to function most efficiently, emotionally and physically. Sleep can eventually be recompensated for, but it can't be done in one really long night's sleep if your daily routine is less than eight hours per day. In other words, one all-nighter can't be made up for simply by getting sixteen hours of sleep the next night.

According to a medical director at Harvard Sleep centers, hours of sleep can't really be made up for until after several months, if sleep deprivation has been consistent for an extended period of time.

Likewise, a study in the scientific journal *Sleep* found that it is not possible to train yourself to be a short sleeper. So, if it takes months to make up for the one hour per night you've been missing throughout your college education, maybe reconsider the tradeoff before your next all-nighter.

Sources: Molly Webster, "Can You Catch Up on Lost Sleep?" *Scientific American*, 2008.

ONE CAN FIND A **SPA** OR MEDICAL WATERING-PLACE FOR MOST COMPLAINTS

Horace Walpole's sardonic "One would think the English were ducks; they are forever waddling to the waters" might apply equally to European visitors to fashionable watering-places. Spas owe their origin to two factors: Roman hygiene in the example of the public bath, and Christian miracle-seeking in the case of miraculous healing springs, Aachen's fame is due to the former; and North Marston (Bucks.) to the latter. Many English springs were suppressed at the Reformation but Spa (in the Belgian Ardennes) gave its name to a new type of watering place, such as Baden, Baden Baden, Marienbad, and Ems. In England the fashion spread to Tunbridge Wells (1606), Scarborough (1622), Epsom (1625), Sadler's Wells (1683), Islington (1685), Cheltenham (1716) and the rest.

Fanciful ideas of the curative powers attributed to these spas were held by many with a vested interest in the commercial success of these spas, and by the gullible, whose cures (if effected at all) were due mainly to a change of air, a simpler diet, and rest. John Wesley, one such misguided advocate of "healthful" watering-places, recommended cold baths for deafness, blindness, and the falling sickness. Many of the medical fallacies connected with watering places can be found in John Camp's *Magic, myth and medicine* (London, 1973, chapter 11).

MAN HAS CONQUERED **SPACE**

Man has of course invented and utilized spacecraft, and begins to know more and more of the solar system. But, as Arthur C. Clarke states "We'll never conquer space," in *Edge of awareness,* ed. by Ned E. Hoopes and Richard Peck (New York, 1966). "We have abolished space here on the little earth; we can never abolish the space that yawns between the stars." One of the difficulties is that messages (still less any material object) can never travel faster than light. Messages can thus take as short a time as twenty minutes between Earth, Mars, and Venus, but even if our spacecraft can be propelled at near enough the velocity of light, it will still take five years to get from Earth to the nearest star, or more than twenty-six years to the brightest star of the northern skies, Vega of the Lyre.

But the number of other suns in our own galaxy is about 10^{11}, or 100,000,000,000, and the relatively poor telescopes that we possess at the present can observe a further 10^9 other galaxies. Moreover, the number of galaxies does not seem to diminish at the extreme limit of observation. Thus we can be sure that, no matter how ingenious man becomes at constructing space vehicles and at powering them, he will never be able to reach the outermost limits of space to the point where it can be truly be said to have been "conquered."

THE DEFEAT OF THE **SPANISH** ARMADA LED TO THE DECLINE OF SPAIN

This idea is believed and taught even now in many schools and colleges, but was dispatched fairly definitively in Garrett Mattingly's *The Armada* (Boston, 1959). Some scholars suggested that the defeat of the Spanish Armada in 1588 caused the decline of Spain and the rise of the British Empire. As Mattingly observes, "it is hard to see why they think so. By 1603, Spain had not lost to the English a single overseas outpost, while the English colonization of Virginia had been postponed for the duration."

To those who argue that the defeat of the Armada transferred control of the seas from Spain to Britain, Mattingly replies that before 1588, "English sea power in the Atlantic had usually been superior to the combined strengths of Castile and Portugal, and so it continued to be, but after 1588 the margin of superiority diminished. The defeat of the Armada was not so much the end as the beginning of the Spanish navy." To those who argue, on the other hand, that defeat dislocated the Spanish economy by the disruption of communications with America, Mattingly retorts, "More treasure reached Spain in the years between 1588 and 1603 than in any other fifteen years in Spanish history."

Similar claims as to the "effects" of certain defeats or reverses in war (or even certain battles) are almost invariably overstated.

IN ENGLISH **SPELLING**, "I" COMES BEFORE "E," EXCEPT AFTER C

Generation after generation of schoolchildren have been taught the above spelling rule, which works with "field" and "ceiling" perfectly well, but it is not a valid *rule*. "Seize" and "leisure" are only two of the many examples which test the "rule" and find it so wanting that it had better be forgotten completely. Now.

SPIDER FALLACIES

1) Everyone Swallows an Average of Four Live Spiders per Year in Their Sleep

Although it is commonly acknowledged as an unsettling fact of life, the statement above is a hoax.

According to legend, the myth began in 1993, when a columnist began collecting common facts that were circulating on the then-new World Wide Web. In order to demonstrate the way people tend to believe whatever information they read on the Internet, this columnist (Lisa Holst) made up her own list of "facts." One of these intentionally misinformed facts was that on average, people swallow 4-8 spiders per year, which Holst took from a 1954 collection of common misperceptions relating to insect folklore.

Appropriately, the factuality of this story is still debated by some, such as author of an *Eight Spiders* blog, who says that despite his great efforts, he was never able to track down the article or the magazine Holst had apparently written for

(Continued)

(*PC Professional*). Regardless, it makes for an interesting tale. Furthermore, according to spider experts, such as Brenda Gilmore, you probably have never swallowed a spider without knowing it.

As much as we hate and fear the idea of these eight-legged critters crawling into our mouths at night, it turns out that spiders themselves also have little interest in ending up there. Believe it or not, spiders have enough sense to avoid the dark, humid holes from which we breathe while they are crawling around, searching for food. Food sources for spiders tend to be bugs like crickets and flies, both of which are attracted to light, so most spiders follow suit. Moreover, the only instance in which a spider might end up in your mouth is if it lost its grip and happened to plunge from its web or from the ceiling straight into the depths of your throat and beyond.

2) Waking Up with Bug Bites Always Means a Spider Bit You in Your Sleep

Scenario: upon waking up from what you thought was a long and healthy night's sleep, you may find small red marks on your legs and arms. You, like most of us, probably immediately assume you have spider bites.

It's easy to blame the spider. These critters are common enough in households that it wouldn't be a stretch to assume that one crawled into bed with you to take a few nibbles of your skin. Also, although people tend to be disturbed and disgusted by spiders, they tend to be happier to say they have spider bites than bed bugs' bites.

However, the spider is much too often the scapegoat. Doctors and researchers for years have over-exaggerated the severity and frequency of spider bites in humans. Most spiders won't bite unless they are provoked, and only the larger species of spiders have fangs sharp and big enough to pierce through human skin. Likewise, they do not feed on human blood, like mosquitoes and bed bugs do, so they have very little incentive to hang around humans, let alone feast on them.

It is much more likely that you would roll over and accidentally crush the spider that somehow ended up in bed with you in your sleep than the spider inflicting harm on you. Besides, spiders' fangs are underneath their bodies, so there's no physical way they could bite a sleeping human if they were being crushed underneath it. Make sense? To conclude, spiders are simply a lot less interested in us than we are in them, so we humans should stop wasting our time hating on a species that has decided actively to ignore us.

3) Spiders Are Poisonous

Poisonous is the wrong word choice. Spiders can't really be poisonous, meaning, they are not toxic to eat, touch, or ingest in any way. Most are, however, venomous.

As mentioned previously, they are not looking to bite humans or to suck their blood. Spiders generally only use the venom from their fangs to paralyze or kill the insects they are planning to eat, or as a defense mechanism, in the event that they are being preyed upon. Humans, being slightly too large for a spider to trap between its fangs or wrap up in its web to eat later, are usually not on the menu.

4) Spiders Are Insects

Actually, they are air-breathing arthropods, belonging to the largest order of arachnids. The main difference between spiders and those of the insect breed is the number of legs: spiders have eight and insects have six. Also, spiders have two segmented bodies and four to eight eyes, while they lack antennae and wings. Thus, they are more closely related to ticks and scorpions than they are to insects like ants and bees.

5) Finding a Spider in Your House Means It Came in to Avoid the Cold Weather

Unfortunately for those of us who like to keep our homes insect free, there are spiders that naturally live and breed indoors. Indoor or "house" spiders come in a variety of forms. The Cobweb spider is the most common in American households. Cobweb spiders are not aggressive, and so even if a human swipes a hand into their cobweb homes that they construct in windowpanes and ceiling corners, they generally won't attack. Other spiders that may be found in a household near you are yellow house spiders, wolf spiders, jumping spiders, or orb weavers. Some of these groups are web-weavers, tending to make webs inside houses, while others will wander inside in search of food or for mating purposes. Most buildings, nonetheless, house spiders that hide in secluded areas such as attics, basements, behind furniture, or in between cracks of floorboards. These spiders, although considered invaders when we find them scurrying across the carpet in our bedrooms, can actually be beneficial to household maintenance, in that they live off of eating the flies and other insects that end up inside our homes. Other outdoor spiders usually end up dying of thirst or being eaten by the indoor spiders when they are unlucky enough to wander inside.

(Continued)

So, think about it this way: out of sight, out of mind, and you'll be well on your way to a peaceful co-existence with your arachnid roommates.

Sources: Michigan State University Extension, "Spiders: Biology and Control," 2003; Washington State University, Gardening in Western Washington, "Spiders"; Dr. Brenda Gilmore, "Spider bite while human is sleeping," Brown Recluse Spider.org; Zidbits, "Do You Really Eat 4 Spiders a Year in your Sleep?" 2011; F. B. Peairs, W.S. Cranshaw, P.E. Cushing, "Spiders in the Home," Colorado State University Extension, 2008; Nick, *Eight Spiders: Don't Swallow Everything* blog, "Why Eight Spiders?" 2008; Geoffrey K. Isbister, MD, "Spider Bites: Addressing Mythology and Poor Evidence," *The American Journal of Tropical Medicine and Hygiene*, 2005.

TARANTULA **SPIDERS** SPIN WEBS AND ARE HIGHLY VENOMOUS

While most spiders spin webs, the four-inch-long tarantula cannot; it depends on its sting to kill small insects, but its venom is not a serious threat to human beings.

Source: *National Geographic School Bulletin,* January 13, 1975, p. 256.

CROSSING YOUR LEGS CAUSES **SPIDER VEINS**

Like a fair amount of other common fallacies, if things were this simple, significantly less people would develop unfavorable physical conditions. In this case, the condition is spider veins. This very name conjures up the image of a sixty-plus-year-old librarian with veins so blue, bruised, and dominating that they can be seen almost transparently through her balled up nylon stockings on her legs.

Maybe our elementary school selves, out of fear, decided it was too late for Ms. Lynch (a woman with traditional manners, nonetheless), and that we would sacrifice our ladylike sensibilities of leg crossing in order to avoid getting spider veins in old age.

Unfortunately, avoidance is not so easy. What we know as spider veins (more properly called "telangiectasias") is actually a less severe condition than varicose veins. Spider veins occur when smaller, more surface level valves inside the veins give out, while varicose veins are due to medium to larger vein dysfunction.

Actually, varicose veins form primarily as a result of excessive standing, experts suggest. The explanation goes, in order to stand, we need not only leg muscle strength but we also need the valves in our leg veins to push upwards, against gravity, to ensure that blood flow keeps on moving towards the heart. So, if a valve stops working, the blood flows back down to the ankles, causing a build-up and leading to swelling. In a minor case, the veins remain surface level as "spider veins," but in more severe cases, the blood pressure falling down from one broken valve weighs down other veins and causes them to give out and plummet down, bunching up by the ankles. The results are unsightly *and* painful.

Other factors which are said to cause varicose/spider veins are heredity, sex (females are more likely), age (childbearing age, whatever that means, and older), hormonal changes, obesity, jobs that require a lot of standing, and sometimes, constricting stockings, tights, or knee highs.

Maybe Ms. Lynch's problem was her choice of leg wear, not her conservative manners that beckoned the early onset of spider leg syndrome after all.

Sources: Kate Griesmann, "Myth or Fact: Crossing Your Legs Causes Varicose Veins," *Duke Health.org*; Rosalyn Carson-De Witt, MD, "Varicose Veins," The Mount Sinai Medical Center.

"SPINET" DERIVES ITS NAME FROM THE ITALIAN "SPINA," A THORN

As late as his second edition of 1945, Karl Geiringer could write in *Musical instruments* (London, 1945) that the plucked keyboard instrument called spinet or virginal derived its English name from the Latin and Italian word *spina* (thorn) through *spinetta* (little thorn).

But A. J. Hipkins, in the third edition of Grove's *Dictionary of music and musicians* (5 vols., 1927), had already reported that Ponsicchi, in *Il pianoforte* (Florence, 1876) quoted Adriano Banchieri's tale, in *Conclusioni nel suono dell'organo* (Bologna, 1608): "The spinet received its name from the inventor of that oblong or tabular form called Giovani Spinetti, a Venetian. I have seen one such instrument in the hands of Francesco Stivori, organist at Montagnana, bearing the following inscription: JOANNES SPINETUS VENETUS FECIT. A.D. 1503." [Translation by Ph.W.]

Spinetti was therefore not the inventor of anything but the physical form in which the Italian form of the virginal was constructed, but it is his name which survives.

A **SPIRAL UNIVERSE**

The "spiral universe," discovered by the American George Francis Gillette (b. 1875), takes as its starting-point the absurdity of relativity. And while Gillette has unbounded admiration for Sir Isaac Newton, he is convinced that he himself has gone far beyond his master in explaining our "spiral universe." This, he explains at some length in four books such as *Orthodox oxen* (1929), consists of indivisible changeless unimotes which make us the "supraunimote" of our universe and the "maximote" of the entire cosmos.

Martin Gardner's essential guide to *Fads and fallacies in the name of science* (New York, 1957) quotes the following paragraph from Gillette as a sample of his expository style on the new cosmology:

"Each ultimote is *simultaneously* an integral part of zillions of otherplane units and only thus is its *infinite* allplane velocity and energy subdivided into zillions of *finite* planar quotas of velocity and energy."

Gillette was one of those fanatics who believe that the whole of the scientific establishment forms a gigantic monolithic conspiracy to keep him silent and unrecognized, comparing himself with the persecuted Galileo and Copernicus. But nothing could be further from the truth.

Specialist scientific journals exist in virtually every field, and with a delay of two or three years every new theory can be tested by the author's peers and accepted if true. Furthermore, if editors of journals have personal or otherwise subjective (or even objective) grounds for rejecting scientific papers, the author is at liberty (at least in the Free World) to have his paper printed privately and distributed to general news magazines such as *Time* or *The New York Times,* or to general science magazines such as *Nature* or *Scientific American.* If this were not enough, it must be allowed by all scientists that never has the state of science been in such a state of excitement and ferment as it is now, especially with interdisciplinary experiments and the overlapping of fields previously considered distinct. New ideas are welcomed nowadays as never before, and it is unlikely that a revolutionary concept can go long unrecognized or misunderstood.

To call "conventional" scientists "orthodox oxen" as Gillette does is a reflection more on Gillette than on the scientists he denigrates.

SPOONERISMS WERE A RECURRENT FEATURE OF THE SPEECH OF REV. DR. W. A. SPOONER

Spooner, Warden of New College, Oxford, heartily denied having spade any moonerisms in his life to a reporter (see *Evening Standard,* July 22, 1924). However, it was fairly early in his career that he is alleged to have announced in chapel the first line of the hymn as "Kinquering Congs their titles take."

When he was asked whether he had made any Spoonerisms, he retorted "It is a lace Bible." And on another occasion, "Ah, come in,

Mr. Smith. I'm afraid I have already detected several prowlers in your hose." It is of Spooner that the legendary account is told of the departure from a station which consisted of kissing the porter and giving sixpence to his wife.

SQUIRREL FALLACIES

1) The More Nuts a Squirrel Hoards, the Severer the Winter Will Be

The more nuts a squirrel hoards, the better the nut-season has been! The old country adage is completely false, as is the idea that all squirrels hibernate completely. Some squirrels hibernate completely, taking no food the whole time; the majority doze for days at a time, and take food at intervals when they wake; and others, especially in the mildest winters, do not go into a torpid state at all, remaining active, and feeding on bark and twigs as normal. During the autumn they devour more food than is necessary, the store of fat being gradually consumed while the animals are asleep.

2) Squirrels Are Shy

I suppose every frightened animal is shy. But tame grey squirrels, such as those in London's Regent's Park, where my family has picnicked a few feet away from inquisitive squirrels, will come very close to pick up offerings such as breadcrumbs. They are equally tame in Central Park, New York.

Source: Richard Lydekker, *A hand-book to the British mammalia* (London, 1895), who also quotes William Macgillivray.

BLACK SQUIRRELS ARE DEADLIER THAN OTHER SQUIRRELS

More on squirrels: black squirrels are not of a different species of squirrel, but rather, they are distinguished by having a "melanistic morpheme," or "color morph"; a relatively rare genetic variation. Black squirrels thus have no defining distinctions in behavior or tendency when compared with gray ones, or any other colored squirrels. *Merriam-Webster Dictionary* defines melanism as, specifically, "an increased amount of black or nearly black pigmentation (as of skin, feathers, or hair) of an individual or kind of organism." This is usually a result of genetic mutation but it can also sometimes be caused by exposure to unpredictable temperature fluctuations during gestation (in the period between conception and birth), industrial elements, and adaptive reasons.

Squirrel behavior varies slightly according to type. For example, fox squirrels in general are less aggressive, more playful, and more

(Continued)

often hunted than predatory squirrels and so therefore are not as dominant as other types of squirrels that coexist in many areas, primarily the eastern grey squirrel. Fox squirrels are tree squirrels while eastern fox squirrels are scatter-hoarders. According to one study, there was no difference in behavior when dogs and humans approached black and gray morphs of the so-called "gray squirrel" (formally, *sciurus carolinensis*) of an urban area in New York. The only differences in aggression were between male and female squirrels (males more dominant at feeding sites and in event of approaching people), but not between black and grays.

Black squirrels can exist in any of these species of squirrel, meaning it's inaccurate to say black squirrels in general are deadlier than other squirrels. Neither type is said to have any mating or, consequently, survival advantages over the other. This also eliminates the theory that the melanism in black squirrels is due to industrialization (because they are also found in agricultural areas), and it doesn't seem to be adaptive. So, it's probably simply an internal genetic mutation in birth that creates this variety.

Also, squirrels as a species as a whole are not especially deadly. There are some questionable reports from park rangers that squirrel attacks have occurred. But there are no direct quotes or particular cases cited so it seems safe to say that squirrels are for the most part harmless to humans, and the black ones are just the same. I mean, any animal *can* be deadly if provoked, or if bored park rangers want to make them seem more interesting.

Sources: *American Midland Naturalist*, "Behavior of Black and Gray Morphs of Sciurus Carolinensis in an Urban Environment," Eric J. Gustafson and Larry W. Vandruff, 1990; *Journal of Heredity*, "The Genetic Basis of Melanism in the Gray Squirrel (Sciurus Carolinensis)," Helen McRobie, Alison Thomas, Jo Kelly, 2009.

THE **STAG** WILL PROTECT HIS ENDANGERED DOE AND FAWN

A tale perpetuated by such writers as Eric Fitch Daglish (*The life story of beasts,* New York, 1931). In fact, as the specialist W. C. Allee emphasizes (*The social life of animals,* New York, 1938), "when danger appears during the rut, the stags make off and rejoin the females when it is past." Much the same fear is felt and shown by all social male animals, according to Allee, except the fully socialized male termites. The popular belief is due to sentimentalism.

CLUB SODA GETS OUT **STAINS**

Some might argue that removing stains is the most recognition that this carbonated water beverage (so-called soda) receives. Drawing from personal experience, many people may very well keep a few cans of it in their refrigerator or garage solely for the purpose of cleaning up stains at the site of the spill.

Again, while the effectiveness of this mess eliminating tactic can only really be proven by demonstration or reported accidents, it seems worthy to say that there appears to be no scientific support for why fizzy water is a better carpet cleaner than regular water.

According to MIT chemist Pete Wishnok, as there is no difference in chemical properties between water and club soda (the latter is just water with carbon dioxide and salt), there should really be no difference in their respective abilities to clean stains.

It is vaguely possible that club soda, containing a weak amount of acid (definitely weaker than that of soda), could be slightly more likely to lessen pigment in stains than straight water. However, according to chemist Pete Wishnok, the likelihood of club soda being able to get rid of a stain is pretty much dependent on what material the stain is on and how quickly post-spill the soda is poured.

All the club soda does is to spread the spill around in its still wet stage so it can more easily be blotted up by paper towels. In which case, water would have the exact same function.

Personally, we think the fizz effect is at the heart of this myth, and no less a powerful visual and psychological illusion for the best of us.

Sources: Pete Wishnok, "How Does Club Soda Remove Red Wine Stains?" *Scientific American*, 2006.

THE **STARS** ARE MADE OF ICE

John Finleyson or Finlayson (1770-1854) was a Scot who published far too many pamphlets with scientific claims and little sense.

Among them was *The universe as it is, and the detection and refutation of Sir Isaac Newton. Also, the exposure and proved fabrication of the solar system* (London, 1830). Finleyson, who claimed that Earl Grey (1764-1845) was a descendant of Uriah the Hittite, also asserted that the stars were made "to amuse us in observing them" and that they are "oval-shaped immense masses of frozen water." The next time you put ice in your drink, just pause: you might be consuming part of a fallen star.

STATISTICAL FALLACIES

1) Statistical Error

This is, according to W. J. Reichmann, "the difference between an actual observed value of a variable and its 'expected' value (i.e., as derived from some assumed basic law or theory), the deviation arising from some chance effect and not constituting a mathematical mistake,"

This is not to be confused with a "sampling error," which I will describe below.

2) If Statistical Samples Are Sufficiently Large, They Are Invariably Correct

Many people are aware that small statistical samples are liable to a high degree of error, but place greater faith in larger samples.

This fallacy was exploded in the U.S. presidential election of 1936, when more than 10 million ballot papers were mailed out by the *Literary Digest*. More than 2.3 million were returned, most of them favoring the Republican candidate Alf Landon. The *Digest* thus predicted 370 electoral votes for Landon, and only 161 for the Democratic candidate. Yet Roosevelt, the Democrat, won 523 votes, and Landon only 8.

This "sampling error" is defined by W. J. Reichmann in his *Use and abuse of statistics* (London, 1961) as "the difference between a population parameter and an estimate thereof obtained from a random sample, the difference arising from the fact that only a sample of values has been observed."

3) Fallacy of Insufficient Statistics

Wesley Salmon's *Logic* (Englewood Cliffs, N. J., 1963) is one of the few works on logic to take account of statistical fallacies.

Salmon notes the problem of insufficient statistics: making an inductive generalization before enough data have been accumulated to warrant such a generalization. Thus, a road traffic survey undertaken *either* only during a rush-hour period *or* only during the middle of the night will give a completely false conclusion.

Salmon also warns against biased statistics: basing an inductive generalization on a sample known to be selective or believed to be selective.

4) In Statistics, Every "One Chance in a Hundred" Must Occur Once in Every Hundred Occasions

No subject except religion occasions more fallacious beliefs than statistics. If "on average" an event occurs once in every hundred events, and the sample covers a thousand events, then that event may occur ten times in ten events, as long as no further event occurs in the other 990 events. Similarly, it may occur not at all in the first hundred, two hundred, or even nine hundred chances and yet still occur "on average" once in a hundred events.

5) Increasing a Figure by 200 Percent Doubles the Figure

Stuart Campbell of Edinburgh kindly submits the popular fallacy that a sum increased by 200 percent is *tripled*, not doubled, as many assume without bothering to work it out. The initial 100 percent is frequently ignored. Thus, 300 prcent of a sum does not treble a given sum: it quadruples it. And so on.

Sources: W. J. Reichmann, *Use and abuse of statistics* (London, 1961, p. 339); Donald R. McCoy, *Landon of Kansas* (Lincoln, Nebraska, 1966).

STERILITY IN MEN CAN BE CAUSED BY CLOSE-FITTING UNDERPANTS OR BY THERMAL UNDERWEAR

"Many infertile couples have been 'cured' by the advice to the man to give up tight underpants," writes J. Cohen in *Reproduction* (London, 1977).

Dr. T. E. Thompson writes in refutation of this widespread fallacy: "Such advice may form part of the advice given to infertile couples during subfertility counselling. Such counselling involves many aspects of human sexuality, and it is not possible to separate later which aspects of the advice given resulted in any success obtained. Subfertility counsellors are not experimenters, nor would their patients wish to be experimented upon. At present there is no sound evidence that the style of underwear worn by a man (unless it actually induces morbidity) can influence his fertility.

The supposed scientific basis of the tale derives from laboratory studies that have established that heat produces detrimental effects on the functioning of the testis. But it is equally well established (see Cockett and Urry's *Male infertility, workup, treatment and research,* New York, 1977) that cold stress may harm the functioning of the testis. No mammalian organ system will continue to function properly if subjected to extreme temperature stress: this is not a peculiarity of the testis.

Further experimental information has been provided by a survey of the effects of deliberately excessive exposure of a team of volunteer students of medicine to the Finnish sauna bath. Twelve subjects used the sauna eight times in two weeks, the temperature in the bath being 77-90°C, considerably above the normal body-temperature which rarely reaches 40°C. The total sperm count was studied for a period of two months after the period of exposure to the high temperature of the sauna. The only deleterious effect noted was that a negligible drop in sperm counts occurred between the 30th and 39th days after the beginning of the experiment. The truth of the matter is that the blood circulation of the body, which penetrates the testis just as it does nearly all the other organs of the mammal, is ample to smooth out local fluctuations in the temperature of individual organs. The testis is little more at risk in the sauna than is the nose or the pancreas."

Sources include: Procopé, "Effect of repeated increase of body temperature on human sperm cells." In *International Journal of Fertility,* vol. 10, 1965, pp. 333-9.

STILL WATERS RUN DEEP

The common saying is reflected in Anthony Trollope's novel *He knew he was right* (1869, ch. 35): "That's what I call still water. She runs deep enough . . . So quiet, but so—clever."

But Trollope had given no more thought than any of his predecessors to the inherent fallacy: *still* waters do not run at all!

THE **STOIC** CLASSIFICATION OF FALLACIES

One is not to trust Sextus Empiricus (2nd-3rd century) on the Stoic classification of fallacies, for he was hostile to the Stoics (or, "Dialecticians" as he calls them in his *Outlines of Pyrrhonism,* Book II), but there is no other source at all.

"Now the Dialecticians assert that an argument is inconclusive owing to inconsistency or to deficiency or to its being propounded in a bad form or to redundancy. An example of inconsistency is when the premisses are not logically coherent with each other and with the inference, as in the argument "If it is day, it is light; but in fact wheat is being sold in the market; therefore Dion is walking." And it is a case of redundancy when we find a premiss that is superfluous for the logic of the argument, as for instance "If it is day it is light; but in fact it is day and Dion also is walking; therefore it is light."

And it is due to the bad form in which it is propounded when the form of the argument is not conclusive; for whereas the really syllogistic arguments are, they say, such as these: "If it is day, it is light; but in fact it is day; therefore it is light"; and "If it is day, it is light; but it is not light; therefore it is not day"—the inconclusive argument runs thus: "If it is day, it is light; but in fact it is light, therefore it is day."

And the argument is faulty by deficiency, when it suffers from the omission of some factor needed for the deducing of the conclusion: thus, for instance, while we have, as they think, a valid argument in "Wealth is either good or bad or indifferent; but it is neither bad nor indifferent; therefore it is good," the following is faulty by way of deficiency: "Wealth is either good or bad; but it is not bad; therefore it is good."

C. L. Hamblin, a foremost writer on logical fallacies, makes three main observations on these words of Sextus Empiricus. Firstly, the four kinds of "inconclusiveness" are regarded as involuntary lapses of reasoning, and not as sophistical tricks. Secondly, two of the "inconclusive" arguments are formally valid. The second type merely possesses a superfluous premiss, while the fourth type has a valid argument but a false first premiss. Thirdly, the statement by Sextus is not an explanation of a fully grown logical system, but a brief catalogue of some types of fallacy. The books of the major Stoic logician, Chrysippus, do not themselves survive—though we have an impressive list of them by Diogenes Laertius—except for fragments in the *Stoicorum veterum fragmenta* edited by H. F. A. von Arnim (4 vols., Stuttgart, 1903-24), vol. 2, pp. 89-94.

Sources include: C. L. Hamblin, *Fallacies* (London, 1970).

STOLISOMANCY

Divination by the observation of another's mode of dressing.

The Emperor Augustus, a prey to numerous forms of superstition, was convinced that a military revolt could be predicted by the fact that one of his manservants had buckled his right sandal to his left foot.

Life is neither that simple; nor—judged from a second point of view—that complicated.

THE **STOMACH** WORKS HARDEST DURING SLEEP

A number of the informants with whom I have spoken are quite convinced of the above notion, but no doctor I know will admit a possibility that it might be true. The stomach "works" away without taking any notice whether the person is sleeping, sitting and thinking, or just sitting.

STONEHENGE

There are numerous fallacious theories about the Neolithic people who built England's most celebrated monument (Stonehenge I) and the Beaker people who may have converted Stonehenge to a temple with celestial orientations, adjusting the probably haphazard axis of the old ring. The standard *Stonehenge* (1956) by R. J. C. Atkinson has not been superseded or significantly amended by the imaginative theories of the historically naive, represented here by the most intelligent, Gerald Hawkins (*Nature,* October 1963 and June 1964, expanded in his tendentious book *Stonehenge decoded,* 1965) and Fred Hoyle (*Antiquity,* 1966, p. 262).

Atkinson, who writes that "a high proportion [of the huge mass of literature on Stonehenge] is the product of that lunatic fringe of archaeology to which Stonehenge has always acted, and still acts, as an irresistible magnet," reviewed Hawkins' full-length book in *Antiquity* (1966, 212) and exposed with great patience the fallacies involved.

Hawkins decided to use a computer to analyse the "positions" formed by "stones, stone holes and mounds" belonging to successive periods at Stonehenge and the relations between those positions and other points selected by various criteria as being significant.

While agreeing that the arrangement of the alignments was not a random one, Fred Hoyle *(Nature,* 1966) parted company with Hawkins on the Aubrey hole "computer," suggesting that those holes represent the ecliptic and were used with stones representing the sun, moon, and the nodes of the moon's orbit. He suggested that priests, observing that the old divinities were eclipsed whenever the stones representing the divine sun and moon were closely associated with the stone representing the invisible nodes of the moon, would conclude that the third unseen god was the most powerful. This might be the origin of the invisible, all-powerful God of Isaiah. It might have destroyed sun-worship and originated the doctrine of the Trinity.

The principal fallacy of the Hoyle approach is not that it is intrinsically impossible, but that it demands of the builders of Stonehenge an intellectual prowess astonishing (as Hoyle himself confesses) among primitive farmers without any other known tradition of learning. "A veritable Newton or Einstein must have been at work," says Hoyle, though the term "must" seems extraordinarily questionable.

Atkinson attacked Hawkins for his numerous archaeological howlers, the arbitrary selection of his "positions," his failure to differentiate between the various building periods, the inaccuracy of the plans used, the faults in his method of calculating the validity of his statistics, and his insistence on taking the "positions" F, G and H to be man-made, whereas they are in fact natural tree holes. Other specialists contributing to *Nature* declared that the 56-year eclipse cycle "known" to the builders of Stonehenge according to Hawkins does not even exist; D. H. Sadler suggested that eclipses could be more easily predicted from forty-seven marks.

Criticism of Hoyle was more restrained, due to his achievement in other fields, but Newham, who worked for many years on the astronomical interpretation of Stonehenge, suggested that "if Professor Hoyle had been made aware of all the facts his approach would be entirely different." Eleven of Hoyle's twenty-three readings have been questioned.

The most exhaustive criticism of the Hawkins-Hoyle opinions has been made by Jacquetta Hawkes in *Antiquity* (1967, pp. 174-180), who concludes that "it is enormously improbable that [the builders] had script or numbers . . . ; Stonehenge was intended primarily as a sanctuary, and the intention behind the great horseshoes and circles of stone was architectural and not mechanical, [and] what went on there was mainly ritualistic and not intellectual."

STOP, DROP, AND ROLL

We were all taught how to react to fires in school. Besides getting out of the house and leaving all your valuable possessions behind (plus arranging a meeting place with your family), there is always the good old-fashioned "Stop, Drop, and Roll" technique for when one catches a spark or two. But is this method reliable?

"Stop, Drop and Roll" is a fire prevention technique taught to children, emergency persons, and workers in big factories as part of their health and safety training. The method is generally used to put out a fire on a person's clothes or hair. But, do people ever really think to do this if they are on fire? The question as to whether young children are really able to apply what they learned in school to a real fire situation has been raised. For example, Kathy Foye, teacher and parent of young kids, points out that playing with fire is the number one cause of death to children under five in the United States. Thus, there are other precautions that need to be stressed aside from stop drop and roll itself, such as making sure children know what a toy is and what is not, to not fear firefighters, etc.

At the same time, others emphasize that learning to abide by the "Stop, Drop and Roll" procedure is useful for children as a psychological tool, making them feel as though they will have some way to protect themselves in the event of a fire.

Furthermore, on a variety of online forums, the general opinion on this topic seems to be something along the lines of: "it works better than just standing there and doing nothing."

Source: *Mpf.org / firesafety*

STRANGER DANGER

In elementary schools today and for several decades past, lessons on "Stranger Danger" have been taught incessantly to young children. Who hasn't heard the all too common to be considered parental warning, "Don't talk to strangers"? But where did this term come from? And how threatening to children are strangers, really?

The first time this catchy phrase was used was in the United States was in the 1960s. The phrase arose in various campaigns and later spread to other countries, despite the fact that these campaigns reportedly had little success and received lots of criticism. So, why has the phrase carried over until now?

Being cautious of strangers was intended to be a means for schools to educate children not to trust people they don't know, implicitly, to the degree that they would trust someone they do know. In reality, kidnapping, sexual harassment, and other crimes on children are significantly higher when they are committed by relatives or people

(Continued)

the child knows, while the same statistics for strangers are much lower. According to the National Center for Missing & Exploited Children, in a one year period, 203,900 children were the victims of family abductions, 58,200 children were the victims of non family abductions, and only 115 children were the victims of "stereotypical kidnapping" where the kidnapper is a stranger to the child.

Some experts in psychology or sociology fields have said that the Stranger Danger mentality is starting to create a hostile world. Following this theory, in her article in *Amsterdam Social Science*, Mary Stokes explores the way in which Stranger Danger has somewhat evolved into a social construct, i.e. a large scale misguided fear. She refers to a 2002 data poll of child abduction offenders between 1993 and 1995 which found that 82 percent of offenders were "non-familial." However, non-familial does not necessarily mean they were strangers. In other words, they very likely could be acquaintances. Stokes also notes that in a poll of children and teenagers in 2008 who lived in urban areas, they were more likely to talk about pedophiles and "known" people in their community whom they feel are more dangerous than strangers.

Despite the wisdom of the very teens and children schools and parents are trying to protect, for the most part, the danger of strangers remains a staple concern. Anxious mothers continue to blame the anonymous and therefore untrustworthy stranger for their irrational fears that their child will get lured into an unmarked van with candy while waiting to be picked up outside the parking lot of their elementary school.

Sources: *missingkids.com*; Mary Stokes, Amsterdam Social Science, "Stranger Danger: Child Protection and Parental Fears in the Risk Society," 2009.

THE LAST **STRAW** BREAKS THE LADEN CAMEL'S BACK

Charles Dickens quoted this absurd fallacy in *Dombey and Son* (ch. 2, 1848), without realizing that no camel ever rose from its haunches with a burden too heavy to carry. Camels are too cautious to be overloaded, and will lie down until some of the unfair weight has been removed.

The regular load of a camel is 400 pounds, but H. E. Cross states that before World War I the natives of the Raj loaded their camels with up to 800 pounds and big camels in good condition have been known to carry 960 without excessive discomfort.

Source: H. E. Cross, *The camel and its diseases* (London, 1917).

STRESS CAUSES HAIR TO GO GRAY MORE QUICKLY

To suggest humans are vain is also a way to admit that we're afraid of getting older and, moreover, afraid of how it's going to look. In line with this way of thinking, the popularity of American speculation about President Obama "going gray" due to his immense professional stress levels makes sense. The before and after photos of our country's leader, zoomed in on his hair, have flooded the media, portraying the topic as a prominent and genuine element of public focus.

In reality, Obama's salt and pepper look is entirely appropriate at age 47. According to various sources, the average gray hair onset for men is roughly age 30, for women age 35, and typically no later than 50 for either gender. Although African Americans and Asians do tend to turn gray a little later than whites, at middle age, not having any natural gray hair is actually fairly abnormal.

As everyone's hair follicles inevitably stop producing pigment at some point, these cells experience the only real "distress," while psychological stress as a factor or acceleration of the process is purely myth. At the same time, a study published in the *New York Times* has also shown that the onset of gray hair apparently has no other real correlation with other signs of aging, such as wrinkles and baldness. So, perhaps being young and gray will someday start to be viewed as feasible, and as progressive as our current president is, at least in hindsight.

UNITED STATES UNIVERSITY STUDENT RIOTS IN THE 1960S MADE FOR WIDER STUDENT PARTICIPATION IN RUNNING THE UNIVERSITIES

This is still popularly believed to be the case, yet Michael Davie's *In the future now* (London, 1972) reports that, despite widespread demands for more contact between students and faculty, professors spent less time with their students at the University of California at Berkeley in 1970 (9.3 hours per week with 3rd- and 4th-year students) than in 1960 (12.8 hours); students still have no say there in the appointment of teachers (and some teachers they favored have been silently removed); and the curriculum remains much the same as it was.

The American Council of Education, in its five-yearly review published in 1970, still put Berkeley at the top of its list of American universities, as "the best balanced, distinguished university in the nation."

SUBSTANTIALISM

An anti-Newtonian theory propounded by a Methodist minister, Alexander Wilford Hall (1819-1902), in his oft-revised *The problem of human life* (New York, 1879), which is predominantly an attack on evolution.

All forces, including the force of gravity, are in fact "substances" according to Rev. Hall, even if they are composed of atoms much smaller than those comprising "material" substances. Light, heat, electricity and magnetism and even sounds and odors have "substance" in the view of Rev. Hall, who pursued his theories through two magazines: *The Microcosm* (1881-92) and *The Scientific Arena* (1886-88). These journals failed to elicit detailed refutation from the scientific establishment. In order to erect a scientific hypothesis, it is however a courtesy to effect an agreed demolition of prevailing opinion, and this the Reverend Hall did not feel obliged to do. He attacked not only Darwin, Huxley and Haeckel, but also Tyndall, Helmholtz and Mayer. He was a bitter opponent of the wave theory of sound. His dissent from Newtonian gravity hinged on his disbelief that the action upon a body outside of a sphere is the same as if the mass of the sphere were concentrated in a single particle at its center, and the distance between the bodies were to be accounted as the distance from the center of the sphere. Hall wrote all this in bad verse.

SUCCULENTS NEED LITTLE OR NO WATER

"The old idea that cacti [and other succulents] need little or no water dies hard, but this is far from true," write Edgar and Brian Lamb in their *Pocket encyclopaedia of cacti in color* (Poole, 1969). "Cacti may be able to go without water for a considerable period without looking too unhappy, but they enjoy a 'good drink' as much as most other plants. Even so, we find with the many growers we meet each year that there is still a general tendency to under-water rather than over-water. Another mistaken idea is that cacti should only be watered at the base, and never from above; after all, rain falls directly on and around species growing in the wild!"

Walther Haage confirms this view in his *Cacti and succulents* (London, 1963). "After all," he writes, "no plant, not even the most drought-resisting, can exist without any water for long."

EATING SUGAR LEADS TO CRIME

We are indebted for the above fallacious generalization to the "organic" food cultist Jerome Irving Rodale, publisher of the magazines *Organic Gardening* and *Prevention* with a combined circulation, at one time, of over 1.75 million readers. Some of the observations in these magazines are sensible enough, but Rodale gets out the hobbyhorse and rides it to the realm of fantasy in *Natural health, sugar and the criminal mind* (New York, 1968). The book starts off with the conclusion that there is a causal connection between a high rate of sugar consumption and a tendency towards crime and even psychosis. We are interested to learn that "Hitler was a typical example of sugar addiction relating to a tendency towards crime ... The evidence is there. There can be no question about it. Hitler must have suffered from low blood sugar due to an over-consumption of sugar." Addiction to sugar, Rodale asserts, is responsible not only for the rising crime rate in America, but also for the high suicide rate in Denmark. Well, Cuba has a rising rate of sugar consumption but a falling suicide rate. One of the fallacies here is the irrelevant analogy: one might as well say that a rising rate of sugar consumption leads to an increase in the birth-rate. The two phenomena might concur, or they might not, but they are unconnected causally in either case.

HIGH FRUCTOSE CORN SYRUP IS WORSE FOR YOU THAN REGULAR **SUGAR**

We all know things that are full of sugar are generally full of things that are bad for you if not taken in moderation. So, for reasons of "health" and reasons of cost, we have begun adding sweeteners to processed foods and drinks, the most prominent being high fructose corn syrup.

When we first began adding high fructose corn syrup to our foods as a sugar substitute (about forty years ago), it was a cheaper alternative, but it was also motivated by the rise in popular opinion that sugar was evil and "high fructose corn syrup" was a healthy alternative. As of recently, that perception has flip flopped, and as obesity continues to grow in America, Americans and American food companies have started advertising sugar as the pure and natural ingredient that is meant to be consumed, while high fructose corn syrup is unnatural and the culprit of our health problems.

While studies have been done proving that high fructose corn syrup is much more harmful for health than products that fall under the category of "artificial sweeteners," research has been done to prove that corn syrup and cane sugar are actually quite similar in their biological makeup.

Refined sugar, also called sucrose, is made up of two molecules: carbohydrate glucose, which is bonded to another molecule of carbohydrate, fructose. These two molecules mixed together are the sole ingredients in what we know as regular sugar, evenly distributed (50/50). High fructose corn syrup is made up of exactly the same two ingredients: 55 percent fructose (which makes it slightly sweeter than sugar), and 45 percent glucose. Because both of these "sugars" are made up of the same two molecules of carbohydrates, they break down in our systems exactly the same way.

As pointed out by leading childhood obesity specialist Robert Lustig, the question is not whether high fructose corn syrup or

(Continued)

413

sugar is worse for you, the question is how much of it is being consumed and is sugar, in and of itself, toxic?

Essentially, we are putting too much sugar (which he considers interchangeable with corn syrup) into our diets. Sugar has no protein, vitamins, minerals, antioxidants, or fibers, and therefore does not make for a good substitute for other high calorie but more nutritional foods. Plus, it has been found that fructose, if consumed frequently and quickly, will be turned into fat by the liver. This leads to a condition called insulin resistance, which is now proven to be the leading cause of obesity, a big factor in heart disease, and in type two diabetes.

According to the FDA's official definition of HFCS, it is a "sweet, nutritive saccharide mixture," making it, for all appearances sake, a simple sugar.

In light of the section below (See ARTIFICIAL SWEETENERS), we could certainly question the validity of the FDA's official labels for food products. Or, we could rest easy at night, assured that eating pop tarts for breakfast is no worse for you than having a few dark chocolate strawberries for dessert.

Sources: Hilary Parker, "A sweet problem: Princeton researchers find that high-fructose corn syrup prompts considerably more weight gain," Princeton University news, 2010; Gary Taubes, "Is Sugar Toxic?" *New York Times Magazine*, 2011; Erin Johansson, *The Health Hawk* blog, "Top 20 Myths & Facts About High Fructose Corn Syrup," *masterofpublichealth.org*, 2010; U.S. Food and Drug Administration, "CFR – Code of Federal Regulations Title 21," "Sect. 184.1866 High Fructose Corn Syrup," 2011.

SUNDAY IS THE SABBATH

The Sabbath is the "seventh" (Hebrew) day of the week. Sunday, however, is the first. Yet the common confusion of identity persists, the Jews maintaining Saturday as their Sabbath, or day of rest, and the Christians maintaining Sunday as theirs. The Muslims take their day of rest on Friday.

THERE IS A SUN-SPOT CYCLE EVERY 11.2 YEARS

There seemed until very recently to be no question about this "observation," but it has been proved fallacious. The outer layers of the sun are not constant in rotation or in the number of spots, and the period roughly 1625-1695 has been identified as having experienced few sun-spots. There has been no agreement on the coincidence of that period with the reign in France of Louis XIV, the "Sun-God," but the designation of the period as "the little Ice Age" may well have been factually inspired.

Source: Professor John Jack Eddy, High Altitude Observatory, National Center for Atmospheric Research, Boulder, Colorado.

ARTIFICIAL **SWEETENERS**

1) Aspartame

Aspartame is an artificial sweetener that was approved by the FDA in 1981. Despite recent public controversies over the safety of the sugar substitute, the FDA stands strongly by its acceptance and approval of aspartame. There have been a huge amount of accusations made about aspartame causing health problems such as multiple sclerosis, vision alteration, headaches, tiredness, and even Alzheimer's Disease.

However, there is little concrete proof that frequent aspartame consumption and people developing cancer is a cause and effect relationship. Of course, like most artificial substitutes for the foods and drinks we consume, the main chemical ingredients in aspartame, phenylalanie and aspartic acid, can be dangerous if taken at a very high dose. But research shows that regular aspartame "users" only consume 4-7 percent of the acceptable daily intake of the FDA's standard for aspartame.

Like everything else, aspartame has been accused of causing brain tumors/cancer. But if being disease free means quitting chewing our favorite gum that is 180 times sweeter than gum made of regular sugar, then some of us will just have to grin and bear it.

2) Saccharin

This artificial sweetener is one of the older ones. The most notable product that is made primarily of saccharin is Sweet n' Low. Another claim to fame is that it is also used in combination with aspartame in Diet Coke. Saccharin is much sweeter than sugar and is comprised of different chemicals, and it can go directly through the system without being digested or broken down. However, it can still lead to a release of insulin in the liver, as does aspartame.

In the 1970s, saccharin was linked to the development of bladder cancer, as a laboratory test done on rats proved. Therefore, a government warning label about health risks on all products that contained saccharin became mandatory and in 1981, the sweetener was listed in the U.S. National Toxicology Program's Report on Carcinogens. However, several decades later it was found that the bladder tumors that developed in rats after consuming

(Continued)

saccharin was caused by a biological mechanism that does not exist in humans. Thus, as of 2000, saccharin products no longer contain warnings and hopefully, don't contain cancer either.

3) Acesulfame Potassium, Sucralose, and Neotame

Aside from Aspartame and Saccharin, these three are the remaining artificial sweeteners that have been approved by the FDA and, presumably, are moderately okay for you.

Acesulfame potassium was approved in 1988, Sucralose in 1999 (also known as "Splenda," the yellow sugar packet at restaurants), and Neotame in 2002.

4) Stevia

Stevia, which is also recognized as "sweetleaf" and/or "sugar leaf" is a native South American genus of natural herbs and plants. The sweetener was used in Paraguay and Brazil for centuries by indigenous groups before it came to Japan and then to the West in the 1970s. Although stevia had been generally considered safe for many years, the FDA banned the sweetener in the U.S. in 1991, in response to a study that was published in 1985 that indicated stevia caused liver damage in rats.

Although there were three different petitions to try and overturn the ban, the FDA denied them all due to lack of evidence that stevia was safe to put in foods. Interestingly, stevia was not the only herbal additive that became banned in the '90s in the United States. In response from the vitamin and herbal product manufacturers and notable support from the American public, Congress passed the Dietary Supplement Health and Education Act in 1994. This act specifically excepted products that could meet the statuary definition of "dietary supplement" from the FDA's food additive policies.

Most importantly to note, the passing of this act meant that products that were labeled as "food additives" or "dietary supplements" suddenly did not require premarket approval, and the safety issues became solely determinate on whether the FDA approved them.

So, ironically, although probably not many would try to argue that a natural herbal sweetener is more toxic than those made from chemicals, stevia and vitamins are still called "supplements" while aspartame and saccharin are labeled as "sweeteners."

Sources: John Henkel, "Sugar Substitutes: Americans Opt for Sweetness and Lite," *FDA Consumer Magazine*, 1999; National Cancer Institute FactSheet, "Artificial Sweeteners and Cancer," 2009; Lisa Burnett, "Sweetness Lite?: Artificial Sweetener Controversies from Saccharin to Sucralose," *webcitation.org*, Harvard Law School, 2008.

YOU HAVE TO WAIT THIRTY MINUTES BEFORE SWIMMING AFTER EATING

Another fallacy enforced to this day by paranoid mothers everywhere! Although it's not especially groundbreaking, we're here to confirm that it is in fact a-okay to go swimming right after that last bite of grilled cheese. In one news article that discusses the invalidity of this safety precaution, head of gastroenterology at the University of Alberta Hospital, Dr. Richard Fedorak, is quoted with the proclamation: "That's a myth, and we need to myth bust."

The legend developed because apparently, at one time or another, people believed that the process of digestion in the stomach would require oxygen that would otherwise be necessary to the muscles involved in swimming. But according to modern scientific findings, there is enough oxygen stored in the body to operate both actions at once.

On the other hand, drinking alcohol before swimming is probably not the safest choice. According to a study of adult Californians cited in the *New York Times*, 41 percent of drowning deaths were alcohol related. Additionally, a study in the *Journal of Pediatrics* reviewed 100 adolescents who drowned in Washington, and found that 25 percent of them had been intoxicated. Maybe the next generation of mothers can kill two birds with one stone when they warn their children against the risks of alcohol and swimming on a full stomach.

Sources: Anahad O'Connor, *Really?* Blog, "The Claim: Never Swim After Eating," *New York Times*, 2005; CBC News, "'No Eating Before a Swim' Rule Holds no Water," 2005.

SYMBOLIC MAGIC

The occultist A. O. Spare claimed to have invented a new system of magic. "Like all magicians he believed that any desire deeply felt in the inmost centre of human consciousness was capable of fulfilment." His method was to compress his desire into the shortest possible sentence; cross out letters, so that each letter occurs once only; combine the remaining letters to form a sign; and concentrate on the sign by staring at it intently and allowing it to sink into his subconscious.

One such experiment was to cause freshly cut roses to fall from the air by concentrating on symbolic drawings around the room and repeating "roses" with his face screwed up. At that moment the overhead plumbing exploded, deluging Spare and his observer with sewage.

Since there can be no conceivable relation between words or letters and physical phenomena such as roses or sewage, the fallacies inherent in symbolic magic need not surely be underlined too humorlessly!

Source: Francis King, *Ritual magic in England* (London, 1970).

NATURE IS **SYMMETRICAL**

J. Robert Oppenheimer described as a "gay and wonderful discovery" the classic paper *Question of parity conservation in weak interactions* by the Chinese-Americans Tsung Dao Lee and Chen Ning Yang in the *Physical Review* of October 1, 1956.

The discovery reported in their paper was the subject of an experiment by Madame Chien-Shung Wu. They questioned the hypothesis, long taken for granted, that Nature has a perfect left-right symmetry. Before the results were known, the great theoretical physicist Wolfgang Pauli wrote his pupil at Massachusetts Institute of Technology: "I do *not* believe that the Lord is a weak left-hander, and I am ready to bet a very high sum that the experiments will give symmetric results." Dr. Pauli was duly proved wrong and "parity" was observed to be overthrown. Doctors Lee and Yang were awarded the Nobel Prize in 1957. The nuclear system is now known to be asymmetrical, though the fallacy of symmetry has not by any means been completely eradicated from the popular mind.

Source: Martin Gardner, *The ambidextrous universe* (New York, 1964).

A **SYMPATHETIC POWDER** CAN ASSIST
RECOVERY FROM WOUNDS

The famous "sympathetic powder" described by Sir Kenelm Digby in *A late discourse . . .* (London, 1658) was applied not to a wound, but to the weapon by which the wound was inflicted. The wound was closed up and no further attention paid to it. It was found to be a quite satisfactory method of dealing with the problem until some adventurous thinker tried closing up the wound without applying the sympathetic powder to the weapon. The result was identical.

SYPHILIS WAS IMPORTED TO THE OLD WORLD
FROM THE NEW

This fallacy is so prevalent that it recurs in the otherwise entirely reputable *Penguin medical encyclopedia* (2nd ed., 1976): "There are no recognizable accounts of syphilis earlier than about AD 1500, but after the return of Columbus from the New World the disease spread as a plague from the Mediterranean across Europe. *Nobody can prove that Columbus and his men imported syphilis* (my italics), but it seems likely." In fairness to Peter Wingate, he does immediately confess that

"There is, however, a considerable weight of contrary opinion, some of it well informed."

The problem is one of nomenclature, since the name "syphilis" was not coined until 1530 (by Fracastorius, in his poem *Syphilis, sive Morbus Galticus),* when it was fancifully derived from an unfortunate shepherd, one Syphilus, who cursed the sun during a heatwave and was punished with the "new" disease.

Numerous characters in history have had what one might assume to have been syphilis if only the name had been applied earlier: Herod, king of the Jews, is said to have died of a malignant disease of the genitals, and the same applies to John of Gaunt (d. 1408).

Source: Howard W. Haggard, *Devils, drugs and doctors* (London, 1929, pp. 244-5, as reprinted in 1975).

T

"To know that we know what we know, and that we do not know what we do not know—*that* is what is meant by *true* knowledge."

—CONFUCIUS

"Truth is as poor as Job, as barren as the desert sand, and as boring as an old second-hand-bookseller. But falsehood is as rich as the Pope in Rome! Falsehood builds up monuments that can stand for millennia and give millions of people a home where they feel happy and secure."

—HJALMAR SÖDERBERG, *Jesus Barabbas v* (Stockholm, 1928)

TABOO

The fallacy of the "taboo" action or thing is based upon a combination of fear and ignorance. H. G. Barnett, in his important *Innovation: the basis of cultural change* (New York, 1953, p. 369) writes: "Taboos that have divine sanction carry with them the threat of supernatural vengeance for their infraction; and negativistic mores, sometimes called taboos, are observed because ignoring them brings social sanctions to bear that can be as frightful as divine punishment. When individual Palauans, Hawaiians, and Tahitians decided to break their dietary taboos, they did so in defiance of an awful penalty. Contrariwise, threats to unbelievers and heretics have brought many converts into religious congregations through fear of personal harm."

YOU CAN MAKE YOUR WIFE **TALK** IN HER SLEEP

The 16th-century Neapolitan prodigy Giambattista della Porta lived in a period, like the present, when the sciences were being attacked as reactionary by pseudo-scientists. Whereas the 20th-century scientist is subjected to irrational claims from those who claim experimental validity for parapsychology and flying saucers, the 16th-century seeker after truth was assailed by those claiming the reality of alchemy, prophecy, and witchcraft.

Della Porta was not a charlatan, but was taken in by alleged miracles. His field was optics, and he was easily led astray by claims for extraordinary discoveries in fields other than his own. Della Porta's

Magiae naturalis, sive de miraculis rerum naturalium libri iiii (Naples, 1558) contains so many more "miracles" than "natural things" that one could effortlessly produce A *Book of Common Fallacies* consisting solely (and uncharitably) of his own mistakes. The *Magiae naturalis* went into dozens of editions, and became one of the most widely read books of the time. An English translation, *Natural magick* (London, 1658), shows that its attractions were not confined to southern Europe, and to those who could read Latin. "How to force a woman to babble in her sleep whatever we desire to know of her secrets" is a technique that perhaps the English language did not need to acquire. Della Porta advises the curious reader to wait until his wife is sound asleep, and then to place over her heart the tongue of a frog or of a wild duck, for these animals "give tongue" at night! After waiting for the magic to take its effect, one asks the questions to be answered. If your wife does not answer at once, wait and repeat the questions. Ultimately, all will be revealed.

How long ago did rational men stop believing such nonsense? Dear friend, if you will open your daily newspaper at the horoscope page, or open such magazines as *Fate,* similar wonders of gullibility will be revealed. Not yesterday only—not today only—but also tomorrow, and for as long as men continue to surrender their powers of independent thought to the mass media, to advertisers, to political parties, to religious groups, and to exclusive societies of whatever nature. Della Porta was no greater a victim of his times than we are of our own. Let us beware.

THE BITE OF THE **TARANTULA** SPIDER CAN ONLY BE CURED BY DANCING THE TARANTELLA

A hysterical malady, tarantism, characterized by an impulse to dance, was common in Apulia (southern Italy) from the 15th to the 18th centuries. The city of Taranto was particularly connected with outbreaks of tarantism, which by folk etymology was confused with *Lycosa tarantula,* a spider found in the Taranto area. Confusion was so rife at one time that some thought that the dance was a cure for the spider's venomous bite, and others that the dance was *caused* by a bite! The tarantula spider is, however, entirely unconnected with the phenomenon of tarantism, which recurred in patients summer after summer. Tarantula spiders still exist in the Taranto region, as does the tarantella dance. The playwright Oliver Goldsmith (in *Animated nature)* described the hoax played on visitors by the Tarantese. For a fee paid by a credulous traveller, a peasant would be "bitten" by a spider, simulate collapse, and then be restored to health by the music and dancing of the tarantella. The "explanation" of the Tarantese was that the sweating caused by dancing exuded the poison of the spider's bite!

Sources include: Theodore N. Savory, *Arachnida* (2nd ed., London, 1978).

SCOTTISH **TARTANS** HAVE BEEN FIXED FROM TIME IMMEMORIAL

A. E. Haswell Millar has devoted nearly two pages to demolishing this error in the Historical Association's *Common errors in Scottish history* (London, 1956). The salient points are as follows:

1. The "tartan" pattern type, far from being truly Scottish, is a simple design known to be native to many parts of the world, including Latin America and the Far East. A tartan has been identified in a fifteenth-century Sienese painting, and others appear commonly in the Japanese prints of the 18th and 19th centuries.

2. Those people bearing certain Scottish surnames claim the right to wear a given pattern as an exclusive right. But the assigning of certain patterns to certain clans in a more or less systematic manner is a phenomenon of the 19th century, and can indeed be roughly dated from 1822, when George IV visited Edinburgh and was seen in a form of Highland dress. At the same time Sir Walter Scott's novels were endowing the Scottish Highlanders with a spuriously "romantic" past far removed from the historical truth, and the so-called Sobieski Stuarts—two brothers claiming descent from "Bonnie Prince Charlie"—were "transcribing" (if that is the word, the original never having been traced) a manuscript in their possession which the elder Sobieski Stuart alleged laid down all the correct clan tartans. Nothing supports this claim. On the contrary, no tartan found on the Grant portraits at Castle Grant is found repeated, and not one is close to the "Grant" tartan known today. Other families (the Murrays, say, and the Macdonalds) fail to show consistent use of a single tartan on family portraits as early as the 18th century.

"All the pictorial evidence suggests that the Scottish gentleman or lady regarded the patterns in their clothing in the same spirit as we select the material of our suiting today: they simply fancied a certain color and design.

"To sum up, the presumed heraldic or "family badge" significance of the tartan has no documentary support, and the establishment of the myth can be accounted for by a happy coincidence of the desires of the potential customer, the manufacturer and the salesman."

Sources: M. M. Haldane, "The Great Tartan Myth," in *The Scots Magazine,* September-November 1931; *and* A. E. Haswell Millar, "The truth about the tartan," in *S.M.T. Magazine,* November 1947.

TASTE IS ACQUIRED

In a certain way, one's tastes can change. However, it is not such a gradual and natural process as the word acquiring seems to indicate it is.

First of all, taste itself is a broad term. In this case, we are referring to taste as mainly flavor. One *American Scientist* writer claims that taste can incorporate texture, temperature, smell, and other elements in food or drink or spices. He argues that the taste of some spicy foods, such as Mexican food, would be quite bland if the whole body wasn't reacting to a kind of pain in the mouth that its spices induce. Meaning, in a sense (no pun intended) that someone might not like the taste of a certain food, when really the main problem is their dislike for the texture, or their personal physical sensitivity to really hot or really cold beverages.

There does not seem to be much evidence how, why, or if people ever really acquire tastes for certain foods and/or drinks over time. It doesn't appear to be linked to development of maturity, meaning it doesn't necessarily prove to be true that children don't like coffee and then suddenly become coffee lovers in adult life because their palates have changed.

In other theories, a person's desire for or repulsion to certain tastes can definitely be dependent on associations with that taste. In one example, there are people who are repulsed by the taste of ice cream because they ate some right before going into chemotherapy, where as other people favor the taste of a certain kind of medical water (generally not considered tasteful) because they may have drank it after recovering from an illness. But these preferences are extreme and circumstantial, seemingly caused by out-of-the-ordinary traumatic experiences, not gradual and acquired.

Even more radically, it has been suggested that "acquiring taste" in food or drink is not biological, but is really just the same as developing a preference for anything else one may not instinctually care for, for social or personal reasons. This can be a healthy and certainly normal thing for people to do, as seeking out new tastes can mean expanding one's horizons or overcoming personal challenges. However, acquired taste can also be a double-edged sword, because if we fool ourselves into liking what we inherently do not, we can become victims of consumerism and culture. Not sure if this is totally so relevant to taste for food and drink (at least in America) as it is to academics, music, and other forms of art. But then again, maybe those of us who have never

(Continued)

423

tried to force down a vermouth drenched olive at a cocktail party are really missing something.

Sources: *American Scientist*, "Taste, its Sensory and Motivating Properties" and "Flavor-Illness Aversions"; Kevin Melchionne, *Contemporary Aesthetics*, "Acquired Taste," 2007.

THE AVERAGE AMERICAN HAS BETTER **TASTE** THAN THE AVERAGE BRITON (OR VICE VERSA)

Sadly not. The Duke of Bedford, England's most successful country-house showman, remarked to Walter Knott, the owner and operator of Knott's Berry Farm and Ghost Town in California advertised as "truly one of America's most unusual and enjoyable dining, shopping and entertainment attractions, half-an-hour's drive from Los Angeles" after examining Mr. Knott's gift shop: "We have one thing in common. The uglier the things are, the better they sell."

The "things," in Knott's case, included wall plaques of Bizet, and plaster groups of singing nuns, one of them clasping a guitar.

Sources: Michael Davie, *In the future now: a report from California* (London, 1972, p. 164).

TATTOOS INTERFERE WITH MRIS

These days, many people have tattoos. It's no longer unexpected or shocking to catch a glimpse of a small star on your high school guidance counselor's ankle, or a phrase written in small black font in Latin on the philosophy obsessed perfectionist in your college seminar. Tattoos are no longer just religion-based, nor are they just symbols of punk rock/counterculture lifestyles, or for strictly those considered "low class."

A survey by the Pew Research Center found that 36 percent of people between the ages of 18 and 24 had tattoos, and even more significantly, 40 percent of those 26 to 40 years old have been inked. As tattoos didn't really become popular (or at least, considered a kind of art form) until recently, it seems tattoos are not just a young person's thing either.

MRIs (magnetic resonance imaging) are common procedures that older people may go through in order to check for brain tumors and other health issues. As the younger generation of tattoo wearers gets older, there has been concern that they may be in danger of harmful side effects while going through an MRI procedure. This is also because supposedly, tattoo ink has traces of metal that may be picked up on during MRI scanning.

However, the consensus on a variety of health sites and surveys has been that MRIs have little to no effect on tattoos. At least, there is very little risk involved, in the words of the FDA. Not surprisingly, health sites and, well, the government, still don't condone the vast popularization of tattoos in America, probably in attempts to keep up what they consider to be a clean and respectable public image, but reportedly to keep undiscovered health problems at bay.

The real concern people with tattoos undergoing MRIs should have is not for their health, but for the state of their body art, as the radiation reacting with the metal in the ink could cause the images to become slightly altered for the worse. So, before you get a tattoo, make sure to weigh out the pros and cons.

Source: fda.gov/Radiation-EmittingProducts/

TAURINE COMES FROM BULL SPERM

Natural supplements such as taurine and guarana, which are meant to have stimulating effects alongside caffeine in popular energy drinks, sometimes get a bad rap. Namely, taurine, urban legend says, is made from bull semen, and therefore is unnatural and moreover, unsanitary for humans to consume on any sort of regular basis.

This rumor has slight variations: taurine is extracted from bull testicles; taurine is taken from bull urine; taurine pumps testosterone into your bloodstream. None of these are correct. Taurine is an amino acid which naturally occurs in the human body, though it is more prominent in other animals and in food.

The reason this mistaken idea of taurine's origins is so widespread is, aside from the fact that people are keen to jump on any opportunity to justify why energy drinks are so gross, is because taurine was actually first discovered in ox bile in 1826. Additionally, some sources say that another root of the myth is that the word taurine originated from the Latin word *taurus*, meaning bull.

Furthermore, an ox is generally castrated, making its role as a "draft" animal, or animal used for transportation, easier. Incidentally, Red Bull does not carry the equipment necessary

(Continued)

to provide for prepubescent boys to get hopped up on aggressive animal testosterone.

Sources: Woojae Kim, "Debunking the Effects of Taurine in Red Bull Energy Drink," *Nutrition Bytes Journal*, University of California, 2003; Sonal Patel, "Taurine + Energy Drinks: Meant to Be or Doomed?" Vanderbilt University, Health Psychology Home Page, 2006; *Online Etymology Dictionary*, "Taurine"; Tess Taylor, "On Small Farms, Hoof Power Returns," *New York Times*, 2011.

MORE **TEA** IS DRUNK PER CAPITA IN BRITAIN THAN IN ANY OTHER COUNTRY

Tea consumption in the Republic of Ireland was 7.76 lbs. (1200 cups) per head in 1973, surpassing all other countries in the world producing official statistics, including Great Britain and Northern Ireland.

Source: Official statistics.

THE BRITISH HAVE BAD **TEETH**

Well, kind of, at least in comparison to Americans, on a public level in particular. But there are reasons for the difference, and a lot of it has to do with the fact that the British public has never really put oral hygiene (dentistry) as a priority over other types of nationalized, accessible health care.

Dentistry is a very profitable profession to go into, but it's definitely not necessarily affordable for lower income U.S. citizens. In Britain, it seems, most people are able to get publically accessible dental care, but the way in which the system operates is that the dentist can't really spend more than a few minutes on each patient. So, therefore, there are a lot of people who don't get the same standard, every-six-months thorough teeth cleaning that is so regular for Americans. But at the same time, in America, there are a lot of people who can't afford dental health care at all, probably because it's pretty much only run by private practices.

So, yes, Americans are generally seen as having beautiful pearly whites, depicted in movies, politics, and in people who receive a lot of public attention and who are more or less wealthy. But it's certainly not everyone that has perfect teeth. And as much criticism as the American writer of *Politics Daily* article gives the structure of dental hygiene practices in Britain, it does seem a little silly that Americans are so obsessed with having spotless perfect teeth—more obsessed, perhaps, with saving face than saving lives via affordable public health care.

Sources: Alex Berenson, "Boom Times for Dentists, but Not for Teeth," *New York Times,* 2007; Delia Lloyd, "When Health Care Rationing Fails: The British and Bad Teeth," *Politics Daily*, AOL News, 2009.

TEILHARD DE CHARDIN

In *Le phenomène humain (The Phenomenon of Man,* London, 1959), the French Jesuit Pierre Teilhard de Chardin (1881-1955) brought to a head (though not then to a conclusion) his meditations on the nature of man.

The book was hailed in France on publication in 1955 as the Book of the Year, and even the Book of the Century. Its sensational sales, increased by news of its author's death just previously the same year, were made to the general public as well as to the scientific public at which it was nominally aimed. "Yet the greater part of it," writes P. B. Medawar in *Mind* (January 1961), "is nonsense, tricked out with a variety of tedious metaphysical conceits, and its author can be excused of dishonesty only on the grounds that before deceiving others he has taken great pains to deceive himself. P. B. Medawar, a great immunologist and Nobel Prize-winner, dissects the style of Teilhard, which is sufficiently obscure to conceal in many places the paucity of ideas and the laxity of logical structure. He places *The Phenomenon of Man* in the tradition of German *Naturphilosophie,* which "does not seem even by accident (though there is a great deal of it) to have contributed anything of permanent value to the storehouse of human thought. French is not a language that lends itself naturally to the opaque and ponderous idiom of nature-philosophy, and Teilhard has accordingly resorted to the use of that tipsy, euphoric prose-poetry which is one of the more tiresome manifestations of the French spirit."

Teilhard's theory is founded on the belief that the fundamental process in the entire universe is *evolution,* that "general condition to which all theories, all hypotheses, all systems must bow . . . a light illuminating all facts, a curve that all lines must follow." Or, to put it in another Teilhard way, evolution is "the continual growth of 'psychic' or 'radical' energy, in the course of duration, beneath and within the mechanical energy I called 'tangential'"; evolution then is "an ascent towards consciousness." Medawar infers that evolution, in Teilhard's view, must have a "precise *orientation* and a privileged *axis*" at the topmost pole of which stands Man. Teilhard leaves his "scientific" argument for a metaphysical argument which is very simple: our present consciousness must culminate in a Supreme Consciousness, which apparently assimilates to itself all our personal consciousnesses, and is known in Teilhard as "Omega." Although already in existence, "Omega" is added to progressively. In Teilhard's words: "All round us, one by one, like a continual exhalation, 'souls' break away, carrying upwards their incommunicable load of consciousness," and so the end-product is "a harmonized collectivity of consciousnesses equivalent to a sort of super-consciousness."

Teilhard is a typical example of those for whom "life" and "nature" are governed by one principle and only one principle, which would be interesting and even significant if the "Only One" believers would for a moment agree on what that single principle is. For Lévi-Strauss it is deep structures, for Freud it is sexuality. "Like all things in the universe," for Teilhard, "life is and can only be a 'size' of evolutionary nature and dimensions . . . This is the fundamental fact and . . . the evidence for it is henceforward above all verification, as well as being immune from any subsequent contradiction by experience."

P. B. Medawar has denounced the lack of sense, of logic, and of scientific rigor throughout Teilhard's best-known work. How, then, has it become so popular? Sir Peter explains that "just as compulsory primary education created a market catered for by cheap dailies and weeklies, so the spread of secondary and latterly of tertiary education has created a large population of people, often with well-developed literary and scholarly tastes, who have been educated far beyond their capacity to undertake analytical thought." The attractions of Teilhard's woolly theoscience include the following points:

1. *The Phenomenon of Man* attacks scientists as shallow beings interested only in materialistic proofs. As Sir Peter explains: "Laymen firmly believe that scientists are one species of person. They are not to know that the different branches of science require very different aptitudes and degrees of skill for their prosecution. Teilhard practiced an intellectually unexacting kind of science in which he achieved a moderate proficiency. He has no grasp of what makes a logical argument or of what makes for proof. He does not even preserve the common decencies of scientific writing, though his book is professedly a scientific treatise."

2. The book's style is almost totally unintelligible, and new terms are introduced to define concepts which remain undefended. The opacity of Teilhard's style is construed as evidence of the author's profundity, which is a *non sequitur* familiar to all who make a habit of scanning (dare one say it?) crank literature.

3. Teilhard diagnoses a terrible "malady of space-time," and proposes a remedy so obscure that anyone can claim to practice it. [Sure enough, a Phenomenon of Man Project has been set up in 1962, at 8932 Reseda Blvd., Suite 204, Northridge, California 91324 and there is now a Pierre Teilhard de Chardin Association of Great Britain and Ireland.]

4. Sir Peter Medawar "read and studied *The Phenomenon of Man* with real distress, even with despair. Instead of wringing our hands over the Human Predicament, we should attend to those parts of it which are wholly remediable, above all to the gullibility which makes it possible for people to be taken in by such a bag of tricks as this. If it were an innocent, passive gullibility it would be excusable; but all too clearly, alas, it is an active willingness to be deceived."

Source: Sir Peter B. Medawar, (review article), *Mind,* January 1961.

WATCHING **TELEVISION** CAUSES HARM TO EYESIGHT

There are a number of reasons why parents worry about their children sitting in front of the television or computer screen for hours on end, often rightfully so. However, it has long been proven that staring at virtual entertainment boxes does not actually do any damage to eyesight.

According to a *Scientific American* article, studies show that there has been no harm in eyesight since 1968. Apparently, the stigma about television hindering eyesight dates back to the sixties, when a company called General Electric produced a bunch of color TV sets that emitted as much as 100,000 times more radiation than federal health officials deemed as safe. Although the company recalled the products immediately and re-created newer and safer TVs, the initial reputation remains in the minds of the American public, at least for some.

Watching a lot of television can, according to doctors, cause strain and fatigue in eyes. But this is easily cured, simply by turning off the TV and resting one's eyes. Till tomorrow night's *American Idol*.

WILLIAM **TELL** SHOT AN ARROW THROUGH AN APPLE ON HIS SON'S HEAD

A stone in the Washington monument in the United States, contributed by the Swiss Government, bears the inscription, "This block is from the original chapel built to William Tell, in 1338, on Lake Lucerne, Switzerland, at the spot where he escaped from Gessler."

The Historical Society of Switzerland has diffidently pointed out to both governments concerned that both Tell and Gessler are wholly fictional characters, but the common fallacy persists. As long ago as August 1890 the canton of Schwyz ordered the Tell legend to be expunged (as nonhistorical) from the cantonal school textbooks. The events are usually placed in the 14th century and are first found in writings of the 15th century. Similar legends of marksmen shooting at an object on the head of a man or child are found in many countries, notably in England (William of Cloudesley) and Norway (Egil).

Source: Sir Paul Harvey, *The Oxford Companion to English Literature* (4th ed., Oxford, 1967).

ANIMALS OBEY THE **TEN** COMMANDMENTS

This is not a Moody and Sankey tale or a Billy Graham joke: it was stated seriously by Ernest Thompson Seton in *The natural history of the Ten Commandments* (New York, 1907), a latterday collection of moralistic animal tales in the same vein as the Greek *Physiologus* familiar throughout medieval Europe in a Latin translation. There is some justification for an ignorant scribe with a religious message to impart to describe a panther as "an amiable beast, friendly to all creatures but the dragon" (the panther symbolizing Christ in the Christianized rewriting of the *Physiologus)*; but for a 20th-century writer to claim that incidents from animal life in any way "represent" the sins of covetousness, adultery and murder is an outrageous fallacy.

As a reviewer wryly remarked in *The Brooklyn Eagle,* even Mr. Seton was unable to obtain zoological support for monotheism and opposition to perjury. He also omitted the prohibitions against swearing and working on Sunday.

SETTING THE **"THAMES"** ON FIRE

This common error began circulation when the name "temse" was changed to "sieve." A laborer working with a sieve (or temse) would be urged to shake it so vigorously that the sparks would fly from it, and one exercising too little effort would be rebuked: "You'll never set the temse on fire." It is only comparatively recently that the nonsense "Thames" element crept in.

LEFT BRAIN VS. RIGHT BRAIN **THINKING**

This theory, although proven to be generally untrue, is an interesting one. It somehow allows for both equality and inequality at the same time. Right brain thinkers (or those said to use the right sides of their brains more often than the left) are said to be people who are creative, emotional, intuitive, and visual/spatial, while those who are left brain dominant are logical, rational, verbal, and scientific.

This rumor probably to some degree served to make students who were better at math and science in school feel like there was a reason why they weren't as creative as their artistic friends, while kids who might be spacey or in academia but excelled in piano or theatre could feel justified in failing calculus.

Luckily, this simple classification of people into one of two types of "thinkers" is just as inaccurate as trying to divide people into being either introverts or extroverts like Jung thought we could.

There is a slight difference between one side of the brain and its counterpart. For instance, language is proven to definitely be concentrated in the left side. According to the 1960 Nobel Prize-winning scientist's findings, when patients lost brain power in the left but not right side of the brain, they were significantly less able to use language effectively. They were able to correctly associate a written word with an object by reading the former and pointing to the latter, but they were unable to remember the names of objects just by looking at them, without the word given to them.

While the right brain is proven to be more effective in some areas than the left, such as in identifying melodies and detecting facial emotions, there is a subtle difference between right and left. And their functions are mostly intertwined.

So, even though kids might have different learning styles in school, the simple division between right brained kids who will want to draw a diagram and left brained students who would prefer to discuss linguistically is essentially only a metaphor.

Sources: Daniel Willingham, "Willingham: Left/right brain theory is bunk," *The Washington Post*, 2010; *Psych* Blog, "Two Brains for the Price of One?"

THOUGHT FORMS ARE VISIBLE

This is one of the fallacies deriving from the error that thoughts are really things, not of course hard, solid and opaque but ethereal, vaporous and colored. Visible thoughts are said to be symbolic, not pictorial, so that for example a pink fluffy cumulus-cloud effect is "seen" to emanate from a person who is happy and at peace with the world, whereas a brown-green snakelike effect is caused by thoughts of jealousy.

Source: Annie Besant and Charles W. Leadbeater, *Thoughtforms* (London, 1905).

TIBERIUS INHERITED HIS DRUNKENNESS FROM HIS NURSE

This absurd error in Roman history and heredity is only one of the hundreds such that litter the pages of Benjamin Walker's *Encyclopedia of esoteric man* (London, 1977), issued by a reputable publisher. Walker does not believe in group thought, and questions the powers of Uri Geller as reported in the mass media. But he seems to believe in the medicinal and aphrodisiac powers of bone and bone-powder; that ectoplasm smells of ozone; that dimples on the chin are a sure sign of a flirt; that a nude female in a room wards off disease; and that an anal fixation is manifested in obstinacy and a desire to collect stamps, antiques, and money.

He also appears to credit the "findings" of Sister Justa Smith, a Franciscan nun and biochemist, that healing rays from the hands of Oskar Esterbany, a Hungarian-born "healer," consider-ably increased the activity of enzymes.

As C. Vita-Finzi concluded his review of the book in the *Times Literary Supplement* (July 22, 1977), "Esoteric is perhaps the right word after all. The initiated will welcome this book. The outsiders are likely to find their minds even narrower after reading it."

IT IS POSSIBLE TO TRAVEL THROUGH TIME BY OTHER THAN THE USUAL METHOD OF GETTING OLDER

It is one thing to enjoy H. G. Wells's splendid *Time machine* (1895) and similar science fiction, but quite another to postulate the real capacity to travel suddenly and quickly forward or backward in time, as many authors have done, among them Johannes von Buttlar in his *Journey to infinity: travels in time* (London, 1975), translated from the German original of 1973. Even if unintentionally, however, Buttlar confuses the issue by bringing in the alleged "elixir of life" which gives those who use it a longer life than those who do not and introduces the "Comte de Saint-Germain" who is claimed to have lived for 245 years; by bringing in dreams, unidentified flying objects, Lunan's hypothesis of interstellar contact, hypnosis, and mummies, none of which is related to the central and inescapable problem that nobody at any time and in any place is known in practice to have travelled forward in time at any pace other than that of our human clocks, or to have travelled backward in time at all, despite numerous claims such as those of C. A. E. Moberly and E. F. Jourdain in their best-selling Versailles tale, *An adventure,* first published under their pseudonyms Elizabeth Morison and Frances Lamont (London, 1911), which has at last been exposed, if a little sadly, by Joan Evans, in *Encounter* (October 1976, pp. 33-47). Dame Joan comes to the conclusion that the two ladies had inadvertently strayed into a rehearsal for a *tableau-vivant* and did in fact see everything they claimed to see (it was not a willed mirage as claimed by Jastrow) but merely misinterpreted the evidence of their senses.

J. W. Dunne stated in *An experiment with time* (London, 1927) that time is "the fourth dimension," just as Einstein had done, but the difference is that Dunne holds that human beings in their sleep move freely along this fourth dimension, and so are enabled to foresee the future . . .

Dunne's theory and H. G. Wells's hasty (and hoaxing?) endorsement of it (as the author of *The time machine)* is, in the view of Eric Temple Bell *(The search for truth,* 1935, p. 36), "as hopeless a muddle of woolly thinking by means of metaphors and far-fetched analogies as any of the more childish efforts of the perpetual motion cranks to do the impossible."

Further fallacies pepper Dunne's subsequent *Serial universe* (London, 1934) and *The new immortality* (London, 1938).

TIN FOIL AND ALUMINUM ARE THE SAME THING

Maybe it's simply because the word "aluminum" consists of too many syllables to pronounce every time you just want to ask your wife if there's anything you can use to wrap up a leftover sandwich, but regardless, the words aluminum and tin foil are considered to be interchangeable. Factually, they are not the same.

According to chemistry professor Robert L. Wolke of University of Pittsburgh, tin was made into foil first in the 19th century by Thomas Edison in his phonograph machine invention. In the 20th century, tinfoil was used commonly as a way to preserve food and drugs. But by mid 20th century tinfoil was essentially entirely replaced by aluminum foil.

The word *aluminum* was first coined by English chemist Sir Humphry Davy in the early 1800s. Both aluminum and tin are metals found from natural resources, but aluminum is more prominent and less malleable and generally found in igneous rock, clay, and soil. While aluminum is used in combination with other metals to make up certain aircraft parts, tin is very often used in alloys, such as bronze, and as a noncorrosive coating on steel. Tin foil is made with an alloy of tin and lead, where as aluminum foil is made with approximately 98.5 percent pure aluminum metal.

Sources: Robert L. Wolke, "Tin, Aluminum, Chronium," *Washington Post,* 2006; *Etymolonline.com,* "Tin Foil" and "Aluminum"; Dictionary.com, "Tin" and "Aluminum," *Collins English Dictionary - Complete & Unabridged 10th Edition*, HarperCollins Publishers.

TOAD FALLACIES

1. Toads Do Harm in a Garden, and Tortoises Do Good

Toads are good for a garden, because they are insectivorous, and especially like to eat slugs and snails. Tortoises do not, and though often bought for their ability to keep down garden pests, are in fact exclusively herbivorous. It is possible that black beetles avoid them if possible, and consequently leave the garden of their own volition when tortoises are brought in, but there appears to be little evidence on this question either way.

2. Toads Are Connected With Toadstools

Dr. Werner Broch writes from Basle that *Tod* is the German for "death" and *Stuhl* the German for "chair" or "seat," thus bringing together with some force the poisonous nature of the fungus, which the English "toadstool," comically omits. The Early English origin is "todestole."

The modern German word for the toadstool is *der Giftschwamm,* literally "the poison fungus."

MAN IS THE ONLY ANIMAL THAT CAN ACTUALLY MAKE TOOLS

Chimpanzees have long been known to be able to *use* tools in such activities as cleaning their bodies after diarrhoea (with leaves), cleaning teeth (with a twig) or weapon-throwing (with a stick). It was consequently asserted that Man differed from the apes in his ability to *make* tools. This fallacy has been exploded by Jane van Lawick-Goodall; her *In the shadow of Man* (London, 1971) describes how chimpanzees strip leaves from a stem to make a tool suitable for "fishing" for termites. Leaves, made more absorbent by chewing *for that purpose,* are used as a sponge to sop up rainwater that cannot be reached with the lips.

So far, however, there is no indication (despite encouragement) that chimpanzees can use tools to make other tools, the next achievement in the technological cycle.

TOP HAT FALLACY

The celebrated "Top Hat Fallacy" has been restated by Conrad Waddington in *Tools for thought* (London, 1977, p. 139):

"It is important to realize what a correlation between two variables means and, in particular, what it does *not* mean. It means that, in the population studied *(not* necessarily in all populations), there is a tendency, whose strength is expressed in the correlation coefficient, for the measurements of the two correlated characteristics on the same individual (say, its height and weight) to vary together; the more one measurement departs from the average, the more the other will do so too. This does *not* mean that one characteristic causes the other; it may do so, but the fact that they are correlated is not good evidence to reach that conclusion. They can both be caused by something else, and have no essential causal relation to each other. This is a very basic point of warning about the misuse of statistics. It is usually enshrined in an old parable, known as the "Top Hat Fallacy"—and the fact that it is out of date sartorially should not make you forget that it is still bang-on in what it implies. I quote it in the words of a former President of the Royal Society, in his memorandum about how to do operational research: "statistical investigation of the population of many cities would show that the wearers of top hats are significantly taller than the average. The missing causally effective variable here is clearly the higher average income of the top-hat-wearing group."

MUSSOLINI MADE THE ITALIAN **TRAINS** RUN ON TIME

A common defense of Italian fascism was that regimentation and efficiency replaced an easygoing life and inefficiency. However, questioning of people who actually lived in Italy between the March on Rome (October 22, 1922) and the execution at Como in 1945 bear witness to the fact that Italian railways were no more careful of timetables than they are today.

HEINRICH SCHLIEMANN DISCOVERED HOMERIC **TROY**

No: the city excavated by Schliemann from 1870 to 1873 was the pre-Achaean city, long antecedent to any Troy known in Homeric times. But the site, Hissarlik, was the correct one, as predicted in Schliemann's extraordinarily percipient *Ithaka, der Peloponnes und Troja* of 1869. His *Trojanische Alterthümer* (Leipzig, 1874) appeared in the year that Schliemann started the equally fruitful campaign at Mycenae, on the Greek mainland.

It was Schliemann's successor Dörpfeld, working with money endowed by Schliemann, who finally uncovered the walls of the sixth stratum at Troy (contemporary with the height of the Mycenaean excavations) which Schliemann had wrongly believed to be Lydian.

TRUTH WILL PREVAIL

In 1390, John Gower seemed to believe that "Trowthe mot stonde atte last," and many writers and politicians, lawyers and policemen have either believed the fallacy that truth will always emerge in the end, or at least wanted their readership at large to believe the fallacy.

John Stuart Mill has indicated that the adage has frequently been contradicted by harsh experience: "The dictum that truth always prevails over persecution is one of those pleasant falsehoods which men repeat after one another till they pass into commonplaces, but which all experience refutes. History teems with instances of truth put down by persecution. If not suppressed forever, it may be thrown back for centuries."

Examples that rush to mind include that of Galileo whose views were vindicated by the Roman Catholic Church as late as 1820 (by Pope Pius VII), and the *Gulag Archipelago* revelations by Alexander Solzhenitsyn which demonstrated the existence of concentration camps not only during Stalin's period, but right up to modern times.

TRYPTOPHAN IN TURKEY AND WARM MILK MAKE YOU SLEEPY

1) Turkey
If at no other occasion, turkey is certainly the star of the table at Thanksgiving dinners all across America. This lovely bird was killed in its prime in order to give us all the juiciness, fats, and hardiness we crave upon the approach of winter with its little daylight, bleak cold, and plenty of holiday cheer.

After saying thanks for the surplus of food and feasting till we're nearly in a coma, we often feel exhausted enough to fall right asleep. Why, many of us have asked? Blame it on the turkey, of course. As turkey contains the so-called sleep-inducing nutrient tryptophan (one of twenty naturally occurring amino acids), we get tired after eating an excess of it.

True, tryptophan is obtained through eating turkey. However, there are not typically higher contents of this essential acid in turkey than in other types of meat (less crudely, food protein). The perception that tryptophan leads directly to fatigue comes from the connection between tryptophan and serotonin in the brain. Serotonin is a neurotransmitter, said by some researchers to bring about "slow-wave" sleep in humans.

But there is a catch. As mentioned earlier, there are twenty kinds of natural amino acids. Turkey, in addition to other meats and foods with heavy protein content, has many of these acids, tryptophan actually being one of the rarest amongst them. Tryptophan never occurs in food proteins without the presence of other amino acids, which is problematic, as it competes with these other acids to get into the brain. These acids need to be transported from the blood stream to the brain by specific proteins (which have this particular function assigned to them). Tryptophan has less of these proteins and competes with five other acids for the same transporter, thus making the direct cause and effect link between tryptophan and serotonin in the brain quite unusual.

Interestingly, the more likely explanation for why sleepiness occurs after eating Thanksgiving dinner is due to the consumption of sugar and carbohydrates. For instance, eating something like pumpkin pie causes the cells in one's pancreas to secrete insulin. Insulin is a hormone that turns most amino acids into tissues. But this is not the case for old, stubborn tryptophan. However, in eliminating some of the acids that tryptophan competes with, eating carbs after eating turkey sort of indirectly allows for tryptophan to be more influential on serotonin and thus, supposedly, tranquilization.

Still, there is little evidence that turkey has much to do with post-food overdose doziness. More likely, it's the wine.

2) Warm Milk

If turkey is known widely to cause sleepiness after eating a lot of it, milk is said to have the same, if not stronger role as a sleep aid for the restless. But the two are more related than you may have thought. The sole reason for milk's reputation as a sleep-inducing beverage is, once again, its heavy presence of tryptophan.

Again, this claim is moot, as tryptophan cannot easily enter the brain through the bloodstream while tryptophan's more prominent and aggressive rivals (amino acids) get absorbed significantly more often. As studies have predicted that one would need to eat roughly forty pounds of turkey in order to actually become noticeably tired from consuming tryptophan, we can safely assume that one glass of milk will not do much in the way of sedating either.

Why so many seem to stress that it's not just milk, but warm milk that puts you to sleep, we cannot so easily explain.

Sources: Coco Ballantyne, "Does Turkey Make you Sleepy? Stop Blaming the Bird for your Turkey Daze," *Scientific American*, 2007; Anahad O'Connor, *Really?* Blog, "The Claim: A Glass of Warm Milk will Help you get to Sleep at Night," *New York Times*, 2007.

TURKEYS ORIGINATED IN TURKEY

Turkey-fowl originated wholly in the American continent, and were first imported into Europe shortly after the first invaders entered Mexico in 1518. However, they were confused at that time with the guinea-fowl which entered Europe from Africa via the Turkish colonies (Eric Partridge makes the same error in his *Origins,* 4th ed., London, 1966) and when the two species were subsequently differentiated, it was—inevitably perhaps in a world so inclined to error—the *American* bird which acquired the designation "turkey."

Sources: *Oxford English Dictionary.*

TWINS ARE USUALLY IDENTICAL

The first detailed study of this subject has still apparently not been absorbed by the popular mind. *Inquiries into human faculty* (1883) by Sir Francis Galton stated that "one would have expected that twins would commonly be found to possess a certain average likeness to one another; that a few would greatly exceed that average likeness, and a few would greatly fall short of it. But this is not at all the case. Extreme similarity and extreme dissimilarity between twins of the same sex are nearly as common as moderate resemblance. When the twins are a boy and a girl, they are never closely alike; in fact, their origin is never due to the development of two germinal spots in the same ovum."

The fact that the same point has been made in numerous publications over the succeeding ninety years has made little difference to the common lore on twins.

AN OBJECT CANNOT BE IN TWO PLACES AT ONCE

"But an electron suffering diffraction can. It also seems clear that though size and position is infinitely variable, everything shares the same time; but, as Einstein showed, this is not so. We must check our intuitive ideas all the time."

Source: B. K. Ridley, *Time, space and things* (Harmondsworth, 1976, p. 40).

U

"The utmost that can be said on behalf of errors in opinion and motive, is that they are inevitable elements in human growth. But the inevitable does not coincide with the useful, Pain can be avoided by none of the sons of men, yet the horrible and uncompensated subtraction which it makes from the value and usefulness of human life, is one of the most formidable obstacles to the smoother progress of the world. And as with pain, so with error. The moral of our contention has reference to the temper in which practically we ought to regard false doctrine and ill-directed motive. It goes to show that if we have satisfied ourselves on good grounds that the doctrine is false, or the motive ill directed, then the only question that we need ask ourselves turns solely upon the possibility of breaking it up and dispersing it, by methods compatible with the doctrine of liberty."

—JOHN MORLEY, *On compromise*
(London, 1886, pp. 83-4)

"The universal and everlasting craving of humanity—to find something to worship."

—FYODOR DOSTOEVSKY.
The Brothers Karamazov

SWIMMING IS DANGEROUS WHERE THERE IS AN **UNDERTOW**

There is no objective "undertow" in water that is not immediately reversed. An active and persistent seaward underflow at the bottom demands the occurrence of a correspondingly active and persistent shoreward flow at the surface. Except under doubly specialized conditions of wind direction and shore configurations, "undertow" does not exist and never has, outside the imagination of frightened swimmers. The intermittent seaward pull as each wave slides back from the beach is reversed every few seconds by an equally temporary shoreward movement of the next wave.

Source: William H. Davis, in *Science,* February 20, 1925, pp. 206-8.

UNIDENTIFIED FLYING OBJECTS (UFOS)

After thousands of reported sightings by enthusiasts, mainly in the United States, a study was carried out under the auspices of the University of Colorado from 1966-68 under the leadership of Dr. Edwin U. Condon. Over nearly 1,500 pages of analysis of the evidence, the Condon Report refuted the allegedly extraterrestrial origin of phenomena generally categorized as UFOs. Its general conclusion was that "nothing has come from the study of UFOs in the past 21 years that has added to scientific knowledge. Careful consideration of the record as it is available to us leads us to conclude that further extensive study of UFOs probably cannot be justified in the expectation that science will be advanced thereby."

A UNIVERSITY EDUCATION IS AN EDUCATION FOR LIFE

The cliche which exhorted all serious young people to obtain tertiary education has been replaced since World War II by the Unesco policy of lifelong education. Furthermore, the rapidity of technological obsolescence, and the speed with which new discoveries and inventions are made combine to force the engineer, doctor, and all other professionals and academics to keep abreast of the literature, to attend refresher courses, and generally to treat their few years of university education as a preparation for learning rather than as an educational end in itself.

V

"El vivïr en medio de errores, y estar satisfecho de ellos, y transmitirlos de generación en generación, sin hacer modificación ni mudanza, es propio de aquellos pueblos que vegetan en la ignorancia y envilecimiento: alli el espiritu no se mueve, porque duerme" (To live in the midst of errors, and to be content with them, and transmit them from one generation to the next without change or correction, is characteristic of those peoples who stew in ignorance and degradation: there the spirit does not move, for it lies sleeping).

—JAIME BALMES (1810-1848)

"Veritatem laborare nimis saepe, aiunt, extingui numquam." (It is said that truth is often eclipsed, but never extinguished).

—LIVY, *Annates,* XXII, 39

PASTEUR'S THEORIES OF VACCINATION ARE UNIVERSALLY ACCEPTED

Inoculation against smallpox created an enormous outcry among the ignorant when it was introduced, and there are still millions who reject the theory and practice of vaccination as somehow "unnatural." Current medical opinion advises vaccinating infants at the age of six weeks, and every seven years thereafter.

To take a sample of the effectiveness of smallpox vaccine, in Sweden the decline in smallpox mortality has been phenomenal since compulsory vaccination was introduced in 1816, having enjoyed its widespread practice since 1801. In 1800 there were 2,049 deaths per million population; an average of 623 per million from 1802 to 1811, and an average of 1 per million in the years 1890 to 1899. Vaccination against other diseases has proved equally effective.

Perhaps the most celebrated opponent of smallpox in recent years was George Bernard Shaw (who also objected strongly but fallaciously against pasteurizing milk), but the funniest book advocating the abolition of vaccine is *The blood poisoners* (Croydon, 1965), by Lionel Dole.

Mr. Dole feels strongly that instead of vaccine what we need are fresh air, clean living, fruit, and vegetables. John Sladek, in *The new apocrypha* (London, 1974), shows that "across America, healthy, sturdy, suntanned farm children were struck down by polio every summer (when they were getting naturopathic medicines of all types)" before the introduction of the new polio vaccines. It is of course true that vaccinations do not always "take" and that some vaccinations (such as that against smallpox) do not guarantee lifelong immunity. But the shortcomings of the vaccines that are available should not blind the independent observer to the crucial benefits brought to mankind by those who have developed vaccines.

NATURE ABHORS A **VACUUM**

This idea of Aristotle was universally accepted until Torricelli (1608-1647) showed that if a tube closed at one end is filled with mercury and inverted, the mercury will stand up to the top of the tube only if the tube is less than thirty inches long; evidently Nature's abhorrence of a vacuum is limited.

Source: W. F. G. Swann, *Error in physics,* in Joseph Jastrow, *The story of human error* (New York, 1936).

"**VIKING**" RHYMES WITH "LIKING"

It rhymes on the contrary with "licking," as *vik* (Icelandic) means "creek, inlet, or bay," and *ingr* (in Icelandic; in Anglo-Saxon *ing*) means "people of," or "belonging to." The Anglo-Saxon word *wicing* is therefore a borrowing from Scandinavia.

If it is argued that long incorrect usage makes the incorrect into the correct, it should be remembered that a language as far removed from Scandinavian as Italian has always employed the correct pronunciation in *vichingo*. The correct pronunciation appears in the Scottish coastal town of Wick, and all such compounds as Lerwick.

Source: Walter W. Skeat, *An etymological dictionary of the English language* (Oxford, 1888).

MODERN MAN'S **VIOLENCE** IS A RESULT OF HIS DESCENT FROM THE FEROCIOUS AUSTRALOPITHECINE "APE-MAN"

The above view is stated by the popularizer Robert Ardrey in his best-selling *African genesis* (London, 1961) and is very widely believed.

However, relics found near Lake Rudolf in Kenya have shown that the ancestor of Man and Australopithecus were two distinct species, and while modern man can be said to be violent in some senses of the word, it is fallacious to state the cause in Ardrey's terms.

VITALISM

We owe to the Hippocratic school of medicine the interesting fallacy that a mystic demon or *archeus* controls the bodily functions. The school of Democritus held, correctly, that the operations within a living body are controlled by the same mechanical laws of atomic action as prevail elsewhere in the known universe.

Vitalism was common not only in Greek and Roman antiquity, but passed with no diminution of strength to medieval medicine and philosophy, then to Paracelsus, van Helmont, and the eminent Swedish chemist J. J. Berzelius (1779-1848), who claimed that it was impossible to synthesize in the laboratory the organic compounds that are produced in plants and animals.

Proof that organic compounds are *not* formed solely by a vital force was given in 1828 by Woehler (1800-1882), who synthesized the organic substance urea (secreted in the urine) by heating ammonium isocyanate.

Even now, however, occultists refuse to credit the proof, despite the fact that many other compounds of plant and animal origin have been synthesized in the laboratory from a variety of inorganic substances.

Sources include: Charles A. Browne, "Errors in chemistry," in Joseph Jastrow *(ed.)*, *The story of human error* (New York, 1936).

YOU CAN NEVER HAVE TOO MUCH **VITAMIN C**

As we have seen, for the most part, there is basically no reliable cure for the common cold. Nonetheless, people still try and invent their own remedies, or swear by the ones that seem to have done the trick for others. But what about vitamin C? If nothing else, we drink orange juice or take vitamin C pills, in sickness or in health, as an extra precaution or a hopeful defense against flu and cold symptoms. Why has vitamin C become such a staple of healthy living?

Apparently, the hype surrounding vitamin C really took off in the 1960s, after Nobel Prize-winning chemist Linus Pauling claimed that taking super high doses of this vitamin was beneficial to health. A megadose of vitamin C, Pauling claimed, could potentially cure cancer, and would definitely cure the common cold.

Vitamin C originally came about some number of decades after a plague hit Europe in the 1500s, when scurvy was killing a whole lot of sailors. Then it was found that vitamin C is necessary for human survival, and that it needs to be obtained

(Continued)

outside the body itself, through vegetables, fruit, milk, sunlight, etc. It is needed for healing wounds, re-enforcement of the cartilage needed to keep ligaments functioning, blood flowing, and maintaining teeth and bones.

Once we realized how great vitamin C was, we figured, why not ingest as much of this life boosting formula as possible? According to one doctor interviewed on NPR, taking megadoses of vitamin C was one of the biggest hoaxes ever pulled on the American public. And according to sources almost across the board, taking more than the recommended dose of vitamin C per day (60-90 milligrams) will not have any effect on reducing cold symptoms. The only proven way in which vitamin C helps against illness is when it is taken regularly every day for at least a year. Following this regimen, duration of the common cold *may* be reduced by up to one day. But taking double or triple the amount of vitamin C upon onset of cold symptoms is completely useless.

According to studies done, ironically, by the Linus Pauling Institute (along with others), cell tissues can't use more than 200 milligrams per day. This is a fifth of the amount that many Americans believed for years was the appropriate amount of vitamin C needed to sustain healthy bodies.

Although there is no real danger in over dosing on vitamin C pills, as they are water-soluble and eliminated through urine if the body is unable to use it, there is really no point in spending money on excess supplements of it, when you can easily get your daily dose of the high and mighty C via fruit salad or in a single yellow bell pepper.

Sources: Patti Neighmond, "The Vitamin C Myth," NPR, 2006; University of Maryland Medical Center, "Vitamin C (Ascorbic Acid);" Depaul University, "History of Vitamin C;" Hemila H. "Vitamin C Supplementation and the Common Cold—Was Linus Pauling Right or Wrong?" US Library of Medicine, National Institutes of Health, 1997.

THE NAME **"VOLTAIRE"** IS A PSEUDONYM

Numerous writers make the mistake of thinking that François Marie Arouet the Younger's pen-name "Voltaire" is a pseudonym. It is, however, an *anagram* for "Arouet l.i." (Arouet *le jeune*).

VULGAR ERRORS

1) Browne on Vulgar Errors

Sir Thomas Browne, the great English stylist of *Religio medici* (authorized ed., 1643) and *Hydrotaphia* (1658), is to be credited with the first attempt at a comprehensive survey of vulgar errors (as opposed to a classification of them) in *Pseudodoxia epidemica: or, enquiries into very many received tenents, and commonly presumed truths* (London, 1646), a book usually referred to as *Vulgar errors*.

Pseudodoxia epidemica is divided into seven books, the most interesting being the first, which is introductory. This deals with the fallibility of human nature as a source of fallacies, including credulity, false deduction, supinity, adherence to antiquity, tradition and authority. Browne considered himself absolutely free from heretical opinions as a Christian (the *Religio medici* appeared in Paris, where he was thought a Roman Catholic), but the Vatican placed the work on the *Index Expurgatorius* to be on the safe side. Browne gives a list of those authors to be treated with caution. Among them is Pliny, whose *Historia naturalis* is condemned in words that really demand to be reproduced: "there is scarce a popular error passant in our dayes, which is not either directly expressed, or diductively contained in this worke, which being in the hands of most men, hath proved a powerfull occasion of their propogation . . ." It is worth mentioning, for those readers skeptical of Browne's wholesale disapproval, that Howard M. Parshley echoes Browne's view in *The story of human error* (New York, 1936) edited by Joseph Jastrow: "Pliny's *Historia naturalis* was so stuffed with errors of the time that it undoubtedly takes the palm as the greatest single repository of misinformation known to man."

Book two of Browne's work is devoted to errors concerning minerals and vegetables; book three is on animals; book four on man; book five is on "many things questionable as they are described in pictures" and on various superstitions; book six on geographical and historical fallacies; and book seven on religious errors, and a potpourri of such picturesque errors as those "that the Army of Xerxes drank whole rivers dry" and "of the wandring Iew."

Like all writers on fallacies, Browne knew that he was fallible, and added a caveat in his preface that "we are not Magisteriall in opinions, nor have wee Dictator-like obtruded our conceptions, but in the humility of Enquiries or disquisitions, have only proposed them unto more ocular discerners." Again, like all writers on fallacies including myself and beyond, he was credulous about some beliefs which later ages exposed as fallacious and, to his discredit, gave testimony at Norwich in 1664 which led to the death of two "witches," the wretched Amy Duny and Rose Cullender.

"Thomas Browne Redivivus" is the pseudonym of Caroline Frances Cornwallis, whose *Exposition of vulgar and common errors* was published in 1845.

2) Cornwallis on Vulgar and Common Errors

Under the pen-name of "Thomas Brown[e] Redivivus," Caroline Frances Cornwallis (1786-1858) wrote *An exposition of vulgar and common errors adapted to the year of grace MDCCCXLV by Thomas Brown [sic] Redivivus* (London, 1845).

Caroline Cornwallis was an endearing lady, "large-featured, tall and thin," and with a sparkling sense of humor to irradiate her scholarship. This is one of many "Small books on great subjects" which she and her friends wrote pseudonymously.

The first part of her *Exposition* ridicules a number of proverbs and popular sayings which may possibly be correct in a certain context but, as a general guide to behavior and good sense, leave a very great deal to be desired. These sayings are: "A young man must sow his wild oats," "A good fellow, nobody's enemy but his own," "We must do as others do," "he that spareth the rod spoileth the child," "A boy should be manly," "A man is not responsible for his belief, "Women have no concern with politics," "Marriage is a lottery," "You can't put an old head on young shoulders," "Ne sutor ultra crepidam" (Let not the cobbler go beyond his last), "A little learning is a dangerous thing," "I will retire from business, and prepare for another world," and "It is only a white lie."

Miss Cornwallis added essays on fallacies concerned with genius, evil spirits, "An enquiry if ignorance be requisite to women" (as a persuasive feminist and educator her answer is a resounding "no!"), "Of errors in grammar" (including the difference between "shall" and "will" which causes quite as much difficulty 135 years later), "Of certain errors current in regard to disease and medicine," and "Of the condition of society and touching the female sex."

The influence of Miss Cornwallis and her circle was directly and indirectly a cause of much improvement in the treatment of women in politics, business, and public life, and in the home. The gentle polymath was firm in her rejection of received errors, and well deserved her chosen pen-name.

3) Fovargue on Vulgar Errors

Stephen Fovargue's *A new catalogue of vulgar errors* (Cambridge, 1767) is a collection of thirty-six essays, some of them discursive and a few even digressive, which indicate some of the commonest fallacies of the mid-18th century in England. I append a complete list of Fovargue's fallacies.

1. That the more ammunition is put into a fowling piece, the farther it will do execution.

2. That the heron makes a hole in the bottom of her nest, through which her feet hang, when she sits upon her eggs.
3. That the bittern puts his bill or beak into a reed, and that the reed gives, by the breath and motion of the beak of the bird, that deep and low note which we so frequently hear him make as he lies in a Fenn.
4. That the tone of a violin is to be brought out, by laying on like a blacksmith.
5. That the farther you go south, the hotter is the climate.
6. That exactly under the Aequator is always the hottest climate on the globe.
7. That the more hay is dried in the sun, the better it will be.
8. That the violin is a wanton instrument, and not proper for psalms; and that the organ is not proper for country-dances, and brisk airs.
9. That the Organ and Harpsichord are the two principal instruments, and that other instruments are inferior to them in a concert.
10. That every key in music ought to have a different effect or sound.
11. That a piece of music which has flats set before it, is in a flat key on that account, and vice versa with sharps.
12. That apparitions or spectres do exist, or that the ghosts of men do appear at, before, or after their deaths.
13. That bleeding is proper for a patient, who is apt to be sick in a morning. [On scurvy.]
14. That no thing which moves upon the surface of the earth, is so swift as the wind. ["Even pigeons and swallows can go faster."]
15. That there is now, or ever was, such a science as astrology. [Fovargue would be astonished to find this error still widespread two centuries later.]
16. Most Londoners are mistaken when they think that they have wit enough to impose on countrymen. [Wrongly phrased; Fovargue does *not* think this a fallacy; he himself was a Fen-man.]
17. That a pointer, if he lifts up his foot, when he comes upon game, does it in order to shew his master the spot where the birds lie. [It is coincidental.]
18. That the way to make boys learn their books, is to keep them in school all day, and whip them.
19. That clogging their parts with long grammar rules, will make them bright scholars.
20. That teaching boys Bawdy Books will make them religious men and good clergymen. [The "Bawdy Books" are by that "Master of Intrigue" Ovid and that "Libertine" Horace.]
21. That the present age is a duller Age, and less ingenious, than those which are past.

22. That the musical composition of this present age is inferior to that of the last.
23. That the hearing of musical performances, is apt to soften men too much, and by that means to give them an effeminate manner.
24. That the Italian operas consist of effeminate musick
25. That nothing is poetry but what is wrote in rhyme.
26. That kicking up the heel behind, and twisting round upon one leg, is fine scating.
27. That using hard words and long sentences, in discourse or in writing, is an indication of scholarship.
28. That the way to get a sailing boat off the shore, when she is fast by any accident, is to let go both or all the sails, and stand at her head, and push with a sprit.
29. That planting aquatics upon banks of the Fenns will preserve and strengthen them, so as to render them more able to resist the force of a flood.
30. That those who lived 2000 years ago, were larger than the present race of mankind.
31. That bleeding in May will preserve the constitution against illness during the ensuing summer.
32. That negroes are not a part of the human species. [Refutes with the aid of Locke's *Essay concerning human understanding*].
33. That negroes are the descendants of Cain, and that the color of their skins is that mark which was set upon Cain, after killing Abel.
34. That Love is nothing but concupiscence to a high degree, or that love and lust are the same thing.
35. That the Hedge-Hog is a mischievous animal; and particularly that he sucks cows, when they are asleep in the night, and causes their teats to be sore.
36. That a person is the better or the worse for being of any particular calling or profession.

"The whole history of civilization is strewn with creeds and institutions which were invaluable at first and deadly afterwards"

—WALTER BAGEHOT

"We spoke already of lying and I gave a possible definition of psychology as 'the study of lying.' So one of the first and most important things for you to observe is lying. Very much akin to lying are our illusions, things about which we deceive ourselves, wrong ideas, wrong convictions, wrong views and so on. All these must be studied because until we begin to understand our illusions we can never see truth."
—P. D. OUSPENSKY, *The fourth way* (London, 1957)

WAGNER IS MAD

"Wagner est évidemment fou," wrote Berlioz in a letter dated March 5, 1861. D.-F.-E. Auber, cited in *Le Ménestrel* (September 27, 1863) declared: "Wagner, c'est Berlioz moins la mélodie."

Max Kalbeck described Wagner in the *Wiener Allgemeine Zeitung* (April 28, 1880) as the artistic incarnation of the Anti-Christ.

These three judgments commit the fallacy of forming a judgment before a phenomenon (such as the new musical style of Wagner) can be fully assimilated, understood, and appreciated. It would have been possible to compile a book twice as long as the present dictionary with erroneous value-judgments by journalists and hack reviewers on major writers whose contribution was undervalued principally because it exceeded the horizons of the day in terms of imagination, style, or "daring" content.

In art, major errors have been committed in attacking (usually for the wrong reasons) Picasso, the French Impressionists, abstract art, Whistler, Neizhvestny and indeed all Russian artists failing to conform to the doctrine of socialist realism, Jackson Pollock and other action painters, the surrealists, Courbet and Corot . . . The list is endless because it is *normal* for artistic taste in the public to lag at least a generation behind the achievement of the artists. In music, Debussy, Stravinsky, Webern and Berg have been bitterly attacked, while Puccini was condemned almost universally during his early years for operas which now grace every opera house in the world. In literature, Byron, Dylan Thomas, Dostoevsky, Balzac and James Joyce have all been insulted. *Blackwood's Magazine* called Keats' *Endymion* "drivelling idiocy." Even now it is impossible to buy more than one or two of the novels of Benito Pérez Galdós in paperback in Spain, though the wealthy (hence presumably the non-revolutionary) can buy expensive hardback editions. The fallacy here is that the criticism of human nature is potentially or actually deleterious to the society thus criticized; in fact, the stifling of criticism (as in Czarist Russia) is usually more dangerous to a state's stability.

WALT DISNEY'S BODY AND/OR HEAD IS FROZEN

There are a lot of mysteries revolving around Walt Disney, particularly in relation to his death. For instance, his passing seemed rather sudden to outsiders, being frozen as a mode of preservation was on the rise, and his will was intentionally kept very secret from the private eye.

However, the popular urban legend that Walt Disney was "cryogenically frozen and stored beneath the Pirates of the Caribbean ride at Disneyland" is extensively proven to be, sadly, incorrect. Disney was actually cremated on December 17, 1966 in Glendale California. Instead, the man who was frozen (the first ever human to undergo this procedure) was James Bedford. He was frozen roughly a month after Disney's death (Jan. 1967).

Rumors claiming it was actually Disney who was frozen stem from several circumstances:

1. Cryopreservation was on the rise in popularity at the time of Disney's failing life/impending death.
2. Ten years before his death, Disney publically stated that he didn't want to have a funeral.

However, he did tell his family he wanted to be cremated. But, all the same, there are no written records that Disney had a specific plan for the preparation of his body after death. In other words, instructions for his funeral and burial were not included in his will and thus unavailable to public, so the people were therefore free(r) to make up rumors about him.

The earliest printed version of the myth appeared in the magazine *Ici Paris* in 1969, already several years after his death. Regardless of the impossibility in fact of Disney's body hiding frozen under a legendary theme park ride, waiting to be resurrected at any moment and grab the 21st century by the horns, considering some of Disney's quirkiness and the context of his life and death, to believe in this myth is not so farfetched.

WAR IS CONDUCIVE TO PEACE

Long before George Orwell's *1984* and *Animal farm*, Friedrich von Bernhardi is alleged to have stated: "It is a matter of humanity to wage ruthless, pitiless war, in order that war should be concluded more rapidly." This is one of the most fearsome of fallacies.

Sources: Pierre Loti, *L'horreur allemande* (Paris, 1914). There is an English translation of Bernhardi's original work by K. von Donat *(On war of today,* 2 vols., London, 1912-1913).

PRISON OFFICERS ARE TECHNICALLY KNOWN AS **"WARDERS"**

J. Crane of Morecambe, Lancashire., has written that the term "warder," still used ubiquitously in radio, television, and books, was officially banned in the year 1921, when the term was changed to "prison officer."

YOU ALWAYS NEED TO USE **WARM** WATER WHEN WASHING YOUR HANDS

Washing your hands with plenty of soap under water is undoubtedly the best way to prevent the spread of diseases and germs, and to avoid contracting a number of illnesses. Cleanliness is the key when you consider how many things you touch and people you come in contact with every day that are potentially really dirty.

Moreover, we have been trained to believe that it is warm water, not cold, that truly eliminates the hands of any trace of bacteria or dirt that may have taken up residence in the palms temporarily. But does it really make much difference whether the water is warm or cool? Does anyone really want to wait a solid five minutes for the hot water to take effect, when rinsing off with a quick cool splash seems a favorable alternative?

As of late, the always-wash-with-warm-water myth has been re-evaluated. According to a study by scientists from the Joint Bank Group, there was no difference in bacterial reduction on hands of subjects between temperatures ranging from 40 to 120

(Continued)

degrees Fahrenheit. These scientists added that as there was no benefit to using warm water over cold, one should really just base the water temperature on what is most comfortable for him or her, as you are supposed to keep hands under there for at least twenty seconds.

Perhaps the reason old wives and medical literature alike have continued to see warm water as better than cold is because truly hot water is used for sterilization purposes. However, for water to be as hot as it would need to be in order to get rid of all bacteria, it would be impossible to keep hands under the faucet for half a minute multiple times a day without experiencing unpleasant burning on skin.

Government regulated disease prevention sites have mixed reviews, seeming to want to hold onto the idea that warm is better than cold more out of habit and/or stubbornness than as a result of reasonable evidence. According to the Center for Disease Control and Prevention, the "right" way to wash your hands includes a number of specific directions, while choosing between cold and warm water is listed as optional. Also, hand sanitizer is not as effective as washing with cold or warm water, as it only cleans the outermost layer of hands rather than getting down to the nitty gritty that lathering allows for.

Importantly, don't forget the soap. And don't forget to rub hands together for at least twenty seconds. If you need a timer, one helpful source suggests humming "Happy Birthday" in full two times before rinsing and drying off. So for those of you counting up to twenty "Mississippi's," post-pee, it's more than enough, but hey, better safe than sorry when it comes to public bathrooms, you know?

Sources: US National Library of Medicine, "Hot Water for Hand Washing—Where is the proof?" *Journal of Occupational and Environmental Medicine,* 2005; Centers for Disease Control and Prevention, "Handwashing: Clean Hands Save Lives" and CDC via Morbidity and Mortality Weekly Report (MMWR), "Appendix C: Hand-Washing Recommendations to Reduce Disease Transmission from Animals in Public Settings," 2007.

WASHINGTON CUT DOWN A CHERRY TREE BELONGING TO HIS FATHER

Mason L. Weems's biography of George Washington relates the now-celebrated story that the boy cut down a cherry tree belonging to his father and, when asked if he had done it, admitted the deed, adding

"I cannot tell a lie." Despite the fact that Weems's fabrication of this entirely apocryphal incident was exposed shortly after its publication, Newnes' *Pictorial Knowledge* (vol. 2, London, 1947, p. 159) repeats that "George Washington is known as "The boy who could not tell a lie . . . ," and countless children repeat the fairytale as fact. Another error is to think of the boy Washington as a pacifist. On the contrary, he was praised as "first in war and first in peace" after a successful military and political career.

WASPS AND HORNETS SHOULD BE KILLED

This pernicious belief should be killed instead. Both wasps and hornets destroy many garden pests, and only a few of the many varieties of wasp or hornet sting.

They should not be destroyed unless they build nests in your attic rafters, porch corners, or where children habitually play.

Source: Alma Chesnut Moore, *How to clean everything* (New York, 1972).

WATER ALWAYS FREEZES AT 32°F (0°C, 273.15K)

"Freezing point" is not always exactly what it seems, as you can easily test experimentally, by reducing the temperature of pure, still water. Only when it is shaken, at a few degrees below freezing point, will the water turn rapidly into ice. Alternatively, one could make ice quickly by adding some ice-crystals or other solid matter.

Another fallacy is to assume that all ice must be at the same temperature. Modern low temperature research ought to have corrected the popular view, for the range now possible is from 32°F (0°C, 273.15K) down to 1 in 5.46×10^8 of the melting point of ice.

A third fallacy concerning low temperatures is the notion that it is possible to record absolute zero, equivalent to -273.15°C or -459.67°F.

EVERYONE SHOULD DRINK EIGHT GLASSES OF WATER PER DAY

Sure, eight glasses a day has always sounded a bit intimidating. Even if it is just water, it's difficult to figure out how to even schedule in eight times during the day where you are finishing an entire glass of water without having to chug it. Not to mention, drinking that much water means releasing that much more liquid from your bladder throughout the day. Technically, urinating counts as at least double the interruption to your everyday life alongside water breaks.

(Continued)

But as a prescription from doctors everywhere as a part of sustaining a healthy life, who hasn't been told that eight full glasses of H_2O a day is not a necessary one, but certainly indisputably recommended? After all, it's only water. Water dominates our world, literally. And it is commonly known that in a dire situation, humans can survive longer without food if they have access to a water source. So, if water is what we need to keep us alive, what could be the harm in drinking as much of it as possible?

Well, it seems our illusions have been shattered. Studies in the past decade or so have been conducted and concluded to verify the fact that eight glasses of water a day is fine, but a bit over the top, and definitely not a requirement for optimal health conditions.

For instance, Dartmouth Medical School doctor Heinz Valtin has researched a number of studies that have determined there is no medical benefit or reasoning for drinking eight glasses of eight ounces of water every day. His findings appear in the *American Journal of Physiology*. He has done his homework well, covering everything from the history of the myth, our biological makeup, and observing the way in which doctors, health specialists, as well as the general public religiously abide by this so called "eight by eight" rule.

Valtin admits that drinking eight glasses of water can be beneficial for people with certain health problems, namely kidney stones, as well as in the circumstance of long exposure to very hot weather, long airplane rides, and post-rigorous physical exercise. On the flip side, there can be such a thing as too much water. In some not so rare cases, the kidneys can become overwhelmed with too high and frequent water intake and can't process quickly enough. Most commonly, this is the case in ecstasy users, who inadvertently drown themselves by drinking more water than they think they need while feeling the heightened sense of dehydration caused by the drug.

He also debunks the idea that being thirsty is a sign of dehydration, which has begun before thirst came on. Thirst is actually quite normal, and not a warning sign. Also, the concept that dark urine signals dehydration is discredited, as blood levels at normal urinary volume are present but not anywhere near as dark as can be seen in the urine of genuinely dehydrated people.

Another doctor of Pennsylvania University puts it in a more clear cut way: if you are thirsty, drink water. If you are not thirsty, there is no reason to drink water.

Sources: Dartmouth Medical School, "Drink at Least 8 Glasses of Water a Day – Really?" 2002; Nancy Cordes, "Busting the 8-Glasses-A-Day Myth," CBS News, 2009.

"ELEMENTARY, MY DEAR **WATSON!**"

I may be blind, forgetful, or merely careless, but I have read all the Sherlock Holmes stories of Sir Arthur Conan Doyle, and cannot remember ever having come across on one single occasion the phrase which is allegedly characteristic of the great detective. It crops up, though not as a quotation, on page 100 of Hesketh Pearson's *Conan Doyle: his life and art* (London, 1946), but not—so far as I know—in the works of Doyle himself. Can any reader prove the contrary?

WATT INVENTED THE STEAM ENGINE

James Watt (1736-1819) is the familiar hero of the tale you heard at your mother's knee: holding an egg-cup in steam from the spout of a kettle, he saw the steam condense on it, scalded his fingers, dropped the egg-cup which caused it to break and his granny to scold him for his idle daydreaming.

The steam engine was apparently first designed by Edward Somerset, Marquis and Earl of Worcester, in 1655 and patented by Robert Hooke in 1678. The pumping steam engine was invented by Sir Samuel Morland in 1682. A model pumping steam engine was first exhibited by Denis Papin in 1685. Still before Watt's birth, Thomas Newcomen erected the first practical working steam engine at Tipton, Staffordshire, in 1712. Watt's achievement was a great improvement in efficiency by condensing the steam in a separate closed vessel instead of in the cylinder itself: he also closed the top of the cylinder and used low-pressure steam instead of cold air to drive the piston down.

There goes another childhood fantasy! Sources include: L. T. C. Roll's article "Steam engine" in *Eureka!* (ed. by Edward de Bono, London, 1947, p. 71).

WEATHER CAN BE PREDICTED
100 PERCENT ACCURATELY

1) **Meteorologists**

Partly as a result of widespread publication of forecasts, it is almost universally believed that meteorologists can predict what the weather will be with a great degree of accuracy. This is completely irresponsible. Meteorologists study the "motions and phenomena of the weather" *(Shorter Oxford English Dictionary)* and the connection of this scientific study with forecasting the weather is no closer than the study of philology with forecasting the languages or linguistic developments of the future. As Richard Inwards, President of the Royal Meteorological Society, wrote in *Nature,* August 15, 1895, "all the great authorities agree that in the present state of our knowledge no human being can correctly predict the weather, even for a week to come." Techniques of more accurate forecasting since Inwards' time, including radio-sonde balloons, airplanes, rockets and man-made satellites, have made his statement less comprehensively accurate, since it is possible to forecast, depending on present conditions, certain weather changes (based upon current awareness of similar conditions) over a very limited period. However, fraudulent "long-range weather forecasts," often issued with the best intentions to assist farmers or seamen, should be ignored as guesswork.

2) Changes in the Weather Can Be Predicted by Observing the Behavior of Plants and Animals

No changes in the weather can be predicted with complete accuracy since, outside the realms of (some) pure science and experimental physics and chemistry, nothing whatever can be predicted with complete accuracy, for the unforeseeable can intervene.

E. J. Lowe, F.R.S., the meteorologist, tested signs generally "accepted" to indicate change and carefully noted what happened after each sign. He did not state that *all* indications from animals and plants are useless, since he did not test them all, but those he did test seemed to fail the test.

He took the well-known signs of bats flying about in the evening, many toads appearing at sunset, many snails about, busy bees, fish rising more than usual in lakes, locusts appearing, cattle becoming restless, flies and gnats becoming troublesome, crows congregating, and ducks making more noise than usual. In 361 observations of the above signs, they were followed 213 times by fine weather, and only 148 times by wet weather; even after prognostications for rain, there was a greater preponderance of fine weather.

Even when swallows fly low, they are not an indication because, as Mr. Lowe regretfully points out, they almost invariably skim the surface of the ground in late summer and autumn. There is a possibility that animals can sense the onset of a heavy rainstorm or any other sudden and highly contrasted change in the weather, but then so can man. The pimpernel and marigold do in fact close their petals before rain, because the air is getting damper, so this is not a fallacy; but it is an error, though almost universal in the countryside, that a large crop of hips, haws and holly-berries indicates a severe winter to come, "Nature" thus providing food for the birds. As if the sight of birds dying of starvation were not sufficient to disprove this!

Source: A. S. E. Ackermann, *Popular fallacies* (4th ed., London, 1950, pp. 733-5).

PEOPLE WITH AGING JOINTS CAN PREDICT
BAD **WEATHER** PATTERNS

As we get older, our joints hurt more frequently and sadly, probably more severely, hence why most sources online have found only that a person who already has arthritis or other types of chronic joint pains and/or the elderly report that certain weather conditions make their pain worse.

Although many people, including doctors, swear that older people with more sensitive bones can really predict storms and other types of bad weather, they haven't been able to prove this scientifically.

The only reasonable explanation for this theory is that barometric pressure causes joint pain, as it acts like air pressing down on you like on airplanes and elevators. However, skeptics dispute this explanation, as air pressure from inside planes is not severe enough to cause serious physical discomfort. Moreover, you would not be feeling the effects of the weather from inside an airplane, nor are pressure swings from weather and atmospheric change on land anywhere near as drastic as they are at the altitudes of in-motion airplanes or in cars driving over mountains. Indicatively, in the formerly mentioned situations, you may have to pop your ears, where as when you're just walking around and suddenly an unexpected cloudy haze comes over the area, you do not.

Plus, arthritis or rheumatism patients, despite cold and damp weather generally having a negative effect on their joints, are not have not reported significant relief after moving to drier climates.

Additionally, the wetness effect on bones seems unlikely, as people do not report feeling worsened joint pain in baths or showers. In terms of humidity entering the respiratory tract and affecting the bones as a factor, again, not likely, as patients are often given humidifiers to breathe in hospitals and there are no reports of this making arthritis conditions worse. And, once again, showers would probably be a lot more generally avoided by arthritis sufferers and probably complained about much more if general cleanliness was causing them painful symptoms.

Experts have been studying this supposed correlation between joints and aching joints for decades and they really haven't discovered much to back this theory up or provide a scientifically fathomable explanation for this sensation. In many attempted surveys or studies, the correlation between weather and joint pain is too mild to be considered credible.

Moreover, people most likely continue to assert personal anecdotes as truth because the theory can't really be properly

(Continued)

disproved or proved scientifically ever, really, as conducting a blind trial without bias when exposure to weather is involved is fairly impossible. In other words, people can still sense and feel the temperature while wearing a blindfold.

Sources: *Scientific American*, "Does Damp or Wet Weather Really Make Arthritis Pain Worse? If so, How?" Donald A. Redelmeier, 2005; *Oxford Journals*, "Osteoarthritis pain and weather," F. V. Wilder, B. J. Hall, J. P. Barrett, 2002; *USA Today*, "Scientists Still Mulling Causes of Weather-Related Pain," 2005.

WELSH RAREBIT IS A CORRUPTION OF WELSH RABBIT

Welsh rabbit is toasted cheese. Skeat dealt with the above fallacy in his *Etymological dictionary* by pointing out that those who were too dense to see the joke of calling toasted cheese "Welsh rabbit" pretended that the name is a corruption of "Welsh rabbit, which is as pointless and stupid as it is incapable of proof."

It may have arisen because the original jokers thought that there were no rabbits in Wales, because in Australia there was a dish called "colonial goose" (mutton cooked with stuffing) from the times before geese were introduced there. Similar nonsense names used in cooking include "Irish apricots" or "Munster plums" for potatoes; "Gravesend sweetmeats" for shrimp; "Essex lion" for veal; "Glasgow magistrates" for herrings; and "Fieldlane duck" for baked sheep's head.

WEREWOLVES

Technically "lycanthropes," or those affected with lycanthropy, a kind of insanity in which the patient imagines himself to be a wolf, or, loosely, a beast of any kind (*Shorter Oxford English Dictionary*). The fallacy occurs when a gullible observer takes the experience to have an occult or supernatural significance. All primitive and peasant societies have such beliefs, and it is only in the last century or so that a belief in werewolves as beings different from humans has begun to die out, though in Sicily and parts of Greece the belief is still found. Secret societies in Africa use such beliefs to their own advantage by dressing in skins of the wild animal they represent (whether it be leopard, crocodile, or another), leaving appropriate tracks in the soft ground, and tearing the flesh of victims to imitate the teeth- and claw-marks of the alleged perpetrator.

The aberrations of lycanthropes are often accompanied by degeneracies such as necrophilia (sexual assaults on corpses), sadism, cannibalism, or zoerasty (sexual relations with animals). The tiger-men of Assam and northern Burma come to associate themselves with a particular tiger in the vicinity and they believe that when that tiger is caught and killed their own death will shortly follow, a belief known as *thanatomania*.

Source: D. H. Rawcliffe, *Illusions and delusions of the supernatural and the occult* (New York, 1959).

WESTMINSTER HAS AN "ABBEY"

Not since the dissolution of the monastery, or abbey, by King Henry VIII. The official title of Westminster "Abbey" since 1560 has been "The Collegiate Church of St. Peter, in Westminster." Queen Elizabeth I replaced the Abbot by a Dean.

Source: Violet Brooke-Hunt, *The story of Westminster Abbey* (London, 1902).

WHALES SPOUT WATER THROUGH THEIR BLOW-HOLES

Whales breathe through their lungs and, being unable to separate air from water as fishes do, must rise to the surface to breathe. The "spouting" of the whale, which is commonly mistaken at a (safe) distance for water, is in fact the ordinary act of breathing out that any mammal has to perform, but in the case of the whale the intervals between breathing out are longer and the action therefore seems to be more dramatic. If the breathing out takes place under water of course it is water that is ejected, but this is relatively rarely seen, and the observer usually sees the ejection of air (highly charged with watery vapor) mixed with mucous matter.

Source: Frank Thomas Bullen, *The cruise of the "Cachalot"* (London, 1898, pp. 188-9).

WHISPERING PRESERVES VOICE

Maybe you woke up with a sore throat from screaming your heart (and vocal chords) out at the concert the night before, or you may have just come down with a case of strep and/or laryngitis. It is quite natural to think that as your throat is sore and swollen and probably in some pain, talking in a quiet whisper is a good way to continue to communicate with others without the risk of worsening the problem.

It turns out that whispering and talking "softly" are not at all synonymous. In reality, studies have shown that whispering

(Continued)

can actually be just as damaging to the voice as yelling. This is because when you whisper, you are putting a good degree of strain on your vocal chords. More specifically, if you are practicing a "stage whisper" (classified as so by the Voice and Swallowing Institute), which is essentially the only degree of whispering that will be understood by others who cannot read lips, you are producing a significant amount of pressure and air flow, plus exerting a lot of muscle tension. Trying to keep your voice essentially inaudible while still making noise through your mouth requires forced constriction of blood vessels which is not good for cell tissues. Furthermore, use of too much air pressure and muscle tension is not a healthy way to develop voice, and clearly has more adverse effects on both normal and damaged vocal regions.

In the event of a sore larynx, the best way to communicate is to speak softly on the exhale, trying to relax the muscles in the throat rather than exert them. And next time you are at a party trying to gossip with your friend over loud music, best to speak at a low volume directly into his or her ear, as the attempt to get what you're saying across through a loud whisper looks just as unsubtle from the outside as it feels on your insides.

Sources: Rebecca N. Gaughan, "How do you get Laryngitis?" *Scientific American*, 2002; The Voice and Swallowing Institute, New York Eye and Ear Infirmary, "FAQs about Voice Therapy"; US National Library of Medicine, National Institutes of Health, "Laryngeal hyperfunction during whispering: reality or myth?" Lakeshore Professional Voice Center, 2006.

A BREED OF **WHITE ELEPHANTS** EXISTS

No true white elephant has ever yet been reported, but Dusit Zoo in Bangkok usually exhibits a salmon-pink (albino) elephant, which is sold to the Royal Family when born since "white" elephants are a rarity even in Asia.

The veneration of the Thais for white elephants is shown by a marvellous description written by a Siamese ambassador at the Court of Queen Victoria who wished to evoke the respect due to her in the following gallant terms: "One cannot but be struck by the deportment of the revered Queen of England. She clearly comes of a divine line of warrior kings and conquerors of the world. Her eyes, her complexion, and above all her fascination are those of a splendid and majestic White Elephant."

Source: Philip Ward, *Bangkok* (New York, 1974).

PUTTING A WET FINGER TO THE **WIND** IS A SUREFIRE WAY OF TELLING WIND DIRECTION

This age old method of figuring out which way the wind is coming from has been a staple to sailors, kite fliers, and curious young physicists alike. Although this strategy may give us a general idea of where the wind is coming, it seems as though in these types of situations we may need a compass or, ideally, other modern instruments to accompany the finger in order to come up with accurate findings.

Here's how this old-fashioned navigation tactic works: upon licking your finger and holding it up in the air, you will be able to determine the direction of the wind by feeling which side of your finger dries more quickly and furthermore, becomes colder quickest.

Although the fans and users of the wet finger strategy are diehard, there seems to remain no real proof of its accuracy besides hearsay and personal experience. Some sources admit that this method of wind direction determination is primitive and likely not very useful, but for those who have written books that highlight the glorious and irreplaceable sensation of the open sea air on the body while sailing, the wet finger is sticking around till the ship goes down.

Sources: William H. Shellenberger, "Cruising the Chesapeake: A Gunkholer's Guide," 2001; "About Wind," Nassau County Skywarn; C. Donald Ahrens, "Essentials of Meteorology: An Invitation to the Atmosphere," 2008.

AN ORGANIZED SOCIETY OF **WITCHES** EXISTED IN MEDIEVAL AND EARLY MODERN EUROPE

In *Europe's inner demons* (1975), Norman Cohn has sought to discover and to expose the origins of this curiously persistent fallacy. Earlier writers traced the origin to the Inquisition's campaigns against the Cathars in southern France and northern Italy during the 13th century, but their conclusions were based on forgeries and hoaxes now exposed by Cohn. In a review of two other books in *The Times Literary Supplement* (July 23, 1976, p. 903), Cohn declares that "we still do not know why the great witch-hunt happened when and where it did. However . . . I myself once . . . advanced a tentative hypothesis: I pointed out that at the end of the Middle Ages and in the early modern period witchcraft acquired a new meaning, as the supreme expression of apostasy, and I suggested that the witch might thereby have acquired a new psycho-social function, as a scapegoat for an unacknowledged hostility to Christianity. I did not at that time know that French scholars, inspired by the researches of Jean Delumeau of the Collège de France, were already beginning to examine how in certain parts of Europe a new, more individual, more demanding type of Christianity was imposed on the laity between the fifteenth and the seventeenth centuries; how this produced, especially among the relatively privileged, an intenser, more personal sense of guilt; how the devil grew in stature, as a symbol of everything that might oppose or rebel against these developments; and what bearing that might have on notions of witchcraft and on the treatment of suspected witches."

WOLVES HUNT IN PACKS

Not outside the realms of the popular movie or children's adventure story. As Stefansson remarks in *The standardisation of error* (London, 1928), *zoological* wolves go in pairs or families, never above a dozen.

Stefansson tracked down all reports of wolf-packs over a period of twenty years, and not one had been authenticated. Neither is there a single authenticated account of a wolf's having attacked and eaten a human being. This fallacy persisted so strongly that the Biological Survey in Washington carefully checked up on every published account of the killing of human beings by wolves in both the United States and Canada, and "without a single exception they proved to be purely imaginary." This might not seem so surprising, were it not for the fact that between January and March 1929, the *New York Times Index* showed reports of wolves devouring sixteen Austrians, five Poles, an aged Bulgarian priest and many Czechoslovaks. They also "menaced Constantinople," whatever that might mean.

THERE IS NO DIFFERENCE BETWEEN
A WOOD-CUT AND A WOOD-ENGRAVING

The two terms are used interchangeably by the careless, but "strictly speaking, a *wood-cut* is cut with a knife along the plank, while a *wood-engraving* is cut with a graver or burin on the cross-section, usually of a piece of box-wood. The latter makes for harder wood and therefore permits a much greater delicacy in the design. But the terms are used indiscriminately by most cataloguers (and many other people) for any illustration printed from wood as distinct from metal."

Source: John Carter, *A B C for book-collectors* (3rd ed., London, 1961).

IF A WORD FOR A THING EXISTS,
THEN THAT THING ALSO EXISTS

E. R. Emmet deals with this hoary error in *The use of reason* (London, 1960). He first quotes John Stuart Mill: "The tendency has always been strong to believe that whatever receives a name must be an entity or being, having an independent existence of its own: and if no real entity answering to the name could be found, men did not for that reason suppose that none existed, but imagined that it was something peculiarly abstruse and mysterious, too high to be an object of sense."

Emmet adds: "To take a simple case, it is not necessarily true that because the words "unicorn," "centaur" exist there are in nature animals for which the words stand. This seems obvious to us now, but it was not always so.

Or again, to take a more complex example, though it may be convenient and intelligible to talk of a man having a strong Will or a good Memory, or a powerful Reason, it is generally agreed by psychologists today that this division of the personality into departments such as "Will," "Memory," "Reason" is erroneous and misleading and that these words cannot rightly be thought of as standing for real entities."

COMMON ERRORS IN ENGLISH **WORD** USAGE

There are many sets of words or words alone which people believe they are using correctly, but in reality, are misusing. We couldn't list all of them if we tried, but we thought we would provide a (relatively) short list of words used erroneously that even we, as "dictionary" authors, were surprised to find:

1) Backwards vs. Backward

It is appropriate to use either "backward" or "backwards" as an adverb. For instance, "walking backward/backwards." However, only "backward" can correctly be used in a sentence where it serves as the adjective, such as in the phrase, "a backward motion."

2) A while and Awhile

"Awhile" as one word is really only effective when it serves as an adverb, and refers to time. So, if you were requesting for someone to "stay awhile," you would use the one word version. By contrast, if it becomes an adjective, or in any case, if there is a preposition before it, then "a" and "while" must be separated. So, you could change "stay awhile" into "stay for a while."

3) Closed-minded

While this phrase is often used in this way to describe someone who is stubborn and narrow in their beliefs, the original/traditional spelling is actually "close-minded." Though there is some debate that close-minded is a less extreme form of closed-minded (meaning, not receptive to new ideas in the former and inflexible to other ideas or lacking tolerance in the latter), they are categorized by most sources as having the same basic meaning, and as close-minded was the original version, though seemingly less logical in its spelling, that is the correct way to use the term.

(Continued)

4) Could care less

It is completely insensible, as a phrase, when you think about it for even a second. Indeed, there are so many catch phrases like this in American culture, which have lost meaning in both a logical sense, and because they are so over used. Saying you could care less about something means, in actuality, that maybe you don't care all that much, but you could, in fact, care less than you do. This is quite different from "could not care less." It is also not especially ironic, because in literal terms, it's kind of a middle ground between caring and not caring, rather than the adverse of "could not care less," which would be something more like "I care so much."

5) Discreet vs. Discrete

Interestingly, the double "e" spelling of the word is the more common one. To be discreet means to be prudent, well-behaved, inconspicuous, or circumspect. In other words, to respect someone's privacy is to be "discreet." On the other hand, "discrete" means distinct, or separate. "Discrete" in mathematics means separating distinguished parts or numbers into different groups. This can be applied to the social world as well, as if putting smokers and nonsmokers, for instance, into two "discrete" groups.

6) Hanged and Hung

The origin of the unique word "hanged" is actually quite interesting. While the two words originally meant the same thing and could be used interchangeably, "hanged" became the one to use only in a particular circumstance. We can all probably see why "hanged" means something as harsh and unpleasant sounding as its name: being put to death by hanging. This special term was coined in its present definition in 1887, though it probably originated in years before this, during one of the many series of commonplace public hangings throughout history. "Hung" refers to all other past tense forms of "to hang." Somewhat surprisingly, the term "hung" in reference to a male with impressively sized genitals dates all the way back to the 1640s. In regards to the relation between "hung" in this alternative sense and "hanged," we'd rather not speculate.

7) Connote vs. Denote

Distinguishing between these two words is difficult. The literal meaning of "denote" is easier to put simply, as a word's denotation, appropriately, is its literal meaning. Somewhat confusingly, a word's connotation is less easy to define, but it refers to a wider association that certain words have. Two words can have the same denotation but have different connotations. For instance, both "wise" and "smart" denote intelligence. But the former has connotations that may refer to wisdom, the elderly, one who has been through a lot in a lifetime and therefore has culminated a great deal of knowledge; the latter may just refer to someone who does well in school, or in a negative sense, being "smart" might negatively connote being snide or unpleasant.

8) Cliché vs. Clichéd

Who would have guessed that cliché is not the correct word to use when describing something boring, cheesy, or conventional? In fact, the grammatically correct way to use the clearly not even English at its roots word is in the past tense. So, rather than saying "I can't believe he gave her roses on Valentine's day, that is so cliché," you would tack a friendly letter "d" to the end of the last word. However, it is right (we believe) to describe something as "a cliché" if it is a noun. So, your teacher might say to you, "don't use this intro, it is a cliché," and he would not be wrong. So, best to not correct him.

9) Nauseous vs. Nauseated

It is commonplace to say that when you are feeling sick to your stomach, or more appropriately, when you need to vomit, that you are feeling nauseous. However, the traditional word that one would use in order to describe this sensation would be "nauseated." Technically, being nauseous is considered by traditionalists to mean being the source of what makes other people nauseated. Kind of like, contagious?

10) Premises and Premise

These two seem like they could be the plural and singular forms of one another. However, they are quite different in meaning. "Premises" refers to an area surrounding a particular location. So, for example, the grounds surrounding a central building or set of buildings are its premises. A premise (also spelled "premiss") is the statement or proposition which is meant to support a conclusion. In logic, two premises can exist in order to support the whole, or the conclusion. But a premise or the main premise can never be used to describe a central, or any other singular part of the premises as a whole.

Sources: Paul Brians, *Common Errors in English Usage*, (online version), 2nd edition, 2008; *The Online Etymology Dictionary*.

ONE **WORM** BECOMES TWO SEPARATE WORMS WHEN CUT IN HALF

It's an old playground tale that cutting a worm in half means that it will not die, but instead become two new worms. We have the pleasure of letting those of you know who never tried it in your childhood that the majority of worms do not have these special abilities.

However, even earthworms are generally totally able to stay alive after half of their bodies have been cut off. Jealous?

Apparently, the worm's ability to regenerate a tail is part of its biological makeup. To elaborate, a worm's anatomy is broken into segments. After twenty-one sections, a new segment will begin, which is more or less a repetition of the same first segments. In each of these parts, the worm has vital organs it needs to survive, such as the pharynx. So, as long as the worm is cut so that it still has at least one full set of twenty-one, it can survive and heal itself.

Others argue that the vast majority of worm species will not grow back a head if it is amputated. Therefore, that uninvited worm you found in your bathroom which you stepped on will not suddenly come back to life from the dead to haunt you with twice the army it started with, assuming you crushed it in its entirety.

Sources: "Why do worms grow back when you cut them in two?" *Lansing State Journal*, 1995; Jen Fong and Paula Hewitt, "Frequently Asked Questions About Worm Composting," Cornell Composting; Alan D. Tomlin, "Earthworm Biology," *Earth Worm Digest*, Pest Management Research Center, 2006.

XYZ

"Zeale without knowledge is sister of Folly:
But though it be witlesse, men hold it most holly."
—JOHN DAVIES, *The scourge of folly* (1611)

"You sit there, you plump beauty, still buying neckties from sidewalk sharpies, still guessing which walnut shell contains the pea, still praying along with Elmer Gantry. America, sometimes I worry about you."

—MIKE MCGRADY,
*Stranger than naked, or how to
write dirty books for fun and profit*
(New York, 1970)

FACULTY X

The fallacy that man has a mysterious faculty "X," responsible for his involvement with the paranormal, is the main thesis and conclusion of Colin Wilson's *The occult* (London, 1971). Faculty "X" is defined as "that latent power that human beings possess to reach beyond the present . . . it is the power to grasp reality, and it unites the two halves of man's mind, conscious and subconscious." [It is not proven that man's mind is divided into two halves, however.]

According to Wilson, faculty "X" is found in the spiritualistic seance, in the casting of runes, the fall of the Tarot pack, the predictions of Nostradamus, and the ramblings of characters like Ouspensky and Gurdjieff. One fallacy is in assuming that whatever one cannot understand is ultimately intelligible, and another that all otherwise unintelligible phenomena have the same explanation. In mathematics, "x" can usefully be taken to mean anything, but in the history of ideas the notion of "X" is of no help at all.

YAWNS ARE CONTAGIOUS

There's a certain satisfaction in a yawn. And despite what a pair of new childhood friends might want to believe, yawns are not actually contagious in any physical or medical sense. The reason people yawn in groups (i.e., a chain of yawns occurring almost

(Continued)

like a wave during read-aloud time in a classroom circle) is social, psychological, and technically voluntary.

Since the '70s, a number of studies have been conducted which prove that this so called yawning "epidemic" is really just the normal way in which children, and to some degree adults, emotionally communicate and empathize with one another. The consensus on these findings is that while children normally start developing this social quality around age four, kids with Autism don't typically demonstrate the same behavior.

Generally, children are conditioned to hypothetically catch yawns from their peers, somehow almost subconsciously learning the mechanism in which to imitate the initial yawner and carrying it in a toned-down form into adult life. Although this is perhaps an important part of development and in forming healthy social environments, such as learning how to adapt, scientists and neurologists have continued to find that the reaction remains totally (though interestingly) behavioral.

Sources: *Cognitive, Affective, and Behavior Neuroscience Journal*, "An Investigation of Auditory Contagious Yawning," 2009; Emily Sohn, *Discovery News*, "Why is Yawning Contagious?" 2010.

METCHNIKOV AND THE POWERS OF **YOGURT**

A Russian pathologist, Ilya Metchnikov, who died at the age of seventy-one in 1916, is cited by Benjamin Walker (in his *Encyclopedia of metaphysical medicine,* London, 1978) for a belief (unchallenged by Walker) that man does not die or age naturally, but poisons himself by autointoxication. His large intestine is submitted to continuous putrefaction, a process that can be arrested. Metchnikov's method of obtaining immortality is not the medieval Philosopher's Stone, but— yes, you've guessed it—yogurt. His theory was that the lactic-acid bacillus present in yogurt would, if taken in large enough amounts, stop putrefaction. His example of longevity (not very convincing, statistically) was that of the Bulgarian peasants, whose staple diet was alleged to be kumiss, fermented mare's milk.

Metchnikov's ideas were followed blindly throughout much of Europe in the early years of this century, and were taken up again by Gayelord Hauser in such books as *Look younger, live longer* (London, 1951).

Unhappily for Metchnikov, Hauser, and all those others who teach much the same thing, or follow the faddists, the large intestine is *not* submitted to continuous putrefaction, for our intestinal bacteria are by and large a necessary part of our biological structure. The parts of the body do not all age at the same speed, but they *do* all age. There goes our dream of human immortality again!

It is equally fallacious—and many young girls who live on yogurt and little else seem to be unaware of it—that yogurt contains no nutrients whatsoever other than those in milk.

ENGLISH MONARCHS HAVE ALWAYS BEEN ADDRESSED AS **"YOUR MAJESTY"**

The first English monarch whom we know to have been addressed as "Your Majesty" was Henry VIII. The mode of address varied from reign to reign so that, for instance, we have records of "Your Grace" (Henry IV), "Your Excellent Grace" (Henry VI), and "High and Mighty Prince" (Edward IV).

ZOOLOGICAL FALLACIES

That inbreeding causes degeneration (it causes the intensification of known characteristics); that ants and bees are intelligent; that certain fly larvae, living as guests in ants' nests, are molluscs; that selection can gradually change the nature of an hereditary factor, or gene; that toads at the breeding season find ponds through an ability to sense water from a distance; and that fishes can sense a current as such and swim against it when unable to see or feel the bank or bottom of the stream . . .

THE LAST FALLACY

Or perhaps better to say "the first fallacy." To assume that, in every single case where I, in my ignorance, have selected what I have thought the best available advice, there is consequently no room for error. A glance behind my shoulder to similarly assured lists of popular delusions over the centuries is enough to persuade me that more than one of my foregoing assertions is incorrect, and that the reader should consult this book no less than any other with a skeptical air, as if to say "this too may be wrong—let me never trust what is offered as fact, truth, or wisdom without testing it in the light of experience and observation."

The Book of Common Fallacies, like any other book, is a fallible compilation carrying, despite the author's best intentions, its own defects and misconceptions. *Caveat lector.*

Select Bibliography

This bibliography omits standard works such as encyclopaedias and dictionaries which mention fallacies only in passing, as well as works written to support the fallacies which are listed and analyzed in the entries concerned. The following entries supplement the hundred-odd sources offered there, omitting general dictionaries and encyclopaedias which mention fallacies only in passing as well as works written to support the fallacies listed and analyzed in the body of the book.

Aarnodt, Sandra and Wang, Sam (both Ph.D), *Welcome to Your Brain*, 2008.

Abelard, Pierre. Dialectica. Ed. by L, M. de Rijk. 2 vols. sen, 1956.

Abelard, Pierre. Logica ingredientibus. *In* Peter Abelards Philosophische Schriften. Ed. by B. Geyer in *Beiträge zur schichte der Philosophie und Theologie des Mittelalters,* vol. XXI, .-3 (1919-27). [Both works by Abelard reproduce and discuss the sixfold classification of fallacies of Boethius, q.v.]

Ackermann, A. S. E. Popular fallacies. 4th ed. London, 1950.

Adams, *Sir* John. Errors in school. London, 1927.

Adelung, Jean Christophe. Histoire des folies humaines; ou, biographie des plus celèbres necromanciers, alchimistes, devins . . . Leipzig, 1785-9.

Ahrens, Donald C. *Essentials of Meteorology: An Invitation to the Atmosphere*, 2008.

Agricola, Rodolphus. De dialectica inventione. 1497. [Facsimile of the 1539 ed., entitled 'De inventione dialectica lucubrationes,' Nieuwkoop, 1967]

Allport, Gordon W. *and* Postman, Leo. The psychology of rumor. New York, 1965.

[Anon.] The common errors, in the education of children, and their consequences, with the method to remedy them. London, 1744.

[Anon.] Fallacies concerning the deaf and the influence of such fallacies in preventing the amelioration of their condition. 1883. [There is a reprint, by Scholarly Reprints Inc., New York, 1976]

[Anon.] Fallacies on Poor Laws. *In London and Westminster Review,* January 1837.

Arnauld, Antoine. La logique, ou l'art de penser. 1662. [Trans. by James Dickoff and Patricia James as 'The art of thinking (Port Royal logic),' New York, 1964]

Aristotle. On fallacies, or the Sophistic! Elenchi. With a translation and commentary by Edward Poste. London, 1866.

Atkinson, D. T. Magic, myth and medicine. New York, 1956.

Averroes. See Ibn Rushd, Muhammad bin Ahmad.

Ayer, A. J. The problem of knowledge. Harmondsworth, 1956.

Bacon, Francis. The advancement of learning. London, 1887-1902. [This work, originally published in 1605, and expanded in 'De augmentis' (1623), suggests the compiling of a *Calendar of Doubts* to be sifted and resolved, and of a *Calendar of Popular Errors,* "chiefly in natural history, such as pass in speech and conceit . . . that man's knowledge be not weakened nor imbased by such dross and vanity"]

Bacon, Roger. Opera hactenus inedita. Ed. By Robert Steele. Oxford, 1909. [Fascicule 15 contains the 'Sumule dialectices' of c. 1245]

Bacon, Francis. Novum organon. Edited by T. Fowler. Oxford, 1878. [For the *idola* see i. 38-9]

Barnum, Phineas Taylor. The humbugs of the world. London, 1866. [Especially amusing on the 'spiritualists' of the time].

Barry, B. Austin. Errors in practical measurement in science, engineering and technology. New York, 1978.

Beaty, John Y. Nature is stranger than fiction. London, 1943.

Bechtel, Guy and Carrière, Jean-Claude. Dictionnaire de la bêtise et des erreurs de jugement. Paris, 1965.

Beers, Yardley. Theory of errors. 2nd ed. New York, 1957.

Bell, Eric Temple. The last problem. New York, 1961. [On Fermat's problem, q.v.]

Bell, Eric Temple. Numerology. New York, 1933.

Bell, Eric Temple. The magic of numbers. New York, 1946.

Bell, Eric Temple. The search for truth. New York, 1935.

Belnap, Nuel Dinsmore, jr. An analysis of questions. Santa Monica, Calif., 1963.

Bentham, Jeremy. The book of fallacies. London, 1824. (Rev. ed. By Harold A. Larrabee, Baltimore, 1952). [Political fallacies]

Berkusky, H. 'Regenzauber'. In Mitthellungen der Anthropologischen Gesellschaft in Wien, 1913. [On concepts of magical rainmaking in some primitive groups]

Bessy, Maurice. Histoire en 1000 images de la magie, Paris, 1961. (Trans. by M. Crosland and A. Daventry as "A pictorial history of magic and the supernatural", London, 1963).

Black, Max. Critical thinking: an introduction to logic and scientific method. 2nd ed. Englewood Cliffs, N.J., 1953.

Black, Max. Margins of precision: essays in logic and language. Ithaca, N.Y., 1971.

Bochenski, Innocentius M. A history of formal logic. Notre Dame, Indiana, 1961.

Boethius, Anicius Manlius Torquatos Severinus. De syllogismo categorico. Introductio ad syllogismos categoricos. In Migrie, J.-P., Patrologiae cursus completus, ser. latina, vol. 64, cols. 761-832. Paris, 1860.

Bombaugh, Charles C. Facts and fancies for the curious. London, 1905.

Bombaugh, Charles C. Oddities and curiosities of words and literature. New York, 1961.

Braithwaite, R. B. Scientific explanation. Cambridge, 1953.

Brecht, Bertolt. Fünf Schwierigkeiten beim Schreiben der Wahrheit. Berlin, 1949. [First published in a German newspaper in Paris, and distributed illegally in Nazi Germany. The 'five difficulties in conveying the truth' are that one must have courage to write it; the sagacity to recognize it; the craft of using it as a weapon; the judgment to realize in whose hands it will best work; and the cunning to ensure its correct dissemination].

Breland, Osmond P. Animal facts and fallacies. London, 1950.

Brians, Paul. Common Errors in English Usage, (online version), 2nd edition, 2008

Bronowski, Jacob. The origins of knowledge and imagination. New Haven, 1979.

Browne, Sir Thomas. Pseudodoxia epidemica. London, 1646. (In Works, Edinburgh, 1927). [This is the work m usually known as "Vulgar errors"]

Budge, Earnest Alfred Wallis. Amulets and talismans. New York, 1961.

Burks, Arthur W. The logic of fixed and growing automata. Engineering Research Institute (University of Michigan), 1957.

Burnam, Tom. The dictionary of misinformation. New York, 1976.

Camp, John. Magic, myth and medicine. London, 1973.

Caradec, François and Arnaud, Noel. Encyclopédie des farces et attrapes et des mystifications. Paris, 1964.

Carnap, Rudolf. The logical syntax of language. London, 1937.

Carrington, Richard Temple Murray. Mermaids and mastodons: a book of natural and unnatural history, London, 1957.

Carroll, Dr. Aaron E. and Vreeman, Dr. Rachel C. Don't Swallow Your Gum!: Myths, Half-Truths, and Outright Lies About Your Body and Health, 2009.

Cavendish, Richard, ed. Encyclopedia of the unexplained: magic, occultism and parapsychology. London, 1974. [Strong bias in favour of most phenomena discussed]

Chaplin, James Patrick. Rumor, fear, and the madness of crowds. New York, 1959.

Chase, Stuart. Guide to straight thinking; with thirteen common fallacies. London, 1959.

Chase, Stuart. The tyranny of words. London, 1938.

Christopher, Milbourne. Mediums, mystics and the occult. New York, 1975. [Written "to give those not familiar with deceptive techniques a better understanding of what too often are called 'unexplained phenomena'"].

Clark, C. E. The mistakes we make. London, 1898.

Clark, C. E. More mistakes we make. London, 1901.

Cole, Richard. 'A note on informal fallacies'. In *Mind,* vol. 74, 1965, pp. 432-3.

Corliss, William R. The unexplained: a sourcebook of strange phenomena. New York, 1976.

Cornwallis, Caroline Frances. Exposition of vulgar and common errors, by 'Thomas Browne Redivivus'. London, 1845.

Cramp, A. J. Nostrums and quackery and pseudo-medicine. Chicago, 1936. Cuénot, L. 'Sciences et pseudo-sciences'. *In Revue Scientifique,* vol. 78, no. 1, January 1940, pp. 3-11.

Crawshay-Williams, Rupert. The comforts of unreason: a study of the motives behind irrational thought. London, 1947.

De Bono, Edward. The five-day course in thinking. New York, 1967.

De Morgan, Augustus. A budget of paradoxes. London, 1872. (2nd ed., 2 vols., Chicago, 1915).

Dodds, E. R. The Greeks and the irrational. Berkeley, Calif., 1951.

Draper, J. W. History of the conflict between religion and science. London, 1922.

Dunham, Barrows. Man against myth. London, 1948.

Dudeney, Henry E. Amusements in mathematics. New York, 1917.

Dudeney, Henry E. The Canterbury puzzles. New York, 1919.

Duncan, Ronald *and* Weston-Smith, Miranda. The encyclopaedia of ignorance. Oxford, 1977. [2nd ed. is announced for publication shortly]

Eaton, Ralph M. General logic: an introductory survey. New York, 1931.

Eisler, R. The royal art of astrology. London, 1946. [One of the few useful titles in this immense field]

Elson, Louis Charles. Mistakes and disputed points in music and music teaching. 1910. [There is a reprint, by AMS Press, New York, 1974]

Emmet, E. R. The use of reason. London, 1960.

Erasmus Roterodamus, Desiderius. [Encomium Moriae] Praise of folly, and Letter to Martin Dorp, 1515. Trans. by Betty Radice. Harmondsworth, 1971.

Evans, Bergen. The natural history of nonsense. London, 1947.

Evans, Bergen. The spoor of spooks, and other nonsense. London, 1955.

Evans, Christopher. Cults of unreason. London, 1973.

Eysenck, Hans Jurgen. Sense and nonsense in psychology. Harmondsworth, 1958.

Fearnside, William Ward, *and* Holther, William Benjamin. Fallacy, the counterfeit of argument. Englewood Cliffs, N.J., 1959.

Festinger, Leon, *and others*. When prophecy fails: a social and psychological study of a modern group that predicted the destruction of the world. Minneapolis, 1956.

Finley, M. I. The use and abuse of history. London, 1975. [For 'Myth, memory and history' see pp. 11-33]

Fischer, David Hackett. Historians' fallacies. New York, 1970. [A valuable typology of historiographical fallacies]

Fishbein, Morris. Fads and quackery in healing. New York, 1933.

Fishbein, Morris. Shattering health superstitions. New York, 1930.

Flacelière, Robert. Devins et oracles grecs. Paris, 1961.

Flaubert, Gustave. Le dictionnaire des idées reçues, ed. E.-L. Ferrère. Paris, 1913. (The 1951 ed. also includes the *Catalogue des idées chic),* The translations into English include "A dictionary of platitudes", by Edward J. Fluck, and "A dictionary of accepted ideas", by Jacques Barzun (both London, 1954).

Fontenelle, Bernard Le Bovier de. Histoire des oracles. Paris, 1686. [There are English translations by A. B., London, 1688, and by S. Whatley, Glasgow, 1753, and a critical edition by L. Maigron, Paris, 1908].

Foote, G. W. Infidel deathbeds. London, 1888. [False accounts of deathbed 'conversions' listed]

Fort, Charles The book of the damned. New York, 1919. [Fort's overriding aim was to ridicule both orthodox and unorthodox scientists and his books, of which this was the first and most readable, are content to record the absurd, with virtually no serious analysis]

Fovargue, Stephen. A new catalogue of vulgar errors. Cambridge, 1767.

Furneaux, Rupert. Fact, fake or fable? London, 1954. [Fourteen essays: 'The money pit' (on Oak Island, Nova Scotia), 'The escape of John Wilkes Booth, assassin of Lincoln', 'Drake's plate of brass', 'The Casket Letters of Mary, Queen of Scots', 'The place of a skull: where was Golgotha?', 'Raleigh's lost colonists', 'The donation of Con-stantine', 'The silent stones of Tiahuanaco', 'Ney, the man who lived twice', 'The Protocols of Zion', 'The Kensington rune stone', 'Constantine Simonides', 'The Old Stone Tower at Newport, Rhode Island', and 'The Zinoviev Letter']

Furneaux, Rupert. Myth and mystery. London, 1955. [Fourteen essays: 'The Creation', 'The Deluge', 'The Exodus', 'Myth versus mathematics' (on Velikovsky), 'Lost Atlantis', 'British Israel', 'Prophecy in stone?' (on Pyramidology), 'The Argonauts', 'King Arthur', 'The inscrutable faces of Easter Island', 'A mystery of the sea' (on the *Marie Celeste),* 'Flying objects', 'Sherlock Holmes — a myth?' and 'The curse of the Pharaohs']

Gardner, Martin. Fads and fallacies in the name of science. New York, 1957.

Gardner, Martin. Mathematical puzzles and diversions, London, 1961. [Includes seven mathematical fallacies, but the rest of the book is an equally exuberant celebration of the pleasure to be derived from paradox in mathematics]

Gautama. Nyayasutras. Ed. And trans. From the Sanskrit by Ganganatha Jha (2 vols., Poona, 1939). [Fallacies in ancient Indian logic].

Gilby, Thomas. Barbara Celarent: a description of scholastic dialectic. London, 1949.

Glanvill, Joseph. The vanity of dogmatizing. London, 1661. [Reprinted by the Facsimile Text Society, New York, 1931]

Goldsmid, Edmund. Un-natural history, or myths of ancient science. Edinburgh, 1886.

Gombrich, Ernst Hans. Art and illusion. London, 1960 (2nd ed., London, 1962).

Gould, George M. and Pyle, Walter L. Anomalies and curiosities of medicine. Philadelphia, 1897.

Gould, Rupert T. Oddities: a book of unexplained facts. London, 1929.

Grillot de Givry, Emile. Picture museum of sorcery, magic and alchemy. New York, 1963.

Guinchant, J. 'La science nouvelle du pendule n'est qu'une nouvelle science occulte.' *In Revue Scientifique,* vol. 74, 1936. [Against radiesthesia]

Haggard, Howard W. Devils, drugs and doctors. London, 1929 (Reprinted Wakefield, 1975).

Haldane, John Burdon Sanderson. Fact and faith. London, 1934.

Haldane, John Burdon Sanderson. Science and life. London, 1968.

Hall, Carl William. Errors in experimentation. Letchworth, Herts., 1978.

Hall, Trevor H. New light on old ghosts. London, 1965.

Hall, Trevor H. The spiritualists. London, 1962.

Hall, Trevor H. The strange case of Edmund Gurney. London, 1964.

Hamblin, C. L. Fallacies. London, 1970. [On logic].

Hawton, Hector. The feast of unreason. London, 1952. [Indicates the fallacious ideas in the thought of Pascal, Kierkegaard, Nietzsche, Sartre, Heidegger, and others in the same traditions]

Hawton, Hector. The thinker's handbook. London, 1950. [Controversies viewed from both the religious and the secular positions, favouring the latter]

Hazlitt, William. The plain speaker. 2 vols. London, 1826. [The *Everyman* edition of 1928 contains the full text of 'Essay XIV: On Dr Spurzheim's theory', concerning phrenology]

Hempel, Carl Gustav. 'Studies in the logic of confirmation'. *In Mind,* vol. 54, 1945, pp. 1-26 *and* 97-121.

Herbert of Cherbury, Edward, *Lord*. De veritate. London, 1624. [The translation by Meyrick H. Carré, Bristol, 1937, omits the extra treatise 'De causis errorum' appended to late editions in the 17th century]

Hering, Daniel Webster. Foibles and fallacies of science. London, 1924.

Heuvelmans, Bernard. Sur la piste des bêtes ignores. Paris, 1955. (English trans., "On the track of unknown animals," London, 1958). [Discusses animals which are thought to exist but may well not].

Hirsch, Steven R. *Schizophrenia*, 2003

Historical Association. Common errors in history. London, 1945.

Historical Association. Common errors in history. 2nd ser. London, 1947.

Historical Association. Common errors in Scottish history, ed. by Gordon Donaldson. London, 1956.

Hodges, Wilfrid. Logic. Harmondsworth, 1977. [An excellent modern textbook, with answers to the exercises]

Hoffer, Eric. The true believer: thoughts on the nature of mass movements. New York, 1951.

Hogben, Lancelot. Dangerous thoughts. London, 1939.

Hogben, Lancelot. The retreat from reason. London, 1937.

Holbrook, Stewart Hall. The golden age of quackery. New York, 1959.

Holder, C. F. and Jordan, D. S. Fish stories alleged and experienced. London, 1909.

Huff, Darrell. How to lie with statistics. London, 1954.

Huff, Darrel. How to take a chance. London, 1960.

Ibn Rushd, Muhammad bin Ahmad. Tahafut at-Tahafut (The incoherence of the incoherence). Trans. from the Arabic by S. van den Bergh. 2 vols. London, 1954.

Ingersoll, Robert Green. Some mistakes of Moses. London [n.d. but c. 1890]

Inhelder, Bärbel *and* Piaget, Jean. The early growth of logic in the child. New York, 1964.

Jahoda, Gustav. The psychology of superstition. Harmonds-worth, 1970.

Jameson, Eric. The natural history of quackery. London, 1961.

Jastrow, Joseph. Effective thinking. London, 1932.

Jastrow, Joseph. Error and eccentricity in human belief. New York, 1935.

Jastrow, Joseph. Fact and fable in psychology. London, 1901.

Jastrow, Joseph. *ed*. The story of human error. New York, 1936.

Jastrow, Joseph. Wish and wisdom. New York, 1935.

Jauvais, Gregoire. Erreurs scandaleuses des théories officielles en matière de santé. Paris, 1970.

Jeffrey, Richard C. Formal logic: its scope and limits. New York, 1967.

John of Salisbury, *Bishop of Chartres*. The Metalogicon: a twelfth-century defense of the verbal and logical arts of the Trivium (1159). Trans., with an introduction and notes, by Daniel D. McGarry. Berkeley, Cal., 1962.

Jones, Abel J. In search of truth. London, 1945.

Jones, John. Medical and vulgar errors refuted. London, 1797.

Jones, William, F. S. A. Credulities past and present. London, 1880.

Jordan, David Starr. The higher foolishness. London, 1927.

Jordan, David Starr. The stability of truth. London, 1911.

Joubert, Laurent. Erreurs populaires et propos vulgaires, touchant la medecine et le regime de sante. Bordeaux, 1579.

Kaiser, Walter. Praisers of folly. London, 1964.

Keene, M. Lamar. The psychic mafia. New York, 1976. [An expose by a former medium].

Keith, Sir Arthur Berriedale, The place of prejudice in modern civilization. New York, 1931.

Kemmerich, Max. Aus der Geschichte der menschlichen Dummheit. Munich, 1912. [Anecdotes of human foolishness].

Kemmerich, Max. Kultur-Kuriosa. 3 vols. Munich, 1910-1936. [Absurdities of human behavior].

Kennaway, Sir Ernest. Some religious illusions in art, literature, and experience. London, 1953.

King, Francis. Ritual magic in England. London, 1970.

Kneale, W. C. and Kneale, M. The development of logic. Oxford, 1962.

Kubizek, August, The Young Hitler I Knew, 2006, London

Lamont, Corliss. The illusion of immortality. London, 1936.

Larrabee, Harold A. Reliable knowledge. Boston, 1954.

Lawrence, Robert Means. Primitive psycho-therapy and quackery. Boston, 1910.

Lee, Henry. Sea monsters unmasked. London, 1884.

Leff, Gordon. Heresy in the later Middle Ages. Manchester, 1967.

Leroy, E. B. Les visions du demi-sommeil (Hallucinations hypnagogiques). Paris, 1926.

Levenson, E. Fallacy of understanding. New York, 1972.

Lever, Ralph. The arte of reason, rightly termed Witcraft: teaching a perfect way to argue and dispute. London, 1573.

Ley, Willy. Salamanders and other wonders. London, n.d. but c.1958.

Littlechild, S. C. Fallacy of the mixed economy. Levittown, New York, 1978.

Locke, John. Essay concerning human understanding. London, 1690. [The best ed. is that by John W. Yolton, 2 vols., London, 1961].

Loewenfeld, Leopold. Über die Dummheit. 1913. [Human stupidity in the fields of sex, race, economics, politics, art, literature and science]

Lum, Peter. Fabulous beasts. London, 1952.

MacDougall, Curtis D. Hoaxes. New York, 1940 (2nd ed., New York, 1958).

Mackay, Charles. Extraordinary popular delusions and the madness of crowds. London, 1852. (2nd augmented ed. of "Memoirs of extraordinary popular delusions," London, 1841).

Malina, Robert M. and Bouchard, Claude. Growth, Maturity, and Physical Activity, Second ed., 2004.

Maple, Eric. Magic, medicine and quackery. London, 1968.

Maxwell, E. A. Fallacies in mathematics. Cambridge, 1959.

McCracken, Robert D. Fallacies of women's liberation. Fort Collins, Colorado, 1972.

McGlashan, Alan. Gravity and levity. London, 1976. [A psychiatrist's view of uncertainty in knowledge]

Mcintosh, Christopher. The astrologers and their creed. London, 1969.

Merton, Egon Stephen. Science and imagination in Sir Thomas Browne. New York, 1949.

Mill, John Stuart. A system of logic, ratiocinative and inductive: being a connected view of the principles of evidence, and the methods of scientific investigation. 2 vols. 2ⁿᵈ ed. London, 1946. [Fallacies are dealt with in book V].

Minty, Leonard Le M. The legal and ethical aspects of medical quackery. London, 1932.

Montagu, M. F. Ashley *and* Darling, Edward. The ignorance of certainty. New York, 1970.

Montagu, M. F. Ashley. Man's most dangerous myth: the fallacy of race. 4ᵗʰ ed. Cleveland, 1964. [Somewhat overstates a generally tenable position].

Montagu, M. F. Ashley *and* Darling, Edward. The prevalence of nonsense. New York, 1967.

Montaigne, Michel de. Essais. 2 vols. Bordeaux, 1580. [A third volume was added in 1588. The greatest essay is the 'Apologie de Raimond Sebond' (Vol. II, ch. XII), the most eloquent attack on fanaticism ever published. The most accessible modern edition is that by Pierre Michel in 'Le Livre de Poche', Paris, 1965. There is an English ed. by Donald M. Frame, London, 1958]

Moore, J. Howard. Savage survivals. London, 1933. [How man's rise towards reasoning behavior is impeded by factors in his ancestry; deals also with domesticated animals, but this section is outdated].

Morley, John. On compromise. London, 1886. [Ch. II treats "Of the possible unity of error"].

Morus (*pseud. Le.* Richard Lewinsohn). Animals, men and myths. London, 1954.

Naess, A. Scepticism. London, 1968.

Nesfield, John Collinson. Errors in English composition. London, 1903.

Northrop, Eugene P. Riddles in mathematics: a book of paradoxes. London, 1948.

Oesterle, John Arthur. Logic: the art of defining and reasoning. 2nd ed. Englewood Cliffs, N. J., 1952.

Ong, Walter J. Ramus: method and the decay of dialogue: from the art of discourse to the art of reason. Cambridge, Mass., 1958.

Palfreman, Jon. 'The seances and the scientist'. In *New Society,* 21 June 1979, pp. 709-11. [On the various phases of spiritualist activity in Britain since 1848]

Palmer, A. Smythe. The folk and their word-lore: an essay on popular etymologies. London, 1904.

Parish, E. Hallucinations and illusions. London, 1897.

Parsons, J. Population fallacies. London, 1977.

Partridge, Eric. Origins: a short etymological dictionary of modern English. London, 1958 (4ᵗʰ ed., London, 1966).

Petrus Hispanus, *later* Pope John XX or XXI. Treatise on the major fallacies. MS. Clm. 14458, fol. 1^r – 28^r in the Bavarian State Library, Munich.

Phin, John. Seven follies of science. New York, 1912.

Pitkin, Walter Boughton. A short introduction to the history of human stupidity. London, 1935.

Plato. Republic. Translated by H. D. P. Lee. Harmondsworth, 1955. [For the *idola* see vii, 516A]

Plato. Theaitetos. Translated by John Warrington in Plato's *Parmenides* . . . London, 1961. [A Socratic dialogue on the definition of knowledge].

Poole, Stanley B.-R. Royal mysteries and pretenders. London, 1969.

Popkin, Richard H. The history of scepticism from Erasmus to Spinoza. Berkeley, Ca., 1979.

Popper, *Sir* Karl R. Conjectures and refutations. London, 1963.

Popper, *Sir* Karl R. The logic of scientific discovery. Rev. ed. London, 1968.

Popper, *Sir* Karl R. Objective knowledge. 2nd ed. London, 1979.

Popper, *Sir* Karl R. On the sources of knowledge and ignorance. London, 1961.

Porter, Eugene 0. Fallacies of Karl Marx. El Paso, Texas, 1954.

Powys, Llewelyn. Damnable opinions. London, 1935. [The tradition of Epicurus, Lucretius, Lucian, Machiavelli and Voltaire as 'heretics' viewed against the orthodoxy of their times]

Price, Harry. 'Exposure of brothers' false seances'. *In Empire News,* 16 September 1934. [On the fraudulent brothers Craig and George Falconer]

Price, Harry. 'Exposure of Jan Guzik, Warsaw'. *In Journal of the American Society for Psychical Research,* February 1924.

Price, Harry. 'Facts, frauds and fallacies of psychical research'. *In Journal of the Midland and Birmingham Society for Psychical Research,* May 1924. [But note the corrective autobiography, *Search for truth,* London, 1942].

Primrose, James. De vulgi in medicine erroribus libri IV. London, 1638. [There is a 2nd ed., Amsterdam, 1644, and an English translation by R. Wittie, 'Popular errours, or the errors of the people in physick', London, 1651].

Proctor, Richard Anthony. The borderland of science. London, 1873. [The last three chapters are 'Gambling Superstitions', 'Coincidences and Superstitions', and 'Notes on Ghosts and Goblins'. In connection with ghosts (on pp. 427-8), the author concludes that "Real sights and sounds are modified by the imagination, either excited or diseased, into seemingly supernatural occurrences"].

Quine, Willard van Orman. From a logical point of view: nine logico-philosophieal essays. 2nd ed. Cambridge, Mass., 1953.

Quine, Willard van Orman. Philosophy of logic. Englewood Cliffs, N. J., 1970.

Radford, Edwin *and* Radford, M.A. Encyclopedia of superstitions. London, 1948. (Revised ed. by Christina Hole, London, 1961). ["Time, and the disappearance of the religion or philosophy that gave them birth, have made [superstitions] meaningless, and therefore irrational, but have not always deprived them of the power to influence men's lives"—C. Hole]

Rameau, Jean-Philippe. Erreurs sur la musique dans l'Encyclopédie. [A facsimile edition, Paris, 1971. The *Encyclopédie* in question is that of Diderot and d'Alem-bert, 17 vols., Paris, 1751-65]

Ramus, Petrus. Dialectique. [Critical ed. by M. Dassonville. Geneva, 1964]

Ráth-Végh, Istvan. Az emberi butaság kulturtörténetébol. Budapest, 1938. ['The cultural history of human stupidity' has been translated from Magyar into Spanish by F. Oliver Brachfeld, Barcelona, 1950]

Ráth-Végh, Istvan. Új butaságok az emberiség kultur-történetéböl. Budapest, 1939. ['New stupidities from the cultural history of mankind']

Ráth-Végh, Istvan. Vége az emberi butaságnak. Budapest, 1940. ['An end to human stupidity']

Rawcliffe, D. H. Illusions and delusions of the supernatural and the occult. New York, 1959.

Rescher, Nicholas. The development of Arabic logic. Pittsburgh, 1964.

Richet, Charles. Idiot man. London, 1925. [Analyses such human follies as fashion, superstition, customs tariffs, slavery, feudalism, the martyrdom of pioneers, and addiction to alcohol, nicotine and opium]

Rijk, Lambertus Marie de. Logica modernorum: a contribution to the history of early terminist logic. 2 vols. in 3. Assen, 1962-7. [Vol. 1 contains "Glosses on the Sophistical Refutations", "Parvipontanus fallacies", "Summa of Sophistical Refutations" and "Viennese fallacies" ; Vol. 2 contains "London fallacies", "Dialectica Monacensis" and "Tractatus Anagnini"]

Robinson, Philip. Fishes of fancy. London, 1884.

Rogers, Clement F. Verify your references: studies in popular apologetics. London, 1938. [A publication of the Society for the Promotion of Christian Knowledge and thus strongly biased, the book is nevertheless sound on the basic principle of confirming assumptions, even if the practice is less than perfect]

Rose, Louis. Faith healing. Harmondsworth, 1971.

Rostand, Jean. Science fausse et fausses sciences. [Translated by A. J. Pomerans as 'Error and deception in science,' London, 1960]

Rousseau, Pierre. Voyage au bout de la science. Paris, 1963. [There is an English translation, 'The limits of science', London, 1967].

Rowe, William Leonard. 'The fallacy of composition'. *In Mind,* vol.71, 1962, pp. 87-92.

Rudolph, Dr. Marvin J. *Pop Rocks The Inside Story of America's Revolutionary Candy*, 2006.

Russell, Bertrand Arthur William. Let the people think. London, 1941.

Russell, Bertrand. Human knowledge: its scope and limits. London, 1948.

Saleeby, C. W. Some fallacies about war. *In Pall Mall Gazette,* 29 December 1913.

Salgues, Jacques Barthélemy. Des erreurs et des prejudges répandus dans la société. 3rd ed., 3 vols. Paris, 1818. [Vol. 4, 'Préjugés des reputations', appeared in 1830]

Samour, Patricia Queen and Helm, Kathy King, "Milk and Mucus," *Handbook of Pediatric Nutrition*, 2005.

Sanchez, Francisco. Tractatus de multum nobili et prima universali scientia, quod nihil scitur. Lyons, 1581. [There is a translation into Spanish by Marcelino Menéndez y Pelayo, 'Que nada se sabe', Madrid, 1923?, and another into Portuguese by B. de Vasconcelos and M. Pinto de Meneses, 'Tratados filosóficos', vol.1, Lisbon, 1955]

Schopenhauer, Artur. Essays from the Parerga and Paralipomena. Trans. by T. Bailey Saunders. London, 1951. [For "The art of controversy"]

Sears, C. E. Days of delusion: a strange bit of history. Boston and New York, 1924.

Senna, Carl. *ed.* The fallacy of I.Q. New York, 1973.

Sextus Empiricus. Works, with a translation by R. G. Bury. 4 vols. London, 1933-49. [See vol. 2 for "Against the logicians"]

Shellenberger, William H. *Cruising the Chesapeake: A Gunkholer's Guide*, 2001.

Sidgwick, Alfred. The application of logic. London, 1910.

Sidgwick, Alfred. Distinction and the criticism of beliefs. London, 1892.

Sidgwick, Alfred. Fallacies: a view of logic from the practical side. London, 1883.

Sidgwick, Alfred. 'The localisation of fallacy'. *In Mind,* vol.7, 1882, pp. 55-64.

Sidgwick, Alfred. The process of argument: a contribution to logic. London, 1893.

Sidgwick, Alfred. The use of words in reasoning. London, 1901.

Simoons, Frederick J. Eat not this flesh. Madison, Wis., 1961.

Sladek, John. The new apocrypha: a guide to strange sciences and occult beliefs. London, 1974. Sparkes, Alonzo Clive W. 'Begging the question'. *In Journal of the History of Ideas,* vol.27, 1963, pp. 462-3.

Stcherbatsky, Theodore. Buddhist logic. 2 vols. New York, 1962.

Stefansson, Vilhjalmur. The standardisation of error. London, 1928.

[Stephens, John] The errors of men personated in sundry essaies: and their passions deciphered in honest characters. [British Library shelf-mark Mic. A. 605]

Sully, James. Illusions. London, 1881 (4th ed., 1895).

Tabori, Paul. The art of folly. London, 1961.

Tabori, Paul. The natural science of stupidity. Philadelphia, 1959.

Taylor, F. Sherwood. The alchemists. London, 1952.

Thomas Aquinas, *Saint*. De fallaciis ad quosdam nobiles artistas. *In* "Opuscula philosoph-ica" (Turin), no. 43, 1954.

Thomen, August Astor. Doctors don't believe it: why should you? New York, 1935.

Thouless, Robert Henry. Straight and crooked thinking. 2nd ed. London, 1959.

Timbs, John. Things not generally known. London, 1860. Topping, J. Errors of observation and their treatment. 3rd ed. London, 1962.

Trench, Richard Chenevix. A select glossary of English words used formerly in senses dif-ferent from their present. London, 1906.

Vayson de Pradenne, A. Les fraudes en archéologie préhistorique. Paris, 1932.

Vidyabhasana, Mahamahopadhyaya Satis Chandra. A history of Indian logic. Calcutta, 1921.

Voltaire, François Marie Arouet de. Dictionnaire philosophique, Paris, 1764.

Walker, D. P. The decline of Hell: seventeenth century discussions of eternal torment, London, 1970.

Walker, D. P. Spiritual and demonic magic from Ficino to Campanella. London, 1958.

Wang Ch'ung. Lun Heng: philosophical essays. Trans. by A Forke. 2 vols. 2nd ed. New York, 1962. ['Discourses weighed in the balance' are civilized, erudite essays written in A.D. 83 by a great Chinese sceptic]

Ward, Henshaw. The psychology of conviction. Boston, 1918.

Watts, Isaac. Logick, or the right use of reason in the enquiry after truth, with a variety of rules to guard against error, in the affairs of religion and human life, as well as in the sciences. London, 1725.

Webb, James. The flight from reason. Volume 1 of 'The Age of the Irrational'. London, 1971. [An excellent, unbiased account of the occult and spiritualism in American and West European intellectual history from the Foxes at Hydesville, N.Y., in 1848]

Webb, James. The flight from reason, London, 1971 (US edition entitled "The occult revival", New York, 1973).

Westaway, Frederic William. Obsessions and convictions of the human intellect. London, 1938. (2nd ed., entitled "Man's search after truth", London, 1942).

Wheatley, Harry B. Literary blunders. London, 1893.

White, Andrew Dickson. A history of the warfare of science with theology in Christendom. New York, 1896. (2 vols. in 1, London, 1955).

Whitehead, Alfred North. Adventures of ideas. Harmonds-worth, 1942.

Witherspoon, Alexander M. Common errors in English: how to avoid them. 1943. [Reprinted London, 1979]

Wittgenstein, Ludwig. Über Gewissheit. On certainty. Edited by G.E.M. Anscombe and G. H. von Wright. Trans. by Denis Paul and G. E. M. Anscombe. Reprinted with correc-tions. Oxford, 1975.

Young, J. Z. Doubt and certainty in science. Oxford, 1951.

Zabaleta, Juan de. Errores celebrados. Madrid, 1972. [17th-century moral lessons drawn from anecdotes of classical antiquity]

Zaehner, R. C. Drugs, mysticism and makebelieve. London, 1972.

Ziman, John. Reliable knowledge: an exploration of the grounds for belief in science. Cambridge, 1978.

Zöckler, Otto. Geschichte der Beziehungen zwischen Theologie und Naturwissenschaft, mit besondrer Rücksicht auf Schöpfungsgeschichte. 2 vols. Gütersloh, 1877-79.

Index

INDEX